Second Edition

CORRECTIONS

CORRECTIONS

A Concise Introduction

Second Edition

James F. Quinn

University of North Texas

WAVELAND

PRESS, INC.

Long Grove, Illinois

For information about this book, contact:
  Waveland Press, Inc.
  4180 IL Route 83, Suite 101
  Long Grove, IL 60047-9580
  (847) 634-0081
  info@waveland.com
  www.waveland.com

CONTENTS

4   Probation   73

5   Intermediate Sanctions   95

PREFACE

Years of study and direct observation have convinced me that corrections is the most neglected and misunderstood aspect of the justice system. Our neglect of corrections ultimately springs from its success in keeping offenders out of public sight. The system itself is kept largely out of public salience as well, which makes it vulnerable to abuses of all types. Most people think about corrections only when the system fails or becomes a political pawn in some larger game of policy. The system is poorly understood because most law-abiding citizens have their own rational, fully socialized definitions of effective and fair crime control. This view is unlikely to induce positive change in a criminal population that is poorly socialized, largely lower class, and often emotionally driven. My goal in writing this text is to enlighten voters and future correctional professionals on crucial issues so that I might retire in a safer society than the one in which I now live.

The horrors of modern crime are too often paralleled by those of imprisonment. Increasing the use of imprisonment is a reflexive response to public fear of crime that drains resources from health and educational agencies that could help to dissuade people from crime. Simultaneously, we ignore the many programs that are effective in reintegrating large numbers of offenders into society because we are told only of their occasional failures and not of their successes. As we abandon hope for prevention and rehabilitation, we resign ourselves to a system based on retribution and incapacitation. The result is the inefficient use of limited resources to support unprecedented rates of imprisonment. This kind of justice cannot undo the negative effects of crime but it can bankrupt society, corrupt our sense of decency, and frustrate our progress as a nation. Public resignation to a "punish and confine" strategy presumes that punishment will change people for the better. All the evidence, however, says that encouragement, support, and development of new skills are required to bring about positive change in offenders.

Although few of us realize it, we are constantly encountering former offenders as we go about our daily lives. They have been reintegrated into society in spite of their experiences with the justice system. Some are rehabilitated due to the talents of the professionals who gave them the help and respect they needed to make the transition. Many more, however, continue to consume tax dollars because society and practitioners take an attitude of "millions for punishment but not one cent for treatment or assistance!" The cost of this attitude is too enormous to be tolerated by a society that cherishes human rights and financial conservatism.

My interactions with students, practitioners, and citizens were critical in culling the available material into the concise form it takes in this book. I cannot enter a correctional facility within a hundred miles of my home without encountering former students. Listening to their thoughts about their training encouraged me to eliminate many frills. Students have also taught me to be succinct in my analyses of the processes that create and perpetuate the problems of corrections. This is not achieved by neglect of material or perspectives, but rather by avoiding unnecessary glitz. This book directly addresses the most crucial questions and concerns of the field while challenging the stereotypes that guide our current policies. The correctional issues that trouble and intrigue us, the conundrums that baffle us, and the ideological details over which we argue provide a framework for future analysis and insights.

The book contains several unique features designed to encourage critical thought among readers. A series of ethical dilemmas are presented with sensitizing questions that cut to the core of the dilemmas faced in modern corrections. Entitled "Ethics on the Line," these vignettes are based on cases faced by professionals that have been altered just enough to assure the anonymity of the participants. Many are amalgams of remarkably similar stories told by different friends and acquaintances. They underscore the difficulties of practitioners as they simultaneously strive to minimize harm, remain faithful to both agency policy and personal conscience, and protect the interests of self, agency, and client. Calm consideration of such choices in a text allows readers to more fully prepare themselves to deal with similar dilemmas later, in more confused and hectic professional settings.

Policy also is given special treatment in features that bring practical and moral correctional issues into focus. Sections entitled "Policy Matters!" help readers focus attention on the consequences of our search for efficiency and fairness. All corrections texts point out the contradictions between retribution–punishment and treatment–reintegration. But this idea must be taken a step further: the main contradiction lies in the conflicts between the need to be efficient and the desire to assure justice. The situations described in "Policy Matters!" highlight the points at which these goals collide most dramatically, while stimulating readers to think critically. They also encourage readers to respect, if not accept, perspectives distinct from their own.

"Comparative Views" describe particular aspects of corrections in other nations. They illustrate the range of responses to crime found in modern cultures. Many suggest alternatives to those used in our society; others simply provide a context for examining the beliefs and values on which corrections can be based.

These insets broaden readers' comprehension of how culture and human nature affect the control of socially injurious behavior.

Special care has been taken to assure that these boxed features inform readers without distracting from the flow of the text's core material. All are designed to elucidate the book's central themes, and each may be characterized as a critical thinking exercise. I invite instructors to employ them as stepping-off points for writing assignments and class discussions.

As with all such ventures, this book owes its existence to many people, only a few of whom can be named here. My wife Carla was essential to the project. Not only did her love and support give me the strength to finish this book but her insights and criticism were invaluable to the quality of the final product. A Unit Supervisor for the state parole division who handled sex offender and super-intensive supervision caseloads for ten years, Carla was my professional advisor and proofreader as well as friend, lover, and confidante. Carol Rowe, Waveland co-owner and editor, also deserves much of the credit. Her positive attitude, consistent support, and erudite critiques contributed much to the final product. She knows more about criminal justice than do many professors and is one of the most delightful people I have ever met. Her husband Neil, Waveland publisher, also made many contributions to the production process. Along with many others on the Waveland team, he is an unsung hero of the creative process that led to the book's publication. Karen Chapman, Parole Supervisor, and the staff of the Denton District Parole Office made direct and indirect contributions as well. Above all, however, I must acknowledge the influence of the many students, correctional professionals, and reformed felons who have taught me so much over the years and to whom this work is dedicated.

The Goals of Correctional Policy

Corrections is the term used to describe the set of agencies created to control the behavior of people accused or convicted of a criminal offense. The goals and methods of the jails, prisons, probation departments, and parole agencies that make up our correctional system are the product of political processes that reflect society's moral and practical concerns. They are also the product of our beliefs about what constitutes fair and efficient social control at a particular time.[1]

Social control is any set of methods designed to encourage or to force people to obey norms. Crime control is just one area of social control. Families, peers, and communities have much more impact on individual behavior than could any criminal justice agency or policy. The criminal justice system is the last resort for social control in a democracy. It is a bureaucratic approach designed for use only after all other control systems have failed. Because criminal justice agencies have absolute power over the life and liberty of citizens, they must be closely regulated if freedom is to be preserved.

The belief that crime is one of the biggest threats to our society makes social control an increasingly important political issue.[2] It affects all elements of the criminal justice system: the police who arrest offenders, the courts that decide guilt or innocence, and the four types of correctional agencies that administer confinement, supervision, and treatment. Jails, prisons, probation, and parole agencies are spread across local, state, and federal jurisdictions and are a vital part of the criminal justice process.

Society's long struggle with how to handle criminals is part of an ongoing attempt to balance efficiency and fairness. Efficiency concerns focus on how to keep society as safe as possible from law violators at minimum cost to taxpayers. Fairness is a fundamental value that is basic to our morality and sense of justice. Tension between the demands of fairness and efficiency lies at the base of most complaints against the justice system. These goals will always be in conflict because no process designed and operated by humans can ever be completely fair and efficient. The process is only as good as the people who work in it. Many of the requirements of fairness, such as thorough trials, are inefficient and many attempts to be efficient strike people as unfair. These conflicts affect every aspect of criminal justice but are most obvious in the processes of sentencing and punishing offenders.

To fully understand corrections, one must be familiar with (a) its content, the components that make up the system; (b) its context, the situation in which it operates; and (c) its goals or mission. The many interrelated components of corrections are discussed in the chapters that follow. Here we will look at the context and the goals of modern corrections.

Defining the Study of Corrections

Content	Criminal offenders; jails, prisons, probation/parole agencies, and their staffs
Context	The politics of a democracy; especially the legislative enactments that guide sentencing and control agency budgets
Goals	(1) Efficient crime control, low rates of recidivism, and public safety (2) Fair and thorough treatment of each person and case

---

THE POLITICAL CONTEXT OF CORRECTIONS

Government attempts at crime control in a democracy can never be extremely efficient for two reasons. First, democratic values stress the fair and equal treatment of individuals over efficient social control. Most social control issues are left to informal institutions like the family. The justice system is designed to deal only with the occasional failures of the family and community. Second, democracies assume that each citizen is law abiding until it is proven otherwise. Authoritarian governments make the opposite assumption and have highly efficient social control systems because all citizens are under constant suspicion.

It is vital to understand that correctional agencies have little real control over their own activities. Agency resources, workloads, and priorities are set by politicians. Police and prosecutors decide what kinds of offenders will be handled by the courts. Working under rules set by legislatures, trial courts set the type and length of correctional control an offender will experience. The executive branch appoints the policymakers within most correctional agencies. The agencies must then handle the offenders assigned to them by courts in the manner dictated by the legislatures that control them. Legislative control is exercised in three ways: (1) designing sentencing structures for the courts, (2) describing each agency's legal powers and duties, and (3) setting each agency's budget. In addition, appellate courts interpret legislative enactments and apply them to agency activities. While legislatures often stress efficient crime control and manage the government budget, the courts strive to assure fairness. Thus, the tension between fairness and efficiency is constant. The balance is tipped toward one or the other, depending on the methods favored at a particular time or the groups that have the power to influence policy.

DEFINING MODERN CORRECTIONAL GOALS

Most correctional agencies are designed to control and to punish offenders. Attempts to change offenders' behavior are secondary to these goals. Control makes the public feel safer, and punishment appeals to the current sense of fairness. Even so, many voices emphasize that reforming offenders is more cost effective in the long run. Like fairness and efficiency, the contradiction between punishment and reform is at the core of many of the problems faced by the correctional process. Punishment may be fair, but reform offers the greatest hope of long-term efficiency. To illuminate this contradiction, we will outline the difference between punishment and discipline in changing behavior.

Punishment means to inflict a penalty for wrongdoing by deliberately causing someone to experience pain. It is usually justified as a method of assuring justice and satisfying the emotions of those who are injured or offended by an act. While punishment can sometimes help to shape behavior, usually it is resented and results in bitterness toward those felt to be responsible for it. People act on the basis of their own perceptions and beliefs rather than on the basis of what society believes. We must therefore look at the world through the eyes of the offender if we are to change his or her behavior. While we see punishment as just, offenders usually feel victimized by it and may use their anger to justify further criminality. The experience of imprisonment simply confirms and intensifies their beliefs. Even though such a reaction results from distorted thinking, it is nonetheless seen as valid by the offender and can provide a basis for further crime. Punishment satisfies demands for justice but is often very costly in the long run. Punishment is also a poor method of shaping behavior because it does not address the cause of the criminal act. It has little impact on motivation beyond creating fear and thus merely teaches the person to avoid the cause of the pain (i.e., the police or mainstream society), to rationalize his or her behavior, or to "stubbornly do nothing."[3] Rewards, on the other hand, actually (re)organize the emotional centers of the brain that motivate behavior and are thus much more powerful in controlling behavior.[4]

To be truly efficient, corrections must assure that offenders learn the kind of self-control required for a productive life. This is a matter of discipline. *Discipline* is training designed to assure obedience to a set of rules. It instills the sort of self-control that assures law-abiding behavior. Being able to think about the long-term consequences of one's actions, to understand and appreciate the needs of others, and to respect society's rules are its key goals. Honesty with self and others is crucial to the development of self-discipline. So is respect for the rules one is expected to obey. Respect, in turn, is most easily achieved when loyalty and warmth toward the source of the rules are the dominant emotions. However, it is hard for people to be loyal, warm, and respectful to that which they have experienced primarily as a source of pain. Compare criminal punishment with the discipline provided by good parents.

Children get love and are provided with the necessities of life by their parents; punishment is a relatively unusual event. The parent-child relationship is based on warmth and support; punishment is accepted because it occurs in this context. Offenders, on the other hand, see the government or mainstream society as oppressors that deny them their dignity and freedom. Many believe their poverty, failed relationships, and other misfortunes are the result of their position in society and society's treatment of them. By the time they are processed by correctional agencies, they usually have a very negative attitude toward society.

Many will take issue with this view, claiming that democracies try to offer support to all citizens and to minimize oppression. While this may be true, it is irrelevant because the perception of the offender, not the truth of the situation, guides the offender's behavior. In the final analysis, we need to admit that we punish criminals to satisfy our own emotional and safety needs. In doing so we may actually be reducing our ability to bring their behavior into conformity with the law. Punishment may be fair since criminals have often committed heinous wrongs, but it is inefficient when it weakens our ability to establish self-discipline in offenders.

The impulse to punish is undeniably strong. Most people feel that wrongs must be repaid. Devoting large amounts of time, money, and effort to changing the behavior of offenders would deprive us of the sense of justice that punishment affords. It could also be defined as unjust because what is spent on offenders could have been used to help law-abiding citizens. Many Americans argue, for example, that convicts should not get job-skills training for free when law-abiding citizens have to pay for it. The *principle of least eligibility* asserts that offenders should never receive any service or product that is not equally available to nonoffenders. Offenders should be placed in circumstances less comfortable than those of our poorest citizens according to this view.[5] The opposing position, sometimes called *normalization*, maintains that offenders should be treated as much like ordinary people as possible except for the deprivation of liberty implied by their sentence.[6] The idea of approximating normality in prison in an attempt to teach offenders to behave responsibly reduced Missouri's recidivism from 33% to 19% in a six-year trial period.[7]

Punishment requires that the status of the offender be reduced in some way; it often drives offenders out of society as outcasts. By lowering the status of the offender and making him or her a deprived outcast, we achieve a form of fairness known as *retributive justice*. An alternative approach, *restorative justice*, tries to assure that the situation of the offender, victim, and community are better off after the crime than they were before the crime. This approach focuses more on preventing future crimes than responding to those of the past.[8] Most restorative justice programs are designed for community-based agencies because of their emphasis on restitution. This has resulted in problems for some departments due to the tendency of officers to resist change and the new routines and power structures that come with it.[9]

To be efficient, corrections must put offenders back into society as productive citizens. This often requires that we improve their status or skills through the development of self-discipline or through other means, so that they have a reason to seek society's approval. However, helping offenders strikes many people as unfair. They view the help as a reward for violating the law and feel that taxpayers are being forced to correct someone else's mistakes. This is the root of the contradiction between punishment and treatment that has plagued corrections for more than two hundred years.

Ethics on the Line
The Media and the Public's View of Crime and Corrections

The media stresses rare and dramatic types of crime, such as shootouts and serial murders, while ignoring more common offenses like burglary and spouse abuse, because: (1) only unusual events are considered newsworthy, and (2) violent street crimes are simple but dramatic and therefore can easily be described in quick newscast formats. Further, communications technology is so efficient that crimes from all over the nation get instant and detailed coverage. The focus on especially heinous crimes causes a higher level of fear than is appropriate and leaves viewers with the impression that these acts are common and widespread. Even coverage of the executions of unusual killers dwarfs that of more typical death cases.[10] Media attention to murder stories increased 473% between 1993 and 2001 while the number of homicides dropped 33%.[11]

Similar dynamics affect media portrayals of corrections. It is the media's job to investigate the failures of government agencies and to expose their abuses or incompetence. It is rare, however, that publicity is given to their successes. While the fact of recidivism deserves discussion, publicizing the fact that a successful member of the community is a former prison inmate might destroy that person's future. On the other hand, the failure to recognize the successful reintegration of offenders leads to a biased view of the correctional process. This leads to a loss of faith in treatment in particular, and in the entire justice system in general, that may not always be justified by the facts. The same is true of most public agencies: when they do right, few notice, but when they do wrong, few forget. Correctional agencies are working to improve their relationships with the media while assuring security and avoiding undue costs by establishing policies to allow limited media access to facilities and inmates. This is done by creating specific policies and public information offices while sensitizing officials to the need for interaction with the media. Much remains to be done in this area however, if the public is to be properly informed about correctional norms and issues.[12]

Questions to Consider

1. How much fear of crime is based on sensationalized media reports? Does the fact that we hear so much about unusually brutal crimes occurring all over the world distort our view of reality? How are these trends likely to affect crime-control policies?

2. How much effort should agencies devote to publicizing their successes? What could be done to interest the media in more typical, and therefore policy-relevant, events?

MORAL AND UTILITARIAN VIEWS
OF THE CORRECTIONAL MISSION

Correctional priorities change with the dominant beliefs of society but can be roughly grouped into two categories. *Moral arguments* focus on the search for fairness and try to compensate for the wrongs done by crime. *Utilitarian arguments* focus on the practical goal of reducing crime while spending as little as possible. Moral arguments tend to look backward in time to the crime and are concerned with fairness rather than the future behavior of the offender. They are matters of conscience that cannot be scientifically evaluated. Efficiency is of secondary concern to those who rely mainly on moral arguments. Utilitarian arguments, on the other hand, look forward to the future safety of citizens and the costs of various practices. Because they strive for efficiency, they can be scientifically evaluated. Most definitions of the correctional mission can be classified as primarily utilitarian or moral in theme.[13]

The power of various arguments for what should be the main goal of corrections changes with society's social and political climate. Economic factors are a critical influence on public opinion, but so are political ideologies, media influences, and the amount of fear created by crime. This means that agency practices are more closely tied to politics than to the science of behavior change.[14] However, the currently favored ideas of science are often used to justify selected practices, and utilitarian rhetoric is often employed to justify what are really moral goals. For example, it has been argued that many deterrence supporters actually favor retribution but find the idea of deterrence more socially acceptable because it is a utilitarian goal. This is part of the reason that deterrence remains popular despite its failure to reduce significantly many types of crime.[15]

A number of approaches to corrections are commonly accepted by Western societies. Each emerged at a particular point in history and takes a different view of human nature and the causes of crime. Each is based on a specific set of moral or practical values and leads to a different set of concerns for the legislatures and courts that guide the activities of correctional agencies. We now need to evaluate each of them in terms of how they contribute to the correctional process.

Retribution

Probably the most ancient rationale for punishment, retribution, calls for inflicting pain on the offender that is equal to, or slightly greater than, the harm that has been done to the victim. Retribution is based on the desire for revenge. Its main idea is to "even the score" with the offender. Those who believe in this view often feel that fairness demands the life of the murderer in exchange for that of the victim. In theory, retaliation-in-kind may also have deterrent value, but assuring that the offender's welfare is less than that of the victim's is the goal of retribution. Society's responsibility is to make sure that the punishment does not excessively outweigh the harm done by a crime and that inequalities do not result from differences in the power or popularity of the victim or offender.[16]

Critics of retribution believe that it draws attention away from attempts to determine what policies and practices are most effective in reducing crime. They argue that while people's sense of fairness may be served, the social and economic price of retribution is far too high. Indeed, the costs of punishment do outweigh those suffered by victims.[17] Further, beliefs about what is "fair" punishment vary with personal and social characteristics so there is rarely widespread agreement as to the appropriate level of punishment for specific crimes.[18] The philosophy of retribution does not claim to protect society or change behavior. It cannot be evaluated by science because its arguments are entirely moral.[19] Many people see the idea of "vengeance" as too primitive an idea to guide modern correctional practices. The philosophy of "just deserts" uses similar moral arguments but replaces retaliation as the underlying principle.

Just Deserts

The *just deserts* philosophy maintains that punishment should be used to assure a sense of fairness in society. While similar to the idea of retribution, it stresses social justice rather than revenge. The moral justification for just deserts demands equal penalties for similar crimes. The emphasis is on making punishment certain and consistent, but concern is focused on society's sense of fairness rather than the status of the victim or offender. In practice, upper and lower limits are set on punishment, and its nature and magnitude can be affected by the particular needs of both victim and offender.[20] Both retribution and just deserts use punishments thought to have deterrent value.

Deterrence

Deterrence tries to use the threat of punishment to influence how people make decisions. It is a utilitarian complement to retribution and just deserts that attempts to minimize crime by influencing our rational, conscious choices. If people know that certain behavior will be punished, it is assumed that they will avoid that behavior. Laws should therefore be designed to guide people's decisions in directions that will benefit society. To be an effective deterrent, punishment must be a relatively *certain* result of committing a crime, be administered *swiftly* after the crime has occurred, and be reasonably *severe*. If punishment is not relatively certain, then offenders can always hope to avoid being caught. If a long period of time intervenes between crime and punishment, then the cause of the punishment will be blamed on factors other than the criminal act. If punishment is too mild, then it will not discourage the offender from future crime. If punishment is too severe, it may inspire rebellion in offenders or society. The maximum effect is achieved when most criminals are quickly caught and punished. It is the potential offender's perception of the certainty and swiftness of punishment that is critical to its effects, not the objective reality of the situation.[21] Even long-standing supporters of this philosophy agree that it is the certainty of punishment that accounts for most of the impact on crime rates, not the severity of the punishment. While severity is easily altered by political action, the costs of such policies should be carefully considered prior to their implementation.[22]

Deterrence-based policies try to influence individual choices by giving people a reason to want to obey the law. Even though they could profit from crime, it is hoped that they will recognize that the costs of punishment will outweigh any gain. The fact that criminals obtain many rewards from crime before being caught can undermine attempts at deterrence.[23] Social rewards for crime may outweigh any reasonable legal punishments, and imprisonment is even a method of earning status in some subcultures. More important, both deterrence and retribution assume that (1) crime results from a rational calculation of the expected costs and benefits of various acts; and (2) this calculation can be affected by legal penalties. Deterrence is not effective in controlling many types of street crime because its assumptions are often false.[24] Many crimes, especially violent ones, are impulsive, unplanned acts in which no mental calculations are performed. People are most affected by their perception of the certainty of being caught and punished, but they are more likely to believe that others will be caught, rather than themselves.

Personal experience with a behavior weakens the perception of certainty that is crucial to deterrence. A person who has used drugs, for example, is less likely to fear arrest than one who has never used.[25]

Similarly, the more present oriented a person's thinking, the less likely he or she is to respond appropriately to deterrence.[26] An inability to think in terms of future consequences is a common trait among street criminals, making them less likely than the average citizen to be deterred by harsh penalties. The distorted thought patterns of many offenders lead them to believe that they have the "street smarts" to avoid being caught, which means deterrence is unlikely to affect them while it may be more effective with nonoffenders.[27] On the other hand, there is evidence that premeditated crimes like burglary and planned violence can be deterred by increasing the certainty and severity of punishment.[28] A review of domestic-violence studies shows that the mandatory arrest policies reduce subsequent assaults by 30%.[29]

There are two types of deterrence. ***General deterrence*** punishes one offender in an effort to discourage others from committing crimes. Its goal is to persuade potential criminals to avoid crime by making an example of known offenders. It

Chain gains illustrate how deterrence and retribution may be combined. Inmates shackled together cannot work efficiently and often have medical problems as a result. The practice is degrading and painful to those on whom it is inflicted. It is popular in many states as a method of punishing teens and adults because it sends the kind of message desired by deterrence advocates to the offenders and those who see them. Critics note that the practice has been, and still is, associated with abuses and racism even though several states currently use it.

does not attempt to change the known offender. The idea of general deterrence suggests that well-publicized punishments create fear in observers that discourages them from committing crimes. *Specific deterrence* suggests that punishing a particular offender will discourage that individual from committing crimes in the future. Its goal is to teach offenders that crime leads to unpleasant consequences.[30] Most discussions of deterrence focus on the general form, and its advocates seem to assume that most people would commit crimes if they did not fear punishment. This is probably true for some offenses such as traffic infractions but appears less valid an assumption as more serious acts are considered.

Boundary Setting

Societies have always identified some behaviors as criminal in order to set boundaries that distinguish one group from another. Members of a society cannot feel united as a "we" unless there is some readily identifiable "they" with whom to contrast themselves. By defining some acts as criminal, a group sets itself apart from others and limits the behavior of its members. This is known as the ***boundary-setting*** function of punishment. Those who break the law are cast out in order to alert others to what the rules are and which ones are most important at a given point in time. Punishment reinforces the moral standards that define the group and are reflected in its laws.[31] It sanitizes society by removing criminal members. This philosophy supplies one of the mechanisms by which retribution and deterrence operate.

Punishment helps to demonstrate that certain behaviors must be avoided by those who want to remain full-fledged members of society. It lets people know

Punishment segregates and isolates those who break the law.

what acts they must avoid if they want others to accept them as "good citizens." If laws are not upheld, the group itself is endangered because its boundaries are unclear. Public rejection of criminals creates and maintains the boundaries of respectable society. Criminals are outcasts from the group or society. Under this philosophy, the punishment of crime is important to assuring unity and stability in society.[32] Boundary setting focuses attention on society's welfare rather than on the behavior of known or potential offenders. Because offenders become outcasts, however, it may also have some deterrent value. Boundary setting and deterrence are not concerned with the victims of crime. This is the goal of restitution.

Restitution

Restitution repays the victim for material and financial losses suffered as a result of crime; its concern is more with the victim than with the offender. Restitution focuses on material losses, while retribution is more concerned with suffering and moral symbolism. In cases involving property crimes, restitution requires the offender to restore the victim's property to its original value or to pay for it. In cases of physical injury, restitution applies to medical costs and counseling needs. Restitution can be accomplished through civil suits, arbitration, or criminal sentences and is often required as a condition of probation or parole.[33]

Victims of violence can usually apply for compensation from a special fund operated by the state. Offenders are required to make payments into that fund as part of their probation or parole. Money from fines and tax dollars are also placed in these restitution funds. Payments to the victim may be handled by the local prosecutor or a special state agency. Regardless of which agency handles the money, the process assures that there will be no contact between victim and offender.[34] When restitution is the main goal in prosecuting a criminal case, community-based sentences are preferred because they allow offenders to maintain their earning potential. When the crime is nonviolent, financial arrangements are usually made through the court or probation office. Paying restitution is common as part of probation or parole, but the ability to pay varies widely among offenders. Judges are most likely to assign restitution when the costs of the crime are easily and clearly translated into a specific sum of money. Offenders who must repay a business are more likely to complete this aspect of their sentence than those whose debt is to an individual.[35]

Restitution is often used to punish minor crimes. When there is no readily identifiable victim, service to the community can be used as a form of restitution. *Community service* is a form of restitution because "victimless" crimes disturb the peace and order of society, lower the quality of life, or offend public morality. The labor required for community service is usually hard and requires no special skills. In some jurisdictions the labor is controlled by the government, while in others offenders are given a list of charities from which they can choose. In all cases, this labor is devoted to jobs that would not otherwise be accomplished due to lack of funds. While restitution helps to keep offenders busy and tired, it has not been shown to reduce recidivism. Nevertheless, advocates of restitution hope that knowing the cost of repayment will deter some offenders while others may develop ties to the law-abiding community through community service.

Incapacitation

Incapacitation prevents offenders from committing further crimes by making it physically impossible for them to do so. This is particularly important when serious crimes, like serial murder, are involved. In Western societies incapacitation is now achieved primarily by imprisonment. However, this ignores the fact that prison inmates commit crimes against one another and against prison staff. More important, this approach overlooks the fact that many will be more dangerous when they leave prison than when they entered it.[36]

Incapacitation is a utilitarian approach to preventing crime that "warehouses" offenders in the belief that age and/or deterrence will discourage them from continuing their criminal careers when released. Many studies suggest that it is the main, or perhaps even the only, utilitarian effect we can expect from incarceration.[37] Incapacitation is often justified as the surest means of safeguarding society from habitual offenders. A Florida study showed that the incapacitative effects of lengthy sentences on repeat offenders reduce slightly the incidences of rape, robbery, assault, burglary, larceny, and auto theft.[38] A national study suggested that the incapacitative effects of imprisonment may help reduce the rate at which women are killed by husbands and lovers.[39] Virtually all who have empirically studied this issue feel the relationship between recidivism and incarceration is so complex that policies based on broad generalities should be avoided.

Incapacitation often results in warehousing offenders.

Legal Approaches to Incapacitation. The need for incapacitation is based on the idea that a small percentage of chronic offenders are responsible for much of the nation's serious crime. Habitual offenders, who have been convicted of two or more felonies, can be incapacitated with special laws allowing increased punishment. ***Habitual offender laws*** have been used for decades throughout the nation. However, up to one-third of those incarcerated under such laws are "false positives" who would not have actually continued their criminal career if left in society.[40] The financial and moral implications of this fact disturb many analysts who believe we lack the ability to predict future criminality that these laws presume.[41]

Habitual offender laws may be used for any set of felony convictions. In contrast, ***sentence enhancements*** add one to ten years to a sentence only if the offender has one or more prior convictions for a particular crime. Sentence enhancement is most often used for drunken driving, sex offenses, and violent crimes. Enhancement may also be used for certain aggravating circumstances, such as use of a firearm or victimizing a child or elderly person.

Habitual offender laws are designed to cut the crime rate by incapacitating serious recidivists. Being convicted under a habitual offender statute is treated as a distinct offense in forty-three states. The offender is sentenced for both the third (or additional) felony and for being a habitual offender. The decision as to when to use habitual offender laws is generally left to the prosecutor. There is evidence that prosecutors are often haphazard in their use of this incapacitation strategy. Serious criminals may escape the additional penalty, while petty offenders who present little threat to the public are imprisoned for long periods under habitual offender laws.[42]

"Three-strikes" laws are a modern version of habitual offender laws that handle a variety of felonies in the same manner. Sentences under these laws are often considerably longer than those required by the older habitual offender laws. California was the first state to enact such a law in 1994. Studies show that the law has little effect on crime and is not used consistently by different prosecutors.[43] In November 2002 (*Lockyer v. Andrade*) the American Civil Liberties Union argued before the U.S. Supreme Court that a potential life sentence for petty theft under the "three strikes" law constitutes "cruel and unusual" punishment.[44]

Sentences of life without parole have a similar intent; they are designed to incapacitate the most dangerous offenders by assuring that they are never released back into society. Only four states—Kansas, New Mexico, and Texas (death penalty states) and Alaska (a non-death-penalty state)—do not have life-without-parole laws.[45] Federal law also provides this penalty for certain types of murders. Life without parole differs from other life sentences in two ways. First, most life sentences permit parole after a period of years has been served. Second, parole boards and legislatures often change the rules about how various forms of early release are to be used. Loopholes in these laws have led to the release of some very dangerous offenders. Life-without-parole sentences reduce the likelihood of such problems. In a few states it is a special sentence in itself. More commonly, trial court judges control if and when an offender will be eligible for parole with much the same effect.

Sentence enhancements, habitual offender laws, and three-strikes legislation deal only with the sentences received by convicted offenders. Many jurisdictions allow the *preventive detention* of habitual and/or heinous offenders before they have been convicted to assure they commit no further crimes. Those who have committed a crime while out on bail may also be kept in jail under this approach. Sometimes offenders who seem likely to commit further serious crimes can be denied bail. More commonly, their bail can be set high enough to assure confinement prior to trial. Though some feel that this is a form of economic discrimination against the poor, the practice has been upheld by the Supreme Court for both juveniles and adults.[46] While legal, the efficiency of this approach to crime control is seriously questioned by many experts.

The Prediction Problem

All laws targeting repeat offenders presume that we can predict which offenders will commit new crimes with a reasonable degree of accuracy. At present we do not have the ability to accurately predict who will offend again and who will not. This is both a moral problem and a utilitarian issue that results from overconfidence in the ability of science and law to predict human behavior. Many scholars refer to it as the "prediction problem." This is particularly a problem for presumptive sentencing structures which rely on a combination of prior record and offense seriousness. Research is increasingly casting doubt on the ability of these variables to accurately predict which offenders most need to be incapacitated.[47]

Certain types of offenders (e.g., forgers, drug addicts) are extremely likely to be recidivists, even though they are not especially dangerous. On the other hand, many who commit serious crimes (e.g., murderers) are often guilty of only one or a very few offenses.[48] Knowledge of such general patterns does not lead to accurate predictions of recidivism at the individual level. It is estimated that for every true recidivist jailed under preventive detention laws, two or three "false positives" are unnecessarily incarcerated.[49] Some may have been ending their criminal careers when last arrested. Our ability to predict who will commit further serious crimes is critical to both the efficiency and morality of incapacitation. The goal of incapacitation should be to select carefully those most likely to commit further serious crimes. The result of most legal incapacitation strategies, however, is a gross increase in the rate of imprisonment with little or no effect on the crime rate.[50]

Treatment–Reintegration

Correctional treatment is an attempt to convert offenders into law-abiding citizens. It is supported by the same utilitarian logic that urges efficient crime prevention. Treatment is the method of this approach, while reintegration into society as a taxpayer is the goal. Programs make prisons easier to manage, decrease recidivism, and improve the life quality of offenders, their families and their communities.[51]

Most treatment advocates believe that crime occurs because of some sort of mental, spiritual, educational, or vocational inadequacy in the offender. If the inadequacy is corrected, criminal behavior will cease. Crime is a symptom of some greater problem within the individual. The unique problems of the individual, not the act he or she has committed, are the focus of attention here. Therefore, the length of treatment cannot be set by law; it will vary with the individual and the circumstances. Changing behavior patterns generally requires the reeducation or

Correctional Philosophies		
Philosophy	**Focus**	**Goal**
Retribution	Inflicting pain on offender	Justice/revenge
Just deserts	Inflicting pain on offender	Social justice
General deterrence	Future behavior of potential offenders	Reduce crime by discouraging potential offenders from illegal acts
Specific deterrence	Future behavior of known offenders	Reduce crime by discouraging known offenders from illegal acts
Boundary setting	Definition of group and behavior required to assure membership; moral outrage at crime and desire for punishment	Deter crime and reinforce social stability through loss of group membership; create/enhance a sense of unity among citizens
Restitution	Financial compensation	Restore victims' welfare
Treatment–reintegration	Future behavior of known offenders	Reduce crime by changing offenders' behavior
Incapacitation	Offenders' ability to act	Enhance public safety by reducing number of people capable of crime

even resocialization of the offender. To do so however, requires programs that empower inmates rather than degrade them. This prerequisite for reintegration runs counter to the demands of retribution and offends many citizens' sense of justice. When the appropriate investment is made, however, such programs can be remarkably, though not entirely, successful.[52]

Some who favor this philosophy also take a deterministic view of the causes of crime. If crime is the result of social organization or inequalities, then society has a responsibility to help reintegrate offenders. Further complicating the issue is a growing body of data suggesting that the brains of offenders often differ from those of others in various ways ranging from abnormalities in areas critical to morality and judgment[53] to the influence of skull injuries[54] and genetic deficiencies.[55] Ignoring the free-will aspect of human behavior, however, is problematic; offenders must choose to avoid crime by changing the way they think and act. Criminal history is static but other factors influencing criminal behavior such as substance abuse, antisocial attitudes, and associations are changeable.[56] Offenders who want to change may be helped by treatment programs. Treatment is usually associated with science and efficiency, while punishment attempts to correct a wrong. These two views form the basis of most sentencing practices.

CORRECTIONAL DECISION MAKING

There have been two primary approaches used in setting goals for corrections. Each originated during a specific period of history and reflects the beliefs about human behavior, law, or science that were dominant at the time. Many contradictions within our modern justice system are due to their intermingling over the last century as laws, policies, and practices developed. The legal orientation is associated with the *justice model* that originated in the 1700s. It is the basis of the U.S. Constitution as well as attempts to control crime through deterrence. The *scientific model* or *"medical" model* grew out of attempts to improve the quality of human life that were associated with political reform movements in the late 1800s. By the 1940s its ideas had become central to most sentencing laws in the nation. This view was traditionally associated with liberalism. However, its scientific logic can be used by any ideology that seeks to justify its political goals, and this approach has been adopted by some conservatives. In the final analysis, its main goal is efficient crime control. The justice model regained popularity in the late 1970s, and many jurisdictions began to change their sentencing laws to reflect those values. Conservatives hoped it would make punishment harsher, while liberals believed it might end discrimination in sentencing. The current trend is to favor the sentencing practices recommended by the justice model, but most state laws still rely heavily on the scientific model.[57]

	Legal and Scientific Approaches to Corrections	
Criteria	**Legal Approach**	**Scientific Approach**
Core belief	Individuals are equal in their ability to make rational choices	Science can and should be used to solve human problems
Subject	Role of law and government in a free society	Causes of crime
Values	Justice and individual rights	Efficiency and public safety
Goal	Fair punishment	Prevention/reduction of future crime
Focus of Attention	Criminal Act	Criminal person
Preferred Method	Determinate sentences	Indeterminate sentences
Central Philosophy	Deterrence	Treatment/prevention

The Scientific Approach

The scientific model holds that the courts should judge each offender as a unique individual. This judgment can stress the offender's culpability, dangerousness, treatment needs, and/or other factors. This view suggests that some people are less able to avoid crime than others and thus questions the idea that crime is always a product of free will. Factors believed to cause criminality, such as slum environments and violent norms, are seen as diseaselike influences that can be identified and dealt with through scientific procedures. Supporters of this model note that most offenders will someday return to society. If they return as productive citizens, then everyone benefits. If not, taxpayers must again bear the costs of crime and imprisonment.[58] However, its more recent use has focused on the need to incapacitate certain especially dangerous offenders, such as sexual predators, permanently. In either case, the concerns of the scientific model focus on efficiency rather than on fairness.[59]

The scientific model argues that offenders should be sentenced on the basis of their backgrounds, psychological traits, and the circumstances of their crimes. Because each offender is unique, the level of danger posed and the amount of time required for treatment cannot be predicted solely on the basis of the crime for which he or she was convicted. Because people who have committed similar crimes may have very different reasons for and degrees of control over their behavior, they should not receive the same level of punishment. These views lie behind the use of indeterminate sentencing in the United States.[60]

Indeterminate Sentences. These sentences allow judges to sentence offenders to a broad range of years (e.g., 5 to 20). The minimum amount of time assigned is that needed for retribution and deterrence purposes. Part of the sentence may be served in prison, and the rest under supervision in the community. The offender's actual date of release is left to a parole board or to prison authorities, who use the inmate's previous record and prison behavior to set the length of incarceration. Release dates are also likely to be influenced by the degree of crowding in the state's prisons.[61]

The idea behind indeterminate sentencing is that punishment should be based on the dangerousness and treatment needs of the criminal rather than the type of offense. Indeterminate sentences were originally designed to make offenders "earn" their release through hard work at treatment; they also encourage inmates to obey the prison's rules. Very few prisons have enough guards to control their inmates physically. Sentencing structures, parole rules, and other procedures are therefore needed to encourage prisoners to cooperate with prison authorities. This same principle is behind the widespread practice of taking time off a prison sentence for good behavior. The credit earned toward early release is called "good time" and is set by the legislature in most states.[62]

Good-Time Laws. Laws that allow inmates to earn early release on parole through good behavior and hard work have been in use since the 1850s. The amount of "good time" awarded varies from state to state, but the concept is the same: a certain number of days are subtracted from inmate sentences for each month that they do not get in trouble with prison authorities. Drug offenders are the most likely to earn early release under such laws,[63] but others may also be eligible depending on how state laws are written. Good or "merit" time encourages offenders to follow prison rules and make prisons cheaper to run. Because good time can be adjusted to relieve crowding, it has become a popular "back door" for reducing prison populations. "Good time" reductions of sentences often increase as prisons become overcrowded and more costly to operate.[64] Inmates keep careful watch on such changes, but the public is rarely aware of them. Legislators can increase the length of criminal sentences to appear "tough" on crime, while at the same time changing good-time laws to relieve crowding.

Several states do not allow good time because they want to use a tougher approach to corrections. In other states, certain types of offenders who are felt to be especially dangerous cannot earn good time until half or more of their sentence has been served. Good-time laws, like indeterminate sentencing, are a result of the scientific model's emphasis on efficiency. They are, however, offensive to many who prefer the certainty of the justice model.

The tension between justice and efficiency is at the root of the two contradictory descriptions about what should be the top priority of corrections. The scientific model wants to achieve efficiency by treating each offender as a unique case, with the goal of returning that person to society as a productive citizen. The justice model, on the other hand, tries to assure that sentencing is fair, while demonstrating society's moral outrage against crime.

The Legal Approach

The legal approach is based on the justice model, which presumes that each person has a natural dignity and value that requires respect because they rationally choose each of their actions.[65] It argues that law should be used to encourage people to make socially desirable choices by using punishment to deter crime. This view assumes that people will act in largely selfish or even antisocial ways, unless they are threatened with consequences. Retribution and/or just deserts are seen as appropriate expressions of social beliefs that set boundaries for society. This model holds that people who commit similar crimes should receive similar punishments. The "seriousness" of the crime is the only relevant factor in justice-based sentencing. "Seriousness" is defined in terms of the offender's blameworthiness and the amount of harm done by an act. Past offenses are considered relevant because they reflect past attempts at deterrence and reintegration and thus affect blameworthiness. The focus of punishment is on the crime, not the criminal, as is the case with the scientific approach. Little or no attention is given to predictions of future behavior.[66] Justice model sentencing is based mainly on moral arguments and gives priority to fairness rather than efficiency. There are several ways in which this can be accomplished.

Determinate Sentences. Penalties are determined solely by the person's crime and prior record. Judges choose from a range of years set by the legislature. For example, burglary can be punished with a sentence of anywhere between two and five years. While one offender may get two years and others four or five years, each knows exactly how long he or she must serve when being sentenced. Only good time can reduce the length of an offender's sentence under this approach. This type of sentencing tries to fit the punishment to the crime and the offender's legal history. Its goal is to assure certainty about the level of punishment received by each offender. Five states have this type of sentence for at least some crimes. However, it is the least popular type of justice model sentence because it allows judges to use their personal discretion in deciding how much punishment each offense deserves.[67]

Mandatory Sentences.   These sentences give judges virtually no discretion. Everyone convicted of the same crime gets exactly the same sentence under this approach. Sentences are set at the moment of conviction under these laws. The

Under determinate sentencing, the judge handles each case as a unique event.

legislature controls the penalty for crimes punished with a mandatory sentence. Prosecutors gain power because they decide what offenders will be charged with what crimes. Most mandatory sentencing laws prohibit the use of suspended sentences and require imprisonment. They are most common for weapons and drug offenses but are also imposed for certain types of violent offenses in some states. This is the type of sentencing favored by a strict interpretation of the justice model.

Some states and the federal government require mandatory minimum sentences for certain crimes such as drug offenses and drunken driving. A recent study of people convicted in Kansas City shows that the imprisonment of drug offenders actually increases their future criminality,[68] while an Arizona study found that these laws had no impact on DUIs because the laws failed to address the "irrational nature" of the crime. This report criticized the legal approach to drunken driving as ineffective and recommended a return to scientific sentencing.[69] Mandatory minimums for drug offenses have increased the proportion of minorities in federal prisons without impacting drug use.[70] Other studies suggest that mandatory sentences may have a small impact on index crimes and domestic homicides, however.[71]

The main difference between mandatory and determinate sentencing is who has the power to set a sentence—legislators or judges. Determinate sentences give this power to the judge who has heard all the facts relevant to the particular case, so that each case can be handled as a unique event. Mandatory sentences are set by legislators who look only at the type of crime; the unique features of the offender or situation are deliberately ignored by this approach. Presumptive sentences are determined by a commission and are a compromise between determinate and mandatory sentencing.

Presumptive Sentences.   The federal system has used presumptive sentencing guidelines since 1987; they are also employed by a growing number of states. Federal sentencing guidelines are set by a commission of judges appointed by the president. The commission began by setting a narrow range of time to be served based on the average of sentences assigned for each crime under the older indeterminate structure. This range is based on (1) the severity of the offense for which the person was convicted and (2) salient factors in that person's legal history that predict recidivism. *Salient factors* are determined by the commission and reflect research on legally permissible predictors of recidivism. (While race and economic status contribute to scientific attempts to predict criminality, their use in setting punishments is illegal.) Number of prior arrests and convictions, age at first incarceration, addiction to drugs, and similar facts are assigned values and summed to a salient factor score, which is then used to select a sentence from the guidelines. Judges assign sentences within these guidelines. Exceptions to guidelines may be permitted if the judge finds aggravating or mitigating factors. All exceptions must be explained in writing by the trial judge and approved by the commission. The commission can reject the exception and force the judge to resentence the offender within the guidelines.[72] In many states with presumptive sentencing the legislature controls the sentencing commission, but a few put this power in the hands of the governor or courts.

Truth-in-Sentencing Laws.   These laws assure that people convicted of certain offenses must serve a minimum amount of the sentence before they can be

Types of Sentences

Type of Sentence	Who Sets Release Date?	Amount and Location of Discretion
Determinate	Trial court judge	Judges work within limits set by legislature
Indeterminate	Parole or prison authorities	Wide discretion for judge, legislature and parole board
Mandatory	Legislature	The legislature has complete control
Presumptive	Sentencing commission	Very little if decision is within guidelines; exceptions must be justified in writing and approved by commission

released. Most deal only with violent offenders. Like other justice model sentences, truth-in-sentencing laws reduce the discretion of judges and parole authorities. Legislatures determine how much time will be served, and there is little room for individualized sentences. Most require that people convicted of certain offenses serve 50% or more of the maximum sentence before being considered for release. Some deny or limit "good time" for certain violent offenses. The Massachusetts version is probably the broadest yet; it requires all felons to serve at least two-thirds of their sentence before becoming eligible for release. An evaluation of the law's impact, however, found that it wasted prison resources on nonviolent drug offenders and inflated the percentage of imprisoned minorities.[73] The *Violent Crime Control and Law Enforcement Act of 1994* provided financial incentives for states to pass truth-in-sentencing laws. By 1998 27 states and the District of Columbia had done so. Today, most of the nation's violent offenders must serve 85% of their sentence as a result of these incentive grants.[74]

The main problem with these new sentencing laws is economic. Some experts warn that the inflexibility of these laws could drive states into bankruptcy by forcing them to expand their prison systems.[75] It is also feared that the overcrowding caused by these laws could result in the early release of dangerous offenders who were sentenced before this trend took hold, as happened in Florida.[76] In Virginia, however, the anticipated population expansion problems never materialized, even though parole was abolished and inmates have to serve 85% of their sentence. The national decline in crime rates that occurred just as the new law took effect is thought to be responsible for these findings. The law's coverage was also somewhat narrower than that of states that had adopted earlier versions of truth-in-sentencing laws.[77] A few states limit sentences to the amount of time that the state believes it can afford to impose. However, this approach has not been popular with those who want to "get tough on crime." The combination of increasing the length of criminal sentences and cutting government budgets leads many to fear the long-term impact of these new laws.[78] To what extent public concepts of "justice" and fear of crime will lead to longer periods of confinement is a related, but separate, question.

The Impact of Justice Model Sentencing

Mandatory, presumptive, and determinate sentences are all attempts to assure equality in sentencing. Each of these approaches to sentencing attempts to assure fair punishment. Treatment is not taken into account in any of them; their focus is entirely on making sure that punishments "fit the crime." They are currently popular because they make early release difficult and are thought to be harsher than the indeterminate approach. Each came about in response to public demands for tougher punishment, and thus far they seem to be accomplishing this goal to some extent.[79] The average violent offender released from prison in 1996 had been sentenced to serve 85 months in prison but was paroled in less than 50 months. However, increased severity in sentencing adds far more nonviolent offenders to American prisons than it does violent ones.[80] Justice model sentences have extended that to an average of 88 months under federally supported truth-in-sentencing grants to states.[81] Prison spending has increased nearly as fast as the overall rate of imprisonment as well. Offenders are serving a larger percentage of significantly longer sentences in prison as a result of these laws but also have higher recidivism rates than those incarcerated under indeterminate sentences.[82]

Supporters of the justice model believe that longer prison sentences are partly responsible for the drop in the crime rate noted in the mid-1990s.[83] Most studies suggest that this drop was due to factors unrelated to sentencing, such as the number of young people in society, improved economic opportunities, better policing methods, greater community cooperation with police, and tougher gun laws.[84] Some studies have shown that these new laws have caused prison populations to swell,[85] while others claim that no such effect can be shown.[86] There is also some evidence that prison crowding continues to influence sentencing decisions despite these new laws.[87] A recent examination of federal mandatory minimum sentences found that patterns of sentencing varied with the specific law and type of offense.[88] In general, most authorities find that these new laws have had little effect on crime[89] and are more the product of conservative lobby groups, media hype, and public fear than the realities of crime.[90] Many states are questioning their usefulness, and some have begun to reverse the trend toward severe sentencing for financial reasons. [91]

CONTRADICTIONS AMONG CORRECTIONAL GOALS

Different methods of sentencing develop out of different justifications for punishment, which, in turn, reflect fundamentally different beliefs about human nature. However, some very serious contradictions exist between the basic goals of sentencing and those of the correctional process. Polls show that the public believes in retribution and deterrence but also feels that offenders should receive treatment.[92] There are few contradictions between incapacitation, deterrence, and retribution. Each is oriented mainly to punishment rather than "correction" and relies on the infliction of pain. While compatible with one another, these justifications of punishment conflict with the requirements of treatment and thus frustrate attempts to reintegrate offenders back into society. This is the most fundamental contradiction in corrections; punishment and reintegration cannot be combined in a way that will satisfy the demands of both efficiency and justice.

It is practically impossible to develop the kind of environment required for treatment while inflicting misery on people. The practical contradictions between punishment and reintegration are well illustrated by their effects on the offender's status. Punishment drives offenders out of society as outcasts; treatment pulls them back into society. Retribution reduces the status of the offender or deprives him or her in some way. Reintegration requires improving the status or skills of the offender, usually through academic or vocational training. The principle of least eligibility argues that convicts should not get a free education while law-abiding citizens have to work for one. Treatment advocates note that if we do not help offenders to become productive, they will continue to commit crimes after being released.[93] Our sense of justice demands punishment, but our desire for efficiency seeks reintegration.

Growth of the U.S. Prison Population[94]

The graph shows the rate of incarceration (the number of persons imprisoned per 100,000 people in the general population) for the U.S. prison population serving sentences of one year or more from 1925–2001. Note the decreases in incarceration associated with World War II (1941–1945) and the period around 1970. Note the dramatic increases in prison populations since 1980, even more pronounced in the late '80s as new sentencing laws took effect. Only at the end of the century does the rate decline again and then level off. The number of people held in U.S. prisons has increased more than 100% since 1985, an unprecedented jump in the nation's rate of incarceration.

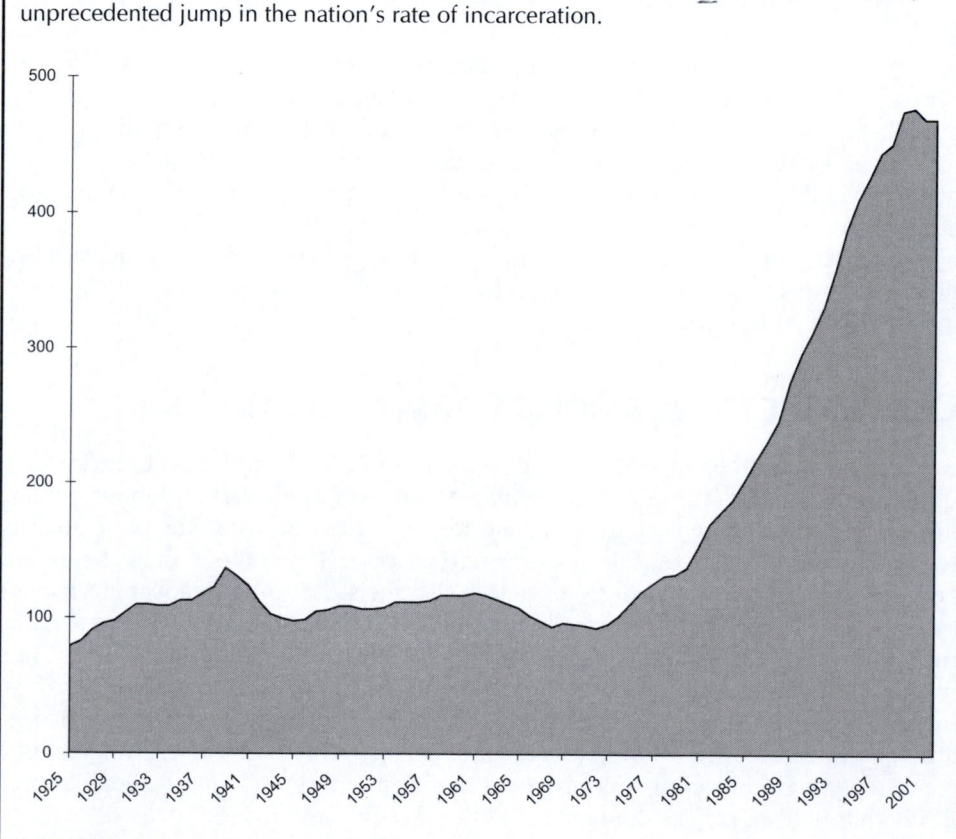

SUMMARY

Political processes based on attitudes about punishment at a particular time determine correctional goals. Attitudes are the product of beliefs about crime and human nature supported by the science and ethics of an era. Just as we laugh at the beliefs in demonic possession that guided crime control in the 1500s, future societies will probably find many of our beliefs absurd.

Understanding the linkages between the assumptions of a philosophy and the policies to which they lead is critical to the study and practice of both criminology and corrections. A better understanding of the causes of crime will lead to more effective correctional practices. The value of utilitarian versus moral arguments is a matter of personal ethics and beliefs. The scientific and justice models summarize the application of various philosophies as well as their origins and methods.

Beginning in the mid-1970s, the philosophies of incapacitation and just deserts have dominated. Determinate sentencing is becoming more common, and mandatory sentences are increasingly popular for some crimes. The scientific model is still in use, probably more for beliefs about its economic and administrative efficiencies than in response to public opinion or objective evidence. Polls reveal that the public expects reintegration as well as retribution from its correctional system but does not recognize the contradictions between these philosophies.[95]

The problems facing modern corrections are both moral and utilitarian. The philosophies that guide our attitudes toward punishment often overlap with and contradict one another. It is doubtful that any human creation can be both efficient and fair, but society alternates between these two contradictory goals in its attempts to control crime. It is not possible to imprison more offenders than ever before while reducing taxes at the same time. Prison spending outstrips that for higher education in many states, despite the fact that it is cheaper to educate people than it is to imprison them.[96] The United States already imprisons a larger percentage of citizens than any other industrial society except Russia. It may be convenient simply to build more prisons, but this may not be the wisest approach. Moreover, our assumption that imprisonment is the best response to crime is almost 200 years old and should be revisited.

QUESTIONS FOR DISCUSSION AND REVIEW

1. What kinds of arguments are used to justify the practice of punishing offenders? What values are at the root of each?

2. What are the concerns and values of the justice and scientific models? Upon what does each focus? What does each set as the goal of corrections? What does each assume about human nature?

3. How are moral arguments for punishment affected by an individual's view of the "causes" of criminal behavior? Relate this to the notions of free will and determinism.

4. Which philosophies of punishment are compatible with the justice model? Which fit the assumptions of the scientific model? How do these models influence the way we sentence offenders?

5. What assumptions do retribution, deterrence, and treatment make about human behavior? To what degree do these assumptions affect the efficiency of each philosophy?

6. What are the main arguments for the incapacitation approach to crime control? What are the central arguments against it? What assumptions underlie this philosophy? To what degree are these assumptions correct?

7. Why are the demands of retribution and rehabilitation incompatible?

TWO

THE HISTORY OF PUNISHMENT

Many policies introduced over a century ago remain unquestioned today. Reliance on imprisonment as our main form of punishment is one of these. Knowing where and why these practices began can help us to understand why the system works the way it does today. Each idea appeared in a unique social and political setting and must be examined in light of both past experience and the current situation. The focus of this chapter is on the issues and problems that have guided corrections to its present state. The main concern is with how the needs of society are translated into specific practices that create both opportunities and problems.

THE ORIGINS OF PUNISHMENT

Early tribal societies did not recognize the idea of punishment beyond what was required to satisfy offended gods or families. Virtually all social control relied on religious leaders or families. In these cultures, families were usually large, clan-like groups that exerted strict control over their members. The welfare of the group, not the quality of justice received by an individual, was their main concern. Crime as we know it today was rare. When a wrong occurred, the victim's family sought vengeance. This often created a history of bloody feuds between clans. As cities developed, the family weakened as a primary source of social control. Crime increased and lawlessness threatened to disrupt society. This led to greater reliance on government efforts to control individual behavior. As crime became a problem, punishment became important as a method of controlling individuals, and formal legal codes appeared.[1]

The **Code of Hammurabi**, written in Mesopotamia about 1700 B.C.E., is one of the most famous of the ancient criminal codes. It used the principle of *lex talionis* (equivalent retaliation) to limit the amount of revenge that could be taken by families. Many ancient cultures, such as those in India and Egypt, used this principle as a basis for punishment. A similar idea is found in the Bible: "An eye for an eye, a tooth for a tooth." Although used today as a justification for severe punishment, the original purpose was to limit vengeance to a retaliation that matched the offense. This principle helped to control feuds but did not eliminate them.

Ancient societies had ideas about fairness that were very different from ours. The status of the victim and offender were vital in setting the level and type of punishment until about the time of the American Revolution. Crimes by slaves were always more severely punished than those of freemen; acts that hurt the nobility were treated more harshly than those that injured peasants. These distinctions were seen as perfectly natural by their creators because they reflected the organization of those societies and their religious beliefs.

Punishment in Ancient Societies

Most punishments in ancient times were corporal, financial, or capital: *corporal punishment* involves inflicting physical pain on the offender; fines and other economic penalties were sometimes used as a means of *financial punishment*; and *capital punishment* refers to use of the death penalty. In addition to these, banishment or exile from the group was common in many societies. It was a kind of social death. In most early civilizations, however, punishment meant killing or hurting the offender. Imprisonment was rarely used to punish; it was simply a method of controlling someone who might otherwise flee.

The ancient Greeks believed that punishment should serve as more than mere vengeance. It should encourage reform among criminals and deter others from crime. Athens used jails to punish those who refused to pay their fines and to hold those awaiting trial or execution. The Greeks restricted the use of fines to citizens. Slaves were stoned, burned alive, strangled, poisoned, or banished for their crimes. The Romans used fines, loss of property, death, and exile to punish offenders. Slaves and conquered peoples received the most severe punishments, such as mutilation, branding, and death by burning or crucifixion.[2] This reflects the class structure of ancient Greek and Roman society; most modern legal codes reflect the structure of their societies as well.

Little reliable information is available on the facilities used to hold prisoners during ancient times. Historians feel certain, however, that various types of cages were used by many cultures; some also used abandoned stone quarries to house prisoners. The Romans built Mamertine Prison underneath Rome's main sewer system in 64 B.C.E. to detain prisoners and to apply corporal punishments.[3] When Christianity became the state religion, the view of human nature—and of appropriate punishment for criminals—began to change.

Christianity and the Medieval Era

The use of social isolation to punish criminals began in the Roman Empire during the fourth century C.E. after Christianity became the state religion. Unlike pagans, Christians believe their God is entirely good. Therefore, divine explanations of criminal acts are not accepted by most Christians. At the same time, the quality of mercy is very important to Christians. Confinement in monasteries became an alternative to death, especially for powerful people in the early days of Christian Europe. These sanctuaries provided an environment in which it was hoped that criminals could rehabilitate themselves through expiation. *Expiation* uses social isolation to encourage offenders to reflect on their actions, recognize the wrongness of their acts, and repent.

After 529 C.E. most European countries used some form of the Justinian Code, which listed all recognized crimes and provided a specific punishment for each offense. Corporal punishment could be avoided by paying a fee to the victim or his or her family. These early penal codes were based on the social class of the offender. Those who were too poor to pay for serious crimes could be executed, while the rich often paid small fines for serious felonies. Throughout the Middle Ages, the severity of punishment increased as cities grew and crime became more of a problem. Deterrents, such as blinding or the amputation of hands, nose, or ears, had been reserved for slaves but were eventually applied to freemen in an attempt to slow the rising tide of crime.[4]

Castle dungeons were more similar to our jails than to modern prisons. Their primary purpose was to hold people awaiting trial. As gunpowder came into use, castles became useless for military defense and were increasingly used to imprison political prisoners. These offenders often had enough power to make rulers uneasy about executing them. Long-term denial of freedom was beginning to be recognized as a form of punishment by the end of the Middle Ages. For most offenders, however, punishment remained corporal and capital. Furthermore, the living conditions for most people at this time were brutal, and punishments reflected the norm of society in which they occurred.

English jails were called *gaols* and were controlled by the sheriff. Most sheriffs were nobles who did not want to trouble themselves with prisoners, so they allowed private businesses to run these facilities. Sanitary conditions were terrible, even by the standards of that era. Men, women, children, felons, debtors, unwed mothers, and the insane were housed together; the strong routinely preyed upon the weak. Most of the people in gaols were debtors. They were incarcerated as the result of a civil process. The purpose was to secure the debtor until the debt was paid, not to punish.

Payment for operating the gaols was the main concern of the businessmen who ran them. They charged inmates for room and board, charged admission fees for visitors, and used whatever means they could to profit from their position. Accused persons might be found innocent but die in the gaol years later because they could not pay their bill. On the other hand, wealthy prisoners could have liquor and prostitutes brought to them if they were willing to pay for such luxuries.[5] These inequalities were rarely questioned during this era; it was unthinkable to treat the wealthy in the same way as peasants.

Roman law was a major influence in England for more than four hundred years before the Anglo-Saxons invaded in 500 C.E. Unlike Roman law, Anglo-Saxon law was unwritten and based on tribal customs. The laws of the Anglo-Saxon tribes eventually merged with those of the Romans to form a medieval justice system. Two of the most important principles were: (1) the King's Peace; and (2) the idea that the king was entitled to compensation for any injury done to a free man. The **King's Peace** promised the use of the monarch's power to provide peace, security, and order to his subjects. In return citizens owed the king their loyalty.

Monarchs were thought to be God's appointed rulers. Therefore, any misconduct in the king's presence was an extremely serious crime. This notion grew to include any offense that disturbed the peace of the kingdom. Since all citizens were under the king's protection, the king should be paid for any harm inflicted on any one of them. This reasoning led to the state being defined as the injured party in criminal cases. Victims soon became little more than witnesses in the criminal justice system.[6]

Knights were appointed to enforce the King's Peace throughout the land, but they often abused this power. In 1215 King John was forced to sign the **Magna Carta**, which put formal limits on the king's power. This document gave many rights and powers to local governments, prohibited punishment without trial, limited the severity of punishments, and provided methods of redressing wrongs by government through the courts. It gave many powers to minor nobles rather than to the people, but it was the beginning of popular control of government powers that was to become unique to the English-speaking world.[7] This English tradition of placing strict limits on government powers was brought to the North American colonies, where it grew even stronger.[8]

Growth of the Cities

Europe was rapidly urbanizing between 1500 and 1800. The use of violence to settle disputes was common. Punishment was inflicted in public to deter others from committing similar acts. Hangings, floggings, and similar spectacles had been major sources of public entertainment for centuries. Punishments, especially executions, were public events that drew large crowds on a regular basis. The public was often allowed to help punish offenders. Passersby threw rotten food or stones at people in stocks and pillories. Despite these severe measures, crime continued to increase. Banishment had been a common means of removing disruptive people. As cities grew, banishing vagrants from one area caused problems in another. The obvious failure of pain and death to deter crime, and fear of the crowds attracted by public punishments, forced authorities to find other ways to punish offenders. Fines were not effective for those too poor to pay. Bondage, punishment that restricted a person's freedom and forced labor, was one option.

The poor were the first to experience bondage as a punitive sanction. Authorities saw the poor as a threat to the stability of society and needed a way to supervise this threat.[9] Bondage was originally a disciplinary rather than a criminal sanction. It was intended to resolve the problems presented by the poor and marginal members of society. Bondage had been used on galley ships since the fifteenth century. Another form of bondage, public work, had been used to punish those convicted of a crime. Forced labor in mines, working on roads, or collecting human waste was used as punishment in Spain beginning about 1550.[10] The idea spread through Europe and continued through the seventeenth and eighteenth centuries, where it gradually was associated with imprisonment.

European workhouses were the result of the problems created by the dramatic growth of cities. The industrial revolution changed the nature of society. People left rural farmlands and flocked to cities in search of jobs. When unsuccessful at finding work, they took up begging or crime as a way of life. The family was no longer able to control individual behavior. Urban society had to find some way to control the increasing numbers of jobless and homeless poor congregating in the cities.

Religious beliefs at the time strongly supported a work ethic. Begging, gambling, and prostitution were considered immoral. Work was one way to reform this behavior. In 1556, Bishop Ridley converted Bridewell Palace to a workhouse to keep criminals, beggars, and the insane off the streets while teaching them to be productive workers. As similar places of detention were opened, they were known as **Bridewell Houses**. They were designed to teach the value of hard work and discipline. Humanitarians hoped that a change from punishment to discipline would help curb crime. However, Bridewells quickly became places to isolate criminals and other social misfits from the rest of society. In 1597, Parliament authorized the building of houses of correction, and by 1609 each county was required to have such a facility.[11] Gaols, Bridewells, and houses of correction were the ancestors of our prisons today.

The idea that inmate labor should be used to make a profit goes back to the ancient practice of enslaving offenders. France began leasing convict labor to private businesses early in the 1700s. The state was responsible for keeping the convicts healthy enough to work in factories, and the items they produced were sold to the state. In 1703 the **Hospital of St. Michael** opened in Rome under the control of Catholic monks. Young offenders, orphans, and the sick were housed in solitary cells so that they could reflect on their sins and repent.

Inmates worked silently in groups in experimental prisons.

Labor was important to these experimental prisons. Inmates worked silently in groups to produce goods for the church. Solitary cells, work, and religious training were used as reform methods.[12] However, there were very few of these church-run facilities. The growth of colonial empires provided a more popular way to remove those who offended society.

The fourth type of bondage, transportation, was introduced as a penalty by King James in England in 1615. Each of the European powers had a place of exile for serious offenders during the 1700s and 1800s: Spain had African colonies; French convicts were sent to South America or to remote Pacific islands; England could choose between North America and Australia. Up until the American Revolution in 1776, more than 30,000 convicts had been transported to Colonial America. Growing opposition from Australian colonists to the use of their islands as penal colonies soon followed. As the transportation of convicts to colonies ended, the English turned to the use of prisons.[13] Although the Bridewell originated as a social policy, it soon affected criminal policy. The Bridewells and houses of correction marked a shift in attitudes from a public spectacle of corporal and capital punishments to labor and serving a fixed amount of time.

THE AGE OF ENLIGHTENMENT

A new view of human nature, and the role of law and government in guiding behavior, appeared in the 1700s. This view rejected the idea that kings had a divine right to govern others. Instead, it stressed the unique value and dignity of each individual. The idea that all people are "created equal" surfaced during this era. This new outlook rejected supernatural explanations of crime based on spirit possession and similar ideas. Instead, the notion that law should serve the welfare of the majority became the basis for punishment. These ideas encouraged democracy and led to our beliefs in equality, deterrence, and personal freedom. This view of human nature and government originated in the *Age of Enlightenment* and became the basis of our Constitution and Bill of Rights. These views of law and crime control led to the classical school of thought and the "justice model" that was discussed in chapter 1.

Enlightenment thinkers wanted to create and run a society based on personal freedom and equality. They believed that behavior results from conscious choices for which only the individual is responsible. They questioned the idea that nobles were superior to the rest of the population. They rejected the idea that punishment should vary with social status and focused on how a society of equals could govern itself. If actions were the responsibility of the individual, then each person should take full credit for his or her achievements and full blame for his or her wrongs. At first these principles were applied only to white males who owned land, but they were slowly expanded to include all adults. The Age of Enlightenment is the source of the personal freedoms that make our Constitution unique and lead us to grant a few rights even to convicted offenders. However, enlightenment thought cannot be classified as "liberal" in today's use of that term because it also provided the basis for belief in deterrence.

Cesare Beccaria and the Classical View[14]

Cesare Beccaria was an Italian scholar who summarized much of the enlightenment philosophy. He saw law as a contract between the people and the state in which individuals must give up some freedom to assure peace and security for the society. It was vital that people understand and respect the laws they were expected to obey. Governments must justify their actions and serve the largest number of people possible if they were to remain partners in this contract. Fear of punishment helped insure that each person kept his or her part of the social contract. The punishment for each crime must be justified by the harm done by the crime. The classical school was based on the idea of **utilitarianism**, which insists that laws be designed to bring the greatest good to the greatest number of people. This idea, rather than humanitarianism, was the guiding principle of the classical school.

Beccaria fought to abolish torture. He also questioned the frequent use of the death penalty because he believed that it was the certainty of punishment, not its severity, that deterred crime. He feared that capital punishment would put offenders in a position where they had "nothing to lose" by committing further crimes. For example, if robbery was punished by death, then robbers would have no reason not to kill their victims.

Enlightenment thinkers believed that people made decisions based on a calculation in which the possible costs of an act (punishment) are compared with its likely rewards.[15] This **greatest happiness principle** assumes that people make choices that will help them avoid pain and obtain pleasure. Laws must encourage people to make choices that will benefit society as well as themselves. This is the basis for using punishment to deter crime. We sacrifice a few criminals to deter others and keep society as safe as possible for the law abiding. These ideas of free will, equality, and deterrence led to the idea of due process and to the justice model of crime control. They also encouraged the use of confinement as the main way of punishing offenders.

London was the largest city in the world during this era, and crime was its worst social problem. During the 1800s, the English created a system of prisons in hope that loss of individual freedom would deter crime. These prisons were modeled on the military. They emphasized labor, discipline, and separation from society. These principles symbolized society's idea of a good and orderly life. Prisons were seen as harsher than transporting prisoners to the colonies, and it was hoped that they could reform offenders.[16]

Overcrowding soon became a major problem for English jails and prisons. Many cities temporarily solved the problem by using old buildings as prisons in which criminals, women, children, and the mentally ill were held in group cells. Overcrowding also led to the use of old ships as prisons. These hulks, often called "Hell Holds," were filthy, rat infested, and unventilated. Inmates performed degrading labor on these ships while townspeople paid a fee to be entertained by their misery. Disobedience was punished with flogging. The use of prison ships lasted until 1875. Ironically, almost exactly one hundred years later, three states seriously considered using old U.S. warships as prisons as a solution to prison overcrowding.[17]

Prison ships were a convenient solution to overcrowding but increased the misery of inmates confined in them.

REFORM AND THE BIRTH OF MODERN CORRECTIONS

In 1777 an English sheriff named John Howard exposed the filth and brutality that were typical of jails at that time. He felt that religion, labor, and humane surroundings could be used to reform most criminals. As a result of his efforts, England passed a law calling for four major prison reforms: (1) prisons should be secure and sanitary; (2) prisons should be regularly inspected; (3) inmates should not be charged for basic services; and (4) prison administration should become professional. Howard's reforms eventually led to the separation of criminals from other social outcasts in English institutions and a decrease in the use of execution.[18] By the 1850s use of the death penalty was restricted to first-degree murder and treason in England. In the 1860s executions were moved behind prison walls because the crowds they attracted threatened public order.

Punishment and Law in Colonial America

Colonial America followed the English tradition of using corporal and capital punishments for serious crimes. Milder forms of public punishment were used for minor offenses, and "women's crimes" were handled differently from those of men. Gossips were punished by "dunking" in a pond, and sexual misbehavior was punished by shearing off the woman's hair. Crime was not a serious problem because there were few large cities, and offenders were easily encouraged to "go west," an informal continuation of the practice of banishment. The main developments of the colonial era were in the laws that controlled punishment.

William Penn, a Quaker leader who founded the colony of Pennsylvania, established a penal code in 1682 that led to major correctional reforms. As a Quaker he was opposed to violence of any kind and objected to the use of corporal and capital punishments, especially for minor crimes. This rejection of violence had a dramatic impact on attitudes, and Pennsylvania was a leader in the early development of North American corrections.[19]

NORTH AMERICAN PRISONS

In 1787, Benjamin Rush, an author of the Constitution, helped found the Philadelphia Society for the Alleviation of the Miseries of Public Prisons. He felt that the humiliation of public punishment alienated offenders from society and led to even worse criminality. He wanted to create a system that would encourage offenders to rejoin society.[20] It was believed that crime was the result of the evil influences of society. The penitentiary was seen as an institution that could isolate offenders from corrupting influences, instill the discipline they lacked, and provide the time to reflect on their misbehavior and be reformed into a useful citizen. Lawrence Friedman described the idea of the penitentiary—a "grim, total, silent monastery for criminals"—as winning many converts.[21]

Philadelphia's Walnut Street Jail was the first real penal institution in North America. In 1790, the Pennsylvania legislature converted a wing of this jail into a penitentiary for convicted felons. Prior to this, felons were incarcerated along with misdemeanants and those awaiting trial in workhouses and jails. At first, the Walnut Street Jail kept prisoners in solitary confinement and did not allow them to work. This was very expensive and had a disastrous effect on inmates, leading to suicides and mental breakdowns. As a result, prisoners were eventually allowed to work and to receive religious instruction.[22]

Thomas Eddy took over New York City's Newgate Prison in 1797. He introduced many new policies, such as evaluating the need to imprison each inmate. He concluded that no more than 10% of offenders actually required the kind of security provided by the prison. Job descriptions were required for all prison staff positions; hiring was based on the abilities of applicants rather than on friendship or political favoritism. Inmates' diets were planned to be nutritionally adequate, and the menu changed daily. For the first time, the services of a physician and pharmacist were made available to inmates. Newgate was the first prison with policies that promoted professionalism and brought basic services to inmates.[23] However, these efforts were limited to facilities for men.

Prior to the 1800s, female offenders were few in number and were seen as especially depraved. They were held in unused areas of male prisons, such as attics, where they were separated from male inmates but guarded by men. Women were seen as inferior to men in all ways. They had few rights, and it was commonly believed they could not learn or change as easily as men. Therefore, little attention was paid to them by society. Elizabeth Gurney Fry's work at Newgate Prison in the early 1800s showed that even the most hardened women could be rehabilitated. Fry proposed separate facilities for women, staffed by females, with humane treatment as their central philosophy. Like John Howard, she argued for the use of work, education, and religious training instead of punishment. Her efforts established the theoretical and practical bases for many modern correctional practices and helped to bring humane conditions to U.S. prisons.[24]

The two central goals of the prison were also established in this era. The first—assuring custody of prisoners—meant giving top priority to preventing escapes. Second only to this goal was maintaining control of inmates within the prison's walls. Despite the reforms at Newgate, humane conditions or treatment were a distant third at best. Prisons were designed to keep inmates isolated and powerless. During the first half of the 1800s, policy was often based on the belief that solitary confinement could lead to repentance and reform. Crime was seen as a product of the evils of city life so rural settings were chosen to encourage inmates to contemplate their sins. Silence was used to enforce separation from others and to encourage penitence. Extreme discipline was thought to have rehabilitative effects, and labor was required to replace idleness.

These three assumptions about the requirements of rehabilitation—separation from society, hard work, and extreme discipline—became the basis of prison organization. People believed these factors would prevent exposure of prisoners to additional kinds of criminal behavior. Two types of prisons—Pennsylvania and Auburn systems—developed during this era. The main difference between the two was in how they tried to control and reform inmates.[25]

The Pennsylvania System

Pennsylvania built the Western Penitentiary in Pittsburgh in 1826 and the Eastern Penitentiary in Cherry Hill in 1829. The Pennsylvania system extended the concepts of the Walnut Street Jail. It was believed that solitary confinement would reduce violence because inmates would not be in contact with each other. Fewer guards would be required. Upon arrival at the prison, inmates were considered "dead to the world" and were told to expect little human contact while serving their sentence. "Social death" was part of the penalty for crime during this era, and convicts had no rights. Letters and visits from outsiders were almost entirely forbidden. Only clergy and a few citizens approved by the Pennsylvania Prison Society were allowed to see inmates. Religious education and services were offered as treatment; Bibles were the only permitted reading material.[26]

Being allowed to work was a reward for cooperative inmates that helped break the boredom of complete isolation. In theory, this led them to see labor as a reward rather than something to be avoided; in practice, it helped keep prisons from draining the state budget. The Pennsylvania system was not profitable, however, because prisoners working by themselves were not very productive. The separation of prisoners, called the *segregate system*, was eventually abandoned. The problem of financial support for the prison was never solved, and mental breakdowns among inmates were common. Despite these problems the Pennsylvania system was copied throughout the world, and some nations built similar institutions as recently as the 1960s.[27] Due to financial problems and overcrowding, Pennsylvania finally adopted the *congregate system* that had been developed in Auburn, New York.

Early prisons in the United States were modeled on the British system. Both were based on the idea of expiation and required that inmates be as socially isolated from each other as possible.

The Auburn System

The Auburn system began in 1816. It was also based on the philosophy of expiation and enforced a "code of silence" among inmates. Prisoners worked in groups during the day and were confined to separate cells at night. Communication between inmates was restricted to the minimum required for work, and rule violations were quickly punished by guards armed with bullwhips. These prisons were actually profitable for the states that used them because they made better use of inmate labor.

Elam Lynds was the warden who made Auburn profitable during the 1830s. He believed that prisoners deserved to be whipped as often as possible and designed procedures and clothing to be as humiliating as possible. His cruelty was also felt by staff members, who described him as a sadistic dictator. The state government was pleased to see the prison make a profit but was so embarrassed by his sadism that he was finally forced to resign.[28]

Supporters of the Pennsylvania system claimed that Auburn's use of the whip to enforce the code of silence naturally led to the sort of cruelty for which Lynds became famous. They also felt that allowing inmates to work together was too great a temptation to violate the "code of silence." Advocates of the Auburn system pointed out that it was more profitable and led to fewer mental problems than the segregate system. Auburn-type prisons were also cheaper to build. Passionate debates between supporters of these two models raged for much of the early 1800s, but most U.S. prisons had adopted the Auburn approach by 1860. Auburn's code of silence was abandoned, however, as overcrowding made its enforcement impossible.[29]

Regional Influences on Prisons

In the mid-1800s crowding led to the building of large prisons, designed to hold as many inmates as possible. The era of the "big house" overlapped with that of the Auburn and Pennsylvania systems but lasted into the early twentieth century. There was little interest in reforming criminals during this period. These huge institutions emphasized large size, efficiency, and production. All these values were admired by early industrial societies. Having a huge prison was a source of pride for many states during this period, just as having the most prison beds today is seen as beneficial.

During this period, state governments in the North and West took control of prisons away from cities and counties. In the South, control of convicted felons remained in the custody of county governments until the early 1900s. While industry provided the model of work and discipline in the North, slavery filled this role in the South long after the Civil War.[30]

The South did not adopt the penitentiaries so popular in the North. Older public punishments, such as whipping, shaming, or hanging, remained prominent during this period. Race influenced punishment in the South. Killing slaves while "disciplining" them was not a serious crime in the Southern states. The death penalty was used for many felonies if committed by slaves, but whites who committed the same offense only received prison time. After the Civil War, prisons became more common in an attempt to control ex-slaves. The Thirteenth Amendment freed African Americans from slavery but allowed the use of convicts as slave labor for state and local governments. White inmates were given clerical jobs, and some even served as guards or foremen. African Americans worked 10- to 12-hour days on plantations and chain gangs.[31]

The Reformatory Prison

Between 1870 and 1900, science replaced religion as the guiding principle for changing offenders. At least in theory, treatment had become a primary goal. This period saw the introduction of academic and vocational training, indeterminate sentencing, and parole. The remedial prisons of this era tried to use scientific knowledge to reform inmates.[32] It was at this point that the rhetoric of reform began to guide corrections. Reform described the process of using all available, ethical, and humane methods to change offender behavior patterns. The belief was that linking privileges to good behavior and hard work would help offenders achieve goals set by the authorities. The basic idea of reform had appeared much earlier in the efforts of Maconochie, Crofton, and Brockway.

Alexander Maconochie served as warden of the Norfolk Island penal colony near Australia between 1840 and 1844. He required convicts to earn their room and board by working in small groups. The foundation of this system was the indeterminate sentence. Convicts could earn early release by working hard and behaving well. It was hoped that the disciplined habits learned in this structured environment would continue to guide offenders when they returned to society. This idea was adopted in Ireland by Walter Crofton. Crofton's system was based on a series of stages through which prisoners passed to earn their release. Inmates were first assigned to solitary confinement and boring work under close supervision but could earn the privilege of being involved in more pleasant projects. If they continued to follow the rules, they were removed from solitary confinement and given work that was not supervised. Eventually they could win conditional release into the community. The modern practice of parole began in this way. By 1869, 23 states had passed good-time laws to encourage reform and good behavior among inmates and to relieve the overcrowding that again troubled U.S. prisons.[33]

A corollary to the idea that offenders could earn early release from prison was that some offenders were incorrigible—incapable of reform. Reform based on offering rewards had to have a balancing punishment. Habitual criminal laws had been used even in colonial days. In the late 1800s, laws were passed to treat recidivists much more harshly than first-time offenders.[34]

Early in the 1870s, Zebulon Brockway used indeterminate sentences to reduce crowding at Detroit's House of Correction for Women. In 1876 he was asked to manage the state prison at Elmira, New York. This was the first "reformatory," and it became a model for most of the prisons built between 1876 and 1913. This was a revival of an older practice of allowing inmates to earn early release with "good time" that had been introduced by Samuel Howe in 1847.[35] Brockway tried to emphasize the value of education and hard work as a method of earning one's freedom. However, lawsuits based on the capitalist demand that the state not compete with private companies soon forced him to replace labor with military drills and recreation. Inmates who were kept busy were much easier to control than those who remained idle regardless of the activity they performed. This remains the central purpose of prison recreation to this day.

The practice of granting judicial reprieves had been used in England in the late 1700s to reduce jail and prison crowding. A reprieve was a suspension of sentence granted for offenders who were felt to be worthy of lenient treatment. Once released, these offenders were not supervised but if they reappeared in court, the original sentence could be reimposed. This practice was adopted by many American judges, especially in Massachusetts, and was used mainly with minor first offenders. Reprieves were found to violate the separation of powers principle in the Constitution in 1916, but their popularity during the 1830s led to the development of modern probation.[36]

In 1841 a Boston shoemaker named John Augustus began asking the local court to release certain drunks, prostitutes, and other petty offenders to his custody. Augustus tried to help them rehabilitate themselves, and he at first allowed them to stay in his home. Later he and his wife opened a shelter to house these men, women, and children. If offenders cooperated and managed to lead decent lives before their trial, Augustus would request that the charges against them be dropped.

Local officials profited from jail crowding because they were paid on the basis of the number of inmates in their facility. Augustus was a threat to their profits. However, municipal judges chose to cooperate with him, and he continued this activity until his death in 1859. He is thought to have taken in over two thousand offenders and was often successful in reforming them. His example inspired volunteers from all over Massachusetts to work with petty offenders and juveniles. In 1878 the state legislature created the position of probation officer and formalized the system.[37] Three forces motivated the gradual expansion of probation systems throughout the nation: (1) an increasing concern with juvenile delinquency; (2) growing faith in the power of scientific treatment; and (3) financial problems caused by prison crowding.

Parole traces its origins to Maconochie, Crofton, and Brockway. The same pressures that led to the expansion of probation also encouraged the growth of parole. Parolees were rarely minor offenders, however. They had experienced imprisonment and were generally more hardened than probationers. Today parole usually is controlled by the executive branch at the state level. This encourages communication between prison officials and parole officers. It also allows some states to give parole officers limited police powers over their charges. Probation, on the other hand, works closely with the local court system.

The principles of the reformatory, which still guide some correctional practices, were outlined in Cincinnati, Ohio, at the 1870 meeting of prison experts from throughout the nation. This group called for an emphasis on treatment to replace that of punishment. They argued for standardized but indeterminate sentencing, parole services, the use of rewards to control inmate behavior, and the creation of a single national correctional system. Most striking was their belief that society was partly responsible for crime and therefore should develop crime prevention programs.[38] However, such progressive ideals were accepted only in the North and Midwest. In the South, dealing with the damage caused by the Civil War and controlling freed slaves were still the major concerns.

Positivism and the Medical Model of Criminal Justice

In the late 1800s such disciplines as psychology and sociology appeared, and their value was quickly recognized by Western society. Science promised solutions to problems caused by large numbers of people immigrating to the United States. The positivists were concerned mainly with the use of science to improve the quality of life. They believed that human behavior is guided by family and environmental circumstances and/or biological conditions such as genetics and hormones. Because different people come from different situations, positivists felt that people have varying degrees of control over what happens in their lives. In other words, some people are less responsible for their actions than others according to this school of thought. Positivists believe that punishment should be designed to fit the specific offender and the forces that caused him or her to commit crime. They also felt that each offender must be dealt with as a unique individual; some would need more time to change their behavior than others. Sentences should be based on the cause of the criminality rather than on which law was violated. Positivism stressed efficient crime prevention and treatment through use of the medical model that was introduced in chapter 1.

Positivism and the reform ideology were ignored in the Southern states where the Civil War had destroyed the economy and most prisons. Southern jurisdictions adopted a lease system that allowed private businesses to rent convict labor from the state or county. A contractor took custody of the inmates and made them work long hours under terrible conditions. This system was modeled on slavery; the prison, not the convict, was paid for the labor.[39] The lease system made many prisons profitable but led to terrible abuses of human rights. Conditions at many convict-lease operations were so bad that the bureaucrats assigned to inspect them refused even to enter the facilities. Illegal deals and outright bribes added to their corruption. Objections to convict leasing by the federal government and labor unions led to the collapse of this system at the turn of the century.[40]

As we move today toward increased reliance on private prisons, the abuses of the lease system must be remembered. Issues such as the morality of making a profit from human misery and the conflict between the profit motive and decent living conditions are very relevant today. The abuses of the lease system eventually forced Southern states to take control of prisons away from the counties. They were also one of several forces that led to the creation of the Federal Bureau of Prisons.

The Federal Bureau of Prisons

Until 1895 there were no federal prisons for civilians. Persons convicted under military law were confined at Leavenworth, Kansas, or Portsmouth, New Hampshire. Civilians sentenced to a year or more were housed in state prisons; those with shorter sentences were kept in local jails. The federal government simply paid the state or county for the room and board of these prisoners. This was a problem in the South because U.S. law prohibited the leasing of federal prisoners, but Southern jurisdictions routinely ignored these laws. By 1890 prison crowding was again a major concern, and many jurisdictions were reluctant to continue housing federal inmates.

At the same time, federal law was expanding to cover more offenses, so the number of federal prisoners was also rising. These problems led to the creation of the federal prison system. Construction of the federal prison at Leavenworth, Kansas, began in 1896 but the facility did not open until 1928. The U.S. penitentiary at Atlanta, Georgia, opened in 1899 and the territorial jail at McNeil Island, Washington, became a federal prison in 1907. A federal facility for women opened in West Virginia in 1927. These prisons were immediately overcrowded because of the federal government's increasing involvement in criminal law enforcement.[41] All of these facilities are still in operation today. In 1930 these prisons were combined into the Federal Bureau of Prisons, which is part of the U.S. Department of Justice. Many consider the Federal Bureau of Prisons to be the most professional and modern prison system in the world. Its early development was guided by a reform mood that swept the nation at the turn of the century.

The "Progressive" Era

The reformers who were active between 1870 and 1930 were called "progressives." They were optimistic about the ability of science to deal with social problems.[42] Many of their ideas, such as humane treatment, diagnosis, and classification, have become basic parts of our correctional system. Other progressive

ideas, however, like democratic government of prisons by inmates, met with failure. Thomas M. Osbourne, the warden at Sing Sing and Auburn prisons in New
York, felt that regulating all inmate behavior and providing all essential needs
made offenders less responsible than ever before. He allowed inmates to elect representatives who created rules for the prison and sentenced violators. His reforms
increased industrial production and reduced violence, but the idea of democracy in
prison seems to have worked only because of Osbourne's unique personality. Nonetheless, his work was typical of the Progressive Era because he questioned popular
beliefs and tried to change traditional ways of doing things.

This was also a time of change in the status of women and juveniles. Until the
late 1800s juveniles were handled in about the same way as adults. Progressives
created special juvenile courts and facilities. Many progressives were women who
volunteered their services. While some worked with immigrants from urban slums,
others devoted themselves to reforming female offenders.[43]

During the Progressive Era, science was used to support the idea that females
were more passive and less dangerous than men. Women's prisons, therefore, had
more freedom to experiment with programs. Many modern prison programs such
as libraries, work release, and behavior-based classification systems were first used
in women's prisons.[44]

Despite attempts at reform, imprisonment remained the basic way to punish
those convicted of serious crimes. "The great penitentiaries were not pulled down.
There they stood—corrupt and brutal; warehouses for convicts." [45] The reforms
tested in some of the large prisons had no effect on county and local prisons and
jails. Thousands arrested for drunkenness or vagrancy were subjected to filthy conditions and had little recourse. Lawrence Friedman states, "In general, prison and
jail conditions everywhere in this county were a scandal"—hidden lesions and
sores on society. They were also a lesion on the meaning of race, poverty, and lack
of power—and the terrible indifference of respectable people to the miseries of life
underneath their feet.[46]

This era was far from progressive so far as civil rights for minorities were concerned. Although people of all races were treated badly by justice practitioners,
minorities were handled with special savagery. The period between 1882 and 1903
saw the lynching of nearly two thousand African Americans who had committed no
crime. Legal executions were also used in a very racist manner during this era as
well; more than 90% of those executed for nonfatal rapes and burglaries were people
of color. The huge majority of those executed for murder were minorities as well.[47]

The "Warehouse" Prison

The stock market crash of 1929 signaled the end of the Progressive Era. Economic problems led to gross neglect of the correctional system during the Great
Depression that followed. The loss of prison industries that had begun in the late
1800s was hastened by the economic panic of the Depression. In 1929 the
Hawes-Cooper Act subjected all items produced by prison labor to the laws of the
state to which they were shipped. The 1935 Ashurst-Sumners Act further restricted
the sale of prison products, and a 1940 amendment to this law stopped the sale of

items produced with inmate labor. These laws were written to protect businesses and the jobs of their employees from competition with prison industries. License plates and furniture for government offices were the only items that prisons could continue to produce and sell.

Prison riots had been a major problem in the early 1800s but faded as the reformatory movement and prison industries took hold. This was largely because treatment and labor kept inmates tired and busy. Riots began again in 1930 as prisons lost these industries, governments cut treatment funding, and crowding worsened. Idleness, filth, and overcrowding again became the norms of prison life. The early 1940s were relatively quiet due to the Second World War, but riots recurred after the war ended and continued into the 1950s. Boredom, poorly trained staff, crowding, huge institutions, haphazard sentencing, poorly designed parole policies, and politically controlled management led to serious problems in most U.S. prisons.[48]

Riots in the 1950s led to the study of prison organization and the effects on inmates. The economic recovery after World War II and the emphasis on public education created an atmosphere in the 1950s that renewed the emphasis on rehabilitation and individualized treatment. The medical model was once again prominent. There was a renewal of interest in prisoner welfare. Model penal codes were developed in an attempt to make criminal punishment more efficient. Attention during this era focused on sentencing, the use of probation, good time, and parole release.[49] Treatment based on the needs of the offender, rather than punishment to fit the crime, was the focus. At the same time, a heroin epidemic led to severe anti-drug laws throughout the nation.[50]

Social upheaval in the 1960s reinforced this trend and led to reforms in the civil rights of prisoners, but rising crime rates soon hardened attitudes about the goals of corrections. President Johnson tried to reduce crime by attacking the causes of social and economic inequality in the mid-1960s. He appointed a special panel of experts to study the problems of the U.S. justice system. The need for crime prevention programs, sensitivity to minority rights, and improved practitioner training were major themes of their report.[51] Increases in the crime rate and a series of riots during the late 1960s led to renewed concern with crime control. Racism was so widely accepted that many agencies had no minority employees whatsoever, and the justice system was still seen as a tool of racial oppression by most minority citizens.[52] It was at this time that the Supreme Court began to demand that the Constitution be enforced by all levels of government. This shift in judicial philosophy is known as the due process revolution.

The Due Process Revolution

Up until the 1960s a variety of legal doctrines were used to keep the courts from becoming involved with the operation of prisons. The constitutional separation of powers between the three branches of government was used to argue that judicial oversight of prisons could undermine the powers of the legislative and executive branches. The idea of federal abstention suggested that federal courts had no authority to interfere in the operation of state prisons. Fear that giving inmates legal rights would threaten the authority of prison officials and the safety of their staff provided another reason to avoid hearing the complaints of convicts. Apprehension that frivolous inmate suits would overwhelm the courts had a similar effect.[53]

Many of the courts' reasons for avoiding suits about prison conditions and practices were summarized in the *rights-versus-privileges doctrine*, which is still recognized in a limited form today. This doctrine holds that "rights" are protected by the Constitution but "privileges" are controlled by the agency. Until the due process revolution, conviction meant the loss of all rights; anything given to inmates

---

Prison Designs Follow Philosophy and Security Demands[54]

The physical layout of an American prison reflects both the philosophy under which it was built and the security concerns that were uppermost in the minds of authorities at that time. Most facilities were adapted to uses for which they were not originally intended, posing further problems for administrators. Blind spots, long distances between staff areas and inmate living or activity areas are common in the oldest U.S. prisons that were built when inmates moved about only rarely or in groups. More recent prisons have converted what was once staff areas to cell space, which means that unsecured vents and wall segments can be removed by inmates, posing security threats.

Pennsylvania system facilities used a *radial design* with a central control area for staff and cell blocks running off it like the spokes of a wheel for inmates. The exterior was castle-like and foreboding to symbolize the power of the state to control and discipline.

Auburn prisons were more economical in their use of space. They were composed of back-to-back tiers within a hollow building with cell doors that faced an open area and outer wall. Virtually all space was devoted to cells or work areas. Interaction between staff and inmates was discouraged by this design as well as that used in Pennsylvania. Auburn prison exteriors were Gothic in style but were just as symbolic and foreboding as those of the Pennsylvania system.

Reformatories used a *telephone-pole design* in which a single long corridor (the "pole") was crossed by shorter cell blocks (the "cross-ties"), administrative areas, and dining halls. Each cell block had its own control center. This design served the more complex classification systems of the era but was often so large that staff had to use bicycles to travel the long corridor. Later variations tried to make the facility more compact by having three or more corridors branch out from a single point.

In the mid-twentieth century, smaller institutions were built with the goal of eliminating the need for an outside wall or fence. This was done by using the building's outer wall as the facility's perimeter. In the late twentieth century crowding and riots became the main challenges to security, and prisons grew smaller so inmates could be controlled more readily. Bars gave way to shatterproof plastic windows, and dormitory rooms replaced cells as closed-circuit television was used to cut staff costs.

Current trends include experimentation with underground high-security units and consideration of skyscraper prisons. However, pre-manufactured *podular units* can be erected quickly at minimum cost; they dominate modern correctional architecture and help authorities keep pace with burgeoning inmate populations. A typical "pod" consists of an open area surrounded by cells and holds about 50 inmates. *Direct supervision* is also typical of modern medium- and minimum-security prisons; staff are in constant face-to-face interaction with inmates and can thus prevent trouble before serious incidents occur. Maximum-security units are technologically controlled and employ isolation cells.

beyond food, shelter, and clothing was a privilege. The due process revolution, however, led to the belief that a felony conviction limited rights but did not strip people of all constitutional protections. For example, convicts have less control over their privacy and property than ordinary citizens, but they should be assured sufficient rights to keep their basic human dignity.

Prison administration was defined as largely beyond the jurisdiction of the courts because no civil rights were felt to be involved during the hands-off era. Courts sometimes examined the legality of confinement but rarely heard complaints about prison conditions. These were seen as administrative issues beyond judicial control.[55] The Supreme Court began to reconsider these ideas in *Monroe v. Pape* (1961), which involved an illegal police search. This decision held that claims that federal rights had been violated by a state or local official should allow the victim to be heard by federal courts without first going through the state courts. In 1964, *Cooper v. Pate* made it clear that this right of access to the federal courts was available to state prisoners.[56]

This granting of limited rights to prisoners encouraged inmates to file suits seeking other constitutional rights. The Eighth Amendment ban on cruel and unusual punishment was applied to the conditions within prisons. The Fourteenth Amendment's guarantee of equal justice and due process was applied to prison disciplinary decisions and soon became the basis for much judicial intervention in U.S. prisons. The suits that followed established a number of rights for inmates in the areas of religion, speech, medical care, and due process.[57] Sixth Amendment rights to a fair trial and Fourth Amendment rights to privacy, however, were withheld from inmates.[58]

The 1970 case of *Holt v. Sarver* was an important turning point in due process reforms. A U.S. district court ruling found the entire Arkansas prison system to be in violation of the Eighth Amendment because: (1) some inmates guarded others; (2) the prisons' design encouraged violence; (3) isolation cells were unsanitary; and (4) there were no treatment opportunities for inmates. This ruling was strengthened and clarified by *Pugh v. Locke* (1976), which made the "totality of conditions" rather than any one aspect of the prison the central issue in Eighth Amendment cases. The Pugh decision touched on most of the problems in modern prisons: overcrowding, poor classification procedures, unsanitary conditions, racial discrimination, and the use of violence by guards. Prison officials had allowed their facilities to be overrun with insects; one prison housed more than 200 men but had only one toilet for inmates. Conditions like these violated the Constitution and constituted cruel and unusual punishment.[59]

The courts ruled that a prison procedure was unconstitutional if it debased the human dignity of inmates, if it was worse than the crime committed, or if it was unfair and/or shocking to the public conscience. Most of the case law that guided these decisions was written long before the 1960s when it was finally enforced.[60] Within a few years, the conditions and policies of prisons in many states had come under court control as a result of illegal practices or conditions. It was the *Ruiz* decision, however, that led to most takeovers of state prisons by the federal courts.

Ruiz v. Estelle (1980) was a Texas case in which a federal court defined overcrowding as a violation of the Eighth Amendment ban on cruel and unusual punishment.[61]

This allowed the courts more or less to take control of prisons in nearly three-quarters of the states. The *Ruiz* decision also put an end to the practice of giving some inmates power over others, which had been common throughout the South. These powers were often badly abused, and the practice has been condemned by virtually all U.S. courts and correctional associations.

Idealism similar to that of the Progressive Era became dominant again during the late 1960s, and the notion of democratically operated prisons reappeared. These interactive prisons were sensitive to the power of guards, treatment staff, and inmates but were also dramatically affected by the media and courts. The goal of the interactive prison was to imitate the outside world so that inmates could rejoin society more easily when released. However, these reforms made prisons as dangerous as the city streets from which the inmates had come, and the idea of the interactive prison did not last long.[62]

THE ANTI-CRIME BACKLASH

In the 1970s some researchers claimed that most treatment programs had failed to reduce recidivism.[63] Simultaneously, crime—especially homicide—grew at an unprecedented rate, and conservative ideology dominated national politics. Fear of crime continued to increase, even after crime rates declined in the early 1990s.[64] Both the news and entertainment divisions of the media continued to focus attention on crime; a new genre of "reality" television shows also appeared during this period, adding to public fears.[65] These factors led to a resurgence of retribution and incapacitation as dominant strategies. The federal courts became increasingly conservative, and many of the rights granted prisoners in the 1970s disappeared or were severely limited in the 1980s and 1990s.[66] While overcrowding remains illegal, crowding is permitted, and the ability of prisoners to sue has been restricted by both legislative and judicial actions.

The 1980s were characterized by massive prison construction campaigns in many states. Indeed, the national prison capacity increased by more than 100% between 1985 and 2000.[67] Simultaneously, the federal government slashed spending on education and other social programs, and states faced "taxpayer revolts." This combination of factors forced many states to cut school budgets to finance prison operations.[68] Crime rates have a small but significant effect on the expansion of prison populations; the states with the worst crime problems tend to have the largest amount of growth in imprisonment. Fear and stereotypes, along with economics and politics, have been the driving forces behind the increase in prison populations.[69] Disproportionate numbers of African Americans and other minorities have been imprisoned, resulting in "invisible punishments," such as disenfranchisement. Some analysts fear that these trends could threaten "the future of (meaningful) minority participation in the democratic process," a fear that has grown along with prison populations.[70]

By the mid-1990s the newly expanded prison systems were inadequate to house the increased numbers of prisoners, and there were severe cutbacks in programs and staffing.[71] Conditions in prisons today are generally harsher than they have been since the 1950s. Texas, California, and Florida have the largest prison populations in the nation while Louisiana, Texas, and Mississippi have the highest rates of imprisonment.[72]

The foundation of this trend is more political than scientific. A panel of experts concluded that "there is no systematic evidence that . . . incapacitation has had or could have a major impact on crime rates." This panel noted that the increased use of imprisonment is due largely to the way in which the war on drugs is being fought and the increasing severity with which the justice system responds to minorities and women.[73] There is considerable evidence from several different sources that race plays a major role in both the war on drugs and the use of criminal punishment in the United States.[74] It is likely that ideology also plays a role, because data also show that large increases in prison populations usually occur under Republican presidents. Bill Clinton, an exception to this generality, however, supported the incarceration policies of the Reagan-Bush administrations.[75] This severity, and the desire to limit agency responsibilities as agency budgets shrink, is at the root of the increasingly dominant approach to the correctional mission known as the "new penology."

THE NEW PENOLOGY

One of the most striking changes in modern corrections is the introduction of new norms for assessing correctional agencies and practices. Traditional penology, based on law and criminology, emphasizes punishment and rehabilitation. The *new penology* focuses on risk management and administrative efficiency. Its central goal is to incapacitate high-risk offenders for as long as possible. Risk estimates are made using *actuarial methods* based on factors that predict violence or recidivism for broad categories of people, such as drug or sex offenders.[76] Some states will not consider certain types of offenders for discretionary release; some use commitment laws to hold sexual predators after they have served their full sentence.[77]

Critics of the new penology feel that it ignores the personal problems and social conditions that foster criminality and emphasizes only the efficient use of agency resources. Because our concepts of justice focus on the actual behavior of individuals, many criticize the new penology's focus on groups as unfair. There is also concern that efforts to control high-risk groups will replace the goals of justice and reintegration. The new penology does not try to eliminate or reduce crime; it simply tries to improve the coordination of the social control system.[78] Most states have adopted some elements of this approach, and others seem to endorse it fully.

SUMMARY

The history of corrections shows how our reliance on government control of individual behavior has grown over time. As society became more urban, the family and community lost much of their ability to control individuals. As informal social control became less able to regulate behavior, governments took more responsibility for controlling individuals. Dissatisfaction with society's ability to control crime resulted in a series of reform movements. These movements were alternately driven by fear of crime, humanitarian ideals, economic problems, and new ideas about how to control behavior. Each led to major changes in corrections, but none significantly reduced the level of crime in the long run. All suffered from a failure to question basic beliefs about human behavior.

The prison began as a humane alternative to corporal punishment. The segregate system, however, proved worse than flogging for many prisoners. Overcrowding led to the collapse of the silent system and later frustrated the goals of the reformatory. It also contributed to the creation of the Federal Bureau of Prisons, which is generally seen as the most modern correctional system in the world. Warehousing of offenders under horrible conditions was routine until the due process revolution when the courts demanded that the basic dignity of inmates be respected. Throughout history, economic pressures, overcrowding, and faith (or lack thereof) in treatment have shaped correctional policies and practices. Crowding and other problems continue to plague U.S. prisons as states alternate between expanding their prison systems and reducing their prison populations. These problems, however, are usually unrelated to the crime rate but rather are driven by political trends within society where prisons remain the easiest way to control criminals and to keep them out of sight. Economics also play a large role in setting correctional policies and are a large part of the motivation for both the new penology and restorative justice programs.

QUESTIONS FOR DISCUSSION AND REVIEW

1. How did early societies respond to crime? What factors led to the invention of the prison as we know it today? What kinds of punishments did the prison replace? Why did people feel the need to replace these sanctions with imprisonment?

2. What were early prisons designed to accomplish? What popular beliefs guided their creation and development? How do current ideas about efficiency and fairness affect modern prisons? What should be the goals of the modern prison?

3. What was the lease system? Where was it used? What goals did it serve? What led to its collapse? What lessons should we learn from this as we again look to the private sector to assist with prison overcrowding?

4. How did parole and probation develop? What were their original goals? What problems did they address?

5. How has the doctrine of *lex talionis* affected the development of North American corrections? How do public opinion and politics affect the definition of what is a reasonable punishment for a given crime?

6. How have the classical and positivist schools of thought influenced modern corrections? What contradictions in our policies and practices can be traced to the differing concerns and assumptions of these views? Can these contradictions be reconciled? How?

7. What ideas about human nature drove the Progressive Era? What methods of handling offenders originated in this period? Were these changes the result of

scientific progress or optimistic emotions? Are similar events occurring today in prison policy making?

8. How and when did the due process revolution impact our correctional system? What legal doctrines and Supreme Court decisions were pivotal in defining the relationship between the courts and the correctional system? What was the substance of these changes? By what legal methods do courts affect prison operation? What does society gain from this?

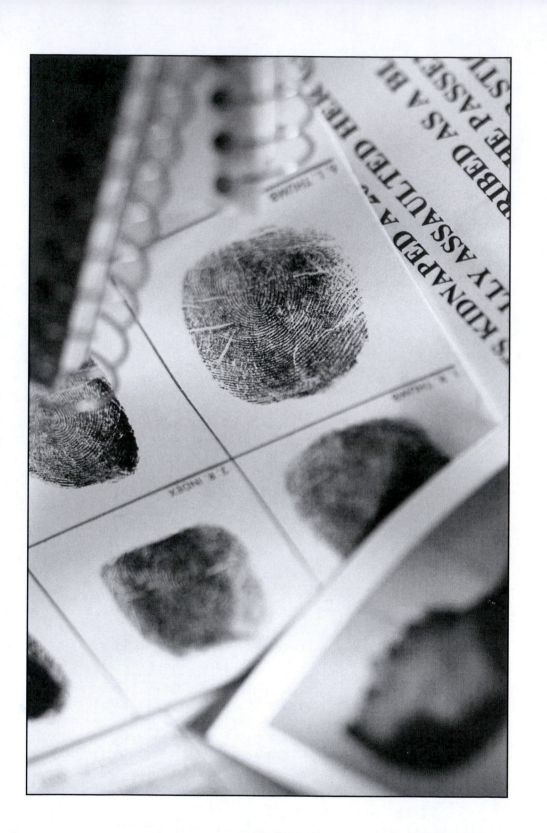

JAILS

Any facility with cells to hold people accused of a crime may be called a jail. City or county governments operate most U.S. jails, but in a few areas they are under state control. Many of these facilities are too small to hold prisoners for more than a day or two. They are essentially *holding facilities* where suspects are detained for up to forty-eight hours. After that, they must either be released or be transferred to a facility that can provide long-term custody. In contrast, other jails often hold fifty or more people for weeks or months.

All elements of the justice process use, or are affected by, jails. Federal, state, and local law enforcement officers use jails to detain suspects and may go there to question them as well. Hearings to set bail or to revoke probation/parole are often held at the local jail. In addition, jail crowding puts pressure on both trial courts and prison systems to move inmates through the process. Throughout history, jails have held social misfits alongside dangerous offenders. Despite their importance, however, they are one of the most neglected areas of study in criminal justice.

MODERN JAILS

Few scientific studies have examined jails, so little can be said with certainty about them. The available studies focus mainly on: (1) physical conditions; (2) management problems; (3) inmate rights; or (4) reform efforts. This lack of interest in jails is partly because they house few dangerous criminals for long periods. Jails are also hard to study because their populations are constantly changing. Many people suspected of minor crimes are released soon after their arrest, and convicted felons are usually transferred to prison within a few weeks of being sentenced. Further, a different agency controls each jail so getting access to them can be very time consuming. However, most jails have similar design features.

Jail Capacity, Crowding, and Costs

Figure A compares the number of people jailed with the holding capacity of U.S. jails. Jail crowding was not a national problem until 1988, when the number of inmates exceeded the capacity of jails. Forty percent of the increase in jail populations between 1983 and 1989 was due to the war on drugs. In 1992, capacity caught up with the number of inmates due to construction projects throughout the nation. The average growth since midyear 1995 has been 25,591 beds every 12 months. At midyear 2001, the capacity of local jails was estimated at 699,309; the number of inmates was 625,966 (90% of capacity).[1] The increase in beds has been costly, however, as is shown in figure B. Jail costs rose 60% as the war on drugs began (1983 to 1988) and grew another 47% over the next five years (1988 to 1993) before slowing.[2]

National statistics often fail to describe accurately the situation faced by particular jails at the local level. A federal survey in the late 1990s found that 35% of jails were over-crowded, meaning that they were at least 10% over their rated capacity. This was an improvement over the 52% that reported serious crowding in 1990. The reduction in over-crowding is largely due to massive prison and jail construction projects in many states. However, many of the largest jails in the nation are also the most overcrowded. Eighteen of the nation's 50 largest jails are currently operating at more than 100% capacity; the number of inmates and staff affected by this problem is massive. Small jails are much harder to track at the national level but often suffer from physical neglect as well as crowding. Drugs, pro-bation/parole violations, domestic violence, longer misdemeanor sentences, and convicted felons being held in local jails because of prison space shortages remain the central causes of overcrowding.

Figure A   Jail Capacity and Number of Inmates, 1978–2001

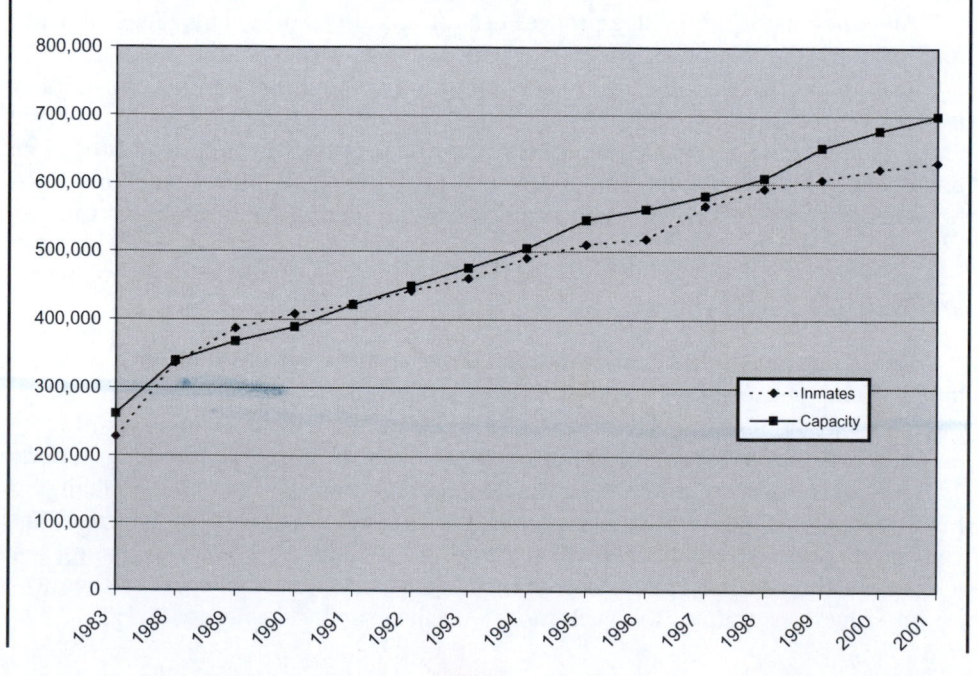

Figure B   Jail Costs, 1983–1999

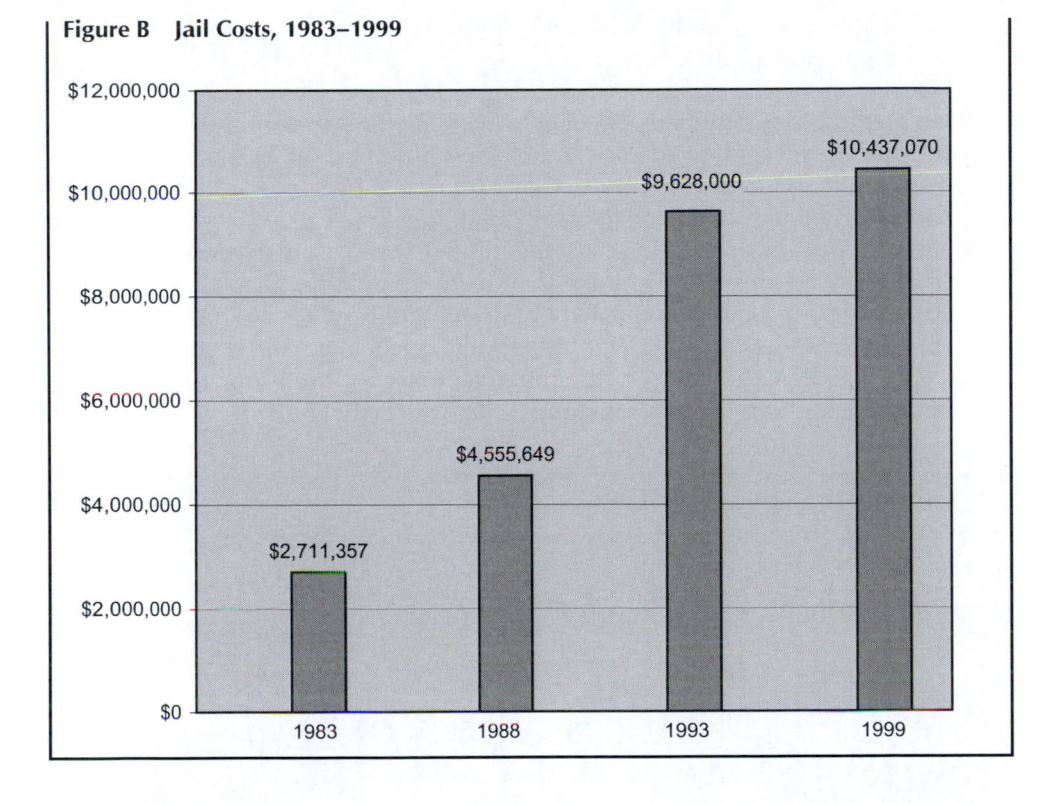

Design and Organization

The basic organization of most jails is similar. The entrance used by police officers to bring prisoners into the facility is called a *sallyport*. This is a secure area into which vehicles can be driven. The sallyport door is opened and closed by remote control from inside the jail when requested by the dispatcher. Guards can enter the sallyport to assist police with combative suspects when needed. There is usually a set of lockers in the sallyport where officers must place their guns before entering the jail. Firearms are prohibited in jails and prisons to prevent inmates from getting control of them and escaping or taking hostages.

Close to the sallyport is the *booking area*, where fingerprints and mug shots are taken. Close to this area are rooms for frisk searches, Breathalyzer tests, and other functions related to arrests. Basic information about suspects and the charges against them are recorded by jail staff during the transfer of custody. Some of this information is required to insure that inmates are healthy when admitted. Jailers should never accept custody of suspects who appear to be sick or injured unless a medical professional has certified that the individual is healthy enough to be jailed. Suspects claiming to be sick or injured must be examined by a medical professional. Some jails have an infirmary staff who can perform this duty as well as care for anyone who becomes sick or injured while in custody. Suspects who express suicidal thoughts or are afraid of being assaulted should be identified during intake. Suspects are allowed to make one or more phone calls unless they are combative or highly intoxicated.

After being booked in, suspects are placed in a large holding cell. Called the **bullpen** or **tank**, this cell holds prisoners who will be released within a few hours or who will be transported to some other location. The tank is usually equipped only with a drain in the center of the room. Intoxicated persons are left here until they are sober enough to be booked and either released or placed in the jail's general population. Tank areas are usually the filthiest part of a jail because large numbers of drunks pass through them. For their own safety, intoxicated persons cannot be released or placed in the main area of the jail until they have sobered up.[3]

Segregation units consist of one-person cells for inmates who require disciplinary action, special treatment, or close observation. They are usually located near the main booking area so that inmates can be watched closely by jail staff. As in

After entering the jail, suspects are taken to the booking area where fingerprints and mug shots are taken.

prisons, there are two basic reasons for segregating individual inmates. *Punitive* segregation is solitary confinement for disciplinary reasons; these inmates are assaultive, have tried to escape, or have otherwise threatened the security of the facility. Before they can be assigned to such a cell there must be a hearing before a neutral person or board.[4] Administrative or *protective* segregation is for inmates who are suicidal, mentally ill and disruptive, or who may be harmed if placed in the general population of the jail (e.g., informants). Persons awaiting disciplinary hearings can also be placed in administrative segregation if they are a threat to themselves, others, or the order of the facility.

The rest of the jail is organized into a series of cells, pods, or cell blocks. In the more professionally managed jails, prisoners are classified according to legal status and dangerousness. Their classification is used to decide where they will be housed and how much freedom they will have within the jail. Classification systems vary widely in their value and utility. Many jails have little or no classification system and treat all inmates the same.[5]

Jail classification systems often do little more than separate felons from misdemeanor offenders and the convicted from pretrial detainees. A few, however, carefully sort prisoners by the level of risk they pose for violence and escape. Those thought to be assaultive or escape risks are placed in high-security areas deep within the jail. Older offenders and homosexuals are usually separated from other prisoners for their own protection.[6] New prisoners are treated as though they require maximum security until they are classified and placed in a cell suited to their security needs. The color of the inmate's jail uniform is sometimes used to signify his/her classification status. The brighter the color, the higher the security level required by the inmate.

Inmates who have shown that they pose no threat to security may be assigned *trustee* status. Trustees get special privileges in exchange for working around the jail or on projects in the community. They are often housed in a separate, minimum-security area but may also be dispersed throughout the jail. Most trustees work as janitors, in food service, or help with maintenance. They are vital to the operation of most jails because they perform unskilled, routine labor at virtually no cost to the facility. Being a trustee is a much-desired status because these inmates have more freedom to move about the facility than others.

Convicted misdemeanor offenders may be housed in a *stockade* facility that is built for minimum security standards. Work programs, such as highway cleanup crews, often operate out of these facilities, as do some work release programs. *Work-release programs* allow inmates to leave the jail for their normal job each day. If they do not return immediately after work, they are considered escapees. Although these programs present some inherent threats to security, they also reduce recidivism.[7] Stockades are usually under the same administration as the jail but located in a different, often more rural, location.

Jail Administration

There are 3,360 jails holding 631,240 inmates in the United States at the beginning of the twenty-first century.[8] These institutions vary greatly in size, the largest having a capacity of more than 8,000. Roughly 20% of U.S. jails are city managed. Although only about 500 jails are in this category, they include some of the largest facilities in the world, such as those serving New York City and Los Angeles. Most jails, however, can hold no more than 50 inmates at once. Besides city and county jails, there are more than 13,500 other holding facilities (e.g., lockups, drunk tanks, and so on).[9] Jail administrators have little direct control over who is admitted to the jail or the length of stay. However, they can influence policies that affect overcrowding such as access to pretrial services to help speed the processing of defendants.[10]

Some jails are very old and badly neglected, while others represent the "state of the art" in correctional design and planning. The highly variable conditions reflect the range of financial and crime problems in the United States. In 44 states, a county agency operates jails and must compete with schools and roads for funding from local governments.[11] Most jails are operated by the county sheriff, even though sheriffs are usually trained in law enforcement rather than corrections. Likewise, most sheriffs' department employees are oriented to police work rather than corrections. Thus, jails are often operated by people who know little about running correctional facilities or handling their diverse populations.[12] Furthermore, few counties provide civil service protection to jail employees, so political connections are often the only qualification needed to be appointed as a supervisor or guard.

Most of the 3,360 jails are managed by the city or the county.

Some counties have addressed these problems by separating jail administration from the sheriff's office and hiring jail managers to operate their facilities. These managers are correctional professionals who answer to the county commissioners. This approach was pioneered in New Mexico, where half the counties use such a system. Texas has both local and state-run jails. The latter hold minor felons for up to two years and try to coordinate their services with local probation agencies.[13] Texas' local jails are operated by either the county sheriff or a private company and fulfill the traditional mission of the jail.

Besides county and city facilities, the Federal Bureau of Prisons operates eleven federal detention centers. These facilities hold prisoners who are awaiting trial in federal courts or facing deportation as illegal immigrants. Due to the focus of federal law on organized crime, drug trafficking, bank robbery, and white-collar offenses, the populations of these facilities contain a higher percentage of whites and males than do local jails. Several of these facilities serve primarily as holding areas for aliens facing deportation. It costs an average of $22,773 to hold an inmate for a year in one of these facilities, while in a local facility the cost would be $14,667. The higher cost of federal jails is due to the fact that they are in central locations of large cities, and their employees are better trained and paid than those at most local facilities. These facilities were operating at 139% capacity in 1999.[14]

Inmate Populations

Modern jails serve four purposes: (1) pretrial detention, (2) dumping ground for social misfits, (3) local penal institution, and (4) holding facility for convicted felons awaiting sentencing or transportation to prison. Most jail inmates are **pretrial detainees** who have been charged with a crime and cannot make bail while awaiting trial. Many pretrial detainees are charged with minor offenses, and most are released soon after their arrest. However, those with little money are likely to remain in custody. Other detainees have been denied release because they are accused of serious offenses or are considered poor risks for pretrial release. Pretrial detainees make up 58.5% of the national jail population.[15]

Jails have always been used to control social misfits, most of whom are members of the underclass. They are more visible to police than other groups and are less able to remove themselves from the justice system once arrested. Many are homeless, addicted to drugs or alcohol, or mentally ill, and most lack the stable ties to the community required for release prior to trial.[16] Few members of the underclass are truly hardened or dangerous offenders. Jails serve as penal institutions; they hold inmates sentenced to short terms.[17] Persons convicted of misdemeanors can be sentenced to jail for up to one year in most states; but most jail sentences are for 10 to 90 days.[18] Jails also house convicted felons awaiting sentencing and/or transfer to a state or federal prison.

Crowding creates a constant source of tension between county and state governments. When state prisons get crowded, prisoners awaiting transportation remain in the county jails and cause overcrowding there. In 1993, convicted felons awaiting transfer made up more than 12% of all jail inmates; the percentage has fallen since many states opened new prisons. This figure changes depending on the number of people sentenced.

In 1983, 7.1% of jail inmates in the United States were women; by 1990 women made up 9.2% of the jail population, and by 2001 this figure had grown to 11.6%.[19] Women make up a larger percentage of jail than prison inmates because of their involvement in petty theft and drugs, crimes for which jail time is most often imposed. Jails are thus confronted with issues related to pregnancy and sexual harassment. Because of these problems, women are more expensive to hold than men. The increasing rate at which women are being jailed threatens the financial health of many local governments.

Drug charges account for more a third of the women in jails but only one-fifth of the men. The growing percentage of women in American jails is largely due to the war on drugs. There are no significant gender differences in property, public order, and other crimes but twice as many males are jailed for violent offenses. This means that women are far more likely to be held for nonviolent offenses than men. Most women imprisoned are young, poor, and from the inner city; over one-third of these women have children under the age of 18.[20]

Legal Status of Jail Inmates[21]

All jail inmates can be placed into one of five categories. Some of these categories are only rarely encountered (e.g., material witnesses) while others make up the bulk of the jail's mission (e.g., pretrial detainees). Almost half (41.5%) of all jail inmates have been convicted of a crime.

1. *Pretrial detainees* (including persons awaiting parole/probation revocation hearings (58.5%);

2. *Convicted misdemeanor offenders* serving their sentences;

3. *Sentenced felons* awaiting transportation to state/federal prison;

4. *Convicted felons* awaiting sentencing; and

5. *Material witnesses* being held under court order to (a) assure their safety or (b) assure their appearance at trial. (A judicial order is required to hold a material witness and it is a very rare practice. This group makes up less than 1% of the jail population.)

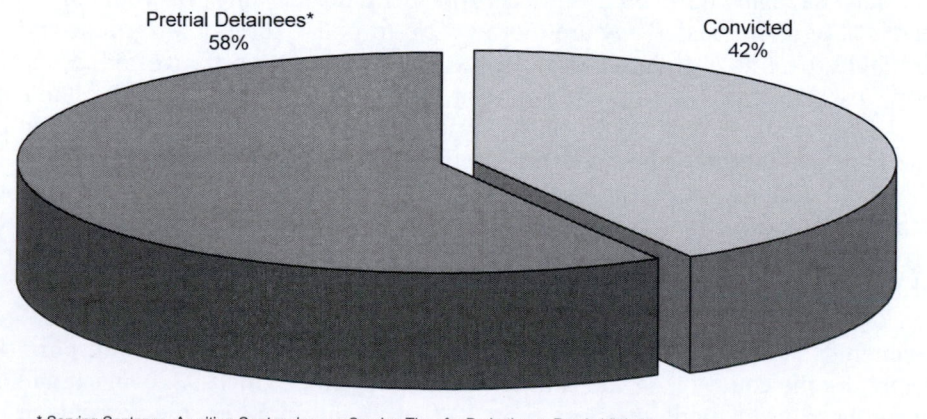

Pretrial Detainees*
58%

Convicted
42%

* Serving Sentence, Awaiting Sentencing, or Serving Time for Probation or Parole Violation

Demographics of the United States Jail Population[22]

Gender		Education	
Males	88.4%	High School Dropouts	41%
Females	11.6%	High School Graduates	59%
Race		**Employment**	
African American	40.6%	Employed	41%
Hispanic	14.7%	Unemployed	59%
White	43.0%		
Other	01.7%	**Marital Status**	
		Married	21%
Median Annual Income	$5,486	Unmarried	79%

Race and the Jail Rate[23]

It is estimated that more than ten million people are jailed annually; over 625,000 are in jail on an average day—a larger percentage of the nation's population than ever before. In 1983 the rate of jailing was 96 per 100,000, but by 1997 this figure had risen to 212 and in 2001 it reached 222. The jail rate for whites in 1985 was 68 while for African Americans it was 138. By 2001 the white rate had reached 138, while that for African Americans had risen to 703. While African Americans make up 41% of jail inmates, they are only 13% of the overall U.S. population. Most criminologists believe that the war on drugs is a major reason for disproportionate minority confinement.

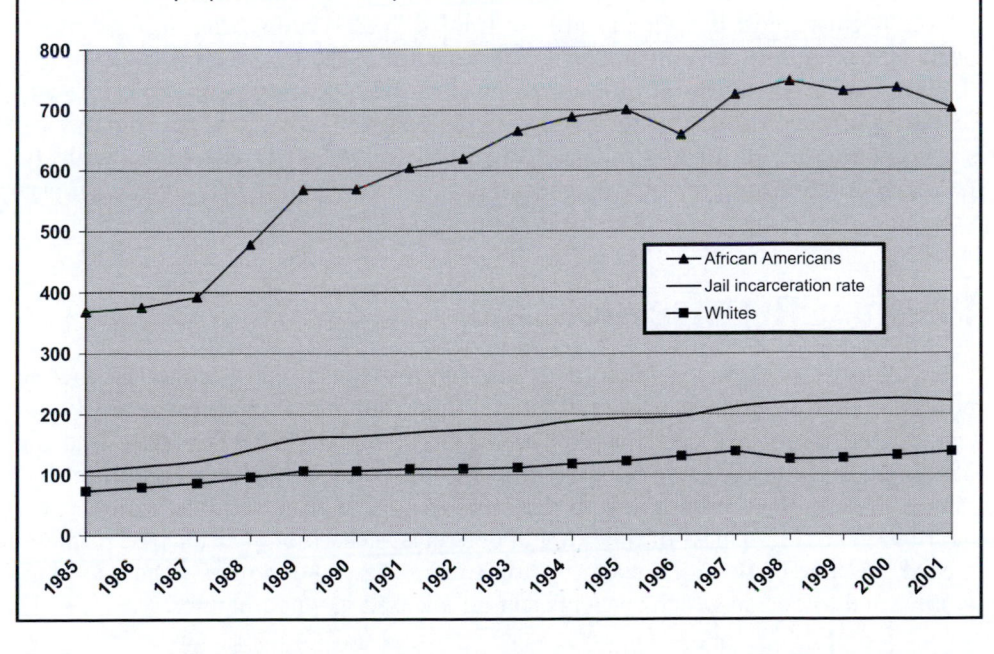

Jail Programs

Several characteristics of jail populations affect efforts to provide programs for inmates. First, the time spent in jail is usually too brief to allow for effective offense-related counseling, basic education, or vocational training. Most job training programs require 25 to 30 weeks of training, and other types of counseling often take even longer. Overcrowding and high turnover among staff and inmates are also barriers.

Studies show that anywhere from 10% to 33% of jail inmates have a serious mental, alcohol, and/or drug problem. In 1998 an estimated 7 in 10 local jail inmates had used drugs regularly or had committed a drug offense.[24] Treatment programs aimed at this population of alcoholics and addicts appear to be effective in cutting their recidivism as well as the frequency with which they violate probation for "technical" reasons.[25] It is increasingly common for inmates to suffer from mental illness along with a substance abuse problem. Addicts are often drawn to drugs because of other conditions for which they have not been treated, and some mentally ill persons have co-occurring mental or physical disabilities. Few jails have the space or funding for programs to serve the mentally ill and chemically dependent, even though these groups make up a significant part of most jail populations.[26]

Seventy-eight percent of jails screen for mental health problems at intake.[27] However, only about 25% of all jails have any educational or treatment staff, and even these employees rarely are trained to deal with serious mental health, alcohol, or drug problems. Jail staff usually see their role as simply keeping inmates in custody and under control. When jails do offer programs they must usually deal with very basic skills like literacy, hygiene, and high school equivalency (GED) education. Because most jail officials are not trained in corrections, these programs get even less attention than in prisons. The security problems created by outdated facilities, poor classification procedures and fear of appearing "soft" on crime add to the reluctance of many sheriffs to provide programs for inmates. This has led some experts to call for less reliance on jails for minor offenders. Along with the financial problems faced by local governments, crowding nonetheless makes it necessary to release many low-risk suspects prior to trial.

PRETRIAL RELEASE FROM JAIL

Only 36% of felony defendants, primarily those accused of violent crimes or probation/parole violations, are held in jail from the time of their arrest until their trial.[28] Pretrial release decisions are based largely on the need for space and the likelihood that the accused will appear in court as ordered. Most courts will release minor offenders with strong ties to the area on a mere promise to return for court hearings. The seriousness of the crime a person is accused of, his/her past criminal record, his/her history of appearing for court dates, and similar facts are commonly used to decide which suspects can be released in what manner.

Most jail inmates are pretrial detainees who cannot afford to post bail.

Bail

Traditionally, suspects have had to provide **bail**, a sum of money held by the court to guarantee that a person will return for his or her trial. Bail is available to most suspects in all jurisdictions. Only 7% of defendants are denied bail.[29] If the suspect appears at all required court hearings, bail is returned even if he or she is convicted. Bail is set by a judge or magistrate at the suspect's initial court appearance, usually within 24 hours of arrest. A range for bail for each offense is set by the penal code. Judges may set bail anywhere within this range based on their estimate of what is needed to assure that the suspect will appear for later court hearings. The Eighth Amendment forbids use of "excessive bail." The meaning of this term, however, varies with the judge, the seriousness of the crime, the suspect's wealth, and the stability of his/her lifestyle. Bail may be set higher than usual if the suspect is felt to be at high risk of fleeing or poses a threat to victims, witnesses, or the public. However, the use of bail as punishment is prohibited. In large cities, about 34% of pretrial releases require financial release.[30]

Bail for felonies is usually several thousand dollars or more per charge. The most common type of financial release is a surety bond, which involves the services of a commercial bail bond agent. **Bail bondsmen** post the required amount of money with the court to obtain the suspect's release. Bondsmen charge 10 to 20% of the bail for this service. This money is the bondsmen's profit and is not returned after the case has been handled by the courts. If a person is jailed on a charge for which the judge sets a bail of $10,000, it will cost $1,000 to $2,000 to obtain release through a bondsman. The bondsman retains the fee and risks losing the full amount of the bail if the suspect does not return for trial. Other types of financial release are full cash bonds and property bonds; these are posted directly with the court.[31]

Release on Recognizance

The use of cash bail bonds was questioned in the 1960s. It was viewed as a form of economic discrimination. Developed as an alternative to bail, **release on recognizance** allows a judge or magistrate to free a suspect on his or her promise to return for court dates. Thirty percent of defendants released in large urban areas are released on recognizance.[32] Sometimes called a PR or personal recognizance bond, it is used with minor offenders with strong ties to the local area. Homeowners and those whose families live nearby are much more likely to be released on recognizance than are the homeless or those who are "just passing through" the area. Although people released on recognizance are no more likely to fail to appear for trial than those who use cash bonds to obtain release, the eligibility criteria used in recognizance decisions are often not related to the probability of failure to appear for later court dates.[33] Release on recognizance helps relieve overcrowding by freeing suspects who pose little threat to the community. It also helps suspects obtain their own legal counsel, keep their jobs, and support their families in the months between arrest and trial. While created to help avoid the potential for discrimination inherent in bail, recognizance has been criticized for excluding the underclass; favoring whites, women, and Hispanics; and inadequately controlling offenders at high risk of recidivism.[34]

Conditional Pretrial Release

The expense of holding accused people in jail must be balanced against the likelihood that they will commit new crimes if released or fail to appear for their court date. Approximately 16% of released defendants committed a new offense before trial, and 24% failed to appear in court.[35] A wide variety of *conditional pretrial release programs* have sprung up around the United States to relieve jail crowding. Thirteen percent of felony defendants in urban areas received conditional release.[36] These programs impose restrictions on the defendants released prior to trial. Some are designed to make release on recognizance tougher, while others are used with defendants who would not otherwise qualify for such a release. Others use social service referrals to help offenders adjust to a law-abiding life in the community.[37] New technologies like urine testing and electronic monitoring are often used to assure that defendants obey the conditions of their release. House arrest can now be used to incapacitate suspects awaiting trial without sacrificing cell space.[38]

The need to release nonviolent suspects is especially pressing because of the war on drugs, but judges are also sensitive to the public's fears that dangerous offenders will be released. Probation officers are trained to do background checks on offenders and estimate the risk they pose to the community. They are also uniquely equipped to supervise people who are free in the community under the control of a court. As probation caseloads increase, however, jail staff are becoming increasingly involved in these programs.[39] Releasees are usually required to check in at least once a week and may also have to submit to drug testing and curfews. These release programs are very similar to the probation and intensive supervision programs discussed in chapters 4 and 5. Their use with pretrial detainees is one approach to cutting jail costs. Programs such as work release, weekend confinement and residential drug treatment being used in many jails are designed to reduce the number of convicted misdemeanor offenders in crowded jails.[40]

Pretrial *diversion programs* are sometimes offered to nonviolent defendants who agree to participate in treatment. Diversion may occur prior to booking or after formal charges are filed. Charges are dropped if the person successfully completes the program so that the negative effects of an arrest on a person's earning potential can be minimized. This approach is most often used with minor, first-time, drug offenders. Another type of diversionary program consists of transferring the mentally ill into mental health facilities rather than jailing them. These programs are usually based on agreements with local mental health treatment facilities that will handle offenders brought to them by the police. Such an approach to controlling jail populations requires police or jailers to be trained to identify the mentally ill.[41] Detoxification centers that provide medical treatment for alcoholics/addicts operate in much the same way. While attractive in theory, these programs are usually overcrowded themselves and have long waiting lists.[42]

ALTERNATIVES TO JAIL

Alternatives to jail for the convicted include fines, restitution, community service, work release, and intermittent sentences. Like pretrial release, these programs are usually run by probation departments and are discussed in detail in chapter 5. The use of fines instead of imprisonment is not a new concept, but several problems limit its effectiveness. On the one hand, financial punishment for offenders who are so poor that they cannot even pay their own bills is not a reasonable alternative. Many impoverished offenders must choose jail instead of a fine because they have no income. On the other hand, fines have little deterrent value for the wealthy.

Day fines address these problems by allowing judges to base the amount of an offender's fine on the basis of the seriousness of the offense and the offender's ability to pay the fine. Each crime is assigned a certain number of "punishment units." For example, disorderly conduct may be valued at 5 to 10 punishment units, while attempted assault may be worth 30 to 45 units. The number of punishment units is then multiplied by the amount of money earned by the offender in a single day. The resulting amount may be adjusted if exceptional family or personal problems are shown to affect the offender's ability to pay. Day fines are very popular in Western Europe but have only recently been introduced in the United States.[43]

Some judges like to utilize *intermittent sentencing* that allows convicted offenders to work during the day and spend nights and/or weekends in jail. They are popular with judges because they punish offenders while allowing them to support their families and repay their victims. However, intermittent sentencing causes jailers much difficulty because it consumes cell space and staff time during periods of peak activity in most jails. It also increases the risk of drugs being smuggled into the jail. These programs have shown mixed results with regard to recidivism rates but may be valuable in helping some offenders avoid the negative effects of the jail environment.[44]

Drug courts are one of the fastest growing methods of diverting nonviolent substance abusers from the justice system. Offenders with little or no prior criminal history are selected for these programs partly for their motivation to stop abusing drugs or alcohol. They must receive intensive treatment in the community, hold a job, submit urine for analysis each week and meet with probation officers and counselors attached to the court to monitor their progress. Other conditions may also be imposed. Drug courts usually meet weekly and each offender's progress is reviewed by the judge in that public setting. Those who do well are praised while those showing signs of trouble may be warned, receive new conditions, be jailed briefly, or be expelled from the program. Assignment to a drug court may occur prior to or after conviction. Expulsion from a preconviction program means the offender must face trial for the offense while postconviction courts may impose the original sentence. This approach requires the close cooperation of defense and prosecuting attorneys as well treatment providers. The entire process is carefully monitored by a judge who should be selected for concern with reforming substance abusers and skill in dealing with them.[45] Experimental programs applying this model to mentally ill offenders are under way in Florida, Alaska, California, and Washington state,[46] and attempts to do the same with drunken driving[47] and domestic violence[48] are also in progress.

THE INMATE EXPERIENCE

The problems encountered by jail inmates are much like those experienced in prisons. Although sentences are shorter, jail inmates spend less time outside their cells than prison inmates and are less likely to work or receive treatment. Both jail and prison inmates suffer three shattering processes.

Degradation consists of humiliating experiences that result from routine jail procedures such as strip searches, delousing, loss of personal items, and separation from the opposite sex. Inmates must refer to guards in a respectful manner, but guards need not return this courtesy. Being forced to associate with other social outcasts is also part of the degradation process. *Disorientation* results from being held in a loud, dirty, and unpredictable environment. Institutional routines and idleness become the norm, and inmates lose track of time and other features of normal life. The *disintegration* process consists of the loss of property, social contacts, and the power to manage one's own life. Being placed in jail is often counterproductive to any hope for reintegration with society because it encourages inmates to take on the values and attitudes of the inmate population.[49] Recently, the situation has been worsened by a number of factors. Most prominent of these is the effect of the growing numbers of mentally ill inmates.

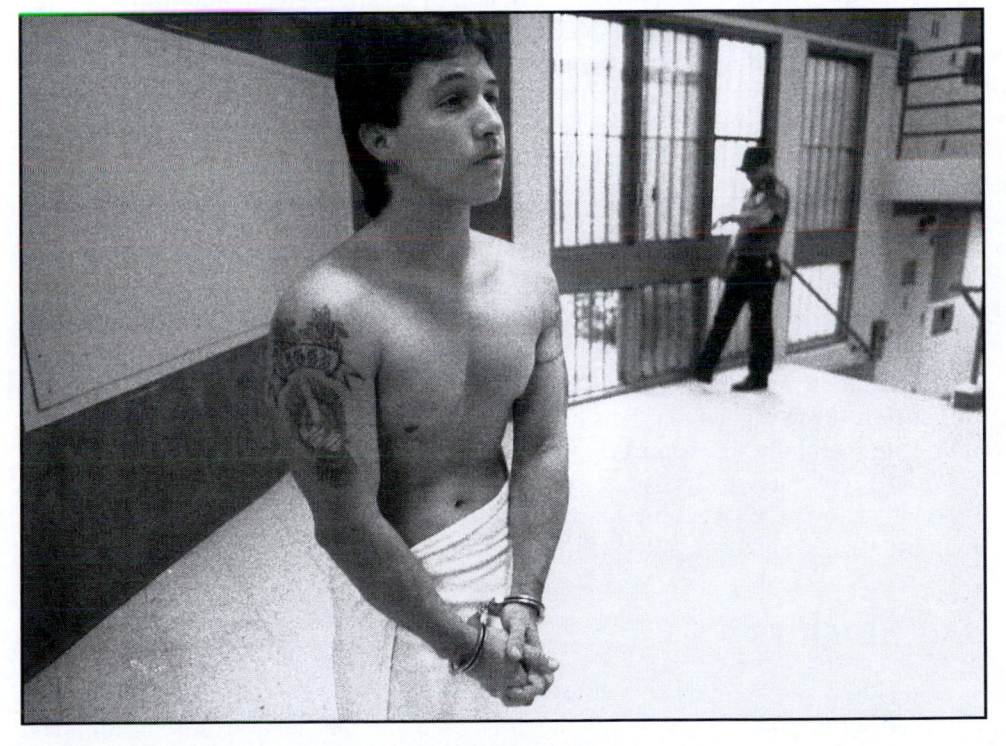

Routine jail procedures contribute to feelings of degradation, one of three processes most inmates experience in jail.

The Mentally Disordered in Jail

In the early 1970s the Supreme Court imposed very strict standards for long-term involuntary commitment to mental hospitals. At the time of these court rulings, scientific data on the harmful effects of living in an institution were growing rapidly as was judicial sensitivity to the rights of disenfranchised people. No one can be confined in a mental institution for more than a few days unless there is *clear and convincing evidence* that they may harm themselves or others in the immediate future. This standard of proof is halfway between the absolute certainty required in a criminal trial and the "preponderance of evidence" used in civil trials. Prior to the 1970s, people could be confined if a physician swore that they were (1) "in need of treatment" and (2) unable to realize it. This was declared illegal in the 1970s, and current law requires that a recent statement or act must clearly indicate a person is dangerous to self or others if commitment is to be legal.[50]

These factors led to a movement for *deinstitutionalization* in the 1970s, which forced the release of many patients. New drug therapies could treat many of the disorders that previously required institutionalization. The movement's goal was to treat these people in the community, where costs were lower and they could more easily be reintegrated into society. However, funding was never provided for community mental health centers; without supervision to make sure medication was taken in the correct dosage and at the right time, drug therapies were useless. As a result of these changes, the percentage of inmates with severe mental disorders rose from less than 1% in 1900 to more than 15% by 1998;[51] in 2002 it was reported that about 16% of the 630,000 people in the nation's jails suffer from some form of mental illness.[52] This means that there are nearly three times as many people with severe mental disorders in urban jails as in the general population. Many of these inmates were homeless prior to being arrested and will return to a life on the city streets when released.[53] The police are permitted to place people in protective custody for a short period if they appear to be mentally ill or highly intoxicated. As a result, addicts and the mentally ill are a major part of jail populations.

The impact of the mentally ill on jails is one of the major problems facing American corrections. There are two questions that must be answered before an effective solution can be found: Do we jail the mentally ill more often than others, or do criminals have higher rates of mental illness than noncriminals? The *criminalization thesis* claims that jails have replaced mental hospitals as places for confining the mentally ill. According to this argument, the mentally ill are jailed for disorderly conduct, trespassing, panhandling, and other minor crimes because there is no other convenient place to hold them. One study of mental patients found that 75% had been jailed while awaiting admission to a psychiatric facility.[54]

JAIL SUICIDES

Suicide is the second most common cause of death in jails and is much more common among jail inmates than in prisons or in the general population. The problem is compounded by the fact that offenders experience the greatest crisis immediately after arrest, before correctional officers have had the time to learn very much about them. Most suicides occur within a few hours or days of a person being jailed. The fear and embarrassment that result from being arrested and jailed can lead to suicide. Being bullied by other inmates is also a common cause of suicidal thoughts, and those at greatest risk of suicide may also be at high risk of being bullied.[55] Inmates who display one or more of the following traits are at high risk: (1) open threats of suicide; (2) history of suicide attempts; (3) intoxication, especially drunkenness; (4) serious mental/emotional disturbances; and (5) expressions of deep depression and hopelessness or hostility.[56] The inmate most at risk of committing suicide while in jail is a 29-year-old single, white, male arrested for public intoxication. Most suicides are by hanging and occur on a Monday.[57] Alcoholics and addicts often attempt suicide while suffering through withdrawal in jail, and the mentally disordered are at very high risk of killing themselves as well. The shock of incarceration is extremely distressing for anyone, and for those with fewer emotional, mental, and social resources it is even more devastating. Most jails try to eliminate opportunities for suicide by removing belts, shoelaces, and

Causes of Death among Jail Inmates[58]

It must be emphasized that fewer than 1,000 people die in U.S. jails each year. Natural causes have become the leading cause of death in jails since 1989. Until then suicide was slightly more common. Serious illnesses, such as tuberculosis, are more common among jail inmates than in the general population because (1) many offenders come from the worst living conditions found in this nation, and (2) many have abused their bodies with alcohol, drugs, and "hard living." AIDS is the third leading cause of death among jail inmates. It accounted for 8% of all deaths recorded among jail inmates in 1999, but its impact is decreasing as improved medical treatments become available. Homicide is the rarest cause of death among jail inmates—only 28 inmates were killed by others (3%). Drug and alcohol overdoses, accidents, attempted escapes, and unknown causes are included in the "other" category. These data underestimate the overall number of deaths because not all jails were able to report complete data on deaths, and information on inmates who died elsewhere (e.g., after transport to a hospital) are often not available.

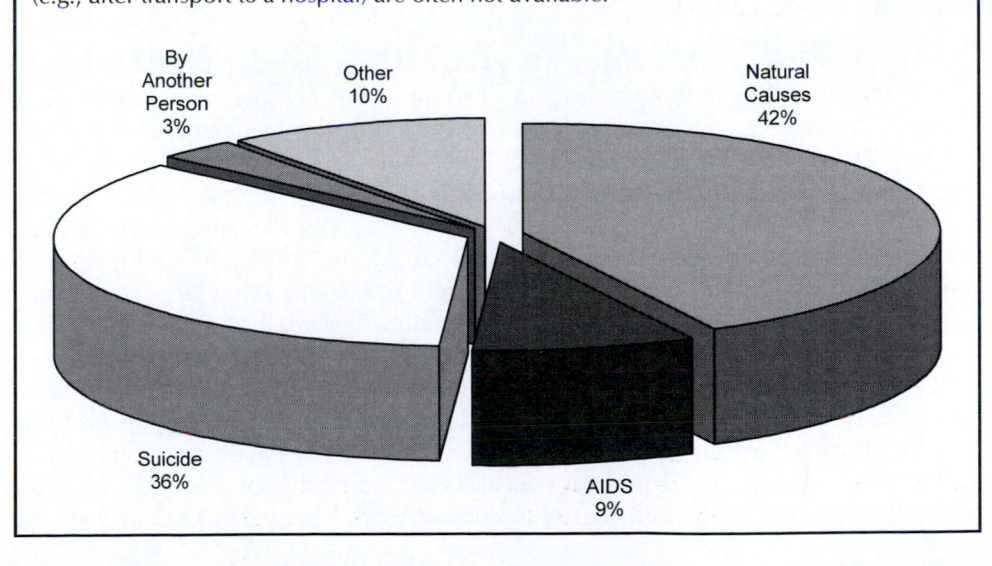

other materials that inmates could use to harm themselves and by closely supervising new prisoners. Those who appear at risk of such behavior are usually isolated in special cells where they can be closely monitored by staff.[59]

Inmate suicides pose practical and ethical problems for jails and their staff members. The welfare and safety of anyone in any form of physical custody is the legal responsibility of the practitioner and agency. Failure to properly supervise inmates can lead to lawsuits against jail administrators and employees. Proper supervision includes preventing injury to inmates by self or others. Jailers must be trained to identify those at risk of suicide. All jail staff must remain alert to the possibility of suicide among inmates and take all necessary steps to prevent it.[60]

LEGAL REGULATION OF JAILS

Jails hold people who have not been convicted of any crime and must be "presumed innocent." The conditions under which they are held, however, are often worse than those for convicted felons in state prisons. In 15 states there are no government standards for jails. Even where legal standards exist, enforcement is often haphazard so jails are plagued with overcrowding, poor sanitary conditions, and other problems. Professional associations such as the American Correctional Association provide guidelines, but they carry no legal weight.

The laws controlling jails and other detention facilities focus on employees to prevent abuse of inmates and to discourage violence and suicides. The federal government requires that all U.S. jails: (1) employ qualified personnel; (2) fire or retrain those who are unqualified or untrained; (3) assign employees to specific duties on the basis of their qualifications; (4) have written procedures for all aspects of operations; and (5) adequately supervise employees at all times. The degree to which these regulations are actually followed varies widely from jail to jail.

DETENTION OFFICERS

Jail guards are usually referred to as detention officers, or DOs. Their main duty is to assure that all inmates remain safe and in custody. They are the least well trained, the lowest paid, and the least educated people employed in corrections. Many want to become police officers and see their DO roles as merely a stepping stone toward that goal. Tight budgets, political favoritism, employee turnover, and other factors combine to keep DOs the least professional of all correctional practitioners. So does the tendency among sheriffs to "dump" problem employees into jail positions.[61] Further complicating the situation is the fact that DOs are becoming more dependent on technology to do their jobs. Jails are increasing their use of electronics for routine matters like opening doors and keeping track of inmates.

Architecture has long been the main method for assuring that a few officers can keep a large number of inmates under constant control. Keeping inmates in small areas that can be sealed off quickly is a basic part of the design of most jails and prisons. Technological innovations like video surveillance and electronically controlled doors allow fewer guards to control more inmates quickly and safely.

Many jurisdictions used technology to cut their staff to a bare minimum in the early 1980s. However, it has been shown that the closer the DOs are to the inmates, the better their ability to keep the jail under control.[62] The potential for positive DO–inmate interactions also encourages this trend. Many believe that because DOs have the most contact with inmates, they should be trained in basic communication and treatment techniques. Most jail administrators, however, lack the resources and desire to do so.

The result of this stress on direct contact between DOs and inmates has been a **new generation** of jails that are designed to be safer and more efficient than older types. The mark of a new-generation jail lies partly in the attitudes and training of the employees and partly in its physical design. The **podular unit** is one architectural hallmark of the new-generation jail. These prefabricated "pods" hold 10 to 50 inmates and include an open area surrounded by cells. Direct supervision places DOs in the pod with the minimum- to medium-security inmates.[63] Because there are no barriers between staff and inmates, problems can be dealt with while they are still minor, and inmates remain aware of staff's presence. Both inmates and staff feel safer in these types of jails and there is less violence and destruction of property.[64] There are also indications that this type of jail may help reduce recidivism.[65] This is an often unrecognized, but nonetheless significant, method of cutting jail costs. However, as governments try to shrink budgets even further, other methods of cost cutting are being implemented in many jails.

CUTTING JAIL COSTS

Concerns with government spending, along with the desire to get tough on crime, have led to many changes in how jails are organized. Much attention has recently been given to the private sector's ability to provide services for jails and prisons. Of special significance to jails are fee-for-service programs that force inmates to pay for some or all of the services they receive while jailed. This should remind us that many "new" programs are really just reinventions of older traditions, such as the fees charged by medieval gaolers. Finally, some jails find it profitable to rent space to out-of-state prison systems or to other counties. The goal of each of these programs is to cut costs. In the short run most of these programs seem to have great promise. However, we must look more closely if we are to anticipate the long-term costs of such changes.

Privatization

Private involvement in jails may take any of four different forms:

- Subcontracting *specific services*, such as medical care or food services;
- Use of *inmate labor to produce goods or services* for private companies through contracts within government-run jails;
- *Privatization of alternatives* to jails, such as detoxification centers; and
- Contracting for *private maintenance and operation* of the jail.

Corrections is a booming area of private-sector growth with services of every type being offered to all jurisdictions. Its recent popularity is due to claims that the private sector can build and run facilities more efficiently and at less cost than the government. Many local governments hire private contractors to take over some or all responsibility for jail operations. This often means that private contractors simply run a particular aspect of the jail, such as food or medical services. A Massachusetts jail has cut its medical costs from an average of $10 per inmate per day to $6 by contracting with local care providers and encouraging continuing care after release. In most cases, contractors restrict their services to the institution and some companies are entirely devoted to providing institutional needs.[66] This kind of arrangement is not new but is getting more publicity as privatization of government services becomes popular.

A few jails allow some inmates to work for private contractors to earn their room and board as well as to earn money for use after release. These inmates may perform industrial, clerical, or other types of unskilled or semiskilled labor. In most cases, convicted inmates produce goods for government agencies in exchange for "good time" credits toward early release, but some programs use pretrial detainees. When jail-industry products are intended for sale in the private sector, inmates are paid the prevailing rate for factory labor to avoid charges of unfair competition with free workers. However, it is rarely cost effective to bring the work into the jail, so inmates who participate in the programs are screened to assure they can be trusted to leave the jail.

In many areas, noninstitutional alternatives, such as detoxification centers, drug rehabilitation centers, and halfway houses, are privately run. Jails or the courts contract with these facilities to relieve crowding and to reduce recidivism. In a few places, however, privately owned facilities are being used instead of jails built with public funds. More commonly, local agencies own the facility and hire a private company to run the jail.

The trend toward privatization raises some sticky questions that are dealt with in detail in chapter 12 but deserve review here as they pertain to jails. Many charge that privatization is an overly simplistic, "quick fix" that is creating a "phantom government" that is not accountable to the public. Cost reductions often come at the expense of quality and programs, while hidden costs are ignored. Jail employees feel threatened because private-sector jobs are often less secure and pay less than government positions.[67] Sheriffs and county governments worry about who is liable for the actions of private contractors. In other words, who pays for medical care and other unforeseen costs? Who will be sued by inmates who feel they have been treated unfairly? In addition, many people are worried about the political power that private correctional contractors will obtain as they become vital to crime control efforts. On the other hand, privatization frees sheriffs to deal with law enforcement and administrative matters instead of correctional ones. It makes life easier for sheriffs but does little to solve the problems of jails.

Leasing Space from Other Jurisdictions

Renting space from other jurisdictions can reduce construction costs when a temporary crowding problem occurs. This kind of arrangement can also be used while a county adds to its jail space. The simplest version of this arrangement is when one county needs jail space and another has more than it can use. Inmates who are expected to be in jail for several weeks or months are moved from one jail to another. The county from which they came pays the county that holds them for their room and board but can avoid having to build a new facility. A more complicated version of this idea occurs when a county jail in one state contracts to hold convicted felons from another state's prisons.

For example, in the early 1990s Oregon and New Mexico had more prisoners than their prisons could hold. Simultaneously, many Texas counties had jail space available. The counties leased the excess cells to Oregon and New Mexico. Because they were convicted felons, the out-of-state prisoners were kept in their own special area of the jails and did not mix with local jail inmates.

Three types of problems can occur when leasing jail space for out-of-state prisoners. First, prisons offer more programs and work assignments than jails, and transferred inmates lose access to those activities. Idleness compounds the problems of imprisonment. Second, placing inmates in out-of-state jails means that they rarely get visits from their family and friends. Contact with noninmates keeps prisoners from becoming totally absorbed in the subculture of the facility and helps to reduce recidivism. Finally, some jurisdictions found that they were holding extremely dangerous inmates from other states in facilities designed for minimum-security inmates. The state transferring its prisoners had lowered their classification from maximum to medium. These inmates were returned to their home state after it was revealed that they were at high risk for escape and violence. Guard training was not adequate to handle some of them, and the facility itself was not built to control such men. These are matters of the contract between the jurisdictions that can be ironed out, but they illustrate the kinds of problems that can be expected of such arrangements. The need for extreme care in negotiating contracts with private contractors cannot be understated because of the long history of problems such as these.

Fee-for-Service Programs

Another method of reducing costs and increasing the retribution value of jails is to charge inmates for various services. The most common of these arrangements are programs that charge inmates for their health care. The goal is to discourage inmates from claiming to be sick in order to avoid work or to relieve the boredom of life in jail. A fee of $3 to $10 is charged for each visit to the doctor or infirmary. While such a fee seems small, it is a substantial amount to many jail inmates, who come from the poorest segments of society. About half the nations' jails have, or are considering, such a program. Critics fear that such fees may lead to some inmates not getting care soon enough, which can greatly increase the costs of medical care in the long run. A few even fear that some jurisdictions may use such fees to deny inmates medical care. However, all fee-for-medical-services programs known to the National Commission on Correctional Health Care have procedures for waiving the fee for inmates who can prove that they are truly indigent. GED programs are always free, but many jurisdictions charge room and board and garnish any wages their inmates receive to pay fines, child support, fees, and related costs.[68]

Some jails force inmates to pay for their own room and board. Many of these programs are designed for inmates who are on work release or who work in jail-based industries, but some force inmates to use any savings they might have to pay the fees. A few even garnish the wages of former inmates after they are released in order to collect these fees. Maine now charges $20 per day for room and board and is considering a law that would increase the fee to $80. Charging inmates for being in jail may be fair. However, it can only increase their bitterness and may drive some to crime by increasing their economic desperation upon release. Because these inmates are isolated from their families, welfare costs for noninmates may rise and families suffer in less easily measured ways, which indirectly contributes to the costs of incarceration.[69] However, both praise and criticism of these programs is premature because their effects on costs and inmate behavior have not yet been evaluated.

Ethics on the Line
Reporting a Use-of-Force Incident

You have worked for four years as a DO in the county jail while completing your college degree. You will graduate in two months and have been told informally that you will be sent to the police academy and hired as a patrol officer shortly after you graduate. This has long been your goal.

The cell block in which you work holds prisoners from another state who are felons. The sheriff has made an arrangement with that state to use empty cell space in the jail. Because they are convicted felons, they are strictly segregated from the rest of the jail and have no contact with other inmates. One day there is a disturbance on the cell block. The inmates are complaining that conditions in the jail are much worse than those in the prisons of their home state. They also claim that this arrangement violates their civil rights. They do not become violent but refuse to obey orders and destroy some jail property. Your lieutenant calls for help and a SWAT team of patrol deputies is sent in to restore order. You are surprised when the team orders the DOs out of the building and dismayed when you hear screams from the cell block. An hour later you return and find that many of the inmates are bruised and bloody. Your lieutenant advises you to keep quiet; the sheriff is running in a close election, and the deal to house these prisoners is very profitable for the county.

Several days pass and you hear the inmates claiming that the SWAT team beat them after they obeyed the officers' commands. Then an old friend who is now a reporter with the local paper calls you seeking information on a rumor about a "riot" at the jail. She assures you that you will never be identified and that she has several sources at the jail. However, none of them has actually been on that cell block except you.

Questions to Consider

1. Should you tell the reporter what you have observed? Why or why not?

2. Should you instead report what you know to the captain of the jail and ask for an official inquiry into the incident?

3. Does the fact that being labeled as a "whistle-blower" could endanger your being sent to the police academy affect your decision?

SUMMARY

Jails have been used to hold people awaiting trial and to remove social misfits from society throughout history. Although the main purposes of the jail remain unchanged, prison crowding has forced jails to hold convicted felons as well. The war on drugs and the increasing severity of penalties for drunk driving add significantly to the overcrowding problems of most jails. As a result, many badly overcrowded jails come under financial and legal pressures to reduce their populations. Drug courts and other diversion programs are one method of reducing populations along with pretrial release supervised by probation officers and the more traditional methods of bail and release on recognizance.

Legal concerns and the physical design of modern jail facilities have recently combined to encourage direct contact between detention officers and inmates. The law requires detention officers to treat inmates in a humane manner and to assure that they do not harm themselves or each other. Inmates must be protected at all times because they do not have the power to protect themselves adequately. Therefore, new-generation jails are changing the role of the detention officer from that of an observer who reacts to problems to that of an active control agent in direct contact with inmates. This presents a challenge to traditional jail guards, who have long been the least well trained of all correctional practitioners.

Jails suffer from serious personnel problems and overcrowding. Lack of money is behind most of these problems. Most authorities believe that we have reached the limits of efficiency in using technology to cut costs and assure safety in jails. If the financial burden of constantly enlarging our jails is to be avoided, society must rethink how it handles pretrial detainees and minor offenders. Alternatives to imprisonment are slow to gain acceptance because fear of crime is high, and tolerance for the underclass is lacking in much of America.

Jails compete with schools and roads for local funding from property taxes in most jurisdictions. This leads to great interest in cost-cutting measures such as fees-for-services, privatization, and space-leasing arrangements. However, little is known of the long-term effects of such programs on costs or recidivism. Part of the problem with U.S. jails lies in the fact that they are run by police agencies that consider them a burden. Therefore, jails will probably continue to be neglected even though they are critical to the operation of the rest of the justice system.

QUESTIONS FOR DISCUSSION AND REVIEW

1. What is the basic purpose of the jail? What secondary roles does it fulfill?

2. What traits make jails hard to study? Can general conclusions be drawn?

3. What problems were associated with privately operated jails in medieval times? What can we learn from these experiences as we again consider privatization in corrections?

4. What type of agency is most likely to manage an American jail? What advantages and problems are posed by organizing jails at this level of government?

5. Into what legal categories can jail inmates be grouped? How does the fact that jail inmates can be at any stage in the justice process affect the operation of jails?

6. Which types of criminal justice practitioners are most likely to use or visit a jail as part of their work routine? Why?

7. What sort of social environment does a jail provide? What social psychological processes do inmates experience as a result of this environment?

8. Why are large numbers of mentally ill persons routinely found in our jails? What sorts of problems do the mentally ill pose for jails?

9. Why is jail suicide of such great concern to jail administrators? What inmate traits are associated with jail suicides? What steps can jailers take to prevent suicide?

10. Why is it difficult to offer treatment to jail inmates? What sorts of programs are most common in jails? What programs are most needed?

11. What are the main alternatives to jail at this time in America? What advantages and problems are associated with each?

12. What methods are being used to cut costs in U.S. jails? What concerns are raised by these methods?

PROBATION

The term probation comes from the Latin word *probatio,* a period of proving or trial and forgiveness. In its modern usage, probation refers to (1) a sentence to supervision in the community; (2) an organization that supervises persons with such sentences; and (3) the process by which offenders are supervised while free in the community. As a sentence, probation means that offenders are under official supervision in the community and must follow special rules set by the court. As organizations, probation departments help trial courts by investigating the backgrounds of offenders awaiting sentencing and enforcing the conditions of release set by the court. After release to the community, the process of probation includes monitoring the offender's activities and coordinating treatment services.

Probation is a contract offered to an offender by the court; there is never a legal "right" to probation. Probation is a form of *conditional release* back into the community that is granted by a judge. It is conditional because the offender must obey the rules imposed by the court in order to remain free. Violations of conditions or commission of new crimes may result in revocation of probation. Conditions of liberty usually include reporting to a probation officer on a regular basis, maintaining employment/school enrollment, remaining in a specific geographic area, avoiding drugs and alcohol, and not associating with known offenders.

THE GOALS OF PROBATION

If supervision of offenders in the community was not a viable option for dealing with people who commit minor crimes, prisons and jails would have additional financial problems and overcrowding. These are two reasons for the continuing popularity of probation sentences: they cut costs and reduce crowding. Imprisonment can also lead to further and greater criminality in many cases. Prison and jail norms discourage the development of social skills and often result in the deepening of anti-social behavior as a means of survival. Removing offenders from the community reduces their ties to the law-abiding populace and links them to the convict subculture as an alternative. Jail and prison life also discourages inmates from accepting responsibility. Every aspect of an inmate's life is structured and controlled by rules. Probationers, on the other hand, are usually required to work, make restitution to victims, and pay part of the costs of their supervision and treatment. It is for all these reasons that probation is essential to modern corrections. Nonetheless, lack of funds and overcrowded community facilities reduce the effectiveness of this vital component of the correctional process.[1]

PROBATION POPULATIONS

Probation is the most common sentence for nontraffic offenses in the United States. This is because most offenses are relatively minor ones. However, probation departments receive less than 10% of the funding given to correctional agencies in the United States.[2] Almost 4 million people, approximately one of every 54 adults in the United States, is on probation. The average length of probation supervision for felons is slightly under four years. The number of people on probation rose an average of 3.2% each year between 1990 and 1999. Washington and California have the highest rate of probation in the nation (3,619 and 3,548 per 100,000) while Montana has the lowest (782). Fifty-three percent of the people now on probation have been convicted of a felony. People convicted of drunk driving make up 18%, and drug offenders account for 25% of U.S. probationers. Over half (55%) are white, 12% are Hispanic and 31% are African American. Twenty-two percent are women. Sixty-two percent successfully complete their sentence in the community while 23% are returned to jail or prison and 4% have fled supervision. The remaining 11% have "other" forms of unsuccessful completion.[3]

IDEOLOGICAL PRIORITIES IN PROBATION

Two rationales are given for the use of probation today. Some see it as a way for society to treat minor and accidental offenders in a humane manner. Probation is a way of giving them a second chance before incarcerating them. The concern here is with minimizing human misery and building the offender's ties to the law-abiding community. This can mean that probation officers (POs) need to become involved more closely with members of the offender's community (police officers, neighbors, friends, etc.) and to solicit the help of people who could be considered a guardian of the offender (parents, wife, etc.).[4] The fact that probation officers usually refer to the people they supervise as "clients" rather than "offenders" or "convicts" illustrates the treatment orientation on which probation was traditionally based. Probation is undergoing many ideological changes, and the nature of these changes varies widely from one place to the next. In some cases, the ideals of restorative justice are increasingly important and the focus is on healing the wounds that result from crime.[5] Efforts to make probation more controlling and punitive are also popular throughout the nation. These two goals are not always mutually exclusive and many agencies interpret "restorative justice" as being concerned only with the welfare of the victim and punishment of the offender.[6]

Loss of public confidence in probation, renewed faith in retribution, and the general trend toward the use of community-based methods in criminal justice have led to what some call a "reinfection" of probation.[7] Most probation departments have changed their priorities to emphasize close supervision, offender accountability and the sharing of information with the public. There is also additional effort made to estimate the risk posed by each offender and set supervision standards accordingly.[8] In many cases the demands of these new priorities have strained probation departments to the breaking point because mid-level managers lack the breadth of skills and training to adjust to them as quickly as political mandates for their implementation require.[9]

Others see probation as an inexpensive method of controlling offenders. It helps reduce prison crowding and allows offenders to repay their victims, support their families, and pay taxes instead of becoming tax burdens while in prison. An average prison cell costs $55,000 just to build, while imprisoning an offender for one year costs an average of $22,000. On the other hand, placing a person under close supervision in the community and providing him or her with treatment averages between $5,000 and $15,000.[10] In addition, probation is necessary if restitution is a central

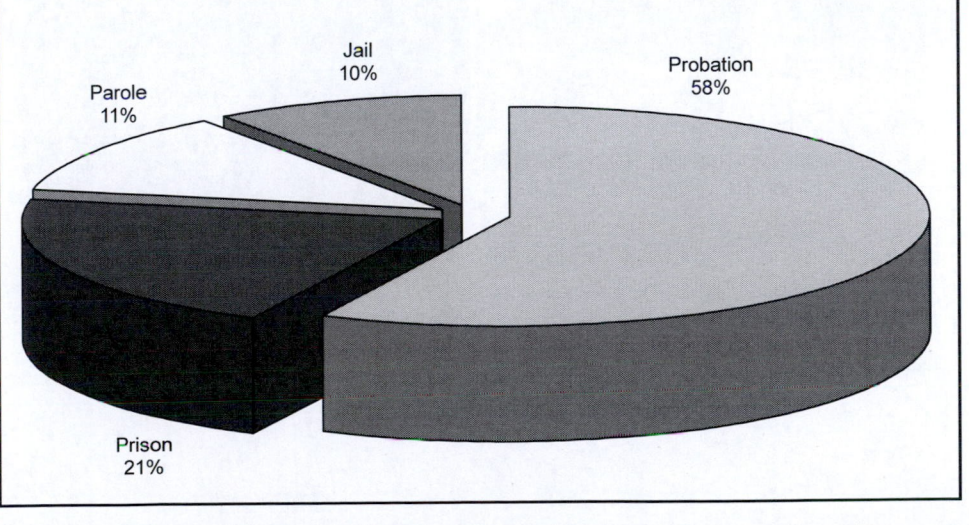

Correctional Populations in the United States[11]

This figure compares the number of probationers with that of parolees and jail and prison inmates. Approximately 58% of all persons under correctional supervision in this country are on probation. Prison inmates account for 21%, and persons under parole supervision constitute another 11%. Known and suspected offenders held in jails compose only 10% of those handled by correctional agencies. Probation is popular because most crimes are too minor to justify imprisonment, but it is often overused because of prison and jail crowding.

Jail
10%

Parole
11%

Probation
58%

Prison
21%

goal of sentencing. Only offenders who are free in the community have a realistic chance of paying back the victim or society.

Objections to probation claim that it does not provide enough retribution, deterrence, or control. The influence of these arguments is readily seen in the more severe terms of probation now used in many jurisdictions. Treatment advocates fear that this increased severity will reduce probation's ability to reintegrate offenders. Everyone seems to agree, however, that probation is best used with minor offenders who have ties to law-abiding society. However, this is not always the case. Probation is often a compromise when prosecutors lack sufficient evidence to assure a conviction. It is also used when there is no cell space for an offender. These issues can only be fully understood after the legal methods of imposing probation have been reviewed.

Offenses of Probationers

This chart describes the most serious offenses of people on probation in 2001. More than 2.1 million adults entered probation supervision in 2001. One in 54 adults is on probation. Fifty-three percent of all probationers had been convicted of a felony and 45% of a misdemeanor. The chart describes the most serious offenses of people on probation in 2001. Twenty-five percent had drug law violations, 18% were sentenced for driving while intoxicated or under the influence of alcohol. Less than 10% were on probation for minor traffic offenses and domestic violence.[12] These data clearly show that serious violent offenders usually get prison while less dangerous offenders are more likely to receive probated sentences. Males are especially prominent among drunken drivers on probation, while females are most often placed under supervision for drug or property crimes.[13]

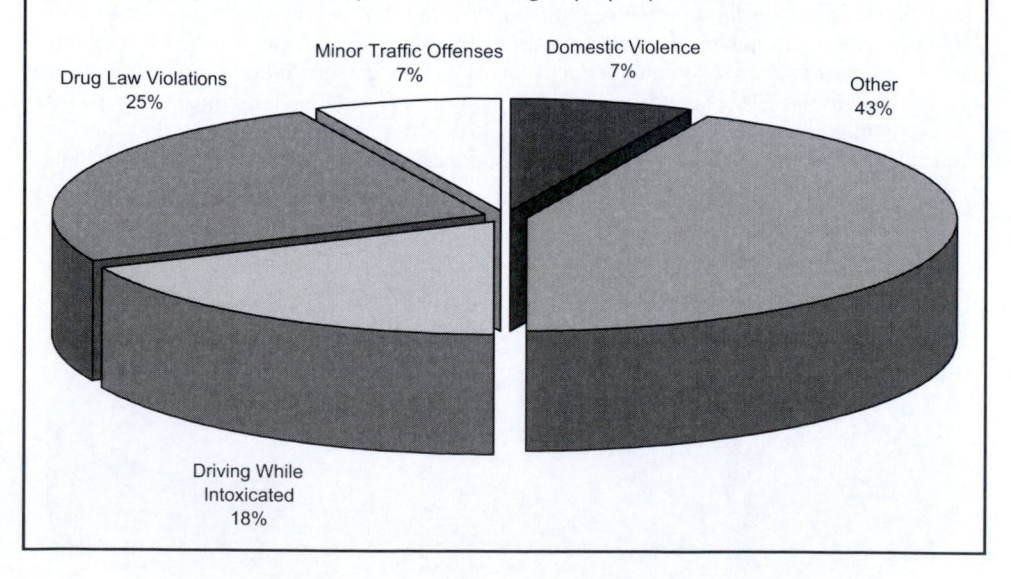

Minor Traffic Offenses 7%
Domestic Violence 7%
Drug Law Violations 25%
Other 43%
Driving While Intoxicated 18%

IMPOSING THE PROBATION SENTENCE

Probation is a sentence created by legislatures and applied by courts. Its success requires the cooperation of the court, probation department, offender, and community. Probation may be imposed in several ways. It can be directly imposed by the court as a sentence following a guilty plea or verdict. In other cases the defendant may be found guilty and put on probation without being formally sentenced. This is known as *suspended imposition of sentence*. Probation may also result from *deferred adjudication*, or suspension of a judgment of guilt. In these cases the court places the defendant on probation for a set period of time without a formal finding of guilt. Those who obey the conditions of release and commit no new crimes can have the charge dropped when the probation period has been completed. This allows defendants to avoid having a conviction on their record. Deferred adjudication is a form of suspended imposition of sentence.

Probation may also be used when a prison/jail sentence has been imposed and then suspended. This attempt to give the offender a "second chance" on probation is known as *suspended execution of sentence*. If trouble occurs, the judge can have the defendant brought back into court for formal sentencing. Probation may also be combined with a jail or prison sentence. This is usually called a *split sentence* or *shock probation*. Split sentences require a brief period of imprisonment followed by probation supervision and are assigned to 11% of all adults receiving probation.[14] This is an attempt to maximize the deterrent effect of imprisonment while minimizing its negative effects. The federal system's presumptive sentencing guidelines and some states with determinant sentencing structures also impose sentences in this way. Most federal offenders are sentenced to a prison term that is followed by a period of community supervision. In the federal system this is called probation. In most states, however, it is called parole.

Terms of Probation

Regardless of how probation is imposed, it is legally defined as a contract between the trial court and the offender. The terms of this contract are called the *conditions of probation*. Enforcing these conditions is the main job of the PO. At a minimum, the conditions of probation should keep offenders accountable to the court while they are under supervision. They should also be designed to protect the community while meeting the reintegration needs of the individual offender. Probation conditions are methods of achieving various goals related to the control and treatment of the offender. Because each offender is different, each set of probation conditions should vary accordingly.

Setting the conditions of probation is a legal matter that can only be done by a judge. Any changes in conditions must also be authorized by a judge. Probation officers merely make recommendations to the court as to what rules should be included in these conditions, and judges rely heavily on the advice of probation officers; they usually approve POs' recommended conditions.

There are two basic types of conditions. *Standard conditions* are imposed on all offenders sentenced to probation in a particular jurisdiction. *Special conditions* can be added to meet the unique demands of controlling and treating a particular offender. Which rules are placed in which category varies with the jurisdiction. A few general statements about standard conditions can, however, be made. Contact with the PO is usually required on a monthly, or even weekly, basis. Offenders must obey all laws and avoid known criminals and/or persons of dubious character. They must live within the jurisdiction of the sentencing court and must get permission from their PO before changing their residence. The PO must also be notified of any changes in employment during their sentence. Out-of-state travel is closely restricted in most cases, and curfews are often imposed. Restitution, community service, fines, supervision fees, and jail time may also be required. Most probationers (84%) receive some type of financial penalty. The most common are court costs (55%), supervision fees (61%), and restitution (30%). Average fees assessed total $1,800. Virtually all probationers make some attempt to pay these fees, but the average amount paid is only 56% of the total assessed against the offender.[15]

Most probationers have one or more special conditions, such as submitting to drug testing, performing community service, receiving counseling, living in a residential treatment facility, making restitution payments, avoiding contact with the

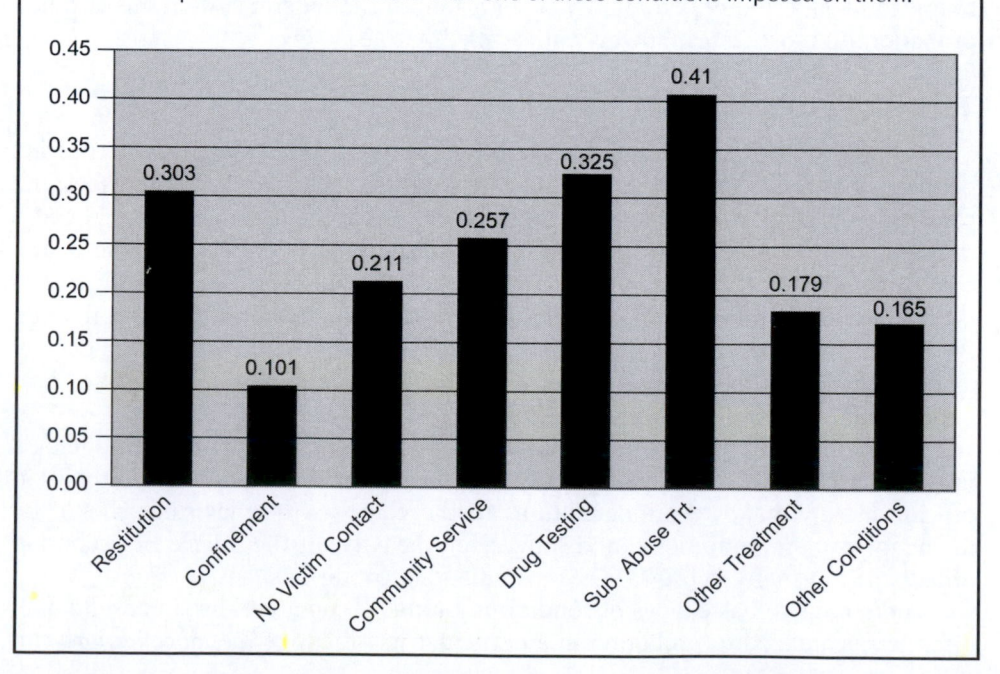

Conditions of Probation[16]

This graph describes the popularity of various conditions of probation. Substance abuse treatment, ranging from 12-step meetings to specialized counseling, is the most common followed by drug testing, restitution, and community service. Some form of confinement was used in 10% of these cases, and various forms of counseling in 18%. Contact with the victim was forbidden in 21% of these cases. The figures in the chart will not total 100% because most probationers have more than one of these conditions imposed on them.

Condition	Value
Restitution	0.303
Confinement	0.101
No Victim Contact	0.211
Community Service	0.257
Drug Testing	0.325
Sub. Abuse Trt.	0.41
Other Treatment	0.179
Other Conditions	0.165

victim, or living under house arrest. Many special conditions involve intermediate sanctions that are discussed in chapter 5. Special conditions are added to standardized probation agreements as a method of customizing the sentence to the offender's particular situation.

Violations of Probation

If the conditions are violated, the contract can be declared void by the court. If this occurs, probation can be revoked and the offender imprisoned. The nature of the violation, the way in which the officer records it, and the frequency with which a person commits violations combine to determine the appropriate response by the officer and sentencing court. A violation of any condition of liberty can result in one of three responses: (1) no action, (2) continued probation with tougher conditions, or (3) confinement in jail or prison. Judges rely heavily on the opinions of probation officers when dealing with probation violators but are not obligated to follow the officers' recommendations.

Two types of violations can lead to revocation proceedings. The first is any new criminal conviction. Second, *technical violations* of probation occur whenever a probationer disobeys a condition of probation without actually violating the law. Technical violations vary greatly in their seriousness. Failure to pay fees or fines is the most common type of technical violation that leads to a revocation hearing, followed by failure to attend treatment.[17] About 20% of all probationers return to court for a disciplinary hearing. This is far more common among felons than misdemeanor offenders. Not all of them have committed serious violations of law or their conditions, however. Thirty-eight percent had been charged with a new offense but an equal number had simply failed to keep up with fine or restitution payments.[18] All technical violations must be recorded by the supervising officer. Although they often appear to be minor "technicalities," they may also represent the development of problems that can be addressed before any new crimes are committed. New crimes by a probationer are usually seen as a major problem requiring revocation, or at least a significant change in the conditions of liberty. Many courts will not revoke probation for "technical" reasons until a fairly long series of violations can be proved. The officer's records are the main source of proof that technical violations have occurred. *Absconding* is an exceptionally serious technical violation in which the probationer intentionally flees or hides from supervision. This usually leads to revocation; 10% of probationers failed to report and could not be located. Absconders increased from 6% in 1990 to 10% in 2001.[19]

Roughly two-thirds of all those placed on probation complete the sentence successfully.[20] When only felons on probation are examined, failure rates range from 12 to 65%, depending on how extensively probation is used instead of prison in the particular jurisdiction. Misdemeanor offenders, however, have far lower failure rates, and it is estimated that about 75% of these offenders successfully complete supervision.[21] Being employed and having a good income are the best predictors of successfully completing a probation sentence. Persons convicted of property and drug offenses are among the most likely to fail to live within the terms of their probation. Because minorities and female offenders tend to be poorer and have less stable jobs than males, even though males more often are probated for drug and property crimes, they tend to have higher rates of failure and revocation than do males.[22]

Revocation of Probation

Revocation of probation requires at least two hearings before a neutral, detached body. These hearings are usually held in the same court that sentenced the offender. The preliminary hearing is to decide if there is probable cause to believe that the terms of probation were violated. This assures that there is good reason to hold the probationer until a general revocation hearing can occur. A second, more thorough hearing is held to review all the available evidence. A sentencing hearing may then be held, or imprisonment may be imposed at the second hearing.

The state may be represented by the probation officer or a prosecutor at these hearings.[23] Probationers may hire an attorney to represent them at revocation hearings but are not entitled to indigent counsel if any sort of sentence was imposed when probation was imposed. Attorneys are often provided when language problems or mental illness/retardation make it hard for probationers to understand the proceedings and to defend themselves.[24]

Prior to the preliminary hearing, several steps must be taken by the probation department. The probationer must be notified in writing of (1) the proceedings against him or her, (2) the nature of the alleged violation, and (3) the nature of the evidence supporting the allegation. Probationers can subpoena their own witnesses unless there is a strong reason to deny such due process. However, no jury is used in these hearings and the standard of proof is less demanding in a revocation

---

Legal Guidelines for Revocation Proceedings[25]

Due process was not required in probation revocation proceedings until late in the due process revolution. Three Supreme Court cases define due process rights at revocation hearings. *Mempha v. Rhay* (1967) outlined when probationers were entitled to indigent counsel and set the basis for other limited due process rights. The 1972 *Morrissey v. Brewer* case actually involved a parolee but was quickly extended to cover probationers as well, in *Gagnon v. Scarpelli* (1973). The minimum due process rights for revocation are given in *Morrissey*:

1. Preliminary and general revocation hearings must be held before an impartial hearing committee or judge, and a third (re)sentencing hearing is also desirable.

2. Written notice of the hearing and specific charges must be provided to the offender prior to the hearing.

3. The nature of the offense and the evidence of it must be described in writing to the defendant.

4. The right to confront accusers cannot be denied without cause.

5. The reasons for revoking liberty must be specified in writing.

In *Gagnon* the Supreme Court ruled that although probation revocation is not a phase of criminal prosecution, it may still result in a loss of liberty. For this reason, the *Morrissey* ruling is applicable to probationers as well as prison releasees.

hearing than in a criminal trial. Because probation is a contract that is a civil matter, revocation requires only that the majority of evidence support the allegations against the offender. This is why prosecutors will plea bargain for probation when they fear their evidence will not stand up in a criminal trial. It is also for this reason that prosecutors will often prosecute an offender for violation of probation rather than for an alleged new crime.

THE PROBATION PROCESS

Good probation practice is based on four elements: investigation, selection, supervision, and treatment coordination. Each is a vital component in the probation officer's job of assuring both the community's safety and the success of the probation client. The investigative aspects of the officer's role center on deciding which offenders have the best chance of succeeding under community supervision. Selecting the right people for probationary sentences is critical to protect community safety and to use resources efficiently. The goal is to identify those offenders who will adapt to supervision and benefit from programs and opportunities available in the community. Investigation is an ongoing process because allegations of misconduct that affect the appropriateness of probation for an offender often after supervision has begun. Supervision of people released to the community is essential for public safety and to assure that effective treatment is actually received. It also gives offenders strong reasons to avoid situations that would tempt them to become further involved in crime. Coordinating treatment means determining the reasons for each offender's criminality and placing him or her in the right sequence of programs.

Presentence Investigations

The probation process usually begins with a presentence investigation (PSI) performed by the probation officer. These investigations make up the majority of the investigative work done by POs. A few jurisdictions are experimenting with PSIs done by private contractors. The quality of these reports varies widely, however, and this is not an area in which privatization has been well accepted.[26] The PSI examines the offender's background and current situation. Its goal is to assess treatment needs and the amount of danger posed to the community. The procedures for conducting a presentence investigation vary with the jurisdiction and the particular offender. Many investigations are done by telephone, especially if the offense is a minor one. In more serious cases, and if time permits, the PO will actually visit the offender's home, neighborhood, employers, and/or school. A written report describing what was found during the investigation is submitted to the judge before a sentence is decided.

Presentence investigation reports usually begin with the official account of the offense followed by the offender's version. Comparison of these two versions of the original crime can reveal the presence of denial, distorted perceptions, or other problems in the offender's thinking. Alternatively, they can indicate the presence of remorse, which often predicts successful community supervision and treatment.

A good presentence investigation report reviews the offender's background, prior criminality, and present circumstances. Data on the offender's family of origin, current living situation, employment history, educational record, military record, and medical condition help the probation officer understand the offender's behavior. Prior encounters with law enforcement will be examined closely. The probation officer may inquire about the offender's character and behavior patterns from neighbors, employers, teachers, and others who know the individual. Similar investigations will also be made after a person has been placed under supervision whenever the PO feels the need. Knowledge of what kinds of programs are available, and their relative quality, is essential to deciding which offenders are most likely to benefit from community supervision.

Because of its traditional association with reintegration efforts, the public tends to view PSIs as a means of justifying lighter sentences. This may have been true in past decades, but recent data show that these investigations are welcomed by prosecutors and judges but are regarded negatively by defense counsel. This suggests that, in keeping with the punitive approach to probation and the new penology, probation officers are clearly "agents of the state" and should be viewed as such by both the courts and the public.[27] Regardless of underlying philosophy, however, choosing people who will succeed on probation is critical to its use in corrections.

Telephone interviews are a starting point for presentence investigations.

Selection of Probationers

The goal of the PSI is to help judges decide which offenders will (1) pose the least danger to the community and (2) benefit most from treatment in the community. People with strong tendencies toward violence or long criminal histories are rarely good candidates for probation. Defendants who have committed well-known crimes may be denied probation to fulfill the boundary-setting function of punishment. Conversely, some offenders who are known to be poor risks for probation will be placed under supervision simply because there is no prison space for them. The legal strength of the prosecutor's case, the willingness of the victim to testify, and other factors may lead to probation via the plea bargaining process. How these factors are handled is largely determined by the sentencing judge. Despite the fact that probation agencies cannot control this aspect of the process, the concept of probation often is blamed when these offenders commit new crimes. This negative publicity does great harm to the use of probation because public support for probation is vital to its success. People must be willing to accept probationers as employees, neighbors, and friends if they are to be reintegrated.

Two sets of concerns must be balanced in the final sentencing decision. Risk to the community, or to specific individuals, must be weighed against the damaging effects of imprisonment. The likelihood that the offender will benefit from services available in the community must also be balanced with the need for boundary setting and deterrence. Offenders with strong ties to the law-abiding elements of their

---

Treatment Concerns in Modern Probation

The most pressing need in modern probation is for additional probation officers to handle the expanding caseloads that are resulting from the war on drugs. Seventy percent of probationers have used drugs, but only 42% receive treatment. Closely related to this issue is the availability of high-quality substance abuse treatment programs. Most drug-abusing probationers who are in treatment merely attend self-help groups, but their POs would prefer more intensive programming for them. Half of all probationers are tested for drugs, but there is great debate about the efficiency of stressing urine testing of offenders.[28] Closely related to drug issues is the fact that offenders are far more likely to have a history of physical and sexual abuse than are other citizens. Nearly 10% of males and 40% of female probationers were sexually and/or physically abused as children. These victims of prior abuse are at higher risk of committing crimes against persons than are other offenders.[29] Many abuse victims suffer from post-traumatic stress disorder, which contributes to their criminality, drug abuse, and responses to authority figures such as probation officers.[30]

The adequacy of the services available to mentally ill probationers is also of great concern. Mentally ill clients need closer supervision and more services than others. While few require hospitalization, most cannot afford psychiatric services and therefore depend on understaffed and overworked public mental health agencies. Treatment for sex offenders is another critical concern in community corrections. While treatment is available, its adequacy is questionable. In all these instances, the problem is partly the availability of programs and partly how to finance treatment for the impoverished. While treatment opportunities are more available in the community than in jails or prisons, their high costs and long waiting lists make a probation officer's job especially demanding.[31]

neighborhoods, those with stable jobs and family ties, and those whose crimes involve mitigating factors are considered good candidates for probation.

Offenders who are alcoholics, addicts, sex offenders, or spouse abusers are at high risk of recidivism and thus are controversial as probation candidates. These kinds of offenders may receive probation because they need many services that are found in the community rather than in prisons and their social skills are already very poor. Prison is likely to worsen the problems that led them to crime in the first place, while employment and family ties are two reasons to keep them in the community. The argument against granting probation is that these offenders are likely to relapse into criminal behavior while under supervision. Data show that probation is most effective in reducing property and drug sales offenses. It is least effective in controlling domestic violence and forgery/fraud crimes.[32]

Probation Supervision

The conditions of probation list specific guidelines for community supervision. Each condition should be tailored to the individual offender. As soon as probation is assigned, the probation officer should explain all the conditions. This helps the officer establish an understanding of the process with the offender-client. The client's responsibilities should be explained in detail, as well as many of the procedures used by the probation officer. This helps avoid misunderstandings and makes it easier for clients to obey the conditions of their release.

Supervision of offenders is the main job of most probation officers. Officers must be able to assure that their clients are obeying the conditions of their liberty at all times. This is done through home visits, urinalysis, periodic checks of the offender's police record (and/or jail records), and interviews with the client and others. Interviews and urine testing are usually done when the client makes required visits to the probation office. Urinalysis is used to discourage drug use and to document relapses by abusers. Although alcohol is more highly correlated with crime than any other drug, testing for alcohol use is very expensive. New electronic technology is available that allows POs to check for alcohol consumption by phone when electronic monitoring is in use. However, it has not yet been legally approved for use in hearings and is cost prohibitive for most agencies.[33]

Checking police records and jail lists is a traditional responsibility of the probation officer to assure that the offender has not been rearrested. Technology is simultaneously allowing law enforcement and probation to share more information than ever before. Some jurisdictions make data from police field interviews available to probation officers. Thus, when police encounter a probationer, all the details of that situation can be available to the probation officer even if no charges are ever filed. Cooperation between police and probation agencies is being stressed in other ways as well. The concept of community policing can be used to assign probation officers to specific communities so that they will be familiar with the offenders' neighborhood and neighbors. This also promotes greater familiarity with local police agencies and officers.[34]

Office Visits.   Most conditions of probation require the offender to report to his or her supervising officer at the probation office at least once a month. Office

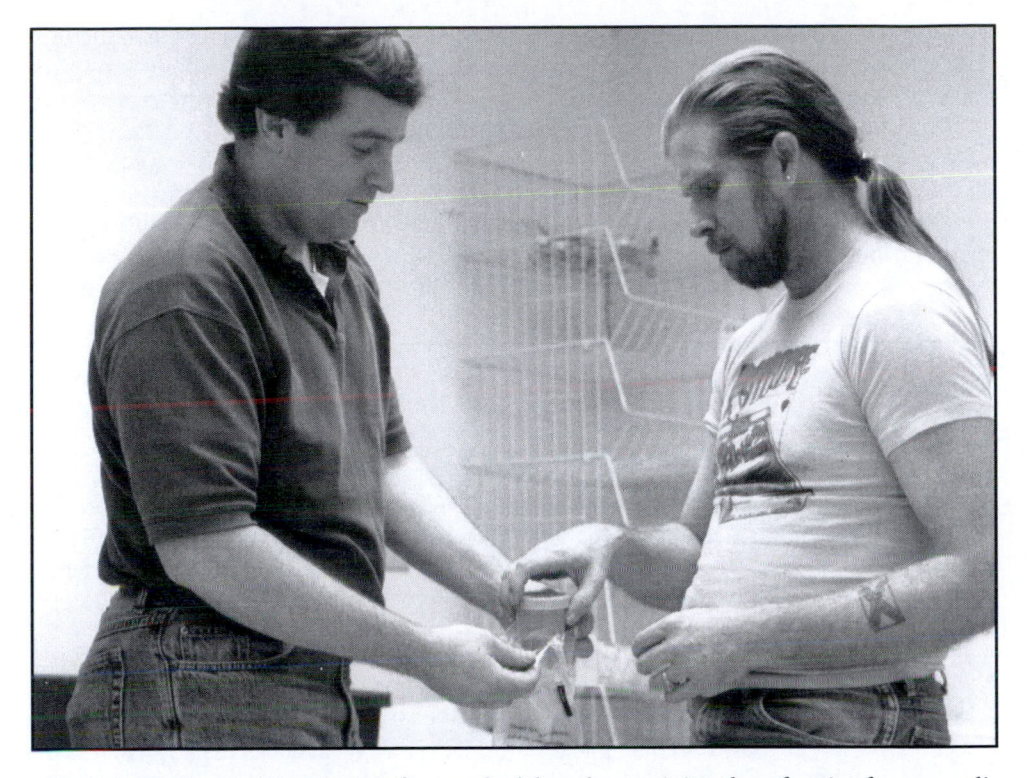

Although the issue of urinalysis is frequently debated, remaining drug free is often a condition of probation. Urine tests may be required during visits to the probation officer.

visits serve two main purposes. First, they provide a convenient opportunity for the officer to collect fees and restitution payments along with materials verifying employment, school attendance, and similar conditions for the client's file. Second, they assure a safe, controlled environment in which to confront probationers about improper behavior and to make demands that are likely to be resented.

Office visits allow a very small number of officers to supervise a very large number of clients in a reasonable period of time. However, simply seeing clients once a month in an office provides little insight on activities and lifestyle. Probation officers may also need to talk with family members, neighbors, and employers in order to check on the offender's behavior. For this reason, many probation agencies are increasing their stress on field visits as a key method of supervision.

Field Visits. Field visits include all situations in which the probation officer goes to an offender's home, place of employment, or other locations in the community. Visits to offenders' homes are the main type of field visit. Home visits allow the officer to see how offenders live and to verify that they have not changed their address. Most of all, they provide officers with the opportunity to check on the routine behaviors of their clients. The presence of alcohol, drug paraphernalia, or other evidence that conditions of probation are being violated should be noted by the officer on a home visit. Officers may not confront the offender about such violations until the next office visit, however, unless it is under their jurisdiction. This protects the officers' physical safety, even though job-related assaults on probation officers are rare. Home visits can also help officers establish more personal relationships with their clients. People are often more open when on their "own turf" than in someone's office.

Talks with counselors, employers, and family members can provide additional insight into the offender's patterns of thought and action. These are called *collateral contacts* because they supplement the officer's knowledge of the offender's lifestyle and provide valuable information about the client's activities and attitude. In

---

Ethics on the Line
Ethics, Confidentiality, and the Threat of AIDS

You handle a caseload of about 90 felony probationers. Your files contain a great deal of confidential information on each client's health and personal behaviors. The records of several of your clients indicate that they have been infected with HIV, but none have full-blown AIDS at this point in time. One man is known to have infected his own wife with the virus. Due to problems in her health, she soon died of the disease. This client was recently arrested for technical violations of probation and is in jail awaiting a revocation hearing. As part of your job you must visit him at the jail to serve him with papers regarding the charges against him. The jail has no screening procedures for diseases among inmates. Only those who request medical treatment receive any sort of medical attention.

After serving the client with his papers, you have a short conversation with a detention officer with whom you've become friendly. This DO casually mentions that this client is a particularly obnoxious inmate. He constantly spits at guards and has been placed in a segregation unit because he has been involved in assaults on both guards and inmates. It is clear from the way this DO speaks that he has no suspicion that the inmate is HIV positive. You want to tell the DO how dangerous this man's blood could be but do not want to violate the ethics of your profession. You do remark that the DOs "ought to be careful of him. He's a very sick guy."

Questions to Consider

1. Have you violated this client's confidentiality with this rather vague statement? All medical information is confidential. Even though you gave no details, you did reveal a medical fact to which the DO would not otherwise have had access. If other inmates discovered he had HIV, he could be assaulted and even killed by them out of ignorance and fear.

2. Is the statement too vague to assure that the DOs will handle this man with proper care? The word "sick" could easily be interpreted as a judgment about his abusive actions rather than his medical condition.

3. Where do you draw the line between your duty to protect the client's confidentiality and your obligation to help protect the DO's personal welfare? What policies should be created to guide your actions?

Probation officers provide both assistance and discipline for their clients. Helping offenders get in touch with agencies that will provide needed services is a critical part of this job role. When clients face a crisis, they may seek advice and feedback from probation officers. Insight into client problems may have created a comfort level with the PO. While the rapport can be a positive sign, officers must be careful not to act as the client's primary counselor. The primary counselor should be a qualified member of the mental health community.

many cases, however, the probation officer will only see the offender at the probation office. In some jurisdictions there is also a desire to minimize the stigma of being under supervision because it could cost clients their jobs or homes.

Increasing emphasis has been placed on the supervision aspect of probation in recent years. If community corrections are to be used to reduce prison costs and crowding, they must respond to public demands for greater control of offenders. It is important, however, that the goal of reintegrating the probationer into the community is not neglected in the effort to assure compliance with the conditions of probation. The degree to which a particular probation office stresses treatment or control should be guided by the nature of the community it serves.

Treatment Coordination

Very few probation officers are qualified to provide direct clinical treatment, and even fewer have the time to do so. In fact, many POs report being unable to coordinate treatment services due to large caseloads and other demands on their time.[35] They should, however, have sufficient knowledge to monitor the offender's progress in treatment. If counseling is a condition of probation, then the probation officer must keep good records on how often the client has attended such treatment. The officer may also insist on access to the therapist. This helps guarantee that the client is cooperating with the required treatment and that treatment is addressing crime-related issues. To discuss a client with a professional therapist, the client must first sign a legal waiver of confidentiality that permits the therapist to discuss the client's progress with the probation officer.

THE PROBATION ORGANIZATION

There are more than 2,000 probation agencies in this country. Probation departments deal mainly with local trial courts, but most are under the control of the state government. Local control of probation gives the sentencing judge the most power, while state control is more likely to assure universal standards for hiring officers and supervising offenders.[36] The extent of state control varies widely from state to state, however. No two states have quite the same administrative system for their probation system.

In most states, probation is a state agency operated by the executive branch. In nineteen states, probation is run by the state corrections department. In twelve states it is controlled by some other state agency. In eleven other states, probation is administered by the superior trial courts. Five states use a mixture of state and local control. Three states place probation powers in a county agency.

Federal probation is organized differently. Each U.S. district court is assigned a certain number of probation officers as part of its basic staff. Unlike most probation officers, federal probation officers supervise both felons released from federal prisons and those whom judges have allowed to avoid incarceration. Persons convicted of federal offenses after 1987 are, in effect, paroled to the supervision of a probation officer.

Regardless of how the agency is organized, the focus for probation officers is the local level because their duties are closely tied to the operation of local courts. As mentioned earlier, both citizens and practitioners are thought to be more satisfied with agencies that reflect the beliefs of their communities. The probation officer's life is simplified by local control. POs employed by state agencies often feel that they serve two bosses at once. They are under the power of their agency's supervisor but must also accept the guidance of local judges. In all cases, it is a judge that sets probation conditions and decides revocation cases. The beliefs of local trial court judges may not always agree with the priorities of the state government. Judicial control of probation eliminates this conflict by giving judges direct authority over the probation office that serves their court.

The Probation Officer

As with all bureaucracies, the quality of probation supervision depends on the training and professionalism of the individual officers. Most states require that probation officers have a bachelor's degree or "equivalent experience." This latter term is rarely defined in a clear way; its interpretation varies with the people and needs involved in each hiring situation. Some states have a number of probation officers with only an associate's degree, and a few will hire people with only a high school diploma. The requirement of a bachelor's degree is by the far the most common, however.

Before being hired as a probation officer, applicants must usually take a civil service exam. While each test is unique, most focus on the applicant's knowledge of law, government organization, offender behavior, and treatment. Communication skills, especially the ability to write reports and memos, are assessed during the hiring process. The applicant's background is usually researched to some degree before hiring to assure the applicant has no criminal history. Some jurisdictions also check credit reports or use psychological tests to screen applicants. An interview with probation supervisors, local judges, or other administrators may also be used.

Many states have special academies to train new probation officers. Much of their curriculum is devoted to the basic legal and administrative aspects of the job rather than the underlying complexities of the role. Entry-level salaries for probation officers average between $20,000 and $31,000 per year, but the extremes range from as low as $16,000 to as high as $54,000. Most probation officers are evaluated several times a year by their supervisors. These evaluations, along with seniority, usually determine the officer's salary.

In-Service Training

A probation officer's training does not end at the academy. Most agencies require 40 hours a year of in-service training for each officer. State agencies, the National Institute of Corrections, and the American Correctional Association offer special programs to update probation officers on topics ranging from legal issues to practical skills like suicide prevention and crisis intervention techniques. In-service training allows probation officers to broaden their skills and keep up with changes in the field. In-service training sessions may be offered at local, regional, or national correctional conventions as well as through state academies, universities, or other institutions. Supervisors also must attend in-service training so that they can assist and evaluate the officers who work under them.

Record Keeping

Probation officers are evaluated on their ability to document the supervision of their clients. The most important of these records is the chronological listing of contacts with, or about, each client; these generally are referred to as "chronos." The officer's records are legal evidence of the offender's compliance with the conditions for community supervision. If records are not well kept, it may be impossible to have an offender's probation revoked despite repeated technical violations. Attorneys representing probationers in revocation hearings are allowed access to these records. If they are not written carefully and precisely, the attorney may use them to discredit the officer in a hearing.

Chronos record all contacts between the supervising officer, the client, and others with an interest in the client. Entries must be brief, and each contact must be recorded in the order in which it occurred. The chrono should note where and when the contact occurred and what occurred during the contact. Evidence of any problem behavior should also be carefully recorded whenever observed. Most officers keep notes on their daily activities and write them up in the case-file chronos at the end of the day or the next morning. Supplementing the chronos are records that verify how the client is complying with the conditions of release. Paycheck stubs are used to verify employment, and bills from counselors document the circumstances, dates, times, and frequency of contact with the client. In addition to keeping track of progress, part of the officer's job is to motivate clients to work at their treatment.

Case Management

Probation officers can use their legal powers to help therapists convince clients that help is needed, however. This can be called the "carrot-and-stick approach" to correctional treatment. The officer provides the "stick" by showing the probationer that incarceration, and other sanctions, will result unless a change in behavior becomes his or her main goal. Simultaneously, the therapist offers the "carrot" of support and assistance in helping the client achieve that change. Both the officer and the therapist must look for signs that the client is ready to seek change. Some of these signs include anxiety, stress, and expressions of guilt. Because these symptoms are uncomfortable to the client, they can be used as devices to encourage change. Major successes or failures in the client's life can play a similar role.[37]

It is vital that officers avoid being manipulated by their offender-clients. To accomplish this they must become aware of their own personal needs, wishes, desires, and insecurities. People who work with offenders should try to understand their viewpoint but establish and maintain appropriate social and psychological distance from them. Discussing decisions with coworkers, especially those who know the client, is helpful in this regard. These insights and practices help officers stay impartial and respond appropriately to each of their clients based on the threat they pose and their rehabilitation needs.

Probation officers are increasingly required to use *case plans* that describe a series of activities that will lead to a goal relevant to the control and rehabilitation of the offender. A case plan describes the goals of monitoring activities, the responsibilities of the offender, and the role of other agencies in handling the case. For example, a case plan might require an offender to find employment within the county so that the officer can directly ascertain that he is working when he claims to be. It would also require the offender to attend an Alcoholics Anonymous group regularly and submit to urinalysis. Consultation with a mental health professional or some sort of vocational training might also be mandated. As these goals are met, others would be added to keep the plan current. The level of risk the offender poses to the public, the methods by which the officer will verify the offender's activities, and the offenders' particular problems are all taken into account in writing a case.

PROBATION CASELOADS

A *caseload* is the group of offenders supervised by a single probation officer.[38] The typical PO supervises more than 90 clients, but average caseloads vary from 30 to 400 clients per officer. The national average is 258 clients per officer, but this figure is misleading because caseload size varies with the type of offenders being supervised. Those handling violent felons or juveniles usually have smaller caseloads while those dealing with minor offenders have the largest. Caseload size is a major issue in modern community corrections. Many authorities argue that a caseload of 35 to 50 clients is best for good supervision.[39] Small caseloads allow closer supervision, which often leads to the discovery of more violations and to higher rates of revocation. If that occurs, smaller caseloads result in probation becoming a stronger form of punishment and control.

Types of Probation Caseloads[40]

Different styles for managing clients must be used with different-sized caseloads. Summarized below are the basic types of caseloads, the number of times the probation officer must meet with each client per month, and the percentage of probationers being handled at each level of supervision. Some jurisdictions may use different terms to describe certain types of caseloads. However, the idea that supervision level is defined by the number of monthly probation officer–offender contacts is fairly universal.

Supervision Level	No. of Monthly Contacts	Estimated Percentage of Probationers
Intensive	9	10%
Maximum	3	32%
Medium	1	37%
Minimum	1 per 3 mos.	12%
Administrative	None required	9%

The critical factor in determining caseload size should be the amount of supervision required by each client. Level of supervision is, in turn, based on the degree to which a client poses a threat to others. This is determined by the charge for which the client was convicted and his/her behavior while under supervision. This is usually accomplished by use of a *risk assessment*, which uses a number of factors from the offenders' legal and behavioral history to determine how great a risk they pose to the public. Each agency uses different factors and assigns weights to them, much like the salient factor scores described in chapter 1. These assessments use only variables that research has shown to predict recidivism and are considered helpful by officials. However, there is no solid "evidence" of their ability to predict future behavior. They are probably best used along with other data to estimate the risk of a particular offender being reinvolved in crime at a particular time.[41] These instruments are one indication of the "new penology's" stress on risk management and administrative procedures focused on actuarial methods of prediction that were discussed in chapter 2.

People convicted of violent and sexual offenses, along with those who have violated the conditions of their probation, usually get intensive supervision. Sex offenders who victimize persons of the same sex are ranked as more dangerous by these methods than those who are attracted to the opposite sex.[42] Persons with a

---

Policy Matters!
Should Probation Punish or Treat Offenders?

As the public becomes more intolerant of crime and as prisons continue to overflow, many probation departments are shifting their emphasis from treatment to control. In particular, agencies are becoming more punishment oriented, and probation supervision is becoming more intrusive. Some probationers must submit to phone calls and even visits at odd hours to assure that they obey their curfews. The amount of fees, restitution payments, and fines assessed to probationers is also increasing. However, probation caseloads are often so large that officers do not have the time to monitor treatment regimens.

In some states POs now work in pairs. "Field contact officers" handle the surveillance of probationers, and some even have the power to arrest any client who violates the conditions of freedom. They do field visits and secretly "check up" on clients. The PO acts as case manager and handles the paperwork associated with each case. Some people fear that as the emphasis on control increases, treatment and reintegration efforts will decrease.

Questions to Consider

1. Should control and retribution be the chief goals of community corrections or should treatment remain a central theme of probation? What facts and concepts of justice support your view? What facts and theories oppose your view?

2. Should probation agencies hire and train officers for a policelike role or should probation officers define their jobs more as case managers and surveillance experts? Why?

3. How should probation officers deal with the contradictions between their roles as law enforcers and as case managers? Can your views stand up to the Fourteenth Amendment's demand that all people in the same legal category be given equal treatment?

4. When retribution stands in the way of reintegration, such as when fines are excessive or probation restrictions make employment hard to find, how should priorities be set?

history of technical violations are also likely to be placed under close supervision. Clients move from one risk level to another based on their history and behavior. Lack of resources often leads to less supervision than officers would like for their most problematic clients. There is also a tendency to reduce the supervision level after months or years of violation-free supervision. Thus people who have an initially high-risk assessment score and supervision level can often "earn" their way into a less restrictive caseload over the course of their sentence. (Sex offenders are often an exception to this general practice.) While this generally serves the agency's efficiency goals, the inability to predict accurately future behavior remains a problem and occasionally leads to tragedies featured in the media.

At the other extreme is administrative probation and minimum supervision. Clients assigned to this low level of supervision usually fall into one of three groups. The first includes minor offenders whose crimes appear to be more or less "accidental." For these clients restitution is often the only goal of probation, and little supervision or treatment coordination is necessary. The second group includes probationers who are assigned to residential treatment programs where they are closely monitored by the private facility; the probation officer simply monitors the documentation. The third group consists of offenders who receive rather long probation sentences. If they perform well for many years under normal supervision, the agency may eventually reduce their level of supervision to reward them and preserve the agency's resources. These probationers usually have completed all of their treatment requirements and have proven that they require little supervision.

It is the quality of the supervision, not its quantity, that makes for good probation practice. Small caseloads can help probation officers increase the time and effort they devote to each offender. If this is high-quality supervision, then the process is improved. Increasing the deterrence, incapacitation, and retribution value of community-based sentences is the goal of a new set of correctional practices that appeared in the 1980s. These new punishments are usually referred to as intermediate or alternative sanctions and are described in detail in the next chapter.

SUMMARY

Probation is a critical part of the criminal justice process. By allowing offenders to remain in the community under legal supervision, probation encourages rehabilitation and saves tax dollars. It can also help relieve prison and jail overcrowding to some extent. The availability of programs and the quality of the probation officers are equally critical to the effectiveness of probation.

Probation officers work closely with the local judicial system. Their activities are guided by elected officials whose goals should reflect the particular needs of the community. This allows each jurisdiction to deal with its offenders in the manner it prefers. Probation officers are in constant contact with service providers from the educational, welfare, and mental health systems. Training in the requirements of the legal system, plus communication skills for interviewing and documenting visits, is essential to good job performance as a probation officer.

Probation is designed to encourage offenders to strengthen their links to law-abiding society. This is done with varying combinations of assistance and coercion by the probation officer. Conditions of probation can emphasize either punishment or treatment as seems appropriate for the offender and community. Communities are increasingly demanding punishment from probation, so the focus of this branch of corrections has changed substantially in the last 20 years. Nonetheless, the ideal probationer is still a nonviolent offender with no prior felony convictions who is likely to benefit from services in the community. Unfortunately many offenders are placed on probation simply because no cell space is available for them and they appear to be less dangerous than others convicted in that jurisdiction.

Although it is often controlled by the state, probation operates primarily at the local level. Its central goal is to encourage minor offenders to rejoin the law-abiding community. For this reason the success of probation depends partly on the public's acceptance of the practice. If the public rejects probationers, the process will ultimately fail to reintegrate them. The leniency that traditionally has been associated with probated sentences demonstrates the humane aspect of our society's legal system.

Probation can be used to serve many goals. It is often used to assure restitution and can have deterrent value. Many judges report that some offenders actually prefer prison sentences to the new forms of probation. These offenders believe that prison terms are shorter than probated ones and require less effort of them. This speaks volumes about the growing toughness of probation in the United States.

QUESTIONS FOR DISCUSSION AND REVIEW

1. Why is probation the most common form of correctional supervision in the United States? How do conservative and liberal justifications for probation differ?

2. In what ways may a probationary sentence be assigned? When might probation be more appropriate than imprisonment or fines? What other sanctions are used in combination with probated sentences?

3. What are the conditions of probation? What is the difference between standard and special conditions of probation?

4. Under what circumstances is probation likely to be revoked? What legal rules govern the revocation of probation? What authorities are usually involved in the revocation process? What role does each play?

5. What is a technical violation of probation? What is an absconder?

6. Describe the process of probation. What are its basic elements? What sorts of investigations do probation officers regularly perform? How does case management differ from counseling? What kinds of contacts should a probation officer have with her or his clients? What is the purpose of each?

7. What sorts of offenders are most appropriate for probation sentences? What sorts of offenders are controversial candidates for probation? Why? How do probationers differ from typical prison populations?

8. What sort of involvement should a probation officer have in offender counseling? Why? What legal and ethical issues are involved in this aspect of probation?

9. What qualifications should a probation officer have? How do these credentials relate to his or her routine activities?

10. What are the goals of probation? How and why do they vary from one jurisdiction to the next? What facts must be thoroughly documented to achieve these goals? What impact has the "new penology" had on these goals?

11. What arguments are made for state control of probation services? What arguments support local control of probation services? How does the organization of federal probation differ from that found in most states?

12. What is a caseload? What factors should be used to set caseload sizes? How does caseload size affect the likelihood of revocation? Why? What is a specialized caseload? What type of supervision is associated with them?

INTERMEDIATE SANCTIONS

Overcrowded prisons, loss of faith in treatment, financial problems, and fear of crime have set the stage for new methods of control that form a continuum between imprisonment and traditional community corrections. Intermediate sanctions are alternatives to prison or jail that are run by probation and parole agencies. Because they are run by existing agencies, they do not require the creation of new bureaucracies that will worsen budget problems. For the most part, they are forms of supervision that appeal to proponents of "get tough" sentiments while reducing the use of jail and prison space for certain offenders.[1]

Imprisonment poses many financial problems for government, contributes to recidivism,[2] and usually makes offenders more dangerous.[3] As public opinion came to favor punishment, traditional probation and parole came to be seen as too lenient. Prison crowding and costs forced a renewed search for alternatives that emphasized control over offenders. The goals of most of these programs focus on incapacitation, restitution and deterrence, but a few have at least the potential to help reform offenders.

The goal is not the same for each sanction or for each offender to which it is assigned, and it varies with the judge or parole board that imposes it. Each program is designed to meet goals set by a particular agency. A few boot camps, for example, have intensive treatment while most provide only control and punishment. Some judges and probation agencies design special combinations of these sanctions to fit the unique problems posed by each offender.

Alternative sanction programs can be used at three different points in the correctional process. They may divert offenders from judicial processing and serve as part of a pretrial release program. "Front-door programs" attempt to reduce prison crowding by allowing secure probation for offenders who would otherwise have gone to prison. Other states use "back-door programs" that allow early prison release for low-risk offenders who are then placed under very strict supervision. Some programs are used to control high-risk offenders who must be released due to the laws under which they were sentenced. All of these programs are meant for offenders whose behavior is problematic enough to suggest jail or imprisonment. When they are used with people whose crimes do not justify incarceration, they unnecessarily inflate correctional costs and reduce personal freedoms.

THE LOGIC OF INTERMEDIATE SANCTIONS

The financial costs of incarceration and prison construction are enormous. We discussed the direct costs of building prison cells and housing inmates in chapter 4. Indirect costs to society include a variety of problems faced by inmates' families, lost earnings, and tax revenues that could have been collected if offenders had remained working members of the community.[4]

In the last 25 years, the public has been concerned primarily with crime control and retribution rather than reform and reintegration. The combination of rising prison costs and the desire for increased control of offenders fueled the growth of intermediate sanctions, most of which are designed to incapacitate and punish. These programs are flexible enough to encourage reform, however, if the unique situation of each offender is taken into account and resources are made available. Six reasons for the use of intermediate sanctions underlie most of these programs:

1. By allowing offenders to remain free and making them work, their sense of responsibility can be increased rather than reduced, as it would be in a jail or prison. Being punished in one's home community is more effective because the family and community are more involved.

2. Punishing offenders in the community makes more treatment and educational resources available while reducing costs.[5]

3. Treatment is more often successful when the community is involved and the offenders' ties to family and employers can be improved rather than disrupted by imprisonment.

4. Restitution can be provided more easily when offenders are held accountable for their crimes in their home community.

5. Offenders can avoid the negative influences of the prison subculture.

6. The fewer people sent to prison, the less cost to taxpayers and the more space for serious offenders.

As with all correctional programs, getting the right offenders in the right programs is critical to the impact they will have on costs and public safety. Indeed, many of the criticisms of intermediate sentencing result more from poor selection procedures than from the nature of the programs themselves; the same is true of traditional probation and parole.

SELECTION OF CLIENTS FOR INTERMEDIATE SANCTIONS

Alternative sentencing works best with nonviolent offenders who have few prior arrests and little or no history of imprisonment. Hard-core recidivists are unlikely to benefit from these programs and may threaten public safety. The same is true of those convicted of serious violent crimes unless release cannot be avoided and the goal is simply to increase the control powers of parole officers through electronic monitoring or similar methods. To be cost-effective, however, these new sanctions should be used mainly with offenders who would otherwise go to jail or prison. While cheaper than imprisonment, these sentences are more expensive than traditional community supervision. They can be used instead of a prison/jail sentence but are often used as alternatives to revocation of probation or parole in borderline cases.[6]

Matching the right offenders with the best program or sentence is very important. When restitution to the victim is a major goal of sentencing, care must be taken to assure that the sanctions used will not affect the offender's employment. Chronically unemployed criminals need to be kept busy and off the streets, however. If the skills required for employment can be acquired, the benefits of the sanction increase accordingly. Day reporting centers can keep offenders under surveillance and teach job-related skills. Because the nation is so unsympathetic to helping offenders become productive citizens, retribution, deterrence, and incapacitation are the themes that currently dictate the popularity of different intermediate sanctions. Although the public perceives intermediate sanctions as lenient,[7] many offenders find them more punishing than imprisonment.[8]

TYPES OF INTERMEDIATE SANCTIONS

Intermediate sanctions vary from one jurisdiction to the next in both their specific details and overall goals. Their breadth and range are limited only by the creativity of the authorities that impose them. Some of the more common programs include intensive supervision programs, electronically monitored home confinement, split sentences, boot camps, day reporting centers, restitution, and community service. Therapeutic communities are still common for drug offenders as well. These methods of dealing with offenders form a continuum between traditional probation and imprisonment that can be adjusted to match the offender's crime and current behavior. Some agencies use the term *graduated sanctions* to describe a series of steps that increase the punishment and intrusiveness of community corrections. This approach has been found to work in reducing the recidivism of drug offenders under community supervision.[9]

Restitution and Community Service

Restitution requires offenders to repay victims or the community for the costs of their crimes with either money or labor. In medieval times, restitution was a popular way of handling all crimes, but as victims became less involved with the justice process after the 1400s it fell into disuse. It resurfaced as a goal of the justice process in the 1960s. It became a significant aspect of correctional practice in the 1980s as different groups lobbied for laws to benefit crime victims and their survivors. Unlike other intermediate sanctions, the use of restitution is popular with both trial court judges and the public.[10] Restitution is a very common condition of community corrections, with 30% of all probationers required to make some form of financial restitution.[11]

Restitution payments may be distributed by the state Attorney General, the probation department, and/or the prosecutor's office so that victims have no contact with offenders. Victims usually apply for restitution through the district attorney's office and must cooperate in prosecuting the offender in order to qualify. Offenders on probation and parole are required to make monthly or weekly payments to the fund. Monies from fines are also used to compensate victims in many states.[12] Some states have had problems with too few victims applying for compensation, perhaps due to the stereotype of an apathetic justice system along with police officers who are too busy, or too poorly informed, to properly advise them of their rights.[13]

In a few cases, victims and offender go through **mediation** sessions in which the victims discuss the impacts of the crime with the offender. A neutral party leads these discussions as they search for ways to repair the damage done by the crime. This victim-centered form of restorative justice results in agreements that are then enforced by police and the courts.[14]

Determining the value of harm done by a crime is a major problem because victims habitually overestimate their losses.[15] In addition, most offenders do not earn enough money to make restitution a realistic possibility.[16] Because many offenders earn barely enough to pay their own bills, **restitution centers** have been set up in more than 30 states. These centers consist of dormitories or barracks that are slightly less secure than a minimum-security prison. They provide for the offenders' needs so that most of their earnings can be used to repay victims. These centers are most appropriate for unmarried offenders who work at low-paying jobs. Restitution centers were initially created to help offenders pay off their debts and to assure continued employment. Much of their popularity lies in the fact that they have some punitive value, however.[17] There is evidence that many restitution centers house primarily minority offenders who stay longer and pay more than white offenders pay in the same jurisdiction.[18]

Community service is a form of restitution in which the community, rather than a specific victim, receives compensation. Compensation takes the form of unpaid labor rather than money. It is especially appropriate for "victimless crimes" in which society is the victim. Most community service work is unpleasant and boring. It often includes picking up trash along roads, cleaning up parks, or stocking shelves at a food bank. Many states prohibit the use of community service where it might threaten the jobs of employees. Probationers are sentenced to a certain number of hours of work supervised by either a governmental authority or a local charity. About one in every four probationers is ordered to perform some type of community service as a condition of release.[19]

Labor has long been seen as rehabilitative, but restitution and community service do not seem to be effective in reducing recidivism. They may, however, have some incapacitating and retributive value. In theory, they could be used to help offenders learn job skills and to handle changes in their lives, but most programs restrict community service to the least skilled, dirtiest jobs available. At present, these programs serve mainly as punishment.[20] Some help to reduce jail crowding while others are imposed as part of a jail sentence and are little different from supervised work crews.[21]

Some scholars worry that community corrections put so many financial burdens on offenders that they may be guaranteeing their failure. Fines, supervision fees, restitution payments, and counseling fees can quickly add up to become the better part of a person's income. These debts can make it impossible for many probationers and parolees to support themselves without turning to crime. By forcing offenders deeper into poverty, these fees may also create the kind of bitterness that leads to crime. Some feel that the financial penalties accompanying intermediate sentences are part of a "perpetual incarceration machine" guaranteeing the failure of parolees and probationers.[22] Supporters of these penalties welcome their retributive value. They also note that these penalties are useful to the community and that offenders' families find them preferable to jail.[23]

Intensive Supervision Programs (ISPs)

ISP is for offenders who are at high risk of recidivism on probation/parole. People in these caseloads get two to four times more supervision than do normal probation or parole clients. If they have no major problems while on ISP, they may eventually be transferred to a normal supervision caseload. Intensive supervision was first introduced in Georgia as a front-door approach to prison crowding. Many other states quickly adopted the idea, and ISP is now a very common sanction in the United States.

When violent offenders are released to the community they are often placed in an ISP caseload. Plea bargaining may lead to probated sentences for serious crimes, when evidence of the crime is weak. Such offenders would be assigned to an ISP.[24] Many states require that paroled sex offenders and others felt to be at high risk for serious recidivism be on ISP for their entire period of supervision. (In practice this type of offender is rarely removed from ISP.) Offenders who do poorly on regular supervision are often placed in an ISP caseload as well but may quickly earn their way back to normal supervision. Differences in how ISP is used result from state criminal procedure codes, judicial sentencing philosophies, and the needs of local agencies.

Officers handling ISP caseloads have fewer clients than other officers and spend more time monitoring each client's activities. Weekly urinalysis, constant curfew checks, frequent home and office visits, and strict enforcement of all conditions are typical of ISP. An average ISP client has to submit to two drug tests and eight PO visits per month. This makes it more likely that ISP clients will be caught if they are violating the conditions of their freedom.[25] Officers supervising these caseloads are also much quicker to file revocation proceedings than are those with normal caseloads. ISP is more expensive than regular supervision but is much cheaper than prison.[26]

Officers handling ISP caseloads spend more time monitoring each client's activities.

ISP clients are more often felons with substance abuse problems than are regular probationers, and this fact predicts that they will have a higher rate of recidivism as well. Those selected for ISP are often "borderline" cases that could have been sent to prison had ISP not been available. Most studies find success rates of about 55% among traditional felony probationers and 40–50% among ISP clients. Unemployment and alcohol problems are the main predictors of recidivism among ISP clients.[27]

ISP does not appear to reduce recidivism or prison crowding. It may even increase the number of people sent to prison for violating probation. More surveillance increases the likelihood of discovering technical violations and thus leads to more revocations of probation. Judges tend to feel that offenders who violate the conditions of probation will also violate the law.[28] Customizing probation/parole conditions to fit each offender, rather than imposing as many conditions as possible, is one possible method of cutting costs and making ISP more effective. Experts increasingly feel that intensive supervision can be effective in the long term if it results in intense involvement in prosocial community and therapeutic activities.[29]

Probation conditions are often imposed without regard to the offender's background, criminal history, or treatment needs. A large number of restrictions on clients makes community corrections more punishing and increases the possibility of technical violations. It also makes participation in prosocial activities impossible. The question is whether punishment or the reduction of crime is the goal of community control programs.[30]

Specialized Caseloads

In many states, officers with special skills handle intensive supervision caseloads. Specialized caseloads include offenders with similar problems that are beyond the training of most probation/parole officers. They may consist of sex offenders, substance abusers, or the mentally impaired. Offenders assigned to specialized caseloads often pose unique risks to the community and/or are at exceptionally high risk of recidivism. In the case of the mentally impaired, the offenders have unique needs that only specially trained officers can fulfill. All of these concerns require that these offenders be given extremely close supervision by an experienced officer trained to deal with their condition.

Another way to improve dramatically ISP's ability to cut recidivism and prison costs would be to increase the emphasis on substance abuse treatment in these programs. Offenders who get counseling, stay employed, perform community service, and make restitution to their victims are arrested 10–20% less than others. Even though most offenders on ISP are classified as "high risk" because of substance abuse, few ISP programs stress employment and counseling. Since good treatment is expensive, most clients simply attend self-help groups such as Alcoholics Anonymous.[31] This leads most observers to believe that incapacitation is the main goal of ISP. ISP does not, however, have nearly the same incapacitation value that imprisonment does. This is overcome with the use of new technologies that allow agencies to make supervision more reliable and community corrections more incapacitating than ever before.

Home Confinement and Electronic Monitoring

Some form of confinement, other than jail or prison, is imposed on 10% of all probationers.[32] Home confinement is a broad term with meanings that range from a curfew to house arrest. Curfews require offenders to be at home during certain hours. Curfews are used to keep offenders off the streets during peak periods of criminal activity such as weekends and evenings; they have long been a standard condition of probation and, in some cases, parole. *Home confinement* describes a number of different conditions but usually requires offenders to stay in their homes except for certain scheduled activities, such as counseling or employment. This is a step above intensive supervision in severity. *House arrest* uses the offender's home as a substitute for a prison cell. Offenders must stay in their homes at all times, except for medical emergencies. For centuries, house arrest was used in Europe to control socially powerful offenders; it is still used in some nations to control political criminals. Most programs in the United States use the less restrictive curfew or home confinement.[33]

Until the 1980s home confinement was rarely used, because it could not be properly enforced and thus lacked incapacitating and deterrent value. Advances in electronics made home confinement viable. Seven states offered programs combining home confinement with electronic monitoring in 1986; by October 1990 all states offered such programs.[34] The newest versions of this technology use global positioning satellites to track the movements of each monitored offender in real time on a computerized mapping system. Other technological advancements allow

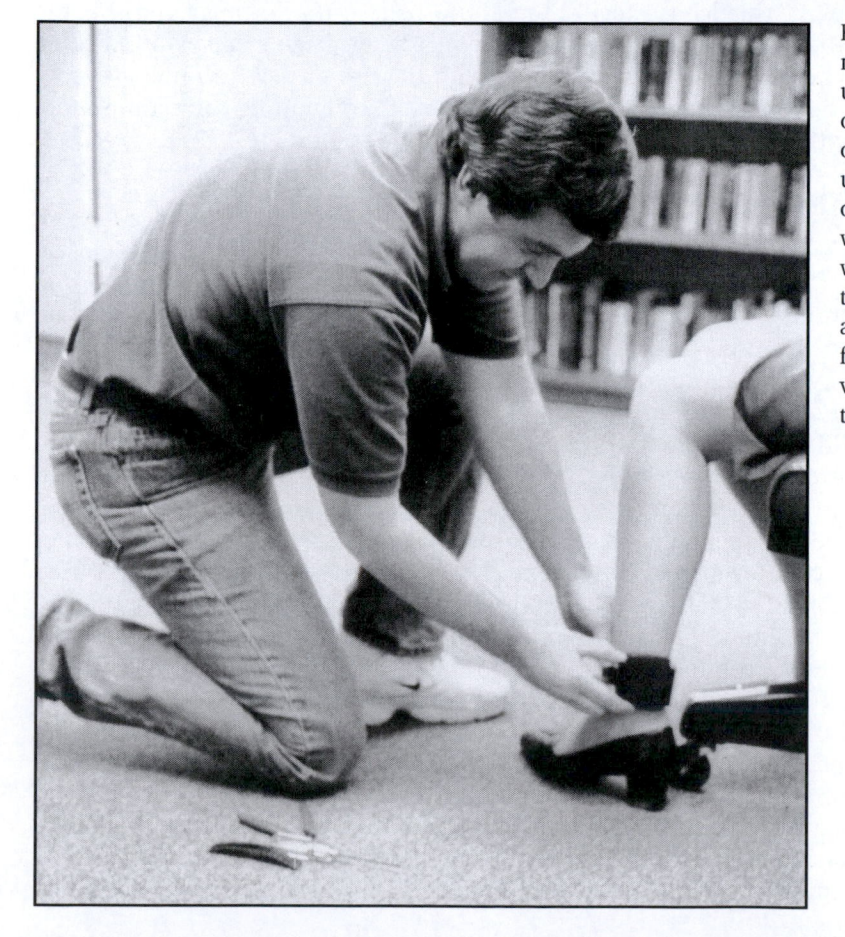

Electronic monitoring uses technology to keep offenders under close observation while they work, care for their families, and help pay for their supervision and treatment.

remote blood alcohol testing. However, neither of these monitoring systems is widely used yet because of their cost.[35]

In a typical electronic monitoring case, a transmitter is attached to the offender's ankle. The transmitter fits into a device attached to the offender's telephone. The probation officer and monitoring company are given a copy of the offender's work and treatment schedule each week. All activities outside the home must be approved in advance and put on the monitoring schedule. This schedule is then loaded into a computer that randomly selects times to call. The offender inserts the transmitter into the device attached to the telephone to confirm that he/she is at home as required by the terms of probation/parole. Offenders must have a home telephone to participate in such a program and must limit their telephone calls to ten minutes. If a busy signal is received, the monitoring company will call back for up to twenty minutes before recording a violation. The offender, and his or her coresidents, must also agree to answer the phone at random times so as to assure the monitor that they are at home. Many of these calls will come in the evening and late night hours. This is known as *random monitoring* and is the most common method used in the United States today.

The *continuous monitoring* approach is increasing in popularity as costs decline. Here, the transmitter sends off a continuous signal that can be monitored from a portable radio carried by the probation officer, a surveillance officer working with the probation officer, or a private company's employee. Instead of random phone calls, the offender is monitored by an officer who simply drives within the transmitter's range (usually about 1/4 mile) and stops to use the equipment. A monitor like that used in random systems assures that the offender remains at home when no approved activities are scheduled. Monitors are also designed to alert authorities to any attempt to remove the device from the offender's body.[36]

Some form of *electronically monitored home confinement (EMHC)* is available to most probation and parole departments. Most contract with a private company for equipment and computer monitoring. Almost half the agencies using EMHC say that their systems need improvement, often due to budgetary restrictions that force them to accept the cheapest reasonable service. One in five agencies refuses to use such systems, while nearly as many agencies say they cannot afford it.[37] Outdated equipment and poor communication between the monitoring company and the parole officer are at the heart of the problem. Poor selection of offenders for these programs has also led to problems in some jurisdictions.

Many states use EMHC programs because they are much less expensive than imprisonment. Like ISP, there are "front-door" and "back-door" versions of house arrest. Some perceive EMHC and ISP as too lenient for most offenders, but polls show that these programs could gain public acceptance by using close supervision to maximize public safety while providing structure for offenders' lives.[38]

Many offenders have said that they would rather do time in prison than submit to this sort of supervision. Their main fear is that supervision is so close that violations seem inevitable and this can prolong their loss of freedom through the revocation process.[39] Many feel it is as painful as spending time in jail. Surveys show that men in general and older, unmarried African Americans who have already experienced incarceration are the most likely to fear ISP and EMHC. Interview data

---

Experience the Sanction

A few critics argue that EMHC is not severe enough to have a deterrent or retributive effect. Before you make up your mind, do the following experiment.[40]

First write a brief statement on whether you feel EMHC is really a punishment and why you feel this way. Then make a schedule of all the things you must do that will take you away from home between the end of class on Friday and the start of class on Monday. Include activities like laundry, grocery shopping, and medical appointments. Give a specific time when you will leave and return for each errand. Do not include visiting friends, going to the library, or studying outside your home. Now follow the schedule as though your free-dom depended on it. When at home, you must stay within 100 feet of your telephone at all times. You may not use the phone for more than 10 minutes at a time.

Record how many times you violate these rules. How many times were you tempted to vio-late them? How did you feel when tempted? Imagine that you had only an old TV and a radio, that you lived in a run-down apartment in a poor neighborhood, and that you had to do this for months at a time. Now write down your new feelings about EMHC. Has this experiment changed the way you look at EMHC? If so, how and why? If not, why not?

---

indicate that many of the "pains of imprisonment," such as loss of autonomy, goods and services, and freedom of movement are also deeply felt by offenders on EMHC. In addition, offenders on EMHC lose money through mandatory fees, see the effects of the sanction on their families, and suffer from the temptations posed by this type of restriction.[41]

EMHC is legally defined as less restrictive than imprisonment and does not infringe on any constitutional rights. EMHC follows the constitutional and case law that guides sentencing and correctional practices. Some studies have shown that the success rates of EMHC are at least as good as more traditional jail sentences.[42] Others, however, have found recidivism rates comparable to those of similar offenders who went to prison.[43] The weight of the evidence suggests that EMHC does little to reduce recidivism in the long run, but results vary with the particular program. One recent study indicates it is not effective with violent parolees.[44] Advocates of EMHC would note that the sanction was not designed for such a pop-ulation despite its increasing use with this sort of offender. Although a punishing sanction, there is no evidence that EMHC has any damaging effects on the mental health of offenders or their families.[45]

Criticisms of electronic monitoring programs focus on (1) the processes by which offenders are selected for participation; (2) the quality of the equipment used and whether it is reliable and tamperproof; (3) the quality of services pro-vided by monitoring contractors; and (4) the possibility that it will unnecessarily increase the number of people under correctional control.

Ignition Interlock Systems

Another technological innovation that is increasingly common in probation and parole is the ignition interlock system. This sanction uses a device that is fitted to the starter mechanism of the car belonging to an offender convicted of drunken driving and requires a breath test prior to starting the car. If alcohol is detected, the car cannot be started. Many interlock systems also force drivers to pull over at random intervals and retest their breath to assure that they are not drinking while driving. Early versions of this technology were sometimes bypassed by offenders with mechanical skills, or by having a sober person blow into the device and then switch places with the offender. Modern interlock systems are designed to prevent these kinds of evasions. When assigned to use an interlock system as a condition of release, an offender must pay $500 to $1,200 for the unit's installation and use. The offenders also must visit interlock service centers on a regular basis to have their interlock equipment checked and recalibrated. While effective in preventing offenders from driving while drunk, these units cannot detect drug use. Some victims groups object to the use of these devices on the grounds that they allow offenders a semblance of normal life and thus help drunk drivers evade punishment. Offenders, however, see the interlock as a significant financial burden. In a quality program, this sanction is accompanied by alcohol education and treatment.[46]

Day Reporting Centers

Unemployed clients are required to attend *day reporting centers* during their hours of operation. Exceptions are made only for job interviews and medical appointments. Client attendance is closely monitored by supervising officers. Day centers have been popular in Europe for many years but only began to appear in the United States in 1986. These centers: (1) make it difficult for clients to become socially involved with criminals or engage in criminal activity and (2) allow probation agencies to make better use of the services available in the community.[47] Some handle persons in pretrial release programs but most are for probationers and parolees.[48]

By requiring offenders to gather in one location during business hours, mental health and educational professionals can quickly provide services for a large number of offenders. Probation officers can visit clients at the center to obtain urine samples, proof of program participation, and other information. Constructive activities for offenders further discourage them from crime by sharpening their ability to assume law-abiding roles in the community. Day reporting centers often focus on building basic skills like literacy and getting a job. Ideally, offenders learn how to function in the community and find jobs. Most studies show that day centers reduce recidivism and encourage supervised reintegration into the community.[49] The amount of time spent in the program and the intensity of its services, along with the intensity of surveillance and the rapidity with which revocation is sought for technical violations, determine the success rates of these centers.[50] These are also the central goals of halfway houses and work-release centers.

Halfway Houses and Work-Release Centers

Work-release centers are locked facilities that confine offenders when they are not at their jobs in the community. Most are only slightly less secure than a minimum-security prison or honor camp. Halfway houses serve similar goals but use rules rather than locks and bars to control their clients. Both bridge the gap between the regimentation of the prison and the freedom of normal life. They are especially crucial for prison releasees who have little money and no place to live while they search for jobs and housing. Some have specially trained staff to help reintegrate the offenders, but most offer little more than supervision, shelter, food, and perhaps a phone. They appear to discourage recidivism in the short run, but their long-term effects are unclear.[51]

Probation and parole authorities have very mixed opinions about these centers. Almost one in three agency directors say that they do not want or need such a center. Some feel that the cost is not compensated by decreased recidivism. Prison administrators, in contrast, take a more favorable view of work-release centers, possibly because they keep inmates busy and help reduce crowding and tension. The "not-in-my-neighborhood" response elicited by these centers (and other correctional facilities) is often very strong and may be a factor in explaining these opinions.[52] This and other factors have led many agencies to utilize existing jails and prisons in their intermediate sanctions programs.

Split Sentences

The terms **shock probation** and **split sentence** have the same meaning. They begin with a short taste of imprisonment that may last from a few weeks to more than six months. Offenders must earn their way out of prison. This is followed by a much longer period of probationary supervision. At first, the supervision is intensive. With continued good behavior regular supervision may replace ISP. Split sentences use imprisonment to shock the offender into a positive and cooperative attitude and were explicitly assigned to 9% of all adults sentenced to probation in 2001.[53] Community supervision may be handled by probation or parole authorities depending on the code of procedure for the particular state. It is estimated that half of probated sentences originally involved some form of shock probation, but the periods of confinement were extremely brief.[54]

Some early studies suggested that shock probation might reduce the reincarceration rate of offenders under community supervision.[55] While more recent analyses have found them to be largely ineffective in achieving this goal, they remain popular in some courts, however, because they appear "tough on crime" despite their relative costliness.[56] The idea of a split sentence originally meant jail or prison time, but over the last decade this sanction has turned increasingly to the use of boot camps.

Correctional Boot Camps

Boot camps are residential facilities that are modeled on military training camps. Rules are strictly enforced, and hard labor is required of inmates. The sentence usually ranges from 90 to 180 days. Boot camps were originally designed to: (1) reduce prison costs and crowding, (2) help younger offenders avoid prison, (3) reduce the costs of imprisonment, (4) deter further crime, and (5) teach offenders self-discipline.[57] They are designed for young offenders with few prior arrests who have been convicted of nonviolent crimes, especially drug offenses. Most are sentenced to prison and then assigned to a boot camp, where they must earn the privilege of release to intensively supervised probation. Offenders who do not obey boot camp rules and neglect to follow orders are usually transferred to a regular prison.[58]

Almost half of all community corrections agencies have a boot camp available to their clients. However, half of the directors of these agencies report that the quality of the boot camps needs improvement. Many seriously question the value of boot camps because their costs are not balanced by reductions in recidivism. The tough, punishing image of these camps appeals to the public and politicians, but their results differ little from imprisonment.[59]

A federally sponsored study of boot camps in eight states compared their clients with similar offenders sentenced to prison: five of the camps had no impact on recidivism, while three reduced recidivism rates. The states in which boot camps reduced recidivism (New York, Illinois, and Louisiana) had camps that lasted longer, offered better treatment programs, and required intensive supervision for six months or more after release. These boot camps held small numbers of inmates and required intensive interaction with staff members. They also took only prison-bound offenders who volunteered for the boot camp experience. It is not yet certain which of these factors is related to the lowered recidivism rate, but the researchers believed that quality of treatment and staff was the most critical determinant.[60]

More recent studies have shown mixed results. Some studies show militaristic camps have higher rates of recidivism than other types of sentences,[61] others describe them as a viable method of reducing prison costs and overcrowding by offering nonserious offenders a chance for rehabilitation.[62] The most comprehensive analysis thus far concludes they have no effect on recidivism.[63] There is so much variation in the design and staffing of these programs that few if any accurate generalizations may be made concerning them. However, a growing body of evidence indicates that they do little to cut recidivism and may even increase it in some cases.[64]

Boot camps have also been plagued by a series of recent scandals concerning the sexual and physical abuse of inmates by camp staff and inmate deaths due to harsh treatment and poor medical care.[65] Despite these abuses, and the generally poor evaluations this approach to curbing criminality has received, boot camps appeal to the public, and some parents have even tried to force their children into them without justice system involvement.[66] On the other hand, some criminologists have concluded that the very nature of the boot camp invites abuses of legal and human rights while encouraging criminality.[67]

Almost all boot camps claim to be therapeutic in design and focus. However, small facilities that stress individualized treatment planning and that select staff for their counseling abilities have the lowest recidivism rates. All punishments in boot camps are called "learning experiences" or "treatment interventions." The ability of staff to communicate what is to be learned and the way in which they handle punishments can have a more positive effect than if they always used the language in policy manuals. Drill instructors who act like prison guards have little effect on recidivism and may even increase it in the long run. Those who take the time to get to know each inmate and approach discipline with a caring attitude are most likely to have long-lasting, positive effects. Aftercare is also critical in helping

Boot camps have great appeal to the public because of the harsh discipline implied by their name, but studies suggest they have little real deterrent or rehabilitative value.

offenders reintegrate.[68] This factor, along with the intensity of treatment offered, is probably why an analysis of the available literature found that therapeutic communities had a significant impact on recidivism while boot camps did not.[69]

Therapeutic Communities

Therapeutic communities (TCs) are long-term residential facilities for people with a common problem, such as substance abusers, sex offenders, or the mentally impaired. The specifics of treatment vary from one community to another, but most use a mixture of counseling, self-help, and education in a homelike atmosphere.[70] The essential idea behind all TCs is that criminal behavior is learned from others and can be undone through similar processes. Synanon, the first TC for offenders in America, was based on the idea that the principles of Alcoholics Anonymous (a self-help, 12-step program) could help ex-convicts avoid crime. Synanon was initially very successful, but its cultlike methods and excessive self-promotion eventually destroyed it.[71] Most American TCs specialize in substance abuse, but many address the full range of problem behaviors presented by clients.

TCs are called "communities" because they strive to develop a sense of pride and loyalty among their inmates and are at least partly closed off from the rest of society. By minimizing other influences on clients, treatment becomes the central focus of staff and clients. Intensive counseling in a supportive and caring setting is the goal.[72] Open and honest client discussion of all fears and feelings as well as traumatic experiences, past failures, and innermost desires is critical to the TC model. Although such self-disclosure is very painful and threatening to most people, especially to offenders, it is essential to the kind of personality development and general maturation on which effective treatment depends.[73] Staff must model prosocial behavior at all times, and attention is focused on reinforcing good choices and appropriate behavior by clients. Twelve-step programs such as Alcoholics Anonymous as well as professional treatment groups and informal interactions are used to promote changes in behavior and attitudes.[74]

People who complete long-term TC treatment have far lower rates of recidivism than others. Former clients are encouraged to remain associated with the program even after they "graduate." Many "drop in" either to act as role models and

Goals, Methods, and Problems of Intermediate Sanctions

Program	Goals	Methods	Main Problems
Intensive supervision	Incapacitation, deterrence, and retribution	Close surveillance and regulation of all activities	High rate of technical violations; expense
Electronically monitored home confinement	Incapacitation and retribution	Technology; cooperation of public agencies and private contractors	Expense; poor selection of clients; equipment/contractor problems
Split sentences	Deterrence, incapacitation, and retribution	Brief imprisonment followed by ISP	Reliance on boot camps, all imprisonment is expensive
Boot camps	Deterrence, incapacitation, retribution, and/or treatment	Use of extreme discipline and military drills to create self-discipline	Potential for abuse; poor client selection; inadequate client-staff interaction
Therapeutic communities	Treatment–reintegration	Multiple types of therapy in closed setting, often based on confronting errors in thinking	Expense, high dropout rate
Restitution/ community service	Restitution and retribution	Financial reimbursement/work at unpaid, dirty jobs	Low earning potential of offenders; PO time in organizing and documenting
Ignition interlock	Incapacitation	Technology	Expense; protects only one vehicle
Day centers	Incapacitation and treatment	Nonsecure facility provides central location for offenders, POs, and treatment providers	Not-in-my-neighborhood response; inadequate treatment and supervision
Halfway houses/ work-release centers	Reintegration	Provides necessities of life and supervision as offenders reestablish jobs and homes	Not-in-my neighborhood response; inadequate treatment and supervision

help others or to get help in avoiding relapse when difficulties arise. Motivation to change seems closely related to completing a TC program, but those who graduate have much lower rates of recidivism than other offenders. Graduation rates range from 20% to 70% of those who enter. These programs are more expensive than other alternative sentences or imprisonment because of high staff and overhead costs, but the savings they reap by cutting recidivism makes them worth the cost in the long run.[75] Attempts to cut costs often threaten the value of TC treatment by reducing the length, quality, and intensity of treatment.[76] The lack of aftercare services for those who graduate from TCs remains a serious problem, especially when the TC is located in a prison as is increasingly common.[77]

Comparative Views
German Alternative Sentences Cut Costs and Recidivism[78]

Western European nations like Germany began using alternatives to imprisonment long before the United States because they are convinced that prisons create more crime. European programs are less concerned with retribution than those in the United States. Day reporting centers, therapeutic communities, and restitution are more in keeping with the Western European style of community corrections than boot camps or intensive supervision. These nations are also less likely to imprison nonviolent offenders, and their prisons offer many more treatment and reintegration services than those in the United States. Social workers are employed by German courts to perform tasks that are similar to those of U.S. probation officers.

During the 1980s the use of short prison and jail sentences gave way to less costly alternative measures: mainly suspended sentences, probation, community service, and day fines. The imprisonment of juveniles dropped more than 50%, and that of adults by nearly 15% between 1982 and 1990, but crime did not increase as a result.

After the fall of communism in 1990 the nation was reunified and the crime rate began to increase. Competition for jobs was intense, and many young adults resorted to theft, robbery, and burglary as a result. At the same time, research was showing that offenders sent to prison had higher rates of recidivism and lower rates of employment than those given intermediate sanctions. Even when it included high-quality job training, imprisonment decreased offenders' ability to find jobs when released. This is also a serious problem in the United States that is linked directly to our high rates of recidivism.

Researchers noted that the attitudes and communication abilities of judges and social workers were important predictors of technical violations and recidivism. (These are jointly referred to as "offender disobedience" by the Germans). Low disobedience rates were linked to officials' faith in the value of rehabilitation and their ability to communicate this to offenders.

- Disobedience was present in only 6.5% of cases where both the judge and social worker were protreatment and expressed hope for the offender.

- Where the judge was pro-treatment and the social worker was dubious about it, 11.3% of offenders were disobedient.

- Disobedience was noted in 14.4% of cases where the judge was doubtful of treatment but the social worker favored it.

- Where both the judge and social worker were doubtful of treatment, 27.3% had further problems.

Most offenders in TCs have been forced into these programs as part of a pre-trial or probation agreement.[79] The evidence is increasingly clear that forcing offenders into extended residential treatment of this sort is effective in reducing substance abuse and related crime.[80] It also appears to reduce violent and sexual offenses, although it is rarely offered to such offenders in the United States.[81] Psychopaths, persons with an especially serious form of antisocial personality disorder, however, are unlikely to complete a TC program because they lack motivation.[82] Many states operate TCs within selected prisons but the quality of the treatment offered at these facilities varies considerably.[83] Nonetheless, staff at these facilities report feeling safer and having fewer job-related problems than employees at similar prisons without a TC.[84]

The image of treatment held by most Americans makes TCs unpopular with the public and politicians. The fact that many TCs employ ex-convicts compounds this "soft on crime" image. In addition, TC designers prefer to locate their facilities in normal communities that are close to 12-step groups, schools, and service providers. This often leads to a "not-in-my-neighborhood" response from local citizens. This is a problem for all correctional facilities, from prisons to probation offices, because of concerns with property values and safety. If such facilities did not exist, however, the offenders they hold would be walking the streets without supervision.

THE EFFECTIVENESS OF INTERMEDIATE SANCTIONS

Different jurisdictions use intermediate sanctions to accomplish different goals. For example, some see boot camps and intensive supervision as rehabilitative, while others emphasize their deterrence value. The goal of reducing prison populations may conflict with decisions to screen participants in certain programs more carefully. Offenders with a history of violence, for example, often fail to meet the admission criteria for therapeutic communities. The many possible combinations of sanctions can also lead to contradictions within particular sentences. One study noted that offenders have been simultaneously sentenced to home detention and community service.[85] Studies of the effects of intermediate sanctions on recidivism show mixed results. The majority of the evidence indicates that most have little impact on recidivism,[86] but the diversity of program goals and approaches makes analysis difficult. The quality of each program's staff also varies widely. Only therapeutic communities have a clear impact on recidivism.[87] Overall, however, these programs appear to save money by reducing the use of imprisonment while helping to control crime.[88] In Connecticut, where public and government support for intermediate sanctions is strong, it is estimated that 150,000 low-risk offenders have been handled through these programs since 1990 at a savings of over $619 million in criminal justice construction and operating expenses alone. No evidence was found to suggest that any aspect of the program resulted in any sort of decrease in public safety. (This does not include lost wages and welfare to offenders' families due to imprisonment, additional crime due to the criminogenic effects of prison, or other indirect costs of imprisonment.)[89]

The original intent of intermediate sanctions was to find new ways to handle offenders who would otherwise be imprisoned. In practice, most offenders assigned to these programs would probably have received regular community supervision had the intermediate program not been available. Imprisonment is costlier than intermediate sanctions, but if participants are not selected from among the prison-bound, the savings disappear. Most intermediate sanctions are more expensive than traditional probation and parole. Also, some fear that the severity of these sentences will increase the number of people sent to prison for violation of probation.[90] More study and further improvements in these programs are needed before we can draw any firm conclusions about their ability to cut costs or recidivism. Perhaps more importantly, each program will have to stand on its own merits.

DANGERS OF INTERMEDIATE SANCTIONS

Political appeal, costs, and recidivism are the standard criteria used to compare intermediate sanctions with imprisonment. However, ethical and legal issues must be weighed against our desire for an efficient correctional system. History clearly shows that many well-intended programs have had unexpectedly disastrous results.

The Growing "Culture of Surveillance"

All correctional programs and procedures should be judged according to how they affect our freedoms as well as whether they reduce crime and save money.[91] The principles established in handling criminals must be carefully controlled, because the number of people to whom these techniques are applied is likely to grow over time. The use of technology to monitor human behavior has especially great potential for both good and evil. Few people object to the monitoring of sex offenders, but what about other violent offenders? Suspected criminals? Traffic violators? If all citizens were monitored, crime control would be much easier, but who would be willing to surrender so much privacy? Following the events of September 11, 2001, public support for surveillance of foreigners increased dramatically. Terror can also be perpetrated by citizens, however, as the Oklahoma City bombing proved. The application of surveillance technologies to political dissidents is controversial. Historical evidence of the abuses of the FBI and other police agencies includes the anticommunist purges of the early 1950s, the civil rights movement of the late 1960s, and the siege at Waco, Texas.

Video cameras, listening devices, and similar electronics can make society safer, but they can also become the tools of a police state. Such a loss of privacy is a slippery slope that leads to the loss of other freedoms and cannot easily be reversed.[92] How much information should be available to the private companies that help correctional agencies with these programs? Can they be trusted to protect the privacy of the people they monitor? How will these companies affect public opinion through their use of the media? How will they use their power to influence policymakers? These questions will eventually have to be addressed by the courts, legislatures, and voters. One of the threats of more effective tools of surveillance is the expansion of the net of state control to deal with social and behavioral problems in the name of public safety.[93]

Policy Matters!
How Far Should We Go in Using Technology to Control Offenders?

Electronic monitoring is becoming a popular method of controlling offenders in the community. The use of technology to control people deserves close attention because of its potential to threaten the personal liberty and privacy of the average citizen. Surgically implanted transmitters could be used to monitor suspects free on bail and offenders on probation and parole. They could also be used to keep track of probation and parole officers in order to assure their safety. Victims could be monitored to assure that they do not accidentally encounter the offender who victimized them. In fact, once the cost of this technology drops, every person in the nation could be monitored via computer. While this sounds like science fiction to some, it is likely that most of us will live to see the realization of these possibilities. What are the ethical, political, and social implications of this technology?

Questions to Consider

1. How much safer would you feel if you knew that computers were constantly tracking each movement of every known criminal in the nation? What about resident aliens? Political extremists?

2. How would you feel about being monitored in such a fashion by your employer? By the government?

3. How could such monitoring be abused by government officials? By private corporations? How much privacy are you willing to sacrifice in order to feel safe from crime?

Expanding the Net of Social Control

Net widening describes the phenomenon in which a program designed to divert populations from imprisonment or institutional placement instead expands control to individuals who previously would not have been "caught." Using a fishing analogy, "the net" that should allow the "small fish" to swim through, thus retaining only the larger catch, instead traps everything. A major fear about alternative sanctions is that they will widen the net of social control by encouraging the supervision of people whose crimes are so minor that they would normally escape supervision. The easier and less expensive it is to supervise people, the more people we will place under supervision if the net of social control expands. It is both a financial and moral issue. The rapidly growing percentage of Americans who are under some form of correctional control indicates that some net widening has already occurred.[94]

Elected officials and practitioners avoid negative publicity by putting mainly low-risk offenders in community programs,[95] which could result in increased costs, net widening, and economic discrimination. Punishing these offenders does not affect public safety but may appeal to the morality of many citizens. The war on drugs, for example, has caused correctional populations to increase dramatically, even though crime has dropped.[96] Net widening could lead a trend toward greater governmental control of all citizens, which would be a major threat to personal freedoms. The programs that are most criticized for inappropriate selection of offenders and excessive termination rates for technical violations also raise the most concerns about net widening.[97]

Discrimination in the Use of Intermediate Sanctions

There is little doubt that some net widening has occurred and will continue to accompany these programs. Who gets what kind of treatment from the courts and corrections is a related issue that needs greater attention. Some fear that net widening will have the most impact on the least powerful groups in society: women, juveniles, and the poor. The point is also made that the same sanction can have varying effects on different people's lives and perceptions. Some offenders shrug off a restitution payment while others find it crippling. Some find EMHC torturous while others see it as mild. Individuals' economic status is often a critical factor in predicting how a sanction will affect them. This is a moral problem related to the justice model's demand of equal punishment for similar crimes.[98]

Others have raised concern with the idea that the quality of a person's lawyer may predict whether he or she goes to prison or into an ISP. The quality of one's lawyer is largely a matter of wealth. Programs such as restitution and electronic monitoring require offenders to pay for their freedom, and this burden is not felt equally by rich and poor. For example, EMHC requires that offenders have a telephone, even though some cannot afford one. A few programs provide special phones that will take calls only from the monitoring company, but this increases the program's cost and not all agencies are willing or able to do it. Because race is closely related to economic status, any form of economic discrimination will have racial impact as well. In addition, some who have studied TCs feel that they are organized around white norms and thus fail to serve other ethnic groups effectively.[99] Similar concern focuses on deciding which offenders will get treatment and which will receive only punishment and control.

Gender-based concerns are also present. It is widely accepted that men do best in competitive settings, while women excel in cooperative ones. This is of special concern to therapeutic communities, boot camps, and other residential facilities. What impact will client gender have on the effectiveness of various programs? The relatively small number of female offenders is also a potential problem. We cannot deny women the same chance to avoid imprisonment as men. However, is it wise to put men and women in the same facility? Would it be economical to have special facilities for women?

Counseling versus Control

At present, the main goal of most intermediate sanctions is to increase agency control of offenders. In theory, none of these sanctions has inevitable conflicts with treatment, but limited agency resources usually assure that treatment is a distant second priority after supervision. Public safety usually comes before the needs of any individual. The question of whether treatment or control is more effective in the long run is difficult to answer, especially when fairness concerns are included in the debate.

The way in which agencies define program goals and procedures is the main factor that must be examined here. For example, boot camps that are designed to control and punish are about as expensive as prisons and have little impact on recidivism. Camps that stress treatment are less punishing but more effective in reducing recidivism. Therapeutic communities might be even more effective but are unlikely to win political support in the near future.[100] Personal contact with the probation officer, even when strictly oriented to supervision issues, cannot be replaced by technology.[101] As with all correctional policy decisions, the two main questions are (1) which offenders should get what kind of sentence? and (2) should corrections stress long-term attempts to reduce crime or support the public's desire for quick and harsh justice?

Risk and Cost Management

Taking calculated risks is basic to the correctional mission. Intermediate sanctions are cost-effective only when used to reduce prison and jail populations, but the public will not support them unless they contribute to public safety.[102] Therefore, many agencies use these programs only with offenders who are unlikely to commit serious, violent crimes. This simply restructures the type of sanction received; it does not test the efficiency of alternative sanctions with a population that previously could be sentenced only to imprisonment. If no risks are taken, there is no gain in terms of reduced prison crowding or correctional costs. We need to study the traits of the offenders in these programs to see what types of people benefit most from which programs. At present, offenders are assigned to alternative programs on the basis of their availability. If we knew what types of offenders would succeed in treatment, control, and punishment programs, we could make more intelligent policy decisions.

Impact on Third Parties

Many intermediate sanctions affect the lives of nonoffenders who live with offenders under supervision. Electronic monitoring entails phone calls in the middle of the night. Intensive supervision can be embarrassing due to frequent visits by a PO and other forms of monitoring. Restitution can take money from the offender's family, which may already be at the poverty level. The effect of community corrections on third parties can often be minimized if POs are sensitive to the intrusiveness of their actions. However, this can reduce the surveillance and punishment value of supervision. This is a practical and moral issue for which no firm rules can be written. These decisions must be handled with professional judgment on a case-by-case basis. At present, little thought is given to third parties by community control agencies because there is no legal reason to do so. The relationships that bind an offender to the law-abiding community, such as those with families, employers, and neighbors, are vital in reducing recidivism. However, the current trend is to permit governmental and private discrimination against felons and their families in a variety of areas under the rubric of enhanced public safety and boundary setting. This means that offenders under supervision, and even some who have successfully completed their supervision, remain outcasts due to the combined effects of government policies and public opinion.[103]

Opportunity Costs

It is important to consider the value of the opportunities that are lost when resources are devoted to one program instead of another. The idea of opportunity costs requires that the benefits of a program be compared with those of others that were not used because of limited resources. For example, if an agency devotes 10% of its budget to electronic monitoring, that money cannot be used for crime prevention, treatment, or prison construction. A program may work well but consume resources that could benefit a much larger number of people. This issue is behind the least eligibility principle as well as every other decision made by correctional policymakers. Each spending question should be evaluated on the basis of how it affects the overall goal of the criminal justice system: crime reduction and the preservation of basic human rights.

Ethics on the Line
What Is a Just and Efficient Sentence for a Drug Offender?

You are a probation officer specializing in presentence investigations. The judge with whom you work almost always follows your recommendations as to sentence and probation conditions. At present you are writing a report on an offender named Mitch. This is his first conviction as an adult, but he was arrested and placed on probation twice as a juvenile. Mitch comes from an upper-class home. He seemed to be a relatively normal youth until his first arrest for possession of cocaine at the age of 15. Shortly after completing a year of juvenile probation, he was arrested for burglary and theft. He admitted that the burglary was part of an attempt to raise money for drugs but denies that he is addicted. He says he just likes to get high and party with his friends. Due to this second juvenile arrest, Mitch spent two weeks in juvenile detention and was on probation until he was 18. He made restitution to his victim and performed 40 hours of community service. When he got off probation he moved out of his parents' home and supported himself by working as a waiter and selling drugs. He is now 20 and has pled guilty to selling "ecstasy."

After his arrest he moved back in with his parents. He works as a construction laborer but is often "between jobs." Despite the fact that both of his parents hold advanced college degrees, Mitch has little interest in getting more education. His parents are very defensive about Mitch's behavior and feel that Mitch is a "follower" who is too easily led by others. Former teachers and his juvenile probation officer support your fear that Mitch would quickly become hardened if imprisoned. There are a few good drug treatment programs in the area, and his parents are willing to pay for his treatment. However, Mitch's father is in poor health and has been advised to avoid stress by his doctors. His parents are therefore reluctant to put up with intrusive control methods like electronic monitoring or intensive supervision. Nor are they willing to cooperate with authorities in controlling Mitch's behavior. The parents are also very fearful of being embarrassed if the neighbors find out about Mitch's situation. What sentence do you recommend? Why?

Questions to Consider

1. How much of a danger does Mitch pose to the community? He has never acted violently, but this could change if he goes to prison. On the other hand, he is clearly a recidivist who has not learned from his past encounters with community supervision.

2. What intermediate sanctions would Mitch benefit from? What goals would they serve? Do they have enough punishment value to fit the crime? Why or why not?

3. If Mitch gets some type of probation, what special conditions would you recommend? Why?

4. Does the economic status of Mitch's parents have any effect on your thinking? If so, what kind of effect? How do you ethically and legally justify this opinion?

5. How do the desires and problems of his parents affect your recommendation?

SUMMARY

Intermediate sentences provide a continuum of sanctions between probation and incarceration. Originally intended as alternatives to prison, intermediate sanctions are frequently used to increase the punishment and control of traditional community supervision. These alternatives emerged in response to fears that prisons actually led to greater criminality, but public dislike of a "soft" approach to crime control led to greater restrictions on probationers and parolees. Boot camps, intensive probation supervision, therapeutic communities, day centers, restitution, and community service are all alternative sanctions. Some are designed to punish, others to control and still others to repay victims or society. A few are focused on making treatment more effective. Lower rates of recidivism and reduced correctional costs are the joint goals of these programs.

Determining whether these sanctions are effective in cutting costs or recidivism will require more study. Failures may be more a result of how the programs are used than of the nature of the programs themselves. In order to cut costs, programs must take clients who would otherwise go to prison or jail. The threat to public safety must be carefully managed—from the selection of who is eligible for intermediate sanctions to supervising the programs that are established. Programs that take only low-risk clients may actually increase correctional costs. They may also widen the net of social control and surveillance while discriminating against the poor. Despite these and other dangers, alternative sanctions offer hope of a fairer and more efficient correctional system.

QUESTIONS FOR DISCUSSION AND REVIEW

1. What are intermediate sanctions? What forces led to their creation? Who runs them?

2. Who is assigned to alternative sanctions programs? How are these assignments made? Why do many people prefer them to more traditional forms of corrections?

3. What is intensive probation/parole supervision? How is it different from traditional methods of community-based control? Does it usually accomplish its goals? Why or why not?

4. Why has home confinement become popular in the last 20 years? What are its effects on correctional costs? Why? Is it effective in reducing recidivism? Why?

5. What is a split sentence? What does such a sentence try to accomplish? What forms might it take? What problems do these sentences pose for correctional facilities?

6. What are correctional boot camps? Why are they so popular? Why are some more effective than others? What does this suggest about our general approach to corrections?

7. What are therapeutic communities? What do they require of their clients? Why? What types of offenders are most likely to go to one? Why do they often fail to meet their goals? What dangers and problems do they pose?

8. What are day reporting centers? What are their goals? Why are they so rare in the United States?

9. What is restitution? How is it handled by correctional authorities? Who benefits from it? Why? How is it different from community service? How is it similar to community service?

10. What are the legal, ethical and practical dangers of alternative sanctions? Can they be overcome? If so, how? How are their failures likely to affect the future of corrections? What can correctional agencies do to avoid these problems?

SIX

POSTIMPRISONMENT COMMUNITY SUPERVISION

People under supervision after being released from prison differ from probationers in two basic ways. First, the fact that they were sentenced to prison by trial court judges implies that they are considered the most serious offenders in their communities. Similarly, even minor offenders (often drug offenders) who did not adapt to the conditions of probation and were then imprisoned are viewed differently because of their imprisonment. Second, prison life teaches a person to avoid intimate communication, to distrust others, and to solve problems with deceit or violence. Social skills are lost as a result of the prison experience, and the stigma of being a convicted felon deeply affects a person's identity, social status, and material welfare. The less time spent in prison, the more likely an offender is to avoid having his/her parole revoked.[1] However, as more people go to prison for longer periods, the challenges of handling the reentry of these offenders into society increase in size and complexity. These offenders are the least well-equipped to survive without turning to crime, suffer from a wide variety of health and mental-emotional problems, are often addicts/alcoholics, and have learned dysfunctional ways of dealing with life while in prison. Therefore both supervision and a range of services must be coordinated for them.[2]

A prison sentence is only part of the penalty for a felony conviction. A felon's loss of civil rights is a matter of state and federal law that has long been upheld by the courts. Which rights are permanently lost varies from state to state, but among the most commonly forfeited rights are (1) the right to own or possess firearms, (2) the right to hold public office, (3) the right to vote, and (4) the right to hold jobs ranging from attorney to hairdresser. Eligibility for certain privileges may also

119

be unobtainable due to a felony conviction. These privileges include the ability to hold a security clearance, enter certain types of job training, become a military officer, and receive a veteran's or civil service pension.[3]

Some of these restrictions are intended to protect the public, while others reduce the social power of felons and extend punishment. The insurance policies of some companies forbid the employment of convicted felons, and many landlords will not rent to people under supervision. A number of moral and utilitarian issues are raised by these restrictions. Some argue that the bitterness and frustration that result simply drives people back to crime. Others feel that it is proper to give more advantages to the law abiding than to known offenders. Regardless of legal restrictions, these restrictions are common to almost every aspect of modern life.[4]

Probation and Parole: Differences and Similarities[5]

Major Similarities

Core Ideas	1. Use of the "least restrictive conditions" that can assure public safety is always preferable in handling offenders. The rationale for this is both legal and economic.
Clients	2. Rehabilitation is most effectively sought in natural community settings where a number of programs that are already being provided to citizens can also be used by offenders.

	Parole	*Probation*
Goal	Convicted felons	Known/presumed offenders (may be felons, misdemeanants or have had adjudication of guilt deferred)
	Supervise/control Reform/rehabilitate	Rehabilitate/reform Supervise/control

Major Differences

	Parole	*Probation*
Nature of offender	Dangerous/ recidivist prisonized	Minor/first offender not prisonized
Legal source of power	Executive branch; governor or board appointed by governor	Judiciary; administered by executive branch (in some areas)
Financial arguments	"Backdoor" relief of prison crowding	"Front-door" relief of prison crowding
Supporting arguments	1. Motivates good behavior and rehabilitative efforts in prison after release	1. Allows offender to maintain ties to law-abiding community
	2. Forces accountability to officials after release	2. Gives minor/first offenders a "second chance"
Failure rate	41%	19%

METHODS OF RELEASE FROM PRISON

There are five methods by which inmates can be released from prison:

- pardon,
- unconditional mandatory discharge,
- conditional mandatory release or mandatory parole,
- discretionary parole, and
- unofficial methods such as escape and death.

Each has unique implications for the likelihood of recidivism and for the degree to which the offender can be controlled after release.

The many methods of release from prison are divided into two basic categories: conditional and unconditional release. **Conditional release** from prison indicates that the offender is under legal supervision in the community. These offenders can be returned to prison for violating the terms of their release. Parole and mandatory supervised release (discussed later in this section) are conditional forms of release. In 1999, 82% of all releases from prison were conditional. Offenders who are not supervised by any legal authority are said to have received an **unconditional release**. These releases account for 18% of those released. Most unconditional releases are classified as mandatory discharges, but a few have been pardoned.[6]

Unconditional Releases

Governors have the power to alter the sentence of anyone convicted in their state, and the president may do the same for those convicted under federal law. **Executive clemency** allows governors and presidents to correct wrongful convictions, act mercifully, or show lenience. This usually occurs when mitigating circumstances are present and/or the offender's guilt is in serious doubt. A **pardon** implies forgiveness of the crime for which the person was convicted and is relatively rare. A pardon may be either conditional or unconditional, but the former is most common. An unconditional pardon restores all of the civil rights lost as a result of a felony conviction and asserts the innocence of the recipient. Conditional pardons restore some civil rights but not all; most forbid the offender to buy or possess firearms. A conditional pardon suggests that the person was guilty of the crime for which he or she was sentenced and may require a period of community supervision. A **commutation** of sentence is another form of executive clemency. When a governor commutes a sentence, he or she reduces the level of punishment in some way. A sentence may be shortened to allow immediate parole, or a death sentence may be commuted to life.

Mandatory discharge occurs when an inmate has completed his/her maximum sentence. It is often called "expiration of sentence." This is the most common type of unconditional release; these offenders have "paid their debt" to society and the state no longer has a legal right to restrict their freedom. Most states require persons with a felony conviction to register with authorities when they take up residence in the jurisdiction. Mandatory discharge usually means a person was a poor risk for conditional release or was a troublemaker in prison. For one reason or another he or she was unable to acquire "good time" credits while in prison. Most inmates, however, are released before the end of their sentence. This type of release increases as sentencing laws have grown more severe and use of discretionary parole has been restricted by legislatures who see it as too lenient.[7]

Conditional Releases

Parole is a privilege extended to convicts that allows them to complete their sentences in the community. It may result from legislation concerning the accumulation of good time (mandatory parole) or it may be granted at the discretion of a board appointed by the governor (discretionary parole). Until 1994 discretionary parole was the most common form of release from prison. However, parole boards are increasingly reluctant to risk early release; mandatory parole has recently

Most of the people sent to prison eventually will be released back into society. The question of release from prison is thus more one of "when" and "how" rather than "if." Almost 600,000 people are released from prison or jail each year. Each person released faces the difficulties of finding employment, housing, and medical or mental health services. Releasees are largely uneducated, unskilled, without a support group—and with the stigma of a prison record. With budgets for treatment and education decreasing, chances are these substantial needs will not be met, and the community faces increased disorganization.

overtaken discretionary parole in frequency of use.[8] Eleven states and the federal system have abolished parole altogether but must still supervise offenders who were released before the decision to eliminate parole. Most states forbid the discretionary release of certain violent offenders.[9] By the end of 2000, 16 states abolished discretionary release from prison by a parole board for all offenders. Other states are considering similar steps, especially regarding discretionary parole.[10] Between 1990 and 1999, state prisoners released by a parole board had less recidivism than those released through mandatory parole. In 1999 54% of discretionary parolees were successful compared to 33% of mandatory parolees.[11] These results call into question the trend for legislatures to take increasing control of the release process.

Methods of Release from State Prison[12]

The pie chart below illustrates the terms under which state prisoners were released in 1999. They apply only to releases that occurred in that year, not to the entire population of former inmates. Certain unusual forms of release, such as unconditional pardons, are not included because they involve so few inmates. Conditional pardons and release to probation supervision are included in the "other conditional" category, as are most commutations of sentence. Expired sentences are more common now than they were a few years ago due to the decline in the public's faith in parole. Many states have added mandatory sentences or mandatory minimums to sentences for certain crimes.

Fourteen states have abolished discretionary parole. Mandatory parole accounted for the largest number of prisoners released in 1999. The legislature determines the amount of time to be served and quantifies credits for good time. Once the term is served (reduced by any earned credits), the inmate must be released. While the discretion involved in traditional parole sometimes resulted in arbitrary decisions, some discretion to individualize cases allows for assessment of changes in behavior or conditions. Mandatory parole removes the possibility for any analysis.

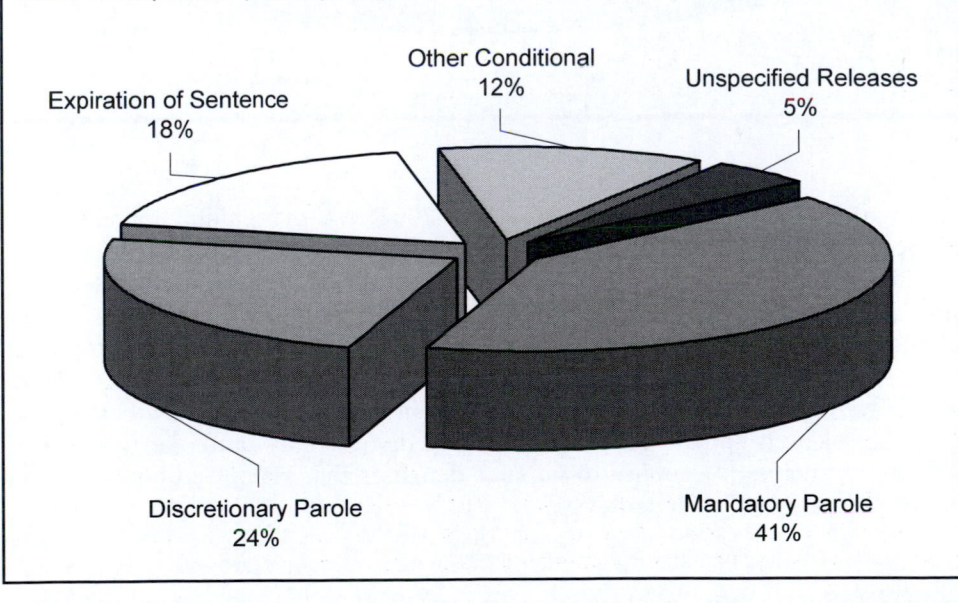

Other Conditional 12%

Unspecified Releases 5%

Expiration of Sentence 18%

Discretionary Parole 24%

Mandatory Parole 41%

124   Chapter Six

Gender, Ethnicity and Offense of Parolees

Figure 6.1 shows the gender of people under parole supervision. While the percentage of female parolees (12%) is much smaller than the percentage of male parolees, it exceeds the percentage of imprisoned women (6.6%).[13] The proportion of women released on parole increased from 8% to 12% between 1990 and 2001.[14] Most of this increase in parole releases was among drug offenders. The female rate of parole has increased faster than that for men because women usually commit nonviolent offenses, which makes them eligible for early parole in most states. Those women who have committed violent crimes usually victimize persons close to them out of passion or fear. They are eligible for early release in many cases, because they do not appear to pose an ongoing danger to society.

Figure 6.1   Gender of Parolees, 2001

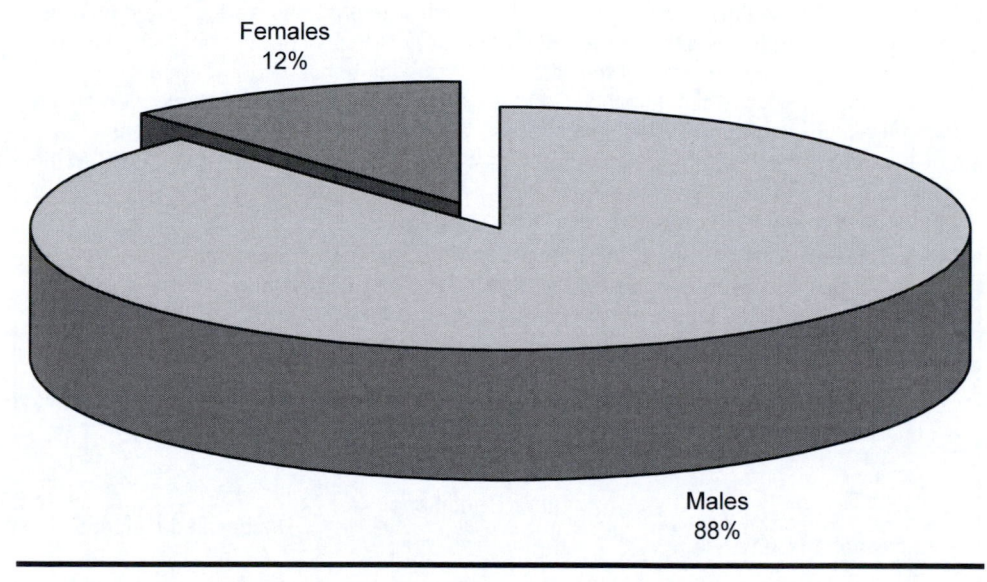

Figure 6.2 shows the race of parolees in 2001. Whether gaining mandatory or discretionary release, African-American offenders served longer than whites.[15]

Figure 6.3 looks at the most serious offense of current persons released from state prison through expiration of sentence. Relative to prison populations, violent offenders are underrepresented among parolees because of reluctance to grant discretionary release to those with a record of violence. Thirty-three percent of those who leave prison due to expiration of sentence are violent offenders, whereas 23% of those released under both mandatory and discretionary parole are violent offenders.[16] This is in response to popular demands that violent criminals serve a larger percentage of their sentence.

Figure 6.2   Race of Parolees, 2001

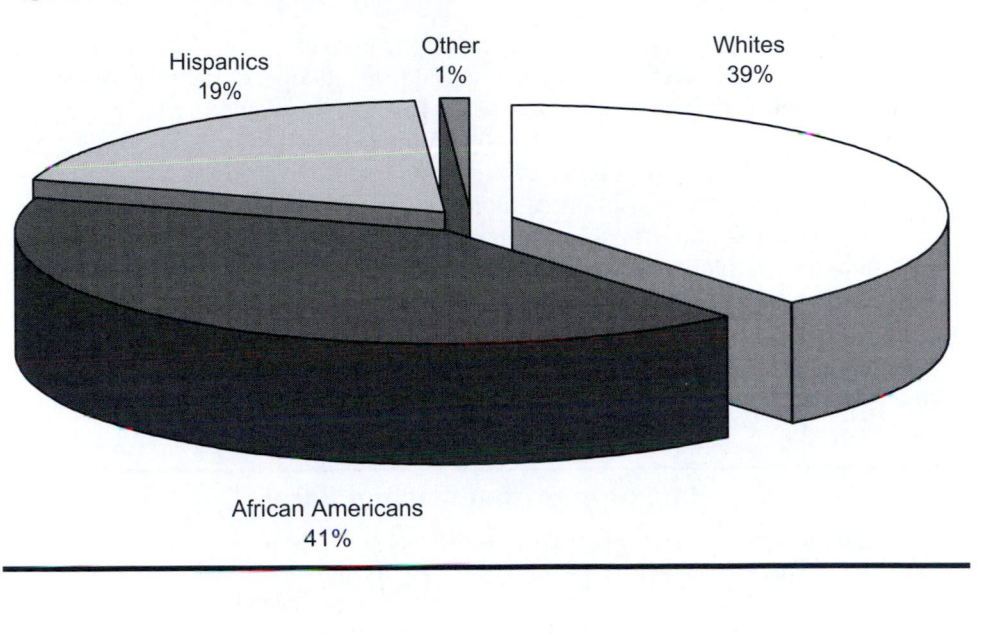

Hispanics
19%

Other
1%

Whites
39%

African Americans
41%

Figure 6.3   Offenses of State Prisoners Released through
Expiration of Sentence, 1999

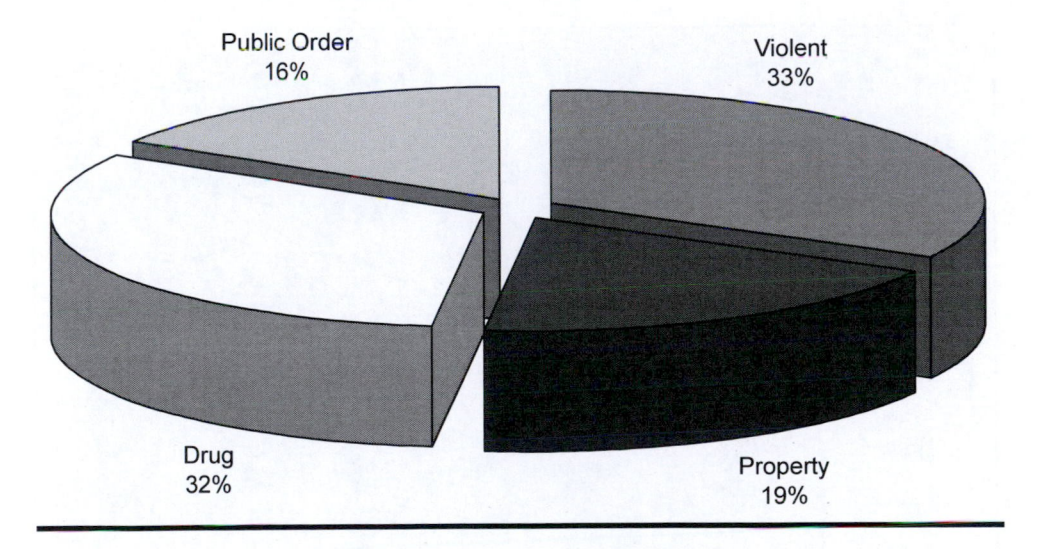

Public Order
16%

Violent
33%

Drug
32%

Property
19%

GOALS OF PAROLE

As it is used today, parole has four main purposes. First, and most important, parole allows offenders to reenter society under legal supervision; releasees must account for their activities on a regular basis. Parole may provide assistance as well as supervision, but the emphasis is usually on the latter.

Unconditional forms of release allow offenders to leave prison without further restraint. Parole supervision imposes many of the restrictions of the prison cell. It can also help to ease the transition from prison to society. The increasing popularity of denying parole to violent and/or recidivist offenders has cut the rate at which parolees return to prison for new crimes but means that these offenders are unsupervised when they finish their sentences.[17]

Parole is a very important method of encouraging good behavior from prison inmates. Because early release partly depends on good behavior in prison, parole

Rate of Imprisonment and Parole

This graph shows how the rate of parole exceeded that of imprisonment between 1990 and 1993.[18] This was probably the result of: (1) the *Ruiz* decision that forced many prison systems to relieve overcrowding by releasing the least dangerous offenders early; and (2) sentencing laws and practices that got tougher during this period of neo-conservative ideology. The rate of imprisonment surpassed that for parole in 1993 just before the parole rate dropped dramatically as a result of (1) additional prison space becoming available due to massive construction projects, and (2) increasingly conservative sentencing laws and release policies. As imprisonment continued to climb between 1995 and 1999, the rate of parole remained almost unchanged, resulting in further crowding of American prisons.

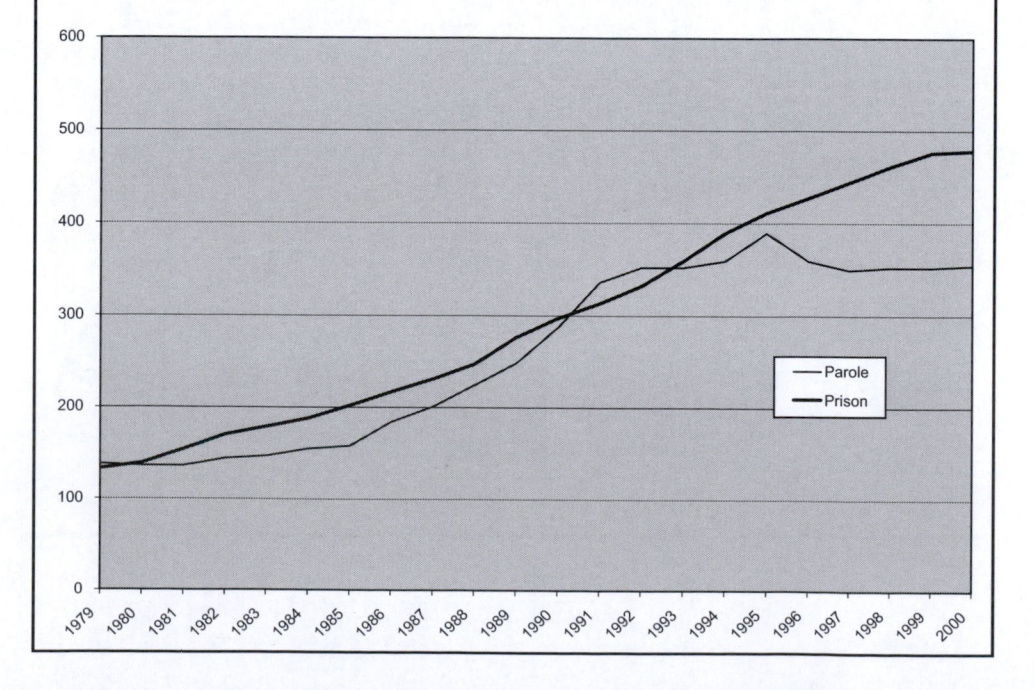

gives inmates a reason to cooperate with prison authorities.[19] Without cooperation from the majority of inmates, prison staff could not maintain control. Parole can also be used to encourage inmates to work at education and to participate in treatment programs while in prison in order to earn early release. However, prisoners increasingly feel that treatment will not help them win early release, so parole functions mainly to encourage good conduct among inmates.[20]

Parole allows the government and politicians to advertise severe sanctions while providing a "safety valve" to relieve prison crowding and financial problems. Offenders can be given very long sentences to satisfy perceived public demand for severe penalties. After this boundary-setting function has been fulfilled, authorities can quietly release some inmates to make room for more serious offenders. This is most often seen with nonviolent, low-profile offenders such as drug offenders. Politicians thus set boundaries that we cannot afford to enforce, while the public is impressed by the fact that they "got tough on crime."

Finally, parole can be used to even out inequalities in sentencing at the state level and is felt to be a less expensive way of doing this than mandatory sentences.[21] Disparate sentences are very common because of the great freedom given to judges by indeterminate sentencing structures. The values of different communities are probably also a cause of disparity in sentencing. When inmates find that others have received more lenient sentences for the same crime they often become even more bitter. This can lead to disruptive behavior, presenting problems for prison authorities. While the judicial branch has this sort of discretion at the local level, parole allows the state to minimize these differences through the parole process.[22] All of these goals of parole are based on the idea that parole authorities will have great discretion in releasing inmates, monitoring them in the community, and revoking their liberty. This level of discretion is justified by the legal theories on which the practice of parole is based.

THE LEGAL BASES OF PAROLE SUPERVISION

Three overlapping legal theories define parole and assure the states great freedom in granting and revoking conditional liberty. Many justify the practice under the *theory of grace*, which maintains that parole is an administrative decision that allows some offenders the privilege of living in society. This privilege may be withdrawn at any time for any logical reason. Closely related to this is the idea of *continuing custody*, under which releasees remain in theoretical custody while free in the community. The releasees' residence is viewed as an extension of the prison cell. Both approaches make parole decisions administrative rather than judicial matters (versus probation, which requires judicial approval for revocation).[23] Releasees have no more rights than do prison inmates, and revocation of liberty is similar to a transfer from one prison to another.

THE ORGANIZATION OF PAROLING AUTHORITIES

While the legal basis of parole varies little from one state to the next, there is little consistency in how parole systems are organized. A few common points in the organization of parole agencies can nonetheless be identified. Most are part of the executive branch of government. Responsibility for parole decisions usually rests with a board whose members are appointed by the state's governor for four- or six-year terms. Most are appointed because they are influential and hold views similar to those of the governor. Only a few states, such as New York, Michigan, Wisconsin, and Florida, require board members to have expertise in criminal justice or criminal behavior.

When the process is handled by an independent agency that reports directly to the governor, it is called an **autonomous** parole system. In some states, parole is handled by the department of corrections, which also includes the prison and probation systems as well. This **institutionally based** model of parole puts parole under the control of prison officials. It presumes that the prison system has the most knowledge of, and access to, the offender and is therefore in the best position to make release decisions. However, the problems of the prison system are likely to be reflected in the decisions of such a system. The **consolidated** model of parole blends these two models into a single system. These boards are part of the department of corrections, but prison officials do not control their decision making.[24]

Parole boards have five basic responsibilities. First, they are usually responsible for establishing the policies that determine which inmates will qualify for discretionary release. Setting the conditions of release for each offender is another important board responsibility. Parole boards have the power to revoke the parole of offenders whose supervising officers report that they have violated the conditions of their release. Some parole boards also define the parole officers' job role and set the priorities for parole supervision, while in other states this is handled by the department of corrections. Finally, the board should advise the governor and legislature on what laws are needed to assure both reintegration of offenders and public safety.

THE PAROLE DECISION

There are three paths to the decision to parole. **Discretionary parole releases** are based on the subjective judgment of the board and do not have to be explained to anyone. The laws under which an offender was sentenced determine when he or she becomes eligible for consideration by the board. Once eligible, the offender's case may be considered by the board either through interviews or, more often, simply through a review of file material. The use of discretion encourages the use of clinical judgments based on the offender's progress in treatment. It also allows parole to function as a release valve for prison crowding problems. It can, however, be used to cover up sloppy or biased decisions.[25]

Second, legislators often enact laws that release inmates who have served enough of their sentence to accumulate an amount of "good time" credit equal to the remainder of their maximum sentence. When this occurs, the board merely sets the conditions that are to be used in supervising these offenders. The **mandatory parole release** is determined by law; the board cannot overrule the release.[26] Parole attracts a lot of criticism because this fact is not well understood by people outside the justice process.

Finally, some states require that parole boards use objective criteria to establish release dates. This is usually done by using an actuarial method based on factors that have been found to predict success among parolees in the past. The most familiar use of actuarial criteria is by insurance companies to predict the likelihood of damage claims among drivers. People in high-risk categories, such as young males, pay higher rates as a result. Actuarial parole decisions are based on studies of other parolees who (1) have already been released and (2) are similar to the inmate being considered for release. These criteria usually fall into two categories: offense severity ratings and salient factor scores.

Offense severity ratings assign a number to each crime to indicate the relative seriousness of that offense. Premeditated murder is always given the highest possible value, while minor crimes like drug possession and simple theft are ranked low. These ratings take public safety, deterrence, and boundary-setting concerns into account. Salient factor scores are computed from aspects of the offender's background that are thought to predict recidivism. These factors often include the number of prior incarcerations and convictions as well as the offender's past failures while on community supervision. Numerical weights are assigned to each factor and summed to produce a score. Salient factor scores and offense severity ratings are then used like a mileage chart to set the length of prison time an offender should serve. This method of setting an inmate's parole date occasionally may be reversed by a clinical override. Overrides allow aggravating or mitigating factors not recorded in objective scores to be taken into account in setting release dates.[27]

Despite these seemingly objective components, the decision to parole is usually a subjective one, and parole boards have some of the broadest discretionary powers of any justice agency. In many states parole boards can only make recommendations to the governor about the use of executive clemency. In these cases, the governor's own policies will also come into play. In California, Governor Gray

---

Commonly Used Criteria in Objective Parole Decisions[28]

At least half of the states that use objective factors in making parole decisions use at least some of the following criteria to determine which inmates should receive parole.

1. Number of prior parole revocations
2. Number of prior convictions
3. Number of prior prison terms
4. History of violent offenses
5. Number of prior felony convictions
6. Number of juvenile convictions/incarcerations
7. Age at time of first incarceration
8. Length of time without conviction prior to last offense
9. Current age
10. History of drug use/addiction
11. Whether on parole/probation at time of last arrest
12. Prison disciplinary record

Davis has refused to parole anyone convicted of murder. Several religious groups have sued on behalf of an apparently rehabilitated inmate on the grounds that, although the law requires that a number of criteria be examined in parole decisions, the governor is using only one: type of offense. The outcome of *In re Rosenkrantz* will have important implications for parole laws in many states.[29]

The central purpose of parole is to allow early release for those inmates who are at the lowest risk of committing new crimes. As previously mentioned, risk of committing new crimes is estimated prior to release to determine release dates. Risk is also assessed at regular intervals after release. Parole officers must complete a risk assessment form every few months on each offender they supervise. Each offender is numerically rated on a series of factors thought to predict recidivism in that state. While most officers would prefer to use their own judgment in predicting risk, these quantitative forms assure impartiality and are seen as a "necessary evil" by most in the field. The first states to implement such policies saw short-term increases in lawsuits over release decisions. Most of these suits either challenged the criteria themselves or their implementation. In most cases, the states' right to use such methods to determine release

---

Ethics on the Line
What Is "Reasonable Protection" for Victims?

As a parole officer, you often make recommendations to the board as to what conditions should be imposed on releasees. State law requires that parole conditions provide "reasonable protection" for victims, witnesses, and their families. The parole board tries to honor requests from victims who fear parolees by making it a condition of parole that the releasee does not enter the county where the victim lives. Today a file arrived on a man convicted of killing his brother-in-law during an argument over a business deal. The man has spent eight years in prison and wants to return to your city. His victim's family, however, has requested that he be forbidden to enter your county and several adjacent ones because family members live or work in these areas. They have also requested that he be banned from entering the only other major city in your state and the counties adjacent to it because there are other, even closer relatives living there. To honor the family's request, you would have to recommend that this releasee never enter any urban or suburban area in your state. Although a convicted killer, the releasee is a first offender and a skilled tradesman. He cannot earn a living in a rural area. His prison records indicate he is remorseful, volunteered for special treatment, and was a model prisoner for the eight years he was imprisoned. As you interview family members, you come to believe that they are more angry than fearful. Some openly tell you that they desire revenge more than protection. One of the victim's cousins is an attorney and has promised to sue you, the parole board, and the state if the family's wishes are not fully honored. The board will probably take the action that you recommend. What geographic restrictions on this releasee will you recommend?

Questions to Consider

1. Is the family's desire for retribution an appropriate reason to make a recommendation that will make it extremely difficult for the releasee to reintegrate himself back into society?

2. What rights should victims have in such a situation? Offenders?

3. What action will best serve the interests of society and your agency?

4. Does your personal view of the punishment thus far received by this man affect your decision? What about your feelings toward the victim's family?

eligibility has been upheld, however. It is hoped that the use of such criteria eventually will make it easier for states to avoid charges of bias when they deny parole.[30]

Denial of Parole

In most states, discretionary parole can be denied for virtually any reason at all. Most parole boards need not justify their decisions so long as they do not discriminate against protected-status groups such as women or minorities. When parole is denied, the board is required only to state a logical reason for its decision. The due process rights that cover probation revocation procedures do not apply to discretionary release decisions. No legal rights are threatened by a parole board decision because the inmate is in prison when parole is considered. Further, parole boards are neutral bodies as required by the Fourteenth Amendment and cannot be presumed to have a prejudiced attitude toward potential releasees. The courts presume that parole boards are mainly concerned with the inmate's potential for successful reintegration into society.[31]

In 1979 the Supreme Court ruled that because there is "(n)o ideal, error-free way to make parole release decisions . . . (and) the whole question (is) the subject of experimentation," estimates of rehabilitation are adequate even though they are subjective. This ruling denied inmates the right to due process in parole hearings. A formal hearing, notice of that hearing, and a statement of the reason for denial are sufficient due process for release decisions. While there is a risk to freedom in revocation proceedings, no such risk exists in the initial parole decision because the state can legally hold inmates until their mandatory parole or discharge date. The idea that release decisions are based on rehabilitation, which cannot be objectively measured, guided these rulings.[32]

Parole boards are often sensitive to public opinion, so heavily publicized crimes by releasees can result in significant, but unofficial, changes in the types of offenders who receive discretionary release. If there is a consistency of denials to all members of a particular category, such as violent or sex offenders, this is perfectly legal. The denial of parole need be justified only by references to the offenders' rehabilitation potential or the threat that release presents to public safety. Boundary setting and deterrence also play a role in some parole decisions. Parole may be denied because authorities have not had sufficient time to estimate the individual's dangerousness, the inmate has a poor record of adjustment to prison life, or because the board feels the inmate needs more time in institutional programs. In general, threats to public safety, institutional discipline, and rehabilitation progress should play key roles in release decisions. Unfortunately, pressures from costs and crowding also impact parole decisions. These pressures can adversely affect the process of release by denying authorities the full range of options to help them assure a smooth transition from prison to community life.

The Release Process

Once an inmate's release date has been set, a four-stage process should begin. First, the inmate and a prison caseworker compose a release plan that describes where the offender will live and support him- or herself until finding a job. The release plan is then sent to the parole office in the community in which the offender wants to live. An officer there checks the plan to make sure that the living arrangements are appropriate. The plan may be accepted, modified, or rejected on the basis of the field officer's investigation. In routine cases, the release plan may be checked by telephoning the parties involved. Release plans for sex offenders and others who pose a major risk to the community should be checked in person, however. Official agency policies usually guide the behavior of the field officer in this regard.

The third step in the parole process should be a transitional phase from institutional to community life. Unfortunately, this step is often neglected, even though studies show that a gradual release process reduces recidivism. The releasee should be assigned to a very low-security facility and permitted frequent furloughs or be placed in a halfway house. Some states have special prerelease centers for this purpose. These practices encourage the releasees to adjust to freedom while being closely monitored.[33] The transition period ends when the offender reports to the parole officer in his or her community. This officer must explain the conditions of release and the procedures for their verification to the releasee and assure that he or she understands them. The PO will also photograph the offender and schedule home and office visits for the next month. Then the process of parole supervision begins.

PAROLE SUPERVISION

The process of parole supervision is much like that already described for probation. Conditions of parole are assigned by the board prior to release, and any changes in them must be authorized by the board. Because parolees tend to have more extensive criminal records than probationers, the conditions of parole will often reflect past offenses as well as the current one. For example, a person on parole for burglary who has a prior record for drug possession may be assigned to a substance abuse caseload. Disciplinary and treatment problems noted during incarceration may also suggest the need for special conditions. A thorough review of the releasee's entire record is necessary for this reason. While this review should be conducted by the board, the supervising officer should double-check to make sure that no major issues were neglected. Releasees usually start out under fairly close supervision. If they appear to adjust well, pay their fees, and meet conditions of liberty, the amount of time devoted to their cases is slowly reduced. All violations of release conditions must be documented in a chronological case record just as in probation.[34]

Officer–Releasee Relations

Each state has slightly different ideas about what mixture of assistance and supervision makes a "good" approach to parole. So does each office supervisor and officer. Each offender is a unique individual with unique needs, problems, and desires. A single parole officer cannot have the same sort of relationship with each person in his or her caseload, nor will POs have the same kind of relationship with a single client over period of months or years. POs must be flexible in handling their clients, but most can be said to have a particular style or ideology of supervision. One typology of these ideologies was developed by Ann Strong in Texas and another by Harry Allen, Eric Carson, and Evelyn Parks (see figure 6.4) for the federal government. Strong's typology focuses directly on the control-assistance continuum,[35] while the one offered by Allen, Carson, and Parks contrasts concern for the offender with concern for the community.[36] They are compatible because concern with the offender implies a treatment orientation, just as concern with the community is associated more with supervision and control. These views can be applied to both probation and parole officers.

Some POs see themselves as law enforcers who coordinate treatment services only when required. They work hard at investigating the releasee's activities and focus on assuring that the offender's punishment continues after release from prison. Very little effort is placed on reintegration efforts. Punitive officers justify their methods with arguments based on public safety. They feel that releasees do not deserve help because they are "criminals" whom society could not or would not fully punish. This comes dangerously close to taking the law into one's own hands but can be effective when limited to being constantly alert to releasees' potential for dangerous behavior.

At the other extreme are welfare workers who focus on assisting the offender in building a happy, productive life. Many presume that happy people do not commit crimes. The investigative and supervisory aspects of the job are minimized in favor of counseling and giving advice. In some cases these officers may even see the releasee as a "victim of society" and play the role of an advocate for the offender. Such an extreme welfare orientation cannot be recommended because most officers lack the training to be counselors; they may open themselves and their agency to lawsuits if they try to act as primary therapists. They cannot be effective as counselors because therapeutic relationships must be based on trust, honesty, and intimacy. It is unlikely that offenders will be completely honest with an officer who has the power to threaten their freedom.[37] By focusing solely on the releasees' needs parole officers may neglect the control aspects of their role and leave the public at heightened risk.

The passive agent is low on all the variables in this typology. These officers like the benefits of a secure government job. Anything that requires much effort will be avoided if possible. POs of this type are the reason that many states have internal

Figure 6.4   Parole/Probation Officer Role Definitions

		Concern with Treatment and Offender's Welfare	
		Low	High
Concern with Public Safety	High	Punitive officer	Paternal officer
	Low	Passive agent	Welfare worker

investigators as part of their community corrections bureaucracy. Passive agent officers have been known to falsify their records to make it appear that they did fieldwork when in fact they were engaged in personal business or relaxing at the office. This behavior is highly unethical, endangers the public, and gives the majority of hardworking POs a bad name. In some cases it may even be criminal.

Finally, paternal officers are high to moderate in concern with both public safety and offenders' welfare. They may lecture and reprimand offenders who appear to be making little effort to lead a productive life but will go out of their way to help those who are trying to become law abiding. These officers take a parental approach to their caseload. By threatening parole revocation for a series of relatively minor technical violations, a paternal PO may persuade a releasee to avoid committing a new crime that will cost him or her many years of freedom. These POs can vary their style from tight supervision to supportive assistance as the situation demands.[38] It is this style of supervision that is best suited to the demands of modern community corrections. It is flexible enough to deal with each individual and situation in a unique way.

The way in which officers define their job role has far-reaching effects on their relationships with clients. POs stressing supervision will not get to know the individuals in their caseload as well as those who stress treatment. Those who focus mainly on offenders' welfare will find it difficult to be effective in their control functions.[39] A certain amount of social distance between PO and client is needed because the officer's main task is to manage the offender's freedom. POs must plan and monitor treatment as well as assure that clients are avoiding crime.

Many offenders belong to a criminal subculture, while POs represent the government and law-abiding society. These two orientations lead to very different ideas on what is important in life. Offenders will try to focus on their priorities, while officers must remain attentive to offenders' potential for crime at all times. Officers and releasees will also differ on what behaviors are appropriate in various situations and may even have very different definitions of key ideas. For example, to the PO "success" on parole means no new crimes or technical violations, but to the releasee it probably means survival with dignity. In many cases it is the PO's job to "convert" the offender from one social world to another. This is a task that is likely to cause friction between officers and releasees, but it is the central purpose of community corrections.

All justice system employees must be careful to avoid dual relationships with their clients. Any financial or romantic involvement with a client, even if the client is in another officer's caseload, is a dual relationship. Dual relationships are unethical, usually violate agency procedures, and destroy the officer's objectivity. They may also be against the law. This means that parole and probation officers should never have any nonprofessional dealings with their clients. For example, a parole officer should not allow a client to fix his or her car even if the client offers to do so. The relationship between officer and client should be strictly professional at all times.

Examination of the PO role makes it clear that highly qualified and dedicated professionals are badly needed if the system is to be fair and effective. Professionalism in every sense of the term is required to meet the intellectual, emotional, and ethical demands of corrections. Unfortunately, however, many qualified people avoid careers in corrections because they do not want to work with offenders, distrust the justice system, or are able to make more money in other fields.

Community corrections agencies often report problems in recruiting enough qualified applicants for open positions. Relatively low salaries are the most common obstacle to recruiting high-quality correctional professionals. Parole and probation officers often have starting salaries between $21,000 and $42,000, which makes it hard for these agencies to compete with private companies.[40] Increasingly tight government budgets limit the number of professionals hired and promoted in a jurisdiction. The poor image of corrections, and the reluctance of many job seekers to work with felons, is more of a problem in parole than in probation. The problem is especially serious among minorities, where the image of the criminal justice system has been damaged by centuries of abuse and neglect. Because the offender population is diverse and minorities are badly overrepresented, it is vital that the correctional workforce also be diverse. All of these problems contribute to the difficulties of finding and keeping qualified professionals in correctional agencies. Keeping experienced professionals in community agencies is critical to the efficiency of parole/probation and thus to public safety. The judgment of the supervising officer is given great weight by many parole boards, especially when the releasee has committed technical violations of his or her release conditions.

Technical Violations of Parole

Response to technical violations may take many forms, depending on the violation. *Absconding* means willfully leaving one's approved residence, making oneself unavailable to the supervising agency, or otherwise physically evading supervision. Absconding is the most serious of all "technical" violations and usually results in revocation. Absconders make up only 9% of all releasees.[41] A recent study suggests that while they are unstable and have a history of technical violations, most parole absconders tend to be low-risk offenders.[42] Nonetheless, parole and law enforcement agencies are devoting increasing amounts of effort to apprehending these offenders.[43]

A variety of sanctions may be used to deal with less serious violations but reincarceration is increasingly common.[44] The PO may simply warn or reprimand the parolee. If this fails to change his or her behavior, the PO's supervisor may further admonish the parolee during what is known as a *case conference*. Letters of reprimand may be issued by agency administrators for minor infractions and the level of supervision can be increased. More troubling situations usually result in the PO filing a request for additional conditions from the parole board. In a few cases the officer or supervisor may have the authority to impose conditions without going to the board.

Unruly parolees may also be ordered to an *intermediate sanctions facility*, which is a locked institution that offers a variety of educational and/or treatment programs. These facilities are less secure than prisons but more so than halfway houses. Some are run by the state, but many are privately operated. Some rehabilitation-oriented states refer to them as "reintegration centers."[45] These facilities are designed for those releasees who have violated the conditions of their liberty or perhaps committed very minor crimes and would otherwise have their freedom revoked. Those who commit new felonies are almost always revoked and reimprisoned. Preventing recidivism is the chief goal of the entire treatment and release process. It is therefore important to examine what is known about recidivism among former inmates.

Parole and law enforcement agencies are devoting increasing amounts of time to apprehend parole violators.

Postrelease Recidivism

About 40% of those released from prison are reimprisoned before completing their supervision under parole.[46] More than two-thirds of those returned to imprisonment have violated parole rules rather than having committed a new crime.[47] Some policymakers are distressed at this and feel that the system is "setting up" parolees for failure.[48] Lack of programs in prisons and the community further compound this problem and contribute to the rate of failure among parolees.[49] Others argue that parole violations often precede or accompany criminal activity and feel this high rate of technical violations demonstrates the ability of parole supervision to prevent crime. Special courts to handle persons facing parole revocation and to oversee the reentry process in general are being used in nine states and are under consideration in others. Some merely hold custody hearings to quicken the processing of parolees charged with new crimes,[50] while others try to help parolees reintegrate. Modeled on drug courts, this latter type is often called a *reentry court*.[51]

Some studies show that young males are most likely to commit new crimes, while others suggest that these traits have no predictive power at all. The earlier in life a person begins his or her criminal career, the greater the chances that he or she will be apprehended for a new crime after release. The fact that criminality declines with age is referred to as *maturing out* of crime. Many studies show that the longer a person has been imprisoned, the greater the likelihood that he or she will recidivate upon release. This is partly because the most serious offenders are held the longest and are the least likely to mature out of crime. Similarly, the more times a person has been arrested and imprisoned, the more likely he or she is to continue a

---

Community Control of Sex Offenders[52]

Sex offenders under supervision in the community are a sensitive issue for corrections. Most have been convicted of fondling children, but some have committed more heinous crimes. The following facts describe how community corrections respond to the challenge of supervising these offenders:

- About one-third of these offenders are supervised as part of a specialized caseload, and various forms of ISP are often used to control them;

- Most agencies require the offender to obtain and pay for specialized treatment;

- Most agencies include a victim-impact statement in the file used by the supervising officer;

- Almost one in three agencies tries to update victims on major changes in the offender's status, and most require releasees to avoid contact with the victim;

- Three out of four parole officers handling sex offenders have specialized training;

- One out of three agencies is part of a multiagency group, usually including police and counselors, that coordinates the control of sex offenders in the community.

Because of increasing concern with sex offenders' use of the Internet, both to obtain pornography and to attract potential victims, one Illinois probation department is experimenting with software that enables tracking of the cyberactivities of some sex offenders. The software records visits to Web sites that may violate programmed guidelines and e-mails copies of them to the supervising officer. The officer then determines if they are appropriate and, if not, what actions should be taken.

criminal career. Postimprisonment crime and recidivism often result from the effects of the prison environment on inmates' thinking and emotions. Some studies indicate that violent offenders are at highest risk of recidivism, while others show property offenders to be at higher risk. Substance abuse, educational achievement, and the stability of a person's employment history are related to recidivism in most, but not all, studies. Many have found prisoners who received treatment and rejoined society gradually do better than others, but such findings have not been universal.[53]

Three different measures of recidivism are commonly used by the authorities: new arrests, new convictions, and new terms of imprisonment. A few generalities can be drawn from the data on releasee recidivism even though such macro-level patterns often fail to predict individual behavior. Women's recidivism rates run about 10% less than those of men (figure 6.5).[54] People over 35 are less likely to commit new crimes than are younger releasees. There is another substantial drop in recidivism after age 45.[55] All racial groups are at equal risk of being reincarcerated (figure 6.6). The higher percentage of rearrest for minorities may be due to police bias or to inner-city lifestyles that expose these releasees to arrest. Level of education helps predict recidivism. High school graduates and offenders with some college are at lower risk of recidivating than less-educated releasees (figure 6.7). Persons convicted of "other" offenses are at the highest risk of being rearrested, followed closely by property offenders, probably because they are the most committed to a criminal lifestyle. Nearly 60% of violent offenders are rearrested, but only 42% are reconvicted and 36.5% reimprisoned, possibly because so many victims of violence fail to prosecute after the offender is arrested. Drug law violators have the lowest recidivism rates of any group. Half are rearrested but less than a third are reimprisoned, a result of their relatively minor violations. The fact that drug offenders are often better educated than property or violent offenders may also be the source of this distinction (figure 6.8).[56]

Figure 6.5 Gender and Releasee Recidivism

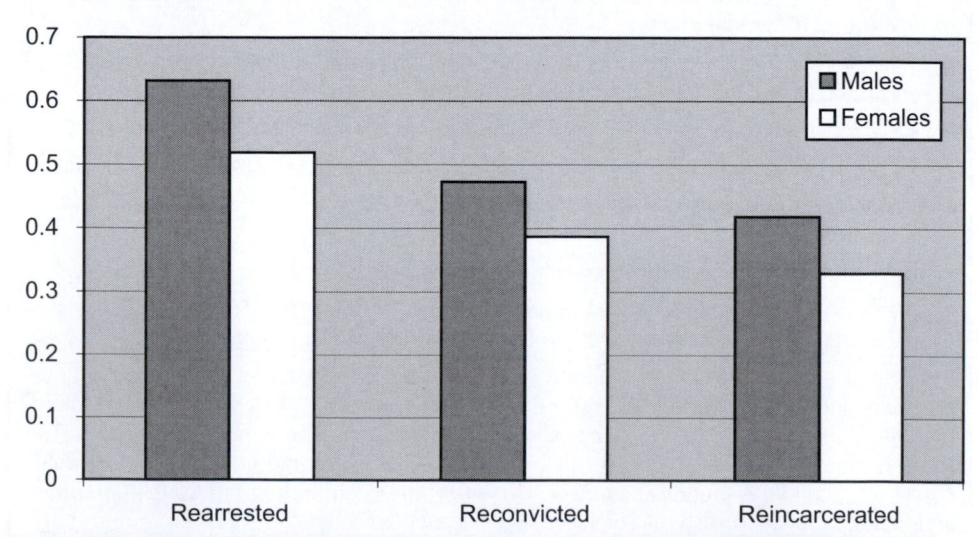

Figure 6.6 Race and Releasee Recidivism

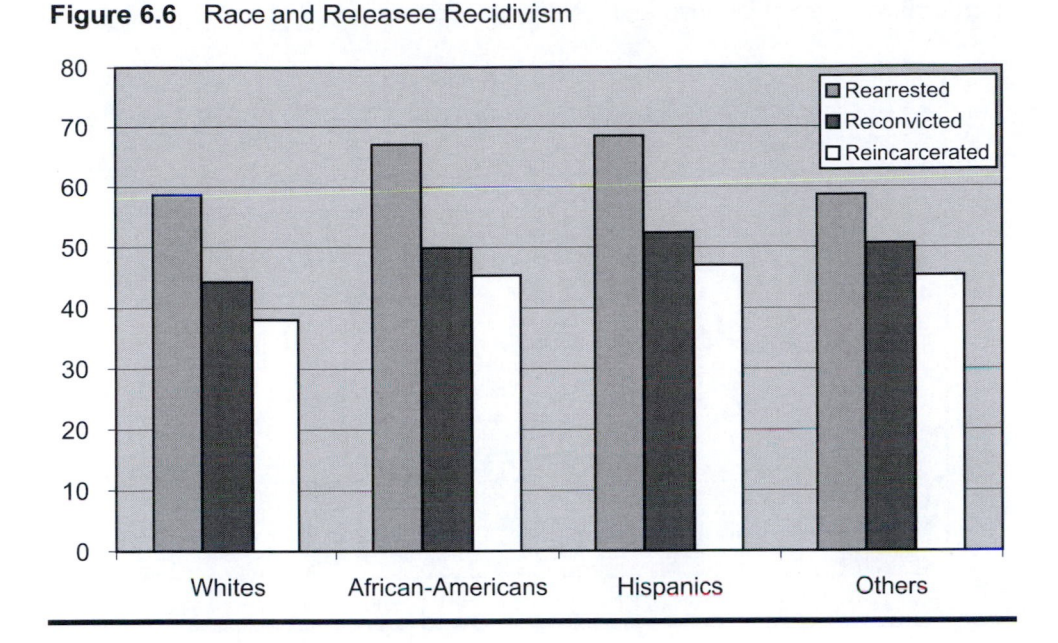

Figure 6.7 Education and Releasee Recidivism

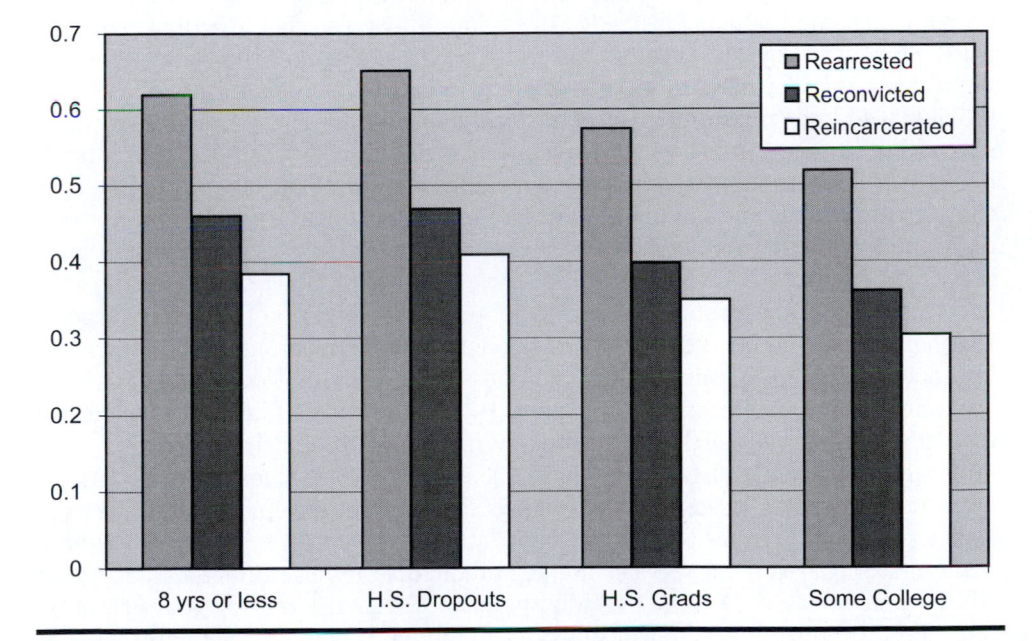

Figure 6.8 Type of Offense and Releasee Recidivism

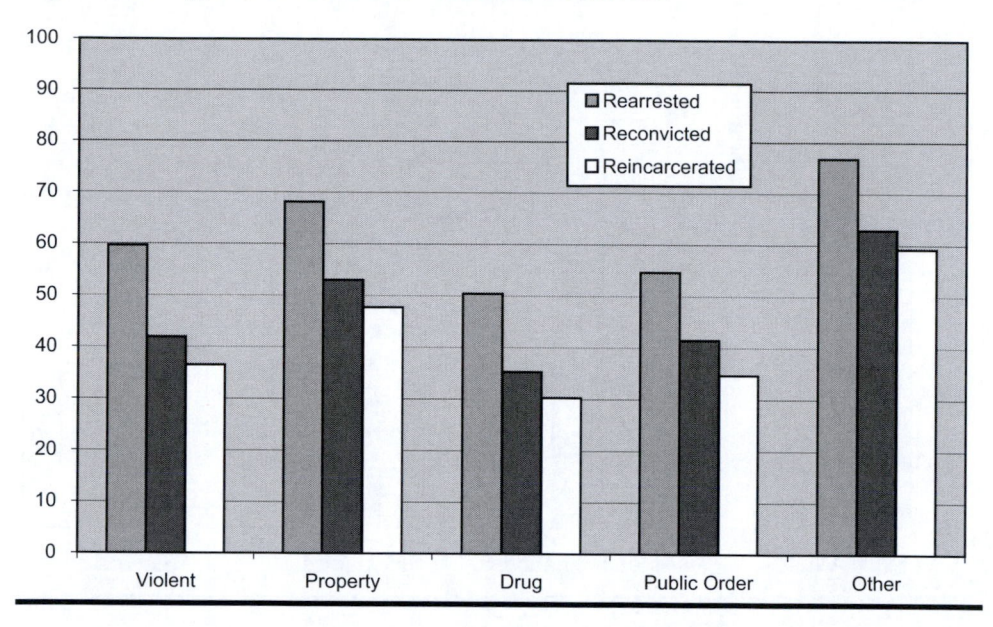

Remember that different researchers have produced contradictory results in attempts to identify traits for use in predicting recidivism. A detailed study of social science methodology is needed to explain fully these contradictions. For now it is sufficient to say that local factors, such as the makeup of the state's offender population, the way particular types of offenses are defined, the nature of the prisons involved, and the number of opportunities for crime in the area, all seem to play a role in determining which traits are associated with recidivism. In general, being over 45 years of age, not being a member of a criminal subculture, having a short arrest record, and having a nonvocational offense (the offender did not rely on crime for his or her livelihood) are probably the most accurate predictors for successful release.

The most serious problems faced by ex-prisoners center on the ability to get a job and to renew family ties. Experts do not agree on the importance of employment in reducing recidivism, but employment and self-esteem are widely held to predict low rates of new crimes among parolees. Helping releasees find jobs quickly can reduce recidivism, especially when other forms of counseling are offered as well. Programs that provide such services have been found to save at least four dollars for each dollar spent on releasees. This savings results from lowered demands on the justice system and reduced levels of victimization in the community. Use of employment and drug treatment services are key predictors of which offenders will avoid crime upon release.[57] Keeping recidivism rates low is the central goal of parole selection procedures and often results in some inmates being denied early release. When these efforts fail and the parolee commits new crimes or serious violations of conditions, the revocation process is used to return her or him to prison.

Policy Matters!
How Much Information on Offenders Should Be Available to the Public?[58]

Many states require that the public be notified whenever a sex offender moves into their neighborhood after release from prison. The first such law was passed in New Jersey after the murder of seven-year-old Megan Kanka by a recently released pedophile. Most of these laws require sex offenders whose victim was under the age of 17 to register with local police within seven days of moving to a jurisdiction. The local police must then publish a notice in the newspaper giving the offender's sex, age, offense, street, city, and zip code. The constitutionality of the law has been upheld by the U.S. Supreme Court, and the idea of publicly labeling offenders is not limited to sex offenders. Some judges allow drunk drivers to use their autos to go to work only if they put a bumper sticker on the car indicating they are under supervision for DWI.

Many people feel safer as a result of these laws and would like to see even more revealed about offenders, such as a photo. They feel that these laws will help parents to protect their children while deterring and incapacitating sex offenders. However, opponents note that fewer than one in five sex offenders commits new sex offenses after release. They fear these laws will inspire vigilantism and could cause the kind of stress in offenders that often leads to sex crimes. Some fear that the social isolation caused by such laws could drive some offenders to recidivism. More important, they fear that notification laws give some parents a false sense of security that may actually endanger children. Relatives and family friends are more likely to victimize children than are strangers.

Questions to Consider

1. Conviction for a felony means that many rights are permanently lost. How much information about a person should become public as a result of a felony conviction? Many parents would like to know if their children's friends have ever been arrested on drug charges. Should that kind of data also be available to anyone who requests it?

2. Do these public notification laws have enough deterrence and retribution value to justify their use? Would you expand their coverage to non-sex offenses for this reason?

3. How much damage could such laws do to the reintegration efforts of releasees who have a sincere desire to conform to social norms? Are they likely to give parents a false sense of safety that could actually make it easier for some child molesters to find victims?

4. If we begin by publicizing information about convicted felons, how far should we go before deciding that some people have a right to privacy even though their actions are distressing to others? Should well-known alcoholics have their autos marked to deter drunk driving before they are convicted of an offense?

Revocation of Liberty

When agency policy or an officer's judgment indicates an offender should be reincarcerated, the PO asks the board to issue a warrant. In some states POs have limited police powers that allow them to arrest parolees after a warrant is issued. In other states, this task is left to the local police. The police may seek out and arrest the releasee, but usually the parole officer must wait until the offender arrives for his or her regular office visit, delay him or her at the parole office, and

Adults Leaving Parole, 2001[59]

The percentage of those returned to incarceration (40) is nearly the same as that for success-ful discharges (46%). In the last decade, the percentage of successful discharges has dropped 5%, while the percentage of those reimprisoned has increased 6%. The proportion receiving new sentences has declined 8% in the same period. These data suggest that the tendency to revoke for technical reasons has had some impact on the number of new crimes committed by parolees. It may, however, indicate that prosecutors are simply letting parole revocation proceedings replace trials in some cases. (If the parolee is revoked, the prosecu-tor can drop new charges that would require a more rigorous series of hearings and even a jury trial. Conviction for a new crime also requires a higher standard of proof than that used in revocation.) "Transfers" have moved to another state but remain under supervision. This is handled through interstate agreements known as compacts. These releasees have been "discharged" to supervision by a different state than the one in which they were sentenced.

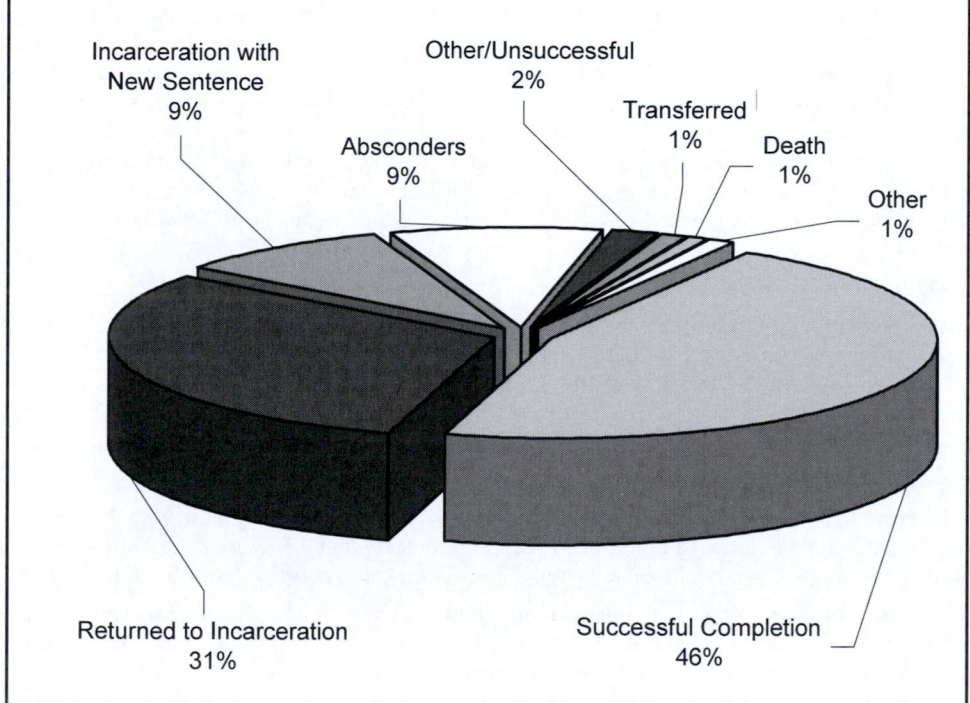

summon police. Once jailed, the parolee is not eligible for bail or other methods of release until a hearing can be held.

Revocation of parole is governed by the Supreme Court's 1972 *Morrissey v. Brewer* decision.[60] Before parole can be revoked, offenders must have a chance to present their case and question the evidence against them in two separate hear-ings. The first hearing is a preliminary hearing to assure that probable cause exists to believe that a violation of the conditions of release has occurred. This hearing reviews the main facts in the case against the releasee, and its outcome determines whether the second hearing is needed. It is, however, often waived by parolees.

The second hearing is similar to a trial except that the PO usually acts as prosecutor. Hearings of both types are usually held at the local jail to avoid having to transport the releasee to a courtroom.

Parolees must be notified in advance of the hearing, and the specific violations must be alleged in writing. They are entitled to a summary of the evidence being used against them and can also issue subpoenas for their own witnesses, which must be served by the parole officer. Representation by counsel is not provided at the preliminary hearing unless the releasee is unable to understand the proceedings. In such cases, which involve retarded, mentally ill, or non-English-speaking releasees, counsel will be appointed. If a parolee can afford an attorney, he or she may have counsel present throughout the revocation process. The decision to

---

Policy Matters!
Should Parole Officers Carry Firearms?[61]

Many believe that the role of the parole and probation officer has grown more dangerous due to the overall level of violence in modern society. Simultaneously, many agencies are stressing the control functions of community corrections over those of reintegration. Some states now require POs to carry firearms and exercise limited police powers such as searching offenders' homes and taking violators into custody. Others simply permit POs to carry weapons for personal protection. Critics of this trend feel that armed POs with police powers undermine community corrections' ability to build the kind of trusting relationship that is needed to reintegrate offenders. They note that most offenders are nonviolent and that police have successfully assisted POs with searches and arrests for decades. Special police units are already used in many states to track down parole violators quickly. Most agencies require that POs work in teams when especially dangerous offenders are contacted in the field. It is also noted that training POs to use firearms is expensive and that many would use them so rarely that their skills are likely to become rusty. Research shows quite clearly that people who are required to carry weapons on the job are at much higher risk of being assaulted than those who are unarmed. While POs frequently encounter verbal abuse and threats, assaults on them are quite rare in states that forbid them to carry weapons. Many POs, and their professional associations, argue that they should have the right to carry weapons because they fear for their safety. Others feel that if even a few POs are armed, all become potential targets both for aggression by the offenders they supervise and for thefts by others.

Questions to Consider:

1. Should POs have police powers, or should they rely on local law enforcement for these tasks? What goals are served by giving POs such powers? What problems do such powers present?

2. Should the feelings of POs be taken into account by the lawmakers who mandate the duties and powers of POs, or should statistical probabilities determine policies on safety issues?

3. Should the safety of the PO or the ability to search and apprehend a parolee or probationer quickly take priority in setting policies?

4. If the option of carrying a gun is given to POs, how should the rights and safety of those who feel weapons are an unnecessary obstacle to the core functions of their job be addressed?

revoke is ultimately left to the paroling authority of the state. The law demands that the hearing be run by a detached, neutral person or committee. If the releasee's freedom is revoked, a written statement of the facts used to support this decision must be provided.[62] Many states maintain a cadre of hearing officers, who travel to various jails to hear revocation proceedings and make recommendations to the board. These hearing officers act much like judges; they rule on the admissibility of various pieces of evidence and control the content of the proceedings. Many hearing officers began their careers as parole officers. This does not violate their neutrality as that term is defined by modern U.S. courts as long as they are supervised by different people than parole officers.

If liberty is revoked, the offender is sent back to prison. In many states, when parole is revoked the releasee also loses credit for the time spent outside of prison. *Street time* is the portion of the sentence served under parole supervision that can be lost as a result of revocation. Thus, parole can actually extend the length of time a person is under the control of correctional authorities if revoked.

Constitutional Issues in Parole Revocation[63]

Each state has its own procedures for revoking parole. However, there are many similarities across states, and many states have similar problems that are likely to inspire constitutional challenges.

1. Differences in the wording of parole board rules and state laws describing the revocation procedure can be a problem. If the state law offers more hope of avoiding revocation than do board rules, releasees may be misled and cannot make informed decisions on how to respond to the charges against them.

2. Waiver of all or part of the revocation process is a problem if the releasee does not have access to an attorney. Many do not fully understand the legal terms in waiver forms, and officers have an interest in avoiding hearings to save time or to evade evidence problems.

3. Even though the releasee has the power to subpoena witnesses, there is no way of enforcing these subpoenas, and officers may not always be conscientious in tracking down witnesses.

4. Hearsay evidence is often used in parole hearings, especially when witnesses cannot be found or do not respond to a subpoena. While this is legal in most states, it denies releasees the right to confront and cross-examine their accusers.

5. Hearing officers may not have expertise in handling evidence such as scientific tests and business records. They frequently lack the training to interpret the case law relevant to the situation before them.

6. In many states, hearing officials merely make recommendations to the board, and neither releasees nor their attorneys have an opportunity to address the board directly.

Some of these issues have been supported by appellate courts, while others have not been examined. None have been fully tested before the Supreme Court.

SUMMARY

Convicted felons who have spent time in prison face many obstacles as they reenter society. They have fewer civil rights than normal citizens, are barred from holding certain types of jobs, and have experienced prisonization. Their ties to their families and friends are often weakened as well. In addition, they may have been among the most serious offenders in the community. For these reasons, most people are supervised by a parole officer after their release from prison, whether they receive parole or a mandatory release.

Early release on parole has four basic functions: (1) it allows offenders to reenter society under supervision, (2) it gives inmates a reason to cooperate with prison staff while incarcerated, (3) it helps cut prison costs and crowding, and (4) it allows the state to reduce sentencing disparities. Despite these important functions, discretionary early release has come under attack in recent years, and several states have abolished it altogether. Given the seriousness of the recidivism problem, however, it seems only reasonable to require a period of monitoring to assure that offenders do not return to crime. As sentences get longer, mandatory parole has become the most common form of release from prison. However, the percentage of offenders who are released unconditionally has also increased dramatically.

Parole is justified by the ideas of continuing custody and grace. Grace defines parole as a privilege granted by administrators, while continuing custody defines the parolee's home as an extension of the prison cell. Most states use aspects of both theories in their parole laws to provide maximum flexibility. Parole decisions are usually controlled by a board that decides which inmates will be released, when they will be released, and the conditions of their release. The boards have great freedom and little accountability in their decisions. Some states require their parole boards to use objective criteria to set parole dates. However, the variables that predict recidivism in one state at one point in time often lack predictive power in other areas at other times.

Both the decision to parole and parole supervision have the same basic goals: to cut recidivism and to reduce prison populations while taking advantage of community treatment opportunities. The threat of revocation gives POs the ability to force clients into treatment. Much of an officer's time is spent checking on the behavior of clients. New crimes are especially serious and usually lead to revocation. Technical violations may be worthy of little more than a brief verbal reprimand, or they may be signs that the releasee is about to return to crime. Parole officers, supervisors, and hearing officers decide how serious the problem is and take appropriate steps to correct it. Such steps may range from a case conference to time spent in an intermediate sanctions facility or to complete revocation of liberty.

QUESTIONS FOR DISCUSSION AND REVIEW

1. How is parole different from probation? How are the organization and priorities of the agencies affected by this? How are the differences in the populations they deal with expressed in their priorities?

2. By what methods can inmates legally be released from prison? Why is parole preferred over these other methods?

3. What rights are lost as a result of a felony conviction? Why? How does this affect releasees?

4. What purposes are served by parole? What are the basic goals of parole supervision? How are they accomplished?

5. What factors determine when an inmate will be paroled? Who makes the decision to parole?

6. What is a salient factor score? An offense severity rating? How are these used to set a parole date? What is a clinical override?

7. What is a parole board? Who controls it? What are its responsibilities? How are its members selected?

8. What steps should be followed in paroling a convict? What is the goal of each step? How is each step accomplished?

9. Why might parole be revoked? What steps must be taken to revoke parole? What rights does the parolee have? How is the final decision made and by whom?

10. What sorts of orientations would you expect to find among parole officers? Which one seems most effective to accomplish the goals of parole supervision?

11. What issues color the relationship between the parole officer and the parolee? How does each affect this relationship?

PRISON POPULATIONS

As laws get tougher, prison populations grow in size and costs rise accordingly. Although different types of people are found in federal and state prisons, both systems face serious economic problems as a result of more inmates serving longer sentences. Problems such as mental disorders and infectious diseases are also found at much higher rates among prisoners than in the general population. In addition, general social trends, like the aging of the population, are affecting prisons in dramatic ways. All of these challenges affect the inmate classification systems that are used to prevent escapes and minimize violence.

PRISON POPULATION GROWTH

The U.S. rate of imprisonment is rising at an alarming rate. More than 2.1 million people are currently held in U.S. jails and prisons. This population has grown by an average of nearly 4% a year since 1995 but may be starting to level off or even decline in some areas. Despite prison construction projects that have increased the number of prison beds by 81% in ten years, the majority of U.S. prisons are operating above capacity.[1] The U.S. rate of imprisonment is the highest in the industrialized world.[2] In 1980, 139 of every 100,000 Americans were prison inmates. By 1995 this figure had reached 411, and by the end of 2001 it had risen to 470.[3] This rate is even higher (690 out of every 100,000 residents) if jail inmates are included.[4] This increase is largely due to drug and violent crimes along with probation and parole violations. At mid-year 2001, one in every 145 U.S. residents was incarcerated.[5]

Until 1995, economists believed the costs of crime and imprisonment were too small to affect the nation's economic welfare. Between 1980 and 1995 the U.S. prison population tripled, and a Nobel Prize winner in economics warned that such a high rate of imprisonment could spell economic disaster for the nation. Prison construction and operation is costly and returns very little to the economy. Further, it is estimated that current unemployment rates for U.S. men would rise by at least 2% if those in jails and prisons were counted.[6] Because a prison term lowers a person's future earnings, the percentage of the population that is underemployed or unemployed will rise as current inmates return to society where most will face chronic problems in finding and keeping a job.[7] Further, the higher a person's income prior to imprisonment, the larger the drop in postrelease earnings. Lowered wages are associated with high rates of recidivism, which means further costs both to victims and to the justice system. We can identify a cycle of low wages leading to crime and imprisonment, which further lowers earnings and thus encourages more crime.[8] Add the destructive effects of imprisonment on the inmate's family and it becomes clear why some penologists refer to "invisible punishment" and feel excessive use of prisons can cause crime.[9]

Prison crowding can be addressed in three basic ways. *Diversion* strategies increase the use of alternatives to imprisonment. Most rely on community-based agencies, especially probation departments. *Population reduction* relies on releasing

---

Imprisonment Rates across the World[10]

The rate of imprisonment is the ratio of inmates to the general population. It is used to control for differences in population size across jurisdictions and time periods. It would make little sense to compare the number of inmates held in American prisons in 1930 to the current number because there are many more people in the nation today than there were in 1930. The same is true for comparisons across jurisdictions. The rate of imprisonment is calculated as:

$$\frac{\text{Number of inmates}}{\text{Number of people in population}} \times 100{,}000 = \text{rate of imprisonment}$$

The figures below are rates of imprisonment for the United States and other nations. Note the extreme difference between the U.S. rate of imprisonment and those of other nations. Compare the U.S. rate of imprisonment first with that of Western European democracies and then with more authoritarian nations such as Belarus and Russia. The United States has the highest rate of imprisonment in the world. One of its closest competitors, Russia, expects its rate to decline as the result of an announced amnesty program to be implemented in 2003. The Cayman Islands have a high rate mainly because of their small population and the fact that they imprison large numbers of noncitizen drug smugglers.

Australia	110	Kyrgyzstan	440
Belarus	575	Netherlands	90
Belize	460	Russia	644
Canada	110	South Africa	400
Cayman Islands	665	Sweden	60
France	90	Switzerland	85
Italy	90	United Kingdom	125
Japan	40	**United States**	**699**
Kazakhstan	495		

the least dangerous inmates early in their sentences. *System expansion* means increasing the number of prison cells by building new facilities and enlarging older ones. Diversion and population reduction are often used as temporary control methods while states search for ways to pay for system expansion. Unfortunately, history shows that expansion is an endless process; many penologists feel that many current inmates could be controlled by less extreme methods in the community.[11]

There is no doubt that building and operating prisons creates some jobs. Corrections is certainly a growth industry and, at least in the short run, the increasing rate of imprisonment is creating a few jobs. However, most economists who have studied the issue believe that investment in virtually any other sort of activity would create more jobs. Prisons are extremely expensive to operate and their costs are a burden, mainly to state governments. For example, California spent only 2% of its budget on prisons in 1980; by 1994 prisons accounted for 9% of its budget. The Rand Corporation, a conservative "think tank," estimated that prisons would devour 18% of California's budget by 2002 if growth did not slow substantially. Educational budget cuts affect inner-city minorities the most, which further increases crime rates in the long run.[12] Similar trends can be noted in many other states. This means that other state-supported services suffer a loss of funds, or citizens must endure a tax hike to pay for the prison construction and operation. While growth may be slowing in many areas, maintaining a prison system the size of those in most states remains enormous. The alternative is to decrease the use of prisons and to devote more resources to crime prevention. However, the forces that are filling our prisons—the war on drugs, the victim's movement, fear of crime, and harsher sentencing laws—show no signs of subsiding, and crime prevention programs are being stripped of funds to pay for prison building and operation.[13]

IMBALANCES IN U.S. IMPRISONMENT PATTERNS

Forty-nine percent of those held in state prisons have been convicted of a violent offense; property offenders make up 20% of state inmates, drug offenders account for 21%, and the remaining 10% are being held for miscellaneous other crimes. The great majority of prisoners are urban, poor, and younger than 40 years of age. The social and economic impact of the current U.S. rate of imprisonment can be seen in the fact that 10% of young African-American men, compared with 2.9% of Hispanic men, and 1.2% of white men were imprisoned in 2001. Prisoners are 94% male. Most were single, unemployed, and substance abusers prior to incarceration.[14]

African Americans are grossly overrepresented among jail and prison inmates. Adult black males are incarcerated 7.6 times more often than whites.[15] Increases in imprisonment for violence and probation/parole violations are virtually equal across the races, but the increase for drug offenses is almost three times greater among people of African descent. This is partly due to the law enforcement emphasis on crack cocaine, the only drug that is more popular among minorities than whites. In the federal system, 14 states have special penalties for crack that are between 3 and 100 times more severe than those for other drugs. While 10% of drug users are African American, 84% of those convicted of crack-cocaine charges

---

Cultural Diversity and Corrections[16]

Respect for cultural diversity means looking at the world in a way that includes every group with a unique heritage as having inherent value. It rejects the idea of assimilation and instead sees the nation as a mosaic of groups with valuable and unique identities that deserve to be passed on to new generations and shared with other groups. Each cultural group in the United States makes a contribution to the national whole. Members of each group can rejoice in and treasure their uniqueness without threatening other groups. Knowledge of, and respect for, the customs, values, and insights of cultures other than one's own is essential to life in a diverse society.

To handle the demands of our mosaic of cultures, each correctional system must examine the array of groups that make up its employees and clients. Correctional practitioners need to learn about the customs and habits of those groups in order to appreciate the behavior of members and respond to it appropriately. For example, many Native Americans will look at the ground when speaking to someone of higher status as a sign of respect in their culture. However, Euro-Americans are accustomed to looking people in the eye when speaking and often misinterpret the Native American sign of respect as evidence of dishonesty. Education is a powerful tool in overcoming such barriers to understanding.

Correctional institutions must also become more sensitive to the religious and cultural beliefs and customs of their inmates. The values and norms of the individual's culture must be thoroughly understood, if staff members are to motivate clients and effectively communicate with them. Special clubs and religious organizations can use ethnic pride to help reintegrate offenders back into their home communities upon release. Similarly, the religious traditions of groups such as Native Americans and Asians can help offenders to reform if they are respected and encouraged by correctional professionals.

---

are from this group. Powder cocaine convictions were more evenly distributed with 58% of defendants being white, 27% black, and 15% Hispanic.[17] Hispanics are imprisoned for drug offenses at 8 times the rate of whites; African Americans are incarcerated 17 times more often than whites.[18] Although the drugs preferred by whites, such as ecstasy and methamphetamine, rapidly are becoming serious public health problems, they have not attracted the kind of attention that consistently is focused on crack cocaine.[19] Authorities explain these discrepancies by referring to the fact that African-American communities are the most heavily impacted by drug use and sales. They also claim that crack is 50 times more addictive than other drugs. Many police administrators feel that it would be discriminatory not to enforce drug laws sternly in communities where drug dealers have destroyed the quality of life. Drug deals in minority areas more frequently occur in public spaces, making it easier for police to arrest and convict.

Treatment for substance abuse problems is much more available to whites than it is to minorities. Part of this discrepancy may be due to economics—whites are more likely to have health insurance that will pay for drug treatment than are minorities. Even when drug treatment is not determined by insurance or quality of legal representation, discrimination seems to exist in legal penalties and sentencing practices.[20]

Most serious violence occurs in minority neighborhoods. Violence is the leading cause of death among young black men but ranks fifth for whites. Sentencing patterns do not reflect this problem, however. Violence against minorities is treated less severely than that which victimizes whites. A Dallas study found that the rape of a white woman resulted in an average sentence of 10 years, while the rape of a Hispanic woman netted an average of 5 years. If a black woman was the victim, the typical sentence was 2 years.[21]

This situation raises a huge dilemma for the justice system. A deterrence-based approach to controlling violence partly depends on harsh penalties. Because most of those affected by this policy would be minorities, some would label such a policy racist. On the other hand, the system's failure to punish fully violence against minorities is often taken as a sign of apathy or bigotry. The justice system needs to find a means of protecting citizens in high-crime areas without depleting those communities of sources of support. The trend toward increasing incarceration has been compared to "an overused antibiotic; it has left the prisoner untreated and unchastened, the community unprotected, and society demonstrably worse off."[22] The best answers seem to lie in increased attention to crime prevention.

Close examination of these issues has led many experts to question whether prisons actually help control crime. For example, Texas' prison system grew faster than those in other states and accounted for 18% of the nations' prison population

The racial inequalities of society have created a situation in which African Americans are grossly overrepresented in correctional populations.

growth during the 1990s, but its crime rate declined the least of all large states.[23] Perhaps the central purpose of imprisonment is to set boundaries on who is acceptable to society and who is an outcast. Thus, prisons serve more to keep the law-abiding feeling good about their obedience than to affect offenders or crime. Throughout history, imprisonment patterns have reflected the economic power structure of the society more than its crime problem.[24] The outcome of this little-recognized dilemma leads to the belief that "the whole law-and-order movement . . . is, in operation, anti-black and anti-underclass. Not in plan, not in design, not in intent, but in operation."[25]

Whether imprisonment rates reflect the crime problem or social prejudices, it is clear that race will haunt discussions of crime control for many years to come. At the federal level, debate centers on the penalties assigned to different crimes, especially in the area of drug laws. At the state level, dealing with addicts and predatory street crimes are the main concerns. This is the result of differences in the legal powers of federal and state governments. These same areas of legal powers also result in major differences in the nature of federal and state prison systems.

FEDERAL AND STATE SYSTEMS

Federal and state prison populations differ in size and the crimes committed by inmates. Federal jurisdiction is limited mainly to crimes that cross state lines or use the mail, large-scale drug smuggling, organized crime, bank robberies, and white-collar crimes. State laws typically deal with street crimes like theft, robbery, and murder. The transfer of prisoners sentenced in the District of Columbia to the federal system was completed in 2001; on December 31, 2001, the federal system held 6,930 inmates from the District of Columbia.[26] Since 1995, state growth rates have dropped while federal rates increased.[27] The federal system holds 157,000 people, while Texas holds over 160,000 and California 159,000.[28] In general, federal inmates are older, better educated, less likely to be from extremely poor backgrounds, and more likely to be from stable families than are state inmates.[29] They are also twice as likely to be "first offenders." Thirty-eight percent of federal inmates and 19% of state inmates had never before been imprisoned or placed on probation. This is largely due to federal drug laws passed during the 1980s that require prison terms for drug offenses.[30]

Federal inmates are almost three times more likely to be imprisoned for a drug offense than state prisoners; 57% of federal inmates in 2000 were serving time for drug offenses (see figure 7.1).[31] Many of these offenders were caught with relatively large quantities of illegal drugs. However, many of those imprisoned by federal authorities are "mules" rather than the people masterminding the operation. Mules are people who are hired to transport drugs and are considered expendable by the organizations that hire them.[32]

State facilities primarily house those convicted of street crimes (see figure 7.2). Note that violent crimes account for almost half of these prisoners. Drug and property offenders are equally represented until gender differences are examined. Drug crimes account for 32% of the women held in state prisons and 20% of the men.[33]

Figure 7.3 charts the most serious offenses of prisoners admitted to state prisons since 1980.[34] Note the increase in drug offenders since the late 1980s. Admissions of violent offenders rose significantly. Figure 7.4 compares some characteristics of prisoners in state and federal prisons.[35] Until 1988 the majority of prisoners were white, but the number of African Americans incarcerated has risen steadily. They now comprise the majority of prisoners even though they make up only about 13% of the nation's residents. Female incarceration rates are substantially lower than those for males, but they reflect similar ethnic disparities.[36] The

Figure 7.1 Offenses of Federal Prisoners, 2000

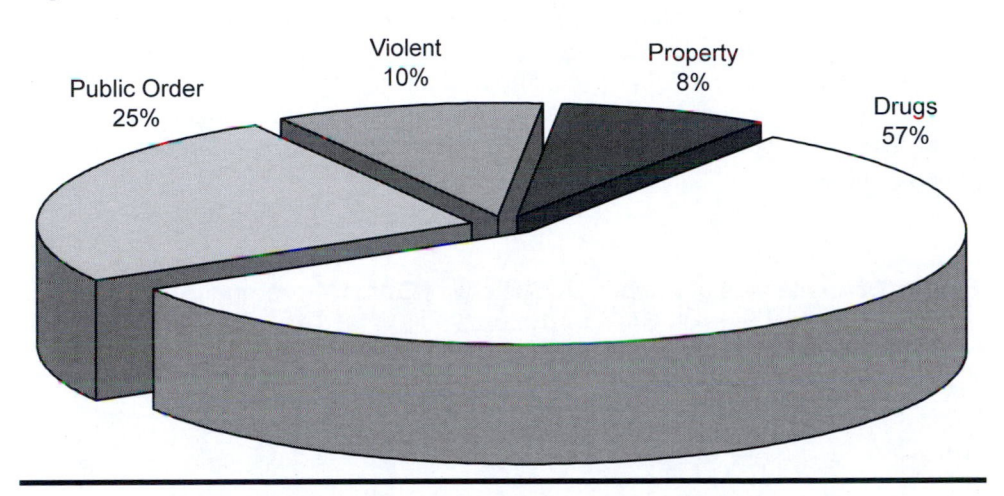

Figure 7.2 Offenses of State Prisoners, 2000

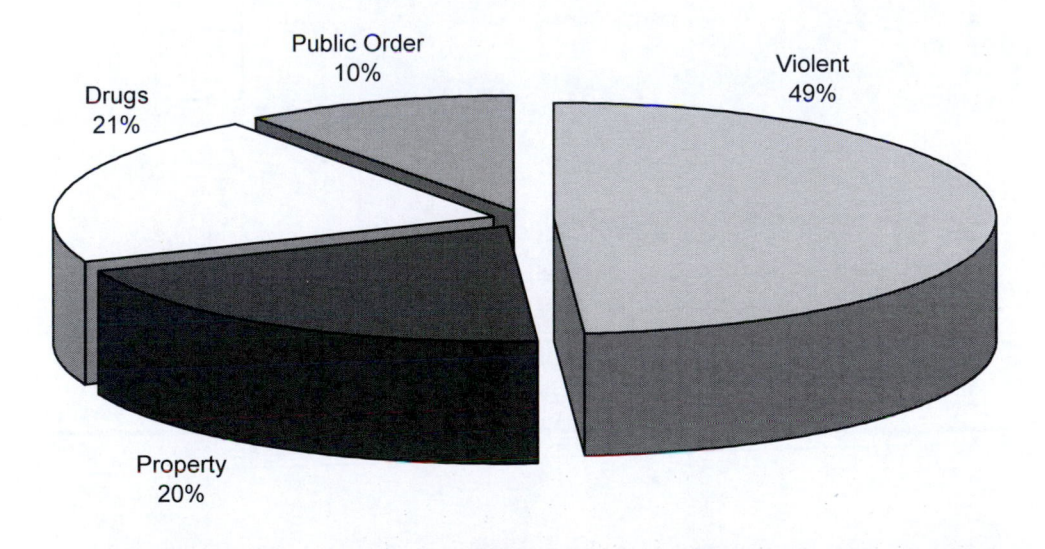

rate of imprisonment has leveled off recently due to (1) declining crime rates, (2) increased use of parole, (3) changes in parole revocation policies, and (4) expansion of drug treatment. These changes are not occurring evenly across the states, however.[37] For example, California has drastically expanded its use of drug treatment alternatives to prison,[38] while Texas has merely adjusted some of its parole policies.[39] There is also growing concern that the imprisonment of nonviolent offenders, especially those found guilty of drug offenses, actually increases recidivism rates.

Drug use, poverty, and lack of education are associated with many social problems other than crime. These social problems have a great influence on the nature of life in prisons and on the lives of correctional practitioners. Health problems are among the most serious of these. Various diseases and disabilities are far more common in correctional populations than in free society. These problems have a very dramatic effect on the economic and ethical dilemmas facing corrections. They also pose serious threats to both correctional practitioners and the general public.

Figure 7.3 Offenses of Persons in Custody of State Correctional Authorities by Most Serious Offense, 1980–2000

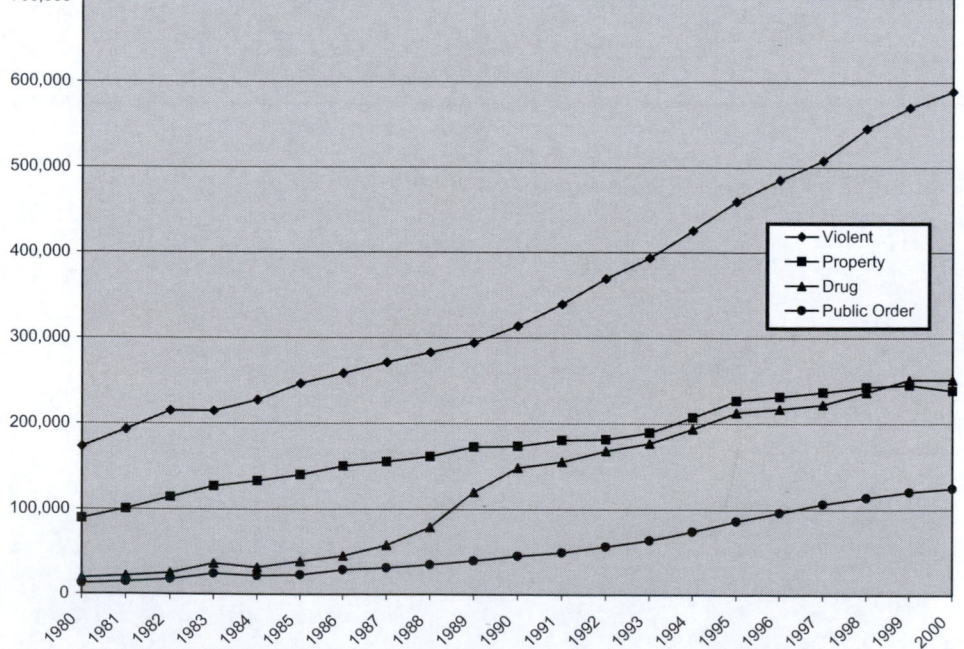

Figure 7.4   Characteristics of Prisoners in State and Federal
Correctional Situations, 1991, 1997, 2001

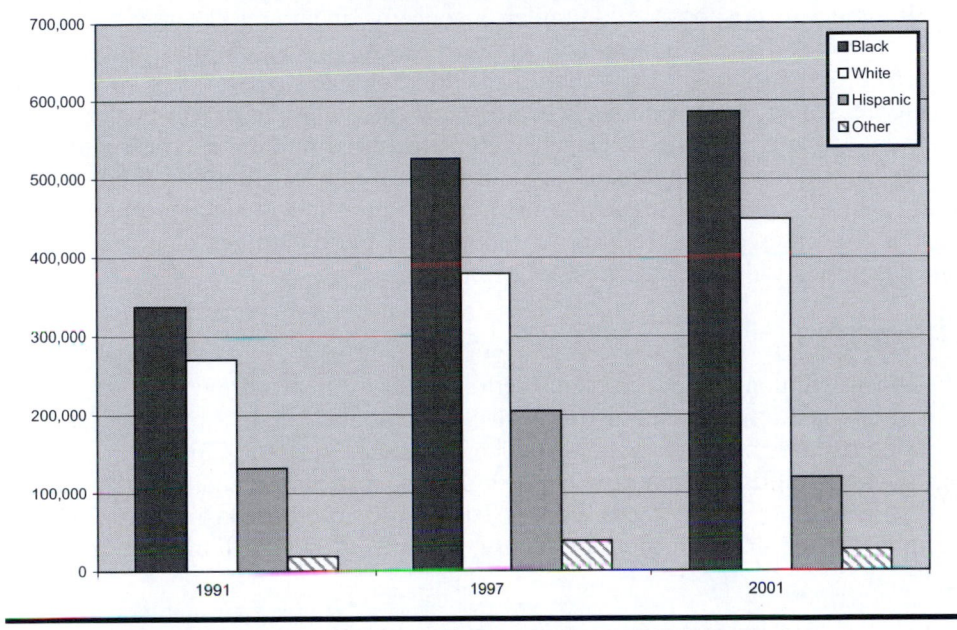

A: Race of Prisoners

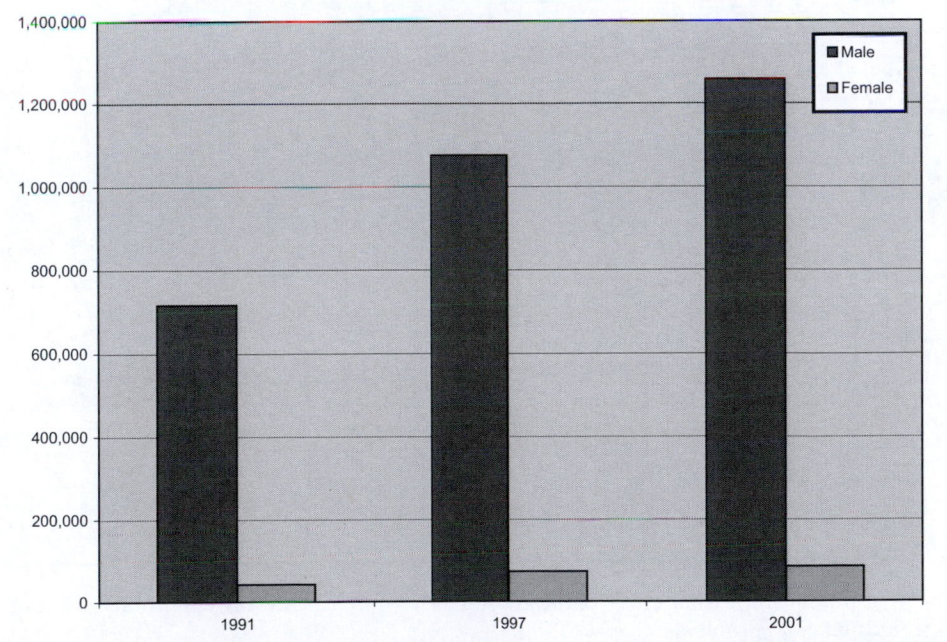

B: Sex of Prisoners

PRISONER HEALTH ISSUES

HIV/AIDS, hepatitis, tuberculosis, and sexually transmitted diseases (STDs) are among the health problems that are overrepresented in prison populations. Health issues in prison raise a number of concerns, including (1) prisoners are in contact with staff who then mingle with the general public, (2) most inmates will return to free society, and (3) the jurisdiction holding a person in a correctional facility must pay for that person's health care. The quality of prison health care is often inadequate, and critics allege that inmates suffer and die needlessly because of neglect. Common problems in prison health care include undertrained medical staff, failure to give out prescriptions properly, and inadequate treatment.[40] The fact that diseases can spread very rapidly in the close confines of a correctional facility further adds to concern about health issues.[41]

HIV/AIDS

Prison populations are infected with the HIV virus at 4 times the rate of the general population, and deaths from AIDS are two and one-half times as common among prisoners as in the general public.[42] Inmates between 25 and 44 years of age who are imprisoned on drug charges are the most commonly infected.[43] There are at least 25,008 HIV cases among federal and state prison inmates, most of them in southern and northeastern states. HIV affects 3.6% of female inmates and

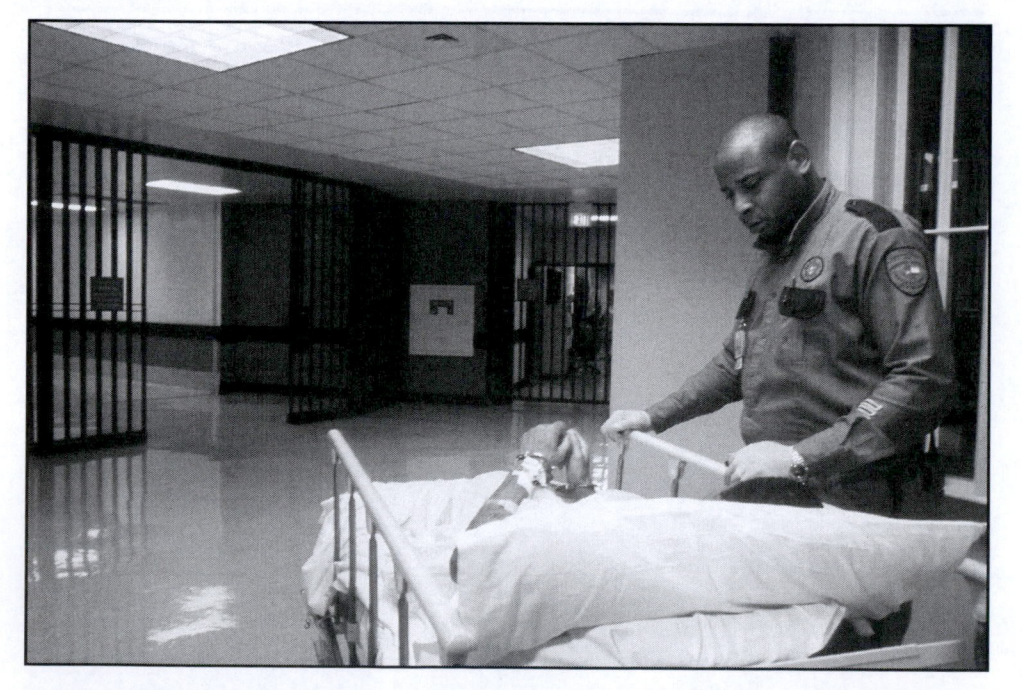

The poor physical health of many inmates combined with prison living conditions can result in serious medical problems.

2.2% of males. Approximately one-fifth of HIV-positive inmates have full-blown AIDS. California, Florida, New York, and Texas held more than half the number of inmates with confirmed AIDS. AIDS-related deaths accounted for 6% of all deaths among state prisoners in 2000.[44] Officials must provide medical treatment for prisoners infected with HIV and help prevent its spread. HIV-positive prisoners often must be protected from assaults because they are feared by many inmates who do not understand how the disease is transmitted.

Prisons screen inmates to determine HIV status. Mandatory initial screening of all or most new inmates was the norm in the late 1980s. However, HIV often does not show up on test results until about six months after a person has been infected, so delayed or repeated testing assures more accurate results. The current trend favors voluntary testing. Most jurisdictions test inmates who have HIV-related symptoms or if the inmates request they be tested. Twenty states reported testing all incoming inmates.[45] Staff are tested only when they are involved in an incident that could infect them with the virus.

Some inmates have sued prisons to require mandatory segregation of HIV-positive inmates; others have sued to remain in general population. The courts have largely refused to interfere with the segregation and testing policies of various prison systems.[46] Most prisons do not automatically isolate HIV-positive inmates from the general inmate population,[47] preferring to deal with each case on an individual basis. Some segregate only full-blown AIDS cases; others allow the inmate to decide whether to live in general or special housing units. By going into special housing, inmates lose access to many recreational, educational, and treatment programs. Many asymptomatic people can lead fairly normal lives for years before they become so ill that they require special care. The more HIV-positive inmates that remain in general population, the smaller the cost to the prison and the better the inmate's quality of life.

Correctional efforts to reduce and treat HIV/AIDS must first reduce anxiety among inmates regarding both their own HIV status and their fears of others who may have the disease. Then attention can turn to teaching offenders to avoid high-risk behaviors. Correctional responses to AIDS have four goals: (1) determine the extent of each inmate's risk behaviors; (2) teach inmates about the disease, especially the methods by which it is transmitted; (3) assure that inmates understand the testing procedures for the virus; and (4) provide education and counseling to inmates that will help them to avoid risk behaviors in the future.[48]

AIDS is usually spread through IV drug use and sexual intercourse.[49] Both of these risk-behaviors are fairly common in prisons. Most U.S. prisons have rejected the idea of distributing condoms. Their argument is that homosexual activity is prohibited in prisons and jails and providing condoms gives tacit approval to homosexuality.[50] Utilitarian thinkers argue that it is less expensive to give away condoms than to pay for the treatment of more AIDS cases. Great Britain allows prison doctors to give condoms to homosexual inmates on request, and Australia advises inmates to clean syringes with bleach if they inject drugs while imprisoned.[51] Some correctional systems in the United States make bleach available to inmates. Although they do not specify a specific use, the likelihood is that if bleach is available, it could be used for syringes.[52] Only six jails and prisons in the United

States (Mississippi, New York City, Philadelphia, San Francisco, Vermont, and Washington, D.C.) provide condoms to inmates.[53] Most U.S. prisons restrict themselves to education and testing efforts, and even these have declined since 1990.[54] Some observers suggest that failure to allow inmates to protect themselves from HIV with bleach, clean syringes, and/or condoms may be a future area of litigation in the United States and Canada.[55]

The high rate of HIV infection among inmates is forcing correctional agencies to educate both employees and offenders. Most prisons and jails provide such training to staff members, and over two-thirds furnish some education to inmates. The necessity for education extends to policymakers. Some correctional institutions exclude HIV-infected inmates from food-service jobs. HIV/AIDS is a health issue, and policies should be based on accurate health information—including the fact that AIDS is *not* transmitted through casual contact.[56] Education focuses on avoiding risk behaviors; it saves money by slowing the spread of the disease. Counseling for people with the virus is important because former sexual partners and others who may have caught the virus should be notified and tested. Counseling is also important to provide psychosocial support to cope with a devastating disease. About two-thirds of prison and jail systems offer support groups led by AIDS service organizations.[57]

Tuberculosis

Tuberculosis (TB) is a bacterial disease that usually affects the lungs but may also impact lymph nodes, kidneys, bones, joints, and other areas of the body. It is spread through the air by the coughing or sneezing of an infected person, but prolonged exposure is usually required for infection to occur. Most people infected with TB never develop an active case of the disease. Symptoms of TB include a low-grade fever, night sweats, fatigue, weight loss, and a persistent cough. Active TB can appear anywhere from two months to years after infection. The risk of active disease lessens as time passes. Carefully monitored drug therapy for 6 to 12 months is required to control the disease.[58]

TB thrives in dirty, crowded situations such as exist in jails and prisons. Few prison and jail ventilation systems meet the standards necessary to prevent infection. The number of TB cases in correctional facilities is 5 times greater than that in the general population. Nationally, the annual rate is about 10 per 100,000; prison officials report a rate of more than 50 new cases per 100,000 inmates per year.[59]

A new form of TB that does not respond to traditional drug therapies is spreading rapidly throughout the world. This drug-resistant strain of TB is very expensive to treat, and the treatment is not always successful. People who stop drug therapy for the older strains of TB too soon are at very high risk of developing the new drug-resistant strain. It is difficult to detect tuberculosis in people also infected with the HIV virus. If a single case goes undetected in a jail or prison, there is the threat of a significant TB outbreak. Thus cooperation between correctional and public health officials is required to protect the public, criminal justice staff, and inmates.[60]

Serious health problems like HIV and TB are of growing concern to correctional personnel as well as to health care professionals throughout society. Less

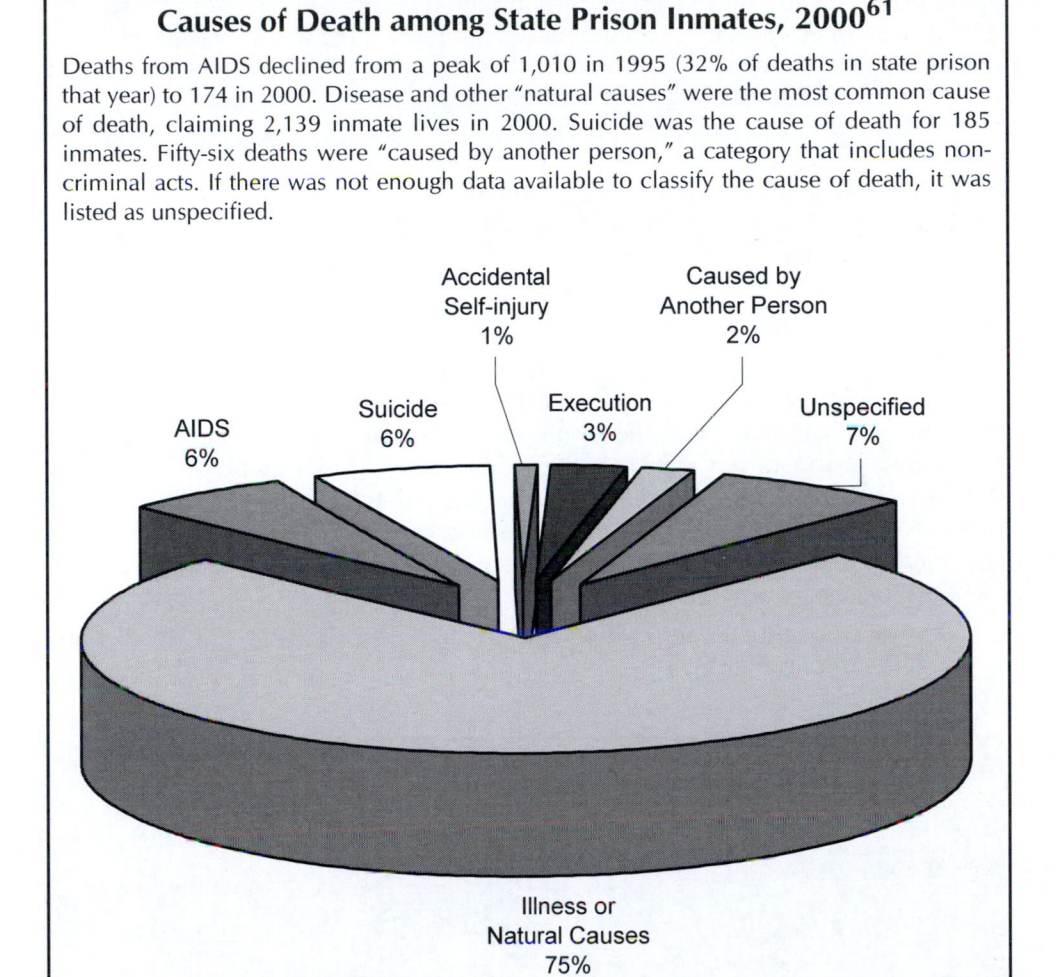

Causes of Death among State Prison Inmates, 2000[61]

Deaths from AIDS declined from a peak of 1,010 in 1995 (32% of deaths in state prison that year) to 174 in 2000. Disease and other "natural causes" were the most common cause of death, claiming 2,139 inmate lives in 2000. Suicide was the cause of death for 185 inmates. Fifty-six deaths were "caused by another person," a category that includes non-criminal acts. If there was not enough data available to classify the cause of death, it was listed as unspecified.

Accidental Self-injury 1%

Caused by Another Person 2%

AIDS 6%

Suicide 6%

Execution 3%

Unspecified 7%

Illness or Natural Causes 75%

serious illnesses and chronic problems are also serious issues for prisons. Many inmates are at high risk because their health has already been endangered by hard living, poor diets, drug/alcohol abuse, and inadequate medical care prior to incarceration. The poor physical condition of many inmates, and the close quarters in which prisons force them to live, make all kinds of disease more of a threat than in free society. In addition, many prisoners suffer from various forms of mental illness that make education and behavior control even harder.

Special-Needs Offenders

Society has always had difficulty deciding how to deal with certain groups of people who cannot fit into socially approved roles because of various mental and physical problems. For centuries, people with mental illness and retardation were imprisoned, as were those with physical disabilities. Little was done to protect the mentally disabled from neglect and abuse until the 1970s, when the legal rights of mental patients were forcefully outlined by the courts.[62] The campaign for civil rights in the 1970s resulted in laws protecting minorities and the aged, but the people with physical disabilities did not receive legal protection until the Americans with Disabilities Act (ADA) was passed in 1990. While these groups are of growing importance in corrections, substance abusers and sex offenders present the most difficult problems for the system because they make up such a large proportion of prisoners.

Substance Abuse

Fifty-seven percent of federal prisoners and 21% of prisoners in state facilities are being held on drug charges.[63] In 1997, 45% of federal inmates and 57% of state inmates had used drugs the month before committing their offense.[64] Nearly one in four prisoners was addicted when incarcerated.[65] Sixteen percent of federal inmates and 19% of state prisoners said that the crime for which they were imprisoned was committed in an effort to obtain money with which to buy drugs.[66] The relationship between drugs and crime is complex. Psychoactive substances such as alcohol, cocaine, speed, and heroin may:

1. affect thought and perceptions in ways that inspire crime (e.g., create irritability or paranoia),

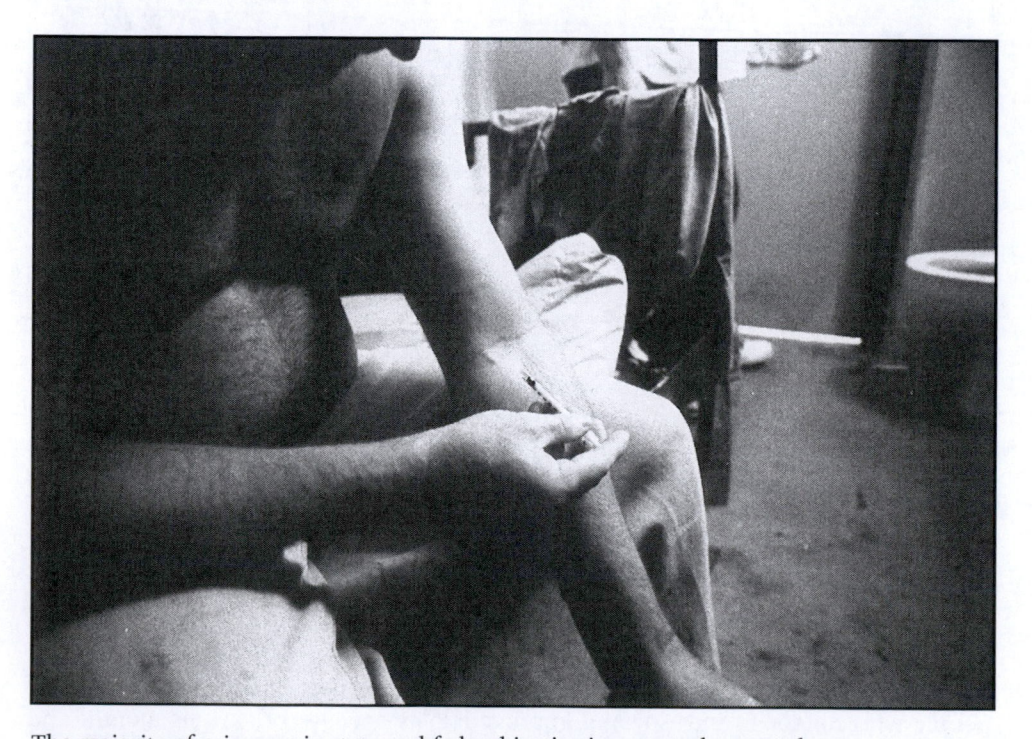

The majority of prisoners in state and federal institutions are substance abusers.

2. be used to facilitate crimes (e.g., render victims less resistant, create sufficient "nerve" to act illegally),

3. create economic needs that lead to crime (e.g., stealing to support a habit), or

4. indicate conformity to a lifestyle based on criminal norms in which contract enforcement and personal status require violent responses.[67]

Further, of those who reported regular use, over half said that this pattern of chemical dependency began after their first imprisonment.[68] Imprisonment forces offenders out of legitimate society into illegal subcultures and discourages their hopes of achieving economic stability. It thus removes many of the barriers to drug use while simultaneously making it easier and more acceptable. Our reliance on imprisonment to control crime may actually be feeding the drug problem and assuring the continued expansion of the crime problem.

Alcohol plays a much larger role in instigating crime than most people realize. Thirty-three percent of state inmates admitted being under the influence of illegal drugs at the time their offense was committed, while 37% admitted drinking at the time of the offense that led to their incarceration.[69] Alcohol is associated mainly with violent and public order offenses, while drugs are linked mainly to property crimes.[70] Alcohol is the only drug recognized by the Justice Department as causing aggression in humans, and it is a factor in at least 60% of homicides. Studies show that about half of all offenders have an alcohol problem.[71] Drugs and alcohol are easy to obtain in many prisons, so even incarceration cannot enforce abstinence from these substances. Correctional authorities must deal with both health and behavioral problems caused by alcohol and drug abuse.

Sex Offenders

While substance abuse is the single most common problem needing attention among offenders, sex offenders cause the greatest amount of public concern. The term "sex offender" covers a wide range of behaviors ranging from exhibitionism to rape and child molestation. More than 9% of state prison inmates are serving time for sexual assault,[72] and many more have been convicted of lesser crimes, such as lewd conduct. Others are technically imprisoned for other crimes or probation/parole violations, but a prior record of sexual misconduct leads authorities to categorize them as sex offenders. These offenders tend to be older than other inmates, are less often part of a criminal subculture, and are usually rather easy to control in prison. Many do not have a prior criminal history. A few sex offenders have serious mental disorders, such as sadism or pedophilia, that cause their offenses, but most sex crimes are due to a combination of substance abuse, poor judgment, and lack of impulse control.[73] According to correctional administrators, sex offender treatment is one of the most pressing needs in most facilities.[74]

Parole boards are reluctant to allow these inmates early release because of the fear that publicity about sex crimes creates in the public, but many are released under mandatory supervision. Contrary to popular belief, most scientific studies of sex offenders have found that 18.5% of convicted sex offenders reoffend within three years of their release. The comparable rate for drug offenders is 25% and for violent offenses it is 30%. With treatment, their reoffense rate drops to 10.5%. The idea that the majority reoffend is a myth begun by the misinterpretation of a scientific study and perpetuated by poorly informed media and politicians.[75] Although treatment can have dramatic effects on the rate of reoffense, sex offenders have no legal right to treatment unless they have a very serious mental disability.

The Mentally Impaired

If the mental condition of inmates meets any of the following criteria, authorities are legally required to provide treatment: (1) those who are so disturbed that they cannot control their thoughts, actions, or emotions (primarily those with psychoses); (2) those who are so retarded that they cannot adapt to the demands of the institution; and (3) those who are at risk for suicide. As many as half of all inmates in U.S. prisons suffer from mental illnesses such as personality disorders, drug/alcohol dependency, depression, and sexual deviations for which they are not legally entitled to treatment. These problems often contribute to criminal behavior,[76] but programs are offered only when budgets permit. Inmates get treatment only if they are lucky enough to be in the right prison at the right time.

Only 2.4% of all offenders are placed in special "mental health" units; the rest live in the general prison population. Nationally, 10% receive special medication but the rate in five states is twice this figure. One in eight receives some other form of therapy for a major mental illness. Regardless of whether they are in a special facility or general population, inmates with mental disabilities are less likely to be housed in prisons with a decreased level of security. Most prison systems screen inmates for these disabilities upon admission but many escape detection. Female inmates have over twice the rate of mental illness as males.[77]

Within the criminal justice system, the condition of mentally impaired offenders may deteriorate due to inadequate treatment; indeed, life behind bars often exacerbates their condition. For example, overcrowding leads to more violence, a lack of privacy, excessive noise, and other stressful conditions that are particularly difficult for those subject to emotional and psychiatric problems. If they are released from prison without arrangements for treatment and services, they are likely to repeat the disruptive behavior that brought them into the system in the first place.[78]

Inmates known to have IQs that indicate developmental disability (retardation) make up 4% of state prison populations. Many more people with undiagnosed cases of retardation are thought to be imprisoned as well. These inmates have difficulty in communicating with others and cannot fully anticipate the consequences of their actions. Many have the mental and emotional abilities of a child and may express themselves in ways that are sometimes violent. This explains not only their crimes but also the kinds of problems that they create for prisons. Some have committed crimes serious enough to require imprisonment while others could be better treated in the community. Much of the problem lies in the failure of the courts to identify and to divert these offenders to intermediate sanctions programs.[79]

Inmates with developmental disabilities are very vulnerable to manipulation by others because they crave social acceptance and approval. Many are unable to adjust to prison routines and are seen as discipline problems by staff. Staff members, however, are rarely trained to identify mental disability, so an inmate's inability to learn prison rules often is interpreted as rebelliousness. This leads to a high number of discipline violations among inmates with developmental disabilities.[80] There is also evidence that they are more likely to be injured accidentally when assigned to work details.[81]

Mental health agencies often consider offenders who are mentally disabled to be the responsibility of corrections, while prison officials see these people as the responsibility of the mental health agencies. Most programs are designed to treat mental illness, *or* the developmentally disabled, *or* people with a chemical dependency.[82] People with multiple conditions, a large percentage of the mentally impaired in the criminal justice system, often have very few opportunities for treatment tailored to their specific needs.

The Physically Disabled

The Americans with Disabilities Act (ADA) requires that all persons with disabilities have access to public facilities and be given all possible opportunities to lead productive lives. As the number of disabled offenders rises, the application of the ADA to jails and prisons is increasingly important. Some predict that it will be a major area of lawsuits in the twenty-first century. Some physical changes to institutions will require

Meeting the Needs of People with Disabilities[83]

The Americans with Disabilities Act (ADA) requires that all public facilities make reasonable changes to their policies, practices, and procedures to avoid discrimination against the disabled. The degree to which correctional facilities will be affected by this law will probably remain unclear until the application of the ADA to prisons and jails is clarified by a series of lawsuits.[84] Many facilities are nonetheless trying to comply with the ADA in order to minimize their legal liabilities. The ADA applies to disabled staff and inmates; failure to comply with it can result in court intervention and damage awards.

Any institution built or modified since 1992 must include features that meet the needs of inmates who are blind, deaf, in wheelchairs, or have artificial limbs. Areas of concern include cells, recreation areas, law libraries, program and disciplinary hearing sites, visitation areas, and work-release rules. Handling the needs of the disabled often requires physical changes in many aspects of prison design. Recreation areas, shower and toilet facilities, law libraries, commissaries, and program areas must be accessible to the disabled. Three to 5% of a prison's housing area, and an equal amount of the visitation area, must be wheelchair accessible. Disabled inmates must have access to all programs and privileges permitted to others in their security category. Telecommunication devices for the deaf (TDDs) must be provided for the hearing impaired.

Correctional agencies must hire qualified people with disabilities and strive to make the facility as comfortable for the disabled as it is for others. In hiring and promotion decisions, the most qualified applicant must be hired regardless of disability status so long as he or she can perform the essential functions of the job with or without the use of accommodation. Physical restrictions may prevent disabled persons from serving in security roles but their ability to serve in clerical and treatment roles will not be affected. Only when a disability presents a "direct and imminent threat" to the safety of the applicant or that of others, or creates undue hardship for the employer, can it be used to discriminate against people seeking a job or promotion.

funds for construction. Ramps will have to be added to some buildings, vehicles will need special equipment, and new services will have to be provided for the hearing- and vision-impaired. For the most part, however, handling the needs of the disabled is a matter of creativity and sensitivity. Guards must learn how to search inmates in wheelchairs and how to handcuff people with artificial arms. Prisoner uniforms may have to be specially tailored to fit some inmates with physical disabilities, and meals must meet the dietary needs of others. Work and treatment assignments appropriate for these inmates also need to be developed.

Some of the basic needs of disabled inmates can be met with help from other inmates. Staff need not always push wheelchairs or guide the visually impaired. However, the inmates chosen to help their disabled peers must be well screened to avoid abuses. They will also have to be trained and supervised by professional staff to make sure that they provide assistance in the right ways. Comprehensive planning using the insights of all prison staff is sorely needed to provide for inmates who are physically challenged as their number grows.[85] Such growth appears inevitable due to the aging of the inmate population. A Pennsylvania study noted that while 1.8% of the overall inmate population required long-term care, the figure rose to 24% when inmates over 65 were examined.[86]

Aging Offenders

The population of older inmates in this nation is small but growing. In 2001, inmates over 55 made up about 3% of all prisoners, but the number of older inmates is 1.5 times greater than in 1991.[87] These increases are due to (1) tough new sentencing laws such as "three strikes" and (2) the aging of the national population as a whole.[88] Most inmates in this age category suffer from conditions related to substance abuse, poverty, and bad nutrition; they are more likely to develop health problems earlier than other citizens.[89] These offenders often have different physical, mental, and emotional needs than younger inmates.

Older inmates can be divided into two categories. Most committed serious offenses in their youth and received long sentences that forced them to grow old in prison. Although these prisoners pose little threat of recidivism when released, they also have little social support and few job skills. The second group consists of people who were convicted of crimes committed relatively late in their lives. These inmates tend to have more contact with noninmates than others.[90] Fifteen percent have committed sex crimes; others were convicted of drunken driving, drug trafficking, or theft. Some of them are "first offenders" while others appear to be career criminals.

People sent to prison late in life are more often convicted for violent crimes, usually conform to mainstream norms, and are less impulsive and hostile than younger offenders. Older inmates experiencing prison for the first time usually have not lived a criminal lifestyle. Further, they seem to adjust as well, or perhaps even better, to prison life than do younger prisoners. Some studies show that older inmates are more dependent on the institution for their basic physical and psychological needs than are younger inmates. As a group, older inmates report having more friends in prison than do younger prisoners and less stress as a result of the prison environment than younger people.[91] Other studies, however, suggest that

Prisons must address the needs of aging inmates and those with physical disabilities.

The Elderly in Prisons[92]

Figure A shows the growth in the number of prisoners over age 55 since 1990. The numbers include persons imprisoned after their 55th birthday and those who turned 55 while serving time. The number of older inmates in 1994 was 27,674; after spiking in 1998, the number decreased to 38,400 in 2001.

Figure A: Growth of the Aged Prisoner Population

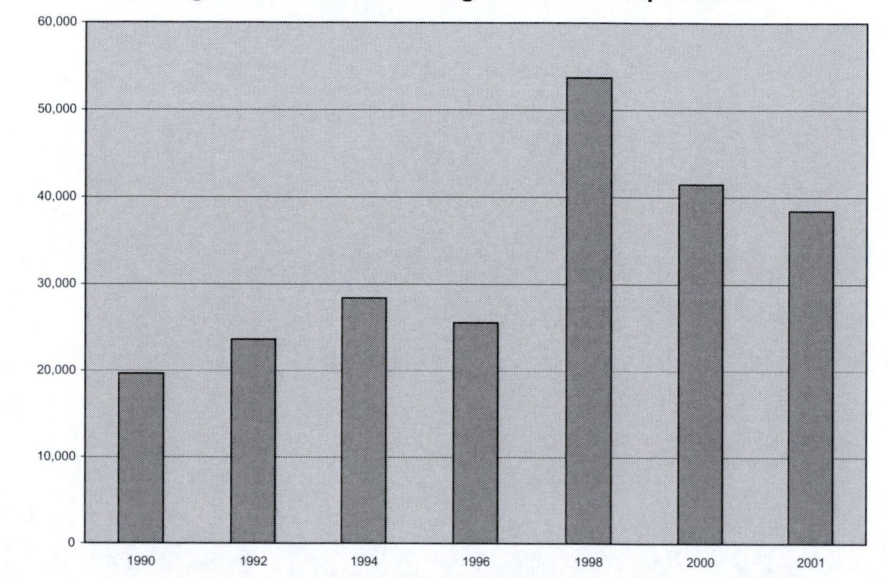

Figure B examines the offenses of persons sentenced to prison after their 55th birthday. Most newly admitted older offenders are classified as violent; the only other age group for which violent offenses are the most common is the one that includes offenders younger than 18 years. Eighteen percent of these older prisoners were convicted of sex offenses other than rape; most of these offenses victimized children. Of those imprisoned for drugs, most were convicted of trafficking charges rather than possession. The majority of public-order offenses committed by these prisoners were DUIs, while most of their property crimes were in the larceny-theft category.

Figure B: Offenses of Prisoners Sentenced after Age 55

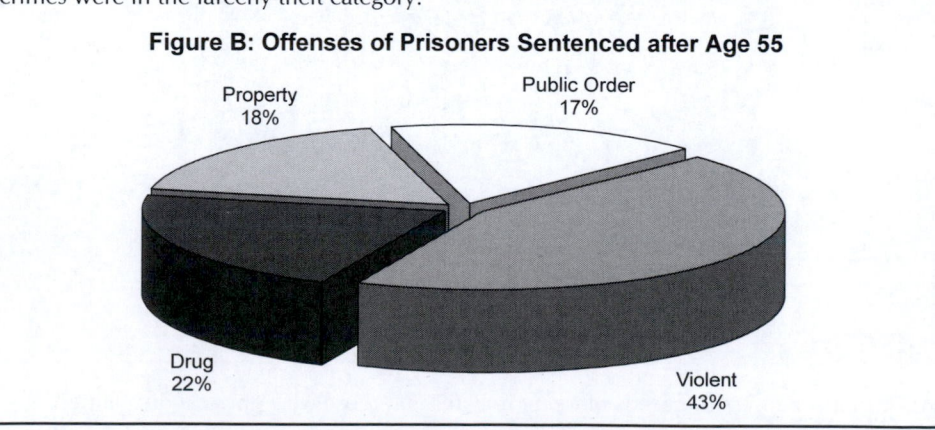

older inmates are more likely to create the impression of adjustment by hiding their stress and anger than are younger inmates.[93]

Most research agrees that as the average age of inmates in a facility increases, the rate of disciplinary problems drops.[94] This suggests that large numbers of older inmates encourage cooperation with prison staff. The social atmosphere of a prison full of younger inmates tends to be more rebellious toward authority.[95] However, studies focusing only on older inmates find that 40% have disciplinary records, which conflicts with the idea that older inmates do not create major problems for prison staff. Prison administrators feel that these differences are best explained by the elderly inmates' prior prison experience. People who go to prison for the first time after age 50 or 55 are more likely to conform than those who have spent much of their lives behind bars. Those who expect to live out their lives in prison, on the other hand, have little to lose from disciplinary violations.[96]

Most prison officials agree that elderly first offenders need to be integrated into prison life differently than older, repeat offenders. The aging of the prison population thus affects classification and security concerns as well as medical and financial planning for corrections. Prison staff must be trained to help these inmates handle a unique set of social and emotional needs as well. Especially critical in this regard are issues related to death and dying. The staff's ability to identify depression is also being given more emphasis because depression is more common in older prisoners. Finally, a process for referring older inmates to community experts is needed. Many of the physical and emotional crises unique to older prisoners must be dealt with outside the prison system. Older people are still rare enough in prison that it would not be economical to hire specialized staff.[97]

Placing special prisons for aging and ill inmates near major hospitals is an increasingly popular way of dealing with the health care needs of the offenders. In other cases, states have built special medical units for the chronically ill or hospices for those whose death is imminent.[98] Nonetheless, while typical health care costs range from an average of $634 per inmate per year in Louisiana to more than $3,000 in Indiana and Florida, total annual costs often reach $70,000 per inmate for aged inmates.[99] By contrast, the average cost of imprisoning the typical inmate is $14,586 and a typical state-supported nursing home costs about $12,000 per year. Unless steps are taken to reduce this population, the number of older inmates could bankrupt many state correctional systems within a few years.[100] Institutions are experimenting with the use of telemedicine, in which medical professionals diagnose and prescribe from a distance using modern communications technologies. Financial concerns plus concern about security issues were the motivating factors for four federal prisons to implement this approach starting in 1996. It is now being pursued as a cooperative federal effort involving the Departments of Justice and Defense as well as NASA.[101]

CORRECTIONAL CLASSIFICATION

The challenges posed by increasing diversity in the age, dangerousness, and disabilities of prisoners during the last two decades have increased the importance of correctional classification. External or *system-wide classification* uses estimates of the threat posed by each inmate to assign prisoners to specific facilities. Internal or *institutional classification* is done later to place inmates in specific housing areas, programs, and work assignments. These systems use predictions of which inmates are at risk of escape and/or violence in order to place them in a specific prison, cell block, and work assignment. They may also be used to coordinate treatment, but getting inmates into the appropriate security level is the main goal of classification. This task is increasingly complex and important as prison populations grow larger, more diverse, and more violent.[102]

The level of security to which an inmate is assigned determines how that inmate will live for the next few years. Security levels dictate prison routines, freedom of movement and, to a limited extent, the type and variety of available programs. Life in a minimum-security facility is much less regimented than life in facilities with higher security levels. Some states allow discretionary release only for inmates who have taken part in treatment programs. If the security level to which an inmate is classified does not offer treatment programs, that inmate has no opportunity for early release. In addition, some inmates are at greater risk of assault from other inmates. Classification is a discretionary matter that the courts

---

Policy Matters!
What Can Be Done about the Rising Rate of Imprisonment?

Economists warn that the rising rate of imprisonment may soon pose a serious threat to the nation's economy. Minority leaders are disturbed that blacks, Hispanics, and Native Americans are badly overrepresented in prison populations. They also point out that violence and drugs are among the most significant problems faced by their communities. The fact that penalties for crimes against minorities are often less severe than those imposed on criminals who victimize whites troubles many as well. Sentences are getting longer for most crimes, especially those involving drugs and violence. Nonetheless, polls show that most U.S. citizens consider crime to be a chief concern. Added to this is the fact that the health care needs of older prisoners may soon threaten to bankrupt some jurisdictions.

As you consider the following questions, keep in mind the opportunity costs; for each new *program*, cuts must be made in other government services or taxes must be raised. Further, for each *person* added to the prison population, additional taxes must be imposed or cuts made elsewhere. In addition, concern with fairness and due process of law cannot be wholly abandoned in the search for greater efficiency in crime control.

Questions to Consider

1. Should the use of retribution and incapacitation in corrections be strengthened? If so, how can we continue to let the rate of imprisonment rise without bankrupting the nation? If not, what alternatives can you propose to satisfy the public's desire for efficient crime control?

2. Should more attention be paid to developing crime prevention programs for high-risk areas and groups? Why or why not? Can government actions strengthen the personal and family controls that discourage people from committing crimes?

3. Should we reconsider how we use the criminal justice system to address problems like substance abuse? How else might we address such moral and behavioral problems?

leave to correctional administrators. The courts require only that prisons use uniform standards in classifying inmates, and each prison system approaches this problem in a different way.[103] For example, some prisons segregate sex offenders into special housing units where other inmates cannot victimize them; others place them in the general population until there is evidence they are in danger.

There are two basic types of classification systems. *Risk-oriented systems* focus on the security issues raised by the offender's background, legal history, and personality. It is used primarily for systemwide placement of the inmate. *Psychological systems* try to predict the inmate's ability to adjust to prison life, to discover the causes of his or her criminality, and to determine treatment needs. Psychological classification requires tests to describe the inmate's personality traits or level of maturity. The information suggests the amount of protection each inmate requires and the nature of his or her treatment needs. Risk-oriented classification dominates the process in virtually all U.S. prisons, but psychological procedures are sometimes used to set the order of treatment programs and to suggest which activities are most appropriate for the inmate. Unfortunately, overcrowding and related problems often override both types of classification, and inmates are moved to lower security levels to make room for other prisoners. There is also a tendency to reserve space in minimum-security facilities for inmates with less than two years remaining before their release.[104]

Reliance on risk-based classification is derived from experiences with male prisons. Women are usually nonviolent offenders with limited criminal histories. Most female inmates pose little danger to staff or other inmates. Classification systems should be modified to take into account risk factors appropriate to women.[105] If distinct classification schemes are developed for women that focus more on their needs, their recidivism rates could be significantly reduced.[106] Idaho, Indiana, Massachusetts, Michigan, New York, and Oklahoma have adopted female-based classification systems; Colorado and Ohio are developing similar systems.[107] Others believe the same system can be used but with gender-specific scoring processes to account for different levels of violence in male and female facilities.[108]

Prison Security Levels

Each correctional system has its own set of terms to describe its levels of security. The Federal Bureau of Prisons rates all of its facilities on a scale from one to six with level six being the most controlled, super-maximum security facilities. Prisons with different security levels will vary in how much effort is taken to control the area around the facility, how guard duties are assigned, the design of cell blocks, and the kinds of staff employed. Some facilities have only one level of security, but many prison complexes have two or three types.

Just over half of all U.S. prisons are *minimum-security institutions* housing prisoners who are low risk for escape and violence or have little time left to serve. Labor is most productive at this level of security, and idleness is less of a problem for these inmates. Furlough and work release programs, when they exist, are usually found at minimum-security facilities. Most states have many small minimum-security prisons, which are surrounded by a fence or wall. A few have guard towers,

In maximum security prisons every inmate is closely monitored by guards and/or closed-circuit television.

perimeter patrols, or electronic devices to detect escapes. Barracks-like sleeping quarters for 20 to 50 are common, but some house inmates in cells like those at other types of institutions.

Almost one-third of U.S. prisons are classified as **medium-security institutions**, and most inmates are held at this level of security for at least part of their sentence. The fences or walls of these prisons are usually higher than those of minimum-security facilities, and two-thirds have gun towers along the walls. These prisons house offenders whose escape risk is either unknown or moderate.

Inmates are under constant observation by guards, and all doors are kept locked at all times. Prisoners must have a pass to move about, and cell blocks can be "locked down" from a main control area. Prisoner counts are made repeatedly throughout the day and evening. Indeed, "the count" is the central method of preventing escapes and controlling prisoners in all jails and prisons. Work is usually less available in these facilities than in those holding minimum-security inmates, although agricultural and industrial production are present in some.

Maximum-security institutions are often the oldest, most isolated prisons in the United States. They are less common than other types of prisons but are larger and house more inmates than other types. Most have several fences and/or brick walls with gun towers as well as perimeter patrols, electronic motion detectors, and electrified fences. Every inmate is closely monitored by guards and/or closed-circuit television. Prisoners are frisked and handcuffed when they have to be moved within the prison, and visits by outsiders are strictly controlled.

Segregation Units

Inmates who are at high risk of escape or violence are held in facilities designed specifically for security and long-term confinement. These units hold about 2% of the U.S. inmate population—mostly those who are believed to be very dangerous. They are increasingly the newest, most automated correctional facilities in the world.[109] The U.S. prison at Marion, Illinois, holds only 200 men while Florence, Colorado, holds 800. California's Pelican Bay is larger and the best known of these new prisons. Super-maximum security units are for prisoners who are extreme threats to institutional or public safety. Some have long histories of serious violence; others are well known "celebrity" offenders (e.g., famous spies) or may be at risk from other prisoners because of their notoriety. These prisons are sometimes called "super seg" or "supermax" units because they hold inmates whom authorities define as hard or dangerous to control within the general inmate population. Some observers challenge that categorization of these inmates, suggesting that more of these facilities are being created simply because the technology is so attractive to administrators.[110]

Prisoners are kept in one-person cells with little sensory stimulation beyond the clang of metal doors and the low mumble of unintelligible words from other cells. Inmates sleep much of the time because there are few activities to occupy their time. However, they get little regenerative (i.e., REM) sleep, so their health and sanity may be jeopardized by these environments. Many supermax inmates display symptoms of mental illness, but any challenge to authority is met with

Segregation units hold approximately 2% of the inmate population, particularly those who could endanger others.

extreme force; security units similar to police SWAT teams handle discipline problems such as refusal to exit one's cell. The extremes of isolation and security found at some of these institutions have led to charges that they violate the basic human rights of their inmates.[111]

SUMMARY

Knowledge of who is imprisoned in each type of correctional facility is essential to correctional policies and practices. A close examination of U.S. prison populations reveals an ugly picture of all the social problems facing the nation. African Americans are disproportionately represented in U.S. prisons. The majority of prisoners are from poor urban backgrounds, with little education and often in poor health due to substance abuse.

Diseases such as AIDS, TB, and hepatitis are much more common among inmates because of their poverty and high rates of risk behavior. Use of drugs to control these diseases and education to reduce risk behaviors are essential in prisons from a public health standpoint. Sex offenders and inmates with mental disabilities often require protection from other prisoners and special programs to treat their problems. Few prisons fully address the needs of these inmates, even though the beneficial effects of programs for these offenders are well known.

Further complicating the economic problems of U.S. prisons is the aging of the inmate population. Some older prisoners received long sentences early in their lives and are growing old in prison, while others committed serious crimes late in their lives. Some states and the federal system are building special prisons specifically for older inmates. Others are placing prisons near hospitals that can care for the inmates. Some experts warn that the costs associated with these inmates could drive some jurisdictions into bankruptcy.

As inmate needs become more complex and prisons grow more crowded, correctional classification becomes increasingly important to meet legal demands that prisoners be protected from disease and from each other. Most states use risk-assessment procedures based on the inmate's past behavior to assign each prisoner to a security level and housing area. Psychological factors may also be used to predict risk and to coordinate treatment. Need for space and the desire to place inmates in low-security facilities immediately prior to release lead many systems to ignore or to devalue the predictions made by their own classification systems.

QUESTIONS FOR DISCUSSION AND REVIEW

1. What is the "rate of imprisonment"? How fast is it changing and in what direction? What factors explain these trends? How, according to economists, does this threaten the nation's welfare? What can be done to address this threat?

2. Why is race such a sensitive issue in discussions of prison populations? Why do some charge that prisons reflect social and economic power structures more than the nature of crime in a society?

3. How do the populations of state and federal prisons differ? Why? What kinds of offenses are behind the increase in prison populations for each type of system?

4. What special problems are faced by inmates who are sick or injured? How do prisons deal with HIV-positive inmates? Why is tuberculosis among prisoners a growing threat to the nation?

5. Why are there so many developmentally disabled and mentally ill people in prisons? What unique problems do they face in the prison environment? What steps should prisons take to meet the needs of these populations? What other segments of the justice process need to pay greater attention to these groups? Why?

6. What is an "older inmate"? Why is the number of older inmates growing? What are the needs of this population? Why is the aging of the U.S. prison population seen as a threat to national welfare? What steps are being taken to address the needs of older inmates?

7. What are the purposes of correctional classification? What methods are used to accomplish these goals? What legal restrictions guide its use? What forces lead prison officials to devalue the predictions made by these procedures?

EIGHT

CONVICT SOCIETY

Prisons were created to control, punish, and reform convicted felons. The terms used to describe these institutions in various eras symbolize the values society placed on these goals at different points in time. The "penitentiary" was designed to rehabilitate through isolation and penance, a fundamentally religious approach. "Reformatories" tried to achieve behavioral change through rewards, punishments, and other "scientific" methods. The "Big House" was a warehouse that sought only to incapacitate. Throughout all of these ideological permutations, the basic purpose of the prison changed very little. Keeping inmates in secure custody is the main goal of these institutions. Preserving order within the facility is the secondary goal. The informal norms of convict society originate partially in opposition to these institutional goals, affect the organization of the prison, and ultimately impact recidivism.

EXPLANATIONS OF CONVICT SOCIETY

Most theories about prison social life and organization focus on either the criminality of the inmates or the effects of being confined in an institution. Importation theory and deprivation theory each illuminate some of the forces shaping adjustment to prison life. Together they explain much of what inmates experience as a result of imprisonment.[1]

Importation Theory

Importation theory asserts that status roles and subcultures of the prison are the products of identities established by inmates before imprisonment. Imported variables originate in subcultures outside the prison and are brought to the institution

175

Prisons were created to control, punish, and reform convicted felons.

by the inmates. Criminal offenders are involved in a wide variety of deviant behaviors and often have exhibited antisocial tendencies before incarceration. These patterns of acting and perceiving are continued and intensified inside the prison walls. Importation theory is especially effective in explaining inmate rule violations, especially assaultive behavior.[2]

Imported roles and behaviors are the basis for the belief that prisons are "schools for crime." This learning may be direct, as when one inmate tutors another on hot-wiring a car. Perhaps even more important are indirect influences, such as the use of violence as a model for dealing with frustration and conflict. Early American prisons tried to address the problem of learning criminal behavior from peers by enforcing a code of silence among inmates. Isolated inmates had no contact with fellow inmates; they were less likely to resist attempts to reform them. As we learned in chapter 2, the practice was too costly both economically and psychologically and was abandoned.

Inmates tend to associate with others who are similar to them in terms of race, age, background, and type of offense. They are often disdainful of other inmate groups. For example, thieves tend to associate with one another and see themselves as "better" than addicts or violent offenders.[3] Members of each clique share their criminal experiences and reinforce each other's tendencies toward antisocial beliefs and behaviors. Prison society rewards inmates for conforming to its norms by providing sources of identity and self-esteem to replace those based on free-world relationships and activities. It can thus encourage further criminality among inmates.[4]

Traditional prison societies were made up of three prison subcultures: (1) the thief subculture of property offenders; (2) the professional criminal subculture of offenders with relatively specialized criminal skills such as safecracker; and (3) the conventional subculture of "Square Johns" who follow the larger society's norms. By the early 1970s new subcultures were appearing in U.S. prisons as the professional criminal faded from importance. A drug-oriented subculture of addicts (hypes in slang) became prominent. State-raised youth who have spent most of their lives in reform schools or other institutions also increased in numbers. For them, release is merely a brief vacation from their institutional home. Hustlers (men who pursue confidence games, pimping, and loan sharking) compose another subculture. Gangs are also an important source of status roles and identity for many prisoners.[5] In short, the nature of crime in the streets of the nation determines the types of behavior of prisoners held in penal institutions. For example, street violence primarily affects African Americans who live in the inner cities; inmates from this background are disproportionately involved in prison violence.[6] As criminals become less specialized and more violent, these changes are reflected in the membership and norms of inmate society. However, there are influences other than imported variables that affect prison life.

Deprivation Theory

Another explanation of the unique social organization of the prison is *deprivation theory*, which alleges that inmate societies develop out of the hardships suffered by inmates while incarcerated. Among the most important of these deprivations are: (1) loss of liberty, (2) loss of access to "normal" goods and services, (3) loss of heterosexual relationships, (4) loss of autonomy, and (5) loss of security.[7] These deprivations contribute to the unique norms of prison society. Deprivation has been linked to the phenomenon of homosexual rape in prisons.[8] In general, the deprivations of prison are most keenly felt by new inmates who are adjusting to prison life for the first time.[9] Part of that adjustment is learning the inmate code of behavior. In 1960 this code was described in terms of five principles:

1. Don't interfere with the interests of other inmates; show loyalty to convicts, not to staff.

2. Don't be nosy, do your own time, and mind your own business.

3. Be cool, don't lose control.

4. Keep your dignity, never show weakness.

5. Don't take advantage of other inmates.

Despite the age of this code, the data indicate that much of it still applies today.[10] Three new factors have changed the way inmates apply the convict code to their lives: (1) toughness is a central part of the convict's identity and is considered by many to be essential to survival; (2) loyalty is expected only to one's own racial group; and (3) extremes of violence are increasingly accepted as normal. The growing lack of unity among prisoners may be the product of racial tensions in mainstream society. Some believe it to be the result of court-ordered changes that reduced abuses by administrators and guards and made prison staff more accountable for their actions. Since inmates have gained greater access to the courts to address their problems, they need not present a united front as they did prior to the due process revolution.

The convict code is largely a response to the unique structure and function of the prison. However, it is clearly influenced by the identities that prisoners bring with them. In other words, the convict code, and much of the problematic behavior seen in prisons, results from the interaction of imported variables with the deprivations of institutional life.[11] Many of these deprivations are the result of the way in which a particular prison is organized. These kinds of influences are called *situational factors*. They are produced by the structure and function of the prison. Situational factors are matters of policy decided by government officials that can be changed whenever society demands it.

The degree to which inmates are able to keep in touch with noninmates is an example of how official policies affect prison life, as is the amount of effort made by authorities to control gangs. The degree to which treatment is stressed in a particular prison is also important. Facilities that emphasize treatment have less violence and happier inmates than those that focus entirely on punishment and control. Also, staff behavior is important; the more forceful and threatening the staff is toward inmates, the more alienation inmates will experience.[12] The amount of alienation experienced by an inmate depends on how situational variables combine with his or her preprison experiences and imported identity.[13] Most situational factors result partly from the fact that prisons are total institutions. The deprivations of institutional life are the best predictor of inmates' adaptation to the convict's way of life.[14]

THE TOTAL INSTITUTION

A *total institution* is a bureaucratically administered facility in which a large number of people with similar statuses live for relatively long periods of time.[15] Prisons are one type of total institution; others include mental hospitals, nursing homes, monasteries, and military boot camps. Adapting to life in a total institution is a process of becoming institutionalized. In the case of imprisonment, it is called *prisonization*. Everything—clothes, meals, medical care, and sleeping quarters—is provided by the facility. Inmates have no responsibilities other than obeying the authorities. Both inmates and staff are clearly affected by prisonization, but the damage is usually more extreme for inmates because staff members can escape the institution at the end of their shift.

Prisonization

Life in an institution is lived almost entirely in the present. Prisonization teaches inmates to avoid thinking about their behavior; they learn to react to events without regard to the past or future. Little attention is given to past errors or taking responsibility for the consequences of one's actions. Survival and maintaining one's dignity on a moment-to-moment basis are the chief concerns of most inmates. This environment encourages escape from the monotonous routines that mark institutional life. The sense of being a victim of the institution can be an important method of saving self-esteem and identity. All of these factors make

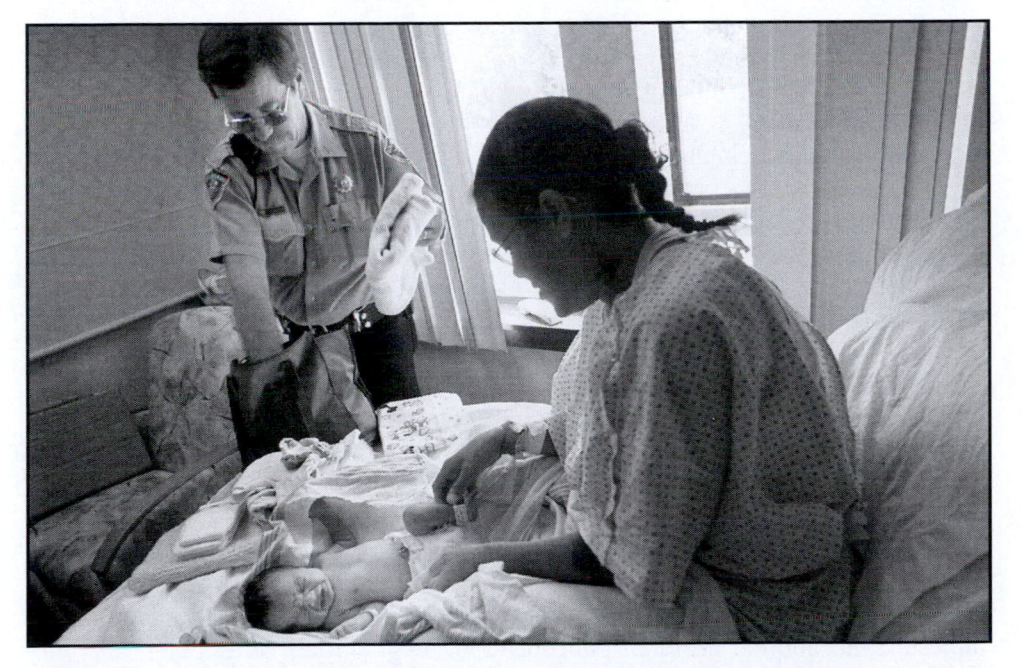

Prisonization affects both inmates and staff members; both can experience difficulty adjusting to the noninstitutional world.

inmates less able to live in free society after imprisonment. Similarly, prison staff members often have difficulty adjusting to the noninstitutional world during off-duty hours. This can disrupt their personal lives and alienate them from society as well.

Prisonization is closely linked to the loss of status that results from being convicted and placed in an institution. While such status changes are inescapable, the treatment that results from that loss of status is a matter of policy that can be altered. The more we know about prisonization, and how imported and situational factors compound inmate's criminality, the more efficient corrections can become.

In general, the harsher and more controlling an institution, the more extensive the impact of prisonization on the identity and behavior of inmates. Because prisonization is affected more by deprivation than imported factors, changes in prison life that reduce its negative effects are likely to make it less harsh.[16] Prisonization is a process that affects different people in different ways and to varying degrees, however. Examination of the process can show how its negative effects occur and can highlight many of the contradictions between effective behavior change and fair punishment.

The Prisonization Process

Being socialized to prison life means learning about the organization, norms, customs, and general culture of the prison while adopting a new identity. It is a process of "desocialization" followed by "resocialization" that affects all inmates and staff to some extent. New inmates are stripped of their identities and behavior patterns by the emotional crisis of being imprisoned and the alien nature of their new environment. Then they are resocialized to prison life with a new, devalued identity as a "convict," which generally means taking one of the many roles recognized by the prison subculture.[17] Although prison staff retain their free-world identities and conventional activities, they are nonetheless affected by the prison environment.

This socialization process teaches inmates to follow norms that are entirely contrary to those of the staff and mainstream society. Inmates learn to accept extremes of violence and hatred as normal and natural; they reject socially "desirable" behaviors in favor of rebellious expressions of contempt for society's values.[18] Prisonization thus increases the likelihood of further criminality.[19] This process is not unique to U.S. prisons; studies have found the same effects among the inmates of many other nations.[20]

In addition to the detailed rules and regulations that govern eating, sleeping, dress, movement, and grooming, prisons also subject their inmates to many personal humiliations that are part of the desocialization process of being placed in an institution. *Degradation ceremonies* are routines that force a person to submit to experiences that most people would find mortifying. In prison, degradation begins with strip searches and delousing upon entry and being referred to as a number. Being forced to associate with others whom one considers "dirty," such as child molesters, is another form of mortification. Degradation ceremonies are very important to the process of detaching someone from a previous identity. Such desocialization must occur before identification with a new subculture can take

---

What Is Prisonization?[21]

Sources of Prisonization

1. Involuntary incarceration
2. Segregation from mainstream society, significant others, and the opposite sex
3. Complex and unique system of social roles in prison
4. Imported antisocial identities and behaviors
5. Degradation ceremonies

Universal Aspects of Prisonization

1. Taking on the devalued identity of "convict"
2. Learning the customs, organization, and general culture of the prison
3. Changing old habits to deal with dangers of prison life
4. Developing new ways of dealing with, and thinking about, people—such as increasing social distance and building an "antisocial" reputation

Factors that Minimize Prisonization

1. Serving a short sentence
2. Having a prosocial cell mate
3. Having a stable personality
4. Maintaining contacts with noncriminals in the free world
5. Avoiding deviant activities within the prison
6. Rejecting the norms of the convict society
7. Serving time in a small, treatment-oriented facility
8. Low levels of security and/or high levels of exposure to the outside world

---

place. The desocialization process is the necessary prelude to resocialization into prison society.[22] Adjusting to a way of living and thinking that is appropriate only in a prison is the central aspect of prisonization. Acquiring a status-role or identity within the convict culture is often a step in this process.

Prisoners usually seek an identity that will get them power, safety, and respect. Antisocial behaviors like violence are often rewarded by convict society; the toughest, most violent inmates are usually leaders who can cover up the crimes they commit while in prison. The desire to earn a reputation as crazy and dangerous is a common adaptation to prison life.

Inmates must develop new habits and ways of dealing with people. Many of these behaviors function to protect the inmate's safety. Sleeping with one's face away from bars, minimizing time in shower areas, and never smiling are several examples. There is a tendency to avoid meaningful contacts with others and never to reveal details of one's personal background. As a result, most leave institutions with a more pronounced criminal identity and outlook than when they entered. Some prominent researchers believe that the state in which inmates leave prison insures that many will be reimprisoned eventually for more serious crimes.[23]

Inmates learn that the environment will provide for them regardless of how they behave. For example, all inmates receive food, shelter, clothing, and exercise regardless of how they behave. This is one aspect of **learned helplessness**, the idea of being powerless to affect one's own life and depending on others for virtually everything. Learned helplessness also means that the individual attributes responsibility for all actions to others.[24] Powerlessness, a closely related concept, is primarily a situational factor and is a strong predictor of prisonization.[25]

The Effects of Prisonization

One of the most famous experiments on the effects of prisonization was conducted by Philip Zimbardo, a social psychologist, in California in 1969. He divided 24 mentally healthy college students into two groups to play the roles of guards and inmates in order to describe the effects of imprisonment on "normal" people. Although the experiment was scheduled to last two weeks, Zimbardo shut it down after just six days because the reaction of the students to their roles was so extreme. Many of those playing the role of guards became highly coercive, and he feared they would soon become violent and injure a "prisoner." Those playing the prisoners became so servile and apathetic that he feared for their mental health. All the subjects were offered counseling immediately after the experiment was halted.[26]

Zimbardo concluded that prisonization (1) affects both staff and inmates, (2) makes people more dangerous and less able to live in free society than ever before, and (3) is so severe that imprisonment should be reserved only for those who are so dangerous that they cannot be controlled in other ways.[27] This is one of two classic studies that penologists use to define and discuss prisonization. The other was conducted by Stanton Wheeler and examined changes in the attitudes of actual prison inmates over time.

Wheeler's U-curve describes the effects of prisonization on inmate attitudes. Prisoners in the first and last six months of their sentences have high hopes of rehabilitation and tend to obey the rules of the institution. Their attitudes are relatively prosocial during these phases. During the middle phase, which is by far the longest, they are more likely to be guided by the norms of prison society. Prisoners in the prosocial phases tend to be oriented to the conventional values of free society. Early in their sentence, many inmates hope to be rehabilitated and want to return to a productive life in society. As they adjust to prison life, they realize that little effort is being made to rehabilitate them, and they adopt the norms of the prison. As their release date nears, they again focus on "making it" in society and become hopeful and prosocial again. The process of prisonization is thus U-shaped over time. The inmates studied by Wheeler served an average of just over four years. Studies of men incarcerated for even longer periods indicate that attitudes may not change back to prosocial.[28]

All inmates experience some degree of prisonization. The degree to which an individual becomes prisonized varies with his or her psychological needs and coping abilities. Since prisonization is a product of social learning, short sentences result in less prisonization than long ones. The length of exposure to prison life, as well as how many times a person has been imprisoned, predicts the degree of prisonization he or she will experience.[29] Short periods of imprisonment allow less time for developing a prison-based identity. This helps preserve the individual's original identity and discourages involvement in the prison subculture.[30] The ability to maintain contacts with noncriminals outside the prison also helps reduce prisonization. Visits from relatives, friends, and clergy help keep inmates in touch with sources of self-esteem and identity that are based on free-world norms. These visits increase inmates' sense of well-being and may reduce recidivism. They are usually infrequent because of the time and expense required for travel. Most inmates come from large cities, but most prisons are located in distant rural areas.[31]

When authorities exercise high levels of control, inmates feel isolated, bored, and victimized. The more security and punishment are emphasized, the more prisonization is experienced. Inmates who participate in work-release programs in minimum-security facilities have relatively low levels of prisonization. Remember that imported variables often overlap with situational ones; minimum security work-release programs are often reserved for the least dangerous offenders and those who are nearing their release date.[32]

Inmates who participate in illegal activities while imprisoned are likely to be highly prisonized. Living by the norms of convict society reinforces the inmate's criminal identity. Involvement in criminal subcultures prior to imprisonment is important in this regard; the more criminal inmates' identity prior to incarceration, the more easily prisonized they are. People imprisoned for drunk driving and murder or manslaughter are the least likely to have serious criminal ties in the free world. They often avoid extreme prisonization by associating with staff more than with inmates. Inmates who used cocaine and heroin often have rather deep levels of involvement in the prison subculture.[33] The social rejection experienced by most drug abusers encourages loyalty to the convict culture. Integration into convict

---

Drug Use in Prison[34]

Drugs are smuggled into jails and prisons by visitors and guards. Smugglers also hide drugs in folded newspapers and other objects mailed to prisoners. Despite attempts to interdict them, the creativity of the smugglers usually assures their success. Nine out of ten prisons now test inmates for drugs and discipline those who test positive. About 1% of federal inmates test positive for marijuana, and one in 250 are positive for cocaine. Among state prisoners the comparable figures are one in 16 for marijuana and one in 28 for cocaine. Most states have drug testing policies that target inmates both randomly and for cause. Most use urinalysis but a few also examine hair because evidence of use remains there longer than in urine. Technologies that use sweat and saliva are also being examined for correctional use. In combination with an emphasis on interdiction, these programs are thought to decrease use among inmates but will probably not eliminate it. The problem is most common at work-release and prerelease centers where inmates spend some time in the free world, but all penal facilities are plagued by drug use.

Some inmates avoid marijuana because it can be detected for at least 60 days after use, while other drugs will not show up after a few days. Many inmates prefer heroin to cocaine because the high lasts longer and creates a more relaxed state. Drug prices in prison are three to four times higher than on the street because of the risks involved in selling drugs in a prison.

society requires having a role that is familiar to other inmates. It leads to participation in various, often illicit, activities. Drug use is the most common of these activities, but virtually all types of crimes occur in prisons.[35]

An inmate's level of involvement in convict society is affected by the character of his or her cell mate(s). When an inmate's closest companions are deeply involved in prison life, it is hard to avoid involvement in the convict subculture and thus prisonization. The stability of the inmate's personality is a major factor as well. People with stable personalities are less likely to adopt the values of those around them. Stable personalities are also more likely to have had positive relationships with noncriminals prior to incarceration.[36] Both of these tendencies help inhibit prisonization among stable personalities. Relationships with staff are often used as predictors of recidivism after release. Relationships within the prison determine the social climate of an institution and affect the dangers it poses to employees and inmates.

Some situational factors can be manipulated to reduce prisonization. Treatment increases inmates' orientation to life after release and helps them keep or enhance social skills. Small prisons, or large ones that are segmented into smaller units, allow better relationships between staff and inmates and should permit less deviant behavior and encourage positive relationships between staff and inmates.[37] Changes in these situational factors help extend the early and late phases of Wheeler's U-curve and reduce the negative effects of prisonization. Unfortunately, any changes designed to reduce prisonization are often perceived as reducing the amount of punishment associated with imprisonment. The current tendency to stress punishment makes it unlikely that the deprivations of prison life will be reduced in the foreseeable future. Also, some of these changes would be expensive, and public opinion discourages both increased spending and attempts to reduce the hardships of prison life.

One of the hardest situational factors to change is the way that time is experienced by prisoners. There is little meaningful activity to occupy inmates in most U.S. prisons and little hope that this enforced idleness will disappear in the foreseeable future. Inmates focus almost entirely on the present, taking one day at a time. Avoiding thoughts about the future helps them escape the boredom and deprivations of prison life. In the words of one prisoner:

> For me, and many like me in prison, violence is not the major problem; the major problem is monotony. It is the dull sameness of prison life, its idleness and boredom, that grinds me down. Nothing matters; everything is inconsequential other than when you will be free and how to make time pass until then. But boredom, time-slowing boredom, interrupted by occasional bursts of fear and anger, is the governing reality of life in prison.[38]

The need to avoid thoughts of the future in order to survive the present is another example of how imprisonment is counterproductive to rehabilitation. Experts consider *time horizon*, a person's ability to examine the future consequences of actions being considered in the present, to be an important predictor of crime.[39] The fact that many offenders have low time horizons is closely related to their desire for immediate gratification and a number of other psychological factors that are linked to criminality.[40]

Prison Slang[41]

Prison slang describes the world experienced by inmates. It is closely related to the street slang of both legitimate and criminal subcultures. Many terms, such as "snitch" or "stool pigeon" and "screw," have passed into common usage. Others, such as "ad seg" for administrative segregation (i.e., the hole or solitary confinement) are short versions or acronyms of technical terms used by prison staff. Like all slang, prison jargon changes rapidly and has many regional variations. The prison slang terms given here were selected for (1) their relative commonality and (2) their ability to highlight the concerns and values of the prison society.

Beef: Criminal charges or a problem with another inmate or guard.

Bit: A relatively short prison sentence.

Books: An official account ledger that lists the amount of spending money available to each prisoner.

Bunkie/Cellie: The person with whom a prisoner shares a cell.

Care package: Food or clothing sent by a friend or relative in the free world.

Catch a ride: To ask a friend with drugs to get you high.

Cell soldier: An inmate who talks tough when the cells are locked.

Check-in: An inmate who no longer feels secure due to pressure, intimidation, debts, etc., and requests assignment to a protective custody (PC) unit.

Ding: A disdainful term for a mentally unbalanced prisoner.

Dry snitching: To inform on someone indirectly by talking loud or performing suspicious actions when officers are nearby.

Fish: A new guard or inmate who has not yet learned the basics of prison life.

Gate time: Any period during which inmates can come and go from their cells.

House: An inmate's cell.

Jacket: Prison file containing information on a prisoner, or a prisoner's reputation.

Jolt: A long prison sentence.

Lockdown: A period during which prisoners are confined to their cells.

Pruno/Hooch: Homemade or cell-made alcohol, which usually resembles wine.

Punk: Derogatory term meaning homosexual or weak individual.

Rapo: Anyone convicted of a sex crime, generally disliked by other convicts.

Short: A prisoner who has little time left to serve before his or her release date.

Slammed: To be placed in "the hole" or administrative segregation unit ("ad seg").

Square John: A prosocial inmate or a law-abiding citizen.

Stand point: To keep a lookout for guards while others engage in some illicit activity.

Street to street: When one inmates' friends or relatives in the free world make payments to the friends or relatives of another inmate for a (drug) transaction within the prison.

Tag/Write-up: A violation of institution rules that is officially acted upon by authorities.

Tom/George: No good/OK. May be spoken or communicated in sign language: to label a person or situation "George" (OK) an inmate strokes an imaginary beard. If the "Tom" sign is given, then the situation is risky or the person is "no good." This is indicated in sign language by tweaking the nose or tugging at the ear lobe.

Turned out: To be manipulated or forced into homosexual activity. To use someone for your own goals.

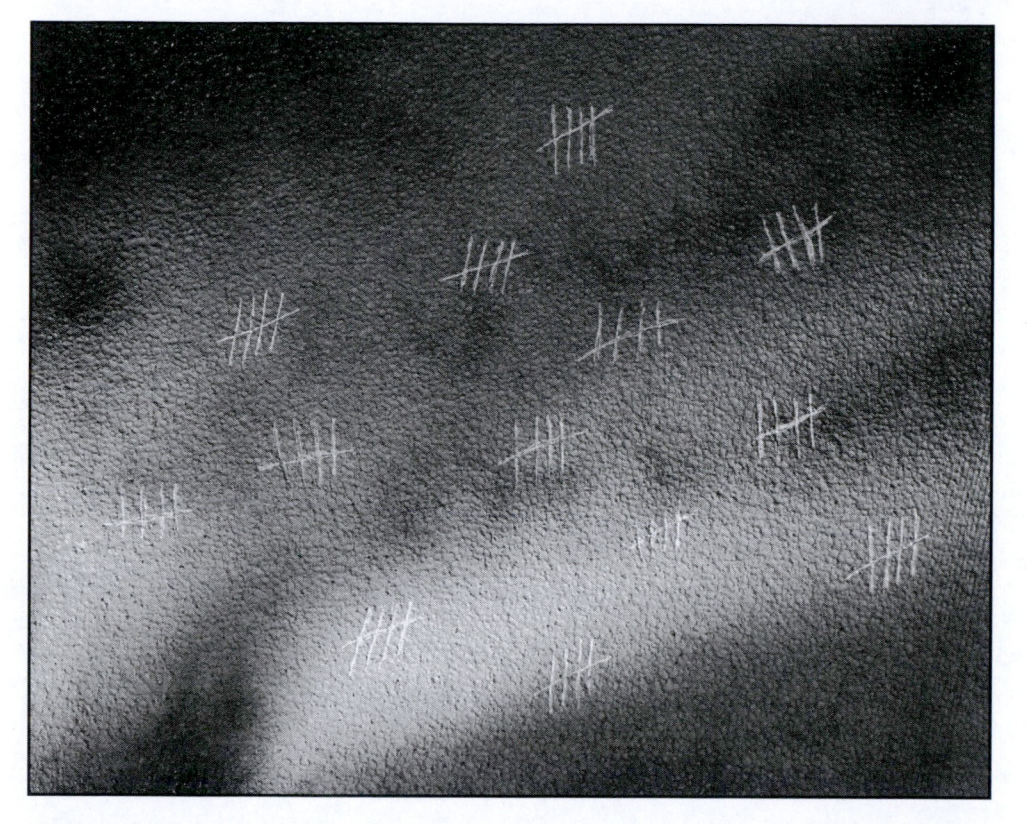

The boredom and monotony of prison life is one of the main challenges that confront prison inmates.

A number of factors influence how inmates adapt to life in prison: length of sentence, the roles chosen in prison, the influence of companions, and the regulations of the institution. Economic status, race, and age indirectly predict which inmates are most affected by this process. Some research suggests that whites lose more self-esteem than do minorities as a result of being imprisoned. This appears to be a result of the fact that (1) minorities often have a devalued sense of self-worth due to racism in society, and (2) there is more social support for minorities in prison because nonwhites are the predominant group in most prisons. Research shows that men of different races adjust to imprisonment in similar ways. However, the more impoverished a person was prior to imprisonment, the more likely she or he is to adjust successfully to prison life.[42] Age is also a good predictor of adjustment. Middle-aged men may adjust to the regimented routines of the institution more readily than younger offenders. This is probably because aging is closely associated with the loss of rebellious attitudes and behavior patterns.[43] It may also be that older offenders simply hide their emotions better than younger ones.

Policy Matters!
What Is the Goal of Imprisonment?

Prisons have three basic goals: incapacitate, punish, and rehabilitate. Research on the effects of imprisonment indicates that these goals are contradictory. To the extent that prisons cause deprivation and misery among their inmates, they also increase their criminality. It is very inefficient to place a person in such a setting. On the other hand, our emotions and current definitions of justice demand retribution. Prisons are relatively effective in accomplishing this goal. Further, we are unable to predict accurately which offenders pose a threat to society if allowed to remain in the community. Many people support incapacitation as the central goal of corrections because they feel that there is no other way to control crime. Therefore, we simply build more prisons. Is this approach really congruent with American values?

Questions to Consider

1. Is retribution morally appropriate as the central goal of corrections? Is it economically feasible? What alternatives would be acceptable? Is your position based on moral or utilitarian arguments? How would those using a different basis respond to your position?

2. Do we owe any significant subgroup of offenders the opportunity to be reformed? (Recall that some criminological theories suggest that society's organization can "cause" crime.)

3. Given our long history of attempting to rehabilitate offenders and predict their future behavior, is it wise to invest in further research on these issues?

TYPES OF PRISONERS

The terms used here to describe types of inmates are based on cultural orientations and prison behaviors among male convicts. The social roles observed in women's prisons are different and are handled in a separate chapter. ***Prosocial inmates*** were not members of a criminal subculture before being imprisoned. They prefer to associate with staff rather than other inmates while in prison. They pose no threat to other inmates, but their rapport with staff means that they get little respect from fellow inmates. The identity of ***antisocial convicts*** was linked to a criminal subculture prior to their incarceration, and it is likely they will return to that lifestyle. Thieves and many street gang members are of this type. ***Pseudosocial inmates*** are those who have many contacts within the prisoner, staff, and free-world cultures but are loyal to none. These are the "politicians" and "merchants" of the prison who manipulate others for gain. Many hustlers fall into this group. Their sociability is a self-serving strategy that allows them to manipulate others. ***Asocial inmates*** have suffered serious emotional damage and have few social skills. Many were "state-raised youths" who have spent more time in institutions than in the free world.

The antisocial inmate is sometimes referred to as a "real man" or "right guy" by other prisoners, and his behavior pattern is idealized by the convict society's code of behavior. The fact that the antisocial inmate is the most desirable role among inmates speaks volumes about the criminogenic nature of prison society. Asocial inmates are feared because they are unpredictable and dangerous. Pseudosocial prisoners are the movers and shakers of the prison, but their activities often cause tension and distrust among inmates.[44]

PRISON GANGS

The criminogenic effects of imprisonment are partly due to the dangers posed by one's fellow inmates. Of special importance to modern corrections is the growth of prison gangs. Among the many problems faced by modern prison officials, gang control is second only to crowding.[45] Membership in prison gangs overlaps with that of street gangs in some areas, and both types of groups are represented in many institutions.

Modern prison gangs can be traced back to the 1950s but caused little concern until the 1970s. In the 1970s, gangs like the Black Guerilla Family, Aryan Brotherhood, and Mexican Mafia took on a major role in prison society. These gangs were organized along racial lines and trace their roots to the California prison system. The modern prison gang is increasingly based on neighborhood or regional loyalties as well as on race. They are controlled by leaders who oversee a council and control most of the drug trafficking within U.S. prisons. Their goals and values are embodied in creed, mottos, and constitutions that justify their criminal activities.[46]

The Aryan Brotherhood and Aryan Circle are the main white gangs. Their ideology is one of racial hatred, especially toward African Americans. "Christian identity" ministries are used to recruit racist whites as new members, as are Viking religions like Odinism. African-American inmates who choose to join a gang usually belong to non-political groups like the Bloods and Crips but may also join the Black Guerilla family or Muslim extremist groups present in some facilities. Chicano gangs arose as extensions of barrio gangs like the Latin Kings. Each Hispanic prison gang draws its members from a different region of the state or nation. *La Nuestra Familia* draws most of its members from Northern California; the Mexican Mafia (*Mexicanemi* or *La Eme*) is more popular with those from Southern California; the Texas Syndicate initially consisted of Texan Hispanics imprisoned in California but is now a major presence in many states.[47]

Some experts feel that gangs set the norms of extreme violence and fear within prisons. Others argue that the general social trend toward increasingly deadly forms of violence has simply been imported from the streets to the prison. In either case, these groups are seen as mutual protection and support groups by inmates struggling to cope with the violence and deprivations of prison life and their own lack of social skills and status.[48] Gangs are most likely to be a major factor in maximum-security prisons where up to one-third of the inmates may be members. Membership is estimated at one in four among medium-security inmates and at 16% among those in minimum security. The proportion of gang members among inmates varies widely from one state to another, partly due to differences in how each system identifies gang members. For example, Arkansas claims 30% of its inmates belong to a gang while neighboring states estimate around 3%. Arkansas (30%), California (30%), Illinois (26%), Mississippi (20%), and New Mexico (47%) report the highest percentages of inmates in gangs. Gangs are most prominent among white prisoners in Maine, among African-American inmates in North Carolina, and among Hispanic prisoners in Texas. Oregon has a significant number of Asian and Polynesian gang members, and Canada reports biker and native aboriginal groups.[49]

Most prison systems have responded to this threat by trying to isolate gang members.[50] Some do this by dispersing gang members across different prisons while others try to segregate all of them into one or a few facilities.[51] Known members of the most dangerous gangs may be placed in administrative segregation for the duration of their sentence, but this can increase the cost of imprisonment by 25% or more per inmate.[52] Another approach consists of offering special assistance to inmates who want to escape the gang lifestyle. Many prison systems offer special programs for those who sincerely want to leave the gang. These prisoners are usually housed in special, gang-free facilities after authorities screen them thoroughly to assure that their desire to leave the gang is sincere and lasting.[53]

Prison gangs are increasingly aligned with similar organizations in the free world. New laws are being passed to allow authorities within and beyond the prisons unprecedented powers to examine the lives of suspected members and to track their whereabouts after their release from prison.[54] Leading experts in the field, however, urge more attention to the treatment and reintegration needs of gang members as the most effective, long-term solution to the problem.[55]

Violence is required as a condition of gang membership and is the main method of gaining status within the group. Many gangs require that an inmate participate in a murder attempt in order to earn membership. This is known as "rolling your bones." Much prison gang violence targets the gang's own members who are suspected of disloyalty or disobedience. Many gangs require that members contribute 10% of their income to the group after they are released from prison. Much of what is said about prison gangs today is speculative, because these organizations are extremely hard to penetrate. Very few prison gang members are willing to admit that the gang exists, and even fewer will discuss their activities.

A few researchers believe that prison gangs emerged to counterbalance the court-imposed ban on the use of inmates as guards or "building tenders," which was ruled illegal in *Ruiz v. Estelle* in 1981. Prior to that, many prisons, especially in the South, gave some inmates the power to control and discipline others when guards were not present. Prison records show that gang activity increased as the use of building tenders ended. While gangs may serve as substitutes for building tenders in some prisons by enforcing convict norms and helping assure stability, the impact of building tenders on overall rates of violence was more one of bookkeeping than objective reality. Building tenders allowed inmates to "fight it out" when staff was not present. Their absence simply means that most fights now lead to disciplinary action whereas before they were unknown, or ignored, by staff.[56] In either case, prison gangs are the result of both imported and situational variables.[57]

SPECIAL ISSUES IN PRISON LIFE

Material and sexual deprivation are high on the list of factors that make prisons different from other settings. The desire for immediate gratification that may have contributed to committing the crime that led to imprisonment can also create other problems. Because many convicts are impulsive and aggressive, violence is a constant concern. Examining the economic norms and sexual behavior of inmates provides insight into prison life, as does a look at the meaning of violence among prisoners.

The Informal Economy of the Prison

Prisons severely restrict the number and kinds of items that inmates may keep in their cells. This conserves space, reduces thefts, and adds to the punishment of imprisonment. Every prison has different rules as to what sorts of possessions inmates may keep in their cells. For example, some allow televisions, toasters, and street clothes; others do not. To cope with the lack of goods and services, an informal economy exists in all but ultra-maximum-security prisons.

Inmates may obtain desired items and services in four ways: (1) as gifts from friends and relatives in free society, (2) from the prison canteen or commissary, (3) through smuggling by staff and visitors, and (4) by stealing and making items within the prison. The first two methods are legal; the latter two are not. Regardless of how they were first introduced to the facility, all sorts of items wind up circulating through the informal economy of the prison.

Prison commissaries allow inmates to buy small personal and food items like deodorant and candy. Inmates are not allowed to possess cash out of fear that it will encourage thefts and aid escape attempts. Any money earned from prison jobs or given to inmates by people in the free world is placed in an account at the commissary. When purchases are made, that sum is deducted from the account; the inmate never handles cash.

Gifts brought in by visitors must be inspected and approved by authorities before inmates may receive them. These sometimes include large, expensive items such as appliances and televisions. Such gifts are often traded to pay off debts or to obtain other goods.

Stealing from work details within the prison is an important and constant source of goods ranging from food to drugs. Those working in industries can make weapons, and those who work in kitchens can steal food. Food is especially common because it is easily stolen and many inmates cannot wait the 15 hours between dinner and breakfast for a meal. Drugs are often smuggled in by staff and visitors but may also be stolen from prison pharmacies. Alcohol may be smuggled in or produced in secret distilleries within the prison.

The informal system of trading among prisoners is important to the operation of convict society. Barter is based mainly on trading noncash items and services that official rules prohibit or restrict. Services ranging from sexual acts to special laundry procedures like starching shirts can be bartered in the black market of most prisons.

In the inmate economy (1) cigarettes and other items are used instead of money, (2) most transactions between inmates are a rule violation, and (3) violence is used to collect debts and settle disputes. Cigarettes are used as money because they are available, easily hidden, and in constant demand among prisoners. Although contraband, cash occasionally supplements barter, especially when drugs are desired. Because the drugs are often smuggled into the prison, cash is required to pay the outside supplier. Bribes, blackmail, and threats are used to coerce the cooperation of staff and visitors in smuggling enterprises.

Drugs and alcohol are almost always available in prison, although they are much more expensive than in free society. As forbidden substances, the risk involved in possessing them leads to hugely inflated prices. Some inmates prostitute themselves for cash, drugs, or cigarettes while in prison. Others sell the services of those indebted to them. Gambling among inmates is popular, and these debts are usually paid with cigarettes. Weapons can be bought on the black market of the prison, as can privileges such as cell or work assignments that are offered by inmates working as clerks in administrative offices. Appliances and clothing are also bought, sold, and traded within many institutions.[58]

Although most of these deals are violations of prison rules, most guards will usually overlook at least some of these transactions as long as drugs or weapons are not involved. The trading of goods and services reduces tension among inmates, provides nonviolent means for them to attain status, and thus makes it safer to live and work in prison. Most inmates make at least a few deals for items they cannot otherwise obtain while imprisoned. Pseudosocial inmates take the role of "merchants" and are almost constantly engaged in "hustling" various items and services. Their ability to obtain goods and manipulate debts can be used to control other prisoners. They are often powerful within the prison but rarely are they popular. Some become leaders within the informal social control system; others work with established convict leaders who use their access to goods and services to assure the loyalty of their followers.[59]

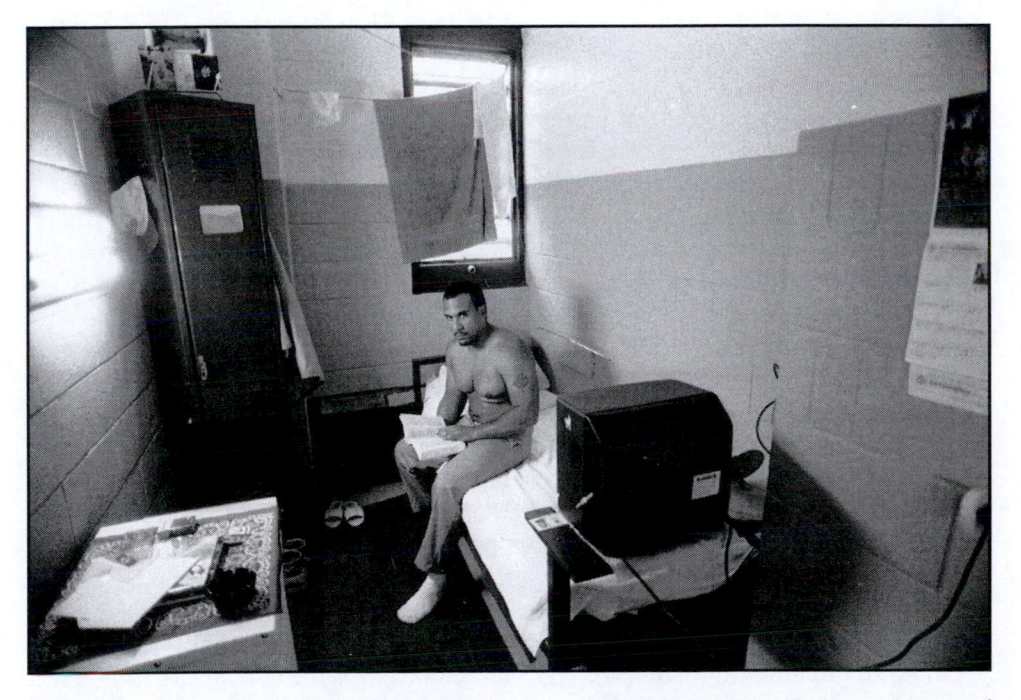

Prisons regulate the type and amounts of items inmates have in their cells, but violations of these rules are common.

Each trade or sale in this hidden economy is a private matter but makes up part of a much larger network of relationships within and between cliques of prisoners. A pharmacy worker may trade stolen drugs for several cartons of cigarettes, which are then used to buy fried chicken, which is traded for sex. Many unspoken norms govern such deals. Cell mates are expected to help one another, and easily stolen items are often shared without charge among clique members. However, prisoners quickly learn to be wary of anything that appears to be a gift. An unfortunate "fish" who accepts the "generosity" of his cell mate may find himself facing a very hard choice: he can immediately pay off the "debt" with cash, cigarettes, or sexual services, or face a severe beating.

The authorities periodically call **lockdowns** to search out contraband and to curtail the illegal economy, but trading resumes as soon as the pressure is off. Official objections to the hidden economy of convict society focus on three issues. First, dangerous contraband (such as weapons, drugs, and alcohol) move through the prison because of the inmate economy. Second, the prison economy threatens the ability of authorities to control all the rewards and deprivations of prison life. This means that certain prisoners whom the authorities would prefer not to have in leadership roles can become powerful by supplying what the inmates want. Finally, dissatisfaction with the goods purchased often leads to violence.

Prison Violence

Prison riots and similar "disturbances" are of special concern because they pose such a great threat to staff as well as inmates. U.S. prisons reported 2,674 disturbances/riots in 2000 (2 were riots) and 2,392 in 2001 (19 were riots). Of the 2001 incidents, 166 were gang related; 59 staff members and 56 inmates were injured as a result of them, but no deaths occurred.[60] Prison violence ranges from simple assault to murder and riots. Prison riots are of special concern because they pose such a great threat to staff as well as inmates. The American Correctional Association believes that enforced idleness, lack of meaningful programs, unpredictable parole policies, inhumane treatment, poor management, and overcrowding are the main causes of prison riots. Extremes of administrative control are more powerful contributing factors to riots than are disruptions of the balance of power among inmates. In other words, high levels of deprivation create extreme tension among inmates, which leads to disturbances.[61]

Most studies show that violence is a response to crowding, inexperienced staff, harsh conditions, and similar factors. Prisons holding more inmates than their rated capacity have more violent incidents than those operating at or under capacity.[62] Social instability, lack of programs, tension, and staff emphasis on control are direct results of crowding that are thought to be major causes of violence. Additionally, the constant intrusions on personal space caused by crowding may worsen the antisocial tendencies of many prisoners. Crowded conditions limit or eliminate treatment, recreation, and effective classification of prisoners that are the chief methods of discouraging violence. This view emphasizes the role of situational factors in producing violence. For example, in the United States, inmate homicides rose by 8.25% between 1996 and 1997, while inmate populations increased by

5.75%. Assaults on staff increased by 7.38%, but killings of staff dropped by one-third. Canada, by contrast, saw a decrease of 2.5% in its prison population and large decreases in killings among inmates (almost 40%). The rate of assaults on staff did not change, but killings of staff declined by 50%. These figures must be interpreted cautiously, however. They involve small numbers of incidents, and percentages can change dramatically when the numbers involved are few.[63]

Other research portrays violence as the natural result of the norms imported from the free world. Mark Mattaini, an associate professor in the School of Social Work at Columbia University, sees violence as functional. "Violence is behavior and people do what they do because it works for them in some way. And in some settings, violence functions to obtain a positive consequence—recognition in the form of attention, approval, or respect."[64] Violence is an accepted means of attaining status within convict society, because most inmates come from subcultures where violence is the chief method of obtaining whatever is needed or desired. One study supports the importation theory by linking the subcultural norms that promote violence among African-American youths and Cuban refugees to prison violence. African-American males were at twice the risk of involvement in violence as whites even after other factors, like prior record, were controlled.[65]

Sexual Behavior in Prison

Masturbation is the primary form of sexual release in prison, but homosexual activity occurs as well. Prison homosexuality can be discussed in terms of two types: dispositional and situational. *Dispositional homosexuality* means that an individual prefers partners of the same sex. These inmates were homosexual or bisexual in the free world and can adapt to the sexual segregation of prison. If identified as homosexual, they are often segregated into special units to discourage sexual relations between them and other prisoners. This is justified by official fears that they will be victimized by other inmates. *Situational homosexuality* is a temporary adaptation to circumstances in which members of the opposite sex are not available. Some otherwise heterosexual inmates will resort to homosexuality until members of the opposite sex are available again. As a result of being deprived of contact with women some inmates feel that their masculinity is threatened. Those who take the dominant role in homosexual acts often convince themselves that their homosexual activity is entirely physical and impersonal. This allows them to keep their heterosexual self-image that is at the base of their masculine identity. In either case, sex in a male prison lacks affection and is often more of a power display than an emotional act.

Coerced sexual activity is a form of rape, even if violence is not present. It is motivated more by a desire for power than for sexual gratification. Prison rapes most often involve white victims and black assailants.[66] Some researchers estimate that more than 20% of all inmates have been coerced or forced into sexual acts. Men were more than three times more likely to report such incidents than women. However, fewer than 4% of these prison rapes are ever reported to administrators, and even fewer are prosecuted. Fear of vengeance and apathy of officials discourage inmates from reporting assaults. Prosecution is rare because of evidence problems and the fact that crimes against prison inmates are given low priority by prosecutors.[67] A recent report by Human Rights Watch charged that the problem was widespread due to the deliberate indifference of prison officials. They cited improper classification of prisoners, crowding, double celling, under-staffing, inadequate response to inmate complaints, and failure to prosecute incidents as violating both the legal and human rights of inmates in 37 states.[68]

Nevertheless, prisons are legally required to do what they can to prevent sexual assaults.[69] Those who are "turned out" (coerced into having sex) are labeled "punks" and are often cruelly treated by other inmates. Punks are often younger, smaller, and weaker inmates who are not socialized to prison life. Fear of rape drives some prisoners to decide to have a homosexual relationship with one man or a few men who will offer them protection rather than risk a group attack. Ignorance of prison norms about paying off debts and favors from others also makes those not yet socialized to prison life vulnerable to being forced into a punk role.[70]

Once raped, a prisoner is likely to become the punk of another inmate in order to obtain protection. Prisoners buy, sell, and loan their punks like property, which deepens their exploitation. The desire to "own" a punk is a frequent cause of conflict among inmates. An inmate who is perceived as weak or insecure by other prisoners is likely to be challenged by someone who does not have a punk. The convict code's emphasis on violence encourages inmates to respond violently to any insult to their masculine honor in order to avoid further problems. The best way to prove such a challenge false is to have a punk or participate in a rape.[71] Regardless of how one becomes a punk, it is an experience that leaves lifelong scars. When victimized men leave prison they may continue their homosexual activities. For this reason, more inmates leave prison as homosexuals than enter it.[72]

Some studies have shown that the harsher prison life is, the more homosexual behavior and drug use will occur. This is probably due to the fact that harsh custodial regimes make inmates more sensitive to their lack of power. This, in turn, can drive them to seek power either by sexually degrading others or through drug-induced escapism. Drug use is more often imported than situational, whereas homosexuality may be either. In other words, inmates who used drugs before prison are most likely to continue use while imprisoned. Some men go to prison with tendencies that favor homosexual activity; others engage in homosexual acts while imprisoned as a method of adapting to sexual segregation. Prisons with relatively youthful inmate populations are more likely to have problems with homosexuality than are facilities with older prisoners.[73]

Despite some alarming statistics to the contrary, some data collected from prisoners shows that sexual activity is not as common in prisons as many believe. Twenty to 30% of prisoners reported having sex with another inmate while imprisoned. Just over 10% reported having had such a contact within the last one or two years. Other studies confirm these impressions, with about 20% of inmates reporting sexual contact within the last year.[74] Rape is even more uncommon than consensual sex, according to self-report studies and reviews of disciplinary records. However, it should be cautioned that such incidents are almost certainly underreported for the reasons cited earlier. Despite the consistency of such reports, most inmates seem to accept the belief that rape is fairly common in prisons. This is despite the fact that they claim not to have personally been victims (perhaps to protect a self-image or to avoid the stigma of being victimized sexually) and say they have never witnessed such an event.[75] When rapes do occur, the attackers are usually heterosexual or bisexual men. Homosexuals are often the targets of such attacks.[76]

Prison administrators do have a few methods of reducing sexual tension among inmates. *Conjugal visits* give prisoners the opportunity for unsupervised social and sexual contacts with their spouses. This practice is common in Mexico, Canada, and some western European nations along with five states in the United States. Conjugal or "family" visits are a privilege earned by minimum- and medium-security inmates through good behavior. Such visits are allowed only once every few months in most of these states, and many test inmates for drug use after such visits. Conjugal visits have been shown to reduce violence and homosexuality. They also aid in preserving marriages and family ties, which helps to minimize prisonization by helping inmates maintain links with nonconvicts. Arguments against conjugal visits focus on the fact that they only serve married prisoners, create many administrative problems, and have no effect on the majority of inmates who are single.[77]

Ethics on the Line
Handling Sexual Assault in Prison

While working as a prison guard supervising a work detail at a minimum-security facility you often gain the confidence of inmates in a way that few other guards can. You notice that an inmate on your detail has suddenly become depressed and withdrawn. When approached he initially reacts with anger but then apologizes. His behavior remains moody and withdrawn, however. You then begin to hear rumors that he is, or will soon become, the punk of a suspected inmate gang leader of his own race. All of this leads you to suspect that he has been the victim of a sexual assault. You carefully choose a time when no other inmates are present to ask him directly if this is the case. He acknowledges that it is; he was attacked by several members of a prison gang simply because he was small, nonviolent, and of a different race than their gang. The victimized inmate is able to identify his attackers but asks you to say nothing. He claims he has "taken care of" the problem himself. You are fairly certain that this statement refers to his new relationship with the suspected gang leader. How do you handle the situation?

Questions to Consider

1. Was it appropriate for you to explore the changes in the inmate's demeanor and its relationship to what you heard about his affiliation with the gang leader?

2. Do you feel bound by the inmate's request that his admission of victimization remain entirely confidential? Why or why not? Does your concern for the inmate's welfare and sense of autonomy overcome your desire to enforce the law within the prison? Why?

3. If you report what you know, experience suggests your superiors will tell you to "forget it" because they see rape as an inevitable part of prison life. Should you report what you know anyway? What will you do if no action is taken?

4 Should you take some sort of informal action such as asking other guards who work in the cell area to monitor the situation? Would this be a breach of ethics? Why or why not?

Although controversial, *home furloughs* have a similar potential for reducing prison homosexuality and are more common in U.S. prisons than elsewhere. Almost all U.S. furlough programs are restricted to minimum-security inmates nearing their release date. However, many of these inmates are recidivists and some have convictions for violence. About 9% of furloughs result in violations, usually for using alcohol/drugs or for returning late.[78] They also add to the risk that an inmate will bring a sexually transmitted disease, such as AIDS, into the prison. Inmates on furloughs are still subject to the rules of the prison. If they misbehave, they can be charged with a new crime, denied parole, or reclassified into a higher level of security as the situation demands.

SUMMARY

The informal social organization of the prison is produced by a combination of situational and imported variables. Life in a total institution leads to a series of changes in a person's outlook and behavior patterns known as prisonization. Prisonization makes people less able to live in society than they were prior to being imprisoned. It also retards any efforts that might be attempted toward rehabilitation. Prisonization is but one example of the contradictions between the demands of fair punishment and those stressing the efficiency of reintegration that are found throughout the structure of the prison. Many prominent researchers believe that we should reserve prison only for the most dangerous. They favor intermediate sanctions for other offenders despite the objections of retribution/deterrence advocates.

Prisoners adapt to institutional life in many ways. The preprison background of each offender is the best predictor of his or her behavior and social role in prison. Antisocial inmates are the type idealized by the "convict code." Asocial prisoners are probably the most feared by other inmates as well as staff. Pseudosocial prisoners are manipulative politicians and merchants who cause tension but can also accomplish things that even the authorities cannot. Prosocial inmates are loyal to the conventional values of staff and avoid their fellow convicts.

Gangs are a response to deprivation and a source of identity for their members. Prison gangs resemble street gangs in many ways but are usually based on inmates' race. They are responsible for most of the drug trafficking in U.S. prisons and much of the serious violence as well.[79] Although created to serve as protection organizations, gangs now fuel racial hatred among inmates. Authorities try to control gangs by segregating their members and offering protection for those who defect, but these groups provide inmates with otherwise unattainable status and identity in the increasingly harsh environment of the modern U.S. prison.

Loss of heterosexual relations is one of the main deprivations suffered by male inmates. Masturbation is by far the most common form of sexual release in prisons, but homosexuality also occurs. Some inmates are bi- or homosexual prior to being imprisoned, while others use homosexuality as a temporary adaptation to imprisonment. Younger, smaller, less violent inmates are most vulnerable to coerced sex.

Sexual acts, drugs, weapons, and other and more conventional goods and services are all available through the informal economy of the prison in which barter arrangements lead to various exchanges. Violence and coercion are used to collect debts and settle disputes over value. Prison authorities try to suppress this informal economy, but it survives because it helps inmates cope with the deprivations of prison life.

QUESTIONS FOR DISCUSSION AND REVIEW

1. What types of variables predict the nature of prison life? Which of these can be affected by official policies and procedures? Why?

2. What two theories are most often used to explain the unique aspects of convict society? What factors does each stress?

3. What is a total institution? How does living in one affect a person? Why?

4. Describe the process of prisonization. How can it be minimized? How does it affect the likelihood of returning to a law-abiding and productive life?

5. Into what four basic types can prison inmates be categorized? To what kind of sub-culture is each most closely tied? How does each relate to staff? Which type best lives up to the norms of the convict code? Which is most feared by other inmates?

6. How are prison gangs organized? In what sorts of activities do they tend to become involved? What factors encourage their growth?

7. What kinds of sexual activity are most common among male prison inmates? Describe the two basic types of homosexuality that are found in prison. How does prison homosexuality differ from that found in the free world?

8. What forms of violence are likely to be encountered in a prison? What factors predict the rate and severity of prison violence?

9. Why does the author feel that most inmates will leave prison less able to adapt to a law-abiding life than when they entered it?

FEMALE OFFENDERS

The treatment of women by justice agencies varies according to beliefs about women in a particular region and time period. Female offenders historically have been subjected to abuse and neglect, stemming from beliefs that: (1) crime was a greater violation of the female sex role than of the male sex role, and (2) women were less valuable than men. In the early seventies, about half the states did not have separate institutions for women inmates.[1] The media reinforce the impression that women who commit crimes are particularly deviant. Rarely do media stories explore the circumstances of many women who commit crimes, such as substance abuse or the lack of resources to avoid victimization. These women often commit offenses of possession of drugs, selling small amounts of drugs, fraud, and prostitution.[2] For most of the twentieth century, fewer than 10,00 women were imprisoned. By 1980, the total reached 12,000, but by 2001, the number was 93,000.[3] Because of the "war on drugs" and "get-tough" sentencing policies, the system that had traditionally ignored women now faced a dramatic increase in the number of women prisoners.[4]

CHARACTERISTICS OF WOMEN IN PRISON

Between 1990 and 2000, drug offenses accounted for 33% of the growth in the number of women state prisoners, compared to 20% for men offenders.[5] Thirty-four percent of women in state prisons were incarcerated for drug charges.[6] In 2000, 66% of federal women inmates were imprisoned for a drug offense. The percentage of women in state prisons in 2000 for the four major categories of offenses were: 11% public order; 25% property; 32% drug; and 31% violent.[7] Most (72%) violent offenses committed by women were simple assault. Crimes of violence committed by women generally can be classified in two categories: (1) assisting males in committing robberies and similar acts and (2) assault of intimates or acquaintances, often as a result of domestic violence.[8] Sixty percent of women in state prisons experienced physical or sexual abuse in the past. Forty-two percent of female felony defendants had no history of prior convictions and were not charged with a violent offense.[9]

Female incarceration rates are marked by ethnic disparities. Black females are 5 times more likely to be imprisoned than whites, and 3 times more likely than Hispanics. The rate of imprisonment for black women is 199 per every 100,000 residents, versus 36 for white women and 61 for Hispanic women. Although monthly drug use by African Americans is consistent with their proportion of the population (13%), 39% of black women in state prisons were convicted of drug offenses compared to 23% of white women; 44% of Hispanic women are serving sentences for drug offenses. Two-thirds of women in prison are women of color.[10]

Women in prison are young; three-quarters of them range in age from 25 to 34. About 40% of the women have a high school diploma or equivalent. Half of those arrested lived below the poverty line and were unemployed. Seventy-eight percent are mothers of dependent children. The explosion in the number of incarcerated

Female Rates of Imprisonment, 1971–2000[11]

This figure shows how dramatically the rate of imprisonment for women has risen in the United States. In 1971, 6 out of every 100,000 women were in prison, while by 1999 this figure had risen to 59, where it remained in 2000. Male rates increased 4.8 times, from 189 to 915, during that same period. The gradual increase during the 1971–1988 period followed by the sharper increase from 1988 to 1999 is similar for all U.S. group rates, as is the leveling off noted in 2000.

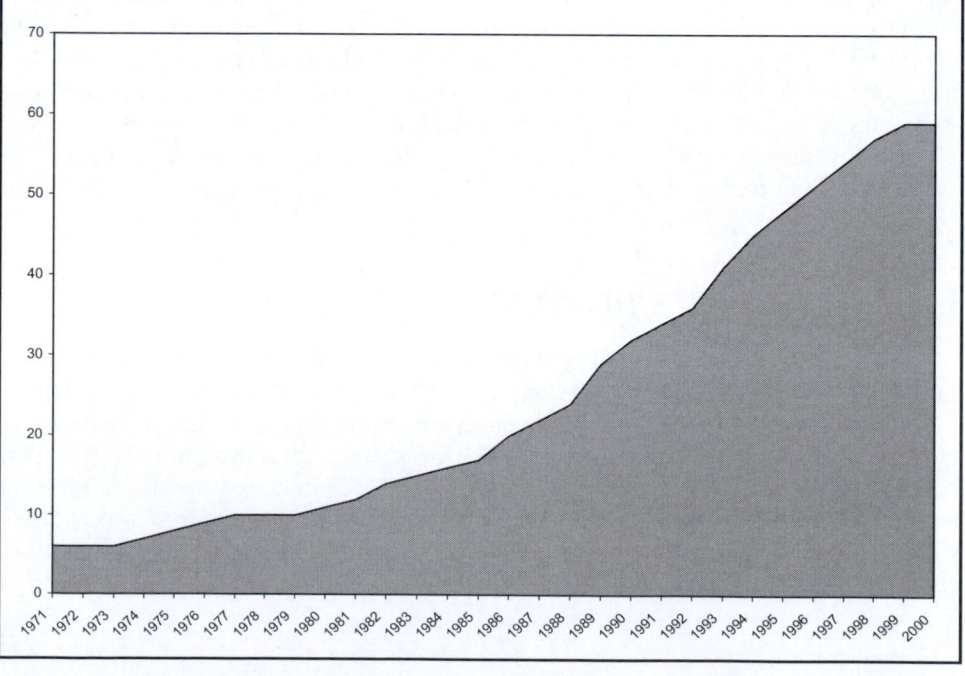

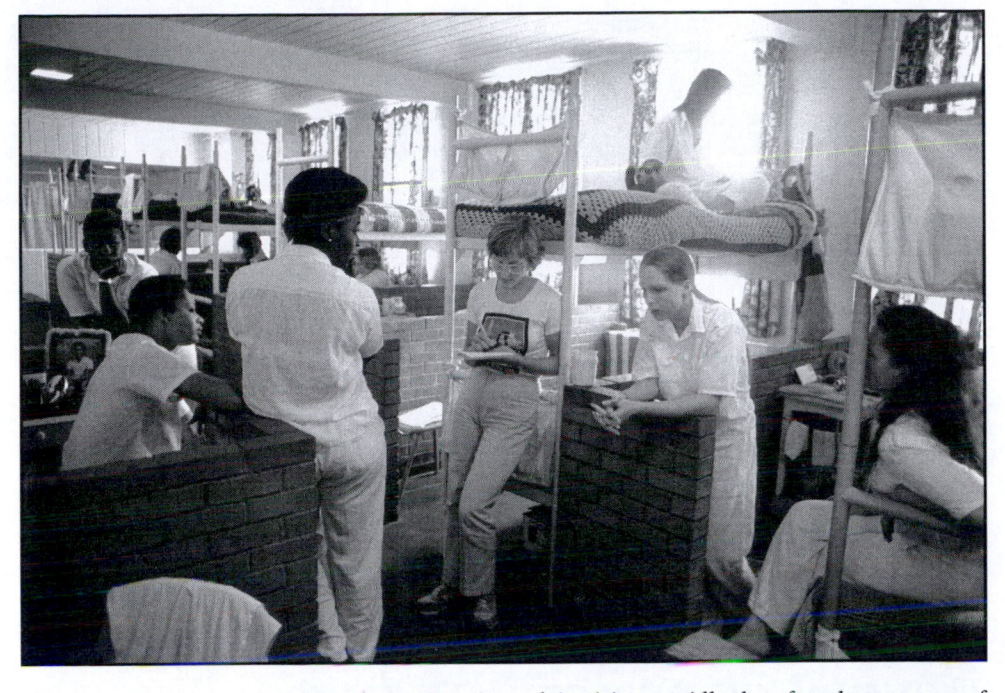

The rate at which women are being imprisoned is rising rapidly, but female patterns of involvement in crime have changed little.

women has created a cycle of crime and punishment. Children of incarcerated mothers are caught in a downward spiral of social disenfranchisement, which often leads to criminal activity and more incarceration. Almost half of women in state prisons report that someone in their family was in jail or prison. Twenty-nine percent of women in state prisons are mentally disabled, a significantly higher rate than for the general population or for male inmates. Ninety percent of women prisoners have a history of drug or alcohol abuse.[12]

FACTORS AFFECTING SENTENCING OF FEMALE OFFENDERS

Research on sentencing generally focuses on several variables (ethnicity, socioeconomic status, type of offense, and prior criminal history) to predict whether a woman is likely to be sentenced to prison and the length of the sentence. Before the 1970s it was accepted that judges would sentence women differently than men. In the 1980s and 1990s, legislation attempted to provide consistent punishment regardless of ethnicity, class, or gender.[13] However, there is evidence that women sometimes are sentenced less harshly than men. A recent Florida study showed that despite the use of presumptive sentencing, judges were more likely to violate the guidelines for women than for men. Florida law allows only downward departures from guidelines and recognizes 12 circumstances that can be used to justify them. These circumstances were often absent in cases where judges went outside the guidelines for women but followed them for male defendants.[14] This tendency to treat women less harshly is known as the **chivalry effect**. Another hypothesis about gender and criminal sanctions, the *evil woman* hypothesis, predicts more severe sanctions for women who violate traditional role behavior. The *dependency* hypothesis predicts less severe sanctions for women who are economically dependent, especially if they have children.

None of the hypotheses consistently predict discrepancies in sentencing. While some women may receive lenient treatment, others do not, even when parental responsibilities and situations are similar. African-American women appear to be more harshly treated than white women.[15] Older women are usually treated more leniently than men of the same age. Girls are more often arrested for minor status offenses like disobedience and running away than are boys, and they are more likely to be confined for offenses that would result in lenient treatment for boys. The sexual activity of women has always been much more regulated than that of men, and the practices of law enforcement are sometimes discriminatory against women. Offenses by women that violate the traditional female sex role are treated more harshly. As drug-related offenses increasingly dominate the statistics on female imprisonment, some have suggested that nonpunitive interventions would be more effective and appropriate methods of changing these women's lives.[16]

WOMEN AS THE "FORGOTTEN OFFENDERS"

Modern scholars label incarcerated women as the "forgotten offenders" for four reasons. First, although the rate of incarceration of women has increased greatly, the number of women in prison is small. Second, female criminals are not seen as particularly dangerous by judges, policymakers, or the public, so their crimes attract little attention. Women are less often involved in violent crimes than men, and when women commit violence it is usually an act of passion directed at someone close to the offender. These crimes are not seen as threatening by the public and receive less attention than those involving strangers. Third, female inmates are less troublesome than males. Women's prisons rarely experience the violence that is common in male facilities; riots are rare at women's facilities.[17] Women are less likely to sue officials. Finally, the variety of training, education, and rehabilitation programs in female prisons is often less than that found in male institutions. Some feminists suggest that the absence of these programs is at least partly because women cause fewer problems for, and therefore attract less attention from, the authorities. Importation theory claims that the female sex role explains both the relative tranquility of women's prisons and the traditional neglect of female inmates. Those favoring situational explanations point out that the small size of female institutions also accounts for the low rate of violence among female prisoners. In all probability, both explanations have some validity.[18]

The law applies the idea of **parity** to the treatment received by male and female inmates. This means substantial equivalence but not complete equality. Some describe parity as a principle of "separate but equal" treatment under which women need not have precisely the same opportunities as men. However, the same types of privileges and comforts must be available to both groups. Differences in the numbers of inmates, as well as in their needs, can be used to justify differences in the treatment of male and female inmates under this doctrine. While the rarity of violence among women and their greater tendency to be cooperative have been used to justify the neglect of female prisoners, that reasoning could just as easily be used to argue that women should receive more resources because they can be returned to society with less likelihood of committing new crimes than men.

FEMALE INMATE SOCIAL ORGANIZATION

While men tend to reenact the violence of the city streets from which they came, most women want to avoid that self-defeating behavior. They tend to form a network of relationships that mirrors a family and helps them avoid negative prison influences.[19] Women also try to remain involved with their children and loved ones in the outside world.[20] At least one prison manager has used these facts to argue that parity for women should be used to make female prisons more reformative. Programs and practices that work well in these facilities could then be adapted for use in male institutions. The low level of violence among female offenders and their cooperative institutional behavior norms also support this view.[21]

Nonetheless, many women offenders follow a version of the "convict code." Imported characteristics like age, criminal history, and experience with prison life predict the degree to which a woman is likely to follow these norms. The extent to which deprivation, a largely situational variable, is experienced as a result of prison life also plays a role, however.[22] While men suffer mainly from loss of autonomy and sexual relationships, the main deprivation felt by women is the loss of family and support networks in the community. In some prisons, women directly attempt to create imitation versions of the family that function as social support groups.

Pseudofamilies

Although women adapt to prison life in a variety of ways, one of the most common appears to be by becoming involved in a pseudofamily membership. In many institutions, incarcerated women form small cliques based on social roles that resemble those of a nuclear family. Older inmates with more prison experience take a parental role in helping younger women adapt to prison life. These cliques function as a family by providing members with both practical and emotional support. Not all women's prisons have pseudofamilies, and the factors leading to their development are unclear. This type of female adaptation to prison is thought to help inmates cope with the deprivations of incarceration that are felt most intensely by women. Pseudofamilies are small, nonviolent groups that are much more easily controlled or eliminated by authorities than are male gangs.

The Social Roles of Female Inmates

Even in prisons that lack pseudofamilies, imported identities have a strong influence on inmate social roles. The literature on women's prisons recognizes three basic social roles. The *square* is a relatively conventional woman, comparable to the prosocial male, with no allegiance to any criminal subculture. She has often been jailed as a result of a violent quarrel with a husband or lover. Her orientation is to conventional society, and she cooperates with authorities to the greatest extent possible. The *cool* is a woman who attempts to get as much pleasure and comfort out of prison life as is possible. She is oriented mainly to prison life and has enough knowledge of institutional norms to manipulate situations to meet her desires. She tries to avoid trouble with the authorities as much as possible. The *life* is a woman who was part of a criminal subculture in the free world. She is likely to be a frequent rule violator who will probably continue her criminal career during and after imprisonment.[23]

Discipline in Women's Prisons

Women's prisons have rules similar to those holding men, and discipline is a constant issue for both staff and inmates. Only a few studies have addressed gender inequities in how discipline is handled in male and female facilities. One comparison of disciplinary reports in male and female facilities in Texas found that women were more often charged with rule violations than men. Despite the fact that most of these violations were of a nonserious nature, the women received harsher punishments than did the men. Sexual stereotypes also seem to play a role in how discipline is applied in female prisons. Certain rules were vigorously enforced in women's facilities but not in those for men. Much of the difference can be explained by the degree to which sex role stereotypes were violated. Male and female prisoners are under the same correctional rules in Texas prisons, but the way in which those rules were interpreted and applied varied with the gender of the inmates and was almost always to the disadvantage of the women.[24]

Mental health researchers have long suspected that psychiatric methods are often used to control women who violate their sex role, and they support their claim by pointing to the higher rate of institutionalization for women suffering moderately severe symptoms.[25] The same tendency also occurs in prisons. When women inmates behave rebelliously, violating gender-role expectations, they are labeled hysterical and are controlled with a mental health intervention, such as confinement in a mental health housing unit.[26] Similar issues have been raised about the use of psychiatric medications to restrain women in jails and prisons.[27]

Race relations in female facilities are usually less tense than in male institutions, but race is still a source of conflict among women. The great majority of minority inmates feel that white prisoners get better treatment than women of color, and 10% of the white inmates agreed with them. Over half of the minority, and almost one in five of the whites, said that racial issues were at the root of most assaults within the prison. Women of color felt the presence of racial conflict more than white women did, but they stopped short of describing the prison atmosphere as racially hostile.[28]

Women's Adjustment to Prison Life

Men adjust to prison life by creating status roles for themselves within the prison culture. This often leads to gang formation, violence, and the smuggling of contraband. While some women do the same, most try to bring the comforts of home to their cells. Women's prisons are kept cleaner than men's because inmates are responsible for janitorial tasks. Where men spend their money on cigarettes, magazines, and candy, women are likely to purchase picture frames, curtains, and similar items. The quality of relationships with peers also gets more attention from women than from men. Each gender is trying to replace what is most missed as a result of confinement.

Descriptions of female adjustment to prison sound stereotypical because traditional domestic concerns seem to dominate. This does not mean that these women have no desire for a meaningful career beyond the family. Because of their greater sensitivity to others and interest in home and family, the atmosphere of women's prisons is less threatening than that of the men's.[29] It is also more easily affected by administrative policies and program offerings.

Adjustment to prison is difficult because of the lack of occupational, educational, and social programs. Programs that provide women with social support and address their psychological needs have been shown to help them adjust to prison life. Such programs must be based specifically on the needs and skills of women. They cannot be operated in the same way as those in male facilities if they are to be effective in addressing adjustment to prison life.[30] The programs that are offered to women are rarely designed for them or for their postrelease needs. Isolated prison locations in rural areas make visits from family rare, and women feel this much more intensely than do men. The adequacy of health and psychological services for women are also very questionable in many areas. In particular, programs that go beyond emphasizing traditional female roles are of great importance in helping female offenders avoid crime after release. Gender-responsive programs empower women to challenge and overcome destructive stereotypes related to sex, ethnicity, and poverty by providing access to resources to help women make changes in their lives.[31]

PROGRAMS FOR WOMEN

Those who design and conduct programs for female offenders need to keep two things in mind. First, women need to leave prison with the ability to provide for themselves and their families in the modern job market. Very few will be released to a middle-class suburb with a husband as sole wage earner. Job skills are therefore of critical importance to women.[32] However, many female offenders have little experience in either managing a home or earning a living. Training in how to interview for a job, set up and follow a household budget, and handle children is thus of great importance to them.

Second, research on education shows that men and women learn in different ways. Men like the challenge of competition and debate. They often prefer to solve problems by themselves, and many thrive on the challenge of interpersonal rivalry. Women, on the other hand, learn better in cooperative, relaxed situations that require teamwork. Where men focus on the number and size of their achievements, women get the most reward from the quality and meaning of their successes.[33]

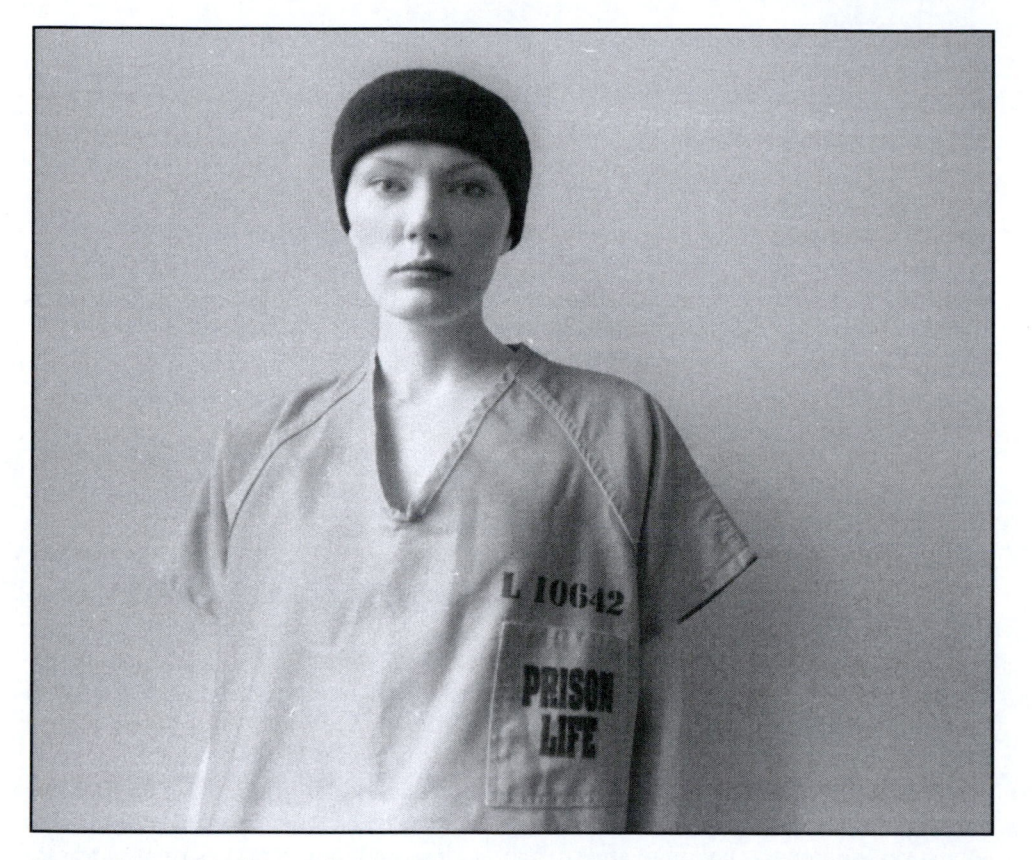

Women have a hard time adjusting to prison life due to the lack of programs designed to meet their needs.

Some Strategies for Effective Reform of Female Offenders[34]

Personal Officers: Each inmate is assigned to, or chooses, a correctional officer who acts as a mentor providing help, advice, and support. This is proposed especially for women serving extremely long sentences. The goal is to link the inmates to the staff in a cooperative manner. Issues of confidentiality, availability, and trust need to be dealt with in a manner similar to that employed in the client–parole officer relationship.

Sentence Planning: To get the most benefit for the least expense, classification procedures for women should stress treatment and family reunification rather than the security concerns that typify male facilities.

Shared Work: Closer ties between prison treatment workers and parole/probation officers in the community need to be developed. Remote prison locations discourage such interaction, but modern technology could easily be used to increase direct communication between these groups of practitioners if their workloads permitted such cooperation.

Awareness of Backgrounds: Most imprisoned women have been physically and/or sexually abused, have dependent children, and tend to have poor relationships with men. Awareness of and sensitivity to inmates' unique backgrounds can foster a cooperative atmosphere.

While the content and goals of treatment and adjustment programs may be the same for both genders, the style with which they are conducted should be different. When programs developed in men's prisons are used in women's facilities they should be modified to (1) address the concerns of women in today's mainstream society, (2) reflect what is known about gender differences in learning styles, and (3) encourage women to take power over their own lives. These same themes should be present in programs designed to assist women with their health care concerns. Like education, science has long neglected the unique needs of women, and female inmates tend to be especially ignorant of their own medical needs. Prisons could save millions in tax dollars just by providing adequate health care programs that address the needs of modern women.

Health Care Issues

Women have many health care concerns that do not affect men. Proper nutrition and activities while pregnant and following childbirth are among these. So are birth control, domestic violence, and menopause. Female inmates are among the least likely to be informed about these issues, and prison provides a unique opportunity to provide education to the most needy segment of the female population in a cost-effective way. Sexually transmitted diseases like syphilis, chlamydia, and AIDS are extremely expensive problems in the United States today. So are the medical problems of newborn infants whose mothers had poor nutrition and health care during pregnancy. Domestic violence is the leading cause of injuries requiring emergency-room care for women.

If prison programs taught accurate and useful information about these problems, they would be cost-effective. Unfortunately, only a few experimental programs really try to empower women to lead productive lives. The most needed programs are usually described as "treatment" because they deal with substance abuse, self-confidence, and assertiveness. Programs that prepare women to enter nontraditional jobs that pay better than jobs traditionally held by women are also needed. However, most programs in women's prisons simply reinforce the sex-role stereotypes that make women vulnerable to domestic abuse, high-risk sexual behavior, and unwanted pregnancies.[35]

Pregnant Inmates

In 1950, thirteen states had laws allowing mothers in prison to keep their infants with them.[36] In 1997, more than 2,200 pregnant women were imprisoned, and more than 1,300 babies were born in prisons. As the rate of incarceration for women in the United States continues to rise, so will the number of children born in jails and prisons. Over three-quarters of these women became pregnant prior to being imprisoned. Some are impregnated by staff members, others during furloughs or conjugal visits or through contacts with men in coed facilities. In most states, babies are taken from their imprisoned mothers almost immediately after birth. Exceptions include California where an eligible pregnant woman may remain with her infant from the time of birth until the end of incarceration (however, there are only 94 openings, and in 1997 there were 381 newborns). In Illinois, qualified inmates may be housed in a residential program for up to 24 months (15 places available in the program in 1997 when 51 babies were born to state female prisoners). In New York, a woman may keep her baby for up to 12 months, in Nebraska up to 18 months, and in South Dakota for up to 30 days.[37]

Many special needs must be met if pregnant women are to have normal pregnancies and deliver healthy children. Prevention of medical problems during pregnancy is far more cost-effective than treatment after birth. A special diet with high levels of protein, vitamins, and minerals is essential along with a level of exercise not usually enjoyed by prisoners. Security practices must also allow for the health concerns of pregnant inmates. Strip searches for women usually include a pelvic examination, which can increase the danger of infection and thus pose a special threat to pregnant women. Use of handcuffs and shackles on pregnant women, especially as they are giving birth, can also be a problem but is permitted in 18 states and Washington, D.C.[38] Work assignments and treatment facilities must also be sensitive to the problems of expectant mothers. Jails especially need to be aware of the dangers that addiction can pose for pregnant women. Pregnant addicts need to begin a special, slow detoxification program within 4 to 6 hours of their last drug use so that withdrawal will not kill or injure the fetus. Information on methods of childbirth and their dangers must also be made available to these inmates. Few prisons have the facilities to deliver a child properly, so transfer to a hospital may be required.[39]

Jails have led the way in providing model programs for pregnant offenders. Many of these programs resulted from lawsuits filed by women who received inadequate care. A well-run facility for women has a medical team able to handle the needs of women inmates. New inmates will be tested for pregnancy early in their incarceration, and a list of pregnant inmates is maintained. Special wrist- or armbands are used to identify pregnant inmates. Pairing each pregnant inmate with another woman who is not pregnant is also helpful. This gives the pregnant woman social and physical support. Prenatal care should include HIV testing, ultrasound examinations, and regular medical checkups. Some programs allow women to have abortions if they so desire, but women should not be pressured to choose this option. Following birth, postpartum care must be provided, often for two or three days. Information on family planning alternatives should be provided, preferably in a private counseling session.[40]

Both family planning and disease prevention require frank and open discussions of sexuality. Because they are usually poorly educated, inmates of both genders often have unrealistic ideas about the risks associated with various kinds of sexual activity. For anatomical reasons, women are more vulnerable to sexually transmitted diseases than are males.

HIV/AIDS Programs for Women

The AIDS epidemic makes it vital that prisons take advantage of opportunities to slow the spread of this lethal virus. While the overall number of HIV cases is relatively small when compared to the number of prison inmates, the costs of this disease remain astronomical. Note that the percentage of infected women is higher than that for males (see figure 9.1). Prostitution, sexual relations with high-risk

Figure 9.1   Gender and HIV Infection among State Prison Inmates[41]

Year	# of HIV- Positive Males	% of HIV- Positive Males	# of HIV- Positive Females	% of HIV- Positive Females
1991	16,150	2.2	1,159	3.0
1992	18,266	2.6	1,598	4.0
1993	18,218	2.5	1,796	4.2
1994	19,762	2.4	1,953	3.9
1995	21,144	2.3	2,230	4.0
1996	21,299	2.2	1,938	3.1
1997	20,608	2.1	2,258	3.5
1998	22,045	2.2	2,552	3.8
1999	22,175	2.2	2,402	3.5
2000	21,894	2.1	2,472	3.4

males, and IV drug use account for most AIDS/HIV cases in women. The percentages of female inmates who test positive for HIV/AIDS are not the same across the United States. The northeastern states have the highest percentage of female inmates with HIV (10.3%). The southern state prisons have the next highest percentage of inmates (3.8%), with the Midwest and the West reporting lower percentages (1.2% and 1.3%, respectively).[42]

Most jurisdictions base prison policies on the needs of male facilities. This is an inappropriate and ineffective way of handling the health care needs of female inmates; HIV education and prevention programs must address the specific concerns of women.[43] In many cases, however, research designed to help the mainstream society understand and deal with HIV/AIDS has ignored the needs of women. One model program was developed and implemented by the inmates of a New York prison. They approached the inmate population as a community and introduced peer counseling and education. This kind of self-empowerment is popular within the women's movement and with treatment experts. However, it often gets a poor reception from prison staff members who feel that inmates should have no power over their lives. (More detailed attention is given to this issue in chapter 11.) The program was found to decrease the stigma of being HIV positive and helped create group support for infected women. This improved the quality of life for inmates with HIV and for those who were affected by it through friendships and family ties. It also reduced tension within the prison and made life safer for both staff and inmates.[44]

To slow the spread of HIV among women, education must go beyond defining high-risk behaviors and partners. It must directly empower women to control the situations in which they are likely to be at risk of catching the virus. In other words, women must learn to break free of the passive, stereotypical sex role that keeps them from asserting their needs to male partners and associates. This is especially important for poor women, women of color, and older women who have not yet been impacted by the women's movement.[45]

Child Custody Issues

One and a half million American children have an imprisoned parent. This figure grew by 50% in the 1990s, largely due to increased arrests of women for drug charges. Two-thirds of incarcerated women have dependent children while less than half of male inmates acknowledge being a parent. (Male parents are most often violent offenders.) When the father is imprisoned it is most often for a violent crime, and the child usually stays with the mother. When mothers are imprisoned it is usually related to substance abuse, and grandparents or other relatives usually become the children's caregivers. These women are most often African American, over 25 years of age, and single at the time they were incarcerated. Twenty percent were homeless at some time in the year prior to their imprisonment, even though slightly more depended on wages from a job than on welfare payments for their income. Most have not completed high school, but 30% have a GED. Most are nonviolent recidivists with a history of drug abuse.[46] This kind of background, and other predictors of female imprisonment, place their children at high risk for substance abuse, mental illness, and criminality.

Female inmates generally come from families with a history of physical or sexual abuse, violence, and drugs. Their children are at risk for crime whether the mother or some other relative has custody of them. A broad range of services in prisons and the community are required to break this cycle. Unfortunately few such programs exist. This means that the children remain at risk while society misses the opportunity to reduce intergenerational cycles of addiction, abuse, and crime.[47]

Separation from their children is an especially traumatic crisis for female inmates; the desire to have contact with their children can motivate them to work toward positive goals. Most (42%) have weekly contact by phone or mail but personal visits average under one per month, because more than half these women are held in facilities that are over 100 miles from the child's residence. Improving the vocational and social skills of the inmate parent and strengthening the parent–child bond should be of special concern in working with female prisoners.[48] The crisis of separation from one's children can open the door to other types of reform designed to reduce recidivism. However, it is crucial that parenting, family reintegration, and child-care services be available to mothers released from prison if this goal is to be achieved.[49]

In order to minimize the damage done to parent–child bonds by a mother's imprisonment, a few states have programs that allow close contact between imprisoned women and their children. These programs take a two-pronged approach to treatment. First, strengthening a woman's bonds with her family, and especially with her children, provides strong reasons to avoid crime in the future. Second, the development of vocational and social psychological skills that will help the woman rejoin and help support her family are encouraged. Social psychological skills usually focus on assertiveness, self-esteem, and personal development, as well as more traditional areas of treatment like anger management and substance abuse. These skills also make women better able to parent in ways that will break the cycle of abuse and crime.[50]

Issues Confronting Imprisoned Mothers[51]

Discussions of imprisoned mothers must bear in mind that the inmate's welfare is not the only factor under the control of correctional authorities. The fate of the children of these women must also be considered. Most jurisdictions try to place inmates' children with relatives, but one in eight must enter foster care. In some jurisdictions a felony conviction can lead to the termination of a woman's parental rights, but others make an effort to maintain the female inmate's relationship with her children. If handled compassionately, bonds to children may discourage recidivism and encourage a productive use of prison programs and parole services. If handled in the traditional, punishment-oriented manner, the children of today's female inmates may lead tomorrow's crime wave. The most pressing problems faced by inmate mothers include:

1. being placed in facilities far from family members, which reduces the strength of family ties and makes it difficult for mothers to see their children;

2. possible resentment of caregivers at having to surrender custody of the children to the mother upon her release, increasing trauma to both child and mother;

3. lack of child-care and parenting programs;

4. visitation procedures and settings that restrict the number, length, and quality of contacts with family members, especially children;

5. lack of parole assistance with family and child-care problems;

6. lack of coordination and communication between correctional agencies, child protective agencies, and foster-care providers during and after imprisonment.

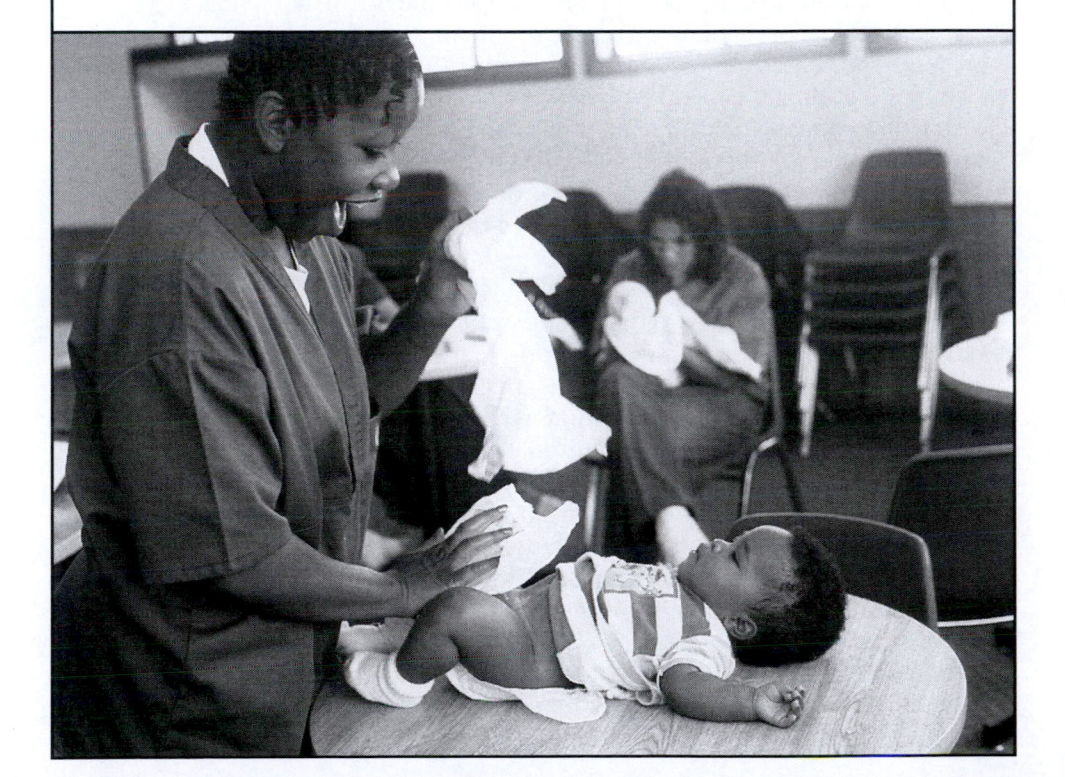

Helping female offenders stay in contact with their children is an area in which community groups and volunteers can make huge contributions. Women in jails often are able to see their children so long as the caregivers will transport them. Prisons, however, are often in rural locations that are very remote from the cities in which the female offender's children live. The relatives taking custody of the children are usually as poor as the offender. They may be elderly parents of the inmate who cannot travel to the prison often enough to assure parent–child bonding. Volunteers willing to transport these children to and from the prison are thus vital, as are organizations willing to collect and donate toys and other items required for child care. The renewal of interest in offenders among charitable and faith-based groups is critical to the success of such programs. A few prisons provide special visiting areas where imprisoned mothers can live with their children for short periods. Where such facilities exist, the furniture, playground equipment, food, and cooking supplies are usually donated as well. Women earn the privilege of having a prolonged visit with their children by cooperating with authorities and working hard at job assignments and treatment programs.[52]

Sexual Harassment and Official Oppression

Wherever females are under the power of men, sexual harassment and exploitation are likely to occur. Sexual harassment is the use of continued and unwanted romantic advances, intimidating behavior, threats, or force to obtain sexual favors of any kind.[53] In general, the lower the status of the woman relative to the men who have power over her, the greater the likelihood of harassment occurring. Thus, harassment of inmates is far more common than harassment of female staff members. The most common context for sexual contact between female inmates and staff is "trading," which involves the women providing a sex act specified by the staff member in exchange for privileges controlled by the facility employee. Sexual contacts ranging from rape to romance are also well documented.[54] Criminal charges against a staff member are also levied in many cases because, under the legal codes of at least 42 states, inmates cannot legally have consensual sexual relations with prison staff.[55] However, the laws protecting female inmates from sexual abuse in 13 states are insufficient by international standards. The federal system and 18 states adhere to these standards only to a limited degree. Thus, only 19 states provide the legal protections for inmates deemed appropriate by internationally recognized human rights standards. Four states allow an inmate to be prosecuted for having sex with a staff member, and Arizona even allows a rape victim to be charged with a crime as a result of being victimized.[56]

Male staff members often offer to use their powers to make life easier for female inmates in exchange for sex or make threats based on force or blackmail. These relations violate the boundary between staff and inmates, exploit the position of the staff member, and threaten facility security. They often result in lawsuits against both the staff members involved and the jurisdiction for failure to properly supervise them. In 1999, at least 22 departments of corrections were responding to litigation based on charges of sexual misconduct by staff. Although only three cases since 1996 received damage awards, departments are beginning to implement policies on officer conduct to prevent future liability.[57]

Ethics on the Line
What Do You Do When Your Training Contradicts the Norms of Your Workplace?

You have recently begun working in a women's prison as your first job after completing college. You know about the special needs of female inmates from your studies, and you know that women respond to the experience of prisonization differently than men do. However, you quickly observe that this information has not been considered in your new place of employment. Virtually everything that occurs is done in a way that contradicts what you know about effective correctional practices for women. What do you do, if anything, and how do you do it?

Questions to Consider

1. What are the ethical conflicts between following the official rules as required by your job and doing things that you understand to be harmful to the inmates by following those rules?

2. As a new employee, how can you introduce needed changes without endangering your livelihood and career? Would it be any easier after you have been an employee of the agency for a while? If so, how do you handle any emotional or moral feelings of guilt that might occur while you wait to take action?

3. Is it your responsibility to try to bring about needed changes in the agency for which you work? If so, why and under what conditions? If not, at what level does such a responsibility become a factor, and how is that responsibility to be recognized and put into action?

When the harassment is entirely private and supervisors cannot be faulted, disciplinary action is, or should be, taken against the involved staff member(s). Many states make it a crime for anyone to use their official position as a government employee to coerce another. Called abuse of authority or official oppression, it is usually punished as a minor felony or serious misdemeanor. Even if no legal action is taken, once discovered, the staff member's career usually ends in disgrace after an investigation shows the activity took place.[58] However, most authorities admit that these investigations are unusual while sexual contact between staff and inmates is fairly common.[59]

Women often note that agencies are reluctant to investigate and prosecute claims of sexual harassment. When no action is taken, harassment often gets worse. Whether the victims are inmates or coworkers, resorting to legal means such as lawsuits is the only realistic option in such cases. The courts are usually able to censure gross instances of harassment but subtler forms are often hard to prosecute successfully. Assuring that women hold a significant number of powerful positions within each agency is one method of reducing sexual harassment.

Co-Correctional Facilities

The increasing number of female prisoners may create renewed interest in female corrections. Issues of fairness, efficiency, and parity plague women's corrections. Co-correctional facilities that house both men and women are one attempt to address these problems. All four branches of the military have such institutions with security levels ranging from maximum to minimum. The Federal Bureau of Prisons has four, all of which are minimum or medium security. The District of Columbia, the territories of Guam and Samoa, and 18 states also maintain co-correctional facilities.[60] At least for the military facilities and those in U.S. territories, the sharing of prison space for male and female inmates is mainly for economic reasons. For example, building a maximum-security prison to house less than 100 women who may need such a level of control would not be economically feasible. Co-correctional facilities offer *economies of scale*, allowing more equality of access to programs to male and female prisoners.

Comparative Views
Woman-Centered Prisons: A Canadian Concept [61]

The Correctional Service of Canada is comparable to the U.S. Bureau of Prisons. Its single prison for women has been under attack by critics since it opened in 1934. A number of task forces and commissions have recommended that this prison be closed and replaced with smaller, regional facilities. Criticisms of the prison for women have focused on the same problems that are found in facilities for women in the United States: sexism in prison planning and practices, lack of programs, too much emphasis on security, distance from families, and insensitivity to the needs of various ethnic groups.

This series of attacks has led to planning what is called a "woman-centered prison." Such a facility would bring what is known about women's problems, needs, and behavior into a cohesive form that could be applied in a correctional setting. A woman-centered prison would be characterized by five principles.

1. *Empowerment* should address (a) the structural inequalities that put women at an economic, political, and social disadvantage in the larger society and (b) the low self-esteem of women that makes it hard for them to direct their own lives and make responsible, rewarding choices for themselves.

2. *Meaningful choices* should allow women to define their needs on the basis of their personal background, select programs on this basis, and learn to take power and responsibility in their daily activities.

3. *Respect and dignity* among inmates, and between inmates and staff members, should replace the current practices that encourage inmates to be passive and servile.

4. *A supportive environment* should be created that encourages inmates to practice empowerment, make choices for themselves, and learn to respect themselves and others.

5. *Shared responsibility* means that inmates, officials, and the larger society recognize that their contributions to crime and the reform of criminals are interrelated; thus solutions to crime must involve the cooperation of offenders, the government, and ordinary citizens.

The woman-centered prison is not yet a reality in Canada. Opposition to this idea focuses on the perceived loss of punishment if these changes were implemented; prisons would be more humane and less painful to live in. This debate is the central obstacle to address behavior that led to crime in order to prevent its reoccurrence. The requirements of behavior change cannot be met in an environment designed to inflict pain on inmates. Confinement is, in itself, painful. Policymakers and voters must decide whether the economy of reform or the feelings of social solidarity and moral superiority that result from punishing others will guide prison practices in the twenty-first century.

Policy Matters!
Gender, Stereotypes, and Correctional Efficiency

Women's corrections has been guided largely by the stereotypical images of women that have dominated society over the last five hundred years. Stereotypes still have much to do with how women are treated and the kinds of programs they are offered in jails and prisons. The women held in modern institutions are those least affected by the women's movement, but many within that movement argue that they are the most victimized by gender stereotypes and discrimination. There is a growing body of research that urges corrections to encourage female inmates to abandon stereotypical behaviors and roles. This feminist perspective encourages assertiveness, self-sufficiency, and pride among female offenders. It often results in a call for training female offenders in nontraditional jobs such as electronics and construction and the use of very different programs for women. Unfortunately, correctional authorities often find it hard to deal with assertive inmates. Their traditional view argues that passivity is to be encouraged in all offenders; the loss of freedom to choose one's own lifestyle and activities is part of the punishment for crime. How should we use the research on gender differences to reform women's prisons?

Questions to Consider

1. How do gender stereotypes influence policy decisions about female offenders? What are the costs of these stereotypes to society? To female offenders? To correctional agencies?

2. What effects would nontraditional vocational training have on female inmates? How might this affect the facilities that hold them? How will it affect their return to society?

3. Is it ethical to use prisons to encourage social changes such as those advocated by feminism? What is the proper role of research data in setting correctional priorities? What role should feminist and traditional ideologies have in these decisions? Why?

There are relatively few such facilities, and their effects on inmate behavior are not yet well understood. Of the co-correctional facilities now in operation, the most successful: (1) have relatively equal numbers of men and women; (2) house only nonviolent prisoners with less than two years left in their sentence; (3) provide furloughs or family visitations in the community; and (4) have strict policies for transferring inmates to single-sex institutions as a penalty for improper behavior.[62] Housing women in the same facility seems to encourage the men to behave less harshly towards one another and staff.[63] However, research suggests that these prisons benefit male but not female inmates.[64]

SUMMARY

Female crime and women's prisons are among the most neglected areas of penology. The treatment of female offenders by justice agencies varies with society's beliefs about women in a particular region and time period. Women have historically been ignored and abused by correctional systems that have stressed the traditional passivity of the female sex role. Nonetheless, many prison reforms began in women's reformatories because their inmates were not as dangerous as males, freeing administrators from security concerns and allowing experimentation with alternatives to standard approaches to prisoners.

Incarcerated women are often referred to as the "forgotten offenders" because they are few in overall numbers; are less troublesome than men; are not seen as dangerous by judges, policymakers, or the public; and rarely have the same number or quality of programs that are found in male facilities. For some, the low levels of violence in women's prisons justifies the neglect of female prisoners. However, it can just as easily be argued that women should receive more correctional resources because they are less likely to recidivate than men. Despite the ease with which they are usually controlled, women are more often and more harshly disciplined than men. Sexual stereotypes predict how rules are interpreted and applied in female prisons.

The goals of treatment programs may be the same for both sexes, but the style with which they are conducted should be different. Programs for women need to assure that they can provide for themselves and their families when they are released. They should also take into account the fact that women learn better in relaxed, cooperative situations. Many will be less crime-prone if they develop the skills required to take power over their own lives.

Women have many unique health concerns, such as pregnancy and childbirth, sexually transmitted diseases, domestic violence, menopause, and osteoporosis, which must be addressed by prisons and jails. Many female prisoners are also mothers. The stress of worrying about their children's welfare and the crisis of being separated from them create an additional hardship on female inmates. The ability of female offenders to stay in contact with their children is largely determined by the contributions of charitable groups and volunteers. The incentive to return to their children encourages reform.

Wherever females are under the power of men, there is danger of sexual harassment. The lower the status of the woman, the greater the likelihood of harassment. Harassment can lead to criminal charges against the staff member and to civil law suits against the staff member and/or agency. Public punishment of offenders and assuring that women hold a significant number of positions of power within each agency seem the best ways of reducing harassment.

Co-correctional facilities can achieve great economies of scale and allow more equitable access to programs for male and female prisoners. It appears that housing women close to men encourages the men to behave less harshly toward one another and staff. There are relatively few such facilities, however, and their effects on inmate behavior are not yet well understood.

QUESTIONS FOR DISCUSSION AND REVIEW

1. To what extent are women represented in the data on arrests and imprisonment? In what sorts of crimes are women most often involved?

2. What aspects of female crime and its processing by the system have changed in the last 30 years? How can these changes best be explained?

3. Why are women described as the "forgotten offenders"? What arguments have been used to justify their neglect? Given the impact of women on the development of corrections, how else could the facts used to justify the neglect of women be interpreted?

4. How are women's prisons different from those holding males? What types of informal social organization would you expect to find in a women's prison? Into what roles would the women be likely to fall?

5. What special health care issues must be dealt with by jails and prisons holding women?

6. What special concerns do female prisoners have with regard to their children? How might these concerns best be handled by correctional authorities?

7. How is sexual harassment different from sex discrimination? What abuses of women are most common in correctional facilities? What can be done to stop them?

8. What is a co-correctional facility? What are the benefits of such facilities? To the jurisdiction? To the prisoners? To staff members?

9. In general, how are the needs of women different from those of men? What aspects of society must be accounted for in correctional programming for women? Why?

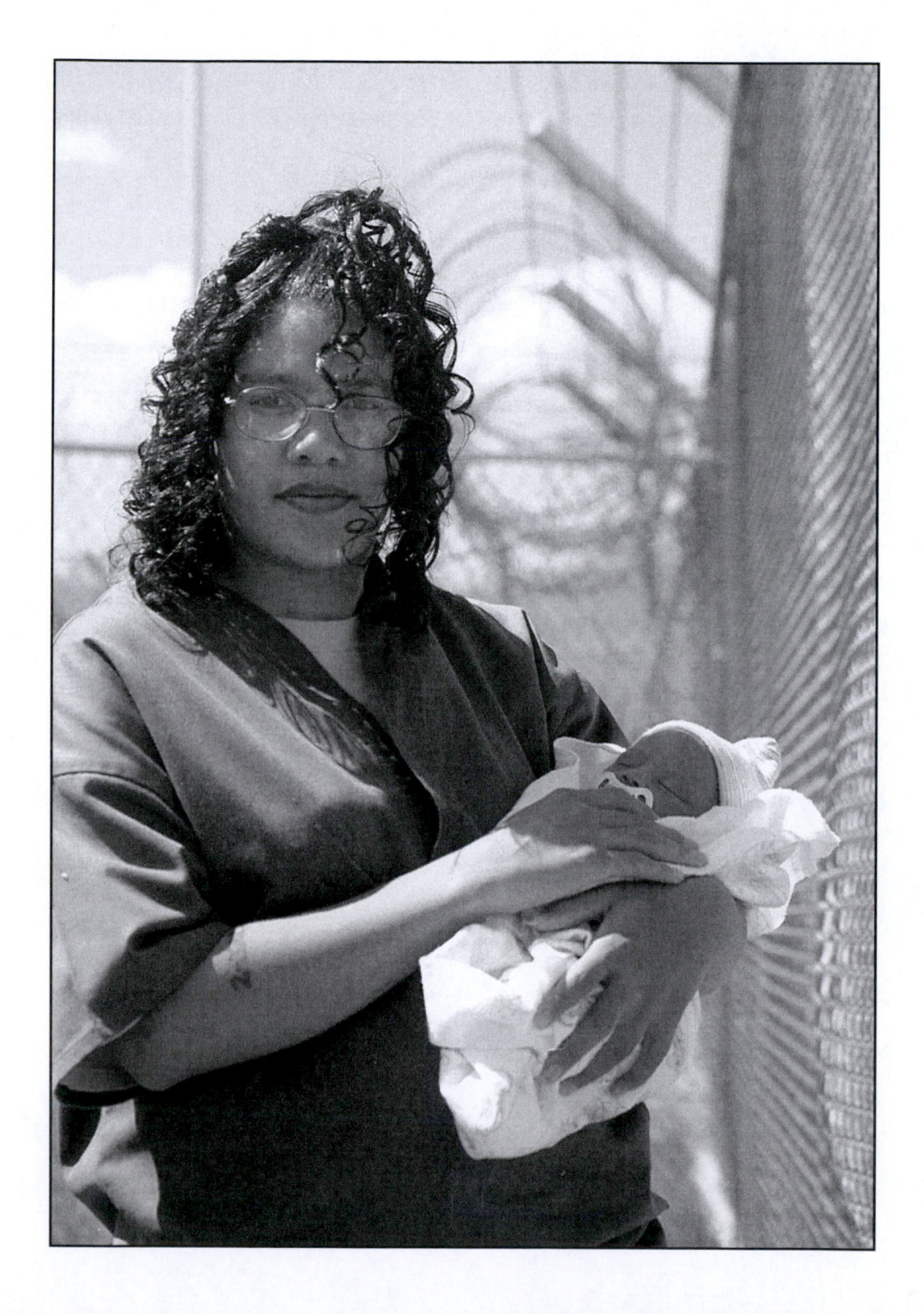

The Legal Rights of Offenders

The courts are responsible for protecting all of the rights and enforcing all the legal duties described in the Constitution and various legal codes. This is a very complicated responsibility, especially as it relates to the rights of prisoners. It is particularly vital because (1) offenders face loss of their liberty, and (2) inmates have little control over their lives once we imprison them.

As defined in chapter 2 the rights-versus-privilege doctrine maintains that "rights" require constitutional protection but "privileges" may be granted or withdrawn at the discretion of the institution. The line between rights and privileges varies with popular definitions of justice and other factors. Until the 1960s the courts observed a hands-off doctrine and did not interfere in prison matters for a variety of reasons.[1] In *Ruffin v. Commonwealth* (1871) Virginia's Supreme Court ruled that inmates were "slaves of the state" whose liberty and personal rights had been lost due to their conviction for a crime. This attitude toward prisons and their inmates was typical of the courts until the late 1960s.[2]

Inmate Access to the Courts

In 1941 the Supreme Court ruled that prisons could not require inmates to submit their court petitions to staff, who could censor them if they were not "properly drawn." *Ex Parte Hull* found this policy to be an unconstitutional denial of the right to access the courts.[3] This decision was never enforced, however. In 1969, *Johnson v. Avery* provided additional support for inmate lawsuits by making it illegal to prohibit inmates from helping one another in preparing legal documents. This decision allowed governments to limit, but not ban, the activities of "jailhouse lawyers" (inmates with legal knowledge who lack a law degree). Bans on jailhouse lawyers are legal only when the state provides a reasonable alternative, such as contract attorneys, for inmates.[4]

Prisoners now use a variety of legal tools to enforce their constitutional rights. Prominent among these are writs of *habeas corpus* and suits based on Section 1983 of the Civil Rights Act of 1871.[5] The courts interpreted *habeas corpus* as one of several ways of asking a federal court to review possible constitutional violations in state facilities. Section 1983 was enacted to protect former slaves from civil rights abuses committed by Klan members who were also government officials. It had not been applied to inmate rights until *Monroe v. Pape* (1961) when the Supreme Court ruled that cases involving constitutional rights could be taken directly to federal courts. This encouraged inmates to file suits because federal courts were felt to be more sympathetic than state courts. The decision to bypass state courts in this process is left to the person bringing the suit.[6] The rights most commonly at issue in corrections are those protected by the First, Fourth, Eighth, and Fourteenth Amendments.

Inmates' rights were extended by the 1977 *Bounds v. Smith* ruling, which forced states to provide assistance to inmates in preparing legal documents. This decision required states to provide "adequate" law libraries for the use of inmates. The details of how this was to be accomplished was left to the individual facilities. A federal district court expanded *Bounds* when it ruled that Arizona had to provide inmates under lockdown access to the law library and provide special help for the

The courts are responsible for protecting the rights of offenders who have little control over their lives once they are imprisoned. The line between rights and privileges varies depending on the current definition of justice.

illiterate and non-English speakers.[7] Many prisons and jails felt that this interpretation of *Bounds* meant that they must create and maintain fully staffed law libraries or provide legal experts to assist inmates in all kinds of legal matters. However, this ruling was reversed in 1996 by a Supreme Court decision that severely limited the legal rights of inmates.

Lewis v. Casey (1996) found that the lower court had exceeded its authority in a "wildly intrusive manner." The Supreme Court ruled that lockdown prisoners could be delayed in accessing the library for security reasons. The *Lewis* decision was based on the idea that inmates must show actual or threatened harm before suing over access to legal assistance. The Court added that *Bounds* requires officials to allow inmates access to the courts but does not give them a right to a law library or any other specific type of legal assistance.[8] *Lewis* is just one of many recent court decisions that limit inmate rights to access the courts. In *O'Sullivan v. Boerckel* (1999), the Supreme Court held that state inmates must bring all issues relating to their case before state courts before addressing them in the federal system.[9] Despite the narrowing of inmates' rights in recent years, some of the cases decided during the due process revolution require mention to show the kinds of conditions that led the courts to become involved in corrections.

The Growth of Court Intervention in U.S. Prison Administration

The 1971 case of *Holt v. Sarver* was the first time a court took control over the correctional conditions and practices of an entire state. This federal appellate ruling found the entire Arkansas prison system to be in violation of the Eighth Amendment ban on cruel and unusual punishment. Inmate trustees guarded other prisoners and abused their powers by allowing rapes and running various rackets. Sanitary conditions were terrible, and there were no opportunities for rehabilitation.[10] Similarly, in Alabama, prisoners provided medical care to other inmates and were responsible for all medical records; wounds became maggot infested, and some inmates died as a result. Dormitory design encouraged violence by creating areas that were hard to monitor, and racial segregation was a matter of policy despite the 1964 Civil Rights Act.[11]

Pugh v. Locke (1976) strengthened and clarified early rulings by making the "totality of conditions," rather than any one aspect of the prison, the central issue in Eighth Amendment cases.[12] Two years later, in *Hutto v. Finney*, the Supreme Court proposed three guidelines for these cases that still guide U.S. courts:

1. the totality of conditions in a prison must be examined to determine if the Eighth Amendment had been violated;

2. each factor that contributed to cruel and unusual punishment must be listed along with the steps required to bring the situation into conformity with the Constitution; and

3. the minimum standards to be met by the prison should be specified by the court.[13]

As the hands-on era began, there were no precedents to guide the courts in deciding which correctional practices were illegal. As cases made their way through the courts, guidelines for the operation of all forms of corrections began to develop. The *Ruiz* decision was particularly pivotal in justifying federal court takeovers of state prison systems.

Ruiz v. Estelle (1980) was a Texas case in which a Federal District court defined overcrowding as a violation of the Eighth Amendment.[14] The court all but took over the management of Texas' prisons for more than twelve years in order to remedy a series of constitutional violations related mainly to overcrowding. *Ruiz* set the precedent for courts to take similarly drastic steps in nearly three-fourths of the states. This decision ended the practice of giving some inmates power over others, which had been common throughout the South despite being condemned by virtually all U.S. courts and correctional associations. The costs of these reforms were not as far-reaching as many imagine. A ten-state study of spending changes during this era showed that judicial decisions affected prison construction costs in only half the states examined. Operating expenses were not significantly affected in any state. The financial costs of these changes were kept to a minimum by changes in how states used available funds and the willingness of the courts to take a comprehensive view of prison reforms.[15]

Although the volume of cases filed in state and federal courts increased dramatically during this period, only a few basic issues had been settled by the late 1970s. Then the Supreme Court started to slow the pace of change in correctional law and granted more freedom to correctional administrators.[16] *Bell v. Wolfish* (1979) marked the beginning of the "one-hand-on, one-hand-off era." Inmates at a federal detention center used the Fifth Amendment to sue over restrictions on receiving books, the widespread use of strip searches, and double celling (placing two inmates in a cell built for one). A federal district court found these conditions violated the due process clause of the Fifth Amendment. Much of that decision was upheld by a federal court of appeals, but the Supreme Court later rejected these rulings. It established a standard that supported restrictions that serve a legitimate government purpose; only practices intended to punish the confined were banned. This gave prison officials wide latitude in setting policies and alerted lower courts to the Supreme Court's growing reluctance to extend the rights of prisoners.[17]

Two years later, *Rhodes v. Chapman* applied similar principles to prison inmates in a suit brought by maximum-security prisoners in Ohio.[18] Unlike *Bell*, *Rhodes* was based on the Eighth Amendment prohibition of cruel and unusual punishment. Again, the lower courts ruled double celling to be illegal, but the Supreme Court disagreed. In *Rhodes* the Supreme Court found that conditions violated the Eighth Amendment only if they (1) inflicted unnecessary or wanton pain or (2) were grossly disproportionate to the severity of the crimes warranting imprisonment. The Supreme Court also told lower courts not to interfere in prison affairs unless conditions were deplorable. The *Wolfish* and *Rhodes* decisions required only that policies be based on legitimate security or treatment concerns.[19] Despite the clear pattern of decisions favoring administrators, the Supreme Court still guards the right of inmates to have full access to judicial review of their complaints.[20] In this way, the individual rights defined in the Constitution and other laws are still protected by the courts. Inmates are no longer slaves of the state, and most of their rights are based on four amendments.

The Constitutional Bases of Prisoners' Rights

The Constitution says very little about crime and even less about corrections. However, the freedoms that make this nation unique are spelled out in the Bill of Rights and the Fourteenth Amendment to the Constitution. The First, Fourth, Eighth, and Fourteenth Amendments are the most critical to the case law on corrections. Combined with these legal rights is the preservation of "basic human dignity" and the ban of conditions that would shock the nation's conscience.

The First Amendment to the U.S. Constitution
Congress shall make no law respecting an establishment of religion, or prohibiting the free exercise thereof, or abridging the freedom of speech, or of the press; or the right of the people peaceably to assemble, and to petition the government for a redress of grievances.

The Fourth Amendment to the U.S. Constitution
The right of the people to be secure in their persons, houses, papers, and effects, against unreasonable searches and seizures, shall not be violated, and no warrants shall issue, but upon probable cause, supported by oath or affirmation, and particularly describing the place to be searched, and the persons or things to be seized.

The Eighth Amendment to the U.S. Constitution
Excessive bail shall not be required, nor excessive fines imposed, nor cruel and unusual punishment inflicted.

The Fourteenth Amendment to the U.S. Constitution
All persons born or naturalized in the United States, and subject to the jurisdiction thereof, are citizens of the United States and of the state wherein they reside. No state shall make or enforce any law which shall abridge the privileges or immunities of citizens of the United States; nor shall any state deprive any person of life, liberty, or property without *due process* of law; nor deny any person within its jurisdiction the *equal protection* of the law. (Italics added.)

FIRST AMENDMENT RIGHTS

The First Amendment protects freedom of speech, access to the press, and the ability to hold and practice one's religious beliefs. It is the basis of our right to assemble and to seek relief from wrongful acts by all levels of government. First Amendment rights can be restricted for free citizens only if there is a "clear and present danger" to government responsibilities. A *prior restraint* is an official attempt to prevent the exercise of a freedom before it has been acted upon. The courts prefer that government take action only *after* these rights have been exercised rather than imposing prior restraints. For example, it is better to allow a newspaper to print a story and then sue over its content than to forbid the printing of certain types of stories. Basic constitutional rights may be limited if they interfere with the state's need to operate a correctional facility safely. Inmates thus lose many of their liberties and people under community supervision lose some, especially if they have been convicted of a felony.[21]

Freedom of Religion

The first major case based on prisoners' freedom of religion was *Cooper v. Pate* (1964), in which the Court overturned a prison rule forbidding inmates to receive religious literature. This was the first use of Section 1983 of the Civil Rights Act of 1871 to sue prison officials. It ended the "slave of the state" attitude toward inmates and placed their religious freedoms under constitutional protection. It also ended the institution's complete control, and an explosion of litigation followed.[22]

It was *Cruz v. Beto*, decided in 1972, that truly established religious liberties for inmates. Texas officials had prohibited Cruz from communicating with other Buddhists and punished him for sharing magazines about his faith with other inmates. The Supreme Court ruled that inmates with unconventional religious beliefs could not be subjected to discrimination and had all the rights possessed by prisoners of any other faith.[23]

The Court has, however, limited the degree to which religious freedoms can be used to affect prison policies. *O'Lone v. Estate of Shabazz* (1987) was brought by Muslims who felt that prison schedules interfered with their ability to attend services at particular times. The Court ruled the prison's schedules to be legal because they were based on "legitimate penological interests" and acquiescing to the prisoners' demands could pose a security threat.[24]

The freedom to *practice* religion is a separate issue from the freedom to hold particular religious and spiritual beliefs. The courts have long held that government discrimination against any religious group or belief is unconstitutional.

Comparative Views
Native American Religion in Canadian Prisons[25]

Most Canadian prisons have "Native awareness programs" in which tribal elders enter prisons as contract employees to perform religious rituals; counsel inmates; and educate them in the beliefs, history, and language of their culture. Prisons often permit indigenous inmates to build "sweat lodges," hold ceremonies, and fast under the guidance of elders. The rehabilitative potential of these activities has been noted by the Solicitor General (the Canadian equivalent of the U.S. Attorney General). Despite the extension of religious freedoms, elders do not enjoy the same privileges as clergy from European religions. For example, medicine bags and ceremonial pipes are often searched by guards while the sacred equipment of priests is untouched.

Several aspects of aboriginal religion have beneficial effects on native prisoners. Sweat-lodge experiences bring peace of mind and increased self-control to inmates, and traditional "healing" practices are better equipped than "scientific treatment" to deal with mental health issues that are unique to native inmates. For example, only elders can provide religious protections against "bad medicine" that many aboriginal prisoners feel afflicts them. Also, dreams are a source of important messages from native spiritual powers and can be interpreted only with the aid of an elder. Elders can help with the identity problems of aboriginal prisoners caused by racism by relating to the feelings and needs of the aboriginal inmates.

The effects of the elders on the prison behavior of aboriginal Canadian inmates seem to be entirely positive, and some native Canadians leave prison better equipped to avoid crime as a result of these religious activities. A recent survey of U.S. prisoners showed that about a third of female inmates classified themselves as partly Native American, and most had positive feelings about that identity. The Canadian experience with the rehabilitative potential of programs based on identification with strong cultural beliefs offers a potential model for similar programs in the United States.

Inmates are thus free to believe whatever they choose; Muslims, Jews, Baptists, and even Satanists share this right equally. How a "religious group" is defined is of critical concern, however. In most cases, the courts use four criteria to determine the legitimacy of a particular group. First, the sincerity of the believers must be judged according to their recent behavior. Past crimes cannot be used as evidence that a person's current religious beliefs are insincere, but recent conduct can be used to justify restrictions on religious practices. Second, the group's belief and practices should be reasonably similar to those of other major religious groups. Third, the longer a particular group has operated as a religion, the stronger its case. Thus, Islamic and Jewish groups that can point to origins in ancient traditions have an advantage over newly invented creeds such as those used by white supremacists. Finally, the costs that would result from allowing the group to have the freedoms it seeks must be taken into account before the courts will force a prison to honor a religious demand.[26]

A practice, omission, or act may not be protected by the First Amendment, even if it is part of a legitimate religious belief system, if it: (1) threatens the security or discipline of the facility, (2) interferes with the legal discretionary powers of institutional authorities, (3) contradicts a reasonable facility rule, or (4) poses an excessive financial burden on the facility or jurisdiction. The application of these principles to specific situations must be addressed by attorneys and administrators empowered to make policy decisions.[27]

In some correctional institutions, inmates who do not pose a security threat are permitted to hold religious services.

While religious practices can be limited for a variety of reasons, beliefs may not be restricted nor may they serve as the basis for discriminatory treatment. Behaviors are always subject to sanction by authorities. Special clothing can be restricted if there are legitimate reasons for doing so. Access to services may also be limited so long as other methods of expressing religious beliefs are available and the restriction serves a legitimate government purpose.[28]

Diet is often a matter of religion, and many facilities provide pork-free meals for Jewish and Islamic inmates. However, especially complex dietary rules, such as those followed by some Rastafarians, could create serious difficulties for prison officials. Some Rastafarian sects forbid eating canned foods or those that have been cooked in metal pots. The complexity of these rules, and the large number of different Rastafarian sects with different beliefs, led the courts to support official refusals to accommodate these diets.[29] Personal appearance norms may also be guided by religious beliefs. Native Americans, for example, obtained the right to keep their hair long in *Gallahan v. Hollyfield* (1982), but headgear may be banned if there is a strong need to do so.[30]

Freedom of Speech

Certain forms of speech can be restricted in virtually all settings; threats, obscenity, and criminal conspiracies are almost always illegal. So are statements that could reasonably be expected to cause unnecessary panic, destruction, or danger. Yelling "fire" in a crowded building when no such danger exists is a classic example of such an act. Noisy speech at inappropriate times without good reason can also be forbidden and punished. False statements that cause harm to others are known as *libel* and are punishable under civil law. Freedom of speech is most ardently protected when political or religious beliefs are involved. Most inmate suits designed to assure free speech concern the right to correspond with others or to receive books or other reading materials.

Prisoner Mail

The regulation of prisoner mail offers another example of the limited rights granted inmates by the courts. In *Procunier v. Martinez* (1974), the Supreme Court ruled that mail could be censored if a "legitimate government interest" was threatened. Mail to people in the free world is given more freedom than that between convicts but can nonetheless be inspected by officials. Complaints or "disrespectful comments" about officials and radical political ideas do not justify censorship unless they are likely to encourage some sort of crime. Inmates possess only "those First Amendment rights that are not inconsistent with (a person's) status as a prisoner" according to this decision.[31]

Prisons and jails routinely examine all items mailed to and by inmates to assure that contraband or escape plans are not being transmitted. Outgoing mail is under less restriction than that sent to prisoners because it poses less of a security threat. The amount of mail received by an inmate in a given period of time can also be limited for reasons of cost and space. Prisons may forbid inmates to correspond with relatives who are imprisoned in other facilities and can refuse to accept books unless they are mailed by the publisher. Security concerns form the basis of these restrictions.[32]

Rehabilitative goals can be used to restrict privileges like correspondence. If any part of a publication poses a threat to security or treatment, the entire publication can be prohibited.[33] For example, all prisons and jails ban mailings from groups that promote adult–child sexual relations.[34] Whenever a package or letter is rejected by officials, both the sender and the intended receiver must be notified and given the chance to protest the rejection.[35]

In *Turner v. Safley* (1987), the court ruled that inmates do not have the right to correspond with, or marry, prisoners in other institutions. The most significant aspect of this case was the four-part "reasonableness test" that resulted from it. This test guides officials and courts in deciding whether "legitimate penological interests" allow interference with constitutional rights. *Turner* is thus much broader than merely allowing regulation of mail. A rule is reasonable if:

1. it has a valid connection with the government interests by which it was justified;

2. there is an alternative method by which inmates can exercise the right in question;

3. exercise of the right has significant effects on prison resources, staff, or inmates; and

4. there are no alternative methods to obtain the result desired by those who created the rule.[36]

Use of this test in *Thornburgh v. Abbott* (1989) resulted in the Supreme Court upholding a ban on publications that were felt to threaten discipline and order by the Federal Bureau of Prisons.[37]

Only one type of mail is exempt from official censorship. **Legal mail** is any correspondence with an attorney, court, or government official. In most cases correctional officials may not read or interfere with the delivery of legal mail. Officials may, however, open and inspect such mail without reading it. Legal mail that appears to contain contraband or be written in a secret code may be seized by officials. These procedures allow officials to protect the interests of the facility without violating the confidentiality of attorney–client communications. However, correspondence between inmates, even if it deals with legal matters, is not protected under *Turner* or *Procunier* because such protection would interfere with the legitimate institutional concerns shielded by *Turner*.[38] At the height of the hands-on period mail from the media had similar protection, but later rulings reassigned media mail to the status of nonlegal correspondence. The Supreme Court, however, has not yet ruled conclusively on this issue.[39]

Freedom of the Press

Freedom to publish is vital to the protection of political freedom, and inmates have a right to publish anything that does not threaten prison security or other government interests. Political statements cannot usually be censored unless they are likely to incite violence. However, because government interests include treatment and crime prevention, inmates can be forbidden to write or read about many subjects. This includes, but is not limited to, sexually explicit or extremely violent writings and pictures. Further, there has never been a constitutional right to profit from crime, and this includes the ability to collect royalties from the sales of articles and books. Some offenders have the right to tell their story to the public, but many states have laws that allow seizure of profits from books written by offenders about their crimes. These profits may go into the jurisdiction's general treasury or be devoted to special victims' funds.

The Right to Assemble

In the 1970s many prisoners tried to form "unions" to lobby for better treatment and other changes in correctional practices. These unions sued for the right to hold meetings and distribute literature, but the courts permitted officials to deny these demands if the denial was based on legitimate concerns. Many jurisdictions place such groups under the same restrictions as prison-sponsored groups like Alcoholics Anonymous; others have completely banned them. According to *Jones v. North Carolina Prisoners Labor Union* (1977) officials need only to show that there is a rational basis for believing that rules restricting inmate meetings contribute to the security of the prison. They need not show that unions have created a security threat. Most prison rules have such a rational basis, and it is very hard for inmates to form unions.[40]

Ethics on the Line
Privileged Communications and Overheard Conversations

You are the sergeant supervising the visiting area of a minimum-security prison. Weekday visits are usually from attorneys, while most weekend visitors are family members. Attorneys always have the privilege of visiting in "contact rooms" to assure privacy. An inmate held on drug trafficking charges is well known for filing suits and has won several minor victories against the prison system. His brother-in-law is an attorney who provides him with advice. One day an officer under your supervision reports that he overheard the attorney brother-in-law mention details of bank transactions as he left the contact room. These statements suggest that the inmate and his brother-in-law are involved in an illegal money-laundering scheme.

Questions to Consider

1. Both you and the officer making the report know that all attorney-client communications are privileged. Should the guard be disciplined for repeating what he overheard? Does the fact that the attorney was careless enough to be overheard affect your thinking?

2. This conversation seems to have had nothing to do with the inmate's legal case. Indeed, it appears that he and his attorney are engaged in a criminal conspiracy. How should this affect the communication privileges involved in the situation?

3. How would you respond if you were told that legal ethics and case law protect even communication about such a conspiracy because these men have a legitimate attorney–client relationship?

FOURTH AMENDMENT RIGHTS

The Fourth Amendment forbids unreasonable searches of homes, bodies, and property. In all situations involving searches, the courts balance the need for the search against the loss of privacy that results from it. This **balancing test** is used to determine who can be searched, how far the searchers can go, and how the search should be conducted. The need for the search must be stronger than the person's expectation of privacy in a particular situation. Expectations of privacy are very limited in a correctional facility and so are the Fourth Amendment rights of prisoners.[41] In fact, someone walking on a public road has a greater expectation of, and therefore right to, privacy than do prisoners, staff, and visitors to correctional facilities.[42]

Reasonableness of a Search

In free society, brief "frisks" and searches with metal detectors require only reasonable suspicion of wrongdoing. **Reasonable suspicion** consists of specific grounds that can be clearly articulated and lead an officer to believe criminal activity may be occurring. Reasonable suspicion can be based on specific information and training possessed by the officer.[43]

Correctional officials, however, do not need any such basis to conduct routine searches of cells or inmates.[44] Only when a prisoner is singled out for special treatment is there a need to justify the search, and this need for justification is based on the inmate's "equal justice" rights, not on the Fourth Amendment right to privacy. Searches of this type must be based on trustworthy information about a specific inmate. Even invasive procedures like strip searches are legal if they are routine for all prisoners in a specific category. Searches are routine for those entering a facility

---

Determining the Reasonableness of a Search[45]

The courts use the following criteria to decide if a search is justified by governmental needs.

1. The *level of privacy a "reasonable" person expects* in a particular setting. Homes are more private than cars and receive more protection from the Fourth Amendment.

2. The *level of justification or cause for the search*. Searches based on "probable cause" have more freedom than those based on routines or reasonable suspicion. The item being searched for is also a factor; more liberty can be taken when looking for a gun than for pornography. Officials' experience and knowledge can always be used to justify security routines.

3. The *location in which the search is conducted*. Nonemergency searches should respect the dignity of the person being searched and avoid embarrassing that person.

4. The *manner in which the search is conducted*. Searchers must act in a professional manner that does not degrade the inmate or unnecessarily destroy private property.

5. The *routine nature of the search*. Inmates with a high-level security classification can be routinely strip searched after contact visits, even with lawyers and clergy, because there is a reasonable suspicion that they might receive contraband during such visits. If only certain inmates are singled out for searches, each search must be individually justified.

for the first time, those returning from a furlough or outside work detail, and those who have had a contact visit with an outsider. In most states, body-cavity searches are controlled by state or agency regulations that may require that they be performed only by medically qualified personnel. Like all searches, they should always be conducted in a highly professional manner.

Prison cells have no "reasonable" expectation of privacy, and inmates need not be present when they are searched. However, officers may not unnecessarily damage property or leave cells in a mess.[46] Even though the reason for a search is legal, it is unconstitutional if performed in a manner intended to harass the inmate.[47] No legitimate government interest is served by using searches to harass inmates.[48] Frisks and pat-down searches are always permitted in jails and prisons, unless particular inmates are specifically targeted without good reason. Likewise, urine testing is almost always permitted.

Persons under community supervision have fewer rights to privacy than an ordinary citizen because they have been convicted and are under government supervision. In *Griffin v. Wisconsin* (1987) the Court ruled that the homes, cars, and bodies of probationers are subject to search if there is a reasonable suspicion that dangerous or illegal items will be found. No warrant is needed, and the "probable cause" standard used by police does not apply in these cases. Agency policy, however, must make explicit provisions for such searches.[49] *Pennsylvania v. Scott* (1998) extended these powers even further when the Court ruled that the exclusionary rule could not be used to declare evidence inadmissible in parole revocation hearings.[50] This principle was even further enlarged in 2001, when the Court ruled that police could search a probationer's home if "reasonable suspicion" existed that evidence of a crime would be found.[51]

Special Needs Beyond Law Enforcement Exception

The rights of prison parolees may be restricted more than those of probationers because parole defines the offender's home as an extension of a prison cell. The agencies supervising these offenders have a "special need" to search that is supported by the courts. (Other examples of special need include searches of elementary and high school students on school grounds or people and baggage at airports.) The *special needs beyond law enforcement exception* to the Fourth Amendment permits these kinds of searches without a warrant or probable cause if authorized by state laws governing the community supervision of offenders. Some states forbid such searches because they might detract from the treatment goals of community supervision and their probation/parole officers are not adequately trained in search procedures. Some mention of the officer's right to search a probationer or parolee's home, car, and person must be made in the conditions of probation or parole to justify such a search.[52] Police also may search the homes of probationers if reasonable suspicion exists that evidence of a crime will be found. The Court's reasoning in these cases is based on the fact that probation follows conviction for a crime and is designed, in part, to facilitate the preservation of public safety.[53]

EIGHTH AMENDMENT RIGHTS

Although the Eighth Amendment ban on "cruel and unusual punishment" is one of the most vague phrases in the Constitution, it is also the most directly relevant to corrections. For example, at the beginning of 2003, the Supreme Court is considering the constitutional rights of prisoners: does restricting certain visits violate the Eighth Amendment's ban on "cruel and unusual punishment"? The Court will decide whether Michigan prison authorities can ban some visits deemed as problematic and whether they can prevent some inmates from visiting with anyone other than lawyers or clergy.[54] Four criteria have developed to guide legal decisions on Eighth Amendment issues. Illegal conditions and practices are those that:

1. shock the conscience of the court and/or violate civilized standards of decency;[55]

2. inflict unnecessary pain in a wanton manner;

3. are grossly disproportionate to the offender's crime;[56] or

4. indicate deliberate apathy to the basic human needs of the inmate.[57]

The final criterion is usually applied to situations involving safety and medical care. The second criterion, "wanton and unnecessary infliction of pain," is the central issue in recent decisions on use of force and conditions of confinement.[58]

Cases involving "conditions of confinement" deal with crowding, food, clothing, safety, sanitation, and shelter. Jails and prisons must provide for the safety and survival of their inmates. They must also provide "reasonable" protection from weather, staff abuses, other inmates, suicide, disease, and accidental injury. For example, the courts usually require a minimum of three to five hours of exercise outside the cell per week. This standard applies to disciplinary segregation units, death row inmates, and the general population. Failure to provide adequate facilities for inmates must be fairly extreme before the courts will act, but deliberately ignoring such conditions can be costly.[59] Deplorable conditions have resulted in federal "takeovers" of entire state prison systems. Fines or damage awards are also possible in extreme cases.[60]

The Obligation to Protect

The duty to protect inmates from one another is an extremely serious one that begins the moment a suspect is arrested and continues until he or she is released from physical custody. This responsibility covers both the general conditions of the facility and threats against particular inmates. Architecture and procedures that encourage or unnecessarily permit violence are illegal. New inmates are usually asked if they fear harm from anyone within the facility. If they claim that they do, special housing arrangements should be made to insure their safety. However, the Supreme Court has ruled that constitutional rights are violated only when negligence, callousness, or recklessness on the part of staff leads to an injury. In *Smith v. Wade* (1983), a youth who had requested special protection after being a victim of violence was placed in a cell with a prisoner known to be violent. After being tortured and sexually assaulted, the youth sued under the Eighth Amendment and

Section 1983 of the Civil Rights Act. The Court ruled that the suit was valid and that the guard could be held liable for monetary damages.[61] Subsequent decisions have established that officials need not act on general fears; the obligation to protect is present only when the inmate presents specific information regarding the alleged threat to safety.[62]

To win a Section 1983 lawsuit, an inmate must show that the injuries resulted from an intentional act of a staff member. In *Davidson v. Cannon* (1986) an inmate sued after telling officials that he feared harm from other inmates; his fears were dismissed and he was subsequently injured. Officials defended their inaction on the basis that they sincerely believed that the man's fears were unfounded. The Court ruled that the lack of intent on their part protected them from legal action.[63] Similar logic led the Court to rule against an inmate who was hurt when he tripped over a pillow left on a stairway by a guard in *Daniels v. Williams* (1986).[64] Both of these cases were based on the Fourteenth Amendment, but their rationale applies to Eighth Amendment cases as well.

Monetary Damages in Civil Proceedings [65]

Monetary damages are the main goal of tort suits. A **tort** is a private or civil wrong that results in injury or loss of money due to someone else's failure to live up to his or her legal obligations. Any failure to take reasonable care to protect others and their property from injury can result in a tort suit. This includes failure to protect inmates from one another, physical hazards, and medical malpractice. Torts can result in financial damage awards within guidelines set by state laws but not injunctions or other court-ordered reforms. Damages beyond the costs of the injury or loss can be added to a settlement to punish the defendant and deter future wrongdoing. These additional damages are known as **punitive damages** while those that repay the victim or "plaintiff" for actual losses are called **compensatory damages**. Damage awards are also used in civil rights litigation. Some states forbid punitive damage awards against government employees, and a few give employees total immunity from tort suits. When an employee acts in good faith and obeys agency policies that are later found to violate the law, a defense of **qualified immunity** may be used (see chapter 12). This is an affirmative defense, meaning that the employee must show that he or she acted in good faith by following an agency rule believed to be legal.

Common Types of Legal Actions in Corrections

Type of Action	Goal of Suit	Jurisdiction
Tort Suit	Compensation for damages and pain. Punitive damages may also be awarded for deterrent purposes.	County, federal, or state, depending on which controls the facility.
Habeas Corpus Petition	Challenge the legal basis on which person is being held.	Federal or state, depending on which controls the facility.
Civil Rights Act Suit	End discrimination based on "protected statuses" like race, gender, or religion.	Federal or state, depending on the statute used.

Medical Care

Inmates have some rights to medical care under the Eighth Amendment. *Estelle v. Gamble* (1976) involved a Texas inmate who was injured while on a prison work detail. He refused to return to work after medical personnel declared him fit and sued on the grounds that the failure to X-ray him was a violation of Section 1983 and the Eighth Amendment. The Court rejected his claim on the basis that "deliberate indifference" was required before such a suit was legitimate. Officials had not been negligent or indifferent to Gamble and thus committed no legal violation.[66]

The "deliberate indifference" standard created in *Estelle* was extended to all Eighth Amendment cases in *Wilson v. Seiter* (1991). Wilson alleged that poor ventilation, heating/cooling, and other conditions violated his Eighth and Fourteenth Amendment rights. The Supreme Court dismissed his claims on the basis that the lack of action by prison officials did not meet the standard of "deliberate indifference." The court also held that inmates must show that officials acted on the basis of a "culpable state of mind" to seek this kind of relief. This precedent makes it very difficult for inmates to sue over prison conditions.[67] Similar suits relating to the spread of TB and the adequacy of care for that disease have also been rejected by the courts.[68]

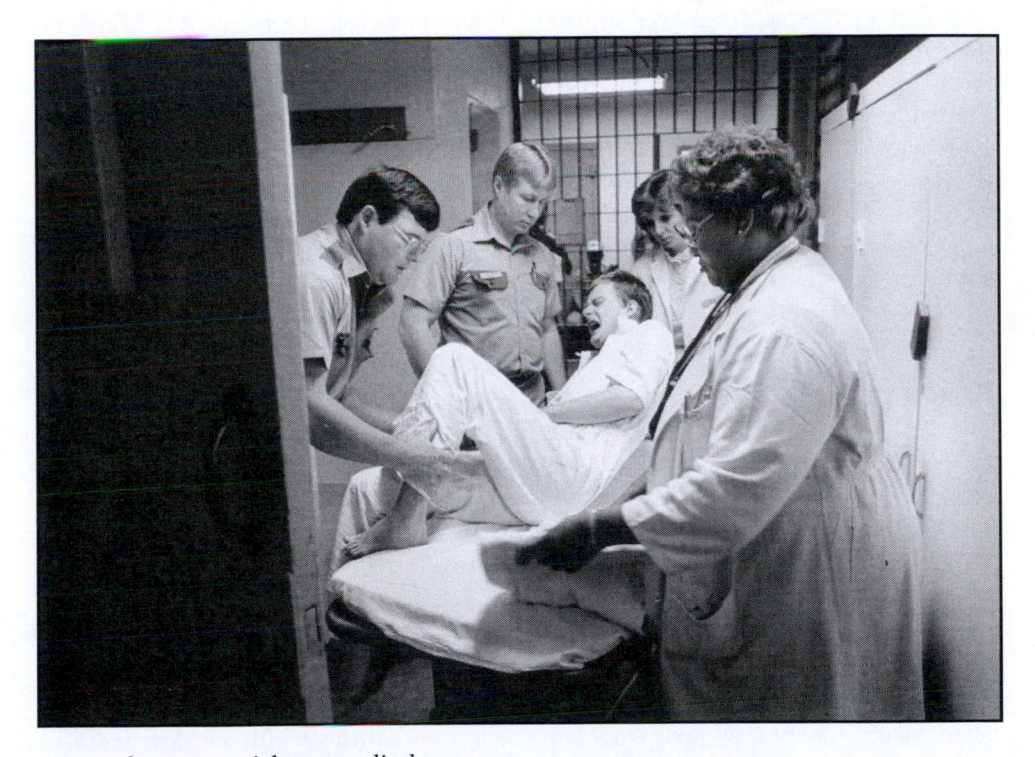

Inmates have some rights to medical care.

Use of Force

The ability to use force against another person must be strictly regulated in a democracy. Peace officers (i.e., police and correctional officers) are governed by the doctrine of *minimum reasonable force*; they may use only the amount of force required to achieve a legal goal. One of the most important cases in this area originated in the use of firearms to rescue a correctional officer who had been taken hostage by several inmates. As officers stormed a building, they fired on another inmate whom they felt posed a threat to them. Because of orders to "shoot low," he was wounded in the leg. The wounded inmate sued, but the Court in *Whitley v. Albers* (1986) rejected his claim, stating that cruel and unusual punishment did not occur unless force was used in a "malicious or sadistic" manner. Even if the force used is later shown to be excessive, if it was applied in good faith to restore order it does not violate the cruel and unusual protection of the Eighth Amendment.[69]

The *Whitley* decision was based on the principle that "unnecessary and wanton infliction of pain" must occur to apply the Eighth Amendment to the use of force by correctional officials. This principle was applied with a different result in *Hudson v. Macmillian* in 1992. Hudson was a Louisiana inmate who was beaten by two guards who were taking him to a "lockdown" area after an argument. One officer held him while Officer Macmillian punched him repeatedly. The trial court ruled in Hudson's favor but was reversed on appeal because Hudson's injuries were too minor to qualify as "cruel and unusual." The Supreme Court rejected this idea on the grounds that the officers deliberately used force that was clearly in excess of that required to control the inmate. This excess was a violation of the Eighth Amendment because injury was inflicted in a malicious and sadistic manner. This established the criteria set forth in *Whitley* as the crucial test of all Eighth Amendment use-of-force cases; force may be used only in good-faith efforts to maintain or restore discipline.[70] The amount of force, however, is usually left to the judgment of the officials handling the particular situation. These judgments should be based on state laws and agency policies, which are often more restrictive than federal case law.

FOURTEENTH AMENDMENT RIGHTS

Many cases based on the First, Fourth, or Eighth Amendment also refer to the reasoning of the Fourteenth Amendment, and many suits are based mainly or entirely on this amendment. The guarantees of due process and equal protection in the Fourteenth Amendment that were highlighted previously bear special attention.

Due Process Procedures

"Due process" is required whenever life, freedom, or property is at stake. *Procedural due process* requires that accused persons be prosecuted and punished according to previously established rules. *Substantive due process* requires that the procedural rules used in such prosecutions obey the principles set forth in the Constitution.

Due process is one way of assuring that everyone is treated fairly in adversarial proceedings such as trials and hearings. The amount of due process required varies with the situation and is based largely on the degree to which a person's freedom is threatened by the proceeding. The state's concern is usually with swiftness and efficient use of resources. The needs of the individual and the concerns of the state must be balanced by the courts in deciding how much due process is required in a particular situation. Most correctional due process issues arise from prison disciplinary proceedings and probation/parole revocation hearings. The Fourteenth Amendment guarantees that the procedures used to punish a person will be those prescribed by law or regulation. This helps to protect property and liberty from unjustifiable government interference. Inmates are entitled to due process in disciplinary proceedings if a significant loss, such as being placed in solitary confinement or revocation of good time, is likely.

Prior to 1974, guards often decided which inmates were to be punished and in what manner. Guidelines for disciplinary hearings were established by the Supreme Court in *Wolff v. McDonnell* (1974). This ruling was based on a state law that allowed revocation of good time as a result of serious disciplinary violations. In creating the right to earn early release, the state also created a **liberty interest** in which discipline violations were protected by due process. A liberty interest may originate in the Constitution, a court order, a state law, or agency regulations and practices. Most are state-created rights.[71]

The *Wolff* decision listed the procedures required to insure due process and equal protection. Inmates charged with serious rule violations have a right to a hearing. Hearings must be conducted by a neutral person or group not involved in the alleged violation and without prejudice against the inmate or special ties to the accusers. High-ranking guards often handle such hearings in jails and prisons. Judges usually deal with probation revocation. The parole board, or its representatives, performs the same role for parolees. Other rights include written notice of charges at least twenty-four hours before the hearing and a written description of how the fact finders reached their decision to revoke freedom. Officials may deny the inmate's right to call certain witnesses or present evidence if such actions would create a hazard to the facility. When this power is used, however, the institution must be able to justify the refusal in later appeals.

Wolff did not give inmates all the rights of free persons. There is no right to counsel in disciplinary hearings, but illiterate or mentally impaired inmates may be represented by a counsel substitute. Assistance may also be provided if the charges are so complex that the inmate cannot comprehend all the issues involved. Assistance may be provided by another inmate, a staff member, or someone from the surrounding community as officials see fit. There is no right to trial by jury in disciplinary proceedings, and the right to confront and cross-examine witnesses can be limited to protect informants.[72] Because the use of witnesses who cannot be cross-examined poses the threat that hearings could be used for vengeance, the Court laid down strict rules for the use of informant testimony. Facts must be presented to show that the particular informant is a trustworthy source of information. The testimony must also be supported by evidence from other sources if it is to be defined as fully credible. Credibility and reliability are determined solely by the hearing officer or board.[73]

Inmates are entitled to meet with their attorney, but in most cases must do so in the presence of a guard.

Inmates facing minor punishments have only a right to be informed of the charges and to speak with a neutral official before being punished. Parolees who have been convicted of new crimes have similarly limited due process rights. In all cases, the officer bringing the charges cannot be considered neutral and may serve only as a witness or prosecutor.[74]

Prisoners rarely have charges dismissed as a result of a hearing because the authorities have wide latitude in determining guilt. *Superintendent v. Hill* (1985) upheld the finding of guilt in a prison assault case even though no witnesses saw the accused person strike the victim. He was merely seen leaving the area where the victim was found. The Court ruled that prisoners could be found guilty and punished on the basis of very limited evidence if the available facts allowed a reasonable person to believe the inmate guilty.[75]

Inmate rights in disciplinary hearings were restricted further by *Ponte v. Real* (1985) where the disciplinary board failed to call three witnesses requested by the inmate. No reason for this failure was offered to the inmate who, like *Hill*, lost a substantial amount of good time and was placed in solitary for over two weeks. The Supreme Court ruled that officials need not explain their reasoning to an inmate but must provide appropriate reasons to a court if the inmate brings suit over their decision.[76]

The due process rights specified by *Wolff* apply only when a substantial liberty interest is at stake, such as the loss of good time or removal to solitary confinement. The definition of such an interest was narrowed by the Court's decision in *Sandin v. Connor* (1995). *Sandin* requires due process only when the changes resulting from a finding of guilt are unusual and lead to significant changes in the conditions of confinement. It focuses attention on the nature of the loss suffered by the inmate rather than the wording of laws and policies. *Sandin* supports the idea that the decisions of correctional officials should be respected by the courts whenever constitutionally feasible.[77]

The *Sandin* ruling is a return to the original logic of *Wolff* and overturns the use of technical issues that were supported in other cases. Under *Sandin*, transfers from one facility to another, removal from the general prison population, and removal from job assignments linked to good time credits are not threats to liberty interests unless the due process procedures outlined in *Wolff* are ignored.[78] There is no right to be held in the general population, and no loss of good time or any other liberty interest is threatened by such a precaution. Detention prior to a disciplinary hearing is permitted because it is defined as a security measure rather than a punishment. Searches that include an inmate's legal papers are also permitted because they do not change the conditions of confinement. *Sandin* does not, however, affect the ability of state courts to identify and protect liberty interests based on their own constitutions or laws.[79]

Forcing Medication on Prisoners

Mentally ill inmates may create a threat to order because they are sometimes disruptive and cannot or will not obey staff commands. Many are the victims of assaults, pranks, and teasing by other inmates and some are suicidal because of

The Development of Case Law Defining Prisoners' Rights

Ex Parte Hull (1941)

Inmates do not need the approval of prison administrators in order to bring complaints to the courts.

Cooper v. Pate (1964)

The idea that inmates are "slaves of the state" is rejected, and prisoners receive limited constitutional protection under section 1983 for the first time.

Johnson v. Avery (1969)

Assistance from other inmates in preparing legal actions can be limited but not banned.

Holt v. Sarver (1971)

Arkansas prisons are found to violate the Eighth Amendment and are taken over by a federal court.

Cruz v. Beto (1972)

Inmates with unconventional religious beliefs have all the rights of prisoners belonging to more popular faiths.

Wolff v. McDonnell (1974)

Due process standards for disciplinary hearings are set, and state-created "liberty interests" become the focus of attention.

Procunier v. Martinez (1974)

Mail censorship policies must be specifically based on a significant government interest that is unrelated to suppressing inmate rights.

Pugh v. Locke (1976)

The "totality of conditions" must be examined to determine if prison/jail conditions violate the Eighth Amendment.

Estelle v. Gamble (1976)

"Deliberate indifference" to inmate medical needs is required before authorities are in violation of the Eighth Amendment.

Bounds v. Smith (1977)

Prisons and jails must provide an adequate law library or comparable assistance to prisoners preparing legal actions.

Hutto v. Finney (1978)

The courts define the criteria that guide judicial decisions intended to change prison conditions.

Ruiz v. Estelle (1981)

A federal court defines gross overcrowding as an Eighth Amendment violation and takes over Texas prisons.

Rhodes v. Chapman (1981)

Conditions violate the Eighth Amendment only if they (1) inflict unnecessary or wanton pain or (2) are grossly disproportionate to the crimes warranting imprisonment. Courts are to avoid interfering in prison operations unless conditions are deplorable.

Wilson v. Seiter (1981)

A "culpable state of mind" and "deliberate indifference" to inmate needs are required to sue under Section 1983.

Hudson v. McMillian (1982)

Excessive force is "cruel and unusual" if administered in a "malicious and sadistic" manner, even if injuries are minor.

Turner v. Safley (1987)

Criteria for judging the "reasonableness" of "legitimate penological interests" are established.

O'Lone v. Estate of Shabazz (1987)

"Legitimate penological interests" may form a legal basis to deny inmates access to certain religious practices.

Thornburgh v. Abbott (1989)

The criteria set forth in *Turner* are applied to the censorship of publications ordered by, or sent to, inmates.

Sandin v. Connor (1995)

The definition of a "liberty interest" is focused on the nature of the inmates' loss instead of the wording of laws and policies.

Lewis v. Casey (1996)

An inmate must prove "actual injury" before the logic of *Bounds* can be applied.

their disability. For all of these reasons, authorities usually want to assure that these inmates receive medication to control the symptoms of their illness. However, many anti-psychotic drugs have serious and uncomfortable side effects, and many mentally ill inmates do not want to take them. *Washington v. Harper* (1990) uses the Fourteenth Amendment to give inmates a liberty interest in avoiding unwanted drugs. Medication can be forced on an inmate if and only if:

1. the inmate is dangerous to self or others;
2. taking the medication is in the best interests of the inmate; and
3. the decision to force medication on the inmate is made in a hearing with the same due process protections as in serious disciplinary proceedings.

The right of authorities to force medication on a prisoner was upheld in 1997 as a rational means to prevent the spread of TB. An inmate won a damage award in that same year, however, when authorities compelled him to take antipsychotic medications that caused permanent neurological damage without using the proper procedural safeguards.[80] Inmates are entitled to assistance from someone who understands the relevant psychiatric issues, and mental health experts must sit on the panel that decides the case. The panel must assure that the inmate is mentally ill, that the illness results in danger to the inmate or others, and that the medication is appropriate. If the panel decides to force medication on the inmate, then regular review of the case is required to assure that forced medication is still necessary.[81] Correctional authorities have the right to treat the mentally ill differently than other prisoners because of their disability. The "equal protection" clause of the Fourteenth Amendment requires that special treatment be justified on substantive grounds and that procedural due process be provided.

Equal Protection under Law

The Fourteenth Amendment outlaws discrimination based on group memberships that have no substantive meaning—that is, memberships that do not predict or reflect behavior. If age, gender, race, or religion appear to influence the way people are treated, Fourteenth Amendment rights are likely to be involved. However, even these statuses may be used to segregate prisoners if the state has "compelling reasons" for doing so. For example, placing inmates of a particular race in segregation is legal only if it can be justified by their involvement in or need for protection from gangs or violent incidents. In *David K. v. Lane*, white inmates sued a Michigan prison because they made up 12% of the prison's population but 40% of those in administrative segregation. These placements were justified because prison officials felt that these white inmates were in danger from black and Hispanic gangs. The court upheld the protective segregation of white prisoners, even though the prison's gang control methods were found to be inadequate.[82] This type of segregation is justified in most cases as long as the measures taken do not constitute "atypical deprivation."[83]

Separate housing for men and women does not violate the Fourteenth Amendment if there is parity in their treatment. Parity, as defined in chapter 9, means substantial, if not exact, equality: the quality and number of programs and facilities must be equivalent.[84] The concept of parity also guides decisions on differences between security levels for prisoners with similar behavioral records. The most sensitive area of concern here is the difference in treatment between inmates in protective segregation and those in the general population. Inmates in protective segregation have done nothing to justify loss of privileges but can be denied access to programs because of the "compelling state interest" in protecting their safety. The conditions under which they are held can be challenged under the Eighth Amendment but not the Fourteenth.[85]

INMATE LAWSUITS

Lawsuits can be used to ask a court to examine any situation that appears to violate the constitutional rights or liberty interests of prisoners. Some prisoner lawsuits are frivolous and seek mainly to harass authorities, but others have exposed intolerable levels of corruption and cruelty. When constitutional issues are at stake, federal law allows U.S. district courts to hear prisoner lawsuits. This does not prohibit the use of state courts, especially when state laws give inmates more rights than do those of the federal government. While the number of appeals to federal courts is increasing faster than those for state courts,[86] the Supreme Court requires that all state appeals be exhausted before an inmate files appeals with federal courts.[87]

Attempts to block access to the courts are defined as retaliation and are illegal. Although many inmate lawsuits are based on weak or nonexistent grounds, it is illegal to discriminate against anyone for filing a legal action. Even if the original lawsuit or petition is dismissed, those who try to take vengeance for a suit can be sued for retaliation. Steps to control frivolous suits can be taken only by the legislature or the courts. On the other hand, correctional staff should not grant special privileges to inmates who are suing them. They must simply go on with their duties in a professional manner that ignores the suit.

Lawsuit defendants can seek compensation for attorneys' fees if the plaintiff loses. The main exception to this is in suits where attorneys' fees cannot normally be recovered. An unsuccessful plaintiff can be charged court costs for bringing a frivolous suit, but this is left to the judgment of the court handling the case. Few inmates have enough money to make such a sanction meaningful, but many jurisdictions will seek judgments in order to hold them symbolically accountable. This occasionally results in some money being returned to the state.

Courts can also refuse to grant inmates the status of *in forma pauperis*, which allows the inmate to avoid paying fees for court actions. By charging inmates a fee for each suit, much litigation can be discouraged. Theoretically, however, the rights of the poorest inmate do not differ from those of the richest, and the courts avoid this sort of action until an inmate has demonstrated that his or her suits have no merit. This situation is rapidly changing, however. The **Prison Litigation Reform Act of 1996** (PLRA) was enacted to reduce the number of lawsuits filed in federal courts by prison inmates. It:

1. forces all inmates filing federal suits to pay a filing fee (other fees may still be waived);

2. limits how much can be awarded in attorney fees when an inmate wins a lawsuit and requires that damage awards to inmates be used to make restitution payments to victims;

3. bars prisoners from suing the federal government for psychological damages unless they have also suffered physical injuries;

4. orders federal judges to screen inmate suits and dismiss those with little merit; telephones and video links are to be used whenever feasible;

Lawsuits by Inmates—from the Frivolous to the Desperate[88]

Many commentators enjoy pointing out that some inmates file lawsuits simply to harass officials and pass the time. Examples of such lawsuits include complaints that:

1. A jar of chunky peanut butter worth $2.50 was ordered and paid for but not received. After complaining to prison officials, the inmate received a jar of creamy peanut butter.

2. The shower area was too far from the cells for comfort on cold days.

3. Inadequate supplies of matches were provided by the prison.

4. The prison needed an interracial chorus but authorities would not sponsor it.

5. The cell block was too noisy to hear the single TV placed in it.

These cases were quickly dismissed for their obvious frivolity. Some of the inmates were also prohibited from filing further suits or had extraordinary restrictions placed on future attempts to file suit. However, many prisoner lawsuits address gross abuses of common decency and human rights. Without court intervention, the following situations might have continued indefinitely.

1. Prisoners restrained in handcuffs and shackles were beaten, scalded, and had their heads bashed into walls and floors by guards. *Madrid v. Gomez* (1995).

2. Confined youths were routinely beaten by facility staff who were also heavily involved in drug trafficking. Sexual relations between staff and youths were found to be common. *D.B. v. Commonwealth of Pennsylvania* (1993).

3. Dozens of women, some juveniles, were forced to have sex with prison employees, including a chaplain. Several became pregnant and were coerced into having abortions by staff members. *Cason v. Seckinger* (1994).

4. A 17-year-old boy, jailed for traffic fines, was tortured for 14 hours and then murdered by other prisoners. Several days before, another teenager had been beaten unconscious by the same prisoners, but authorities did nothing to prevent further violence. *Yellen v. Ada County, Idaho* (1985).

5. Over 400 prisoners were infected when warnings from the Health Department were ignored by prison officials, who failed to use basic tuberculosis detection and control procedures. *Austin v. Dept. of Corrections, Pennsylvania* (1992).

6. A prisoner gave birth on the floor of a jail cell without medical assistance three hours after informing prison staff that she was in labor. Other prisoners had deformed or stillborn babies as a result of getting almost no prenatal care. *Yeager v. Smith* and *Harris v. McCarthy, California* (1989).

7. Single-person cells held four or five prisoners, mattresses placed on the floor were soaked by overflowing toilets, drinking water was contaminated by sewage, and cells were infested with rats. *Carty v. Farrelly, U.S.V.Is.* (1994).

5. allows good time credits to be withdrawn as a penalty for using the courts to harass officials; and

6. prohibits inmates who have had three or more suits dismissed as frivolous from filing again unless they can demonstrate that they are in immediate danger of serious injury.[89]

Perhaps most importantly, the PLRA encourages institutions to use nonjudicial methods of resolving inmate grievances. These include review boards composed of "neutral" staff members (and sometimes inmates), ombudsmen, and third-party mediators.[90] Controlling inmate lawsuits is the legal responsibility of the legislative rather than the judicial branch,[91] and the courts have upheld the PLRA, finding that it does not violate the Constitution's separation of powers doctrine.[92]

Concern with sexual abuse of inmates has caused some to question the appropriateness of the PLRA's requirement of physical injury. Coerced sexual relations

---

Comparative Views
The Adaptation of the Scandinavian Ombudsman to American Prisons[93]

The use of an **ombudsman** to receive, investigate, and report on complaints by citizens against the government and its employees originated in Sweden in 1809. Ombudsmen are independent of other authorities within the bureaucracy to which they are attached. They act as impartial investigators with expertise on government organization and operations. They are accessible to all who deal with the government, but their powers are limited to making recommendations and publicizing their findings. Much of the ombudsman's work consists of identifying improper conduct by employees or problems in the interpretation of policies. Once identified, these issues can usually be handled informally to the benefit of both the inmates and the prison. By cutting through red tape, this office helps avoid use of the courts to settle minor problems.

Most ombudsmen handle complaints about the aspects of government at the same jurisdictional level as their office. Between 5 and 10% of the work of Scandinavian ombudsmen originates with prisoners. In Finland the ombudsman deals only with the activities of the military and the prison system, so at least 25% of his work is related to inmate complaints. Finnish ombudsmen can go anywhere in a prison and have the right to talk with inmates outside the presence of guards or other staff members. Their main role is to let inmates vent their feelings about the prison and its employees. The insight gained on such trips may lead to investigations or formal proposals to improve prison policies and procedures. More often, however, ombudsmen inspire changes through informal chats with prison administrators.

Many countries, such as Canada, Denmark, Guyana, New Zealand, Sweden, and Tanzania, use ombudsmen. American use of ombudsmen has grown in recent years due to legislation encouraging the use of nonjudicial methods of addressing inmate complaints. Some are employed by the prison system or other state agency while others are independent contractors or associated with nonprofit groups. In all cases they are independent of institutional administrators and mainly serve to represent the interests of inmates and their families to the authorities. Formal complaints are not always required for an ombudsman to initiate an investigation, and most are given free access to all areas of the prison as well as to its records. Of the four employed by the state of Texas, three are women who handle requests for public information on prison issues as well as grievances.

rarely involve significant injuries but constitute a form of psychological torture, according to many who have worked with survivors of such assaults. Two federal circuit courts have upheld the PLRA in spite of these objections, while a third has implied that the physical injury provision may not apply to violations of the First, Eighth, and Fourteenth Amendments.[94] As with most such issues, these will require more time to wind their way through the judicial system until they are resolved with either a Supreme Court ruling or new legislation.

In extreme cases where an inmate is known for filing many frivolous suits, the court may place further restrictions on her or his legal rights. Some courts have required inmates to attach copies of all their prior legal actions to new suits. The costs of this requirement are usually sufficient to keep an inmate out of court. In a few extreme cases, inmates (and lawyers) have been completely banned from a particular court for periods of up to five years. Judges are very reluctant to use such severe remedies, however, because the right to redress grievances through the courts is so important.

Policy Matters!
What Will Result from Restrictions on Inmates' Legal Rights?

Both the courts and the legislatures are restricting the ability of inmates to file legal actions against correctional agencies. Their goal is to reduce the crowding of court dockets and to protect the law from being used as merely a game of technicalities. However, some inmate suits have led to badly needed correctional reforms. While we are unlikely to return to a "hands-off" policy, public demands for harsh punishment and the need to reduce the crowding of our courts are leading to changes in legal procedures that will set new norms for corrections.

Inmate legal actions can be roughly divided into two categories. In the first are the many inmates seeking new trials who protest that they are innocent of the charges on which they were convicted. Many of these suits are based on technical legal issues, but others have great factual substance. Since 1963, at least 381 defendants have had a homicide conviction thrown out because prosecutors concealed evidence or presented evidence they knew to be false. Of these defendants, 67 had been sentenced to death. Nearly half of those death row inmates have been released after proving their innocence in long court battles involving multiple appeals.[95] The second and most common type of legal actions challenge prison/jail conditions, procedures, and policies. Some of these suits are clearly frivolous, but others have exposed shocking abuses of power.

Questions to Consider

1. How will restrictions of inmates' legal rights affect the public's trust in the legal system? How might they affect the operation of correctional agencies? Do the restrictions now used allow equal access to the courts regardless of the economic status of the inmate?

2. Should there be a distinction between legal actions protesting a person's innocence and those challenging how a correctional facility operates? Is one type of suit more valuable to society or to inmates than the other? Why or why not?

3. What about state laws that prohibit requests for a new trial after a few weeks or months of the original conviction? Should convicted persons have the opportunity to apply new technologies to their cases after conviction? Do the burdens this would this place on the police and courts outweigh the freedom of a few innocent people?

Use of the courts can be partially offset by the implementation of administrative grievance procedures by institutions and departments of corrections. If these procedures provide a level of due process commensurate with the issue, the courts will not usually intervene. The quality of administrative remedies for minor and frivolous complaints offered by states and institutions is critical to this method of reducing the role of the courts in settling minor issues. As these administrative avenues demonstrate a consistent concern with due process, equal treatment, and basic fairness, the use of the courts by inmates is likely to be slowed further. All such remedies must be used before court intervention is possible, even if those measures cannot grant the inmate the type of relief he or she desires (e.g., financial damages).[96] The ultimate right of inmate access to the courts is unlikely to ever be denied, however.[97] Observers expect judicial intervention in the operation of correctional agencies to continue to decline in frequency, while the professionalization of corrections they caused increases due to the demands of modern society. However, growing prison populations, reliance on new technologies, and privatization are likely to generate new legal questions that will require answers through the litigation process.[98]

SUMMARY

Convicted offenders lose many but not all of the rights enjoyed by free citizens. Which rights are lost and for how long is determined by statutes and court decisions. The right of access to the courts was recognized in 1941, and the right to sue under Section 1983 of the 1871 Civil Rights Act was granted in 1964. The hands-off era, in which many abuses were tolerated, had given way to a "hands-on" era of court intervention by 1971 when a federal court took over the Arkansas prison system. In 1972 inmates won limited religious freedoms, and in 1974 they were granted a few due process rights as well. In the 1980s the Supreme Court restricted the degree to which the courts could dictate correctional policies and the "one-hand-on, one-hand-off" era began.

First Amendment freedoms of speech, religion, and press can be limited if they seriously threaten security, treatment needs, or budgets. Expectations of privacy are very limited in a correctional institution and so are the Fourth Amendment rights of prisoners. States set the conditions under which probation and parole officers can search the homes and persons of their clients. The Eighth Amendment applies when conditions or practices inflict unnecessary or wanton pain. Crowding, medical care, and use-of-force issues are dealt with under this amendment in combination with other laws. Prisons and jails must protect inmates from one another and from physical hazards, but the legitimate concerns of officials must also be respected.

Most disciplinary hearing procedures are based on the due process clause of the Fourteenth Amendment that applies whenever the Constitution or state laws create a liberty interest. If no liberty interest exists, the inmate can only explain his or her side of the story to a correctional official. If a liberty interest exists, the inmate has a few due process rights. The equal protection clause is the basis of the protections given to women, minorities, and older people. Strong reasons, usually based on security concerns, must justify any practice that disproportionately affects a racial, religious, ethnic, or gender group.

Inmates commonly use several methods to bring their complaints to court. Most inmates use the Civil Rights Act to seek relief from oppressive conditions. Tort suits can be used to address civil wrongs that cause injury or loss, but these can only result in monetary damage awards. *Habeas corpus* petitions that challenge the legality of confinement are used to question death sentences, disciplinary segregation, and parole decisions.

When inmate access to the courts is abused, judges can use various fees or court orders to prevent further abuses. Because of the closed nature of correctional institutions and the nearly absolute power of the staff, access to the courts is essential for the survival of democratic values and basic human rights. It is vital to remember that loss of liberty and confinement are the punishments for crime. Prison conditions and staff behaviors should not substantially add to this punishment unless the inmate's behavior justifies it.

QUESTIONS FOR DISCUSSION AND REVIEW

1. When did case law on corrections begin to develop? Through what stages or eras has it progressed? What factors have influenced its development?

2. Why is it important to allow convicted offenders to have access to the courts? To what degree can this access be restricted?

3. What rights are guaranteed by the First Amendment to the Constitution? The Fourth? Fourteenth? Eighth? Which rights are most often lost as a result of imprisonment?

4. What restrictions may be placed on the First Amendment freedoms of imprisoned persons? On prison parolees and probationers?

5. Which Fourth Amendment rights are routinely granted to imprisoned persons? What restrictions may be placed on these freedoms by correctional authorities? What needs must be balanced to determine when and how authorities may search? What criteria are used to determine if a search is "reasonable"? What legal doctrines control searches of the homes and autos of prison parolees and probationers?

6. What obligations are placed on correctional facilities by the Eighth Amendment? How have recent interpretations of these freedoms affected corrections?

7. What are the two most crucial rights guaranteed by the Fourteenth Amendment? How does each affect the operation of prisons and jails? How does each impact community corrections?

8. What is a liberty interest? What case law decisions guide the definition of such an interest? How have recent changes in the way the courts define liberty interests impacted corrections?

9. What legal tools can the courts use to control prison and jail conditions? What methods are available to judges who wish to discourage frivolous lawsuits?

10. What types of legal actions are most often filed by inmates? What is the legal basis of each? What does each seek to accomplish?

CORRECTIONAL PROGRAMS

Offender treatment is the focal point for many of the controversies surrounding the correctional mission. Most offenders will return to an unsupervised life in society, and everyone benefits if they do so as responsible, productive citizens. In order to accomplish this, specialized help is often required, and such services can be costly. The development of a productive lifestyle requires freedom to exercise new skills and the kind of self-respect that will inhibit recidivism. Both of these goals conflict with the desire to seek "justice" by branding inmates as outcasts and inflicting misery on them. Fears about recidivist crime attract more attention than policies that try to balance the cost of programs with the benefits gained.

Correctional programs are found both in institutions and in the community. Recidivism is most directly addressed by educational and counseling programs, but recreation and religion also play important roles in the rehabilitation process. Some offenders need to learn basic life skills such as budgeting, stress management, and literacy. Most must learn to control their emotions and to make better decisions. Many resist treatment because it is a painful process that forces them to deal with deep-set fears and past failures. Fear of ridicule inhibits many from actively participating in treatment beyond what is required to remain free or earn early release. Since participation in treatment is often ignored when release decisions are made, many inmates avoid treatment because they see no payoff in it.[1] However, research has shown that even when offenders are forced to participate in programs, the result is lowered rates of recidivism and a more manageable prison.[2]

Not all experts accept these conclusions, however. They fear that legal officials such as judges and parole officers will play too great a role in clinical decisions. Authorities have increasingly become involved in dictating the type of treatment provided and evaluating whether it has been completed successfully. The danger is that coercive treatment will be ordered for nonclinical reasons. Clinicians who suggest less punishing treatment may feel intimidated and at risk economically for their politically unpopular choices.[3]

Programs for offenders can be roughly divided into two types. **Treatment programs** reshape the offenders' ways of thinking and acting. Inmates in treatment programs learn to think clearly and to make good decisions. **Habilitative services** deal with the basic skills needed for a productive life. They teach inmates to read and write, apply for work, and develop marketable job skills.

HABILITATIVE SERVICES

Four basic types of habilitative programs can be identified. Academic programs teach reading, writing, and arithmetic. Vocational training deals with skills required for particular jobs. Recreational programs can teach teamwork, encourage empathy, help offenders manage stress, and provide healthy ways of building relationships. Religious programs provide a moral basis for thoughts and actions. Basic academic skills must be acquired before most other programs can be effective. These skills are vital if offenders are to find jobs that can provide them with a secure living. Offenders who can't read can't fill out a simple job application.

Academic Programs

All federal prisons and 91% of state prisons offer a few educational programs, compared to 60% of jails. About half of the prison inmates and 14% of jail inmates had participated in a program.[4] However, most prisons have limited classroom space, and inmates have to wait for classes. In Texas, students who read below 6th-grade level and are within two years of release are eligible first, those within five years of release are next; those with more than five years left on their sentences are last on the list. The average student receives roughly one grade level of classroom instruction during incarceration.[5] Since approximately 40% of state prison inmates, 27% of federal, and 47% of jail inmates had less than a high school education (versus 18% of the general population),[6] the need for more academic programs is evident.

Learning disorders are problems in brain function that make it hard to read or to learn. Although these disabilities do not themselves cause crime, failure and frustration in school can lead to lifestyles that encourage crime. These disabilities may also occur together with other biopsychological problems such as hyperactivity. Prison officials should be especially aware that the rate of learning disabilities among inmates is much higher than in the general public and that most of these disabilities are undiagnosed.[7] Some prisons offer special classes for inmates whose disabilities have been identified.

Education reduces recidivism by increasing an offender's postrelease earnings and job security.[8] It also provides the basis for the kind of self-esteem that inhibits crime. Inmates who attend classes to earn privileges or early release show the same levels of achievement as those who simply want to learn.[9] Many studies show that programs aimed at the least educated prisoners have positive effects on prison behavior and recidivism after release.[10] Others find little or no effect on recidivism or employability after release.[11] Most who have worked with such programs stress that including student-prisoners in designing classes is necessary for their success.[12] Some have suggested that "luxuries" such as theater groups are important in producing positive changes in the most hardened offenders.[13]

Education encourages self-discipline and promotes a sense of investment in society that discourages criminality.[14] It is also clear that providing education to prisoners is cheaper than reimprisoning them. Those who earn a two-year college degree are four times less likely to recidivate.[15] It is unclear whether the lowered recidivism rates are due to the effects of classes themselves[16] or their impact on the offenders' postrelease employability.[17] Academic programs seem to reduce the prisoner's desire for social distance. By allowing others to get close to them, inmates develop the emotional skills needed to benefit from treatment, build relationships, and avoid crime. If nothing else, the reduced need for social distance promotes racial tolerance and makes prisons safer.[18] Inmates who take college courses report heightened levels of self-esteem, confidence, and self-awareness. They say that the courses help them deal with the anger, frustration, and aggression caused by their imprisonment. Most also feel that education will help them find employment and avoid committing future offenses.[19]

Literacy Programs.   The ability to read and write is a basic prerequisite to the other skills required for life in modern society. Adults usually hide their illiteracy from others because it is embarrassing. Some have very limited reading skills and can make out just a few words; others avoid situations where they would have

Education is the most highly effective form of treatment.

Self-Esteem and Criminality[20]

For most people, social acceptance is the basis of self-esteem. They have attachments to members of mainstream society and invest their time and effort in socially acceptable activities and goals. Psychological research suggests that low self-esteem is caused by feelings of rejection. This is especially crucial among addicts where the biological basis of their criminality impacts the areas of the brain that deal with hope for the future. These feelings are critical to both self-esteem and self-control. A person's feelings about his or her relationships with others, not the reality of those relations, determine self-esteem. Some people may be more at risk for low self-esteem than others simply because of how they interpret messages from others. Problem behaviors such as substance abuse and aggression can be attempts to gain attention and escape feelings of rejection. Most problem behaviors have the opposite effect, however, and alienate the individual from the group. Gang or group crime is an exception: "Membership may actually raise self-esteem by providing a sense of belonging." This is especially true if the person has high levels of exposure to the gang but is isolated from the mainstream society.

---

to read. The first method of coping can result in misinterpretations of written messages; the latter leads to lost opportunities. The Federal Bureau of Prisons and many states list literacy as a requirement for early release, but these rules are often ignored because of overcrowding and lack of programs. The funding cutbacks that eliminated these programs appear to be political decisions that do not have strong public support.[21]

Literacy programs are found in many communities as well as in prisons and jails. Some use classes similar to those in elementary schools to teach literacy. They differ from regular schools only in the content of what is read. Topics likely to interest adults are preferred, but many prisons can afford only books designed for children.[22] Washington State has an innovative program that uses inmates who have a high school diploma as tutors for their peers who read below fifth-grade level. Tutors work with pupils between classes taught by local community college instructors.[23]

GED Preparation. A General Equivalency Diploma (GED) certifies that a person has achieved the basic skills required for a high school diploma. GEDs are awarded to people who pass a test that covers reading, writing, spelling, grammar, social studies, and science. GED preparation classes rely heavily on individualized instruction and homework. Students work at their own pace with instructors who are sensitive to those who have experienced failure in the past. Some states are experimenting with privately-designed and facilitated "on-line" GED classes as well as certain types of simple vocational training courses (e.g., data processing) and other programs (e.g., race relations).[24]

College Classes. Some prisons still offer a few college-level courses for inmates with the ability and desire to pursue higher education. Furloughs to attend classes are used only occasionally by very few facilities. The most common arrangements are either instruction within the prison or correspondence courses. While literacy and GED teachers are often prison employees, instructors of college-level classes are usually professors or graduate students working a second, part-time job. College classes for inmates were popular in the 1960s, but the public's desire for punishment has created major obstacles to offering these courses for inmates. Pell grants, which fund the college education of many citizens, were available to inmates until 1994. Prisoners accounted for less than 1% of these grant monies and received an average award of $1,500.[25] The elimination of this funding for prisoners greatly reduced the availability of college courses in prisons, and many states now bill parolees for college classes taken in prison.[26] Even under the most favorable circumstances, inmates will take many years to earn even a two-year degree. Few classes are available each semester; summer courses are rare; and specialized upper-level classes are only occasionally offered. Nonetheless, a few inmates have earned four-year degrees while imprisoned.

Vocational Training

Although college work can have dramatic effects on recidivism, providing inmate access to college courses is very unpopular with politicians and the public. In addition, many inmates are unable or unwilling to succeed in or to tackle college-level programs. Training in specific job skills, such as auto or electronics repair, is more common and more popular in most prisons. When it is of high quality, vocational training can reduce prison discipline problems and post-release recidivism. Vocational training must closely resemble real work situations in setting, tone, and equipment if it is to be effective.[27] It must be well organized, and inmates must complete specific programs before release. The pressures of crowding often lead to the release of inmates before they have acquired sufficient skills to compete in the job market.[28]

Vocational training should focus on specific job skills and good work habits.[29] Things like being on time, using time productively, and cooperating with others are skills that should be taught in addition to mechanical/technological skills. Prisons often define any type of inmate work as "vocational training," and many have very limited vocational programs as a result.[30] Much of the work that inmates perform is unskilled, dull, and demeaning. Vocational training can sometimes be combined with prison industries so that both inmates and the prison benefit, but most prison industries are organized simply to occupy the time of as many inmates as possible.

All 50 states have some form of prison industries, but the rate at which inmates participate in them varies widely. So also does the nature and quality of the "industries." Agriculture is still placed in this category by a few systems but most involve some form of manufacturing. Some provide solid job skills; others are mainly sources of revenue for the prison. Most are self-financed efforts that involve partnerships with private companies. Wages range from 20 cents to $1.00 an hour. Most states garnish at least some of these wages for room and board, family support, restitution, fines, and other charges. Only three jurisdictions (Washington, D.C., Utah, and Vermont) report losing money on these ventures.[31] Administrators see prison industries as a way to make money for the institution; voters want their taxes reduced; work supervisors want to stress training; and inmates are driven by the desire to earn money. In many prison industries, inmates find that their wages are unrelated to how hard or well they work. This does not prepare them to rejoin the labor force and may even worsen their work habits.[32]

Prisoners offer low labor costs, require no benefits to be paid, and do not go on strike or engage in collective bargaining. All of these factors are attractive to private industries. These very factors, however, were the basis for arguments to get rid of prison industries early in the twentieth century. Laws that protect businesses from competition with prisons make it difficult to keep inmates occupied or to use vocational training to help manage expenses. The 1979 *Prison Industries Enhancement Act* repealed some restrictions on the sale of products from prison industry and has helped bring private industries into prisons.

Privatization of prison industries in about half the states has brought a few inmates into fields like manufacturing and data processing. However, the costs of insurance and equipment limit this trend. Security concerns also limit the number of programs.[33] Few insurance companies are eager to support businesses that use offender labor because of fears of violence and theft. The equipment used in many industrial programs is ancient and therefore not useful in teaching marketable job skills. Motivating unskilled and uneducated prisoner-employees is another challenge. However, many of these programs have produced significant reductions in the recidivism rates of the inmates who participate in them.[34] There are examples of new programs that offer promise. The Minnesota Department of Corrections offers opportunities for incarcerated offenders to gain marketable skills through

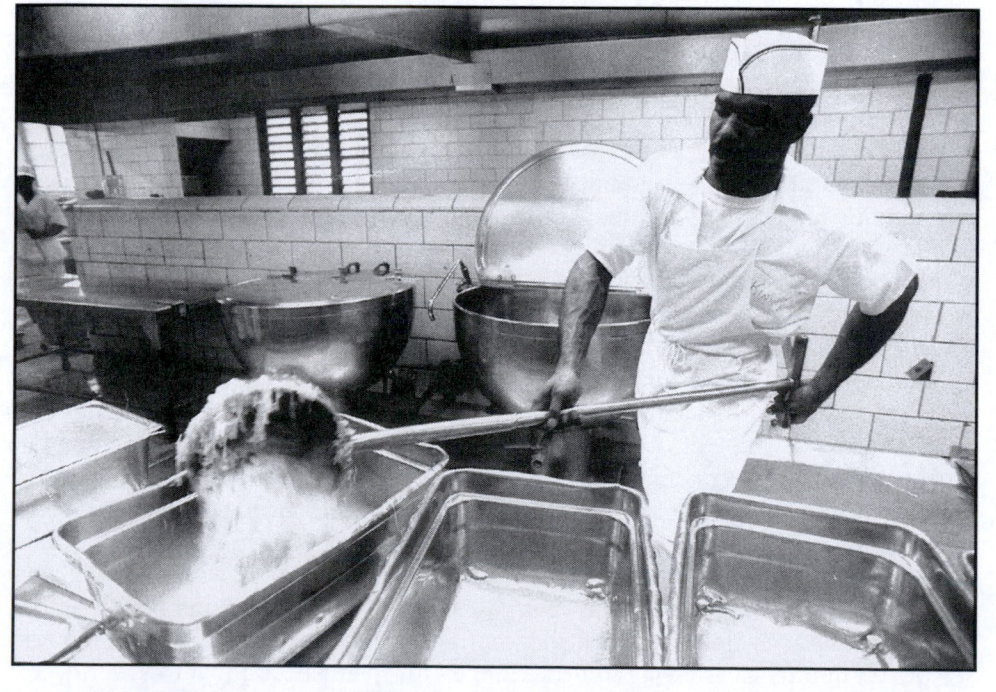

Some prison vocational training programs provide opportunities to learn new skills; others provide labor at low costs.

work programs. Minnesota state colleges and universities are partners in the program, and offenders can earn certificates or diplomas. The AFL–CIO also supports the program and offers apprenticeships.[35]

Securing a job and staying drug free are the best predictors of which offenders will avoid crime after their release. Drug-involved offenders who receive job training while in prison and aftercare upon release are two to three times as likely to succeed as those who do not receive such attention. The quality of the aftercare (support groups and other forms of counseling provided in addition to typical parole supervision) they receive is even more important than the degree to which they are monitored for drug use.[36] While addicts benefit from such programs, those who had decent jobs but sought the high profits associated with transporting or selling large quantities of drugs are probably less affected by job training.[37]

Recreation in Prison

Offenders usually commit their crimes during their leisure hours; few have learned healthy methods of using free time and instead pursue drugs, alcohol, or criminal activities. Cognitive skills training is based on the premise that offenders often have never acquired the necessary "thinking skills" to function productively in society.[38] Training in problem solving, negotiation, assertiveness, anger control, and social skills can help build esteem and the ability to adjust to social conditions. Correctional recreation programs provide another venue for addressing these deficiencies and can teach inmates to use leisure time in healthy ways.[39]

Many believe that offenders commit crimes because of inadequate, faulty, or deviant socialization. Therefore, effective correctional programs must recreate the socialization process in order to resocialize offenders. Recreation can help in this process but is usually offered merely to keep inmates tired and occupied.[40]

Recreational activities can take many forms such as art, crafts and hobbies, team sports, and individual activities like boxing and weight lifting. Most prisons give inmates at least some of these recreational outlets. Exercise is needed to keep the body and mind healthy; it also helps relieve stress and depression that are the most common causes of relapse among substance abusers.[41] It may be for this reason that willingness to exercise is correlated with successful completion of institutional drug treatment programs.[42] Team sports and individual activities are the most popular. Like those in the mainstream society, prison sports are often informally limited to those with special abilities. Those who are not already skilled at the game are unlikely to get a chance to play. Group recreation can be an important part of the socialization process by teaching decision making, teamwork, and empathy while encouraging positive relationships. To accomplish this, however, the goal of winning must be secondary to sportsmanship, cooperation, and participation for all who want to be involved.

Individual activities require no social skills. Many, such as boxing and weight lifting, have a violent image that male offenders seem to prize. Weight lifting is popular among inmates but has been banned in three states and restricted in ten, because of fear that inmates will use the weights as weapons.[43] While individual activities provide outlets for time and energy, they rarely meet the standards of

Team sports and individual activities, such as boxing, are popular forms of recreation.

effective correctional treatment. The same is partly true of activities like arts and crafts. These certainly consume time and energy in a creative fashion and could provide the basis for a healthy sense of self-esteem. However, they do not equip inmates with interpersonal skills and rarely require the kinds of decision-making skills that prisoners need. Nonetheless, any activity is better than sheer idleness. These kinds of activities thus have limited but positive impacts on prison life.

Religious Programs

Religion is the oldest form of treatment offered to prisoners. Some form of religious expression is available in almost every correctional facility in the United States. Faith-based groups have long been involved in a variety of correctional activities and have assumed an even higher profile in recent years. Many offer counseling and mentor programs. At the very least, they provide volunteers who can help offenders with basic social and living skills.[44]

Most prisons have one or more chaplains who represent the major Christian groups in the area. A few also have chaplains for Jews and Muslims. More often, however, a single paid chaplain relies on religious leaders from the community to serve inmates of religions with which he or she is unfamiliar. Many prisons also allow a few trustworthy inmates to serve as assistant chaplains.[45]

Prison chaplains provide three basic kinds of services. They perform traditional religious services for inmates. They also counsel inmates privately about spiritual matters and offer assistance in coping with imprisonment. One prison chaplain describes his role as that of "the release valve on a pressure cooker." He works to assure inmates that they "are somebody in God's sight" to help offset the dehumanizing effects of imprisonment.[46] Finally, it is often the chaplain who serves as a liaison between an inmate and his or her family when especially disturbing events, such as the death of a relative, occur.[47]

The activities of chaplains are often supplemented by volunteers from local congregations who are interested in prison ministry. Volunteers usually teach prisoners about religion and spiritual matters in an effort to give them a moral basis for their lives. Religion makes imprisonment more bearable and can be used to mold ethnic pride into the kind of self-esteem that discourages further criminality.[48] Many sneer at "jailhouse conversions," and some data indicate that their effect on postrelease recidivism is insignificant once more traditional risk predictors are included in the analysis.[49] The effects of special, intensive spiritual training on recidivism seems to be more positive and dramatic. After eight or more years of freedom, offenders who had received such training had recidivism rates that were 11% lower than those for similar inmates who had no such involvement. The reduction in recidivism was four times greater for women than for men. Those with religious training who did commit new crimes committed less serious offenses and avoided crime longer than those without such training.[50]

Life Skills Development

The term *life skills* is used to describe a variety of programs to teach inmates skills that most people acquire through the normal socialization process. Life skills programs teach inmates how to communicate their thoughts and feelings effectively, to form and maintain healthy relationships, to create and live on a budget, and to deal with stress and anger. Literacy, GED, and other "educational" programs are sometimes also included in this category as are some focused on moral reasoning.[51] These programs are very common in U.S. prisons[52] and are sometimes sponsored by community agencies or volunteer groups. Most life skills training involves a combination of classroom and individualized activities. Life skills training tries to make up for the failures of normal socialization that led to crime and combines methods from habilitative and treatment programming. This sort of training has been shown to increase the ability to find a job after release and appears to reduce recidivism.[53]

TREATMENT PROGRAMS

Because most offenders will eventually return to society, changing the behavior that led them into crime should be of great importance.[54] However, a few believe that we should abandon all attempts to change the behavior of prisoners and simply use prisons to incapacitate and punish. Despite much attention to the failures of corrections in reforming offenders,[55] there is ample evidence that some treatment programs work for at least some prisoners.[56] Some believe that treatment programs are valuable regardless of their effect on recidivism because they provide hope to a troubled population and create a more humane environment for staff and inmates.

Between those who argue for punishment and those who embrace rehabilitation is a third approach. Some call this the **responsibility model**, which stresses holding offenders accountable for their choices of behavior both prior to and during imprisonment. This treatment approach forces offenders to participate in programs designed to reduce recidivism.[57] This model is taking hold in many areas for legal, economic, and political reasons, and there is evidence that it is effective in reducing recidivism. This approach is typical of the confrontational style that originated in treating addicts and has become popular in corrections.[58] Some treatment experts question both the effectiveness and the ethics of this approach. They also criticize its tendency to use paraprofessional staff that lack adequate training to administer psychotherapy properly.[59] This latter issue is largely a matter of how we choose to fund and organize offender treatment services.

Approaches to Treatment

There are two basic views of how correctional treatment ought to be organized. **Basic treatment amenability** focuses on the ability and willingness to cooperate with treatment providers. The type of crime committed, the motivation leading to the crime, and personal background are of secondary concern. Criminals are seen as emotionally driven opportunists who do not anticipate the long-term consequences of their actions on their own lives or on those of others.[60] Thus, all programs should focus on these types of attitudes regardless of the crimes committed.[61] Insecure, unsuccessful offenders who have not yet become "hardened" by life in prison or affected by criminal subcultures have the best chance of being reformed. This approach is sometimes described as "one size fits all" because most offenders are assumed to be guided by similar attitudes. They differ only in their willingness and ability to change their behavior patterns.[62] Much of what is in the confrontational style of the responsibility model is based on these assumptions.[63]

Differential intervention strategies claim that offenders must first be classified according to the underlying causes of their criminality. Only then can experts choose the programs that can best deal with their behavior. Thus, offenders with substance abuse problems would get one kind of treatment while sex offenders would receive

---

Forced Participation in SATP[64]

The U.S. Supreme Court heard a case in which Kansas prison officials ordered an inmate who had been convicted of sexual assault to participate in a Sexual Abuse Treatment Program (SATP). The program required inmates to admit responsibility for their crimes and to document their sexual history. The Kansas prison authorities informed the inmate that if he did not participate, his privileges would be reduced and he would be transferred to a potentially more dangerous maximum-security unit. The inmate refused to participate in the SATP on the grounds that disclosing his past history violated his Fifth Amendment rights against self-incrimination and that the impact of the penalties levied for not participating were a violation of his constitutional rights. In the Court's opinion, the fact that Kansas does not offer legal immunity from prosecution for statements made during the course of a SATP does not render the program invalid and Kansas prison officials were not violating the constitutional rights of the inmate by withholding privileges.

another.[65] Some types of offenders can be very disruptive in generalized programs and require special treatment in unique programs. For example, violent psychopaths often must be treated separately from the general population of offenders.[66]

There is some truth in the claims of both approaches. Some offenders seem beyond the reach of any form of treatment; conversely some programs seem to work for a variety of offenders.[67] However, offenders who clearly have problems

---

Offender Thinking Errors [68]

Those who work with offenders often note that they excuse their irresponsible actions with distinctive patterns of thinking and decision making. Some call these thinking errors "offender logic," even though they are common among noncriminals in less extreme form. It is vital that they be brought to the offender's attention whenever they occur if the offender is to be successfully reintegrated into society. Unlike other forms of behavior change, it takes little training to identify these errors and suggest alternatives to them. This is used to justify the widespread use of paraprofessional counselors for offenders and addicts and the intervention of justice professionals in clinical decisions discussed above.

1. *Excuse making or externalizing blame*: blaming situations or others (often the victim) for one's irresponsible behavior in order to avoid accepting one's own faults

2. *Justifying*: redefining a wrongful act as an appropriate one by stressing reasons that support this and thereby avoiding guilt

3. *Minimizing*: reducing the true significance of an antisocial behavior by comparing it with "worse behaviors," denying the effects on the victim, or giving it an innocuous label or name

4. *Victim stance or victim playing*: when confronted with irresponsible behavior, using self-pity and helplessness to portray oneself as the victim to avoid seeing the costs to the real victim or to manipulate others into a desired response

5. *Closed channel*: using secret keeping, closed-mindedness, and self-righteousness to filter incoming information selectively in order to avoid changing attitudes or beliefs

6. *Vagueness*: avoiding specific details of one's behavior to escape having to deal with its consequences, to minimize the negative reactions of others, or to deny the impact of the act

7. *Redefining*: shifting the focus from oneself to another person or changing the subject to a less threatening topic in order to avoid taking responsibility for an action

8. *Fake anger*: using displays of anger to manipulate others in a desired direction

9. *Ownership*: viewing someone or something as a possession over which the offender has control and authority when this is not appropriate

10. *Superoptimism*: establishing unrealistic goals through wishful or "magical" thinking that leads the offender to believe he or she will not be caught

11. *Criminal pride*: believing oneself to be so special that normal rules do not apply

12. *Assuming*: taking things for granted and acting on this belief without checking the facts

13. *Zero state*: seeing oneself as worthless unless things are going perfectly and others are doing as the offender desires

14. *Unwillingness to delay gratification*: refusal to endure discomfort or difficulty to obtain a goal while expecting that one's desires should be promptly met; being unwilling to consider that people sometimes benefit from not getting what they want

15. *Unwillingness to see long-term negative consequences*: having a low time horizon due to immaturity, low verbal IQ, superoptimism, or other thinking errors (This allows offenders to avoid facing the potential consequences of their acts until it is too late.)

16. *Unwillingness to consider alternative courses of action*: failure to see or weigh the potential costs and benefits of various alternatives or to evaluate carefully an attractive course of action (Errors like assuming or closed-channel thinking are often involved because they encourage the offender to avoid considering alternatives.)

17. *Lack of empathy*: failure to consider how others will be affected by an act because they are regarded as objects rather than people (Thinking errors such as blaming, justifying, and minimizing may be used to avoid recognition of this tendency.)

that most others do not share need special treatment. For example, with regard to academic programs, illiterate inmates will not profit from college classes any more than college graduates will gain from literacy programs. On the other hand, most inmates can profit from job counseling. The same is true for treatment. There are many programs, such as those on handling emotions and stress, from which nearly all prisoners (and many free citizens) could benefit. The basic treatment amenability approach seems to dominate in most U.S. correctional programs,[69] but psychologists are increasingly coming to favor the idea of differential intervention, especially in difficult cases.[70] Either or both views can be used to organize treatment for offenders, but they are not the only factors that must be taken into account in setting up treatment. The resources of the agency and the philosophy of available therapists also affect the kind of treatment offered to offenders.

Types of Therapy

Although there are several basic approaches to changing behavior, *cognitive therapies* are the most common in modern corrections. It repeatedly has been shown to reduce recidivism and is congruent with the responsibility model.[71] The goal of these therapies is to bring emotions under rational control by focusing on the conscious thoughts of the client. Clients are encouraged to think about all effective methods of solving each problem that confronts them. They are taught to think about how their emotions affect their interpretation of events. They then work to assure that rational thought, rather than emotions, guides their actions. Cognitive therapies encourage clients to set priorities for their lives and to question beliefs and decision-making methods that have become automatic.[72]

Rather than focusing on a client's thinking or interpretations of events, *behavioral therapies* focus on responses to stimuli. Bad habits are learned responses; those responses can be changed by learning new ones. The therapies attempt to change behaviors through systematic rehearsals of new responses. Prisons allow therapists to manipulate rewards and punishments to affect behavior. Once rewards and punishments are no longer controlled, as in free society, behaviors acquired in this way are likely to disappear. Thus, behavioral methods need to be supplemented with cognitive ones to assure positive postrelease effects. However, behavioral techniques are useful in handling offenders with few verbal skills and should be used to support and extend cognitive therapies for all offenders.

Principles of Therapeutic Discipline

Discipline is critical to the socialization process but must be applied according to certain principles.

1. Time is used constructively to avoid self-pity, frustration, and stress.

2. Constant emphasis on the individual's responsibility for actions should stress how the client's problems have been created or worsened by his or her own choices.

3. Attention must remain centered on the problem behavior. Drifting into other issues allows offenders to play the victim or to manipulate the situation.

4. Always be honest with clients; practitioners are role models who represent the mainstream society.

5. Promote behavior change through rules and structure:

   a. Use fixed and certain penalties to set boundaries for clients.

   b. Set penalties at a level that is punishing but does not alienate clients.

   c. Use "natural consequences" or constructive tasks as penalties for rule violations.

   d. Explain the reasons for each rule so that clients can understand the benefits of complying.

   e. Have a minimum of rules so that clients can experiment with new behaviors and practice making decisions.

6. Recognize and reward *all* client achievements so that they have a clear idea of what good behavior is and can recognize the thought processes that lead to it.

Individual Counseling

Counseling has traditionally used one-on-one sessions between a client and a licensed therapist to bring about behavioral changes. It is relatively unusual in corrections because of its expense. Licensed counselors expect good salaries, and treatment usually requires numerous sessions. Some experts feel that one-on-one sessions make it easier for offenders to manipulate, or become dependent on, the therapist. It can also be hard to convince a client that he or she has a problem in a one-on-one session. A group of people can often more easily accomplish this, especially if the client respects those individuals. A survey of prison therapists showed that they spent nearly equal amounts of time providing individual and group therapies. However, many prison groups are inmate-led, so inmates often spend more time in group than individual sessions. Most of the attention in both types of treatment settings should be focused on substance abuse, stress management, problem solving, and changing personal patterns of perceiving and reacting to events. Special sessions for anger management and sex offenders are often necessary and occupy much of a therapist's time.[73]

Group Therapies

Group counseling methods are much more common than private ones in corrections.[74] Groups are the central method of providing treatment for offenders. They can provide support and advice or be used to confront problem behavior and to practice more responsible alternatives. Ideally, therapy groups consist of 6 to 10 people, but they can sometimes be effective with twice that number. A licensed counselor guides the group, assures that it remains focused on a particular issue, and encourages everyone to participate. Most groups can accomplish their goals in a year or less. However, the "goals" of therapy groups are usually defined in fairly narrow terms. One group may focus on learning how to identify emotions such as anger and depression while another will center on managing anger. Therefore, most correctional clients will need several different groups in order to work through the issues that face them.[75] Weekly or monthly group therapy sessions are sometimes effective but often cannot develop the intimacy and trust required for major changes in perception and behavior. For this reason, therapeutic communities (see chapter 5) are preferred by many experts, but the distrust of officials and public attitudes toward therapeutic communities work against their numbers increasing.

The sharing of perceptions, feelings, and experiences is at the core of most group therapies. For a counseling group to be effective each member must: (1) feel worthwhile and accepted without fearing that what he or she says will be judged, (2) keep focused on the specific goal of the session, (3) take an active role in the group's work, and (4) acknowledge every other member of the group as a

---

Rational-Emotive Therapy [76]

Rational-emotive therapy (RET) was developed by psychologist Albert Ellis and is a basic part of many correctional programs today. Its central concern is with the effects of emotions on reasoning. Internal conversations are the focus of therapy designed to give control of action to the client's rational powers rather than to her/his emotions. The validity of the thoughts that produce particular emotions is closely examined in group and individual sessions under this approach. For example, if a client says, "Everybody hates me," the therapist or group will demand a list of who hates the client and how the client knows that they hate him or her. The goal is to weaken irrational beliefs and to encourage positive behavior. Areas addressed by RET include:

1. excessive need for love and acceptance from others,

2. being overly critical and demanding of oneself,

3. constant pessimism, or defining possible and actual negative events as complete disasters,

4. the belief that one's problems result from forces beyond his or her control,

5. escapism, or avoiding problems rather than dealing with them,

6. focusing on other people's problems in order to avoid one's own,

7. the excessive use of absolute and inflexible standards that lead clients to believe that they can never be "good,"

8. the idea that there is a single "right" answer to every problem and that failure to discover that answer is always unacceptable.

The therapist shows the client that (1) certain feelings and actions are not based on logic or fact and (2) irrational beliefs and actions cause the client's most serious difficulties. Clients are urged to replace the irrational ideas that have guided their choices with healthy alternatives. One of the criticisms of RET is that it oversimplifies mental activity and underestimates the power of emotions.

worthwhile equal.[77] The more open group members are with one another, the more effective the treatment. Group members must take seriously their promise not to reveal what is said in groups, but prison norms make this very difficult to achieve and enforce. The more time group members spend with each other, the greater their ability to help one another.

Twelve-Step Groups.   The twelve-step approach was introduced by Alcoholics Anonymous (AA) in the 1940s. It has since been applied to a wide variety of problem behaviors ranging from eating disorders to sex offenses. Narcotics Anonymous (NA) is based on a similar model and has helped many people addicted to illegal drugs. These groups are especially popular in corrections because they do not require the presence of a therapist and are free. Indeed, AA and NA specifically maintain that members rather than professionals run their meetings.[78] Most prisons and many jails have AA or NA groups, and attendance at these groups is also required of many probationers and parolees. Twelve-step groups presume that people who have managed to handle a particular problem are best equipped to help others do the same. In other words, former drug addicts and alcoholics have more insight into the thoughts and feelings of substance abusers than those who have never had such a problem.[79]

This approach uses stigma as a source of self-esteem by focusing attention on controlling the behavior. An alcoholic who avoids drinking becomes proud to be "in recovery." Peer support is used to link this new identity to self-esteem and

Group counseling can be demanding and painful for participants, but it is the most economical method of delivering many psychological services to offenders.

continued sobriety. Personal stories are told to remind group members of the terrible experiences and feelings to which their addictive behavior led. This keeps clients in touch with the desperation caused by the behavior and helps motivate them to stay straight.

The most effective twelve-step groups are made up of people who share a specific problem and are similar to each other in age, gender, economic status, and ethnicity. In reality, however, correctional self-help groups have a wide diversity of members. In addition, the self-help approach is designed to reinforce a change that has already been achieved rather than to create the motivation for change. Some believe that self-help methods are most effective with middle-aged, middle-class, white males. Others fear that they replace the problem behavior with an addiction to weekly group meetings. Education about the problem behavior is rare in twelve-step groups, and complete abstinence is always seen as the only way of controlling the problem. Spirituality plays a large role in these groups, and some offenders cannot easily accept this aspect of the method.[80] This approach to treatment is the most common in modern America because it is cheap (no professionals are involved) and relies on an aggressive, "in-your-face" style of confronting dysfunctional thoughts and actions. It is also criticized by many experts for these reasons.[81] Federal appellate courts have ruled that offenders cannot be forced to attend 12-step programs because they are "deeply religious" but these rulings have not yet been reviewed by the U.S. Supreme Court.[82]

Specialized Treatment Programs

Certain types of offenders may need specific therapies because of the unique nature of their offense or their mental condition. Some offenders have special needs that are not shared with other offenders. Others must be isolated from other offenders because of their offense (e.g., sex offenders) or their condition (e.g., the mentally ill). The most common forms of specialized treatment are for substance abusers, but prison administrators say that the most pressing need is for sex offender treatment programs.[83]

Substance Abusers. Substance abuse is the most common problem faced by inmates. Alcohol is widely held to be the most criminogenic of psychoactive substances and it is often used along with illegal drugs by offenders. One in three state inmates claims to have been under the influence of drugs or alcohol when he or she committed the crime that resulted in imprisonment. Another 19% said their offense was motivated by the need to get money with which to buy drugs, implying that they were addicted at the time.[84] Chemical dependency is often a ***compulsive behavior***. It is a problem behavior associated with obsessions or ideas that preoccupy the person even though they cause discomfort and shame.[85] The compulsive behavior causes the person to seek immediate physical pleasure despite the consequences of long-term psychological pain. The same basic pattern of thinking is common to all forms of substance abuse, so the methods used to treat alcoholics and drug addicts are the same. However, drug addicts often have had very different experiences as a result of their addiction. For example, they are not always welcomed at AA meetings even when they have abused both alcohol and drugs. The criminal status of drugs, and some of the biological effects of different substances, lead to different treatment needs among addicts.

A complete lack of drug abuse services is most typical of correctional agencies. Only 20% of the offenders who need drug treatment are thought to be receiving it, and the type of treatment received often does not meet the needs of the particular offender. Four basic methods used to address drug abuse in prisons: (1) education and counseling, (2) cell blocks or units modeled on the principles of a therapeutic community, (3) twelve-step groups, and (4) special services for related problems such as anger control and depression. Of these methods, twelve-step groups run by inmates or community volunteers are by far the most common. Educational efforts are also common but tend to be very brief.[86]

In contrast, criteria for federal funding require state programs to last 6 to 12 months; be separate from the general prison population; and develop cognitive, vocational, social, and other skills while enforcing abstinence with routine urine tests. While these model programs use twelve-step groups like Alcoholics Anonymous, they also employ professional counselors and use a variety of therapeutic methods. The greatest failing of these programs is the lack of aftercare available in the community after release. Even so, these programs often drop rearrest rates by more than 50 percent.[87]

The first step in treating many substance abusers is to make them see the need to change their behavior. They must stop denying that they have a problem and come to desire a sober lifestyle. This can be very threatening because substance abuse is often used to escape painful feelings. Severe crises, such as being arrested, may have such an effect. However, it is often necessary to help addicts recognize how the crisis is a direct result of their behavior. Denying the problem is the single greatest obstacle to success in treating these clients. Denial extends beyond the substance abuse to the thinking errors that have developed because of, or caused by, the addictive behavior. These ways of looking at self and others must be addressed along with the substance abuse if treatment is to have lasting effects.[88]

It is important to teach substance abusers about the effects of drug use and withdrawal. Many health problems can result from substance abuse, especially when drugs are injected, and clients are often ignorant of these. Long-term addiction also causes withdrawal symptoms that can persist for many months after drinking or drug use has ceased. Mental cloudiness, anxiety, vague physical discomfort, and slow reflexes are common among recovering addicts. If addicts do not recognize that these symptoms will fade as they stay drug free, they are likely to abandon hope of recovery and return to their addictive behaviors.

Sex Offender Treatment. Self-help and other treatments are more often available to substance abusers than to sex offenders. Where sex offender treatment programs do exist, they are likely to be more thorough than those for substance abusers.[89] While some sex offenders have deviant sexual desires, others are mere opportunists who have trouble controlling their behavior. These differences must be recognized before effective treatment and control strategies can be developed. Counseling for sex offenders requires the therapist to dictate which thoughts, feelings, and actions are proper and which are not. It also requires that therapists not

Methods of Controlling Sex Offenders[90]

Several states have recently adopted legislation that uses radical measures to control sex offenders who prey upon children. These laws range from indefinite psychiatric confinement to chemical methods of lowering the offender's sex drive. Each has highly emotional supporters and opponents. Each is based on research data that are considered flawed by many scholars, showing high recidivism rates for child molesters.

California's "chemical castration" law requires that twice-convicted sex offenders whose victims were less than 14 years of age be injected with **Depo-Provera** as a condition of their release from prison. Those whose first offense is especially serious can also be ordered to undergo this treatment by the sentencing court. Similar laws have been proposed or enacted in several other states. Use of the term "castration" is inaccurate because the drugs used simply reduce an adult's testosterone level to that of a child. The principal male hormone, testosterone, is linked to sex drive and aggressiveness. The effects of the drugs often can be overcome with steroids. A legal alternative to taking the drug regularly at parole offices would be for the offender to volunteer for surgical castration.

Supporters of the California law claim that sex offenders have recidivism rates of at least 90% and prey on the most vulnerable people in society. They cite European studies that claim castration reduces reoffense rates to about 2%. Opponents of the law claim that the European studies are methodologically flawed, that sex offender recidivism rates are "in the teens and twenties," and that counseling can rehabilitate, though not "cure," most sex offenders. The difference in the numbers on recidivism used by the law's supporters and opponents stems from how sex offenders and recidivism are defined. When only hard-core pedophiles are examined over long periods or any new arrest of someone under community supervision is taken as a case of recidivism, very high reoffense rates are found. However, if all persons convicted of sexual crimes are scrutinized and only new sex crimes are examined, the rate of reoffending is far lower.

One expert on sex offenders has called the idea of chronic recidivism among sex offenders a "folk belief" without basis in fact. Some experts fear the law will achieve little because many sex offenders are driven by compulsions that are not entirely sexual. It is felt that chemical treatment will be used instead of more effective counseling treatments. They suggest lifetime supervision with required counseling instead of castration. Constitutional concerns with privacy, the right to reproduce, and the right to control one's own body are also issues raised by opponents of the law.

Civil commitment laws require a mental health evaluation of sex offenders prior to their release from prison. Offenders thought to be a threat to public safety can be indefinitely confined in a psychiatric facility (a practice that is the "flip" side of indeterminate sentencing). Over 1,200 men are now under such confinement in at least 20 states. Most states require that dangerousness be proven without a reasonable doubt. Opponents of the law claim it is a form of double jeopardy and believe that psychiatrists fearing lawsuits will be too quick to confine offenders who have already served their time. Because our ability to predict whether a particular person will reoffend is very poor, the use of expert testimony about the likely future behavior of a sex offender, upon which these laws rely, is seen by many as ethically and scientifically questionable.[91] These laws were initially upheld in a 1997 Supreme Court ruling that it was legal to commit people who had already served a prison sentence if they had mental abnormalities that made it probable they would commit similar crimes in the future.[92] *Kansas v. Crane* (2002) restricted these powers by requiring the state to show that the offender suffers a mental disease that causes serious difficulty with self-control.[93]

believe everything (or even most) of what clients tell them, unless it can be proven by some impartial method. Comparison of what sex offenders say with official records and interviews with family and friends is the easiest and cheapest method of verification.[94] Polygraphs are also used to help verify the truthfulness of what the offender tells counselors and officials, and have helped keep sex offenders away from potential victims.[95] Some therapists use *plethysmographs* to measure sexual arousal while the offender views slides or listens to tapes that depict both normal and deviant sexual acts.[96] There are also several psychological tests that are extremely useful in identifying which offenders are most likely to reoffend.[97]

Most sexual offender groups consist of a variety of sex offenders to prevent specific types of offenders, such as incestuous fathers, from supporting each other and blocking the goals of therapy. Treatment specialists also recommend a mixture of individual and group techniques. Some programs divide inmates on the basis of their personality traits rather than by the type of offense. Such groups might consist of: (1) manipulative or aggressive individuals, (2) the socially inadequate, and (3) average individuals who lack a long criminal history but have shown poor judgment.[98]

Contrary to popular belief, two- and five-year follow-up studies of sex offenders show their recidivism rates to range from 10 to 20%, which is lower than those of most other groups of felons. However, 25-year follow-ups predict that 39% of rapists and 52% of child molesters will reoffend. The issue is more complex than these figures imply. Incest perpetrators have very low reoffense rates, while those who molest young boys are at very high risk of committing further sex crimes. So also are those who victimize strangers. Not only do length of follow-up and type of offense affect these rates, but dynamic factors such as substance abuse, social skills, and attitudes toward the offense behavior have dramatic impact on sexual reoffending. This is why treatment has such a dramatic impact on recidivism rates among sex offenders.[99]

Relapse Prevention

Relapse prevention is the key to long-term success in treating both substance abusers and sex offenders. Twelve-step groups can help to prevent relapses because their members can often identify the facial expressions and activities that often precede relapses. However, close monitoring by correctional officials is an absolute requirement in sex offender treatment. Fantasies about inappropriate sexual acts are defined as near or potential relapses among sex offenders and are treated in the same way as actual relapses among substance abusers.[100] Clients must first learn that potential or actual relapse does not necessarily mean failure. It is vital that all relapses be discussed openly so that offenders learn to control them.[101]

Compulsive offenders often deny the danger of relapse even as they are going through this cycle. Denial must be overcome so that they can be trained to recognize the *seemingly unimportant decisions (SUDs)* that link their rationalizations with actual or near relapses. SUDs are choices that place a person in situations that seem irrelevant to their offense pattern but create opportunities for a relapse. In other words, SUDs seem like reasonable and proper behavior but actually encourage relapse. A recovering addict on his or her way home from work who drives by a street corner where drugs are sold has made a SUD and is at high risk of relapse.[102]

The Relapse Cycle[103]

The sequence of psychological events that sets off a relapse is diagrammed below. It begins with the offender trying to escape stress through fantasies of the illegal act. As the temporary relief provided by the fantasies is enjoyed, the offender convinces her- or himself that she or he is entitled to perform the illegal behavior. This entitlement permits the offender to formulate a plan and carry out the act.

Stress → Fantasy → Entitlement → Plan → Action

Stress relief through fantasies or mere thoughts makes up stage 1 of the behavioral cycle below. Stage 2 consists of rationalizing the act or convincing oneself that it is all right to relapse. In stage 3 the offender commits or at least specifically begins the progression toward performing the act. SUDs are important before and during this stage. Afterwards, in stage 4, the offender pretends that nothing has occurred and that he or she is doing well in treatment.

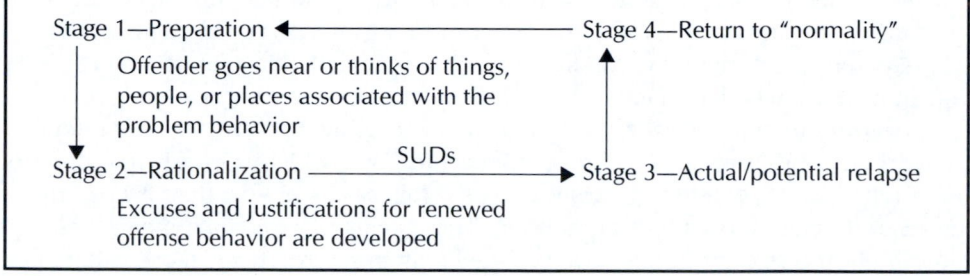

Stage 1—Preparation

Offender goes near or thinks of things, people, or places associated with the problem behavior

Stage 2—Rationalization

Excuses and justifications for renewed offense behavior are developed

SUDs

Stage 3—Actual/potential relapse

Stage 4—Return to "normality"

Contrary to media stereotypes, even sex offenders can learn to avoid reoffending when returned to the community.[104] Effective treatment gives offenders power over their own lives and links their self-respect to productive activities. Prisons, however, are designed to punish offenders by stripping them of self-respect and keeping them dependent on staff for their most basic needs. More important, crowding, administrative convenience, and lack of funds usually combine to assure that few offenders get the treatment that they need.

PRISON POWER STRUCTURES AND THE EMPOWERMENT OF TREATMENT

Traditional prison programs encourage inmates to be passive by stressing obedience and the superiority of staff. In contrast, effective treatment helps inmates become self-sufficient, socially involved individuals capable of responsible behavior. Replacing aggression with assertiveness and teaching inmates to respect others while insisting that others respect them are benchmarks of successful treatment. However, this type of empowerment often conflicts with the goals of prison authorities. Many prison guards would revolt at the idea that they should treat inmates respectfully. More generally, the power structures of most prisons operate to:

1. make employee work routines as easy as possible,
2. reduce public criticism of a "lenient" correctional system, and
3. guarantee the moral superiority of staff over inmates.

The programs best suited to help inmates avoid recidivism teach attitudes that threaten prison and other agency power structures.[105] Once again, the demands of punishment, cost cutting, and control contradict those of effective treatment and are at the root of many correctional failures.

CREATING AN ENVIRONMENT FOR CHANGE: MISSOURI'S PARALLEL UNIVERSE

Life in Missouri prisons has been redesigned to resemble that in free society by promoting decision making, rewarding good behavior, and encouraging ties between inmates and citizens. Instead of staff managing all aspects of life and handling inmates in large "blocks," Missouri inmates earn the power to organize and run their lives while imprisoned. They must work, attend treatment, and use their leisure time for community service, reparation (victim-offender mediation and victim impact classes), recreation, and routine activities such as doing laundry and visiting the library. Each inmate must also develop a relapse-prevention strategy and avoid inappropriate activities involving alcohol, drugs, sex, and gambling. Good conduct is recognized and rewarded with additional opportunities to make choices and guide the direction of one's life within the prison. When possible, families are involved in the change process through visits and letters that update them on the inmate's progress. When the family is nonexistent or involved in problem behavior, involvement with other citizens is encouraged during imprisonment and required as part of the inmate's parole plan.

Policy Matters!
To Treat or to Punish?

Many people blame the current crime problem on repeat offenders, and some feel that we should give up on treating most serious felons and merely incapacitate them. On the other hand, studies show that even a 3% reduction in recidivism makes a program cost-effective. U.S. prisons have never invested heavily in treatment, but many penologists believe that if we designed prisons around the needs of effective treatment we could make a large impact on recidivism. This would make prison life seem more pleasant for inmates, however. How would you balance the requirements of public safety and retribution with those of efficient reintegration?

Questions to Consider

1. How do the requirements of treatment contradict those of punishment in terms of how inmates are handled by prison staff and how correctional priorities are set?

2. Assume that some treatments usually work for certain types of offenders. Would it be fair to treat them differently? What changes in prison priorities would you support under these circumstances?

3. Now make the opposite assumption. What if it were proven that treatment was hopeless for most inmates? What kind of policies would you now support?

4. Review the logic behind your answers to questions 2 and 3. What are you assuming about the causes of behavior? What moral or utilitarian beliefs support these assumptions?

This program promotes tolerance and cooperation among inmates and relieves staff of many minor responsibilities. Inmates are accountable for their decisions and make many of the same routine choices as do people in free society. By handling their responsibilities well (e.g., requesting refills before their medication runs out, seeking new housing if cell mates behave poorly), they earn better work assignments, more visits from family and friends, and the privilege of keeping additional personal property in their cells. In short, making decisions and accepting their consequences is at the heart of the program, which places many choices in the hands of inmates rather than prison policymakers. The program is used throughout the state and has cut recidivism by one-third in a five-year period.[106] This is, however, a form of normalization that violates the principle of least eligibility discussed in chapter 1.

Comparative Views
Japanese Naikan Therapy[107]

Japanese culture emphasizes the welfare of the group rather than the individual. Its key themes—harmony, respect for authority, and social integration—are reflected in its correctional system. In Japan, a system of stages or levels similar to that used by Machanochie and Brockway (see chapter 2) is used to determine which inmates get what privileges. Resocialization is the goal of Japanese prison treatment, and work is the main method of achieving it. *Naikan*, the only form of rehabilitative therapy accepted by the Japanese, is based on Zen meditation and stresses the moral responsibility of the individual. Inmates who choose to involve themselves in Naikan therapy go into isolation to reflect on their crimes, their expectations of others, and their responsibilities to others.

SUMMARY

Many kinds of treatment have been shown to be effective in changing criminal behavior patterns, but they are rarely used in prisons because of economic limits and the public's desire for punishment. Most treatment occurs while offenders are on probation or parole; prisons tend to focus their efforts on academic and habilitative programs, but even these are used by only half of all inmates.[108] Although educational programs ranging from literacy instruction to college classes have been shown to reduce recidivism, they are in short supply and many inmates avoid participating in them. As parole boards place less emphasis on participation in treatment, even fewer inmates are willing to work at changing their behavior. Vocational training is often cited as the most pressing need in modern prisons. Private industry is increasingly used to provide such training, but many hurdles confront these efforts.

Psychological treatment may occur in one-on-one counseling sessions, groups, or therapeutic communities. Cognitive-behavioral techniques are at the core of most current treatment programs. Group therapy is popular because it is both cheap and effective, but twelve-step groups are frequently used because agencies lack the resources to provide professional therapists. People with similar problems can benefit from such groups but the motivation, sensitivity, and insight of each group's members determine its effectiveness. All types of treatment should stress relapse prevention.

Knowledge of one's own pattern of perceiving and reacting to situations is at the base of all behavior change. To be effective, correctional treatment must teach people to make good decisions, believe in themselves, and act on these beliefs. This stands in opposition to the idea of punishment and the power structure of most correctional institutions.

QUESTIONS FOR DISCUSSION AND REVIEW

1. What limits the availability of treatment for prison inmates? For offenders under supervision in the community?

2. What are habilitative services? Why are they so badly needed by correctional clients?

3. What role can private industry play in vocational training? What problems are associated with this practice?

4. How does the concept of basic treatment amenability differ from that of differential treatment? Can these approaches be combined?

5. Why are group methods increasingly popular in corrections? What kinds of groups are used? What are the requirements of effective group therapy?

6. What kinds of treatments are used in programs for sex offenders? How effective are they? Compare these programs with those used for substance abusers.

7. What is relapse prevention? What must offenders learn if they are to avoid crime?

8. Why do prison power structures oppose the most effective forms of treatment? Can treatment be effective when public opinion demands punishment?

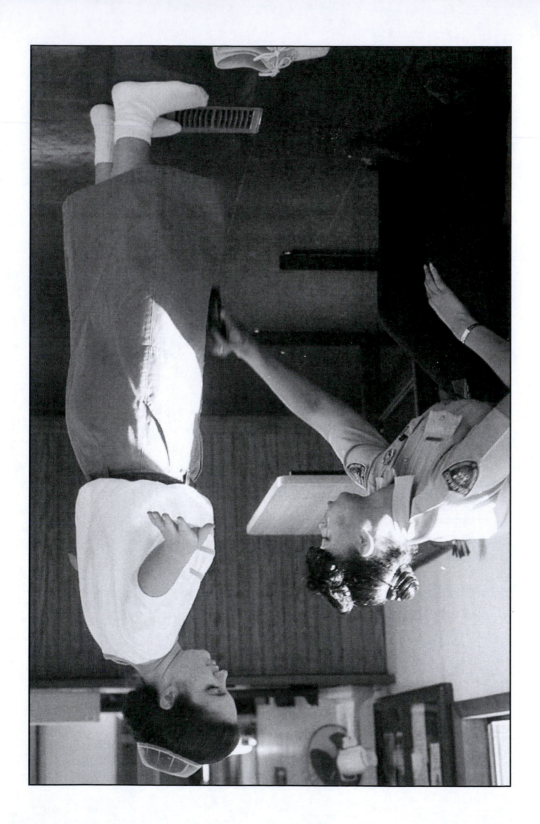

MANAGING THE PRISON

Prisons are miniature versions of urban society in which a variety of social problems are concentrated in a small area. Disease, unemployment, illiteracy, violence, and drug abuse are far more common among inmates than in the general population. Correctional practitioners face most of the miseries of urban society every working day.

Maintaining any large population involves numerous responsibilities. Prison budgets must cover meal preparation, laundry, medical and dental care, building maintenance including plumbing and electrical repairs, and work and leisure programs—plus the personnel to administer all these services. The more crowded the prison, and the fewer staff in it, the more difficult it is to keep up with these demands. All of these challenges confront corrections as it tries to minimize the danger posed by known offenders at the least possible cost.

Assuring custody, maintaining order, and controlling costs are the guiding concerns of modern prisons. Administrators create the rules by which these goals are accomplished, but the correctional staff members are responsible for carrying them out. It is their behavior that determines the atmosphere of each prison.

Correctional agencies compete with all sorts of other government services for money and other resources. They are at a disadvantage in this competition because the public often knows nothing about the goals and responsibilities of correctional agencies and the people who work for them. The media generally ignore policy issues and focus on sensational stories, which shape public attitudes. Public beliefs, in turn, affect politicians who decide what resources will be allocated to various agencies.

PRISON SECURITY

Security is the central concern of the prison that underlies all other activities. Security concerns include both preventing escapes and controlling inmates. Safety

271

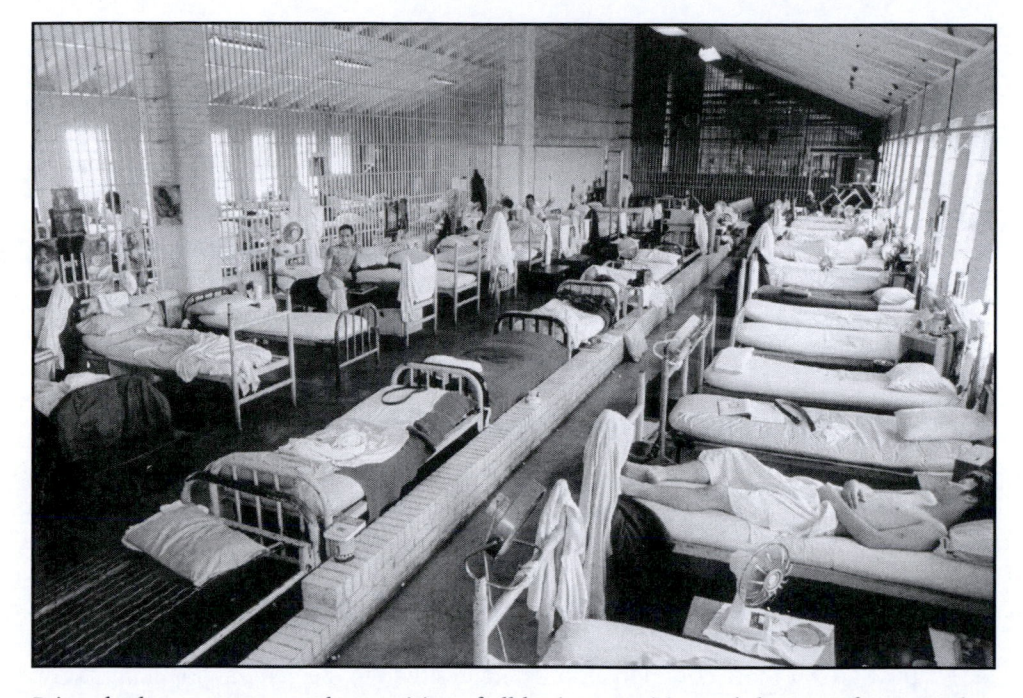

Prison budgets must cover the provision of all basic necessities and the cost of personnel to provide them; the more crowded the prison, the more difficult it is to keep up with demands.

is the paramount concern in most facilities. The quality of security offered by any particular facility is the result of its physical design, the ability of staff to manage the behavior of inmates, its policies and procedures, and the supervision training provided for staff.[1] *Correctional officers* (COs) are the police force of the prison and provide an important link between inmates, the prison, and society. The main function of the CO is to enforce the many rules of the prison.

Prison Rules and Their Enforcement

Prison rules are the product of both bureaucracy in general and the unique problems of the prison. Federal or state laws are the basis of some rules; others, such as those governing inmate cleanliness, reinforce mainstream norms. All are designed to discourage escapes, prevent violence, and protect health. As problems occur, prison authorities write new policies to prevent future incidents. Unusual and extreme cases thus guide policies and procedures, and the regulations of the prison grow over time. This is not unique to prisons; it is found in virtually all bureaucracies.

Enforcing prison rules is an expensive and laborious process; one study found that it cost an average of $970 to deal with a single major rule violation. This includes the time spent reporting the infraction and going through the hearing procedures required to discipline an inmate. The costs of punishing the inmate and holding him or her longer due to loss of good time amounts to another $569. We can be assured that since the time this study was conducted, the expenses

---

Areas Covered by Prison Rules

How rules are written and enforced varies from one prison to the next. The higher the security level, the greater the number of rules, and the more tightly they are enforced. While generalization about rules is difficult, certain types of activity are controlled by virtually all correctional facilities.

1. Inmates must address staff members in a respectful manner and obey lawful commands without argument or significant hesitation.

2. Contacts with people from outside the prison, ranging from mail to phone calls and visits, are strictly controlled.

3. Movement within the facility is controlled by lines painted on the floor or other methods that remind inmates where they cannot go without an escort. Some facilities also restrict the movement of noncustodial staff.

4. Contraband is any item not explicitly permitted by prison officials. Definitions of contraband usually include money, jewelry, weapons, street clothing, and drugs. Many also limit the amount and type of personal property that inmates can keep in their cells.

5. Inmate behaviors, ranging from sexual contact to personal hygiene, are closely regulated. Fighting, gambling, making threats, and using obscene language are forbidden.

---

associated with enforcement have been increased. We can be assured that since the time this study was conducted, the expenses associated with enforcement have increased. Rule violations are common because almost every aspect of inmate life is governed by facility regulations. These rules, and the methods by which they are enforced, are among the main situational factors that affect everyone who lives or works in a prison.[2]

Preventing Escapes

Assuring secure custody of inmates is the chief goal of the prison and an area in which U.S. prisons are quite successful. Escapes are relatively rare in modern prisons; only 492 true escapes were recorded in 2000 while 4,995 inmates "walked away" or were "absent without leave" (AWOL) from furlough or work release situations. Only 9% of these inmates were still being sought by the end of the year.[3] Even if "walkaways," AWOLs, and escapees are combined, these figures amount to far less than 1% of the U.S. inmate population. A New York study found that the typical escapee was a young offender who had served little time on a burglary conviction; 55% were caught within 12 hours, and 82% were apprehended within 72 hours.[4]

Despite the rarity of escapes, security concerns require that COs know exactly where every inmate is at all times. Inmates seek out places and times in which guards will not observe them to engage in illegal activity, such as drug use, gambling, or violence. Thus, the central duty of the CO is to keep track of inmates as they move about the prison. The most common method of keeping track of inmates is the *count*. All activity comes to a halt several times each day as COs verify that all inmates are where they are supposed to be and that none are missing. Counts are also part of the routine for moving groups of inmates from one place to another within the facility.

Corrections and the Media[5]

Most correctional agencies have strict policies covering which employees may speak to media representatives and the topics they may cover. Most have public information officers who specialize in providing routine data to reporters, building relationships with them, and handling press releases when crises occur. The media are an increasingly important part of the environment in which all government agencies operate. Unfortunately, relationships between correctional agencies and the press have never been very good.

Correctional authorities often see the mere presence of any outsiders, including the media, as annoying or threatening because of security concerns, lack of time, and staff shortages. Fear of negative publicity further feeds the desire to avoid the media. The fact that the media often highlight the failures of the agencies and ignore their successes creates tension between officials and reporters. Many correctional officials complain that the media are very poorly informed on correctional topics and that most stories are based on a single visit and a few interviews. The main problem lies in the media's failure to "get the whole story." Press coverage usually focuses on some unique incident or inmate. Reporters work under deadlines that rarely allow enough time to investigate all the background information and to provide an accurate context for the story. Another constraint is the space required to present an adequate discussion of an issue. Whether accurate or not, the perception may be that the public is not interested in background details. The result is often stereotypical treatment of lenient treatment, wasteful spending, or brutal guards.

While the security concerns of institutions make their problems with the press more extreme, community-based agencies suffer much the same fate at the hands of the press. A single major crime by a probationer or parolee will get widespread coverage, while dozens of successes are ignored. Understandably, ex-offenders who have reentered society are rarely willing to risk exposure of their backgrounds; so sensational stories predominate.

Democracy requires a fully informed public to operate effectively. The press is an important part of every agency's environment, and corrections is badly misunderstood because of the failures of both the media and correctional authorities. Both officials and reporters need to rethink their relationships and work together to provide accurate coverage of all correctional issues.

Controlling Contraband

In a prison, *contraband* is any item that inmates are not explicitly allowed to have in their possession. It includes drugs, weapons, certain types of reading materials, and items that might be used in escapes, thefts, or assaults.[6] Anything that might be used to cut through walls or make ropes to climb fences is forbidden, as is anything that might be used to create a disguise. Any item that is desired by but forbidden to inmates is a form of contraband. For example, most states have some sort of restrictions on the use of tobacco, so cigarettes have become a common form of contraband in many prisons.[7] Definitions of contraband vary from one state or facility to the next, but all are based on the security or treatment needs of the facility. (Rehabilitative needs justifiably can be used to ban items like sexually explicit pictures that might inspire antisocial tendencies among inmates.)

Contraband can be roughly divided into two types. Nuisance items, such as gambling equipment and pornography, violate rules that reinforce mainstream morals but do not directly threaten security. Serious contraband consists of items that are illegal

Prison rules control phone calls and other contact with people outside the prison.

in the mainstream (such as drugs) or that pose a direct threat to safety or security (such as weapons and escape equipment). COs will sometimes ignore minor violations involving nuisance items, but only the most corrupt will overlook serious contraband.[8]

COs must constantly be alert for signs of drugs and homemade weapons. Inmates often make crude knives called *shivs* from toothbrushes or scraps of wood, metal, or plastics. Prisoners can be very creative in making weapons, so staff must be constantly alert to the possibility of violence within a prison. Most violent incidents are between inmates, but separating combatants can be dangerous for staff, and direct assaults on employees do occur. Boiling water and lighter fluid can be used to scald or burn others. These are popular weapons in many places.

Shakedowns are thorough searches of cells conducted whenever authorities believe that significant contraband may be found. Warrants are not needed; inmates are felons in custody who have no expectation of privacy and therefore no Fourth Amendment rights. Inmates caught with contraband face disciplinary charges. If the contraband consists of drugs or weapons, they may also face new criminal charges. Staff or visitors caught smuggling contraband will also face very serious charges; bringing contraband into a correctional facility is a crime in all states.

Prison Rule Violators

Punishments for rule violations range from loss of privileges, to solitary confinement, or transfer to a more secure facility. Like crime in general, however, most rule violations are minor and go unnoticed and unreported. Reported violations

---

Methods of Controlling Substance Abuse in Prisons[9]

The following procedures are being employed in many prisons to control the smuggling of drugs, alcohol, and other contraband.

1. Use of ion spectrometers that "smell" minute particles of illicit substances in the air.

2. Restricting inmate footwear and clothing in visiting areas so that visitors' shoes or other clothing with drugs hidden in them cannot be switched with those worn by inmates.

3. Video monitoring and the use of assigned seats so that high-risk inmates can be easily observed by cameras and/or staff.

4. Prohibition of embracing and kissing.

5. Phone-call monitoring.

6. Specialized training of officers assigned to visiting areas. (These officers do not rotate to other assignments so that they remain familiar with inmates and their visitors.)

While these measures have reduced smuggling by visitors, only constant, intensive investigative work within the prison can root out smuggling by staff, which is thought to be a significant, if not the main, source of psychoactive substances.

---

become part of the inmate's record, and rule violations are commonly used to measure an inmate's ability to adjust to the institution. Parole authorities often take the inmate's disciplinary record into account when making release decisions.

Studies based on official records show that known rule violators are most often young, African-American males with many prior convictions. They were usually unemployed prior to being imprisoned and have been incarcerated for a fairly long period of time. The more education an offender obtained prior to imprisonment, the less often he is likely to be involved in violence while incarcerated.[10] Other studies, however, find that black and white inmates are equally likely to violate prison rules but that African Americans are more likely to be reported for doing so.[11] Cultural factors also contribute to prison disciplinary patterns. Most guards come from rural areas while most inmates come from large cities. Two very distinct norm systems interpret the rules differently.[12]

The type of crimes committed sometimes help predict who is more likely to violate prison rules. Property offenders are overrepresented among rule violators, as are those convicted of nonsexual assaults. Property offenders usually are people who feel free to break rules. Having a conviction for a violent offense implies problems in handling emotions or personal relationships. Violent recidivists who have assaulted strangers are at high risk of violent behavior in prison. Drug offenders and those serving time for murder/manslaughter are at low risk of committing major rule violations. Although murder is a violent crime, murderers often do not belong to a criminal subculture but are imprisoned because of a single act inspired by a unique event.[13]

The mental health of inmates appears to predict their capacity for violence better than the type of offense for which they have a record. Inmates with reasonably good mental health, which is usually a product of participation in rehabilitative programs, are not usually involved in violence while imprisoned. Those who are able to receive visits from family and friends on a fairly regular basis also seem to predict noninvolvement in serious disciplinary violations.[14]

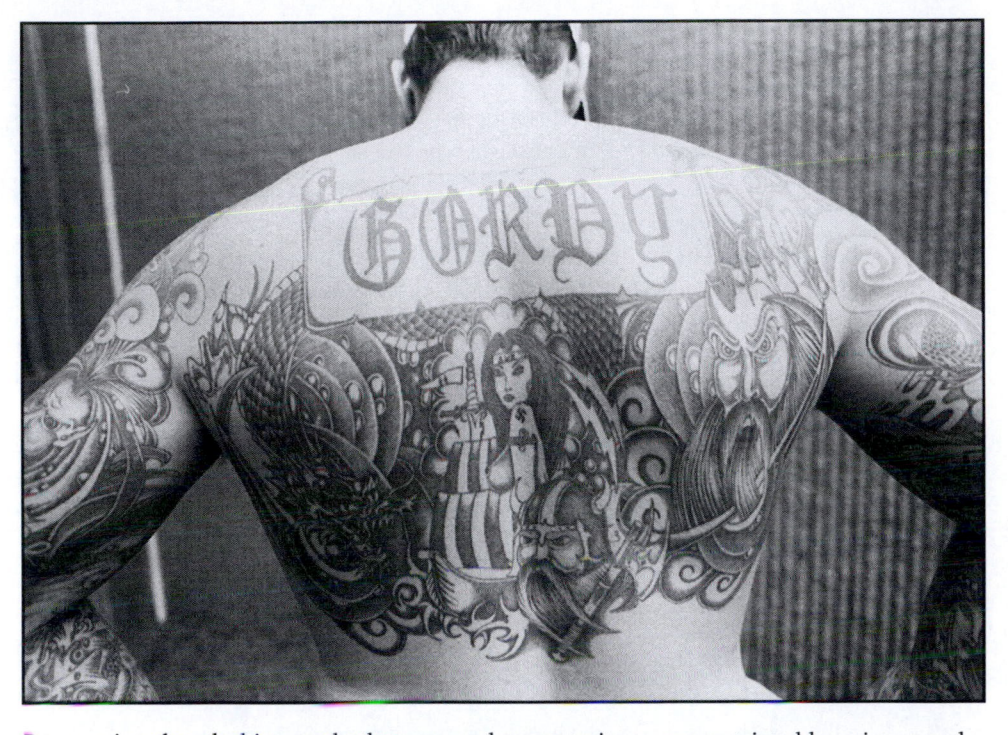

Because jewelry, clothing, and other personal property items are restricted by prison regulations, tattoos are a popular means of expressing one's identity.

Guards may choose to ignore minor rule violations for their own convenience or to win the cooperation of inmates in more important matters. In many cases this is not of great concern and may even make prison life less dismal and therefore safer. For example, a guard who ignores sexually explicit pictures in cells poses little threat to security. However, some COs have clearly been corrupted by various kinds of pressure from inmates. As a result they may smuggle contraband and even look the other way when gangs attack inmates. Their criminal behavior threatens the safety of everyone within and beyond the prison.

Inmate–Correctional Officer Collaboration

In most facilities, COs are badly outnumbered and cannot do their jobs without some cooperation from inmates. As rules multiply, COs sometimes are overwhelmed by the impossibility of enforcing every regulation and may ignore some violations just to avoid paperwork. However, the consequences of not enforcing prison rules can be dangerous. COs can be blackmailed by inmates for failing to report violations. The blackmail leads to more serious activities, such as drug smuggling, going unreported. Guards may be tempted to obtain information or cooperation from certain prisoners in exchange for ignoring rule violations. A few even take bribes to ignore or assist smuggling and other illegal acts. Most COs are honest, dedicated people who make every effort to perform well at a difficult job.

"Unusual Incidents" in New York State Prisons in 1997[15]

Unusual incidents are major rule violations or other events that require formal investigation and extensive documentation by prison staff. Below are some summary data on these reports from 1997 that provide some perspective on the nature of prison violence. In the year reported on here, New York was the fourth largest prison system in the nation with 70,026 inmates.

Total number of Unusual Incident Reports: 8,923

Incident Rate: 128.1 incidents per 1,000 inmates

Location of incident

Maximum-security:	249.8 incidents per 1,000 inmates.	
Medium-security:	76.3	"
Minimum-security:	31.7	"
Shock incarceration:	48.6	"
Minimum-security camps:	48.3	"

Type of Incident

985 inmate assaults on staff

1,860 inmate assaults on other inmates

14.4% of incidents required use of force by staff
(usually in response to an assault on a staff member)

35.1% of these incidents involved weapons used by inmates

221 inmate deaths

4 homicides (3 while the inmate was in community)

14 suicides (1 while the inmate was in community)

193 due to natural causes

10 due to accidents or other causes

CUSTODIAL STAFF RESPONSIBILITIES

Correctional officers are the police force of the prison that directly supervises inmates. Contrary to popular stereotypes, many are committed to the human service aspects of their role,[16] although others see their role as one of punitive coercion.[17] The security level of the facility, the way in which guards are selected and trained, and the methods used to control inmates may explain these differences in attitude. Traditionally, only a high school education was required to become a CO. As the demands of the role grow more complex, many states are seeking applicants with some college courses. While the movement toward "professionalism" is very real in some areas, it is little more than a change in terminology in others.[18]

COs who fear for their physical safety are authoritarian and punitive toward inmates. Nonfearful COs are more flexible and can treat inmates as near equals when their behavior warrants it. Those who are able to develop positive relationships with inmates are less fearful than those who remain distant. Thus, a staff member's attitude toward inmates predicts the nature of his or her experiences, which are then likely to further reinforce that attitude.[19]

COs are usually assigned to a particular shift and area of the prison. Assignments include: a cell block, shop, agricultural area, or school; others work in the yard, the wall posts, or gun towers. Other COs patrol the perimeter or have administrative duties. Only some of these assignments, such as those in cell blocks and work details, place officers in direct contact with inmates. Cell block officers supervise inmates during their leisure time and handle daily routines as well as unusual circumstances like sickness. Shop officers supervise work areas and try to prevent inmates from stealing or making weapons. School officers enforce classroom discipline, assist teachers, and escort inmates to and from classes. Those who guard agricultural work details often ride horses in order to have the advantages of height and speed to discourage escape attempts.

Yard assignments place officers in one of the least structured and most dangerous areas of the prison. The *yard* is an open outdoor area in which inmates gather to exercise and socialize. Yard officers must remain detached from the inmates so that they can break up dangerously large groups and watch key individuals to prevent violence and escapes. Gun tower officers keep watch over the perimeter. These officers, and some who guard work details outside the prison, are the only COs who regularly carry firearms. In other areas of the prison, possession of a firearm is prohibited because inmates might get control of the weapon. Administrative duties include controlling the front gate, escorting official visitors within the prison, or assisting administrators in their jobs.

Gun tower officers are the only COs who regularly carry firearms while on duty.

Those skilled at handling inmates are best suited for cell block, shop, and school assignments. COs who enforce the prison rules with little attention to the uniqueness of the inmates involved will probably perform best in yard or administrative assignments. Unfortunately, COs are usually assigned to specific jobs on the basis of *administrative convenience* rather than personal ability. In other words, administrators do what is easiest for them and pay little attention to the effects of their decisions on staff or inmates. If a CO's job assignment does not fit well with his or her personal style, stress and burnout can occur very quickly.

The nature of the prison population and the monotony of bureaucratic routines create the most stress for employees. This stress can be partially overcome by changes in how staff are treated, but criminal justice agencies are very slow to change. Because they represent society and social control within the prison, racial and gender diversity among correctional officers is vital. As the rest of society becomes more socially complex and technologically demanding, correctional agencies must begin to professionalize their workforce. So far, this trend has had only a minimal effect on state prisons, but the federal prison system is widely held to be a model of correctional professionalism. As with most trends, state governments usually follow the lead of the federal government, albeit reluctantly and often because of legal and financial pressures.

Stress and Burnout among Correctional Practitioners

Correctional officers are routinely confronted by many different sources of stress. Inmates threaten their safety and challenge their authority; administrators demand that they "do more with less"; and lawmakers change budgets and policies for political reasons unrelated to the realities of prison life.[20] These factors can cause high levels of on-the-job stress, which some guards "take home" and thereby affect their family life negatively. Low pay, heavy overtime demands, and rotating shifts create stress at home, which, in turn, impacts their work. Similar problems

---

What Is a "Profession?" Who Is a "Professional?"

Most definitions of a profession emphasize special training or credentials, a distinct mission, adherence to an ethical code, and self-regulation of members' conduct. The American Correctional Association (ACA) works to enhance the training, ethics, and reputation of people employed in corrections but has no real power to regulate practitioners or agencies.

Professionalism is an attitude toward one's work to put forth whatever effort is needed to accomplish goals to the best of one's ability. Excellence in the workplace is always the chief goal. As well-trained specialists, professionals are trusted with a great deal of discretion and autonomy on the job. Autonomy and discretion, however, can open the door to abuse if practitioners do not have a strong sense of ethics.

Autonomy and discretion are limited in criminal justice agencies because of the legal demand for equal treatment of cases. The bureaucratic requirements of uniform record keeping and adherence to procedures also restrict the freedom of correctional practitioners. Within these limits, however, the further professionalization of correctional staff will help to increase both the fairness and efficiency of the system. However, progress toward this goal is painfully slow in most systems.

affect most other types of criminal justice professionals. The results of this dynamic include divorce, finding other types of work, and burnout.[21]

Burnout is the state of emotional exhaustion in which a person feels he or she has accomplished little on the job. Those in the "helping professions"—nurses, teachers, police, correctional officers, and counselors—are the most frequent victims of burnout. In the classic definition of burnout, the professional is overwhelmed by the pain and anger of clients and becomes less able to give of him- or herself as a result. Cynicism and disgust with those one is supposed to be helping are common symptoms of burnout. Correctional staff who get a strong sense of personal accomplishment from their work and feel the support of their coworkers are the least vulnerable to burnout. The sense of commitment that protects against burnout is a significant predictor of job satisfaction among prison staff.[22] A recent study of probation and parole officers, however, found that organizational factors were more important than level of interaction with offenders or personal traits of officers. This study blamed increasing demands for services and heightened emphasis on officer accountability in the context of large caseloads, inadequate treatment resources, and outdated technology for burnout.[23] Both burnout and general job satisfaction have been linked to the inclination among correctional practitioners to seek another type of job.[24]

Job Satisfaction among Correctional Staff

Corrections is one of the fastest growing areas of employment in the nation.[25] However, the remote locations of most prisons, reluctance to deal with criminals, lack of public respect, and low wages make correctional careers unattractive to many people. Community agencies as well as prisons have chronic problems recruiting and retaining high-quality staff members. It is especially hard to recruit qualified minorities because of the legacy of racism in criminal justice. Hiring new workers into an agency means investing in their training, so each practitioner that leaves the field represents an economic loss to the agency as well. Insights into the predictors of job satisfaction are thus of interest to those who run correctional agencies as well as to those considering careers in the field.

While job satisfaction ratings remain fairly high, they seem to be decreasing among prison employees. Among wardens this is due to increasing amounts of control exercised by higher authorities and the growing bureaucratization of the field. Cuts in program funding also play a significant role because they make prisons harder to control.[26] Distrust of administrators, disagreement with official policies, lack of autonomy, and boredom are significant predictors of declining job satisfaction among custodial staff. The longer a CO has been on the job, the more dissatisfaction he or she is likely to express.[27] The same is true of women, minorities, the well educated, those who perceive their job as especially dangerous, and those who feel they lack supervisory support.[28]

Many states have serious problems finding enough qualified people to staff their prisons.[29] As agency staff shortages reach crisis levels in many states, agencies are developing new strategies to attract and retain employees who are well-suited to correctional work as they address issues related to job satisfaction.[30] Escapes and other security problems at various correctional facilities frequently are due to understaffing.[31] Some prisons are trying to professionalize their custodial staff by raising hiring standards, increasing training, providing more benefits, and improving working conditions. While this makes the profession more attractive, it shrinks the available pool of job candidates. In addition, researchers have found that as education increases, job satisfaction falls, probably because of increased awareness of occupational alternatives.[32] Corrections must find a way to balance these contradictions, as knowledge of behavior control techniques and prisoners' rights make education an important requirement for COs. Along with improving staff education and training, greater ethnic and gender diversity among prison employees has become a current trend.

Female Correctional Officers

Women now make up 27.4% of all prison guards in the United States; this figure has increased by about 1% each year over the last five years.[33] Most supervise male inmates. The presence of women is thought to normalize the sex-segregated prison environment and encourage self-control among male inmates by allowing them to preserve their masculine identity.[34]

Male COs traditionally used coercion to enforce rules. In the 1980s, studies showed that women were more likely to persuade rather than coerce inmates. This lowered tension among inmates but was resented by male guards because it differed from their traditional behaviors. Many women felt that they received lower performance ratings from supervisors as a result.[35] More recent studies have found no major distinctions among the methods of controlling inmates used by male and female COs.[36] It appears that both men and women believe that women use a less confrontational approach, but there is virtually no difference in their actual response to various situations.[37] Studies of job satisfaction among correctional officers have found mixed results when the effects of gender on job satisfaction are examined.[38] The data clearly show that women can perform just as well as men in prison settings.[39] Unfortunately, there is evidence to suggest that sexism remains a problem, especially among older male guards.[40]

Covert discrimination, usually in the form of poor job evaluations by superiors, remains a problem in at least some facilities.[41] Although women make up a large part of the prison workforce they hold only a small percentage of supervisory positions. Nearly one in five COs is female, but fewer than one in ten is a supervisor.[42] These inequalities are partly due to the use of seniority in civil service promotion decisions, but discrimination may also play a role. The fact that a higher percentage of women are wardens than supervisors may be due to the tendency to put a few women in highly visible positions to compensate for the lack of women in middle-level management positions. This is a problem, because it is the supervisors who determine the atmosphere of the workplace and evaluate the performance of line staff.[43] Having more women in supervisory positions and promoting greater equality in job assignments are considered effective methods of reducing gender-based discrimination among prison staff.

The privacy issues raised by the presence of opposite-sex guards were once addressed by assigning opposite-sex COs to locations and shifts that would not place them in bathroom, strip search, or sleeping areas.[44] However, this practice has been ruled discriminatory because it limits the employee's usefulness and can hinder promotions. The courts have become sensitive to the need for gender equality in work assignments because it affects job evaluations and promotions. This concern is primarily focused on female guards employed at facilities for men.

Female inmates may benefit from being guarded by female COs—for example, during searches, when there would be a greater possibility of abuse from an opposite-sex guard, or when an inmate has a history of sexual abuse that could make such an invasion of her privacy traumatic. (Searches due to exigent factors, such as the possibility of an inmate having a concealed weapon, are unaffected by guard gender.)[45] Current case law is unclear as to how much freedom opposite-sex officers can have in supervising inmates. There is, however, a clear trend toward making inmate rights secondary to facility needs and gender equality among staff.[46] Prisons must try to preserve the dignity of inmates while avoiding practices that discriminate on the basis of gender in evaluating and promoting staff.

Male attitudes toward their female coworkers are best predicted by the personal relationships they have with female officers and by their overall job satisfaction. Men who are unhappy in their job often blame their female colleagues for their dissatisfaction. Male guards with low levels of education also tend to dislike

Placing women in supervisory positions reduced gender-based discrimination among corrections staff.

working with women, as do those who are more oriented to custody than treatment. This may be due more to the superior education of the women and the changes that they represent than to their gender. In general, the more security oriented the prison, the lower the rating of female COs by male guards.[47] Oddly, inmate perceptions of the competency of female COs rises with security level, however.[48] While the gender issues among prison staff are fairly typical of those in other traditionally "blue-collar" fields, the racial tensions within staff are often similar to those within the convict culture.[49]

Racial Issues among Correctional Officers

Like inmates, guards tend to socialize within their ethnic group and are distrustful of others. African-American officers seem to give each other more support than do whites because of past experiences of discrimination. This is often interpreted as cliquishness and even reverse discrimination by whites. Because they do not socialize together, white and black staff often develop false beliefs about each other, which in turn reinforces stereotypes. A series of incidents that exposed white guards' membership in racist organizations like the Ku Klux Klan have added to the problem over the last few years.[50] Inmates are less likely to feel that racism affects their relations with staff if the administrative structure reflects a proportionate share of minorities. It is therefore important to make sure that minorities are adequately represented among COs, supervisors, and administrators.

A generation ago there were very few minorities employed in correctional agencies. Even today they are slightly underrepresented in management positions and overrepresented among COs.[51] There is also evidence that the increasing racial diversity of the guard force has had a negative impact on the commitment of white officers to the organization.[52] Some people believe that minority officers can better communicate with and understand minority inmates. Others suggest that white COs are more stressed by their dealings with inmates, but that minorities encounter

---

Prison Managers

Prison wardens or superintendents set the management style of the prison. Traditionally they were appointed by the governor or the state agency overseeing corrections, but some states now use merit-based procedures to select people for this role. The warden is responsible for the overall operation of the prison and represents the facility to outsiders. Routine operations are usually left to the associate or deputy wardens who deal specifically with custody-security and programs. In the past there were also assistant wardens for business management and industry/agriculture, but technology and the desire to cut costs have led to central office staff or private contractors taking over these responsibilities.

Deputy wardens for custody are responsible for the prison's security and supervise correctional officers, investigations, visiting procedures, and disciplinary procedures. Deputy wardens for programs focus on the operation of vocational, educational, religious, medical, dental, and treatment services. They must work together, because most decisions involve more than one administrative area but custody concerns supersede all others. For example, a change in program schedules can affect the operation of security procedures, and these procedures usually determine the schedule of any program offered in a prison.

more problems with their superiors. Others have found that job satisfaction among minorities was best predicted by their ability to deal with inmates, while that of white males was related to their relations with their superiors. The fact that the minorities in this study were better educated than the whites may explain why the minority officers reported lower levels of both stress and job satisfaction.[53]

Racial issues among prison staff reflect those in the mainstream. While unity among prison staff is essential, possible disruption caused by an increasingly diverse staff is worthwhile if only to reassure inmates that prison hiring practices are not discriminatory. Racial differences fade in importance, at least among federal prison staff, as guards gain experience.[54] Continued effort is essential to assure fair hiring and promotions in corrections.

STAFF ORGANIZATION

Despite the changes brought about by greater diversity in the prison workforce, the way in which staff are organized has changed little in the last fifty years. Prison staff are managed according to a combination of principles drawn from the military and bureaucracy. While the militaristic aspects of staff organization are decreasing in some jurisdictions, the bureaucratic aspects of the prison seem to be increasing.

Three basic principles guide the organization of all bureaucratic agencies. *Chain of command* describes the flow of commands from administrators to managers, supervisors, and employees. Military ranks are one example of chain of command. This model is used to organize COs in even the most progressive of U.S. prisons. All agency employees, whether or not they are assigned a rank, form part of a hierarchy that stretches from the state capital to individual practitioners. Commands come down from the top of the organization while information is collected at the bottom and sent up. Clarifying the situation of each staff member is the *unity of command* in which each employee has one, and only one, supervisor.

Finally, each manager or supervisor has a particular *span of control* or specific number of people who report directly to him or her. These groups may be based on shift, location, or area of specialization. If a manager's span of control includes more than seven or eight people, communication problems are likely to occur. In small agencies, and among highly professional staff groups, relationships stress equality even between supervisors and subordinates. However, such equality is hard to assure in correctional agencies. This is partly a result of their use of coercion and partly due to their size; the larger the facility or agency, the more likely it is to be hierarchical and bureaucratic.

Bureaucracy

Bureaucracy allows a few practitioners to handle many cases in a short period despite staff turnover and leadership changes. *Bureaucracies* are hierarchical organizations with a specialized division of labor in which rules or policies guide *all* staff decisions. Performance evaluations are based on how well employees follow the rules and keep the records. These specifications are the source of the bureaucracy's efficiency, but they can make agencies and practitioners very insensitive to the people they serve. Keeping the agency's basic goals in mind is crucial to the proper application of rules. Thus, if the communication between hierarchical levels is open and direct, the organization is more likely to operate efficiently.

A clear chain of command consisting of small groups with specific duties allows employees to gain expertise in one or a few areas but discourages them from seeing how they fit into the larger agency or system. Staff must apply general rules from a "procedures manual" to the specific situations they encounter on the job. The better they understand the logic and spirit of the rules, the more likely they are to apply them as intended by administrators.

Because promotions are based on bureaucratic demands about rules and records, employees are more likely to be familiar with the files of their clients than with the unique individuals assigned to them. Correctional staff focus on the criminal acts and legal status of the person and tend to ignore other traits. This is alienating to both the practitioner and the client because it denies each one's full humanity. In a bureaucracy devoted to public safety, solutions to this problem do not come easily. If correctional practitioners allow themselves to be distracted from the criminality of their clients, they can endanger both themselves and the public.

The rules assure that every case processed by an agency gets the same treatment. This keeps decision making predictable and equal by limiting the number of subjective judgments made by practitioners. The amount of discretion given correctional practitioners can threaten attempts to assure fairness and consistency by allowing personal biases to surface. On the other hand, discretion can humanize the process by taking the uniqueness of each situation into account. It is for this reason that the quality of the staff is the most critical aspect of any agency's operation; people are the most important resource of any correctional agency.

Good record keeping is required to keep track of changes in each offender's status. Records allow agencies to replace one practitioner with another so that no one person is essential to the agency's operation. The records also show why and how the rules were applied and are often used as evidence in legal proceedings. They must, therefore, be well written, accurate, and up to date. In focusing on the methods used to make decisions and the demands of up-to-date paperwork, the staff may easily forget their overall goals. All correctional agencies are bureaucracies and operate under these dynamics.

Management styles vary somewhat with the needs of the specific agency. Each agency has a unique mission that is oriented to controlling people and changing their behavior. The particular mission of the agency or facility affects how employees are treated. Maximum-security prisons are usually more rigid in handling staff and inmates than are probation departments. The unique organizational and management features of each agency can be learned only by working in or with that agency. Nonetheless, certain principles of management apply in most or all situations. Much of what is said about managing correctional staff can also be applied to handling offenders. All management principles are based on knowledge of human motivation and the use of power.

THE USE OF POWER IN FORMAL ORGANIZATIONS

The fairness and efficiency of an agency or practitioner depend on how well various types of power provided by legislative mandates are used. The more power people or agencies possess, the more responsibility they have for their actions. Correctional staff have authority over offenders in order to control and change them. In turn, those staff are under the power of their superiors, who ultimately report to elected officials. The use of power always carries with it the threat of abuse, which is worrisome in a democracy. There are three basic types of power, and each has a different impact on human behavior. **Remunerative power** is based on the ability to pay wages or salaries. More generally, remuneration refers to any sort of material gain, from a candy bar to a new home. **Normative power** is the ability to assign symbolic rewards that make one or a few people stand out among their peers. Trophies, titles, recognition ceremonies, and other awards are examples of this type of power, as is a simple "pat on the back" from a supervisor. **Coercive power** is based on the ability to use force to obtain the cooperation of others. This type of power is very dangerous in a free society, because it can quickly become absolute through the ability to confine and kill.[55]

Each type of power leads to a different kind of relationship with the organization that uses it. Coercive power is alienating. The more people are forced to act against their will, the more they will feel distant from and dislike the organization and everything it represents. All organizations need to minimize their reliance on coercive power. This is especially true of the agency's relations with its staff, which are too often coercive. What is effective for staff is also likely to work with at least some offenders. However, few prisons recognize this, and many define coercion as essential to their security and punishment goals. While this strikes many citizens as fair, it is counterproductive from an efficiency standpoint because correctional agencies represent society to the offenders with whom they deal. Coercion makes inmates more helpless and resentful, and thus less able to live in society.

Remuneration is vital to our economy. People depend on their paychecks to survive and enjoy life. However, remunerative power is linked to both mildly positive and mildly negative feelings toward the organization. People who hate their jobs usually find other ways to support themselves, but few love their work so much that they would do it for free. Furthermore, most people never receive as much remuneration as they feel they deserve. Thus, there is often mild resentment toward one's employer.

Normative power builds the greatest loyalty to the organization and its goals. Normative power links a person's emotions to the organization and its goals in ways that impact identity, self-esteem, and values. It can create strong loyalty to and involvement in organizations that use it well.[56]

Correctional employees are motivated mainly by remunerative power. Professionalism sensitizes employees to normative power because of the emphasis on excellence. Offenders are managed largely through coercive power, although remuneration (either in wages or credit toward early release) can play a role. Symbolic rewards can also be used and are vital to habilitative and treatment programs. Unfortunately, prisons are notorious for being coercive toward employees as well as inmates, even though organizational efficiency studies uniformly condemn this approach. Some prisons are trying to minimize coercion and hierarchical relations among staff. This is a long, slow process to change firmly entrenched attitudes in a venue where few are motivated to change.

Management Styles

Most correctional agencies use an **authoritative** style of management that stresses the rank and power of each employee. This style is similar to that of the military and is experienced as coercive by lower-ranking employees. The coercive attitudes toward offenders are often generalized to include employees. When this happens, communication and cooperation among staff usually suffer. There is some movement away from authoritarian management toward methods that encourage employees to participate in the decision-making process.[57] However, correctional agencies are very slow to change; most still use authoritarian techniques, although they may give lip service to other styles. Part of this slowness to change stems from the legal and practical need for a clear system of power and responsibility.

At the other extreme is the professional model of authority, in which employees freely suggest ways to improve their own performance and that of the agency. This approach allows staff members to act without first checking with supervisors because it assumes that they are professionals who will not violate agency policies. This reduces the power of supervisors over line employees and is often resented for this reason. However, professionalism demands that power accompany responsibility, so

---

Unit Management[58]

Unit management is an innovative method of organizing prisons in which each cell block is a partially independent living area for 150–200 inmates. Interaction with inmates from other parts of the prison is minimal under this approach. Inmates assigned to a unit may share a common problem such as HIV/AIDS, old age, or substance abuse or be selected only on the basis of security classification. Units for mentally ill, addicted, or other "special needs" inmates should be smaller than those whose residents come from the prison's general population.

A unit manager coordinates and supervises the activities of the unit's COs, a case manager, a counselor, a teacher, and sometimes a mental health expert. All unit staff cooperate with the manager to create procedures and programs for the inmates. Staff are often **cross-trained**; guards have training in treatment and program staff have training in security. All staff share equally in various shifts and in weekend and holiday duties rather than basing these assignments on seniority.

Unit management reduces escape attempts and assaults while allowing staff to be more efficient. Custodial and treatment staff are unified by their focus on the unit's welfare. The division of inmates into small, easily controlled groups whose members are personally known to staff also promotes efficient security. Close contact over a long period of time by a small group leads to a sense of group identity, which can advance treatment as well as promote safety. Staff members prefer unit management because they can have direct and immediate input on all the decisions that affect them. In addition, the work environment is more relaxed because of easier communication and reduced emphasis on rank and power.

many welcome any movement toward greater freedom for rank-and-file correctional employees. Such *participative management* encourages employees to invest in all of the agency's operations and decisions. At the very least, it recognizes their importance to the organization. At best, it assures their cooperation with new procedures and helps managers make better decisions.

To the degree that correctional roles become more professional, some movement toward participative management can be expected. However, the nature of the corrections mission assures that some degree of authoritarianism will persist in these agencies. The future of corrections depends partly on the way it treats its employees.

PRIVATE PRISONS

The federal government, 32 states, Washington, D.C., Puerto Rico, Great Britain, and Australia allow private companies to build and operate prisons. Most of these private providers are "for-profit" companies but a few are nonprofit organizations. As of 2001, 158 private prisons held 6% of state and local and 12% of federal inmates. The typical private prison is a small facility of less than 800 minimum- or medium-security males located in a southern or western state. Corrections Corporation of America (CCA) and Wackenhut Corrections Corporation control over 75% of all the privately managed prison beds.[59]

From 1991 to 1998, private-prison construction flourished. State legislators seized the opportunity to look tough on crime, to provide employment opportunities, and to appear fiscally conservative by contracting with private companies who presented themselves as highly cost efficient compared to wasteful government bureaucracies. In addition, private companies could build new prisons without the need to obtain voter approval for funds.[60] The process of requesting bids from private contractors and selecting a company to build and operate a new prison can take from six months to two years depending on the complexities of the bidding process. Government standards guide the construction and operation of these prisons, but their management is handled by the contractor, who is paid on the basis of a per-inmate, per-day contract. The more inmates a company holds, and the longer it holds them, the greater its income. The corrections industry and its profits thus grow with the national rate of imprisonment. In fact, CCA built a number of prisons speculating that they would soon win contracts. When state governments cut back on funding for private prisons and the rate of imprisonment slowed somewhat, the companies suffered serious financial losses.[61]

The resurgence of private prisons was based on hopes that they would be more cost-effective than government agencies. Much of the savings attributed to privatization is because these companies' facilities are new, and therefore more efficient, than public ones, many of which are more than 50 years old.[62] Most cost savings, however, are achieved through the lower wages and smaller benefit packages given the staff of private facilities.[63] Supporters of privatization claim that the average private prison costs 5 to 15% less to operate than a similar, government-operated one.[64] Government estimates of savings through privatization are more cautious, however. Rather than the projected savings, the average was 1%.[65] Many states are adopting the cost-reduction strategies of private prisons and reductions in the costs of public prisons are thus expected in many states.[66]

Private prisons are cheaper partly because they usually hold the least dangerous inmates and those who are nearing their release date. There is little private-sector interest in psychiatric facilities or ultramaximum-security prisons that cost much more than ordinary facilities to build and operate. The responsibility for caring for sick inmates in private prisons is often limited while that of the state is not.

Many legal questions about private prison companies and the jurisdictions they serve remain unanswered. Texas was one of the first states to experience unanticipated legal quagmires. In August 1996, private prisons in the state housed about 5,000 inmates from fourteen states. Two Oregon sex offenders escaped from a CCA facility in Houston. Texas officials were unaware that violent offenders from another state were being detained in the minimum-security facility, which usually housed illegal aliens. After the escaped prisoners were recaptured, they could not be prosecuted because there were no laws on the books that prohibited running away from a private prison.[67] All states that contract with private prisons will have to determine who is legally responsible for staff misconduct, accidents, escapes, and other costly events. These laws will undoubtedly be tested in court before clear guidelines and precedents are established. One question is whether a state has the right to control what kind of prisoners private contractors bring into the state. Another is who will be responsible for the costs of searching for escapees—the private contractor, the state that incarcerated them, or the state in which they escaped?[68] These issues illustrate the need for careful review of contracts dealing with private prisons and laws to address potential violations.

Problems with Privatization

Critics note that the promised cost reductions are insignificant and that private prisons are mismanaged. Lack of oversight by state agencies, poor selection and training of staff, transferring inmates to inappropriate security classifications, and understaffing are problems that have surfaced since contracts with private prisons have increased.[69] Private facilities also have higher rates of violence than do public ones (49% more inmate-on-staff assaults and 65% more inmate-on-inmate assaults in a comparison of medium- and minimum-security facilities[70]). Unions fear that private companies will provide fewer benefits and hire fewer workers than governments do. The use of non-civil-service methods for promotion and hiring is a central issue here, along with wages and benefits. Many private prison guards start at little more than minimum wage—considerably less than the starting salary of comparable state employees. Turnover in these facilities is higher than among state employees (41% compared to 15%), meaning that private prisons are often staffed by less experienced personnel.[71]

There has been evidence of illegal treatment of inmates and poor security practices in private facilities. In a nine-month period, four inmate homicides were committed in a Wackenhut facility in New Mexico, and a guard was murdered in 1999. In March 2000, a judge in Louisiana ordered a Wackenhut juvenile facility to be closed because of the abusive treatment of the youths housed there.[72] In August

2000 two prisoners escaped from a CCA prison in Texas. Investigators discovered that doors in the facility had been unlocked, surveillance monitors were not attended, and the staff in the control center simply turned off the security alarm that sounded when the prisoners cut through the perimeter fence. In October 2000, eight guards were injured when prisoners took them hostage in a CCA prison in New Mexico. In December 2000, guards at a CCA prison in South Carolina were convicted of assaulting a youth and fined $3 million.[73]

These deficiencies, abuses, lawsuits, and a slowing in the growth of state prison populations resulted in no state private prison contracts in 2000; some existing contracts were withdrawn. North Carolina, Montana, and California passed laws prohibiting the importation of out-of-state inmates. In contrast, the federal government increased its use of private prisons. The first federal contract was not granted until 1997.[74] However, as the number of federal prisoners increased dramatically, federal prisons were operating substantially over capacity. Less recognized than the impact of drug laws on the increase in federal prison populations is that of federal immigration policies. In 1996 Congress expanded the list of crimes for which a noncitizen could be deported after serving his or her sentence. In seven years the number of noncitizens serving criminal sentences almost doubled, reaching 35,629 in 2001. The growth in this population has been a boon for private prisons. Most of the noncitizen offenders require only low-security facilities. Since the prisoners will be deported, there is little pressure to provide education and counseling programs.[75] In May 2001, the Immigration and Naturalization Service and the U.S. Marshals Service renewed five contracts with CCA estimated at more than $50 million each.[76]

Ethical concerns about private prisons focus on the issue of whether private firms should profit from the government's policy of incarcerating offenders. Private-prison corporations are public corporations obligated to shareholders. There is no incentive for them to consider alternatives to incarceration; public good versus private profit can conflict. Falling crime and incarceration rates, alternatives to imprisonment, changes in drug and immigration laws, and shorter prison sentences could help establish a more equitable justice system, but those very actions would depress the profits of private correction corporations. Choices about public safety, the rights of prisoners, and employee training guided by profit is a potentially disastrous mix.

Another ethical concern involves the power of correctional companies to influence state governments and employees. Just as defense contractors recruit military officers, correctional officials leave the public sector for jobs with private firms. Such career opportunities were much more limited before 1990. The chief operating officer of CCA is a former director of the Federal Bureau of Prisons; another serves on the board of directors at Wackenhut.[77] A professor of criminal justice at the University of Florida resigned his tenured position after he was fined by the Florida Ethics Commission for accepting millions of dollars in consulting fees from the private prison corporations he was researching.[78] The former head of the Texas prison system was convicted of illegal business practices after he retired, formed a private consulting firm, and went to work for a company with which he had dealt while a state official.[79]

As the private corrections field becomes more concentrated and competition between companies is reduced, there are parallels to the defense industry, which has repeatedly been linked to gross overspending, conflicts of interest by officials who move between corporate and government posts, and other abuses. Many writers are already comparing the security-corrections field to the military-industrial complex that became so controversial in the 1960s. "The prison-industrial complex now includes some of the nation's largest architecture and construction firms, Wall Street investment banks that handle prison bond issues and invest in private prisons, plumbing-supply companies, food-service companies, health-care companies, companies that sell everything from bullet-resistant security cameras to padded cells."[80] This **prison-industrial complex** is used mainly to control "surplus populations," such as inner-city minorities and the chronically unemployed, who do not contribute to the national economy.[81]

A recent report by the Institute for Taxation and Economic Policy raises doubts about the ability of private prisons to show a profit without tax subsidies. It noted that politicians and other government officials are increasingly shareholders in private corrections. They suggest that unless formal controls are placed on the relations between government and these corporations, the "prison-industrial complex" will continue to grow at the expense of both taxpayers and minorities. The report also notes that these facilities are cheap and profitable to operate partly because of the subsidies and tax incentives they receive from federal, state, and local governments. No one has studied whether these payments benefit taxpayers, but the report suggests that they may promote reckless spending by at least some of these companies.[82]

Advocates of privatization complain that these companies and their employees have fewer legal protections from lawsuits than do government facilities. Virtually all government agencies have **qualified immunity** from prosecution under section

---

Legal, Moral, and Practical Issues of Privatization[83]

The tension between cost-effectiveness, freedom from crime, the duties of government, and the rights of businesses will be critical to the future of private corrections. Given the past abuses of the lease system, many ethical and practical questions need to be raised about this trend.

1. Should the human misery that is so much a part of imprisonment become just another source of private-sector profits? How will privatization affect the government's ability to make intelligent decisions about the use of imprisonment?

2. What role should private companies have in the creation of correctional policies? Can we trust the advice of these companies on policy matters? How much power should they have in deciding parole eligibility and similar questions related to inmate behavior?

3. To whom do private prisons and their employees owe their loyalty? The public, the agency with which they contract, or their shareholders?

4. How will the privatization of corrections affect the rights of the businesses that provide these services? What should be done to protect their investments in land and buildings? Should they have the same rights as other corporations?

5. Who will be legally and financially responsible for the actions of private prisons? Can they be trusted to put the public good before their own profits?

1983 of the Civil Rights Act (see chapter 10). This immunity protects them from suits over procedures that are not "clearly established" as illegal, allows suits to be dismissed, and protects the agency from paying damages in cases where a new law has yet to be fully interpreted by the courts. In 1997 the Supreme Court found that private prisons can be held liable for damages even if the illegal nature of the procedure has not been established.[84] This means that private companies will have to either raise their fees to compensate for this danger or seek government indemnification as part of their contract.[85]

Indemnification means that if a person or business is sued as a result of performing prescribed duties, they are entitled to (1) the services of the state attorney general as their defense counsel and/or (2) financial protection from court costs and damage awards. These protections are limited to actions made in good faith and justified by contract, state law, or agency policies and training. Those who are improperly trained or act on the basis of a law that is later declared illegal are not liable for their actions. However, if the employee or business violates agency rules, no indemnity is granted. Each jurisdiction has a different definition of what kinds of acts are indemnified. All state and federal practitioners are protected by some form of indemnification. Some employees of local governments are covered by state indemnity laws while others are protected by local rules about indemnity, but a few have no protection at all.[86]

SUMMARY

Prisons must deal with all the problems of a complex urban society. Correctional officers are the police force of the prison. Rule enforcement by well trained, experienced COs and good facility design are at the heart of prison security. Rule violations run the gamut from trivial to life threatening, and guards must often ignore the less serious ones in order to keep tensions manageable. Many jurisdictions are trying to increase the professionalism of their prison staffs through higher standards in hiring and training. Stress and burnout plague prison staff at all levels, but this has not discouraged increasing numbers of women and minorities from entering the prison workforce. Their use of different methods to perform these jobs led both to useful new procedures and to suspicion from white male veterans. Diversification of the prison workforce is one sign of the movement toward the professionalization of corrections. There is evidence that sex discrimination may be declining but racial problems among staff seem more persistent.

The most notable trend in modern corrections is the use of private contractors to save tax dollars. Many questions about the responsibilities of these companies remain, however. Critics fear that many of the problems posed by privatization have yet to appear or are being minimized for political reasons. Many legal and financial issues will also have to be solved before the powers and responsibilities of private firms will be fully known. The ethics of how these companies will deal with the government and the public creates concern among some critics. Others note that if imprisonment becomes too easy and cheap, less attention will be devoted to reducing crime.

QUESTIONS FOR DISCUSSION AND REVIEW

1. Who performs the administrative and managerial tasks in a prison? What are the duties of each prison manager? How has technology changed the administration of the prison?

2. What factors decide the social atmosphere of a prison? What policies and norms are most associated with tension between staff and inmates?

3. What are the responsibilities of a correctional officer? What are the most serious challenges encountered by these prison employees?

4. What are the advantages of increasing the number of women working in prisons? Can women perform as well as men in the harsh, violent setting of the prison?

5. How is increasing racial diversity among correctional practitioners affecting relationships among prison staff members? Is race or ethnicity related to how employees perform their job or the level of satisfaction they get from it?

6. What problems face women and minorities who work in correctional facilities? Is there evidence of gender or racial bias in modern corrections? What forms do they take?

7. Why is interest in and use of private prisons increasing? What problems are foreseen for such prisons and jails?

THE DEATH PENALTY

Capital punishment is an emotional issue; opinions about it are often guided by moral and political beliefs rather than factual knowledge.[1] Most Western nations have abandoned it because they feel that it is barbaric, ineffective, and far too costly. Its American critics feel it is a "dying institution" because it is commonly used only in a few developing nations and several southern states. Concerns with how the penalty is assigned appear to be causing a decline in support for capital punishment in the United States, as groups like the American Bar Association and most major American religious groups take official positions against it.[2] On the other hand, it is supported by people who believe it assures justice, incapacitates the worst offenders, and deters crime.[3] Some of these arguments are based on scientific studies, but most originate in beliefs about justice and efficiency or in the history of the death penalty. Moral and practical arguments overlap with one another in this debate, as do political and legal issues. The same data are often interpreted differently by those who would abolish the penalty (abolitionists) and those who would retain it (retentionists). Part of the ferocity of this debate is due to the fact that capital punishment traditionally has been reserved for the crimes that threaten society the most. The acts that are eligible for the death penalty have changed dramatically over the last two thousand years of Western history.

THE HISTORY OF CAPITAL PUNISHMENT

Tribal societies had few crime problems and recognized only a few offenses as deserving a punishment of death. As empires began to appear, capital punishment was used mainly to control soldiers, slaves, and conquered peoples. It was not until the early Middle Ages, when Christianity became the dominant religion, that use of the death penalty against a nation's own citizens became common. Monarchs depended on the church to support and justify their power, so any challenge to the authority of the church also threatened the power of the state. Therefore, religious crimes like heresy and witchcraft were punishable by death. The revolutionary periods in England, France, Russia, and elsewhere led to dramatic increases in the use of capital punishment. Rulers were quick to use the death penalty to assure their grasp on power.[4] As capitalism began to thrive in England, trade became vital to that nation's welfare, and the number of capital crimes rose from eight to several hundred. Most of the acts added to the list were property crimes. Thieves were executed more often than murderers during the 1700s as part of a desperate attempt to protect English society from skyrocketing rates of crime. By the 1800s the English had lost faith in the idea that executions could control crime and restricted their use to murder and treason.

The American colonies had death penalty statutes but used them less often than did the English. Murder, robbery, rape, rebellion against parents, and religious nonconformity were theoretically punishable by death, but the death sentence was rarely applied. Capital punishment was used more liberally in the southern colonies to control slaves.

Some of the founding fathers of the United States saw capital punishment as a symbol of tyranny, while others feared that too frequent use would weaken its effectiveness. For these and other reasons, its use for crimes other than murder and treason became unpopular in many states. Michigan abolished the death penalty in 1846/7. Wisconsin and Rhode Island followed this example within a few years. However, the execution of slaves continued throughout the South until after the Civil War. Even today, execution is much more common in the southern United States than elsewhere in the nation.[5]

Up until the mid-1830s, executions were public affairs that attracted huge crowds. However, they came to be seen as a threat to social order because of the "animal instincts" they aroused in spectators. Beginning in New York in 1835, executions were moved behind prison walls. New York also introduced the electric chair in 1890, believing that it would be more humane than hanging and less likely to attract rowdy crowds.[6] The last public execution in the United States was a hanging in Kentucky in 1936 attended by more than 20,000 people.[7]

From 1930 until the middle of the 1950s between 120 and 190 people were executed annually. The rate of executions then dropped below 100 per year. Use of the death penalty was expanded to include certain drug offenses in the 1950s, but these laws had little effect on either the drug problem or the rate of execution. By the mid-1960s the death penalty had become unpopular; the last execution for rape occurred in 1964, and only 10 additional executions occurred before use of the penalty ceased in 1967.[8] No one was executed between 1967 and 1972, when the Supreme Court ruled that death sentences were being assigned in an unconstitutional manner.

For the first sixty years of this century, African Americans were executed at an extremely high rate throughout the nation, especially in the South. They were also executed at more youthful ages, for crimes less serious than murder, and with fewer appeals than were whites.[9] More than 3,800 offenders were executed in the United States between 1930 and 1967. Most were murderers, but 12% were rapists and

Increasing Use of the Death Penalty since *Gregg*

States were slow to begin executing offenders after the *Gregg* decision because offenders can only be tried and punished under laws that were in effect at the time of their offense. In addition, the tools of execution had to be certified and the appeals process had to run its course before executions could occur. By 1984 executions were becoming fairly common in the United States and remained at a fairly constant level until the early 1990s, when they began to increase dramatically. By 2000 the rate of executions began to drop for a wide variety of reasons (see Figure A). Death sentences more than doubled between 1977 (137) and 1984 (285). Until 2000 (when the number dropped to 214), approximately 250–300 people were sentenced to death in the United States each year.[10]

Figure A Executions 1977–2002[11]

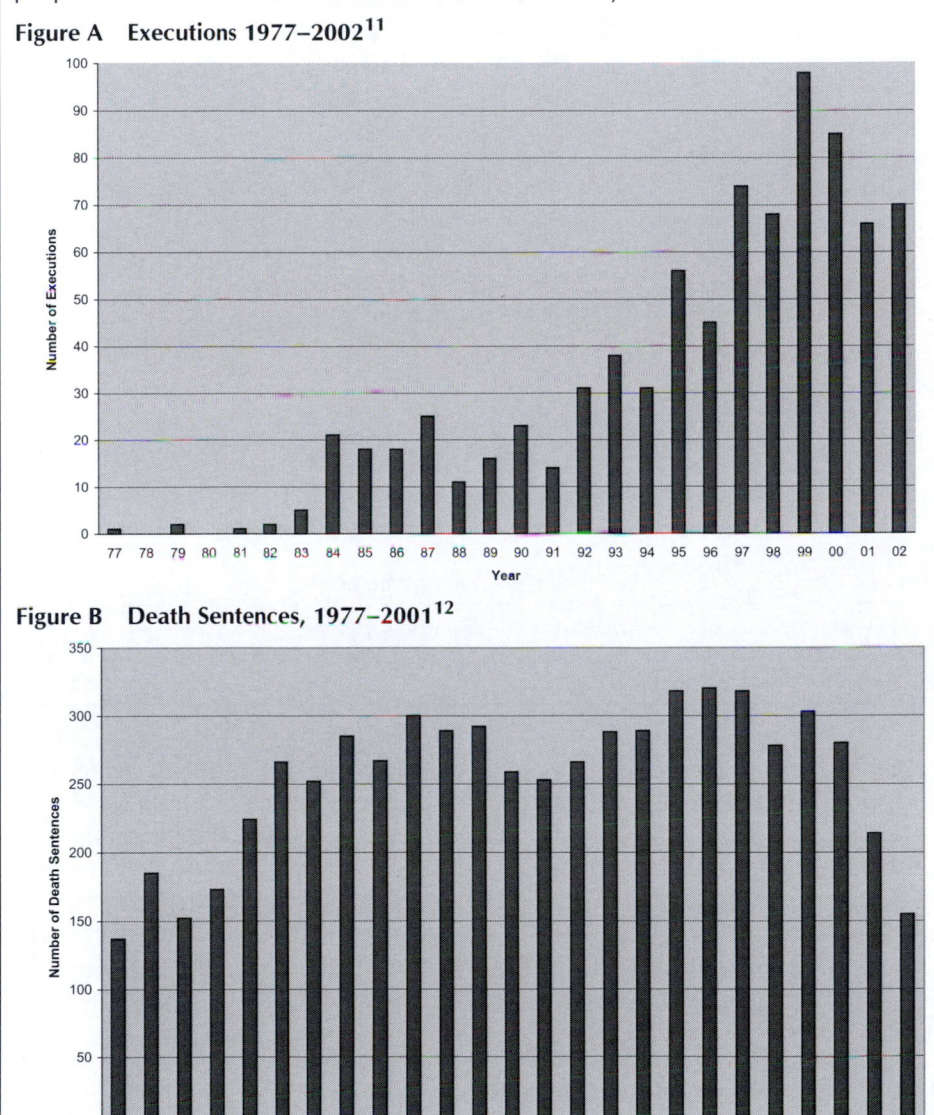

Figure B Death Sentences, 1977–2001[12]

State-by-State Use of Capital Punishment since 1977[13]

Death row populations and specific execution figures are given below for each state. States are listed by the frequency with which they have used the death penalty. Texas, Virginia, Missouri, Oklahoma, Florida, and Georgia lead the United States in executions, but California, Texas, Florida, Pennsylvania, and North Carolina have the largest death row populations.

State*	Number Executed	Number Sentenced	State	Number Executed	Number Sentenced
Texas	289	454	Ohio	5	202
Virginia	87	26	Washington	4	12
Missouri	59	70	Maryland	3	17
Oklahoma	55	119	Nebraska	3	7
Florida	54	386	Pennsylvania	3	244
Georgia	31	120	Kentucky	2	39
South Carolina	28	76	Montana	2	6
Louisiana	27	97	Oregon	2	30
Alabama	25	190	Colorado	1	5
Arkansas	24	42	Idaho	1	22
North Carolina	23	219	New Mexico	1	3
Arizona	22	125	Tennessee	1	106
Delaware	13	20	Wyoming	1	2
Illinois	12	0†	New Jersey	0	16
California	10	613	South Dakota	0	5
Nevada	9	87	Connecticut	0	7
Indiana	9	40	New York	0	5
Utah	6	11	Kansas	0	4
Mississippi	6	69	New Hampshire	0	0
US Govt	2	26	US Military	0	7

*States without capital punishment laws: Alaska, Hawaii, Iowa, Maine, Massachusetts, Michigan, Minnesota, North Dakota, Rhode Island, Vermont, West Virginia, Wisconsin, and the District of Columbia.
†All sentences commuted Jan. 11, 2003.

2% had been convicted of burglary or some other crime. Over 90% of the nonmurder cases involved African-American defendants and occurred in southern states.[14]

Furman v. Georgia (1972) found that laws on capital punishment violated the Eighth and Fourteenth Amendments because they allowed death to be imposed in an "arbitrary and capricious" manner.[15] Evidence that African Americans and other minorities were much more likely to be sentenced to death than whites was critical to the *Furman* decision. In 1976 the Court approved Georgia's new capital punishment law in *Gregg v. Georgia*, and executions resumed a year later with the firing-squad death of Gary Gilmore in Utah.[16]

Eight hundred and twenty people have been executed in the United States since 1977. Thirty-five percent (289) of these have been in Texas and over 81% (668) have been in southern states.[17] Five states have sentenced people to die but have not yet carried out any executions. Although New Hampshire is a death penalty state, it has not invoked the sentence; both Illinois and Maryland had a moratorium on executions in 2002. Twenty-six men have been sentenced to die by the U.S. government, but only 2 have been executed. An additional 7 are on military death rows under federal jurisdiction. Although 38 states have death penalty statutes, only 32 have executed anyone since 1977. As of October 1, 2002, there were 3,697 inmates awaiting execution in the United States.[18]

CRITERIA FOR USE OF THE DEATH PENALTY

Gregg prohibited death penalty laws that were too broad or that might allow discriminatory use of the penalty. Each state had to describe very specific aggravating factors (e.g., multiple victims, intention to kill, or torture) to qualify a case for the death penalty. Capital punishment is now authorized for certain kinds of murder, air piracy, aggravated kidnapping, treason, and rape of a child. Only murderers have been executed since 1977, however, so the constitutionality of some of these laws is open to question.

In *Coker v. Georgia* (1977) the Court found that the death penalty was too severe for nonfatal rapes of adults. The court also ruled that mandatory execution for "first degree murder" was illegal because it was too broad to allow fully for consideration of aggravating and mitigating factors (*Woodson v. North Carolina*, 1976). The use of vague, catch-all phrases like "depravity of mind" was forbidden by the court in *Godfrey v. Georgia* (1980).[19] Along with *Gregg*, these rulings set the standards for new procedures for imposing capital punishment.

Legal Processes in Capital Trials

Cases in which the death penalty may be assigned must use twelve-member juries. Post-*Furman* rulings have encouraged most death penalty states to use a **bifurcated trial process** in which there are two parts to the trial. The first part decides guilt or innocence; the second part is the penalty phase in which the punishment is set. The penalty phase examines the **aggravating** or **mitigating factors** described in the jurisdiction's capital punishment law. These often include the nature of the crime, the defendant's role in it, the likelihood that the offender will continue to endanger society, and the forces that led the defendant to commit the act. On the basis of this evidence, the jury decides if death or some other sentence should be imposed. Jurors can impose a death sentence only if convinced that the aggravating factors outweigh the mitigating ones.[20]

Juror beliefs about the defendant's future dangerousness are critical to jury application of the death penalty.[21] This issue is especially sensitive because many psychiatric experts feel that any or most attempts to predict a person's future criminality are highly questionable and may represent a form of "junk science." When trials rely on expert testimony, there is a danger that psychiatrists and psychologists are actually providing personal values masked in scientific jargon. In the case discussed in the box on page 301, James Grigson, a Dallas psychologist, testified during the jury's penalty deliberations that he could predict with 100 percent certainty that the defendant would engage in future violent acts.[22] The courts have tried to prevent misleading statements by the prosecution or the judge to juries about the penalties they can impose. In *Simmons v. South Carolina* (1994), the Supreme Court held that where a capital defendant's future dangerousness is at issue and the only sentencing alternative to death available to the jury is life imprisonment without the possibility of parole, due process requires that the jury be specifically informed that the defendant will never be eligible for parole. The Court affirmed the *Simmons* decision in *Shafer v. South Carolina* in 2001.[23]

On June 24, 2002, the Court ruled in *Ring v. Arizona* that only juries can sentence a person to death; the decision to impose capital punishment cannot be made by a judge. The ruling overturned death sentencing laws in five states affecting 168 prisoners (Arizona—129, Colorado—5, Idaho—21, Nebraska—7, and Montana—6) and could affect laws in four others (Alabama—187, Delaware—20, Florida—383, and Indiana—39). The decision addressed the basic question: Who decides if aggravating circumstances in a case justify sentencing the convicted offender to death? Twelve years earlier the Court had allowed states to leave the decision to a judge. However, in 2000 in *Apprendi v. New Jersey* the Court ruled that the Sixth Amendment entitles defendants to a jury's decision on whether they are guilty of every element of a crime. Defendants were entitled to a decision by a jury on any fact that would increase the maximum sentence. In her dissent, Justice Sandra Day O'Connor noted the destabilizing effect of *Apprendi* on the criminal justice system. Courts had been "overwhelmed by the aftershocks" of the case that resulted in a flood of petitions in state and federal courts to invalidate sentences. In a separate case, *Harris v. United States*, the Court ruled against expanding *Apprendi* to a jury decision on facts that would increase minimum sentences.[24] There are currently about 3,700 men and women under sentence of death in the United States. It is unclear how many of those sentences will be overturned because of the two decisions.

The Center on Wrongful Convictions at Northwestern University released a study in 2001 identifying the most common factors in wrongful convictions since the death penalty was reinstated. In 33 of the 86 cases studied, eyewitness testimony was the only basis for conviction. In more than half the cases, eyewitness testimony was either mistaken or perjured. Other factors were questionable circumstantial evidence and hearsay (34%), police and prosecutorial misconduct (20%), jailhouse informant testimony (12%), "junk-science" testimony (11%), and false or coerced confessions (9%).[25] The adequacy of defense resources (e.g., funds for independent investigations) and competence of defense counsel are also chronic problems threatening the fairness of these trials.[26]

Because capital trials are extremely expensive and include the possibility of an irreversible sentence, careful review of how verdicts are reached is especially important. An automatic review of death sentences by the state's highest criminal appeals court is required in 37 of the 38 states that permit use of capital punishment. Only Arkansas and the federal system do not require a review. (South Carolina allows convicts to waive their right to review if they have been certified as mentally competent.) The automatic review is similar to an appeal and may examine the conviction, the sentence, or both. Unlike appeals, however, reviews require no action by the offender and bypass intermediate appellate courts in order to save time and money.[27]

Innocent People on Death Row

On November 28, 1976 in a suburb of Dallas, Texas, Randall Dale Adams accepted a ride from a sixteen-year-old stranger, David Harris. Three hours after dropping Adams at his motel Harris, who was driving a stolen car, was stopped for driving without lights. Harris shot and killed Officer Robert Woods and left the scene. After fleeing to Vidor, Texas, Harris bragged to friends about "offing a pig." Police took him into custody. After learning that a ballistics test established that Woods was killed with a gun Harris had stolen from his father, Harris stopped claiming he wasn't involved but said it was Adams who killed the officer. After Harris passed a polygraph test and Adams failed, Harris received immunity from prosecution in exchange for his testimony. Adams was convicted in 1977 and sentenced to death. He appealed to the Texas Court of Criminal Appeals, which affirmed the conviction and death sentence in January 1979. His execution was scheduled for May 8. Adams continued his appeals in the federal courts. Three days before the execution, U.S. Supreme Court Justice Lewis F. Powell Jr. ordered a stay. The Supreme Court then decided that the jury-selection procedure violated *Witherspoon v. Illinois*. That ruling opened the door for a new trial, but the Dallas district attorney instead asked the governor to commute Adams' sentence to life in prison. Adams embarked on another round of appeals for a new trial to prove his innocence. In March 1985, documentary filmmaker Errol Morris took an interest in the case. Morris and Adams' lawyer eventually discovered prosecutorial misconduct including suppressed evidence and witness tampering. The result of this 30-month investigation was the documentary *The Thin Blue Line*, which ended with a confession by David Harris (who was in prison after being convicted of an unrelated murder in 1985). The documentary won a number of awards and stimulated public interest. On March 1, 1989, the Texas Court of Criminal Appeals finally granted Adams a new trial. Three weeks later, Adams was released on his own recognizance; two days later all charges were dropped.[28]

This case is not an aberration. One study found **reversible errors** (legal mistakes in a trial that can be corrected) in 7 out of 10 capital trials conducted between 1973 and 1995.[29] Supporters of the death penalty note that capital trials receive much closer scrutiny than other cases. They claim most retrials still find the defendant guilty but impose a sentence other than the death penalty, concluding that courts are more able to ascertain guilt than to follow the complex laws controlling use of the death penalty. They also note that laws mandating a quality defense for capital defendants are more likely to affect the penalty phase. (The quality of defense available to capital defendants is itself a very controversial issue in many states.) They point to conflict between jurors and elected judges who favor the death penalty and appellate courts that may not.[30] Commuting a sentence is much cheaper than challenging a finding of guilt and thus a more frequent path for indigent death row inmates. As in Adams' case, commutations do not free offenders but remove them from death row.[31]

Since 1977, over 100 people have been freed from death rows in 22 states due to DNA evidence, and at least another 70 have been freed based on other forms of evidence. Many of these men had spent over ten years on death row.[32] Several states are examining their use of the death penalty, and the U.S. Congress is discussing an Innocence Protection Act to assure competent counsel, to assist defendants with DNA testing, and to compensate financially those wrongly placed on death row.[33] More than 20 university-based wrongful conviction projects are operating in the United States.[34] Great Britain abolished the death penalty in 1964 because of the horror felt by citizens when they learned an innocent man had been executed. In an interview with *Texas Monthly* in 2001, Adams said, "In the beginning, I blamed David. But David did not have the power to arrest me, indict me, and sentence me to die. The problem is larger than David Harris. Our criminal justice system, on paper, is the best in the world. But we're human, and so we make mistakes. If you execute and execute and execute, at some point you will execute an innocent man."

Limiting Death Sentence Appeals

The appeals process can be very time consuming; until recently an average case took over eight years to go through a series of appeals, each of which contested a different aspect of the trial or sentencing process. This changed in 1991 with the Supreme Court's ruling in *McCleskey v. Zant*.[35] The Court found that it was legal to restrict offenders facing execution to one *habeas corpus* appeal that examined *all* possible issues related to their trial and sentence. Once this appeal has run its course, only the Supreme Court can grant a stay of execution. Efforts to streamline the execution process were further advanced by the Anti-terrorism and Effective Death Penalty Act of 1996 (ADEPA). This law gives persons sentenced to death one year to assemble and file their federal appeals. In states with approved methods of assuring competent counsel for death cases, the time limit is 180 days. Most federal court rulings on death cases since ADEPA have found problems in the quality of legal representation provided to capital defendants. While the exact legal definition of "adequate counsel" has not yet been resolved, the frequency with which such inadequacies are found is disturbing.[36] The fact that a large proportion of capital defendants are indigent adds to this controversy.

Both the *McCleskey* ruling and the ADEPA are expected to result in more frequent and quicker executions. Supporters of capital punishment applaud this trend, feeling that delays between sentencing and execution weaken the penalty's deterrent value. Critics believe the danger of executing an innocent person is too great without a full appellate process.

The Costs of Capital Punishment

One study estimated that the death penalty costs North Carolina $2.16 million per execution more than the expense of imposing life imprisonment. Another study found that Florida spent $24 million more for each of the 44 executions from 1976 to 2000 than it would cost to house an inmate for life in prison without parole. In Texas, it was estimated that a death penalty case costs an average of $2.3 million—three times the cost of imprisonment in the highest security level for 40 years.[37]

Because local governments finance prosecutors and courts, counties and cities are often left with the bill for capital trials. Local governments meet the unexpected burden of capital trials by raising taxes and by decreasing expenditures on police and highway spending, which has fueled debate about the effectiveness of capital punishment in deterring crime and on whom the burden for the expense should fall.[38] At times the state must intervene with special funding to save local jurisdictions from bankruptcy due to the extraordinary costs of capital trials. This occurred in the case of the "Texas seven," who escaped from a prison in the southern part of that state, killed a police officer on Christmas 2000, and were later apprehended in Colorado.[39] Financial decisions may be a contributing factor to decisions about when to ask for the death penalty. In Illinois, the Commission on Capital Punishment recommended reducing the number of crimes that qualify for the death penalty from 20 to 5.[40]

All the expenses of a trial are magnified in capital cases. There are more pretrial motions. Jury selection takes much longer and is more complicated in death penalty cases. More lawyers and expert witnesses are needed, especially during the penalty phase of the trial. Capital trials also take longer because proof of the crime—and aggravating and mitigating factors—must be debated by experts. Limiting appeals will not help reduce these costs for local governments. The majority of costs of capital cases result from the multiple cases in which the death penalty is *not* imposed. Since the death penalty was reinstated, there have been approximately 6,800 death sentences and approximately 750 executions. Although only 11% of death sentences lead to executions, the extra costs apply to 100% of the cases. Two-thirds of death penalty cases are overturned on appeal; 80% of the defendants retried receive a lesser sentence.[41] Opponents of capital punishment argue that its expense represents a huge **opportunity cost**; money spent on the death penalty would be better used on other crime-control strategies.

SPECIAL GROUPS AND THE USE OF CAPITAL PUNISHMENT

Many of the most disadvantaged groups in society are overrepresented in our correctional populations. The mentally ill, the retarded, and juveniles are sometimes considered less culpable (blameworthy) than others because of their status or condition.

Executions of the Insane

People who are insane when they commit a crime are not usually subject to capital punishment. Similarly, those who are sane when they commit the crime but become mentally ill by the time of their trial can be found incompetent to stand trial. They are confined in a psychiatric facility until they can understand trial procedures and cooperate in their defense. Those who become insane after being sentenced to die compose a third category

In *Ford v. Wainwright* (1985) the Supreme Court ruled it illegal to execute an insane person. Ford's competence and sanity were not questioned when he was convicted, but he began to show signs of psychosis after his arrival on death row. Psychiatrists could not agree on whether or not he was sane. The Court reasoned that the Eighth Amendment prohibited the execution of people who could not comprehend (1) that they had been sentenced to die, and (2) why they had received such a sentence. This ruling was based on the common law principle that for a penalty to be an effective deterrent, the person must understand what is happening and why. The Court added that executions of the insane were offensive to society and criticized Florida's examination of Ford's competence.[42]

The Mentally Retarded

In 1989 in *Penry v. Lynaugh*, lawyers for Johnny Paul Penry claimed that sentencing mentally retarded offenders to death was a violation of the Eighth Amendment ban on cruel and unusual punishment. They claimed Penry had the mental capacity of a seven-year-old when in 1979 he raped and killed a woman after she cut him with a pair of scissors. He was convicted by a Texas court in 1980.

Two legal issues were addressed in *Penry v. Lynaugh*. First, was Penry sentenced to death in violation of the Eighth Amendment because the jury was not adequately instructed to take into consideration all the mitigating evidence and because the terms in the Texas special issues for deciding the death penalty were not defined so that the jury could consider his mitigating evidence in answering them? Second, is it cruel and unusual punishment under the Eighth Amendment to execute a mentally retarded person with Penry's reasoning ability?

The sentencing jury in Penry's trial had been instructed to consider all the evidence in answering three special issues: (1) Was the defendant's conduct committed deliberately and with reasonable expectation that the victim's death would result? (2) Was there a probability that Penry was a continuing threat to society? (3) Was the killing unreasonable in response to any provocation by the defendant? The Court invalidated Penry's sentence because the jury was not adequately instructed to consider potential mitigating factors (such as Penry's abuse as a child and his retardation) and because none of the special issues was broad enough to allow the jury to consider and give effect to those factors. However, the Court ruled against Penry on the second legal issue, stating that there was not "sufficient evidence of a national consensus against mentally retarded capital murderers" of his reasoning ability.

Texas retried Penry in 1990, and the jury again sentenced him to death. In 2001, the Supreme Court in *Penry v. Johnson* again ruled that jurors were not able to give effect to mitigating evidence. A "reasonable juror could well have believed that there was no vehicle for expressing the view that Penry did not deserve to be sentenced to death based upon his mitigating evidence." Penry was convicted a third time in April 2002. His sentencing hearing was not yet completed when the Supreme Court made a decision that will have a bearing on the outcome.

On June 20, 2002, the Supreme Court voted 6–3 in *Atkins v. Virginia* that executions of the mentally retarded are cruel and unusual punishment forbidden under the Eighth Amendment. Writing for the majority, Justice John Paul Stevens cited a 1958 court decision that said "The basic concept underlying the Eighth Amendment is nothing less than the dignity of man. . . . The amendment must draw its meaning from the evolving standards of decency that mark the progress of a maturing society." Reference to the "dignity of man" reflects the logic of the classical school's rationale for civil liberties and deterrence; concern with public opinion is cited as the basis for defining the subjective concept of "decency." Despite ruling in 1989 in *Penry v. Lynaugh* that such punishment was permissible, the Court noted that public opinion in the United States had changed. In 1989, two states (Georgia and Maryland) that had capital punishment banned executions of the mentally retarded; in 2002, the number of states had grown to 18. Justice Stevens cited the "dramatic shift in the state legislative landscape."[43] "It is not so much the number of these states that is significant, but the consistency of the direction of change."[44] A Gallup Poll in May 2002 showed that 82% of the public opposed executing the mentally retarded.[45] Death penalty supporters also believe public opinion as a guidepost for policy establishes a dangerous precedent.

The Court recognized that those with diminished mental capacities are less able to aid in an effective defense, less able to understand fully the arrest and trial procedures, and are more susceptible to making false confessions. "Mentally retarded defendants may be less able to give meaningful assistance to their counsel and are typically poor witnesses, and their demeanor may create an unwarranted impression of lack of remorse for their crimes."[46] The Court also recognized that societal justifications for the death penalty—retribution and deterrence—don't apply to mentally retarded offenders. "This consensus unquestionably reflects widespread judgment about the relative culpability of mentally retarded offenders, and the relationship between mental retardation and the penological purposes served by the death penalty."[47] The high court left it to the states to develop their own systems to determine mental retardation. In his dissent, Justice Antonin Scalia noted that fewer than half of the 38 states that permit capital punishment have banned execution of the mentally retarded. He said the decision would turn capital punishment trials into a game in which defendants would feign mental retardation.

At least 35 mentally retarded individuals have been executed since the death penalty was reinstated in 1976. Critics say the rulings have exposed a basic flaw in the current system. Lawrence Marshall, Northwestern University law professor and legal director of the Center on Wrongful Convictions stated, "The decisions reflect a profound sense that we are making mistakes not only in executing innocent people but in routinely executing people we had no business executing. . . . What do we say to the families now? That we're sorry? That we didn't realize there were 'evolving standards of decency'?"[48]

Juveniles and Capital Punishment

The handling of capital crimes committed by people under the age of 18 is another sensitive topic that will grow in importance as concern with juvenile violence increases. In 1988 the Supreme Court ruled the death penalty illegal for a murder committed by a 15-year-old but upheld it the following year in cases involving 16- and 17-year-olds.[49] The combined effect of these rulings is that people cannot be executed for crimes committed before their sixteenth birthday unless the legislature has specifically authorized a lower minimum age for that state.

Seventeen states permit capital punishment for 16-year-olds, either by an express age statute (7) or by court ruling (10); five restrict the death penalty to those over 17. Sixteen states and the federal government prohibit execution for crimes that occurred before the offender was 18.[50] Eighty-two males are currently on death row in 14 states for crimes committed before their eighteenth birthday and 21 have been executed since 1976.[51]

This precedent has attracted much criticism from the international community. In the last 15 years only seven countries (Bangladesh, Iran, Pakistan, Yemen, Nigeria, Saudi Arabia, and the United States) are known to have executed anyone for crimes committed as juveniles.[52] (It is likely that the Taliban of Afghanistan also did so but this cannot be confirmed.[53]) The majority of these executions have been in the United States. The execution of juveniles has been condemned by the Pope as well as by the U.N. Commission on Human Rights. It is also banned by several international treaties, including the International Covenant on Civil and Political Rights, which the United States ratified in 1992. The Inter-American Court of Human Rights has declared the U.S. refusal to honor this treaty to be a violation of international law and basic human rights. Death penalty supporters are unmoved by these objections. Some counter that youths capable of capital crimes deserve no special treatment, while others claim that U.S. executions of foreign nationals can deter the killing of Americans traveling abroad. They also assert that the United States has a thorough appeals process that assures due process and that its methods of execution are humane.[54]

CURRENT METHODS OF EXECUTION

Five methods of execution are authorized in the United States: lethal injection, electrocution, the gas chamber, hanging, and the firing squad. Fourteen states authorize two methods of execution for practical and legal reasons. If the apparatus for one method is unusable, or its legality is questioned, a legally authorized "backup" method allows them to continue executions without delay.

Ever since the electric chair was introduced in 1890, Western nations have tried to make executions as painless as possible. Lethal injection was invented by Dr. Karl Brandt, a Nazi physician in charge of euthanizing deformed and retarded children and others deemed "unworthy of life" by that regime. (Brandt was executed as a war criminal in 1948, by hanging.)[55] It is now by far the most popular method of execution in the post-*Furman* era, because it is thought to be more humane and foolproof than other methods. When Georgia's Supreme Court ruled that the electric chair violated the state constitution's ban on cruel and unusual punishment it made lethal injection the sole method of execution for those sentenced after the law was passed. Florida's Supreme Court examined the same issues but upheld use of electrocution. The legislature passed a law allowing lethal injection of condemned persons if the electric chair were to be ruled illegal in the future.[56]

The shift toward lethal injection is an attempt to make executions seem as humane as possible. Its dependence on biotechnology has made medical personnel an integral part of the execution process.[57] Data from opponents of capital punishment challenge the idea that lethal injection is humane. Even lethal injection, described by some as "too peaceful" to assure proper retribution, causes paralysis before it kills. Immobilized prisoners cannot move to display their pain, and they may experience some fear and discomfort if the sedative that is administered prior to the injection is not sufficient to render them unconscious. This means that some offenders are likely to endure the pain of feeling their heart and lungs stop while strapped to a gurney.[58]

Methods of Execution in the United States[59]		
Method	# of States Authorizing Use	Executions since 1977
Lethal Injection	36 (+ U.S. Govt.)	580
Electrocution	10	149
Gas Chamber	5	11
Hanging	3	3
Firing Squad	2	2

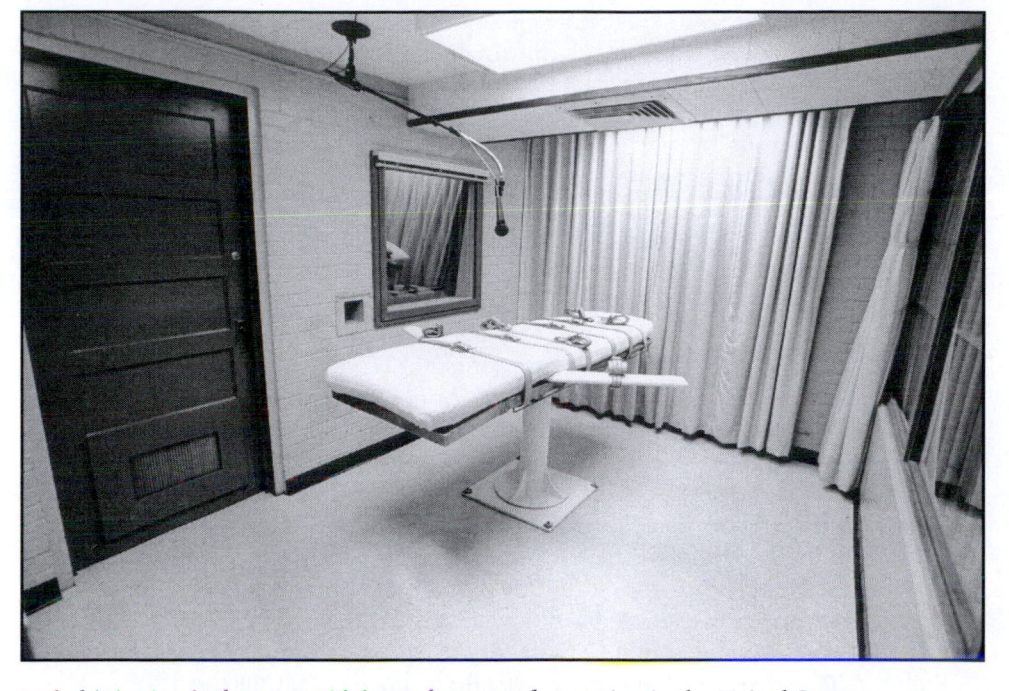

Lethal injection is the most widely used means of execution in the United States.

Thirty-four "botched executions" in 13 states have been recorded by the Death Penalty Information Center: Twenty-four involved lethal injection, 9 involved electric chairs, and 1 involved a gas chamber. Problems with lethal injection include violent reactions to the mixture of drugs and problems in finding a vein that will hold the needle. (The blood veins of ex-addicts are often in such bad condition that the needle cannot be inserted or will not stay in the vein.) At least two condemned men have inserted the needle into their own arms to end the painful procedures. Electric chair malfunctions attract the most attention because of the dramatic plumes of fire and smoke that rise from the condemned person when the apparatus malfunctions. It has taken from eight minutes to more than an hour to complete these executions.[60]

LIFE ON DEATH ROW

In most states, death row is a cell block or building within a maximum-security prison. In thirty states, inmates are usually kept isolated from the general population of the prison and receive the minimum available prison services. Even contact with guards and other death row inmates is minimized in many states. In some states inmates may leave their cells only to shower, exercise, visit the law library, and receive visitors. Even the facilities for these pursuits are minimal in most states. Inmates are shackled much of the time and heavily guarded whenever they leave their cells. They are defined as beyond rehabilitation and are ineligible for most prison jobs or programs. A one-hour period outside the cell is permitted each day for solitary exercise in most states, but a few restrict out-of-cell time to half an hour.[61] In a few states, however, death row inmates have nearly as much access to education and recreation programs as other maximum-security inmates. These death rows are described as ***reformed*** and may even allow inmates to work and take meals as a group.[62]

Observers note that capital punishment kills the offender twice—psychologically while awaiting execution and physically in the death chamber. The constant awareness that the environment is organized entirely to facilitate these inmates' deaths leads to a loss of personality, and even the sense of personhood, in some cases. Guards are discouraged from acknowledging the humanity of these prisoners because they may one day have to help kill them.[63] Inmates have no escape whatsoever from rules, regulations, and oversight. They feel abandoned by significant others in the free world. The extremes of powerlessness and alienation erase any connection to feelings of humanity.

A variety of religious, scientific, and economic arguments have been made as to the value of the death penalty. Many use different interpretations of the same ideas and data: supporters of the death penalty maintain that its origins are Biblical ("an eye for an eye"), while opponents stress "turning the other cheek" and "vengeance is mine, saith the Lord."[64] Opinions on capital punishment are ultimately a matter of conscience, but knowledge of the arguments supporting each view is essential to intelligent discussion of the topic. Each side of this debate tends to support its moral position with practical arguments that, in the final analysis, can be neither proven nor refuted.

Death row inmates are heavily guarded when they leave their cells.

ARGUMENTS FOR THE DEATH PENALTY

Practical arguments for execution usually involve "compelling state interests" in crime control and are important to the courts that rule on the legality of capital punishment. Moral issues are crucial to defining "evolving standards of decency" and therefore are also vital to case law on the subject. These views currently are based on the idea of equivalent retaliation or retribution. Practical arguments for the use of the death penalty focus primarily on incapacitation and deterrence, although executions also have an important boundary-setting function.

Deterrence

Deterrence requires that punishment be certain, swift, and appropriately severe. Supporters of the death penalty believe that it is an effective method of deterring crime. The fact that there was a 100% increase in murders between 1967 and 1977 when no executions occurred is often cited to support the deterrent effects of the death penalty.[65] Those in support of the death penalty also often cite Isaac Erlich, who analyzed data on executions and murders in the United States between 1933 and 1967. After controlling for arrest and conviction rates for murder, unemployment, age structure, and overall level of poverty, he concluded that murder increased as executions declined and estimated that each execution might deter as many as eight killings.[66] Critics objected that changes in morality, handgun availability, and the distribution of wealth explained Erlich's findings better than changing rates of execution. Erlich was also attacked for ignoring regional differences. His analysis looked at the entire United States without regard for which states had the death penalty and which did not. When other scholars examined the same data but looked at trends in each region separately, they found that executions had no deterrent effect.[67] Thus Erlich assumed that an execution in Florida might deter a killing in Alaska while his critics argued that executions in Florida are unlikely to have an effect outside the southeastern portion of the United States.

Stephen Layson's examination of homicide statistics for the period between 1936 and 1977 is more widely accepted by scholars. He found that the probability of arrest is the best predictor of declines in the murder rate followed by likelihood of conviction and then rate of executions.[68] A study by Cameron reached similar conclusions but nonetheless estimated that each execution might deter as many as eight murders.[69] The work of both Layson and Cameron support what has long been assumed about deterrence in general: certainty of punishment is more powerful than severity. However, more recently, many doubt that there is any deterrent effect from sentencing people to death or executing people for homicide.[70] Others argue that if the situation were this simple, then Texas would have the lowest rate of violent crime in the United States. Contrary to the deterrence thesis, it has one of the highest.[71] In one study of capital punishment and deterrence in Texas, researchers concluded that the number of executions was unrelated to murder rates in general.[72]

Some argue that certain offenders pose a particular threat to other prisoners and to prison employees. One Texas study asserts that certain crimes and traits of defendants can be used to predict future dangerousness at the level of certainty required by the courts. These include killing during a robbery/burglary, mass or serial killings, gang membership, and prior imprisonments. This perspective sees executions as necessary to make prisons safer.[73]

A similar line of reasoning fears for public safety if convicted murderers are eligible for parole. While a few famous cases support this position, the majority of the evidence does not. People sentenced to die prior to 1972 had their sentences commuted to life, and were paroled. Studies show that these offenders were no more likely to commit new crimes of violence than were other violent offenders.[74]

Some have called for a return to public executions believing that this would increase the deterrent impact of the death penalty. History does not support this idea (see chapter 2). An experimental study found that support for capital punishment decreased among people who watched a film of an execution.[75] Some opponents of execution have urged televised coverage to impress the horrors of execution upon the public mind, and one death row inmate has volunteered to have his execution televised for this reason. Although many media outlets have said that they would not broadcast an execution, others have indicated an interest. One producer filed a First Amendment lawsuit to gain the right to televise an execution.[76]

The essence of the deterrence argument is that capital punishment is justified by the mere possibility that some innocent victim might be saved by it. The argument can never be "proven" because proof would require measurement of killings that do not occur—an impossible task from a scientific standpoint. However, the utilitarian issues raised by the deterrence perspective often unite with the moral ones of retribution, emphasizing society's "right and duty" to protect citizens and obtain justice.[77]

Justice and Retribution

Some argue that death is the only way society can provide appropriate punishment for especially horrible crimes. Supporters of retribution feel that executions offer the families of murder victims and the public an emotional sense of justice.[78] It is for this reason that at least ten states have laws that explicitly permit the relatives of murder victims to watch the killer's execution.[79] Only New Jersey officially forbids the practice.[80]

Retentionists note that capital punishment is an important symbol for society. They argue that executions draw attention to changes in the level of moral outrage over various acts. Capital punishment laws provide information about new social priorities. This argument has strong historical support, since the definition of which acts deserve death changes with the economics and morality of the culture.

The final safeguard in the system that includes capital punishment rests with the executive branch of government: governors or the president. *Executive clemency* includes the power to grant *pardons* (which invalidate both the guilt and punishment of the defendant), *reprieves* (which temporarily postpone punishment, and *commutations* (which reduce the severity of the punishment). There have been 52 instances of pardons since the death penalty was reinstated. The reasons given for granting the pardons included possible innocence, findings of disproportionate sentence, unfair trials, opposition to the death penalty, and because of mental illness or juvenile status.[81] In January 2003, Illinois commuted all death sentences to life imprisonment without parole (see box pp. 316–317).

Other Arguments for Capital Punishment

The idea that the costs of imprisonment can be reduced by executing some percentage of offenders has great intuitive appeal. However, the costs of due process and secure confinement quickly wreck such notions. The use of due process is presumed by retentionist arguments because it insures fairness. Once again the demands of justice contradict those of efficiency: execution would be cost effective only if we abandoned the safeguards that assure a fair trial.

Some retentionists cite the fact that killings of police officers climbed dramatically just as the number of executions dropped in the 1960s. Opponents of capital punishment believe that the overall level of violence and the availability of guns explain this trend better than does the frequency of executions.

ARGUMENTS AGAINST THE DEATH PENALTY

Moral arguments against capital punishment claim that it lowers society to the level of the criminals it despises and betrays the values that cherish individual lives. Those who want the death penalty abolished also cite the possibility of executing innocent people and claim that its use discriminates against minorities and the poor. Utilitarian arguments against the death penalty fall into two basic categories. Some arguments consist of empirical attacks on the presumed deterrent effects of the penalty.[82] Others are based on fears that executions may actually inspire people to kill others. It is also feared that some offenders will use the death penalty as a form of suicide, just as others attempt "suicide-by-cop" in shootouts with police.[83] All note that the exorbitant costs of executions make it an indulgence of vengeful emotion that society cannot afford.[84]

The Morality of the Death Penalty

At the base of the moral arguments against capital punishment is the belief that the more civilized a society becomes, the less it relies on violence to accomplish its goals. Abolitionists feel it is a regressive form of punishment—the mark of a society more primitive than we claim to be. One writer has described it as an authoritarian form of terror management comparable to human sacrifice.[85] While most executions are attended or even performed by physicians, and many physicians say they would assist in an execution if asked,[86] the American Medical Association has condemned the death penalty as unethical. It is also felt that executions expand the tragedy that results from murder. Some victims' families seek the execution of their loved ones' killers, but others feel traumatized when the murderer is executed.[87] Many victims' families are unable to get on with their lives while the details of the crime are repeatedly dragged through the media as the case is processed. Many report that execution does not bring them "closure" and that the pain and loss endures even after witnessing the execution.[88] Abolitionists believe that retribution is merely a fancy word for vengeance, which is immoral in itself. They feel that the death penalty cheapens human life and lowers the government to the level of the criminal. Additionally, the public attention that capital punishment cases attract may lead some people to seek execution in order to become notorious.

The Brutalization Thesis

The *brutalization thesis* maintains that capital punishment may actually encourage criminal violence. It is thought that potential killers may identify with the state or the executioner and be inspired to commit murder. Government-sanctioned executions are felt to encourage the potential for violence within all people and to make some citizens feel justified in killing those who offend them. Overall, the brutalization thesis maintains that the more violence to which people are exposed, the more justified they feel in using violence to achieve their goals. The more state-approved violence against criminals, the less citizens will value human life.[89]

Some scientific studies suggest that executions may actually increase murder rates. One study found that the homicide rate was 2.4 times higher in the 10-week period following an execution than in the 10 weeks preceding it.[90] Other research has noted that killings by strangers are predicted by the brutalization thesis but that those involving acquaintances and relatives are not.[91] A third more recent study suggests that acquaintance killings may be deterred by executions but increases in the rate of stranger murders seem to last longer.[92] At best the deterrence effect is very weak by most of these accounts. Most analyses have found little or no relationship between homicide rates and executions.[93] Thus, the objective support for the brutalization thesis is only slightly stronger than that for the deterrent effect of executions.[94]

Discrimination in the Imposition of the Death Penalty

Any review of the history of capital punishment shows that it has long been used to control racial minorities and unpopular political groups. The Supreme Court relied on evidence of racial discrimination in its *Furman* ruling. The most recent available data indicates that the race of those executed since 1976 is: 57% white, 35% African American, 7% Hispanic, and 2% other. Since the death penalty was reinstated in 1977, a majority of those executed have been white. African Americans are less prominent among those executed than they are among prison populations.[95]

The U.S. Department of Justice is nonetheless concerned with the possibility of racial bias in federal use of capital punishment. In 1997 the U.S. attorney general instituted a plan to assure that federal death rows would have a racial diversity that reflected the nation's population. This plan resulted partly from the observation that the majority of inmates on federal death rows are African American. "Death penalty committees" directly controlled by the attorney general now decide which cases are appropriate for the death penalty. Previously the prosecutor handling the case made this decision, and the attorney general's approval was needed only for the actual execution. More important, data on the ethnicity of

Race and the Death Penalty in the Post-*Furman* Era[96]

Figure A shows that there seems to be no racial bias in which defendants receive death sentences. The majority of studies show that prosecutors are less likely to seek the death penalty when the victim is not white. Some believe that prosecutors and judges are reluctant to ask for the execution of black defendants out of fear of being labeled racist.

Race of victims in death cases are shown in figure B. Most killings involve victims and offenders of the same race. However, capital punishment is overwhelmingly used when the victim is white. Retentionists argue that killings resulting from robberies and other felonies are more heinous than those motivated by passion and that whites are disproportionately the victims of these crimes. Abolitionists fear that a new form of racism based on the victim's traits rather than the offender's can be seen in these statistics. Only 11 whites have been executed for killing an African American since 1977 while at least 166 blacks have been executed for killing whites. Perhaps most significantly, only 30% of those on death row are blacks convicted of killing other blacks. These figures indicate that white lives are considered more valuable than those of other races. Given the violence problem in minority communities, this message should be of grave concern to all U.S. citizens.

Figure A   Race of Death Row Inmates

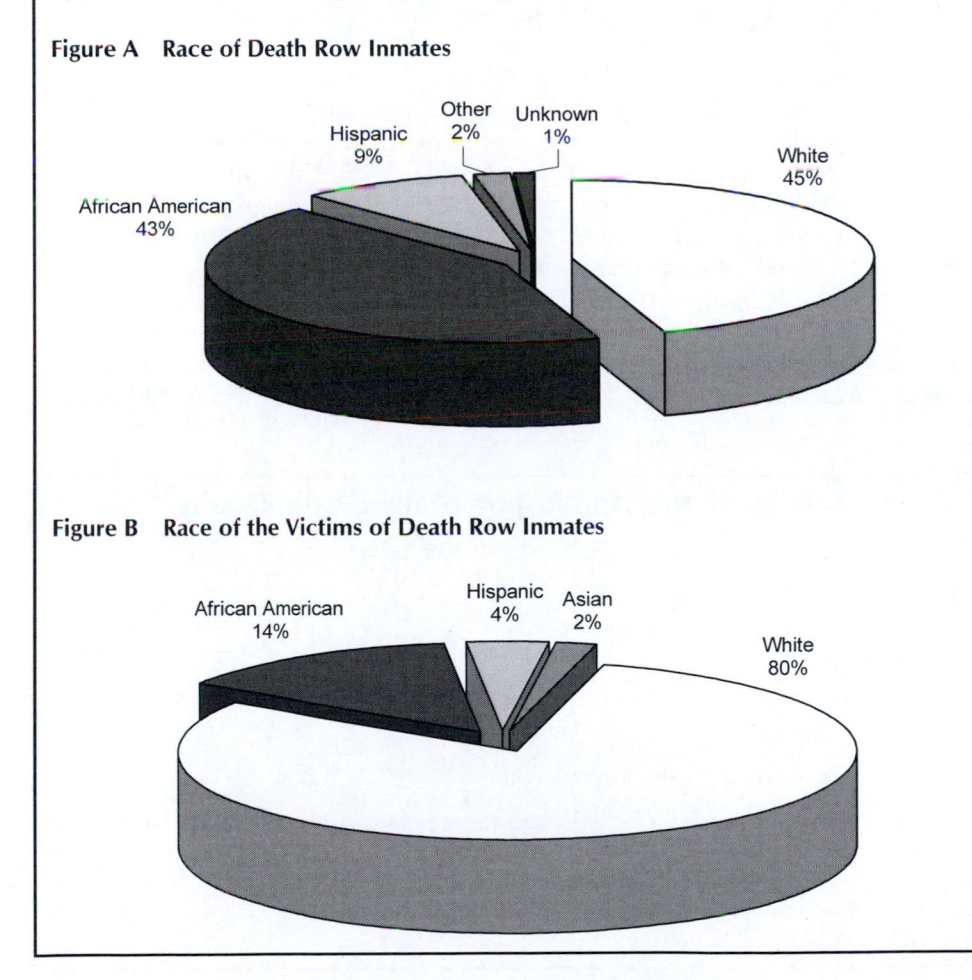

Figure B   Race of the Victims of Death Row Inmates

defendants and victims are now included on the forms reviewed by the attorney general before an execution is authorized. Observers doubt that the new procedures will reduce the frequency with which the death penalty is sought, but some hope it will result in an increase in the proportion of whites on the federal government's death row.[97]

Abolitionists contend that race remains a factor in the use of capital punishment. Killers of whites are three to eight times more likely to be sentenced to die than killers of minorities, depending on the state in which the murder occurs. The race of the offender seems to be irrelevant in this pattern.[98] However, in *McCleskey v. Kemp* (1987) the Supreme Court ruled that this pattern did not violate *Gregg* by making the application of capital punishment discriminatory or arbitrary.[99] Some studies found that even the effect of victims' race declined in the decade following *Furman* decision.[100] More recent analyses suggest that minority defendants may be at increasing risk of being executed in some states.[101] Nonetheless, any suggestion that the deaths of whites get more attention than those of other races should be of serious concern to deterrence advocates.[102]

Abolitionists also charge that the poor are disproportionately represented on death rows across the United States. Closely related to this is the claim that many death row inmates were advised by inexperienced, unskilled, or poorly prepared attorneys at their original trials. Some add that the penalty is still applied in an arbitrary way. Much of this controversy centers on the quality of attorneys provided to indigent capital defendants. In one case, a Texas appeals court found no fault with Calvin J. Burdine's defense attorney sleeping through parts of his capital trial. However, on June 3, 2002, the Supreme Court let stand a district court ruling that awarded Burdine a new trial.[103] Indeed, the American Bar Association called for a moratorium on the death penalty until states can assure that executions are "administered fairly and impartially, in accordance with due process," and with minimum risk of executing the innocent.[104] This argument is supported by three facts: (1) only 1–2% of those eligible for the death penalty actually

---

Factors Predicting Application of the Death Penalty[105]

Predictor	Predictive Value*
Murder with torture	1.9
Grave risk of death to others	1.5
Black defendant	1.4
Caused great harm, fear, pain	1.0
Multiple stab wounds	0.9
Murder in commission of another felony	0.8

* A value of zero would mean a factor had no value in predicting application of death penalty. Use of these values allows ranking of factors found to influence assignment of death penalty in trial processes. The data show being black is significantly more likely to result in capital punishment than is murder in commission of another felony; causing great harm, fear, and pain; or multiple stab wounds.

receive it, (2) the first defendant to deal with the prosecutor is less likely than his or her partner to get the penalty regardless of their roles in the crime, and (3) there is great variation across regions, states, and jurisdictions as to how often the penalty is sought and obtained.[106]

International Issues

Critics of execution are quick to point out that the use of capital punishment places the United States in the same category as many countries that it defines as totalitarian. Many citizens are embarrassed to learn that Texas has recently been cited along with nations like Iran and Iraq as violating human rights because of its use of the death penalty. Western European countries no longer use capital punishment, but it remains popular in nations such as the People's Republic of China and Guatemala—countries that the United States considers to be gross violators of human rights.[107] This is especially true when sensitive issues such as the execution of juveniles or racial discrimination are raised. Those who question retribution-

---

International Status of the Death Penalty[108]

The chart on the next page describes four categories of nations: (1) *abolitionist* nations do not allow the use of capital punishment for any crime; (2) some nations have abolished capital punishment for ordinary crimes but still have the power to use it under *military law*, during a war and/or in highly unusual criminal circumstances; (3) other countries are *de facto abolitionist* because they have not executed anyone in many years even though laws allowing capital punishment are still in their legal codes; and (4) *retentionist* nations have capital punishment laws and have recently executed offenders.

Category	Number	Sample of nations included
Entirely abolitionist	75	Australia, Angola, Bulgaria, Germany, Haiti, Italy, Namibia, Netherlands, Norway, Portugal, Romania, Slovenia, South Africa, Sweden, Uruguay
De facto abolitionist	20	Albania, Bermuda, Central African Republic, Gambia, Grenada, Suriname, Turkey
Only in military during war or other exceptional situations	14	Argentina, Brazil, Israel, Mexico, Peru, United Kingdom
Death penalty retained	86	Afghanistan, Algeria, Chad, Cuba, Ethiopia, India, Lebanon, Libya, Nigeria, Pakistan, Saudi Arabia, Singapore, Thailand, United States, Vietnam, Yemen, Yugoslavia

No western European nations retain the death penalty for ordinary crimes, and the European Union requires abolition of capital punishment for membership. Several eastern European nations allow the penalty for ordinary crimes, but most have abolished it since Soviet domination ended. Many South and Central American nations permit it only in military or wartime cases. Mexico has not executed anyone since 1937, and the Canadian military has not used capital punishment since 1962. Most Moslem nations, and many others in the developing world, retain and use the death penalty.

oriented policies like capital punishment note that the United States has the highest rate of violence in the industrial world and the second highest rate of imprisonment. They suggest that we turn our attention to prevention and avoid the costs of retribution.[109]

On a more practical level, many nations will not extradite drug lords, terrorists, and other fugitives to the United States if they might face the death penalty. This means that many fugitives from the United States can hide in Europe and elsewhere. Mexico's Supreme Court banned the extradition of suspects to the United States, even if they faced only a life sentence, on grounds that such a lengthy period of imprisonment was inhumane. (Mexican courts cannot normally fix a sentence at more than 40 years.)[110] American use of capital punishment has also become a problem early in the "war on terrorism"; Spain was reluctant to extradite suspects in the September 11, 2001, attacks because they would face execution, and France vigorously protested its possible use against one of its citizens, also implicated in the attacks and in U.S. custody.[111] Some nations will extradite fugitives to the United States only if prosecutors agree not to ask for the death penalty.[112] However, public opinion guides use of capital punishment in the United States and is largely unaffected by the beliefs of other nations.

PUBLIC BELIEFS AND THE DEATH PENALTY

Public opinion is one of several factors used by the courts to decide if a punishment violates the Eighth Amendment criterion of "evolving standards of decency." Public opinion also guides prosecutors in deciding when to ask for the death penalty and influences governors' willingness to authorize executions. Over three-fourths of the public believe that scientific studies have "proven" the death penalty to have significant deterrent power. However, a 1996 study found that 90% of criminologists believe that capital punishment has no deterrent value.[113] While scholars are often accused of liberalism, such a charge is rarely leveled at the police; only 1% of police chiefs believe capital punishment is effective in reducing violent crime.[114]

Among the general public, opinions on the death penalty are best predicted by a person's political beliefs and race.[115] The only year in which the percentage of

---

Policy Matters!
Should the Death Penalty Exist?

In January 2003, two days before the expiration of his term as governor, George Ryan commuted the sentences of all 164 inmates on death row in Illinois to life in prison without parole and shortened the sentences of 3 others to 40 years. Borrowing the words of the late U.S. Supreme Court Justice Harry Blackmun, Ryan declared, "Because the Illinois death penalty system is arbitrary and capricious—and therefore immoral—I no longer shall tinker with the machinery of death."[116]

In November 1999 the *Chicago Tribune* reported that half of the nearly 300 capital cases in Illinois had been reversed; 33 death row inmates had been represented at trial by an attorney who had later been disbarred or suspended; two-thirds of the inmates on death row were African American; 35 African-American defendants had been convicted by all-white juries; and 46 inmates were convicted on the basis of testimony from jailhouse informants. By January 2000, Illinois had executed 12 people since reinstating capital punishment in 1977 and had released 13 people from death row after evidence of their innocence. That month Ryan declared a moratorium on executions. He proposed legislation to reform the system by videotaping confessions, restricting the use of jailhouse snitches, creating a centralized review process for prosecutorial decisions to seek the death penalty, and reducing the number of crimes eligible for death. Among the reasons for granting blanket clemency in 2003 was that legislators had failed to take action. "I don't know how many more systemic flaws we need to uncover before they would be spurred to action."[117] In his speech granting clemency, Ryan noted that his actions would be criticized, but he argued:

> Prosecutors in Illinois have the ultimate commutation power, a power that is exercised every day. They decide who will be subject to the death penalty, who will get a plea deal or even who may get a complete pass on prosecution. . . . There were more than 1,000 murders last year in Illinois. There is no doubt that all murders are cruel and wrong. Yet, less than 2 percent of those murder defendants will receive the death penalty. . . . A killing with the same circumstances might get 40 years in one county and death in another county.[118]

The blanket commutation was a dramatic move. It may have prevented an innocent person—like the 17 discovered in Illinois by 2003—from death at the hands of the state, but it also spared the lives of some whose guilt was never in question and who committed gruesome murders. National support for capital punishment is about 70% because many people believe society is safer if people who commit heinous crimes face the same outcome as their victims; politicians see that support and are reluctant to risk voter disapproval. In Illinois, prosecutors and family members of the victims were angry that the decisions of juries and the legislature were altered. Opponents of the death penalty were heartened. Former Illinois Supreme Court Justice Moses Harrison II remarked, "Here's a governor who is pro-death penalty and he recognized the system was broken. No matter how you feel about the death penalty, you have to be willing to examine the system."[119]

Questions to Consider

1. List the pros and cons of capital punishment. Classify each argument as moral, emotional, or utilitarian. Then rank each argument in order of its power. Is there a tendency for one side or the other of this debate to be more moralistic, emotional, or utilitarian than the other?

2. Do you think the granting of blanket clemency will spur more such actions or have the opposite effect?

3. What effect do you think televised executions might have on citizens? Does such a spectacle help deter crime or does it cheapen the value of life even further?

4. To what extent should the wishes of the victim's survivors be taken into account in selecting people for execution? If someone you loved were murdered, would you want to watch the death of his or her killer?

citizens who opposed the death penalty was higher than those who supported it was 1966 (47% opposed; 42% supported). The percentages increased substantially from 1980 to a high of 80% in 1994. In October 2002, the percentage was 70%.[120] Women are less likely to support capital punishment than are men,[121] and support is lower among African Americans than among other racial groups.[122] Other data, however, suggest that high economic status, political conservatism, and a strong orientation to punishment are the core traits that lead to support for capital punishment.[123]

Public support for capital punishment varies with the wording of the question used by pollsters. When the idea of executing a juvenile or mentally impaired person or the alternative of life without parole is mentioned, then support for capital punishment usually drops significantly.[124] In 2002, 26% of the U.S. public supported the death penalty for juveniles, 19% for the mentally ill, and 13% for the mentally retarded. The percentage supporting the death penalty dropped when the questioner asked for a choice between the death penalty and life imprisonment with no possibility of parole.[125] Concerns over executing innocent persons, geographical differences in its application, and racial discrimination were prominent among those with reservations about the use of capital punishment.[126] Beliefs about the frequent use of early parole, usually the result of folk beliefs rather than actual justice system practices, lead many people to support the death penalty.[127]

International studies show that public support for the death penalty has little to do with national rates of violence and murder. Support for capital punishment is high in some nations with low murder rates such as the United Kingdom and Japan. Religion, politics, and culture rather than efficiency concerns play the central role in determining views of the ethics of the death penalty.[128]

SUMMARY

The death penalty is one of the oldest and most controversial responses to crime. As capitalism arose, property crimes were increasingly punished by death but urbanization led to increased levels of crime that executions could not reduce. Most Western nations abandoned this penalty because it was not felt to be effective in controlling crime.

Executions were public spectacles until the late 1800s when they were moved to the privacy of prison death chambers. The invention of the electric chair was especially important in this transition, as was fear that crowds would riot. Racism dominated the use of the death penalty until 1972 when the *Furman* decision declared the use of capital punishment to be so "arbitrary and capricious" as to violate the Constitution. In 1976 the Court approved the core ideas of a new generation of capital punishment laws in *Gregg v. Georgia* that required a bifurcated trial process that examines aggravating and mitigating circumstances.

Moral and utilitarian arguments often use different interpretations of the same ideas and data to defend or attack capital punishment. Retentionist arguments stress retribution and the possibility of deterrence, while abolitionists claim that it is the mark of a regressive, vengeful society. The brutalization thesis suggests that executions may actually encourage people to use violence to obtain what they see as justice for themselves. Evaluating these arguments depends on how one defines concepts like morality, heinousness, and justice. Ultimately, the debate about the death penalty is one of morality, not science.

QUESTIONS FOR DISCUSSION AND REVIEW

1. Describe the history of the death penalty. How was it administered throughout most of human history? What effect did it have on crime as cities developed and industry became dominant?

2. What Supreme Court cases have had the most impact on the use of the death penalty in the United States? What were the central findings of these cases?

3. What legal processes are used to decide who gets the death penalty? What kinds of facts and opinions must be examined in capital cases?

4. Describe the case law that determines how the death penalty is to be used when crimes are committed by juveniles, the mentally ill, and the mentally retarded. Which groups are protected as a class and which are not? Why?

5. What methods are used to execute prisoners today? Which are most and least common? Why are these methods preferred? Are executions really becoming more humane? Does making execution humane defeat the goal of deterrence? Of justice?

6. Which states have the largest death row populations? How do the conditions under which these inmates live differ from those imposed on other prisoners? Which states have actually executed the greatest number of people since 1970?

7. What are the main arguments for the continued use of the death penalty? How does the cost of a trial and execution figure into the debate over capital punishment?

8. How do most other Western democracies view U.S. use of capital punishment? Why? Which nations are most likely to execute civilian criminals? What do these nations have in common? How are they different from the United States?

A young child raises her fist in defiance of the current drug war that sent her mother to prison on a drug possession charge following a drug raid.

FOURTEEN

THE FUTURE OF CORRECTIONS

Elected officials pass laws that determine correctional priorities based on what they feel to be the beliefs of those they represent. Some of those beliefs originate in prevailing concepts of fairness; others are based on efficiency. Fairness is a matter of personal conscience, while efficiency concentrates on public safety and costs. Both are guided by popular beliefs about the "causes" of crime. Correctional policies are more a product of politics than of the crime rate.

The statistics on crime rates and the number of people incarcerated offer telling evidence of the effects of policy. Crime rates have decreased since 1991, while more and more people are housed in the nation's jails and prisons. Some proponents of current policy argue that the decreasing crime rate is the result of increased incarceration—prisons incapacitate offenders and prevent them from committing crimes in communities. However, some scholars estimate that only 25% of the decline in violent crime can be attributed to incarceration.[1] The crime rate has had far less effect on policy than the perception of crime and the manipulation of public fear of crime by the media, politicians, and industries and associations that profit from prisons. The discrepancy between shrinking crime rates and the rising rate of incarceration highlights some disturbing issues. What are the collateral effects of incarceration as the primary means of punishment? What roles do politicians and the media play? Does the United States rely too heavily on imprisonment to combat drugs? Is the prison boom self-perpetuating?

COLLATERAL EFFECTS OF INCARCERATION

After thirty years of increasingly harsh policies, "the land of the free" has imprisoned almost two million people at a cost of nearly $40 billion in annual operating expenses. The United States leads the world in the rate of incarceration. While the general population increased 20% since 1980, the number of people in jail or prison increased 400%. As Jeremy Travis points out, prisons

> are visible embodiments of society's decision to punish criminals. As we punish more people, the number of prisons increases. We can count how many people are in prison, measure the length of the sentences they serve, determine what we spend to keep them there, and conduct empirically grounded analysis of the costs and benefits of incarceration. Because prisons make punishment visible, we can more easily quantify the policy debates over the wisdom of this application of the criminal sanction.[2]

Travis then explains that not all sanctions are visible. He urges that the overlooked consequences of imprisonment—disenfranchisement, loss of benefits, harm to families and communities, increased risk of disease, and so forth—be considered in debates over sentences or any other punishment policy.[3]

It is difficult to determine the precise effect of incarceration on the crime rate—just as it is difficult to quantify the relationship between drugs and crime. In both instances, the contributing factors are complex: individual traits, socioeconomic circumstances, and the state of the economy, to name a few. The easier determination is that both crime and punishment are expensive in human and financial costs.

The discrepancy between shrinking crime rates and the rising rate of incarceration highlights some disturbing issues.

Todd Clear points out that the sustained growth in imprisonment since 1972 has had little relationship to crime rates, economic patterns, or population demographics. Crime rates have increased and decreased in the thirty years; the economy has been through both boom and bust; and the portion of the population most likely to commit crimes has risen and fallen. The growth in incarceration has not been equally distributed. Clear advises us to imagine living "in an area where one in eight parent-aged males is removed for confinement each year, and one in four is locked up at any given time.[4]

> When incarceration reaches a certain level in an area that already struggles for assets, the effects of imprisonment undermine the building blocks of social order. This is, for these neighborhoods a kind of double whammy. First, they suffer the disruptions that occur when large numbers of residents are coercively removed and imprisoned. Then, they struggle with the pressures that occur when large numbers of former convicts return to community life.[5]

Clear refers to a "tipping point" in communities where the effects of large numbers of citizens who have been imprisoned and released contribute to rising unemployment, domestic violence, and crime. Donald Braman warns, "Incarceration is producing deep social transformations in the families and communities of prisoners—families and communities, it should be noted, that are disproportionately poor, urban, and African-American."[6]

Behind the numbers, percentages, rates of incarceration, and quantitative descriptions are people who will rejoin the society that has punished them. "The people society has put out of sight and out of mind continue to exist, and they are shaped—or warped—by the conditions to which we have relegated them."[7] Some local authorities have revisited forms of punishment that had been abandoned as debasing, such as chain gangs, striped prison apparel, and tents to house prisoners in the desert. As Peter Sussman notes, these are "a few of the ways in which already dehumanized men and women have been deprived of whatever individuality they had left and of the inner resources that might help them someday to make a go of it on the outside."[8] Subjecting human beings to such harsh conditions exacerbates violent tendencies and psychological well being.

Even absent extreme treatment, imprisonment has a number of adverse effects. Research by criminologists Cassia Spohn and David Holleran found that offenders sentenced to prison have higher rates of recidivism and commit repeat offenses more quickly than do offenders placed on probation. They found that imprisonment had a greater criminogenic effect on drug offenders than on other types of offenders.[9] Alfred Blumstein has noted that association with other more serious offenders can move a nonviolent petty offender to a higher level of criminal activity.[10] Former inmate Eddie Ellis comments: "If you take someone, lock them up for 10 years, and don't give them any rehabilitative activities, when you let them out you're going to have a failure. They're released back into society, to the same devastated community, with an enormous buildup of anger and frustration."[11]

Families suffer as well as the offender: lost income; social isolation; no support for childcare or daily routines; the added expense of collect phone calls from prison and of visiting distant rural prisons; worry about whether loved ones will survive the prison experience, from the risk of possible violence to the increased risk of disease; the indignities of being searched and watched constantly when visiting.

> Subjection to the coarse cruelties of everyday life in prison leaves an indelible mark on the people whom we cycle in and out of the prison system and on their families. . . . One can learn far more about crime and prisoners by spending time in the endless lines snaking into the visiting rooms of our jails and prisons than by spending an equivalent amount of time poring over budgets, academic reports, or computer databases.[12]

The stigma of having a relative in jail is another burden on families. "While lawmakers may consider shame and injury appropriate sanctions for criminal offenders, the stigma related to incarceration is often borne by the nonoffending relatives of prisoners, something we do not see or hear about because it is in the family's interest to hide it."[13]

An estimated 721,500 state and federal prisoners are parents to 1.5 million children. Black children were 9 times more likely to have an inmate parent than white children, and Hispanic children were 3 times more likely. Sixty percent of state prisoners and 84% of federal prisoners were located more than 100 miles from their last place of residence.[14] After release, parents face enormous obstacles reuniting their families, finding housing, employment, childcare, and medical services. They may have lost the right to vote. If convicted of a drug offense, public housing, welfare benefits, and educational assistance may no longer be available. A criminal record makes finding a job extremely difficult. California prohibits parolees from occupations such as nursing, physical therapy, and education. The jobs available pay approximately half the wages they would pay to people who have not been imprisoned.[15]

> By employing incarceration—the bluntest of social instruments—as the primary response to social disorder, policymakers have significantly missed the mark. The overuse of incarceration harms the families of prisoners as much as, if not more than, the prisoners themselves. . . . That our public policies injure the most vulnerable families and communities in our nation is perhaps an inadvertent by-product of our determination to punish criminality, but it cannot remain inadvertent for long.[16]

THE POLITICS OF CORRECTIONS AND THE MEDIA

The basis for the prison boom has very little to do with the actual crime rate. It is premised on the public's perception of crime and how public fear is manipulated for political and financial gain by politicians, private-prison companies, prison suppliers, and the media. Campaigning against crime is a surefire strategy. Public fears about safety translate into votes.

> Politicians try to outgun one another in their indignant denunciation of crime and criminals and in their passionate support for ever-longer sentences, sometimes for minor offenses that had been featured briefly on newspaper front pages. Once elected, the politicians must respond to the fears and expectations they generated when campaigning for office.[17]

Campaigns against crime aren't limited to politicians; other interests profit from the emphasis on imprisonment. Private prison corporations, a multibillion dollar industry with stockholders, contribute to the American Legislative Council that promotes strict sentencing. The union for California prison guards contributes millions to candidates who support harsh crime control. Other companies profit from providing health care, food, and other supplies for facilities.[18] Prison telephone service is a prime example of how private suppliers profit from services provided to prisons. Inmate class generate about a billion dollars in revenues each year.[19] For security reasons, prisoners may only place collect calls. Something that would cost much less than a dollar outside the walls costs four dollars—and most of the families who face this burden have very limited funds. Rural communities have lobbied successfully for new prisons to increase employment opportunities; 350 prisons have been built in rural communities since 1980.[20] Hundreds of small towns depend on an industry that relies on the continuation of incarcerating large numbers of people. These communities have reaped an additional benefit. Prisoners are counted where they are housed, increasing the population numbers of the rural areas in which most prisons are located. Federal funds are allocated on the basis of population. The predominately black, Hispanic, and urban communities from which the prisoners came lose tax dollars to mostly white, rural regions.[21]

Much of the media's power lies in its ability to direct the public's attention toward certain topics and away from others; this is known as *agenda setting*.

> Whether through social habit, conscious policy, or business focus, the news media often end up mirroring politicians' self-interested stereotyping of prisoners and prison issues. The bulk of the media-consuming public—its attention directed and its perceptions shaped by journalistic coverage—appears to be comfortable with the substitution of simplistic stereotypes for the complex personal and social dynamics of prisons and prisoners. It is far easier to barricade one's fears behind walls of concrete, rolls of razor wire, and reams of clichés than to deal with the realities of criminal experience in our troubled society.[22]

The growth of the cable television market—and the increasing number of stations competing for ratings—has encouraged news, documentary, and entertainment shows to focus on crime. Politicians and the media prefer quick, simple answers that will earn immediate public recognition. Their usual goal is to convince the public that simple solutions can be effective.[23] Government officials sometimes encourage the media to focus on crime to strengthen support for budget increases or to divert attention from other problems.[24] In order to attract attention, the media usually portray heinous acts that can be presented quickly and dramatically. Excessive levels of public fear and badly distorted beliefs result from the media's focus on crimes that are atypical and especially sensational.[25]

From 1990 to 1998, homicides rates dropped 50% but stories about homicides on the major networks increased 400%. Saturation coverage by the media activates public fears. Almost every election campaign includes rhetoric about "more jails, harsher punishment, more executions, all the things that have never worked to reduce crime but have always worked to get votes. It's driven largely, although not exclusively, by television-cultivated insecurity."[26]

Events such as George Ryan's blanket commutation of death sentences in Illinois in January 2003 (discussed in chapter 13) attract media attention. The framing, however, often deflects public attention from the need for reflective thinking to more visceral reactions. John Kass, a *Chicago Tribune* commentator, offered this synthesis of the television coverage of the commutations.

> Ryan has generated extreme emotion in all of us, on all sides of the death penalty issue. It rushes forward, in waves, the rawness of it deliciously attractive to broadcast news, which doesn't deal with context, but rather in pictures and emotion. National TV news audiences will see oodles of drama and Ryan as hero: the mother hugging her son, the ecstatic lawyers, the embittered prosecutors appearing spiteful amid the jubilation, the stunned wife of a forgotten murder victim . . . not knowing whether to demand execution and be cast as vengeful and bloodthirsty; or whether to retreat exhausted and unsure, the ambiguous end to the nightly news.[27]

Information about prisons rarely reflects the uncomfortable realities of life behind bars. Instead, the majority of media stories focus on escapes, riots, or the unrepentant sociopath.

> Prison stereotypes remove all nuance from prisons and prisoners, underscoring the comforting notion that "we" have nothing in common with "them." They underline the menacing violence of prison life and ignore the nobility and pathos that also characterize many prisoners, traits that are familiar to many lawyers, teachers, pastors, and social workers who have spent a lot of time in these remote institutions.[28]

Prison stories that could be useful for a public interested in policy are classified as too dull or too expensive to cover. The media don't have an incentive "to cover communities that are as voiceless, politically powerless, and invisible as those in our prisons."[29]

THE WAR ON DRUGS

For almost a century, exaggerated claims about the evils of drugs and the people who use them have created a dependence on the criminal justice system to provide the solution to the problem of drug use. Politicians, the media, police, correction and parole officer's associations, the military, prison builders, drug-testing companies, antidrug educators, and numerous other interested parties repeatedly link drugs with crime and mutually reinforce their own importance in the battle against drugs.[30]

> Even today, 85 years after the federal government first outlawed narcotics, public and police attitudes toward the dangerousness of drugs are shaped by ignorance of their impact and by mistaken prejudices regarding their users. These are the same irrationalities that led to the criminal prohibition of certain drugs. Individuals taking Prozac . . . or other psychoactive prescription drugs are regarded as patients. Yet millions of our own citizens using heroin, cocaine or marijuana have been and are still regarded as dangerous enough to be caged in brutal prisons, frequently under mandatory sentences more characteristic of a totalitarian society than a democracy.[31]

Studies consistently identify alcohol as the drug most often abused by offenders. Alcohol is especially common in violent crimes and is the only drug with biochemical effects that has been linked directly to aggression in humans.[32] However, the alcohol industry is protected by powerful lobbyists, and the focus remains on illegal drugs. If prison sentences are the primary weapon chosen to combat drugs, the correctional system will need far more resources to cope with the results of that policy.

Drug laws have had little effect on drug use, but they have filled prisons and jails with nonviolent offenders. Since 1980 criminal justice responses to drug offenses have increased dramatically: more arrests and convictions, prosecution of drug offenders in federal courts, and legislation requiring mandatory sentences. The resources allocated to the drug war are enormous. Arrests for drug offenses tripled from 581,000 in 1980 to 1, 580,000 in 2000. The number of inmates incarcerated for drug offenses in state, and federal prisons and jails reached 453,000 in 1999. The cost for incarcerating 251,200 drug offenders in state prisons is $5 billion annually.[33] A substantial number of the prisoners are low-level offenders; 58 percent of drug offenders in state prison have no history of violence.[34] Although drug offenders have violated drug laws, incarceration removes their positive as well as their negative contributions from their community.[35] One-third of the women in prison are serving a drug sentence. The decision to imprison carries multiple consequences, including making 92,000 women and 135,000 children ineligible for public assistance because of the drug conviction.[36]

Using the criminal justice system to combat drugs has resulted in uneven application of the laws. Communities with resources can address their drug problems privately as a health issue, while criminal justice mechanisms are applied to low-income neighborhoods that lack alternatives.[37] In 2000, seventy-five percent of state prisoners convicted of a drug charge were African American or Hispanic. While African Americans constitute 13 percent of drug users, they comprise 56 percent of state drug convictions.[38] The huge disparity between sentences for crack and powder cocaine raises questions about racial bias in the justice system. Eighty-four percent of the people sentenced for crimes involving crack are African American. Drug laws are based on the quantity of the substance rather than the seriousness of criminal behavior. Five grams of crack equals a mandatory sentence of 5 years in prison; 500 grams of powder cocaine equals the same 5 years. Since powder cocaine is required to make crack, the 100:1 disparity seems reversed. Mandatory sentences for the possession of drugs were enacted to reassure the public that the drug problem was under control, but the public is largely unaware of an unintended consequence of mandatory sentencing.

> Another little-known result of prison overcrowding is that wardens throughout the country are routinely forced to grant an early release to violent offenders so that nonviolent drug offenders can serve their sentences in full. This is true because, for the most part, federal law requires that even nonviolent drug offenders must serve their entire sentences; however, there is no such law for bank robbers, kidnappers, or other violent offenders.[39]

The use of incarceration to solve the problem of drug abuse has been ineffective, harsh, and costly. It has diverted resources from prevention, treatment, and alternative sanctions that hold more promise for nonviolent drug offenders.

These unwise sentencing policies which put men and women in prison for years, not only ruin lives of prisoners and often their family members, but also drain the American taxpayers of funds which can be measured in billions of dollars. . . . This is the time to call a halt to the unnecessary and expensive cost of putting people in prison for a long time based on the mistaken notion that such an effort will win "The War on Drugs." If it is a war, society seems not to be winning, but losing. We must turn to other methods of deterring drug distribution and use.[40]

THE COSTS OF CURRENT POLICIES

The 1.96 million people incarcerated in jails and state or federal prisons in 2001 translate to a rate of 690 people incarcerated for every 100,000 people in the population.[41] An additional 4.66 million people are under correctional supervision for probation or parole.[42] How do states and communities cope with the burden on their budgets and the reintegration of releasees?

In 1978, prison and jail expenditures were $5 billion; the total for 2000 was $40, including $24 billion for the incarceration of nonviolent offenders.[43] Between 1980 and 2000, states, counties, and cities built hundreds of new jails and prisons and hired thousands of new correctional officers to contain the millions of new prisoners. The expanding corrections system consumed a large share of the available state and local tax dollars.[44]

During the 1990s, corrections was one of the fastest growing line items in state budgets; by 2000, the average state committed 7% of its resources to corrections.[45] One of the consequences was reduced spending on a number of items, including higher education. As the Justice Policy Institute put it, "The costs of maintaining prisons and universities have collided." Spending to build prisons grew six times faster than spending on higher education. In 2000, nearly one-third more African-American men were incarcerated than were enrolled in higher education programs.[46]

Many states reduced or eliminated educational and treatment programs in prisons to raise funds to operate their new prisons.[47] Some now charge inmates for educational programs, and very few make participation in treatment a condition of early release.[48] As we have seen, crowding, harsh conditions, and lack of treatment increase prisonization and contribute to inmates' postrelease criminality. Crime prevention suffers as well because budgets for education, health, and welfare agencies are cut to pay prison operating expenses.[49] The greater the number of prisoners, the greater the number of releasees who must find a way to overcome the stigma of a prison record. The average length of sentence served in 2001 was over 60 months.[50] Will five years in a prison create a universe of people so scarred by prisonization that they have few options but a return to crime? The prison boom may become self-sustaining by creating more crime in the long run.

Prisons pose a heavy burden for taxpayers, turn minor offenders into more dangerous criminals, and do little to solve the problems that caused the conviction.[51] The economy during the prison boom was robust. Since 2000 states are facing enormous deficits and need to find revenues or cut operating costs. The economic incentive to find more cost-effective corrections alternatives coincides with a slight decline in state prison populations in sixteen states.[52] It costs an average of $25,000 annually for each person imprisoned (not including the cost of prison construction, welfare for the family, or foster placement for children). In contrast, the annual cost for drug and alcohol treatment is about $2,500 and about $6,000 for intensive supervision.[53]

Diverting funds from education, treatment, and crime prevention to build and operate prisons contributes to the recycling of people through the justice system. Supporting and rehabilitating nonviolent offenders in the communities in which they live saves both human and economic capital. The public is beginning to support prevention, rehabilitation, and alternatives to incarceration. If that support is communicated to legislators who then work to repeal mandatory sentencing laws and to allow sufficient discretion so that punishment is proportional to the crime and harm done to victims, communities will benefit from the reduced tax burden and may see their neighborhoods become safer and healthier.

CHANGES IN THE JUSTICE SYSTEM

The activities of the police and courts have dramatic effects on the fairness and efficiency of corrections. For the last decade or so, the higher courts have broadened police search powers to help with the war on drugs. Whether this increases police efficiency is a matter of opinion, but it clearly threatens the basic fairness of the justice system.[54]

There has been a significant increase in the power of prosecutors and a decrease in the discretion available to judges. Prosecutors retain the ability to decide what cases go to trial, but judges are restricted in their ability to decide sentencing, depending on what crime is charged. Similarly, mandatory time-served provisions remove discretion from parole boards. As Franklin Zimring notes, "With the power of release taken away from parole authorities, and judge's discretion also removed, it was left by default to the legislatures to set sentencing policy. Punishment became a political decision."[55]

> Although punishment has always been the defining characteristic of criminal law, it is only in the past thirty years that incarceration has become the presumptive method of punishing lawbreakers. This focus on incarceration coincided with a shift toward incapacitation and retribution and away from rehabilitation and deterrence as the preferred goals of the criminal justice system.[56]

Making institutional life harsher adds to the burdens faced by understaffed facilities. Many fear that the bitterness generated by unrelenting punishment may increase alienation and thus crime rates. Deterrence advocates hope the changes in the justice system will reduce crime, although there is little supporting evidence for that view.

Chapter 9 detailed some of the effects the changes in the justice system have had on women. Meda Chesney-Lind offered this possibility for possible future changes.

> Women in conflict with the law have become the hidden victims of our nation's imprisonment binge. . . . Perhaps, in this new millennium, we could as a nation

choose to chart a course far different from the one that closed out the waning decades of the last. We could begin seriously to reconsider incarceration as a first choice response to crime—a costly, mean-spirited, and destructive course that most of the rest of the civilized world has critiqued for some time. . . . The decarceration of women can begin the much-needed national conversation of how to develop criminal justice policies that heal and treat rather than solely punish.[57]

THE POWER OF VICTIMS

The victim's movement has empowered people who had been neglected, including minorities, women, gays and the disabled. Politicians support victim initiatives; aiding people who have suffered from crime is almost as certain to gain votes as opposing crime. As Gilbert Geis states, the movement

> has influenced the operation of the criminal justice system, sometimes for the better, sometimes for the worse . . . Most importantly, the renewed focus on crime victims has tilted the balance of the scales of justice more toward equity and fairness to all those who participate in and are affected by our system of administration of criminal justice.[58]

The growing emphasis on the need for services for victims of crime offers some indication of a change in focus in the justice system. However, the most measurable effect has been more punishment for the offender. The adversarial relationship is strongly embedded in the criminal justice system. Prosecution vs. defense may have yielded somewhat to victim vs. offender, but the emphasis is still on one party at the expense of the other. Victim services such as restitution, counseling, and help with emotional and financial stress are now available in most states, but attitudes toward offenders have hardened rather than expanded to a recognition of the dual need for services.[59]

Victims' advocacy groups have lobbied for expanded powers allowing victims some participation in pretrial proceedings, plea bargaining, sentencing, and parole decisions. The federal and many state systems require that judges read a *victim impact statement* before sentencing an offender. These statements describe how the crime affected the victim's mental, physical, and financial welfare as well as their family, job, and social relationships.[60] A few states allow victims to address the court directly in addition to, or instead of, providing a written statement. Addressing the court before sentencing may help some victims deal with the trauma caused by the crime. One of the challenges facing corrections is how to balance the concerns of victims with an approach to offenders that allows hope for the future.

The rights of victims to attend and/or to participate at critical points in the criminal justice process can affect prisoner reintegration. The impact does not have to be negative. There are a number of programs that promote victim–offender communication. The goal is to help reintegration by educating offenders about the impact of crime on victims and to repair community relationships damaged by crime.[61] Many of the programs reflect the perspectives of restorative or community justice discussed later in this chapter. One of the challenges facing corrections is how to balance the concerns of victims with an approach to offenders that allows hope for the future. As Emilio Viano advises, "The justice ideal demands a balanced approach to both victim and defendant, respecting the rights and dignity of both."[62]

A few states allow victims to address the court directly.

NEW TECHNOLOGIES

Expanded use of technology to collect, store, and transfer data on offenders has a number of benefits. Computerized data on the legal histories, security classification, and release status of offenders can be sent to other agencies with greater speed, ease, and certainty than ever before.[63] High-security prisons increasingly rely on automated cameras and doors for perimeter security and video surveillance throughout the facility.[64] *Biometrics*—the automated recognition of a person based on unique physiological or behavioral characteristics such as fingerprints, voice, face, eye, and hand geometry—increasingly will be used in both institutional and community-based agencies. This sort of data, along with legal, medical, and other data on an offender, can be stored on *smart cards*, which would be issued to inmates as they enter the system. Smart cards resemble credit cards and offer the same advantages as computerized records. The same card would be used continuously as offenders pass through various levels of supervision.[65]

Many agencies now use computerized information systems to notify victims, prosecutors, and police of changes in an inmate's release eligibility or supervision status. In many cases, it can also be accessed by victims or the public. Moving the data electronically helps assure that it will not be lost and makes it easier to find and update records. Technology also facilitates the training of new staff members. Bulky policy manuals and other documents can be replaced with electronic versions that are easy to access, search, and update. Computer bulletin boards are used by different agencies, administrators, and security staff to exchange data, discuss common problems, and track gang members within and beyond prisons.[66]

Online educational programs that combine video and computer technologies may also make it easier, safer, and cheaper to provide classes for inmates.[67] Institutional security can be enhanced by issuing electronically monitored bracelets to inmates that track movements throughout the facility. This will relieve COs of having to count inmates constantly to assure that each is where he or she is scheduled to be.[68]

As the military downsized in the 1980s and 1990s, many defense contractors began addressing the needs of criminal justice agencies. Puncture- and slash-resistant vests are available to protect officers from attacks with shivs and other sharp objects.[69] Technology like ground-penetrating radar and heartbeat sensors can be reformatted to detect tunnels and inmates hiding in vehicles leaving a prison.[70] While these products offer increased efficiency, all products must be evaluated for the benefits they provide versus costs and for their effects on inmates and staff.

Breakthroughs in biology may also aid corrections in the future. As was noted in the last chapter, many inmates have been released from prison due to DNA evidence just as many have been convicted with it. In addition there are many new drugs being developed that can help control inmates in prison and after release. A deeper understanding of the genetic roots of violence and addiction may lead to new biometric risk assessment methods and control devices. These new technologies could be combined with existing ones to monitor offenders, making that responsibility less labor intensive for supervising officers. To be useful, the innovations must be accompanied by

Online courses increase access to and decrease costs of inmate education.

comprehensive education for the professionals who use them.[71] They must also be analyzed and monitored to insure that they are used ethically and do not infringe on prisoners' rights.

The quick and certain transfer of data from jails, courts, and prisons can help make community-based agencies more efficient. Probation and parole agencies may begin to use global positioning satellite systems to keep track of offenders on home confinement. Effective use of this sanction could help reduce the need for cell space.[72] Some experts have also suggested that low-risk probationers and parolees could report to computerized kiosks. This would free officers to deal more intensively with higher risk offenders.[73] However, it would also reduce personal contact with the offenders who are most amenable to reintegration.[74] "Body alarms," programmed to go off when a sex offender approaches a school or playground, have been proposed to reassure victims that released offenders will not pose a threat to children.[75]

These attempts to improve agency efficiency and to minimize risk parallel shifts in how the duties of the correctional system are defined by officials. The primary concerns are: (1) Will the costs for control technology come at the expense of programs designed to prepare releasees for life outside prison? (2) Can computerized oversight provide an adequate substitute for human interaction and supervision? (3) Will the new technologies be used to widen the net of social control?

Sentencing Decisions

Sentencing decisions have very real consequences for both the people in the system and the society that creates the policies that dictate what happens to people convicted of a crime. Read the following case summaries. Do you agree with the outcomes? What values and concerns guide your thoughts?

In 1974, Alfred Martin was convicted for selling $10 worth of marijuana to a coworker in Martinsville, Virginia. He pled guilty because his attorney told him a jury was likely to respond harshly to a black man who sold drugs to a white woman. Martin was sentenced to ten years in a minimum-security prison, with all but one year suspended. He walked away from the prison farm after serving only two days and fled to Michigan with his wife and infant son. Later that year he was stopped for a traffic violation, and his fugitive status was discovered. Martin hired a lawyer to fight extradition, and Michigan's governor granted him asylum on December 24, 1976. He and his wife raised three children and lived uneventfully for the next twenty-two years. On November 4, 1998, Martin was stopped for having expired license plates. A computer check revealed the old Virginia warrants. Extradition laws had changed, and Michigan had to honor Virginia's request for extradition. Martin was jailed in Martinsville where the prosecutor stated, "Mr. Martin started this by agreeing to sell drugs, and then he ran." The escape was a felony charge, which is usually punished with a five-year sentence.[76]

Is such a sentence appropriate? What goals of punishment are served by such a sentence? What values would encourage lenience? Which do you feel are most important? Should Martin's post-escape behavior be taken into account as his case is considered? Why or why not?

On September 8, 1985, 16-year-old Sean Sellers took a handgun from a friend's grandfather's house and used it to kill Robert Bower, a convenience store clerk. He told his friend that he wanted to know what it felt like to kill someone. The crime went unsolved for six months until Sellers killed his mother and stepfather while they were sleeping. The jury that sentenced Sellers to death was unaware that he suffered from multiple-personality disorder (M.P.D.). The U.S. Court of Appeal noted that M.P.D. was "virtually unknown at the time of Sellers' trial" but could not overturn the state judgment. At the time of the original trial, Oklahoma law limited indigent defense spending to $750. Sellers became remorseful on death row and began an outreach ministry that reached thousands of teenagers with a strong anticrime message. Despite evidence of his mental disorder, his remorse, and his outreach ministry, the Oklahoma Pardon and Parole Board denied his request for clemency and Sellers was executed on February 4, 1999. His lawyers asserted that the "clemency process and procedures were so deficient and arbitrary as to deny Sean Sellers any due process whatsoever."[77]

Bianca Jagger, an Amnesty International activist, eulogized Sellers and condemned the state's decision. "His execution denies the possibility that . . . a child of sixteen can be rehabilitated and redeemed. It is the potential for change and redemption that motivates us all to be better people. Killing the light of that redemption in Sean has killed some of that light in all of us."[78]

Are the defendant's age and mental state sufficient to persuade you against execution? What about the financial limits placed on his defense? Is it appropriate, as most nations have decided, to ban use of the death penalty for crimes committed prior to the offender's eighteenth birthday? How do cases like this affect world opinion? How do you evaluate Jagger's assessment of the meaning of this case? Should the post-conviction behavior of an offender be considered when clemency and related issues are raised? Why or why not?

NEW MODELS OF THE CORRECTIONAL MISSION

Two new ways of defining the goals of criminal justice and organizing the agencies that constitute the system are emerging. They are especially relevant to community-based correctional agencies handling probationers and parolees. The degree to which they will alter the traditional methods of the system remains to be seen, but each is already having some impact in many areas. Fears of racial and economic discrimination and the staggering financial burden imposed by the large-scale use of imprisonment have caused many to reject the retributive approach. The growing power of victim's groups and recognition of local differences in the priority given to punishment, treatment, and incapacitation support and help redefine the organization and goals of the justice process. The types of crime faced by a particular community, its legal and popular concepts of "fairness," and its image of the effect of the crime on its victim are the guiding forces of the community and restorative justice programs springing up throughout the world.[79]

Restorative Justice

Restorative justice is a general label for programs that try to simultaneously assist victims, prevent future crime, and reintegrate offenders wherever feasible. Its primary applications are in community corrections and juvenile justice. It defines crime as victimizing people and communities rather than the state, and it empowers individual communities to become directly involved in all phases of the justice process. Repairing the harm done by a crime is more important than assuring punishment, which is recognized as creating as many problems as it may solve. Some versions acknowledge that many or most offenders were victims of medical, family, or social problems before their offense. Others focus entirely on the current victim and community, blending restitution with retribution in the process. Restorative methods give high priority to repairing all damages suffered by victims; many work equally hard to restore the offender's status within the community. Offenders must be ready to accept responsibility and to apologize for their crimes, while victims must be willing to accept reparations respectfully and to get on with their lives. This view of justice sees punishment as ineffective in changing behavior and strives to hold people accountable for their actions.

Because each community is different, each attempt at restorative justice has unique features. All of these programs share a focus on cooperation between citizens and justice agencies and dialog between community, victim, and offender. Because each attempt at restorative justice strives to balance the needs of all three parties, the approach is often described as "balanced," integrating prevention, treatment, community service, and restitution into a single package. The goals are admirable; the success—and methods for achieving them—are still in progress. [80]

Community Justice

Various attempts to build relationships between local communities and correctional agencies have grown out of the public health approach to crime control. This approach tries to predict and control the growth of crime and the conditions that cause it before serious victimizations result.[81] A variety of programs are classified under this model; most are community based and employ alternative sanctions. Some simply integrate institutional treatment with community supervision to assure continuity of treatment and supervision following release.[82] Others use multiagency task forces, committees, or planning groups to identify problems and to develop strategies for dealing with them.[83] Because it requires close cooperation between agencies within and beyond the justice system, the war against terrorism is likely to expand this community and regional planning approach.

Some agencies have chosen to give local communities direct input into their operation.[84] This can be accomplished through community councils that advise regional administrators and local supervisors while educating the public and assisting in providing services. These councils have the potential to unite citizens and agencies and to avoid possible misunderstandings by establishing quick, informal means of communication between them.[85] In other cases, agencies send representatives to planning councils that control which programs will be funded.[86]

A *"broken windows"* definition of the correctional mission stresses the need for parole/probation officers to identify and address the problems in the community that might cause future crimes before they become too serious. It is the correctional version of community (or problem-oriented) policing that is based on a proactive view of criminal justice rather than a reactive one. Some probation offices have joined forces with community policing efforts to place officers in storefronts and to encourage them to work with the entire community to control and reintegrate particular offenders.[87] While programs like these have been implemented on an experimental basis, it seems unlikely that they will become prevalent in the immediate future because they conflict with the retributive, incapacitative model of corrections that currently dominates the field. The community justice approach places increasing amounts of power in the hands of the line practitioner.[88]

Accreditation

American Correctional Association (ACA) accreditation indicates that an agency or institution follows the highest professional standards in the field. Other associations, such as the National Commission on Correctional Health Care, offer similar, more focused, forms of accreditation as well.

Dozens of ACA manuals are published and revised to keep up with new court decisions and technologies. Over 1,200 agencies use various ACA manuals that set minimum standards and provide guidelines for achieving them.[89] These manuals cover food and health care services, classification, architecture, inmate privileges, and probation/parole supervision. Private and public as well as juvenile and adult agencies are addressed by ACA standards.[90] Although ACA accreditation is strictly voluntary, some courts use these standards to guide the conditions they impose.[91] Accreditation improves staff morale and pride, helps assure quality, and builds credibility in the profession with the courts and the public.

SUMMARY

Rising rates of imprisonment reflect the public's fear of crime and distrust of treatment. The media's focus on heinous crimes and failures of corrections contributes to public support of harsher sentences, the war on drugs, and more punitive approaches to community supervision. The victims' movement often promotes harsh sentencing laws and prison conditions. These trends have created a prison and jail population of 2 million plus another 4.7 million on probation and parole for a total correctional population of 6.7 million people. The economic and social costs of this explosion of incarceration are enormous.

Technology is affecting every aspect of corrections. Agencies can communicate more easily and rapidly with one another, victims, and the public while various monitoring devices add to their incapacitative power. The ways in which technology is used often reflect the values of the new penology, which abandons the goals of justice and reintegration in favor of risk management and administrative efficiency. Alternative approaches based in the community focus on creating an integrated, proactive response to crime that forestalls the development of crime-producing conditions while healing the wounds of crime, rather than making judgments about responsibility and punishment. These approaches often conflict with dominant political models of justice system organization; their concentration of power at the level of line staff contradicts the new penology's stress on administrative accountability. ACA accreditation can improve the efficiency of correctional agencies and help avoid lawsuits.

As we examine various methods of responding to crime, we confront the contradictory demands of justice and efficiency. Massive levels of incapacitation may appeal to our sense of fairness and make us feel safer, but the efficiency of doing so is suspect. Overreliance on imprisonment diverts resources from prevention and treatment. This increases the criminality of some offenders who return to society and commit even worse crimes.

Many penologists believe that we are now incarcerating more people than is necessary because we overestimate dangerousness. The public's loss of faith in reintegration, due in part to erroneous media reports, has led many to feel that we can succeed only in punishing offenders. Although we are unlikely to eliminate crime and recidivism completely, treatment is effective enough to make major contributions to the efficiency of the system. The difficult choices between efficiency and fairness, and between safety and cost control, permeate every policy decision relating to sentencing and correctional issues.

Corrections deals with the most intractable of society's problems. The continuum between punishment and rehabilitation has been well traveled in both directions. A reasonable approach begins with people who are well informed and who are willing to face the challenges posed by conflicting goals. We hope this book has presented a snapshot of the interrelated workings of a system dealt an imposing but vitally important role in the functioning of society.

QUESTIONS FOR DISCUSSION AND REVIEW

1. What forces determine the rate of imprisonment? Do these forces serve the interests of fairness, efficiency, or some other societal need? Is this a rational way to operate a coercive system? What might be done to improve the efficiency and fairness of the system?

2. How do the media affect the public's view of crime and corrections? Are voters responding to the real issues facing the justice system? What changes should the media make in covering crime and corrections? What changes should correctional agencies make to assure better coverage by the media?

3. What goals are served by the war on drugs? Are they worth the financial and social cost? Is the war on drugs effective? Is it moral? Is it racially biased? What alternatives for controlling drug abuse might we want to consider? Why?

4. What are the financial and opportunity costs of our current sentencing and correctional policies? How are these policies likely to affect future levels of crime in the United States?

5. How has the victims' movement affected the way we treat offenders? Who benefits from this? Who is harmed by it? What changes in the laws protecting crime victims do you favor? Are such changes designed to favor fairness or efficiency?

6. List and define the ways in which new technologies are changing corrections. How are these changes likely to affect the lives of practitioners? The efficiency of the system? What dangers do they pose for the system and for society in general?

7. What is accreditation and how does it affect a facility? Who determines which facilities become accredited?

ENDNOTES

CHAPTER ONE

[1] Jess Maghan, "The Dilemmas of Corrections and the Legacy of David Fogel," *International Journal of Offender Therapy and Comparative Criminology*, 41(2) (1997): 101–20; James A. Gondles, Jr. "Living by the Sword," *Corrections Today*, July (2002): 6.

[2] Katherine Beckett, "Political Preoccupation with Crime Leads, Not Follows, Public Opinion," *Overcrowded Times*, 8(5) (1997): 1, 8–11.

[3] B. F. Skinner, *About Behaviorism* (New York: Alfred A Knopf, 1974), p. 62.

[4] Hans C. Breiter, Itzhak Aharon, Daniel Kahneman, Anders Dale and Peter Shizgal, "Functional Imaging of Neural Responses to Expectancy and Experience of Monetary Gains and Losses," *Neuron*, 30 (2001): 619–39; Steven Stocker, "Studies Link Stress and Drug Addiction," *NIDA Notes*, 14(1) (1999): 1–4.

[5] Johannes Feest, "Imprisonment and Prisoners Work: Normalization or Less Eligibility?" *Punishment and Society*, 1(1) (1999): 99–107.

[6] *Ibid.*

[7] Dora Schriro and Tom Clements, "Parallel Universe: A Blueprint for Effective Prison Management," *Corrections Today*, 63(2) (2001): 140–43, 152.

[8] Office of Juvenile Justice and Delinquency Prevention, *Guide for Implementing the Balanced and Restorative Justice Model* (Washington, DC: U.S. Department of Justice, 1998), pp. 1–10.

[9] Frank Domurad, "Who Is Killing Our Probation Officers: The Performance Crisis in Community Corrections," *Corrections Management Quarterly*, 4(2) (2000): 41–51.

[10] Andrew Hochstetler, "Reporting of Executions in U.S. Newspapers," *Journal of Crime & Justice*, 24(1) (2001): 1–13.

[11] Christopher Newton, "Coverage of Minority Crime Skewed, Study Says Murder Stories Jumped 473% in 8 Years, Though Homicides Dropped 33%," *Denver Rocky Mountain News*, 11 Apr. 2001, p. 1-B.

[12] Corrections Compendium, "Survey Summary: Media Access." *Corrections Compendium*, 27(4) (April 2002): 6–7.

[13] Michael Tonry and Joan Petersilia, "Prisons Research at the Beginning of the 21st Century," *Crime and Justice: A Review of the Research*, 26 (1999): 3; Jeremy Bentham, *An Introduction to the Principles of Morals and Legislation* (Oxford: Basil Blackwell, 1948 [1789]), pp. 1–20.

[14] David E. Barlow, Melissa Hickman-Barlow and W. Wesley Johnson, "The Political Economy of Criminal Justice Policy: A Time-Series Analysis of Economic Conditions, Crime and Federal Criminal Justice Legislation, 1948–1987," *Justice Quarterly*, 13(2) (1996): 223–41.

[15] Dan M. Kahan, "The Secret Ambition of Deterrence," *Harvard Law Review*, 113(2) (1999): 413–500.

[16] Anthony Walsh and Craig Hemmens, *From Law to Order* (Baltimore, MD: American Correctional Association, 2000), p. 30; Michael S. Moore, "The Moral Worth of Retribution," in Jeffrie G. Murphy (ed.), *Punishment and Rehabilitation*, 3rd ed. (Belmont, CA: Wadsworth, 1995), p. 130.

[17] James Austin and John Irwin, *It's About Time*, 3rd ed. (Belmont, CA: Wadsworth, 2001), p. 13.

[18] John T. Whitehead and Michael B. Blankenship, "Gender Gap in Capital Punishment Attitudes: An Analysis of Support and Opposition," *American Journal of Criminal Justice*, 25(1) (2000): 1–13; Theodore Caplow and Jonathan Simon, "Understanding Prison Policy and Population Trends," in Michael Tonry and Joan Petersilia (eds.), *Prisons* (Chicago: University of Chicago Press, 1999), pp. 63–120; Travis C. Pratt, Jeffrey Maahs and Steven D. Stehr, "The Symbolic Ownership of the Corrections 'Problem': A Framework for Understanding the Development of Corrections Policy in the United States," *Prison Journal*, 78(4) (1998): 451–64.

[19] Moore, "The Moral Worth of Retribution."

[20] Michael Cavadino and James Dignan, "Reparation, Retribution and Rights," *International Review of Victimology*, 4(4) (1997): 233–53.

[21] Matthew C. Schreider, "Deterrence and the Base Rate Fallacy: An Examination of Perceived Certainty," *Justice Quarterly*, 18(1) (2001): 63–86.

[22] Andrew von Hirsch, Anthony E. Bottoms, Elizabeth Burney and Peter O. Wikstrom, *Criminal Deterrence and Sentence Severity: An Analysis of Recent Research* (Cambridge, United Kingdom: University of Cambridge, 1999), pp. 1–65.

[23] Samuel Walker, *Sense and Nonsense about Crime and Drugs*, 5th ed. (Belmont, CA: Wadsworth, 2001), p. 102.

[24] *Ibid.*, pp. 97–99, 114.

[25] Schreider, "Deterrence and the Base Rate Fallacy: an Examination of Perceived Certainty."

[26] Daniel S. Nagin and Greg Pogarsky, "Integrating Celerity, Impulsivity, and Extralegal Sanction Threats into a Model of General Deterrence," *Criminology*, 39(4) (2001): 865–92.

[27] Sheila R. Maxwell and Kevin M. Gray, "Deterrence: Testing the Effects of Perceived Sanction Certainty on Probation Violations," *Sociological Inquiry*, 70(2) (2000): 117–36.

[28] Alex Piquero and George F. Rengert, "Studying Deterrence with Active Residential Burglars," *Justice Quarterly*, 16(2) (1999): 451–71; Jon L. Proctor and Michael Pease, "Parole as an Institutional Control: A Test of Specific Deterrence and Offender Misconduct," *Prison Journal*, 80(1) (2000): 39–55.

[29] Christopher D. Maxwell, Joel H. Garner and Jeffrey A. Fagan, *The Effects of Arrest on Intimate Partner Violence: New Evidence from the Spouse Assault Replication Program* (Washington, DC: National Institute of Justice, July 2001), pp. 1, 9–12, NCJ-188199.

[30] James Q. Wilson and Richard J. Herrnstein, *Crime and Human Nature* (New York: Simon and Schuster, 1985), p. 494.

[31] Émile Durkheim, *Suicide: A Study in Sociology*, George Simpson (ed.), translated by John A. Spaulding and George Simpson (New York: Free Press, 1951).

[32] Jackson Toby, "Is Punishment Necessary?" in Norman Johnston, Leonard Savitz and Marvin E. Wolfgang (eds.), *The Sociology of Punishment and Correction*, 2nd ed. (New York: John Wiley and Sons, 1970), pp. 362–69; Émile Durkheim, *The Division of Labor in Society*, translated by George Simpson (Glencoe, IL: The Free Press, 1947), p. 89.

[33] Morna Murray and Sterling O'Ran, *Restitution* (Washington, DC: Office of Justice Programs, 2000), pp. 1–20, NCJ-184061.

[34] Office of Justice Programs, *State Crime Victim Compensation and Assistance Grant Programs* (Washington, DC: U.S. Dept of Justice, Office of Justice Programs, Office for Victims of Crime, 2000), pp. 1–20, NCJ-184922.

[35] Maureen C. Outlaw and R. Barry Ruback, "Predictors and Outcomes of Victim Restitution Orders," *Justice Quarterly,* 16(4) (1999): 847–69.

[36] Paul Gendreau, Claire Goggin and Francis T. Cullen, *The Effects of Prison Sentences on Recidivism* (Ottawa, Canada: Solicitor General Canada, 1999), pp. 1–37.

[37] Don M. Gottfredson, *Effects of Judges' Sentencing Decisions on Criminal Careers* (Washington, DC: U.S. National Institute of Justice, 1999), p. 12.

[38] Tomislav V. Kovandzic, "The Impact of Florida's Habitual Offender Law on Crime," *Criminology*, 39(1) (2001): 179–204.

[39] Thomas B. Marvell and Carlisle E. Moody, "Female and Male Homicide Victimization Rates: Comparing Trends and Regressors," *Criminology*, 37(4) (1999): 879–902.

[40] Grant N. Burt, Stephen Wong and Sarah Vander Veen, "Three Strikes and You're Out: An Investigation of False Positive Rates Using a Canadian Sample," *Federal Probation*, 64(2) (2000): 3–7.

[41] Kathleen Auerhahn, "Selective Incapacitation and the Problem of Prediction," *Criminology*, 37(4) (1999): 703–34; James Austin, John Clark and Patricia Hardyman, "The Impact of 'Three Strikes and You're Out,'" *Punishment and Society*, 1(2) (1999): 131–62.

[42] Walker, *Sense and Nonsense about Crime and Drugs*, p. 138.

[43] James Austin and John Irwin, *It's About Time*, 3rd ed., pp. 184–214; Mike Males, Don Macallair and Khaled Taqi Eddin, *Striking Out: The Failure of California's 'Three Strikes and You're Out' Law* (San Francisco: Justice Policy Institute, 1999), pp. 1–11; Kathleen Auerhahn, "Selective Incapacitation and the Problem of Prediction,"; Austin, Clark and Hardyman, "The Impact of 'Three Strikes and You're Out'"; David Shichor, "Three Strikes as Public Policy: The Convergence of the New Penology and the McDonaldization of Punishment," in Stan Stojkovic, John Klofas and David Kalinich (eds.), *The Administration and Management of Criminal Justice Organizations*, 3rd ed. (Prospect Heights, IL: Waveland Press, 1999), pp. 435–36.

[44] *Lockyer v. Andrade*, No. 01-1127 (2002).

[45] http://www.deathpenaltyinfo.org/wop.html

[46] *U.S. v. Salerno*, 481 U.S. 739 (1987), *remanded*, 289 F.2d 345 2d cir., 1987; *Schall v. Martin*, 467 U.S. 253 (1984).

[47] C. Wayne Johnson, "Incapacitation and Deterrent Effects of Incarceration: A Pennsylvania Study," *Corrections Compendium*, 24(12) (1999): 1–3, 16–21; Sara L. Johnson and Brian A. Grant, "Release Outcomes of Long-term Offenders," *Forum on Corrections Research*, 12(3) (2000): 16–20; Melissa Gross, Elizabeth P. Cramer, Jarnett Forte, Jill A. Gordon, Tara Kunkel and Laura J. Moriarty, "Impact of Sentencing Options on Recidivism among Domestic Violence Offenders: A Case Study," *American Journal of Criminal Justice*, 24(2) (2000): 301–12.

[48] Victor E. Kappeler, Mark Blumberg and Gary W. Potter, *The Mythology of Crime and Criminal Justice*, 3rd ed. (Prospect Heights, IL: Waveland Press, 1996), pp. 286–88.

[49] Walker, *Sense and Nonsense about Crime and Drugs*, pp. 128–34.

[50] *Ibid.*, p. 134; Auerhahn, "Selective Incapacitation and the Problem of Prediction."

[51] Daniel Mears, Sarah Lawerence, Amy L. Solomon and Michelle Waul, "Prison-Based Programming: What It Can Do and Why It Is Needed," *Corrections Today*, April (2002): 66–71, 83.

[52] See, generally, Stephen Duguid, *Can Prisons Work? The Prisoner as Object and Subject in Modern Corrections* (Toronto, Ontario, Canada: University of Toronto Press, 2000).

[53] Adrian Raine, Todd Lencz, Susan Bihrle, Lori LaCasse and Patrick M. Colletti, "Reduced Prefrontal Gray Matter Volume and Reduced Autonomic Activity in Antisocial Personality Disorder," *Archives of General Psychiatry*, 57(2) (2000): 119–27; Paul M. Thompson, Jay N. Giedd, Roger P. Woods, David Macdonald, Alan C. Evans and Arthur W. Toga, "Growth Patterns in the Developing Brain Detected by Using Continuum Mechanical Tensor Maps," *Nature*, 404 (2000): 190–93; Jyrki T. Kuikka, Jari Tiihonen, Kim A. Bergström, Jari Karhu, Pirkko Räsänen and Markku Eronen, "Abnormal Structure of Human Striatal Dopamine Re-Uptake Sites in Habitually Violent Alcoholic Offenders: A Fractal Analysis," *Neuroscience Letters, Vol. 253* (1998), pp. 195–97.

[54] J. Grafman, K. Schwab, D. Warden, A. Pridgen, H. R. Brown and A. M. Salazar, "Frontal Lobe Injuries, Violence, and Aggression: A Report of the Vietnam Head Injury Study," *Neurology*, 46(5) (1996): 1231–38.

[55] Kenneth Blum, John G. Cull, Eric R. Braverman and David E. Comings, "Reward Deficiency Syndrome," *American Scientist*, 84(2) (1996); Adriane Raine, P. H. Venables and Mednick A. Sarnoff, "Low Resting Heart Rate at Age 3 Years Predisposes to Aggression at Age 11 Years: Evidence from the Mauritius Child Health Project," *Journal of the American Academy of Child and Adolescent Psychiatry*, 36(10) (1997): 1457–64.

[56] Mark Gornik, *Moving from Correctional Program to Correctional Strategy: Using Proven Practices to Change Criminal Behavior* (Washington, DC: National Institute of Justice, 2001), p. 10, NCJ-017624.

[57] Michael Tonry, "Fragmentation of Sentencing and Corrections," *American Alternatives to Incarceration*, 6(2) (2000): 9–13.

[58] Jeff Glasser, "Ex-Cons on the Street," *U.S. News and World Report* (May 1, 2000): 18–21.

[59] Leon Radzinowicz, *Ideology and Crime* (New York: Columbia University Press, 1971).

[60] John E. Holman and James F. Quinn, *Criminology: Applying Theory* (St. Paul: West, 1992), pp. 48–49.

[61] Brian A. Reaves, *Felony Defendants in Large Urban Counties, 1998* (Washington, DC: National Institute of Justice, 2001), p. 17, NCJ-187232.

[62] National Council on Crime and Delinquency, *National Assessment of Structured Sentencing* (Washington, DC: Bureau of Justice Assistance, 1996), pp. 3–7.

[63] E. Michele Staley, *Merit Time Program Summary October 1997–December 1999* (Albany: New York State Dept. of Correctional Services, 2000), pp. 1–122, NCJ-185648.

[64] William Habern and Gary J. Cohen, "A History of Parole, Mandatory Supervision and Good Time," *Voice*, 25(8) (1996): 21–27.

[65] Eliott Monochese, "Cesare Beccaria," in Herman Mannheim (ed.), *Pioneers in Criminology* (Montclair, NJ: Patterson Smith, 1973), p. 48.

[66] Andrew Von Hirsch, "The Politics of Just Deserts," *Canadian Journal of Criminology*, 32 (1990): 459–76.

[67] National Council on Crime and Delinquency, *National Assessment of Structured Sentencing* (Washington, DC: Bureau of Justice Assistance, 1996), pp. 1–5.

[68] Cassia Spohn and David Holleran, "The Effect of Imprisonment on Recidivism Rates of Felony Offenders: A Focus on Drug Offenders," *Criminology*, 40(2) (2002): 329–58.

[69] Henry F. Fradella, "Mandatory Minimum Sentences: Arizona's Ineffective Tool for the Social Control of Driving under the Influence," *Criminal Justice Policy Review*, 11(2) (2000): 113–35.

[70] Paula M. Kautt, *Separating and Estimating the Effects of the Federal Sentencing Guidelines and Mandatory Minimums: Isolating the Sources of Racial Disparity* (Washington, DC: U.S. Dept. of Justice, National Institute of Justice, 2000), pp. 1–17.

[71] Tomislav V. Kovandzic, "The Impact of Florida's Habitual Offender Law on Crime"; Thomas B. Marvell and Carlisle E. Moody, "Female and Male Homicide Victimization Rates: Comparing Trends and Regressors," *Criminology*, 37(4) (1999): 879–902.

[72] Douglas C. McDonald and Kenneth E. Carlson, *Federal Sentencing in Transition, 1986–90* (Washington, DC: U.S. Dept. of Justice, Bureau of Justice Statistics, 1992), pp. 1–9, NCJ-13427.

[73] "Contract Watch," *Christian Science Monitor*, Mar. 6, 1995, p. 19; Substance Abuse Policy Research Program, *Profile of Anti-Drug Law Enforcement in Urban Poverty Areas in Massachusetts* (Winston-Salem, NC: Substance Abuse Policy Research Program, 1997).

[74] Paul M. Ditton and D. J. Wilson, *Truth in Sentencing in State Prisons* (Rockville, MD: U.S. Dept. of Justice, Bureau of Justice Statistics, 1999), pp. 1–16, NCJ-170032; U.S. Dept. of Justice, Violent Offender Incarceration and Truth-in-Sentencing Incentive Grants: Implementation Report, July 1, 1998–June 30, 1999 (Washington, DC: U.S. Dept. of Justice, Office of Justice Programs), pp. 1–10, NCJ-178910.

[75] G. Pascal Zachary, "Economists Say Prison Boom Will Take Toll," *The Wall Street Journal*, Sept. 29, 1995, p. B.

[76] "Florida's Release of Violent Criminals Upsets Many," *Crime Prevention News*, Mar. 20, 1997, p. 11.

[77] Brian J. Ostrom, Fred Cheesman, Ann M. Jones, Meredith Peterson and Neal B. Kauder, *Truth-in-Sentencing in Virginia* (Williamsburg, VA: National Ctr. for State Courts, 1999), pp. 1–91.

[78] Ronald F. Wright, *Managing Prison Growth in North Carolina Through Structured Sentencing* (Washington, DC: U.S. Dept. of Justice, 1998), pp. 1–6, 20–21; James Austin, "The Effect of Three Strikes and You're Out on Corrections," in David Shichor and Dale Sechrist (eds.), *Three Strikes and You're Out: Vengeance as Public Policy* (Thousand Oaks, CA: Sage, 1996), pp. 155–74.

[79] Melissa E. Fenwick, "Maxxing Out: Imprisonment in an Era of Crime Control," in Wilson R. Palacios, Paul F. Cromwell and Roger G. Dunham (eds.), *Crime & Justice in America: Present Realities and Future Prospects*, 2nd ed. (Upper Saddle River, NJ: Prentice-Hall, 2002).

[80] John Irwin, Vincent Schiraldi and Jason Ziedenberg, *America's One Million Nonviolent Prisoners* (Washington, DC: Justice Policy Institute,1999), pp. 1–16.

[81] Ditton and Wilson, *Truth in Sentencing in State Prisons*.

[82] Sara L. Johnson and Brian A. Grant, "Release Outcomes of Long-term Offenders," *Forum on Corrections Research*, 12(3) (2000): 16–20.

[83] Morgan Reynolds, *Crime and Punishment in America, 1997 Update* (Dallas: National Center for Policy Analysis, 1997), pp. 1–33.

[84] See, generally, Franklin Zimring, "New Politics of Criminal Justice: Of 'Three Strikes,' Truth-in-Sentencing, and Megan's Law," *Perspectives on Crime and Justice: 1999–2000 Lecture Series, Vol. 4* (Washington, DC: U.S. Dept. of Justice, National Institute of Justice, 2001), pp. 1–22, NCJ-188081; Lawrence W. Sherman, Denise Gottfredson, Doris MacKenzie, John Eck, Peter Reuter and Shawn Bushway, *Preventing Crime: What Works, What Doesn't, What's Promising* (Washington, DC: National Institute of Justice, March 1997); Marcus Felson, "A 'Routine Activity' Analysis of Recent Crime Reductions," *The Criminologist*, 22(6) (1997): 1–3; "Deterrence Reduces Crime More than Incapacitation," *Crime Prevention News*, June 19, 1996, p. 9; "Serious Crimes Decline in 1995," *Crime Prevention News*, May 8, 1996, p. 11.

[85] Marc Mauer, "Causes and Consequences of Prison Growth in the United States," *Punishment & Society*, 3(1) 2001: 9–20; Nola M. Joyce, "A View of the Future: The Effect of Policy on Prison Population Growth," *Crime and Delinquency*, 38 (1992): 357–69.

[86] Brian J. Ostrom, Fred Cheesman, Ann M. Jones, Meredith Peterson and Neal B. Kauder, *Truth-in-Sentencing in Virginia* (Rockville, MD: U.S. Dept. of Justice, National Institute of Justice, 1999), pp. 1–9, NCJ-187677; Thomas B. Marvell and Carlisle E. Moody, "Determinant Sentencing and Abolishing Parole: The Long-Term Impacts on Prisons and Crime," *Criminology*, 34(1) (1996): 107–28.

[87] Lisa Stolzenberg and Stewart J. D'Alessio, "The Impact of Prison Crowding on Male and Female Imprisonment Rates in Minnesota," *Justice Quarterly*, 14(4) (1997): 793–809.

[88] Paula M. Kautt, *Separating and Estimating the Effects of the Federal Sentencing Guidelines and Mandatory Minimums: Isolating the Sources of Racial Disparity* (Washington, DC: U.S. Dept. of Justice, National Institute of Justice, 2000), pp. 1–17.

[89] Elsa Chen, *Impacts of Three Strikes and Truth in Sentencing on the Volume and Composition of Correctional Populations* **(Washington, DC: National Institute of Justice, 2000), pp. 1–109, NCJ-187109**.

[90] Vincent Schiraldi and Judith Greene, "Public Opinion Shifts as States Re-examine Prison Policies in Face of Tightening Budgets," *On the Line* (Lanham MD: American Correctional Association, 2002), 25(3): 1–2, 7.

[91] Zimring, "New Politics of Criminal Justice"; Mauer, "Causes and Consequences of Prison Growth in the United States."

[92] Katherine Beckett, "Political Preoccupation with Crime Leads, Not Follows, Public Opinion," *Overcrowded Times*, 8(5) (1997): 1, 8–11; Paige M. Harrison and Allen J. Beck, *Prisoners in 2001* (Rockville, MD: U.S. Dept. of Justice, Bureau of Justice Statistics, 2002), pp. 1–4, NCJ-195189.

[93] Kappeler, Blumberg and Potter, *The Mythology of Crime and Criminal Justice*, 3rd ed., pp. 27–73, 254–57.

[94] Harrison and Beck, *Prisoners in 2001*, p. 3; Kathleen Maguire and Ann L. Pastore, *Sourcebook of Criminal Justice Statistics 1996* (Washington, DC: U.S. Dept. of Justice, 1997), table 6.30, p. 601, table 3.107, p. 352, NCJ-165361.

[95] Christopher Innes, "Recent Public Opinion in the United States toward Punishment and Corrections," in James W. Marquart and Jonathan R. Sorenson (eds.), *Correctional Contexts* (Los Angeles: Roxbury, 1998); Schiraldi and Greene, "Public Opinion Shifts."

[96] Vincent Schiraldi and Tara-Jen Ambrosio, *From Classroom to Cell Blocks* (San Francisco: Center on Juvenile and Criminal Justice, 1997), pp. 1–28.

CHAPTER TWO

[1] Harry Elmer Barnes, *The Story of Punishment*, 2nd ed. (Montclair, NJ: Patterson Smith, 1972), p. 39; Sally Falk Moore, "Law and Anthropology," in Bernard J. Siegal (ed.), *Biennial Review of Anthropology* (Stanford: Stanford University Press, 1969), pp. 252–300.

[2] J. Thorstein Sellin, *Slavery and the Penal System* (New York: Elsevier Scientific Publishing, 1976), pp. 2–29.

[3] *The American Prison: From the Beginning* (Laurel: American Correctional Association, 1983), p. 3.

[4] David C. Anderson, *Crimes of Justice* (New York: Random House, 1988), pp. 179, 230.

[5] Robert G. Caldwell, *Criminology* (New York: Ronald Press, 1965), p. 494; Sean McConville, *A History of English Prison Administration* (London: Routledge and Kegan Paul, 1981) pp. 52, 247–49.

[6] William J. Bopp and Donald O. Schultz, *A Short History of American Law Enforcement* (Springfield, IL: Charles C. Thomas, 1977), pp. 7–9.

[7] See, generally, James C. Holt, *Magna Carta*, 2nd ed. (New York: Cambridge University Press, 1992).

[8] W. Melville Lee, *A History of Police in England* (Montclair, NJ: Patterson Smith, 1970), pp. 19–20.

[9] Pieter Spierenburg, "The Body and the State," in Norval Morris and David J. Rothman (eds.), *The Oxford History of the Prison* (New York: Oxford University Press, 1995), p. 65.

[10] *Ibid.*, p. 67.

[11] Leonard Orland, "Prisons as Punishment," in Kenneth C. Haas and Geoffrey P. Alpert (eds.), *The Dilemmas of Corrections*, 4th ed. (Prospect Heights, IL: Waveland Press, 1999), p. 7.

[12] David J. Rothman, *The Discovery of the Asylum* (Boston: Little, Brown, 1971), pp. xvi–xix.

[13] Michael Ignatieff, "State, Civil Society, and Total Institutions: A Critique of Recent Social Histories of Punishment," in Michael Tonry and Norval Morris (eds.), *Crime and Justice: An Annual Review of Research, Vol. 3* (Chicago: University of Chicago Press, 1981), pp. 153–92.

[14] Cesare Beccaria, *On Crimes and Punishments*, 6th ed., translated by Henry Paolucci (Indianapolis: Bobbs-Merrill, 1977).

[15] Jeremy Bentham, "An Introduction to the Principles of Morals and Legislation," in Joseph E. Jacoby (ed.), *Classics of Criminology*, 2nd ed. (Prospect Heights, IL: Waveland Press, 1994), pp. 61–64; Cesare Beccaria, "On Crimes and Punishments," in Jacoby (ed.), *Classics of Criminology*, pp. 206–7.

[16] Douglas Hay, "Crime and Justice in Eighteenth- and Nineteenth-Century England," in Morris and Tonry (eds.), *Crime and Justice: An Annual Review of Research, Vol. 2* (Chicago: University of Chicago Press, 1980), pp. 45–84.

[17] Dennis Curtis, Andrew Graham, Lou Kelly and Anthony Patterson, *Kingston Penitentiary: The First Hundred and Fifty Years 1835–1985* (Ottawa: Correctional Service of Canada, 1985), p. 2; Hay, "Crime and Justice in Eighteenth- and Nineteenth-Century England."

[18] John Howard, *State of Prisons* (New York: E. P. Dutton, 1929 [1777]).

[19] Hay, "Crime and Justice in Eighteenth- and Nineteenth-Century England."

[20] *The American Prison: From the Beginning*, p. 31.

[21] Lawrence M. Friedman, *Crime and Punishment in American History* (New York: Basic Books, 1993), p. 155.

[22] *The American Prison*, pp. 24–27.

[23] Glenn W. Sheehan, "A Study in 'Progressive Penology,'" *Archeology*, May/June (1992): 44–47.

[24] *The American Prison*, pp. 164–66.

[25] *Ibid.*, pp. 34–45.

[26] Sheehan, "A Study in 'Progressive Penology,'" pp. 44–47.

[27] *Ibid.*, pp. 44–47.

[28] Harry Barnes and Negley Teeters, *New Horizons in Criminology*, 3rd ed. (New York: Prentice-Hall, 1946), pp. 521–23.

[29] Sheehan, "A Study in 'Progressive Penology,'" pp. 44–47.

[30] Sellin, *Slavery and the Penal System*, p. 150.

[31] *Ibid.*, pp. 134–38, 146–48.

[32] Blake McKelvey, *American Prisons: A History of Good Intentions* (Montclair, NJ: Patterson Smith, 1977), pp. 131–48; Charles Stastny and Gabrielle Tyrnaurer, *Who Rules the Joint* (Lexington, MA: Lexington Books, 1982), pp. 12–27.

[33] McKelvey, *American Prisons*, pp. 58–59, 76, 89, 101.

[34] Friedman, *Crime and Punishment in American History*, p. 161.

[35] Dean J. Champion, *Probation, Parole and Community Corrections* (Upper Saddle River, NJ: Prentice-Hall, 2002), p. 262; McKelvey, *American Prisons*, pp. 140–48.

[36] McKelvey, *American Prisons*, pp. 9–10.

[37] Champion, *Probation, Parole and Community Corrections*, p. 136–41.

[38] Stastny and Tyrnaurer, *Who Rules the Joint*, pp. 28–32.

[39] Sellin, *Slavery and the Penal System*, pp. 145–75.

[40] McKelvey, *American Prisons*, pp. 199–204.

[41] Friedman, *Crime and Punishment in American History*, pp. 269–70.

[42] David J. Rothman, *Conscience and Convenience* (Boston: Little, Brown, 1980), p. 5.

[43] *Ibid.*, pp. 206–16.

[44] *The American Prison*, p. 172.

[45] Friedman, *Crime and Punishment in American History*, p. 159.

[46] *Ibid.*, p. 168.

[47] Raymond Paternoster, *Capital Punishment in America* (New York: Lexington, 1991), p. 16.

[48] Sellin, *Slavery and the Penal System*, pp. 171–76.

[49] Michael Tonry, "Unthought Thoughts: The Influence of Changing Sensibilities on Penal Policies," *Punishment & Society*, 3(1) (2001): 167–81.

[50] David Musto, *The American Disease: Origins of Narcotic Control*, 3rd ed. (New York: Oxford University Press, 1999), pp. 231–37.

[51] President's Commission on Law Enforcement and Administration of Justice, *The Challenge of Crime in a Free Society* (New York: Avon Books, 1968), pp. 37–55.

[52] Samuel Walker, *Popular Justice: The History of American Criminal Justice* (New York: Oxford University Press, 1980), pp. 222–24.

[53] Lynn S. Branham and Sheldon Krantz, *The Law of Sentencing, Corrections and Prisoners Rights*, 5th ed. (St. Paul: West, 1997), pp. 280–82.

[54] Courtney A. Waid and Carl B. Clements, "Correctional Facility Design: Past, Present and Future," *Corrections Compendium*, 26(11) (2001): 1–5, 25–29.

[55] *Monroe v. Pape*, 365 U.S. 167 (1961); *Cooper v. Pate* 378 U.S. 546, 84 S.Ct. 1733, 12 L.Ed. 2d 1030 (1964).

[56] Lawrence M. Friedman, *Crime and Punishment in American History*, p. 300; David C. Anderson, *Crimes of Justice* (New York: Random House, 1988), p. 246.

[57] *Johnson v. Avery*, 393 U.S. 483 (1969); *Gilmore v. Lynch*, 319 F.Supp. 105 (N.D. Cal. 1970).

[58] *Holt v. Sarver*, 306 F.Supp. 362 (1970), 442 F.2nd 304 (8th Cir. 1971).

[59] *Pugh v. Locke* (98 S.Ct. 3144), 1976.

[60] *Trop v. Dulles*, 356 U.S. 86, 78 S.Ct. 590, 2d 630 (1958); *Weems v. U.S.*, 217 U.S. 349, 30 S.Ct. 344 L.Ed. 793 (1910); *Lee v. Tahash*, 352 F.2nd 970 8th Cir. (1965).

[61] *Ruiz v. Estelle*, 503 F.Supp. 1265 (S.D. Texas, 1980).

[62] Stastny and Tyrnaurer, *Who Rules the Joint*, pp. 33–39.

[63] Robert Martinson, "What Works?: Questions and Answers about Prison Reform," *The Public Interest*, 35 (1974): 22–54.

[64] James Austin and John Irwin, *It's About Time*, 3rd ed. (Belmont, CA: Wadsworth, 2001), p. 5.

[65] Melissa E. Fenwick, "Maxxing Out: Imprisonment in an Era of Crime Control," in Wilson R. Palacios, Paul F. Cromwell and Roger G. Dunham (eds.), *Crime & Justice in America: Present Realities and Future Prospects*, 2nd ed. (Upper Saddle River, NJ: Prentice-Hall, 2002).

[66] Chadwick L. Shook and Robert Sigler, *Constitutional Issues in Correctional Administration* (Durham, NC: Carolina Academic Press, 2000), pp. 146–49.

[67] Allen J. Beck, Jennifer C. Karberg and Paige M. Harrison, *Prison and Jail Inmates at Midyear 2001* (Washington, DC: Bureau of Justice Statistics, 2002), NCJ-191702; U.S. Dept. of Justice, Office of Justice Programs, *Violent Offender Incarceration and Truth-in-Sentencing Incentive Grants: Implementation Report, July 1, 1998–June 30, 1999* (Washington, DC: National Institute of Justice, 1999), pp. 1–10, NCJ-178910.

[68] Roger Lauen, *Positive Approaches to Corrections* (Lanham, MD: American Correctional Association, 1997), p. xi.

[69] David F. Greenberg and Valerie West, "State Prison Populations and Their Growth, 1971–1991," *Criminology*, 39(3) (2001): 615–53.

[70] Robert R. Preuhs, "State Felon Disenfranchisement Policy," *Social Science Quarterly*, 82(4) (2001): 733–48.

[71] Marc Mauer, *Americans Behind Bars, U.S. and International Rates of Incarceration, 1995* (Washington, DC: The Sentencing Project, 1997), pp. 1–5.

[72] Allen J. Beck, Jennifer C. Karberg and Paige M. Harrison, *Prison and Jail Inmates at Midyear 2001*, (Washington, DC: U.S. Dept of Justice, Bureau of Justice Statistics, 2002), p. 6, NCJ-191702.

[73] James Austin, Marino A. Bruce, Leo Carroll, Patricia L. McCall and Stephen C. Richards, *The Use of Incarceration in the United States* (National Policy White Paper, American Society of Criminology, National Policy Committee), Nov. 2000 (Reprinted in *The Criminologist*, 26[3] [2001]: 14–16).

[74] William N. Brownsberger, "Race Matters: Disproportionality of Incarceration for Drug Dealing in Massachusetts," *Journal of Drug Issues*, 30(2) (2000): 345–74; American Bar Association, *Guilty: There Is Racism in the Criminal Justice System* (Washington, DC: ABA, Criminal Justice Section, 1999), pp. 1–68; Marc Mauer, *Race to Incarcerate* (New York: New Press, 1999), pp. 200–18; Paula Kautt and Cassia

Spohn, "Crack-ing Down on Black Drug Offenders? Testing for Interactions among Offenders' Race, Drug Type, and Sentencing Strategy in Federal Drug Sentences," *Justice Quarterly,* 19(1) (2002): 1–35.

[75] David Jacobs and Ronald Helms, "Toward a Political Sociology of Punishment: Politics and Changes in the Incarcerated Population," *Social Science Research,* 30 (2001): 171–94.

[76] Donald G. Evans, "Actualizing Probation in an Actuarial Age," *Corrections Management Quarterly,* 4(2) (2000): 17–22.

[77] "States Adopting Civil Commitment of Sex Offenders," *Criminal Justice Newsletter,* 28(24) (Dec. 15, 1997): 6.

[78] Malcolm M. Feeley and Jonathan Simon, "The New Penology: Notes on the Emerging Strategy of Corrections and its Implications," *Criminology,* 30(4) (1992): 449–74. See also Evans, "Actualizing Probation in an Actuarial Age," 17–22.

CHAPTER THREE

[1] Allen J. Beck, Jennifer C. Karberg and Paige M. Harrison, *Prison and Jail Inmates at Midyear 2001* (Washington, DC: Bureau of Justice Statistics, 2002), pp. 9–10, NCJ-191702; *Sourcebook of Criminal Justice Statistics 2001,* table 6.14, p. 487, available: http://www.albany.edu/sourcebook/1995/pdf/section6.pdf

[2] Craig A. Perkins, James J. Stephan and Allen J. Beck, *Jails and Jail Inmates 1993–94* (Washington, DC: U.S. Dept. of Justice, 1995).

[3] National Advisory Commission on Criminal Justice Standards and Goals, *Corrections* (Washington, DC: USGPO, 1973), pp. 273–79.

[4] *Wolff v. McDonnell,* 418 U.S. 539 (1974).

[5] James Austin, *Objective Jail Classification Systems: A Guide for Jail Administrators* (Washington, DC: National Institute of Corrections, 1998), pp. 1–72.

[6] Leanne F. Alarid, "Sexual Orientation Perspectives of Incarcerated Bisexual and Gay Men: The County Jail Protective Custody Experience," *Prison Journal,* 80(1) (2000): 80–95.

[7] Olga Skorackyj, "Work Release Programs Help Inmates Succeed," *Sheriff,* 52(4) (2000): 22–25; Timothy Hahn, "Evaluations of the Sheriff's Work Alternative Programs in Madison and Adams Counties," *On Good Authority,* 1(4) (1998).

[8] American Correctional Association, *Vital Statistics in Corrections* (Lanham, MD, 2000), p. 30; Beck, Karberg and Harrison, *Prison and Jail Inmates at Midyear 2001,* p. 1.

[9] Caroline W. Harlow, *Profile of Jail Inmates, 1996* (Washington, DC: U.S. Dept. of Justice, 1998), p. 1, NCJ-64620.

[10] *A Second Look at Alleviating Jail Crowding: A Systems Perspective* (Washington, DC: Bureau of Justice Statistics, 2000), p. 35.

[11] Steve Kemme, "Butler Cancels Projects Fund; Smaller Communities Used It for Roads, Other Improvements," *The Cincinnati Enquirer,* Jan. 21, 2002, p. B-1; Amy Rinard, "School Construction at Center of Budget Fight," *Milwaukee Journal Sentinel–On Line,* May 5, 2001, available: http://www.jsonline.com/news/wauk/may01/rinacol06050501a.asp

[12] Harold B. Wilber, "The Importance of Jails," *Corrections Today,* Oct. (2000): 8.

[13] *Ibid.*

[14] James J. Stephan, *Census of Jails, 1999* (Rockville, MD: Bureau of Justice Statistics, 2001), p. 7, NCJ-186633.

[15] Beck, Karberg and Harrison, *Prison and Jail Inmates at Midyear 2001,* pp. 11–12.

[16] John Irwin, *The Jail* (Berkeley: University of California Press, 1986), pp. 39–41.

[17] Beck, Karberg and Harrison, *Prison and Jail Inmates at Midyear 2001,* p. 8.

[18] Brian A. Reaves, *Felony Defendants in Large Urban Counties, 1998* (Washington, DC: National Institute of Justice, 2001), p. 33, NCJ-187232.

[19] Beck, Karberg and Harrison, *Prison and Jail Inmates at Midyear 2001,* p. 9.

[20] *Ibid.,* table 11, p. 9.

[21] Coordination Group on Women, *Women in Criminal Justice: A Twenty Year Update.* Office of Justice Programs, 1998, pp. 2, 4, 8, available: www.ojp.usdoj.gov/reports/98Guides/wcjspdf.pdf

[22] Beck, Karberg and Harrison, *Prison and Jail Inmates at Midyear 2001,* p. 9; Craig A. Perkins, James J. Stephan and Allen J. Beck, *Jails and Jail Inmates, 1993–94* (Washington, DC: USGPO, 1995), p. 5.

[23] Beck, Karberg and Harrison, *Prison and Jail Inmates at Midyear, 2001*, p. 9; James Austin and John Irwin, *It's About Time*, 3rd ed. (Belmont, CA: Wadsworth, 2001) pp. 7, 17–22, 57–61, 94–95.

[24] Doris James Wilson, *Drug Use, Testing, and Treatment in Jails* (Washington, DC: Office of Justice Programs, 2000), NCJ-179999.

[25] Peter M. Carlson, "Something to Lose: A Balanced and Reality-Based Rationale for Institutional Programming," *Corrections Management Quarterly*, 5(4) (2001): 25–31; Jeffrey A. Bouffard and Faye S. Taxman, "Client Gender and the Implementation of Jail-Based Therapeutic Community Programs," *Journal of Drug Issues*, 30(4) (2000): 881–900; Graduate School, University of Alabama–Birmingham, *Breaking the Cycle* (Rockville, MD: National Institute of Justice, 2001), pp. 1–19, NCJ-188087; Dorinda L. Welle and Gregory P. Falkin, "Preventing 'Violations' Through Drug Treatment," *Women, Girls & Criminal Justice*, 2(6) (2001): 82, 95–96.

[26] Arlene Walsh, "Should Jails Be Messing with Mental Health or Substance Abuse?" *American Jails*, 14(1) (2000): 60–66.

[27] Stephan, *Census of Jails, 1999*, p. 10.

[28] Reaves, *Felony Defendants in Large Urban Counties, 1998*, p. 17.

[29] *Ibid.*, p. iv.

[30] *Ibid.*, p. 17.

[31] *Ibid.*

[32] *Ibid.*

[33] Shelila Royo Maxwell, "Examining the Congruence Between Predictors of ROR (Release on Recognizance) and Failures to Appear," *Journal of Criminal Justice*, 27(2) (1999): 127–41.

[34] Sheila Royo Maxwell and Jessica S. Davis, "Salience of Race and Gender in Pretrial Release Decisions: A Comparison across Multiple Jurisdictions," *Criminal Justice Policy Review*, 10(4) (1999): 491–502.

[35] Reaves, *Felony Defendants in Large Urban Counties, 1998*, p. iv.

[36] Pretrial Services Resource Center, *The Supervised Pretrial Release Primer* (Washington, DC: American University, 1999), pp. 3–24, available: http://www.american.edu/spa/justice/publications/SPR.pdf

[37] T. D. Westerfield, "Why Team Up with Pretrial Release Programs?" *American Jails*, 11(6) (1998): 15, 17–18.

[38] J. E. McElroy, "Increasing Complexity of Pretrial Services," *American Jails*, 11(6) (1998): 8–10, 12, 14.

[39] Belinda R. McCarthy and Bernard J. McCarthy, *Community Based Corrections*, 3rd ed. (Belmont, CA: Brooks/Cole, 1997), pp. 80–81.

[40] Beck, Karberg and Harrison, *Prison and Jail Inmates at Midyear 2001*, p. 9.

[41] Randy Borum, *Jail Diversion Strategies for Misdemeanor Offenders with Mental Illness: Preliminary Report* (Tampa: Department of Mental Health Law & Policy, Louis de la Parte Florida Mental Health Institute, University of South Florida, 1999), pp. 1–25; Jeffrey Draine and Phyllis Solomon, "Describing and Evaluating Jail Diversion Services for Persons with Serious Mental Illness," *Psychiatric Services*, 50(1) (1999): 56–61.

[42] McCarthy and McCarthy, *Community Based Corrections*, pp. 80–81.

[43] Michael Tonry, "Community Penalties in the United States," *European Journal on Criminal Policy and Research*, 7(1) (1999): 5–22.

[44] Champion, *Probation and Parole in the United States* (Upper Saddle River, NJ: Prentice-Hall, 2002).

[45] Richard S. Gebelein, *Rebirth of Rehabilitation: Promise and Perils of Drug Courts* (Rockville, MD: National Institute of Justice, 2000), pp. 1–8, NCJ-181412; Reginald Fluellen and Jennifer Trone, *Do Drug Courts Save Jail and Prison Beds?* (New York: Vera Institute of Justice, 2000), pp. 1–8; Michael W. Finigan, "Assessing Cost Off-Sets in a Drug Court Setting," *National Drug Court Institute Review*, 2(2) (1999): 59–92; Lawrence W. Sherman, Denise C. Gottfredson, Doris L. MacKenzie, Jon Eck, Paul Reuter and Shawn Bushway, *Preventing Crime: What Works, What Doesn't, What's Promising* (Washington, DC: National Institute of Justice, 1998), p. 10, NCJ-171676.

[46] Anne M. Hasselbrack, "Opting in to Mental Health Courts," *Corrections Compendium*, 26(10) (2001): 4–5.

[47] James F. Breckenridge, L. Thomas Winfree Jr. and James R. Maupin; "Drunk Drivers, DWI—Drug Court Treatment, and Recidivism: Who Fails?" *Justice Research and Policy*, 2(1) (2000): 87–105; L. Thomas Winfree Jr. and Dennis M. Giever, "Classifying Driving-While-Intoxicated Offenders: The Experiences of a Citywide DWI Drug Court," *Journal of Criminal Justice*, 28(1) (2000): 13–21; J. Tauber

and C. W. Huddleston, *DUI/Drug Courts: Defining a National Strategy* (Washington, DC: U.S. Dept. of Justice, Office of Justice Programs, Drug Courts Program Office, 1999), pp. 1–46, NCJ-177395.

[48] Lisa Newmark, Mike Rempel, Kelly Diffily and Kamala M. Kane, *Specialized Felony Domestic Violence Courts: Lessons on Implementation and Impacts from the Kings County Experience* (Washington, DC: The Urban Institute, 2001), pp. 1–146.

[49] Dick Franklin, *Culture IS . . . as Culture DOES* (Washington, DC: National Institute of Corrections, 2001), pp. 1–9, NCJ-190435; Irwin, *The Jail,* pp. 45–97.

[50] *Lessard v. Schmidt*, 349 F.Supp.1078, E.D Wis. (1972); *State ex rel Hawks v. Lazaro*, 202 S.E. 2d 109 (W.Va.1974).

[51] Edwin F. Torrey, "How Did So Many Mentally Ill Persons Get into America's Jails and Prisons?" *American Jails*, 13(5) (1999): 9–13.

[52] V. Schodolski, "Jail Suicide Rate Vexes California," *Chicago Tribune*, July 7, 2002, p. 9.

[53] Torrey, "How Did So Many Mentally Ill Persons Get Into America's Jails and Prisons?"; Henry J. Steadman and Bonita M. Veysey, *Providing Services for Jail Inmates with Mental Disorders* (Washington, DC: U.S. Dept. of Justice, 1997), pp. 1–14, 12, NCJ-162207.

[54] Greer Sullivan and Karen Spritzer, "The Criminalization of Persons with Serious Mental Illness Living in Rural Areas," *Journal of Rural Health*, 13(1) (1997): 6–13.

[55] Eric Blaauw, Frans Willem Winkel and Jennifer M. Kerkhoff, "Bullying and Suicidal Behavior in Jails," *Criminal Justice and Behavior*, 28(3) (2001): 279–99.

[56] Cecil Pearson, "Inmate Suicide Prevention," *Corrections Technology and Management*, 5(1) (2001): 52–54; David Meyer, chief deputy director of the Los Angeles County Department of Mental Health remarked, "It states the obvious to say that depression is a mental illness, and many suicides are the result of depression." He added that it is often difficult initially to distinguish between depression caused by an ongoing pathological condition and depression brought on by being incarcerated (Schodolski, "Jail Suicide Rate Vexes California," p. 9).

[57] Melinda M. Winter, "County Jail Suicides in a Midwestern State: A Description of the 'Typical' Suicidal Act from 1980 through Mid-1998," *Corrections Compendium*, 25(1) (2000): 8–23.

[58] Laura M. Maruschak, *HIV in Prisons and Jails, 1999* (Rockville, MD: National Institute of Justice, 2001), table 4, p. 5, NCJ-187456.

[59] Christine Tartaro, "Reduction of Suicides in Jails and Lockups through Situational Crime Prevention: Addressing the Needs of a Transient Population," *Journal of Correctional Health Care*, 6(2) (1999): 235–63.

[60] Cecil Pearson, "Inmate Suicide Prevention," *Corrections Technology and Management*, 5(1) (2001): 52–54.

[61] Harold B. Wilber, "The Importance of Jails," *Corrections Today*, Oct. (2000): 8.

[62] James L. Williams, Daniel G. Rodeheaver and Denise W. Huggins, "A Comparative Evaluation of a New Generation Jail," *American Journal of Criminal Justice*, 23(2) (1999): 223–46.

[63] David M. Parrish, "The Evolution of Direct Supervision in the Design and Operation of Jails," *Corrections Today*, Oct. (2000): 84–87, 127; Allen R. Beck, *Deciding on a New Jail Design* (Kansas City, MO: Justice Concepts, 1999), pp. 1–8.

[64] Williams, Rodeheaver and Huggins, "A Comparative Evaluation of a New Generation Jail."

[65] Brandon K Applegate, Ray Surette and Bernard J. McCarthy, "Detention and Desistance from Crime: Evaluating the Influence of a New Generation Jail on Recidivism," *Journal of Criminal Justice*, 27(6) (1999): 539–48.

[66] Terry Hegarty, "Six Dollars-Per-Day Solution: Good Health Care is Good Public Safety," *Corrections Technology and Management*, 4(5) (2000): 54–57; Tonya Layman, "Happiness Comes in a Quarterly Rebate Check," *Corrections Technology & Management*, 5(4) (2001): 12–14.

[67] "Privatizing and Regionalizing Local Corrections," *Corrections Today*, Oct. (2000): 116–18, 120.

[68] "Inmate Fee-for-Service Programs," *Corrections Compendium*, 23(8) (1998): 7, 16; Susan Clayton, "Fee for Service Programs: Is It Time?" in *On the Line* (Lanham, MD: American Correctional Association, May 1997), pp. 1, 3.

[69] Mark Pogrebin, Mary Dodge and Paul Katsampes, "Collateral Costs of Short-Term Jail Incarceration: The Long-Term Social and Economic Disruptions," *Corrections Management Quarterly*, 5(4) (2001): 64–69.

CHAPTER FOUR

[1] David E. Duffee and Bonnie E. Carlson, "Competing Value Premises for the Provision of Drug Treatment to Probationers," *Crime and Delinquency,* 42(4) (1996): 574–92.

[2] Joan Petersilia, "Probation in the United States: Practices and Challenges," in Kenneth C. Haas and Geoffrey P. Alpert (eds.), *The Dilemmas of Corrections,* 4th ed. (Prospect Heights, IL: Waveland Press, 1999).

[3] Lauren E. Glaze, *Probation and Parole in the United States, 2001* (Washington, DC: U.S. Dept. of Justice, Bureau of Justice Statistics, 2002), pp. 1, 4, NCJ-195669.

[4] Michael E. Smith, "What Future for 'Public Safety' and Restorative Justice in Community Corrections?," *Sentencing & Corrections: Issues for the 21st Century* (U.S. Dept. of Justice, Office of Justice Programs, June 2001), p. 2.

[5] Frank Domurad, "Who Is Killing Our Probation Officers: The Performance Crisis in Community Corrections," *Corrections Management Quarterly,* 4(2) (2000): 41–51.

[6] Edward E. Rhine and Gerald R. Hinzman, "Probation and Parole: The Value of Reinvesting in Community Expertise," *Corrections Management Quarterly,* 4(2) (2000): 61–67.

[7] Dan R. Beto, Ronald P. Corbett Jr. and John J. DiIulio Jr., "Getting Serious about Probation and the Crime Problem," *Corrections Management Quarterly,* 4(2): (2000): 1–8.

[8] Rhine and Hinzman, "Probation and Parole: The Value of Reinvesting in Community Expertise."

[9] Domurad, "Who Is Killing Our Probation Officers: The Performance Crisis in Community Corrections."

[10] Eric Lotke, *Issues and Answers: Does Treatment Work?* (Washington, DC: National Center for Institutions and Alternatives, 1997), p. 4.

[11] Glaze, *Probation and Parole in the United States, 2001,* p. 1.

[12] *Ibid.,* pp. 1, 3, 4.

[13] David E. Olson, Arthur J. Lurigio and Magnus Seng, "Comparison of Female and Male Probationers: Characteristics and Case Outcomes," *Women and Criminal Justice,* 11(4) (2000): 65–79.

[14] U.S. Dept. of Justice, Press Release Aug. 26, 2001, "National Correctional Population Reaches New High" (Washington, DC: Bureau of Justice Statistics), p. 6.

[15] Thomas P. Bonczar, *Characteristics of Adults on Probation, 1995* (Washington, DC: U.S. Dept. of Justice, 1997), pp. 6–7, NCJ-164267.

[16] *Ibid.,* p. 7, table 8.

[17] *Ibid.,* p. 10, table 12.

[18] *Ibid.,* pp. 6–7; Camille Camp and George Camp, *The Correctional Yearbook, 1998* (Middleton, CT: Criminal Justice Institute).

[19] Glaze, *Probation and Parole in the United States, 2001,* p. 4.

[20] *Ibid.*

[21] Petersilia, "Probation in the United States."

[22] Olson, Lurigio and Seng, "Comparison of Female and Male Probationers: Characteristics and Case Outcomes"; David E. Olson and Arthur J. Lurigio, "Predicting Probation Outcomes: Factors Associated with Probation Rearrest, Revocations, and Technical Violations During Supervision," *Justice Research and Policy,* 2(1) (2000): 73–86.

[23] *Gagnon v. Scarpelli,* 411 U.S. 778 (1973).

[24] *Mempha v. Rhay,* 389 U.S. 128 (1967).

[25] *Ibid.; Morrissey v. Brewer,* 408 U.S. 471 (1972); and *Gagnon v. Scarpelli,* 411 U.S. 778 (1973).

[26] David A. Fruchtman and Robert T. Sigler, "Private Pre-Sentence Investigation: Procedures and Issues," *Journal of Offender Rehabilitation,* 29(3-4) (1999): 157–70.

[27] Rodney Kingsnorth, Debra Cummings, John Lopez and Jennifer Wentworth, "Criminal Sentencing and the Court Probation Office: The Myth of Individualized Justice Revisited," *Journal Justice System Journal,* 20(3) (1999): 255–73.

[28] Joan Petersilia, "Probation and Parole," in Michael Tonry (ed.), *The Handbook of Crime and Punishment* (New York: Oxford University Press, 1998), p. 573.

[29] Caroline Wolf Harlow, *Prior Abuse Reported by Inmates and Probationers* (Washington, DC: U.S. Dept. of Justice, 1999), pp. 1–3, NCJ-172879.

[30] See, generally, U.S. Dept. of Health and Human Services, Center for Substance Abuse Treatment, *Substance Abuse Treatment for Persons with Child Abuse and Neglect Issues: Treatment Improvement*

Protocol (TIP) Series 36 (Rockville, MD: Substance Abuse and Mental Health Services Administration, Center for Substance Abuse Treatment, 2000).

31 U.S. Dept. of Justice, *NIJ Survey of Probation and Parole Agency Directors* (Washington, DC: USGPO, 1995), p. 1.

32 Doris L. MacKenzie, Katharine Browning, Stacy B. Skroban and Douglas A. Smith, "Impact of Probation on the Criminal Activities of Offenders," *Journal of Research in Crime and Delinquency,* 36(4) (1999): 423–53.

33 Personal conversation with Lawrence Martin, Account Manager, Digital Products Corporation, Aug. 25, 1993.

34 See, generally, Regional Community Policing Institute of Florida, *Probation-Police Partnerships: Multimedia Training* (St. Petersburg: Regional Community Policing Institute of Florida, 1999); Smith, "What Future for 'Public Safety' and Restorative Justice in Community Corrections?," pp. 1–7.

35 Marilyn Herie, John A. Cunningham and Garth W. Martin, "Attitudes toward Substance Abuse Treatment among Probation and Parole Officers," *Journal of Offender Rehabilitation,* 32(2) (2000): 181–95.

36 *2001 Directory of Juvenile and Adult Correctional Departments, Institutions, Agencies and Paroling Authorities* (Lanham, MD: American Correctional Association, 2001).

37 Keith M. Healey, *Case Management in the Criminal Justice System* (Rockville, MD: National Institute of Justice, 1999), pp. 1–12; Harriet Goodman, "Social Group Work in Community Corrections," *Social Work with Groups,* 20(1) (1997): 51–64.

38 Mark Carey, David Goff, Gary Hinzman, Al Neff, Brian Owens and Larry Albert, "Field Service Case Plans: Bane or Gain?" *Perspectives,* 24(2) (2000): 30–41.

39 Petersilia, "Probation in the United States."

40 Randall Guynes, "Difficult Clients, Large Caseloads Plague Probation, Parole Agencies," in Thomas Ellsworth, *Contemporary Community Corrections,* 2nd ed. (Prospect Heights, IL: Waveland Press, 1996), pp. 108–22.

41 Jan Roehl and Kristin Guertin, "Intimate Partner Violence: The Current Use of Risk Assessments in Sentencing Offenders," *Justice System Journal,* 21(2) (2000): 171–98.

42 Center for Sex Offender Management, *Recidivism of Sex Offenders* (Washington, DC: U.S. Dept. of Justice, Office of Justice Programs, 2001), pp. 4–20.

CHAPTER FIVE

1 Alida V. Merlo and Peter J. Benekos, "Adapting Conservative Correctional Policies to the Economic Realities of the 1990s," in Barry W. Hancock and Paul M. Sharp (eds.), *Public Policy, Crime, and Criminal Justice,* 2nd ed. (Upper Saddle River, NJ: Prentice Hall, 2000); Michael Tonry, "Community Penalties in the United States," *European Journal on Criminal Policy and Research,* 7(1) (1999): 5–22; Joan Petersilia, "A Decade of Experimenting with Intermediate Sanctions: What Have We Learned?" *Justice Research and Policy,* 1(1) (1999): 9–23.

2 Paul Gendreau, Claire Goggin, Francis T. Cullen and Donald A. Andrews, "Effects of Community Sanctions and Incarceration on Recidivism," *Forum on Corrections Research,* 12(2) (2000): 10–13; Cassia Spohn and David Holleran, "The Effect of Imprisonment on Recidivism Rates of Felony Offenders: A Focus on Drug Offenders," *Criminology,* 40(2) (2002): 329–58.

3 Jeff Glasser, "Ex-Cons on the Street," *U.S. News and World Report,* May 1, 2000, pp. 18–20; Michael Tonry and Joan Petersilia, "Prisons Research at the Beginning of the 21st Century," *Crime and Justice a Review of the Research,* 26 (1999): 1–14; Eric Lotke, *Issues and Answers: Does Treatment Work* (Washington, DC: National Center for Institutions and Alternatives, 1997), pp. 1–4.

4 Tonry and Petersilia, "Prisons Research at the Beginning of the 21st Century," pp. 3–5.

5 Petersilia, "A Decade of Experimenting with Intermediate Sanctions," p. 98

6 *Ibid.*; James F. Quinn and John E. Holman, "The Efficacy of Electronically Monitored Home Confinement as a Case Management Device," *Journal of Contemporary Criminal Justice,* 7(2) (1991): 128–34.

7 Brian K. Payne and Randy R. Gainey, "Attitudes Towards Electronic Monitoring among Monitored Offenders and Criminal Justice Students," *Journal of Offender Rehabilitation,* 29(3-4) (1999): 195–208; Michael G. Turner, Francis T. Cullen, Jody L. Sundt and Brandon K. Applegate, "Public Tolerance for Community-Based Sanctions," *The Prison Journal,* 77(1) (1997): 6–26.

[8] Victor E. Kappeler, Mark Blumberg and Gary W. Potter, *The Mythology of Crime and Criminal Justice*, 3rd ed. (Prospect Heights, IL: Waveland Press, 2000), p. 249–51; Peter B. Wood and Harold G. Grasmick, "Toward the Development of Punishment Equivalencies: Male and Female Inmates Rate the Severity of Alternative Sanctions Compared to Prison," *Justice Quarterly*, 16(1) (1999): 19–50; William Spelman, "The Severity of Intermediate Sanctions," *Journal of Research on Crime and Delinquency*, 32(2) (1995): 107–35.

[9] Adele Harrell and John Roman, "Reducing Drug Use and Crime among Offenders: The Impact of Graduated Sanctions," *Journal of Drug Issues*, 31(1) (2001): 207–32.

[10] Morna Murray and Sterling O'Ran, *Restitution* (Washington, DC: Office of Justice Programs, 2000), pp. 1–20, NCJ-184061.

[11] Thomas P. Bonczar, *Characteristics of Adults on Probation, 1995* (Washington, DC: U.S. Dept. of Justice, 1997), p. 7, NCJ-164267.

[12] H. Ted Rubin, "Juvenile Restitution Helps Victims and Offenders but Needs Review," *Victims Report*, 1(1) Mar./Apr. (1997): 1–3; *Crime Victims' Compensation: Meeting the Challenge* (Austin, TX: Office of the Attorney General, Crime Victims' Compensation Division, 1996).

[13] Robert Taylor, James F. Quinn, Eric J. Fritsch, Tory J. Caeti and Sharon Walker, *An Analysis of the Texas Crime Victims' Compensation Fund: Predictors of Access, Utilization and Efficiency*, Technical report sponsored by the Office of the Attorney General, State of Texas (Denton: University of North Texas, 1997).

[14] J. Loconte, "Making Criminals Pay," *Policy Review*, 87 (1998): 26–31.

[15] Maureen C. Outlaw and R. Barry Ruback, "Predictors and Outcomes of Victim Restitution Orders," *Justice Quarterly*, 16(4) (1999): 847–69.

[16] Belinda R. McCarthy, Bernard J. McCarthy and Matthew C. Leone, *Community Based Corrections*, 4th ed. (Belmont, CA: Brooks/Cole, 2001), pp. 231–33.

[17] Norval Morris and Michael Tonry, *Between Prison and Probation: Intermediate Punishments in a Rational Sentencing System* (New York: Oxford, 1990), pp. 8–11.

[18] Evelyn Gilbert, "Significance of Race in the Use of Restitution," in Michael W. Markowitz and Delores D. Jones-Brown (eds.), *System in Black and White: Exploring the Connections Between Race, Crime, and Justice* (Westport, CT: Praeger, 2000).

[19] Bonczar, *Characteristics of Adults on Probation, 1995*, p. 7.

[20] T. Hahn, "Evaluations of the Sheriff's Work Alternative Programs in Madison and Adams Counties," *On Good Authority*, 1(4) (1998); Gail A. Caputo, "Why Not Community Service?" *Criminal Justice Policy Review*, 10(4) (1999): 503–19.

[21] Hahn, "Evaluations of the Sheriff's Work Alternative Programs in Madison and Adams Counties."

[22] Stephen C. Richards and Richard S. Jones, "Perpetual Incarceration Machine: Structural Impediments to Post-prison Success," *Journal of Contemporary Criminal Justice*, 13(1) (1987): 4–22.

[23] Caputo, "Why Not Community Service?"

[24] Eduardo Barajas Jr., *High Risk Offenders in the Community* (Washington, DC: National Institute of Corrections, 2000), pp. 9–19, NCJ-188425; Douglas R. Thomson, "How Plea Bargaining Shapes Intensive Probation Supervision Policy Goals," *Crime and Delinquency*, 36(1) (1990): 146–61.

[25] Michael Tonry, "Intermediate Sanctions," in Michael Tonry (ed.), *The Handbook of Crime and Punishment* (New York: Oxford University Press, 1998), p. 684.

[26] Joan Petersilia and Susan Turner, "Evaluating Intensive Supervision Probation/Parole: Results of a Nationwide Experiment," in Kenneth C. Haas and Geoffrey P. Alpert (eds.), *The Dilemmas of Corrections*, 4th ed. (Prospect Heights, IL: Waveland Press, 1999); Jeffery T. Ulmer, "Intermediate Sanctions: A Comparative Analysis of the Probability and Severity of Recidivism," *Sociological Inquiry*, 71(2) (2001): 164–93.

[27] Kim English, Suzanne Pullen and Susan Colling-Chadwick, *Report of Findings: Comparison of Intensive Supervision Probation and Community Corrections Clientele* (Rockville, MD: U.S. Dept. of Justice, Office of Justice Programs, 1996), pp. 1–70, NCJ-188560; Patrick A. Langan and Mark A. Cunniff, *Recidivism of Felons on Probation, 1986–1989* (Washington, DC: U.S. Dept. of Justice, 1992), pp. 7–8.

[28] S. Christopher Baird and Dennis Wagner, "Measuring Diversion: The Florida Community Control Program," *Crime and Delinquency*, 36(1) (1990): 112–25; Ulmer, "Intermediate Sanctions."

[29] Doris Layton Mackenzie and Robert Brame, "Community Supervision, Prosocial Activities and Recidivism," *Justice Quarterly*, 18(2) (2001): 429–48.

[30] Joan Petersilia and Elizabeth Piper Deschenes, "What Punishes: Inmates Rank the Severity of Prison vs. Intermediate Sanctions," in Thomas Ellsworth (ed.), *Contemporary Community Corrections*, 2nd ed. (Prospect Heights, IL: Waveland Press, 1996).

[31] Douglas M. Anglin and Yih-Ing Hser, "Treatment of Drug Abuse," in Michael Tonry and James Q. Wilson (eds.), *Drugs and Crime*, Vol. 13 of *Crime and Justice: A Review of the Research* (Chicago: University of Chicago Press, 1990); James F. Quinn and John E. Holman, "The Discrepancy between Available and Desired Substance Abuse Treatment Modalities in Felony Probation Caseloads," paper presented at the 1991 Annual Meeting of the Southwestern Criminal Justice Educators Association, San Antonio, TX, October 1991.

[32] Bonczar, *Characteristics of Adults on Probation, 1995,* p. 7.

[33] Tonry, "Intermediate Sanctions," p. 692.

[34] *Ibid.*, p. 693.

[35] Joseph Hoshen and George Drake, *Offender Wide Area Continuous Electronic Monitoring Systems: Project Summary* (Rockville, MD: U.S. Dept. of Justice, National Institute of Justice, 2000), pp. 1–18.

[36] H. J. Hoelter, "Operation Spotlight: The Community Probation-community Police Team Process," *Federal Probation*, 62(2) (1998): 30–35.

[37] *NIJ Survey of Probation and Parole Agency Directors* (Washington, DC: U.S. Dept. of Justice, 1995), p. 2.

[38] Michael P. Brown and Preston Elrod, "Citizens' Perceptions of a 'Good' Electronic House Arrest Program," *Corrections Management Quarterly*, 3(3) (1999): 37–42.

[39] Brian K. Payne and Randy R. Gainey, "How Monitoring Punishes," *Journal of Offender Monitoring*, 12(1) (1999): 23–25; Wood and Grasmick, "Toward the Development of Punishment Equivalencies."

[40] The author of this text assigned this experiment to students in a large corrections class. Initially most students wrote statements saying EMHC was too lenient to have punishment value. After the experiment those in their twenties reported it was harsher than they had ever imagined. Some said it would have been easier to sit in jail. Virtually all younger students violated the terms of the assignment more than once. Only nontraditional students (those over 30) reported few problems. These students described their normal weekends as home oriented.

[41] Wood and Grasmick, "Toward the Development of Punishment Equivalencies"; Brian K. Payne and Randy R. Gainey, "A Qualitative Assessment of the Pains Experienced on Electronic Monitoring," *Journal of Offender Therapy and Comparative Criminology*, 42(2) (1998): 149–63.

[42] Randy R. Gainey, Brian K. Payne and Mike O'Toole, "The Relationships between Time in Jail, Time on Electronic Monitoring and Recidivism," *Justice Quarterly*, 17(4) (2000): 733–52; James Bonta, Suzanne Wallace-Capretta and Jennifer Rooney, "Can Electronic Monitoring Make a Difference? An Evaluation of Three Canadian Programs," *Crime & Delinquency*, 46(1) (2000): 61–75; Quinn and Holman, "The Efficacy of Electronically Monitored Home Confinement as a Case Management Device."

[43] Linda G. Smith and Ronald L. Akers, "A Comparison of Recidivism of Florida's Community Control and Prison: A Five-Year Survival Analysis," *Journal of Research in Crime and Delinquency*, 30(3) Aug. (1993): 267–92.

[44] Mary A. Finn and Suzanne Muirhead-Steves, "The Effectiveness of Electronic Monitoring with Violent Male Parolees," *Justice Quarterly*, 19(2) (2002): 293–312

[45] James F. Quinn and John E. Holman, "Intrafamilial Control among Felons Under Community Supervision: An Examination of Electronically-Monitored Parolees and Their Significant Others," *Journal of Offender Counseling, Services, and Rehabilitation*, 16(3-4) (1991): 177–92.

[46] Darrel L. Longest, "What Is the Future for Ignition Interlocks?" *Impaired Driving Update*, (fall 2000): 77–78; Paul R. Marques, Robert B. Voas and David Hodgins, "Vehicle Interlock Programs: Protecting the Community against the Drunk Driver," in Elsie R Shore and Joseph R Ferrari (eds.), *Preventing Drunk Driving* (Binghamton, NY: Haworth Press, 1998).

[47] Liz Marie Marciniak, "Use of Day Reporting as an Intermediate Sanction: A Study of Offender Targeting and Program Termination," *Prison Journal*, 79(2) (1999): 205–25; Marcus Nieto, *Probation for Adult and Juvenile Offenders: Options for Improved Accountability* (Sacramento: California Research Bureau, 1998), pp. 1–26.

[48] D. J. Williams and Tiffany Amber Turnage, "Success of a Day Reporting Center Program," *Corrections Compendium*, 26(3) (2001): 1–3, 26; Christine Martin, David E. Olson and Arthur J. Lurigio, *Evaluation of the Cook County Sheriff's Day Reporting Center Program: Rearrest and Reincarceration After Discharge* (Rockville, MD: U.S. Dept. of Justice, Bureau of Justice Assistance, 2000), pp. 1–54.

[49] Martin, Olson and Lurigio, *Evaluation of the Cook County Sheriff's Day Reporting Center Program*; Duane McBride and Curtis VanderWaal, "Day Reporting Centers as an Alternative for Drug Using Offenders," *Journal of Drug Issues*, 27(2) (1997): 379–97; Amy Craddock, *Exploratory Analysis of Client Outcomes, Costs, and Benefits of Day Reporting Centers—Final Report* (Rockville, MD: National Institute of Justice, 2000), pp. 1–37.

[50] Williams and Turnage, "Success of a Day Reporting Center Program"; Martin, Olson and Lurigio, *Evaluation of the Cook County Sheriff's Day Reporting Center Program*; Liz Marie Marciniak, "Addition of Day Reporting to Intensive Supervision Probation: A Comparison of Recidivism Rates," *Federal Probation*, 64(1) (2000): 34–39.

[51] Sarah E. Twill, Larry Nackerud, Edwin A. Risler et al., "Changes in Measured Loneliness, Control and Social Support among Parolees in a Halfway House," *Journal of Offender Rehabilitation*, 27(3-4) (1998): 77–92.

[52] *NIJ Survey of Probation and Parole Agency Directors*, p. 2.

[53] Lauren E. Glaze, *Probation and Parole in the United States, 2001* (Rockville, MD: National Institute of Justice, Office of Justice Programs, 2002), p. 4.

[54] Bonczar, *Characteristics of Adults on Probation, 1995*, p. 6.

[55] Andrew R. Klein, *Alternative Sentencing: A Practitioners Guide* (Cincinnati: Anderson, 1988), pp. 242–46; Susette M. Talarico and Martha A. Myers, "Split Sentencing in Georgia: A Test of Two Empirical Assumptions," *Justice Quarterly*, 4(4) (1987): 611–30.

[56] Don M. Gottfredson, *Effects of Judges' Sentencing Decisions on Criminal Careers* (Rockville, MD: U.S. Dept. of Justice, National Institute of Justice, 1999), pp. 1–12, NCJ-17889; Doris Layton MacKenzie and Robert Brame, "Shock Incarceration and Positive Adjustment During Community Supervision," *Journal of Quantitative Criminology*, 11(2) (1995): 111–42.

[57] Dale Colledge and Jurg Gerber, "Rethinking the Assumptions about Boot Camps," in Wilson R. Palacios, Paul F. Cromwell and Roger G. Dunham (eds.), *Crime & Justice in America: Present Realities and Future Prospects*, 2nd ed. (Upper Saddle River, NJ: Prentice-Hall, 2002).

[58] D. T. Wright and G. L. Mays, "Correctional Boot Camps, Attitudes, and Recidivism: The Oklahoma Experience," *Journal of Offender Rehabilitation*, 28(1-2) (1998): 71–87.

[59] Tonry, "Intermediate Sanctions," pp. 688–89.

[60] Ernest Cowles, Thomas C. Castellano and Laura A. Gransky, *Boot Camp—Drug Treatment and Aftercare Interventions: An Evaluation Review* (Washington, DC: U.S. Dept. of Justice, 1995), pp. 1–12.

[61] Jeanne B. Stinchcomb and W. Clinton Terry III, "Predicting the Likelihood of Rearrest Among Shock Incarceration Graduates: Moving Beyond Another Nail in the Boot Camp Coffin," *Crime and Delinquency*, 47(2) (2001): 221–42; Wright and Mays, "Correctional Boot Camps, Attitudes, and Recidivism: The Oklahoma Experience"; Jeanne B. Stinchcomb, "Recovering from the Shocking Reality of Shock Incarceration: What Correctional Administration Can Learn from Boot Camp Failures," *Corrections Management Quarterly*, 3(4) (1999): 43–52.

[62] See, generally, James F. Anderson, Laronistine Dyson and Jerald C. Burns, *Boot Camps: An Intermediate Sanction* (Lanham, MD: University Press of America, 1999).

[63] Doris L. MacKenzie, David B. Wilson and Suzanne B. Kider-Sale, "Effects of Correctional Boot Camps on Offending," *Annals of the American Academy of Political and Social Science*, 578 (2001): 126–43.

[64] Colledge and Gerber, "Rethinking the Assumptions about Boot Camps"; Stinchcomb and Clinton, "Predicting the Likelihood of Rearrest among Shock Incarceration Graduates."

[65] Associated Press, "Abuse Complaints Lead to Removal of Teens," *Fort Worth Star Telegram*, July 23, 2001, p. 4-A; "Inmate Dies During Sentence in Cook County's Boot Camp," *Chicago Tribune*, Dec. 15, 2000, p. 2; Bob Schober, "Tarrant Boot Camp Graduates Final Class," *Dallas Morning News*, July 4, 2001, p. 1-B; Michael Janofsky,. "Desert Boot Camp for Youth Is Shut Down After a Death," *The New York Times*, July 4, 2001, p. A-8.

[66] Lorna Collier, "The Last Resort: As Desperate Parents Try Boot Camp, Critics Claim that Alternative Is Laced with Problems," *Chicago Tribune*, May 27, 2001, p. 13.

[67] Faith E. Lutze and David C. Brody, "Mental Abuse as Cruel and Unusual Punishment: Do Boot Camp Prisons Violate the Eighth Amendment?" *Crime & Delinquency*, 45(2) (1999): 242–55.

[68] Stinchcomb, "Recovering from the Shocking Reality of Shock Incarceration."

[69] Frank S. Pearson and Douglas S. Lipton, "Meta-Analytic Review of the Effectiveness of Corrections-Based Treatments for Drug Abuse," *Prison Journal*, 79(4) (1999): 384–410.

[70] Mary K. Stohr, Craig Hemmens, Diane Baune, Jed Dayley, Mark Gornik, Kristin Kjaer and Cindy Noon, *Residential Substance Abuse Treatment for State Prisoners (RSAT) Partnership Process Evaluation, Final Report* (Rockville, MD: U.S. Dept. of Justice, National Institute of Justice, 2001), pp. 1–129, NCJ-187352.

[71] Richard Ofshe, "The Social Development of the Synanon Cult," *Sociological Analysis*, 41(2) (1980): 109–27.

[72] Mark Gornik, *Moving from Correctional Program to Correctional Strategy: Using Proven Practices to Change Criminal Behavior* (Washington, DC: National Institute of Justice, 2001), p. 10, NCJ-017624.

[73] Darin Weinberg, "Community," *Symbolic Interaction*, 19(2) (1996): 137–62.

[74] Stohr, Hemmens, Baune, Dayley, Gornik, Kjaer and Noon, *Residential Substance Abuse Treatment for State Prisoners (RSAT) Partnership Process Evaluation, Final Report*.

[75] Ricky Taylor, "Seven-Year Reconviction Study of HMP Grendon Therapeutic Community" (Great Britain Home Office, Policing and Reducing Crime Unit, Research, Development and Statistics Directorate, United Kingdom, 2000), pp. 1–4, NCJ-165158; Elizabeth M. Smith, Carol S. North and Louis W. Fox, "Eighteen Month Follow-up Data on a Treatment Program for Homeless Substance-Abusing Mothers," *Journal of the Addictive Diseases*, 31 (1996): 57–72; Michael Eisenberg and Tony Fabelo, "Evaluation of the Texas Correctional Substance Abuse Treatment Initiative," *Crime and Delinquency*, 42(2) (1996): 296–308.

[76] Faye S. Taxman and Jeffrey A. Bouffard, "Assessing Therapeutic Integrity in Modified-Therapeutic Communities for Drug-Involved Offenders" (Rockville, MD: U.S. Dept. of Justice, National Institute of Justice, 2001), pp. 1–35 (also published in the *Prison Journal*, Dec. 2001).

[77] *Ibid.*; Michele Staton, Carl Leukefeld, T. K. Logan and Rick Purvis, "Process Evaluation for a Prison-Based Substance Abuse Program," *Journal of Offender Rehabilitation*, 32(1-2) (2000): 105–27; Patricia A. Kassebaum, *Substance Abuse Treatment for Women Offenders* (U.S. Dept. of Health and Human Services, Substance Abuse and Mental Health Service Administration, 1999), pp. 1–183, NCJ-187313.

[78] Christian Pfieffer, *Alternative Sanctions in Germany* (Washington, DC: U.S. Dept. of Justice, USGPO, 1996), pp. 1–5; Michael Tonry and Joan Petersilia, "Prisons Research at the Beginning of the 21st Century," *Crime and Justice: A Review of the Research*, 26 (1999): 1–14.

[79] Gerald Melnick, George De Leon, Matthew L. Hiller and Kevin Knight, "Therapeutic Communities: Diversity in Treatment Elements," *Substance Use and Misuse: An International Interdisciplinary Forum*, 35(12-14) (2000): 1819–47; Young, Cocoros and Winterfield, *Diverting Drug Offenders to Treatment*.

[80] Taxman and Bouffard, "Assessing Therapeutic Integrity in Modified-Therapeutic Communities for Drug-Involved Offenders"; Douglas L. Polcin, "Drug and Alcohol Offenders Coerced Into Treatment: A Review of Modalities and Suggestions for Research on Social Model Programs," *Substance Use and Misuse*, 36(5) (2001): 589–608.

[81] Taylor, "Seven-Year Reconviction Study of HMP Grendon Therapeutic Community."

[82] Julie Hobson, John Shine and Russell Roberts, "How Do Psychopaths Behave in a Prison Therapeutic Community?" *Psychology, Crime & Law*, 6(2) (2000): 139–54.

[83] Staton, Leukefeld, Logan and Purvis, "Process Evaluation for a Prison-Based Substance Abuse Program."

[84] Michael Prendergast, David Farabee and Jerome Cartier, "Impact of In-Prison Therapeutic Community Programs on Prison Management," *Journal of Offender Rehabilitation*, 32(3) (2001): 63–78.

[85] Dale Parent, Terence Dunworth, Douglas McDonald and William Rhodes, *Key Legislative Issues in Criminal Justice: Intermediate Sanctions* (Washington, DC: U.S. Dept. of Justice, 1997), p. 1.

[86] Paul Gendreau, Claire Goggin, Francis T. Cullen and Donald A. Andrews, "Effects of Community Sanctions and Incarceration on Recidivism," *Forum on Corrections Research*, 12(2) (2000): 10–13.

[87] Parent, Dunworth, McDonald and Rhodes, *Key Legislative Issues in Criminal Justice: Intermediate Sanctions*, pp. 1–8; Doris L. MacKenzie and Robert Brame, "Shock Incarceration and Positive Adjustment during Community Supervision," *Journal of Quantitative Criminology*, 11(2) June (1995): 111–42; Eisenberg and Fabelo, "Evaluation of the Texas Correctional Substance Abuse Treatment Initiative."

[88] Kate Ahern, Craig Cussimanio, Nancy Michel, Laura Parisi, Marylinda Stawasz and Kate Wagner, *Creating a New Criminal Justice System for the 21st Century: Findings and Results From State and Local Program Evaluations* (Washington, DC: U.S. Dept. of Justice, Bureau of Justice Assistance, 2000), pp. 1–107, NCJ-178936.

[89] Patrick J. Coleman, Jeffrey Felten-Green and Geroma Oliver, *Connecticut's Alternative Sanctions Program: $619 Million Saved in Estimated Capital and Operating Costs* (Rockville, MD: U.S. Dept. of Justice, Bureau of Justice Assistance, 1998), pp. 1–16, NCJ-172870.

[90] Parent, Dunworth, McDonald and Rhodes, *Key Legislative Issues in Criminal Justice: Intermediate Sanctions*.

[91] See, generally, William G. Staples, *The Culture of Surveillance* (New York: St. Martins Press, 1997); Gary T. Marx and M. J. Rossant, *Undercover: Police Surveillance in America* (Berkeley: University of California Press, 1988).

[92] John Hagan and Juleigh P. Coleman, "Returning Captives of the American War on Drugs: Issues of Community and Family Reentry," *Crime & Delinquency,* 47(3) (2001): 352–67.

[93] Tony Fabelo, *"Technocorrections": The Promises, the Uncertain Threats* (Washington, DC: National Institute of Justice, 2000), p. 6, NCJ-181411.

[94] Brian K. Payne and Randy R. Gainey, "Electronic Monitoring: Philosophical, Systemic, and Political Issues," *Journal of Offender Rehabilitation*, 31(3-4) (2000): 93–111; Gendreau, Goggin, Cullen and Andrews, "Effects of Community Sanctions and Incarceration on Recidivism."

[95] Tonry, "Intermediate Sanctions," p. 684.

[96] Larry Gaines and Peter Kraska, *Drugs, Crime, & Justice* (Prospect Heights, IL: Waveland Press, Inc., 2003), pp. 9–12.

[97] L. M. Marciniak, "Use of Day Reporting as an Intermediate Sanction: A Study of Offender Targeting and Program Termination," *Prison Journal*, 79(2) (1999): 205–25.

[98] Payne and Gainey, "Electronic Monitoring: Philosophical, Systemic, and Political Issues."

[99] Bridget Dolan, Kevin Polley, Ruth Allen and Kingsley Norton, "Addressing Racism in Psychiatry: Is the Therapeutic Community Model Applicable," *International Journal of Social Psychiatry*, 37(2) (1991): 71–79.

[100] D. A. Andrews, Ivan Zinger, Robert D. Hodge, James Bonta, Paul Gendreau and Francis T. Cullen, "A Human Science Approach or More Punishment and Pessimism: A Rejoinder to Lab and Whitehead," *Criminology*, 28(3) (1990): 419–29.

[101] Eric Tischler, "Does Technology Enhance or Hinder Community Supervision," *On The Line* (Lanham, MD: American Correctional Association, March, 1998), pp. 1, 3.

[102] Michael G. Turner, Francis T. Cullen, Jody L. Sundt and Brandon K. Applegate, "Public Tolerance for Community-Based Sanctions," *The Prison Journal*, 77(1) (1997): 6–26.

[103] Hagan and Coleman, "Returning Captives of the American War on Drugs."

CHAPTER SIX

[1] Timothy A. Hughes, Doris James Wilson and Allen J. Beck, *Trends in State Parole, 1990–2000* (Rockville, MD: National Institute of Justice, 2001), p. 12, NCJ-184735.

[2] John J. Larivee, "Returning Inmates, Closing the Public Safety Gap," *Corrections Compendium*, 26(6) (2001): 1–3, 10.

[3] *Felony Disenfranchisement Laws in the United States* (Washington, DC: The Sentencing Project, July 2001), pp. 1–3; Office of U.S. Pardon Attorney, *Civil Disabilities of Convicted Felons: A State by State Survey* (Washington, DC: USGPO, 1996).

[4] Shelley Albright and Furjen Denq, "Employer Attitudes Toward Hiring Ex-Offenders," *The Prison Journal*, 76(2) (1996): 118–37.

[5] Bureau of Justice Statistics, *Correctional Populations in the United States, 1997* (Washington, DC: U.S. Dept. of Justice, 2000), pp. iii–vi, 9, 112, NCJ-177613.

[6] Hughes, Wilson and Beck, *Trends in State Parole, 1990–2000*, p. 12.

[7] *Ibid.*, pp. 1–4.

[8] *Ibid.*

[9] Corrections Compendium, *Parole*, 26(6) (2001): 8–22.

[10] Horn, Martin F., "Rethinking Sentencing," *Corrections Management Quarterly*, 5(3) (2001): 34–40.

[11] Hughes, Wilson and Beck, *Trends in State Parole, 1990–2000*, p. 1; Louisa Coates, "International Conference Targets Worldwide Need for Parole," *Let's Talk*, 25(3) (2000): 6–9.

[12] Hughes, Wilson and Beck, *Trends in State Parole, 1990–2000*, p. 4.

[13] Paige M. Harrison and Allen J. Beck, *Prisoners in 2001* (Rockville, MD: National Institute of Justice, 2002), p. 1, NCJ-195189.

[14] Lauren E. Glaze, *Probation and Parole in the United States, 2001* (Washington, DC: U.S. Dept. of Justice, 2002), table 7, p. 6, NCJ-195669.

[15] Hughes, Wilson and Beck, *Trends in State Parole, 1990–2000*, p. 7.

[16] *Ibid.*, table 4, p. 5.

[17] "Drop in New York Parolees' Recidivism," *Corrections Compendium*, 27(1) (2002): 5.

[18] Hughes, Wilson and Beck, *Trends in State Parole, 1990–2000*, table 1, p. 2.

[19] Dean J. Champion, *Probation, Parole and Community Corrections* (Upper Saddle River, NJ: Prentice-Hall, 2002), pp. 265–67; Jon L. Proctor and Michael Pease, "Parole as Institutional Control: A Test of Specific Deterrence and Offender Misconduct," *Prison Journal*, 80(1) (2000): 39–55.

[20] Mikail Muhammad, "Prisoners' Perspectives on Strategies for Release," *Journal of Offender Rehabilitation*, 23(1-2) (1996): 131–52.

[21] Champion, *Probation, Parole and Community Corrections*, pp. 266–68.

[22] *Ibid.,* pp. 265–67.

[23] Ira Blalock, "Parole Guidelines," in Forst (ed.), *Sentencing Reform: Experiments in Reducing Disparity* (Thousand Oaks, CA: Sage, 1982), pp. 91–112.

[24] Paul F. Cromwell and Rolando Del Carmen, *Community-Based Corrections: Probation, Parole and Intermediate Sanctions*, 5th ed. (Belmont, CA: Wadsworth, 2002), pp. 187–89.

[25] President's Commission on Law Enforcement and Administration of Justice, *Task Force Report: Corrections* (Washington, DC: USGPO, 1967), pp. 184–85.

[26] Bill Habern and Gary J. Cohen, "A History of Parole, Mandatory Sentencing and Good Time," *Voice*, 25(8) Oct. (1996): 22–27.

[27] Champion, *Probation and Parole in the United States*, pp. 143–46.

[28] Joan Petersilia and Susan Turner, "Guideline Based Justice: Prediction and Racial Minorities," in Don Gottfredson and Michael Tonry (eds.), *Prediction and Classification* (Chicago: University of Chicago Press, 1987).

[29] *In re Rosenkrantz* (2000) 80 Cal.App.4th 409.

[30] A. L. Schneider, L. Ervin and Z. Snyder-Joy, "Further Exploration of Risk/Need Assessment Instruments Supervision Decisions," *Journal of Criminal Justice*, 24(2) (1996): 109–22; Rudy Haapanen and Lee Britton, "Drug Testing for Youthful Offenders on Parole: An Experimental Evaluation," *Criminology and Public Policy*, 1(2) (2002): 217–44; Ric Curtis, "Quality of Life Obsessions and the Micromanagement of Behavior," *Criminology and Public Policy*, 1(2) (2002): 245–50; Gary Zajac, "Knowledge Creation, Utilization and Public Policy: How Do We Know What We Know in Criminology?" *Criminology and Public Policy*, 1(2) (2002): 250–54.

[31] *Menchino v. Oswald*, 430 F.2d 403, 407 (2d Cir.1970), *cert. denied*, 400 U.S. 1023, 91 S.Ct. 588, 27 L.Ed.2d 635 (1971).

[32] *United States ex rel Campbell v. Pate*, 401 F.2d 55 (7th Cir.1968); *Palerno v. Rockfeller*, 323 F.Supp. 478 (S.D.N.Y. 1971); *Monks v. New Jersey State Parole Board*, 55 N.J. 238, 277 A.2d 193 (1971); *Greenholtz v. Inmates of the Nebraska Penal and Correctional Complex*, 442 U.S. 1, 60 L.Ed.2d 668, 99 S.Ct. 2100 (1979).

[33] Daniel P. LeClair and Susan Guarino-Ghezzi, "Prison Reintegration Programs: An Evaluation," *Corrections Management Quarterly*, 1(4) (1997): 65–74.

[34] *Parole Supervision Procedural Manual* (Austin: Paroles and Pardons Division, Texas Dept. of Criminal Justice, 1990), p. 4.

[35] Ann Strong, *Case Classification Manual, Module One: Technical Aspects of Interviewing* (Austin: Texas Adult Probation Commission, 1981).

[36] Harry E. Allen, Eric W. Carson and Evelyn C. Parks, *Critical Issues in Adult Probation: Summary* (Washington, DC: U.S. Dept. of Justice, 1979).

[37] *Parole Supervision Procedural Manual*, pp. 5–6.

[38] *Ibid.*

[39] *Ibid.*

[40] "Parole," *Corrections Compendium*, 26(6) (2001): 20–22.

[41] U.S. Dept. of Justice, Press Release Aug. 26, 2001, "National Correctional Population Reaches New High" (Washington, DC: Bureau of Justice Statistics), p. 6.

[42] Frank P. Williams, Marilyn D. McShane and Michael H. Dolny, "Predicting Parole Absconders," *Prison Journal*, 80(1) (2000): 24–38.

[43] "Crackdown on Illinois Parolees," *Corrections Compendium*, 26(12) (2001): 7.

[44] James Austin, "Prisoner Reentry: Current Trends, Practices, and Issues," *Crime and Delinquency*, 47(3) (2001): 314–34.

[45] *Parole Supervision Procedural Manual*, pp. 24–25, 44, 65–69, 71–73, 124–26.

[46] Jeff Glasser, "Ex-Cons on the Street," *U.S. News and World Report*, May 1, 2000, pp. 18–20; Bureau of Justice Statistics, *Correctional Populations in the United States, 1997*, table 6.5, p. 116.

[47] *Correctional Populations in the United States, 1997*, table 6.5, p. 116.

[48] Christy Hoppe, "Law Makers Fault Parole Procedures," *Dallas Morning News*, May 25, 2000, p. 1-A; Glasser, "Ex-Cons on the Street."

[49] Joan Petersilia, "When Prisoners Return to Communities: Political, Economic and Social Consequences," *Federal Probation I*, 65(1) (2001): 3–8.

[50] Reginald A. Wilkinson, "Offender Reentry: A Storm Overdue," *Corrections Management Quarterly*, 5(3) (2001): 46–51; Thomas Herzog and Martin Cirincione, "Reducing the Number of Parole Violators in Local Correctional Facilities in New York State," *American Jails*, 15(1) (2001): 58–63; National Drug Court Institute, *Reentry Drug Courts* (Alexandria VA: U.S. Dept. of Justice, Office of Justice Programs, Drug Courts Program Office 1999), pp. 1–52.

[51] Jeremy Travis, *But They All Come Back: Rethinking Prisoner Reentry* (Washington, DC: National Institute of Justice, 2000), pp. 1–5, NCJ-181413.

[52] Kim English, Susan Colling-Chadwick, Suzanne Pullen and Linda Jones, *How Are Adult Felony Sex Offenders Managed on Probation and Parole?* (Denver: Division of Criminal Justice, Colorado Department of Public Safety, 1996), pp. 2–8; "Sex Offenders' Use of Computers Monitored," *Fort Worth Star Telegram*, Dec. 31, 2001, p. 5-A.

[53] Paul Gendreau, Claire Goggin, Francis T. Cullen and Donald A. Andrews. "Effects of Community Sanctions and Incarceration on Recidivism," *Forum on Corrections Research*, 12(2) (2000): 10–13; Sara L. Johnson and Brian A. Grant, "Release Outcomes of Long-term Offenders," *Forum on Corrections Research*, 12(3) 2000: 16–20; *State Repeat Offender Rate Declines Sharply* (Lansing: Michigan Department of Corrections, 1996) pp. 1–2; Tennessee Sentencing Commission, *Recidivism Study* (Nashville: Tennessee Sentencing Commission, 1996), pp. 1–3.

[54] Patrick A. Lanagan and David J. Levin, *Recidivism of Prisoners Released in 1994* (Washington, DC: Dept. of Justice, Bureau of Justice Statistics, 2002), p. 7, NCJ-193427.

[55] *Ibid.*

[56] American Correctional Association, *Vital Statistics in Corrections, 1998* (Lanham, MD: American Correctional Association, 1998), pp. 48–50.

[57] Harry K. Wexler, "Integrated Approach to Aftercare and Employment for Criminal Justice Clients," *Offender Programs Report*, 5(2) (2001): 19–20, 32; Mary K. Shilton, *Increasing Offender Employment in the Community* (Rockville, MD: U.S. Dept. of Justice, Bureau of Justice Assistance, 2000), pp. 1–38, NCJ-189824; Maria L. Buck, *Getting Back to Work: Employment Programs for Ex-Offenders* (Philadelphia: Public-Private Ventures, 2000), pp. 1–36; Jeffrey E. Nash, *Final Report of Outcomes for the Ozark Correctional Center Drug Treatment Program* (Rockville, MD: U.S. Dept. of Justice, National Institute of Justice, 2000), pp. 1–36.

[58] Eric Lotke, *Issues and Answers: Does Treatment Work?* (Washington, DC: National Center for Institutions and Alternatives, 1997), p. 2; Robert A. Prentky, "Community Notification and Constructive Risk Reduction," *Journal of Interpersonal Violence*, 11(2) (1996): 295–98.

[59] Glaze, *Probation and Parole in the United States, 2001*, table 7, p. 6

[60] *Morrissey v. Brewer*, 408 U.S. 471 (1972).

[61] Alvin W. Cohn, "The Arming of Parole and Probation Officers May Not Be Necessary," *Corrections Management Quarterly*, 1(4) (1997): 44–54.

[62] *Morrissey v. Brewer*, 408 U.S. 471 (1972).

[63] William T. Habern and Gary J. Cohen, "A Defense Lawyer's Perspective of Constitutional Due Process Problems in the Parole Revocation Process," *Voice for the Defense*, 25(1) (1996): 34–38.

CHAPTER SEVEN

[1] Paige M. Harrison and Allen J. Beck, *Prisoners in 2001* (Washington, DC: U.S. Dept. of Justice, Bureau of Justice Statistics, 2002), table 10, p. 9, NCJ-195189.

[2] The Sentencing Project, *U.S. Continues to Be World Leader in Rate of Incarceration* (Washington, DC: The Sentencing Project, 2001), p. 1.

[3] Harrison and Beck, *Prisoners in 2001*; Bureau of Justice Statistics, *Sourcebook of Criminal Justice Statistics 2001*, table 6.23, p. 494, available: http://www.albany.edu/sourcebook/1995/pdf/section6.pdf

[4] Harrison and Beck, *Prisoners in 2001*, p. 4.

[5] *Ibid.*, p. 2.

[6] Bruce Western and Katherine Beckett, "How Unregulated Is the U.S. Labor Market? The Penal System as a Labor Market Institution," *American Journal of Sociology,* 104(4) (January 1999): 1030–60.

[7] Joan Petersilia, "When Prisoners Return to the Community: Political, Economic, and Social Consequences," *Sentencing & Corrections: Issues for the 21st Century* (Washington, DC: Office of Justice Programs, 2000), p. 3.

[8] Marc Mauer and Meda Chesney-Lind, *Invisible Punishment: The Collateral Consequences of Mass Imprisonment* (New York: The New Press, 2002).

[9] Michael Tonry and Joan Petersilia, "Prisons Research at the Beginning of the 21st Century," *Crime and Justice: A Review of the Research*, 26 (1999): 1–14; Bruce Western, Jeffrey R. King and David F. Weiman, "The Labor Market Consequences of Incarceration," *Crime and Delinquency*, 47(3) (2001): 410–27.

[10] The Sentencing Project, *U.S. Continues to Be World Leader in Rate of Incarceration*, pp. 1–3; John Pratt, "Globalization of Punishment," *Corrections Today*, 64(1) Feb. (2002): 64–66.

[11] Michael Tonry, "Community Penalties in the United States," *European Journal on Criminal Policy and Research*, 7(1) (1999): 5–22; Joan Petersilia, "Decade of Intermediate Sanctions: What Have We Learned?" *Justice Research and Policy*, 1(1) (1999): 9–23; Franklin E. Zimring, "Lethal Violence and the Overreach of American Imprisonment," in *Two Views on Imprisonment Policies* (Washington, DC: U.S. Dept. of Justice, National Institute of Justice, 1997).

[12] Justice Policy Institute, "Cellblocks or Classrooms?: The Funding of Higher Education and Corrections and Its Impact on African American Men" (Washington, DC: Justice Policy Institute, 2002). http://www.justicepolicy.org/coc.pdf

[13] *Ibid.*, pp. 13–14.

[14] Harrison and Beck, *Prisoners in 2001*, pp. 1–14.

[15] *Ibid.*, p. 12; Marc Mauer, "The Crisis of the Young African American Male and the Criminal Justice System," prepared for U.S. Commission on Civil Rights, Washington, DC, April 15–16, 1999.

[16] Gary Cesarz and Joyce Madrid-Bustos, "Taking a Multicultural World View in Today's Correctional Facilities," *Corrections Today*, 53(7) (1991): 68–71.

[17] Michael Coyle, "Race and Class Penalties in Crack Cocaine Sentencing" (Washington, DC: Sentencing Project, 2002), available: http://www.sentencingproject.org/policy/mc-crackcocaine.pdf

[18] William Brownsberger, "Race Matters: Disproportionality of Incarceration for Drug Dealing in Massachusetts," *Journal of Drug Issues*, 30(2) (2000): 345–74.

[19] Larry Gaines and Peter Kraska, *Drugs, Crime, and Justice,* 2nd ed. (Prospect Heights, IL: Waveland Press, 2003), pp. 7–8, 66–68, 70–73.

[20] Mauer, "The Crisis of the Young African-American Male and the Criminal Justice System," pp. 1–18; Steven R. Donziger, *The Real War on Crime: The Report of the National Criminal Justice Commission* (New York: HarperCollins, 1996), p. 120.

[21] Donziger, *The Real War on Crime*, p. 120.

[22] William Raspberry, "Prison Paradox," *The Washington Post*, Oct. 14, 2002, p. A29.

[23] Dana Kaplan, Vincent Schiraldi and Jason Ziedenberg, "Texas Tough? An Analysis of Incarceration and Crime Trends in The Lone Star" (Washington, DC: The Justice Policy Institute, 2000), pp. 1–12.

[24] Tonry and Petersilia, "Prisons Research at the Beginning of the 21st Century," pp. 2–3; S. Christianson, *With Liberty for Some: 500 Years of Imprisonment in America* (Boston, MA: Northeastern University Press, 1998); George Rusche and Otto Kirchheimer, *Punishment and Social Structures* (New York: Columbia University Press, 1939); Michel Foucault, *Discipline & Punish* (New York: Vintage Books, 1979), pp. 232, 272.

[25] The Continuing Crime of Black Imprisonment, The Committee to End the Marion Lockdown, Mar. 27, 1995, available: http://www.uuix.oit.umass.edu/~kastor/ceml_articles/continuing.html

[26] Harrison and Beck, *Prisoners in 2001*, p. 4.

[27] Allen J. Beck, Jennifer C. Karberg and Paige M. Harrison, *Prison and Jail Inmates at Midyear 2001* (Washington, DC: Bureau of Justice Statistics, 2002), p. 3, NCJ-191702.

[28] Harrison and Beck, *Prisoners in 2001*, table 3, p. 3.

[29] Bureau of Justice Statistics, *Sourcebook of Criminal Justice Statistics 2001*, table 6.29, p. 499, available: http://www.albany.edu/sourcebook/1995/pdf/section6.pdf; Caroline Wolf Harlow, *Comparing Federal and State Prison Inmates, 1991* (Washington, DC: U.S. Dept. of Justice, 1994), pp. 1–3, NCJ-145864.

[30] Allen J. Beck, "Trends in U.S. Correctional Populations: Why Has the Number of Offenders under Supervision Tripled Since 1980?" in Kenneth Haas and Geoffrey Alpert (eds.), *The Dilemmas of Corrections*, 4th ed. (Prospect Heights, IL: Waveland Press, 1999), p. 53.

[31] Harrison and Beck, *Prisoners in 2001*, table 20, p. 14.

[32] Howard Abadinsky, *Drugs: An Introduction* (Belmont, CA: Wadsworth/Thomson, 2001), pp. 271, 314.

[33] Harrison and Beck, *Prisoners in 2001*, p. 12.

[34] *Ibid.*, table 17, p. 13; *Correctional Populations in the United States, 1997*.

[35] Bureau of Justice Statistics, *Sourcebook of Criminal Justice Statistics 2001*, table 6.29, p. 499, available: http://www.albany.edu/sourcebook/1995/pdf/section6.pdf; Harrison and Beck, *Prisoners in 2001*, p. 12.

[36] Harrison and Beck, *Prisoners in 2001*, p. 12

[37] The Sentencing Project, "New Prison Population Figures Show Slowing of Growth, but Uncertain Trends" (Washington, DC: The Sentencing Project, 2001) pp. 1–5.

[38] Don Thompson, "Treatment Beats Jail on Ballot, California to Implement Proposition 36 for Drug Addicts," ABC News.com, Nov. 13, 2000, available: http://abcnews.go.com/sections/living/DailyNews/drug_propthreesix001113.html

[39] Texas Board of Pardons and Paroles, *Revised Parole Guidelines* (Austin: Texas Board of Pardons and Paroles, Sept. 18, 2001), pp. 1–5, available: http://www.tdcj.state.tx.us/bpp/parole-guidelines.html

[40] Mike Ward and Bill Bishop, "Deadly Inadequacies Plague Inmate Wards," *Austin-American Statesman,* available: www.austin360.com/aas/specialreports/prisons/16prisonmain.html

[41] United States Department of Health and Human Services, Centers for Disease Control and Prevention, "Tuberculosis Outbreaks in Prison Housing Units for HIV-Infected Inmates—California, 1995–1996," *MMWR Weekly,* February 5, 1999, available: http://www.cdc.gov/nchstp/od/mmwr/tuberculosis_outbreaks_in_prison.htm; California Department of Corrections, "Staff and Inmates to be Tested for Tuberculosis at California State Prison—Solano," press release Oct. 18, 1999, available: www.cdc.state.ca.us/news/1999/99-13.htm

[42] Laura M. Maruschak, *HIV in Prisons, 2000* (Rockville, MD: U.S. Dept. of Justice, Bureau of Justice Statistics, 2002), pp. 1–7, NCJ-196023.

[43] Caroline W. Harlow, *HIV in U.S. Prisons and Jails* (Washington, DC: U.S. Dept. of Justice, 1993), pp. 1–8; *1992 Update: HIV/AIDS in Correctional Facilities, Issues and Practices*, January 1994, NCJRS, DD14333980H.

[44] Maruschak, *HIV in Prisons, 2000*, p. 1.

[45] *Ibid.*, p. 10.

[46] Mark Blumberg and J. Dennis Laster, "The Impact of HIV/AIDS on Corrections," in Haas and Alpert (eds.) *The Dilemmas of Corrections*, 4th ed., pp. 583–86.

[47] Theodore Hammett and Patricia Harmon, "Housing and Correctional Management," *1996–1997 Update: HIV/AIDS, STDs, and TB in Correctional Facilities* (Washington, DC: National Institute of Justice, 1999), p. 63, NCJ-176344.

[48] Dorothy E. Merianos, James W. Marquart and Kelly Damphouse, "Examining HIV-Related Knowledge among Adults and Its Consequences for Institutionalized Populations," *Corrections Management Quarterly*, 1(4) (1997): 84–87.

[49] Blumberg and Laster, "Impact of HIV/AIDS," p. 575.

[50] *Ibid.*, p. 581.

[51] Kate Dolan, Alex Wodak and Wayne Hall, "HIV Risk Behaviour and Prevention in Prison: A Bleach Programme for Inmates in NSW," *Drug and Alcohol Review,* 18(2) (1999).

[52] *Ibid.*; Theodore Hammett and Patricia Harmon, "HIV Transmission and Risk Factors, Precautionary and Preventive Measures," *1996–1997 Update: HIV/AIDS, STDs, and TB in Correctional Facilities,* p. 49.

[53] *Ibid.*, p. 49

[54] *Prisons Slipping in HIV Education Efforts* (Philadelphia: Critical Path AIDS Project, 55, May 1996): 1–2.

[55] James F. Anderson, J. Burns and L. Dyson, "Could an Increase in AIDS Cases among Incarcerated Populations Mean More Legal Liabilities for Correctional Administrators?" *Journal of Crime & Justice,* 21(1) (1998): 41–52; R. Jurgens, *HIV/AIDS in Prisons: Final Report* (Montreal, Quebec: Canadian HIV/AIDS Legal Network, 1999), pp. 1–176.

[56] Hammett and Harmon, "Counseling and Testing Confidentiality and Disclosure," *1996–1997 Update: HIV/AIDS, STDs, and TB in Correctional Facilities,* p. 54.

[57] Hammett and Harmon, "Medical Treatment and a Continuum of Care," *1996–1997 Update: HIV/AIDS, STDs, and TB in Correctional Facilities,* p. 74.

[58] Theodore Hammett, Patricia Harmon and Laura M. Maruschak, *1996–1997 Update: HIV/AIDS, STDs and TB in Correctional Facilities* (Washington, DC: National Institute of Justice, 1999), pp. viii–xv, NCJ-176344.

[59] Michael F. Kelly, MD, *Tuberculosis in Correctional Facilities, Annual Statistical Report* (Austin: Texas Department of Criminal Justice, 1994); "Corrections," *New York Times,* Mar. 4, 1995, p. 2-A.

[60] Theodore Hammett, *Public Health/Corrections Collaborations: Prevention and Treatment of HIV/AIDS, STDs, and TB* (Washington, DC: National Institute of Justice, 1998), pp. 1–19, NCJ-169590.

[61] Maruschak, *HIV in Prisons, 2000,* table 5, p. 7.

[62] The Sentencing Project, "Mentally Ill Offenders in the Criminal Justice System: An Analysis and Prescription" (Washington, DC: The Sentencing Project, 2002), p. 4.

[63] Harrison and Beck, *Prisoners in 2001,* pp. 11, 14.

[64] Christopher Mumola, *Substance Abuse and Treatment, State and Federal Prisoners, 1997* (Washington DC: U.S. Dept. of Justice, Bureau of Justice Statistics, 1999), p. 1, NCJ-172871.

[65] *Correctional Populations in the United States, 1997* (Washington, DC: U.S. Dept. of Justice, 2000), tables 4.14, 4.15, 4.16, pp. 61–62, NCJ-177613.

[66] Tina Dorsey, Marianne Zawitz and Priscilla Middleton, *Drugs and Crime Facts, 2000* (Washington, DC: Office of National Drug Control Policy, 2001), p. 5.

[67] James F. Quinn, "The Complex Intertwining of Drugs and Crime," in Clifton Bryant (ed.), *The Encyclopedia of Criminology and Deviant Behavior, Volume VII* (London, England: Taylor & Francis, 2000), 493–506.

[68] *Drugs and Crime Facts, 1994* (Washington, DC: U.S. Dept. of Justice, Bureau of Justice Statistics, 1995), p. 7.

[69] *Correctional Populations in the United States, 1997,* table 4.16, p. 62.

[70] Dorsey, Zawitz and Middleton, *Drugs and Crime Facts, 2000,* pp. 3–45; *Correctional Populations in the United States, 1997,* table 4.14, p. 61.

[71] Dorsey, Zawitz and Middleton, *Drugs and Crime Facts, 2000,* pp. 5–37.

[72] Harrison and Beck, *Prisoners in 2001,* table 17.

[73] Center for Sex Offender Management, *Recidivism of Sex Offenders* (Washington, DC: Center for Sex Offender Management, May 2001), pp. 1–11; Eric Lotke, *Sex Offenders: Does Treatment Work?* (Alexandria, VA: National Center on Institutions and Alternatives, 1996), pp. 1–6.

[74] *NIJ Survey of Wardens and State Commissioners of Corrections* (Washington, DC: U.S. Dept. of Justice 1995), pp. 1–2.

[75] Eric Lotke, *Issues and Answers: Does Treatment Work?* (Washington, DC: National Center for Institutions and Alternatives, 1997), p. 2; Frank Zimring, quoted in Gina Kolata, "The Many Myths about Sex Offenders," *New York Times,* Sept. 1, 1996, p. 10-B.

[76] Adrian Raine, Todd Lencz, Susan Bihrle, Lori LaCasse and Patrick Colletti, "Reduced Prefrontal Gray Matter Volume and Reduced Autonomic Activity in Antisocial Personality Disorder," *Archives of General Psychiatry,* 57(2) (2000): 119–27; National Institute of Mental Health, "Child and Adolescent Violence Research" (Bethesda, MD: National Institute of Mental Health, Apr. 2000), NIH-00-4706; Maurizio Fava, Katharine Davidson, Jonathan E. Alpert, Andrew A. Nierenberg, John Worthington, Richard O'Sullivan and Jerrold F. Rosenbaum, "Hostility Changes Following Antidepressant Treatment: Relationship to Stress and Negative Thinking," *Journal of Psychiatric Research,* 30(1) (2000): 617–726; Jiri Modestin, Andreas Hug and Roland Ammann, "Criminal Behavior in Males with Affective Disorders," *Journal of Affective Disorders,* 42 (1997): 29–38.

[77] Allen J. Beck and Laura M. Maruschak, *Mental Health Treatment in State Prisons, 2000* (Rockville, MD: National Institute of Justice, 2001), p. 1, NCJ-188215.

[78] The Sentencing Project, *Mentally Ill Offenders in the Criminal Justice System: An Analysis and Prescription* (Washington, DC: The Sentencing Project, January 2002).

[79] Debra Jasper, "Retarded Offenders Lost in Courts: Overwhelmed and Embarrassed, Many Get No Help and Much Trouble," *Cincinnati Enquirer*, Apr. 8, 2001, p. B-1; Joan Petersilia, "Unequal Justice: Offenders with Mental Retardation in Prison," *Corrections Management Quarterly*, 1(4) (1997): 36–43.

[80] *Ibid.*

[81] T. L. Mawhorr, "Disabled Offenders and Work Release: An Exploratory Examination," *Criminal Justice Review*, 22(1) (1997): 34–48; Joan Petersilia, "Justice for All? Offenders with Mental Retardation and the California Corrections System," *Prison Journal*, 77(4) (1997): 358–80; *Ruiz v. Estelle*, 503 F.Supp. 1265 (S.D. Tex. 1980).

[82] The Sentencing Project, *Mentally Ill Offenders*, p. 12.

[83] Darlene Van Sickle, "Avoiding Lawsuits: A Summary of ADA Provisions and Remedies," *Corrections Today*, Apr. (1995): 104–6; Susan W. Campbell, "Facility Design Can Help Welcome Disabled Staff," *Corrections Today*, Apr. (1995): 110–13; Rodney Isom, Kerry Boyle and Pat Smith, *ADA Compliance System* (Atlanta, GA: Elliot and Fitzpatrick, 1992), pp. 2–3, 14–15.

[84] See, for example, *Armstrong v. Wilson*, 942 F.Supp. 1252 (N.D. Cal. 1996) aff'd 124 F.3d 1019 (9th Cir. 1997); *Clark v. California*, 123 F.3d 1267 (9th Cir. 1997); *Pennsylvania Dept. of Corrections v. Yeskey* (1998), 524 U.S. 206.

[85] Herbert A. Rosefield, "Enabling the Disabled: Issues to Consider in Meeting Handicapped Offenders' Needs," *Corrections Today*, 54(7) (1992): 110–14.

[86] Cynthia Massie-Mara and Christopher McKenna, "'Aging in Place,' in Prison: Health and Long-Term Care Needs of Older Inmates," *The Public Policy and Aging Report*, 10(4) (2000): 1–5.

[87] Harrison and Beck, *Prisoners in 2001*, p. 12.

[88] Ryan S. King and Marc Mauer, *Aging Behind Bars: "Three Strikes" Seven Years Later.* (Washington, DC: The Sentencing Project, August 2001).

[89] William Rhodes, Patrick Johnston, Quentin McMullen and Lynne Hozik, *Unintended Consequences of Sentencing Policy: The Creation of Long-Term Healthcare Obligations* (Washington, DC: National Institute of Justice, 2000), pp. 1–87, NCJ-187671.

[90] Joann Brown Morton, "Implications for Corrections of an Aging Prison Population," *Corrections Management Quarterly*, 5(1) (2001): 78–88.

[91] Elaine M. Gallagher, "Emotional, Social, and Physical Health Characteristics of Older Men in Prison," *International Journal of Aging and Human Development*, 31(4) (1990): 251–65.

[92] Harrison and Beck, *Prisoners in 2001; 2001 Directory of Juvenile and Adult Correctional Departments, Institutions, Agencies and Paroling Authorities* (Lanham, MD: American Correctional Assoc., 2001), p. 46; *1998 Directory of Juvenile and Adult Correctional Departments, Institutions, Agencies and Paroling Authorities* (Lanham, MD: American Correctional Assoc., 1998), pp. xxx–xxxi; Bureau of Justice Statistics, *National Corrections Reporting Program, 1992* (Washington, DC: U.S. Dept. of Justice, USGPO, 1994), p. 15, NCJ-145862.

[93] Manuel Vega and Mitchell Silverman, "Stress and the Elderly Convict," *International Journal of Offender Therapy and Comparative Criminology*, 32(2) (1988): 153–62.

[94] Pamela Steinke, "Using Situational Factors to Predict Types of Prison Violence," *Journal of Offender Rehabilitation*, 17(1-2) (1991): 119–32; Stephen C. Light, "The Severity of Assaults on Prison Officers: A Contextual Study," *Social Science Quarterly*, 71(2) (1990): 267–84.

[95] Joseph L. Paulhus and Delroy L. Paulhus, "Predictors of Prosocial Behavior among Inmates," *Journal of Social Psychology*, 132(2) (1992): 233–43.

[96] Ronald H. Aday, "Golden Years Behind Bars: Special Programs and Facilities for Elderly Inmates," *Federal Probation*, 58(2) (1994): 47–54; Marilyn D. McShane and Frank P. Williams, III, "Old and Ornery: The Disciplinary Experiences of Elderly Prisoners," *International Journal of Offender Therapy and Comparative Criminology*, 34(3) (1990): 197–212.

[97] Brian Shapiro, "America's Aging Prison Population: Issues & Alternatives," *Offender Programs Report*, 5(2) (2001): 17–18, 25–27; Aday, "Golden Years Behind Bars."

[98] Helen K. Branson, "Hospice in Prison," *Corrections Technology & Management*, 5(2) (2001): 22–25; Felicia Cohn, "Ethics of End-of-Life Care for Prison Inmates," *Journal of Law, Medicine & Ethics*, 7(3) (1999): 252–59.

[99] Massie-Mara and McKenna, "'Aging in Place.'"

[100] Morton, "Implications for Corrections of an Aging Prison Population."

[101] Peter L. Nacci, C. Allen Turner, Ronald J. Waldron and Eddie Broyles, *Implementing Telemedicine in Correctional Facilities* (Washington, DC: National Institute of Justice, 2002), pp. 1–76, NCJ-190310; Diane Connors, "Telemedicine: The Future of Correctional Health Care?" *Corrections Compendium*, 25(3) (2000): 4–6.

[102] Sammie Brown, "Are Inmate Classification Systems Addressing the Diverse Inmate Population?" *Corrections Today*, June (2002): 104–5.

[103] Patricia Hardyman, James Austin and Owan Tulloch, *Revalidating External Prison Classification Systems: The Experience of Ten States and Model for Classification Reform* (Washington, DC: National Institute of Corrections, 2002), p. 1, available: http://www.nicic.org/pubs/2002/017382.pdf

[104] Courtney A. Waid and Carl B. Clements, "Correctional Facility Design: Past, Present and Future," *Corrections Compendium,* 26(11) (2001): 1–5, 25–29.

[105] *Ibid.*, p. 2; James Austin, Patricia Hardyman and Sammie D. Brown, "Critical Issues and Developments in Prison," *National Institute of Corrections* (Washington, DC: U.S. Dept. of Justice, Federal Bureau of Prisons, 2001), p. 2.

[106] Kathryn Ann Farr, "Classification for Female Inmates: Moving Forward," *Crime & Delinquency,* 46(1) (2000): 3–17.

[107] Austin, Hardyman and Brown, "Critical Issues and Developments in Prison."

[108] Miles D. Harer and Neal P. Langan, "Gender Differences in Predictors of Prison Violence: Assessing the Predictive Validity of a Risk Classification System," *Crime & Delinquency*, 47(4) (2001): 513–36.

[109] Gerald Berge, Jeffrey Geiger and Scot Whitney, "Technology Is the Key to Security in Wisconsin Supermax," *Corrections Today*, 63(4) (2001): 105–9; Roy D. King, "Rise and Rise of Supermax: An American Solution in Search of a Problem?" *Punishment & Society*, 1(2) (1999): 163–86.

[110] King, "Rise and Rise of Supermax: An American Solution in Search of a Problem?".

[111] Hans Toch, "Future of Supermax Confinement," *Prison Journal*, 81(3) (2001): 376–88.

CHAPTER EIGHT

[1] Angela R. Gover, Doris Layton MacKenzie and Gaylene Styve Armstrong, "Importation and Deprivation Explanations of Juveniles' Adjustment to Correctional Facilities," *International Journal of Offender Therapy and Comparative Criminology*, 44(4) (2000): 450–67; Brent A. Paterline and David M. Petersen, "Structural and Social Psychological Determinants of Prisonization," *Journal of Criminal Justice*, (27)(5) (1999): 427–41.

[2] John M. MacDonald, "Violence and Drug Use in Juvenile Institutions," *Journal of Criminal Justice*, 27(1) (1999): 33–44; Jon Sorensen, R. Wrinkle and A. Gutierrez, "Patterns of Rule-Violating Behaviors and Adjustment to Incarceration among Murderers," *Prison Journal*, 78(3) (1998): 222–31.

[3] Randall McGowen, "The Well-Ordered Prison," in Norval Morris and David J. Rothman (eds.), *The Oxford History of the Prison* (Oxford University Press, 1995), p. 99.

[4] John Irwin and Donald R. Cressey, "Thieves, Convicts and the Inmate Culture," *Social Problems*, 10 (1963): 142–55.

[5] Jessie L. Krienert and Mark S. Fleisher, "Gang Membership as a Proxy for Social Deficiencies: A Study of Nebraska Inmates," *Corrections Management Quarterly*, 5(1) (2001): 47–58; Mark S. Fleisher and Scott H. Decker, "Going Home, Staying Home: Integrating Prison Gang Members Into the Community," *Corrections Management Quarterly*, 5(1) (2001): 65–77; Robert Koehler, "Organizational Structure and Function of La Nuestra Familia within Colorado State Correctional Facilities," *Deviant Behavior*, 21(2) (2000): 155–79; Ronald Maki, "Psychological Profile of a Gang Member," *Corrections Compendium*, 25(4) (2000): 8–9, 23.

[6] Miles D. Harer and Darrell J. Steffensmeier, "Race and Prison Violence," *Criminology*, 34(3) (1996): 323–54.

[7] Wayne D. Osgood, Enid Gruber, Mark A. Archer and Theodore Newcomb, "Autonomy for Inmates: Counterculture or Co-optation," *Criminal Justice and Behavior*, 12(1) (1985): 71–89.

[8] Gordon James Knowles, "Male Prison Rape: A Search for Causation and Prevention," *Howard Journal of Criminal Justice*, 38(3) (1999): 267–82.

[9] Werner Gruninger, "Criminal Maturity, Prison Roles, and Normative Alienation," *Free Inquiry*, 3(1) (1975): 38–63.

[10] Matthew Silberman, *A World of Violence* (Belmont, CA: Wadsworth, 1995), p. 34; Kathleen Engel and Stanley Rothman, "Prison Violence and the Paradox of Reform," *Public Interest*, 73 (1983): 91–105.

[11] Gover, MacKenzie and Armstrong, "Importation and Deprivation Explanations"; MacDonald, "Violence and Drug Use in Juvenile Institutions"; Brent A. Paterline and David M. Petersen, "Structural and Social Psychological Determinants of Prisonization," *Journal of Criminal Justice*, (27)(5) (1999): 427–41.

[12] Carol F. W. Smith and John R. Hepburn, "Alienation in Prison Organizations: A Comparative Analysis," *Criminology*, 17(2) (1979): 251–62; Ronald L. Akers, "Type of Leadership in Prison: A Structural Approach to Testing the Functional and Importation Models," *Sociological Quarterly*, 18(3) (1977): 378–83.

[13] Dennis J. Stevens, "The Depth of Imprisonment and Prisonization: Levels of Security and Prisoners' Anticipation of Future Violence," *Howard Journal of Criminal Justice*, 33(2) (1994): 137–57.

[14] Paterline and Petersen, "Structural and Social Psychological Determinants of Prisonization."

[15] Erving Goffman, *Asylums* (Garden City: Doubleday, 1961).

[16] Michael D. Reisig and Yoon Ho Lee, "Prisonization in the Republic of Korea," *Journal of Criminal Justice*, 28(1) (2000): 23–31; Paterline and Petersen, "Structural and Social Psychological Determinants of Prisonization."

[17] James Rosenfield and Margaret W. Linn, "Perceptions of Penal Environment and Attitude Change," *Journal of Clinical Psychology*, 32(3) July (1976): 548–53.

[18] John D. Wooldredge, "Inmate Experiences and Psychological Well-Being," *Criminal Justice and Behavior*, 26(2) (1999): 235–50; Dennis J. Stevens, "The Impact of Time-Served and Regime on Prisoners' Anticipation of Crime: Female Prisonisation Effects," *Howard Journal of Criminal Justice*, 37(2) (1998): 188–205; Matthew Silberman, "Violence as Social Control in Prison," *Virginia Review of Sociology*, 1 (1992): 77–97.

[19] Ronald L. Akers, Norman S. Hayner and Werner Gruninger, "Prisonization in Five Countries: Type of Prison and Inmate Characteristics," *Criminology*, 14(4) (1977): 527–54.

[20] *Ibid.*; Reisig and Lee, "Prisonization in the Republic of Korea."

[21] Stevens, "The Depth of Imprisonment and Prisonization"; Lynne Goodstein, "Inmate Adjustment to Prison and the Transition to Community Life," *Journal of Research in Crime and Delinquency*, 16 (1979): 246–72; Donald Clemmer, *The Prison Community* (New York: Holt, Rinehart, 1958), pp. 298–304.

[22] Harold Garfinkel, "Conditions of Successful Degradation Ceremonies," *American Journal of Sociology*, 61 (1956): 420–24; Rosabeth Moss Kanter, *Commitment and Community* (Cambridge: Harvard University Press, 1972), pp. 74, 103–11.

[23] Paul Gendreau, Claire Goggin, Francis T. Cullen and Donald A. Andrews, "Effects of Community Sanctions and Incarceration on Recidivism," *Forum on Corrections Research*, 12(2) (2000): 10–13; Michael Tonry and Joan Petersilia, "Prisons Research at the Beginning of the 21st Century," *Crime and Justice: A Review of the Research*, 26 (1999): 3–5; Michel Foucault and John K. Simon, "Michel Foucault on Attica: An Interview," *Social Justice*, 18(3) (1991): 26–34; Harold E. Pepinsky, "Abolishing Prisons," in Lawrence F. Travis, Martin D. Schwartz and Todd R. Clear (eds.), *Corrections: An Issues Approach*, 3rd ed. (Cincinnati: Anderson, 1992), pp. 131–46; Stevens, "The Depth of Imprisonment and Prisonization."

[24] Robert Johnson, *Hard Time: Understanding and Reforming the Prison* (Monterey, CA: Brooks/Cole, 1987), pp. 55–70; Lynne Goodstein, Doris Layton MacKenzie and R. Lance Shotland, "Personal Control and Inmate Adjustment to Prison," *Criminology*, 22(3) (1984): 343–69.

[25] Darren P. Lawson, Chris Segrin and Teresa D. Ward, "The Relationship between Prisonization and Social Skills among Inmates," *The Prison Journal*, 76(3) (1996): 293–309.

[26] Philip G. Zimbardo, "Pathology of Imprisonment," *Society*, 9(2) (1972).

[27] *Ibid.*

[28] Stanton Wheeler, "Socialization in Correctional Communities," *American Sociological Review*, 26 (1961): 699–712.

[29] James Bonta and Paul Gendreau, "Reexamining the Cruel and Unusual Punishment of Prison Life," *Law and Human Behavior*, 14(4) (1990): 347–72.

[30] Thomas J. Schmid and Richard S. Jones, "Ambivalent Actions: Prison Adaptation Strategies of First-Time, Short-Term Inmates," *Journal of Contemporary Ethnography*, 21(4) (1993): 439–63.

[31] Wooldredge, *Inmate Experiences and Psychological Well-Being*; Johnson, *Hard Time: Understanding and Reforming the Prison*, pp. 64–65; Penny Jackson, Donald I. Templer, Wilbert Reimer and David LeBaron, "Correlates of Visitation in a Men's Prison," *International Journal of Offender Therapy and Comparative Criminology*, 41(1) (1997): 79–85.

[32] Stevens, "The Depth of Imprisonment and Prisonization."

[33] L. Thomas Winfree, G. Larry Mays, Joan E. Crowley and Barbara J. Peat, "Drug History and Prisonization: Toward Understanding Variations in Inmate Institutional Adaptations," *International Journal of Offender Therapy and Comparative Criminology*, 38(4) (1994): 281–95.

[34] Jennifer Wyn, "Junk in the Joint: The Real Dope on the Prison Drug Scene," *Prison Life Magazine*, Jan.–Feb. (1996): 46–51, 54–55; Thomas E. Feucht and Andrew Keyser, "Reducing Drug Use in Prisons: Pennsylvania's Approach," *National Institute of Justice Journal*, Oct. (1999): 10–15; Allan Turner and Becky Lewis, "Stopping Drugs in the Mail," *Corrections Today*, July (2002): 112–14.

[35] Stevens, "The Depth of Imprisonment and Prisonization."

[36] Mitchell Silverman and Manuel Vega, "Reactions of Prisoners to Stress as a Function of Personality and Demographic Variables," *International Journal of Offender Therapy and Comparative Criminology*, 34(3) (1990): 187–96.

[37] Robert Homant and Douglas Dean, "The Effect of Prisonization and Self-Esteem on Inmates' Career Maturity," *Journal of Offender Counseling, Services and Rehabilitation*, 12 (1988): 19–40; Stevens, "The Depth of Imprisonment and Prisonization."

[38] Norval Morris, "The Contemporary Prison 1965–Present," in Morris and Rothman, (eds.), *The Oxford History of the Prison* (Oxford University Press, 1995), p. 228.

[39] James Q. Wilson and Richard J. Herrnstein, *Crime and Human Nature* (New York: Simon and Schuster, 1985), pp. 53–54, 167–72, 217.

[40] Samuel Yochelson and Stanton E. Samenow, *The Criminal Personality: A Profile for Change* (New York: Jason Aronson, 1976), pp. 104–5, 246–372.

[41] Leonard Hystad, *Glossary of Prison Slang*, Computer Printout (name = "topgloss"), December 28, 1995.

[42] Kevin N. Wright, "Race and Economic Marginality in Explaining Prison Adjustment," *Journal of Research in Crime and Delinquency*, 26(1) (1989): 67–89; John Irwin, *The Jail: Managing the Underclass in American Society* (Berkeley: University of California Press, 1986), pp. 45–97.

[43] Alan R. Rowe, "Race, Age, and Conformity in Prison," *Psychological Reports*, 52(2) (1983): 445–46.

[44] John Irwin, *The Felon* (Englewood Cliffs, NJ: Prentice-Hall, 1970), pp. 7–35.

[45] Mark S. Fleisher and Scott H. Decker, "Overview of the Challenge of Prison Gangs," *Corrections Management Quarterly*, 5(1) (2001): 1–9; U.S. Dept. of Justice, *NIJ Survey of Wardens and State Commissioners of Corrections* (Washington, DC: U.S. Dept. of Justice, 1995), pp. 1–2.

[46] Fleisher and Decker, "Overview of the Challenge of Prison Gangs."

[47] Mark Pitcavage, *Behind the Walls, Intelligence Report* (Montgomery, AL: Southern Poverty Law Center, 2002), pp. 24–27; *Dallas Morning News*, "Texas Prison Gangs," *Dallas Morning News*, July 16, 2001, p. 5-A.

[48] Jessie L. Krienert and Mark S. Fleisher, "Gang Membership as a Proxy for Social Deficiencies: A Study of Nebraska Inmates," *Corrections Management Quarterly*, 5(1) (2001): 47–58; Robert Koehler, "Organizational Structure and Function of La Nuestra Familia within Colorado State Correctional Facilities," *Deviant Behavior*, 21(2) (2000): 155–79.

[49] George W. Knox, "A National Assessment of Gangs and Security Threat Groups in Adult Correctional Institutions: Results of the 1999 Adult Corrections Survey," *Journal of Gang Research*, 7(3) (2000): 1–45; "Gangs Inside," *Corrections Compendium*, 25(4) (2000): 9–19.

[50] Fleisher and Decker, "Overview of the Challenge of Prison Gangs."

[51] Peter M. Carlson, "Prison Interventions: Evolving Strategies to Control Security Threat Groups," *Corrections Management Quarterly*, 5(1) (2001): 10–22.

[52] Ed Timms, "Breaking Out: Texas Inmates Get Help Escaping Prison Gangs," *Dallas Morning News*, July 18, 2001, p. 3-B.

[53] *Ibid.*

[54] Texas Office of the Attorney General, "Is Time Running Out for Texas Gangs?" *Criminal Law Update*, 8(2) (2000): 4–11.

[55] Mark S. Fleisher and Scott H. Decker, "Going Home, Staying Home: Integrating Prison Gang Members Into the Community," *Corrections Management Quarterly*, 5(1) (2001): 65–77.

[56] James W. Marquart and Ben M. Crouch, "Reform and Prisoner Control: The Impact of *Ruiz v. Estelle* on a Texas Penitentiary," *Law and Society Review*, 19(4) (1985): 557–86.

[57] C. Ronald Huff and Matthew Meyer, "Managing Prison Gangs and Other Security Threat Groups," *Corrections Management Quarterly*, 1(4) (1997): 10–18.

58 David B. Kalinich, "Contraband: The Basis for Legitimate Power in a Prison Social System," in Stan Stojkovic, John Klofas and David Kalinich (eds.), *The Administration and Management of Criminal Justice Organizations*, 3rd ed. (Prospect Heights, IL: Waveland Press, 1999).

59 Virgil L. Williams and Mary Fish, *Convicts, Codes, and Contraband* (Cambridge, MA: Ballinger, 1974), pp. 42–44.

60 "Riots, Disturbances, Violence, Assaults, and Escapes," *Corrections Compendium*, 27(5) (2002): 6–19.

61 Bert Useem and Michael D. Reisig, "Collective Action in Prisons: Protests, Disturbances, and Riots," *Criminology*, 37(4) (1999): 735–60; Gerald G. Gaes, "Prison Crowding Research Reexamined," *Prison Journal*, 74(3) (1994): 329–63.

62 Glenn D. Walters, "Time Series and Correlational Analyses of Inmate-Initiated Assaultive Incidents in a Large Correctional System," *International Journal of Offender Therapy and Comparative Criminology*, 42(2) (1998): 124–32.

63 "Violence/Riots/Escapes: Violence in U.S. and Canadian Prisons Fairly Stable over Last Two Years," *Corrections Compendium,* 23(6) (1998): 7–20.

64 Quoted in Gerry O'Sullivan, "Violence and Institutions: Mapping the Ecology of Danger," available: http://www.Columbia.edu/cu/21stC/issue-1.2/Institutions.htm; Sheldon Ekland-Olson, "Crowding, Social Control, and Prison Violence: Evidence from the Post-Ruiz Years in Texas," *Law and Society Review*, 20(3) (1986): 389–421.

65 Harer and Steffensmeier, "Race and Prison Violence."

66 Knowles, "Male Prison Rape: A Search for Causation and Prevention."

67 Cindy Struckman, David Johnson, Lila Rucker, Kurt Bumby and Stephen Donaldson, "Sexual Coercion Reported by Men and Women in Prison," *Journal of Sex Research*, 33(1) (1996): 67–76.

68 See, generally, Joanne Mariner, *No Escape: Male Rape in U.S. Prisons* (New York: Human Rights Watch, 2001), pp. 1–394.

69 *Farmer v. Brennan*, 114 S.Ct. (1970).

70 Julie Kunselman, Richard Tewksbury, Robert W. Dumond and Doris A. Dumond, "Nonconsensual Sexual Behavior," in Christopher Hensley (ed.), *Prison Sex: Practice and Policy* (Boulder, CO: Lynne Rienner Publishers, 2002), pp. 27–47; Mary Dallao, "Fighting Prison Rape: How to Make Your Facility Safe," *Corrections Today*, Dec. (1996): 100–2, 104, 106.

71 Kunselman, Tewksbury, Dumond and Dumond, "Nonconsensual Sexual Behavior"; Silberman, *A World of Violence*, pp. 15, 73–74.

72 Mary Koscheski, Christopher Hensley, Jeremy Wright and Richard Tewksbury, "Consensual Sexual Behavior," in Christopher Hensley (ed.), *Prison Sex: Practice and Policy* (Boulder, CO: Lynne Rienner Publishers, 2002), pp. 111–31.

73 Charles W. Thomas and Robin J. Cage, "Correlates of Prison Drug Use: An Evaluation of Two Conceptual Models," *Criminology*, 15(2) (1977): 193–210; Ronald L. Akers, Norman S. Hayner and Werner Gruninger, "Homosexual and Drug Behavior in Prison: A Test of the Functional and Importation Models of the Inmate System," *Social Problems*, 21(3) (1974): 410–22.

74 Christine A. Saum, Hilary L. Surratt, James A. Inciardi and Rachael E. Bennett, "Sex in Prison: Exploring the Myths and Realities," *The Prison Journal*, 75(4) (1995): 413–30; Richard Tewksbury, "Measures of Sexual Behavior in an Ohio Prison," *Sociology and Social Research*, 74 (1989): 34–39.

75 *Ibid.*

76 Christopher Hensley, Sandra Rutland and Phyllis Gray-Ray, "Conjugal Visitation Programs: The Logical Conclusion," in Christopher Hensley (ed.), *Prison Sex: Practice and Policy* (Boulder, CO: Lynne Rienner Publishers, 2002), pp. 143–56.

77 Christopher Hensley, Sandra Rutland and Phyllis Gray-Ray, "Inmate Attitudes toward the Conjugal Visitation Program in Mississippi Prisons: An Exploratory Study," *American Journal of Criminal Justice*, 25(1) (2000): 137–45; Jill Gordon and Elizabeth H. McConnell, "Are Conjugal and Familial Visitations Effective Rehabilitative Concepts?" *Prison Journal*, 79(1) (1999): 119–35.

78 Christopher Birkbecj, Nora Campbell Wilson and Michelle Hussong, *Furloughs Granted to Minimum-security Inmates in New Mexico* (Albuquerque: New Mexico Criminal Justice Statistical Analysis Center, 1996), pp. 1–13.

79 *Fort Worth Star-Telegram*, "Mexican Mafia Leader's Death Sentence Upheld," Sept. 20, 2001, p. 5-B; Fleisher and Decker, "Overview of the Challenge of Prison Gangs, 2001"; *Dallas Morning News*, "Texas Prison Gangs."

CHAPTER NINE

[1] Meda Chesney-Lind, "Imprisoning Women: The Unintended Victims of Mass Imprisonment," in Marc Mauer and Meda Chesney-Lind (eds.), *Invisible Punishment: The Collateral Consequences of Mass Imprisonment* (New York: The New Press, 2002), p. 78

[2] Merry Morash and Pamela Schram, *The Prison Experience: Special Issues of Women in Prison* (Prospect Heights, IL: Waveland Press, 2003), p. 20.

[3] Paige M. Harrison and Allen J. Beck, *Prisoners in 2001* (Washington, DC: U.S. Dept. of Justice, Bureau of Justice Statistics, July 2002), NCJ-195189

[4] Chesney-Lind, "Imprisoning Women," p. 80.

[5] Harrison and Beck, *Prisoners in 2001*, table 18, p. 13.

[6] Patricia Allard, *Life Sentences: Denying Welfare Benefits to Women Convicted of Drug Offenses* (Washington, DC: The Sentencing Project, 2002), p. 25, available: http://www.sentencingproject.org/allard/lifesentences.pdf

[7] Harrison and Beck, *Prisoners in 2001*, table 17, p. 13.

[8] Tonia L. Nicholls and Donald G. Dutton, "Abuse Committed by Women Against Male Intimates," in Barbara Jo Brothers (ed.), *Abuse of Men: Trauma Begets Trauma* (Binghamton, NY: Haworth Press, 2001), pp. 41–57; Jody Miller, "Gender and the Accomplishment of Street Robbery," in Patricia A. Adler and Peter Adler (eds.), *Constructions of Deviance* (Belmont, CA: Wadsworth, 2001), pp. 502–20.

[9] Lawrence A. Greenfeld and Tracy L. Snell, *Women Offenders* (Washington, DC: U.S. Dept. of Justice, Bureau of Justice Statistics, revised October, 2000), p. 1, NCJ-175688.

[10] Allard, *Life Sentences*.

[11] *Sourcebook of Criminal Justice Statistics 2001*, table 6.35, p. 501, available: http://www.albany.edu/sourcebook/1995/pdf/section6.pdf

[12] *Women in Prison Project* (New York: Correctional Association of New York, 2002), available: http://www.correctionalassociation.org/images/Fact_Sheets_2002.pdf; Amnesty International, *Not Part of My Sentence: Violations of the Human Rights of Women in Custody* (New York: AI-USA, 1999), available: http://www.amnestyusa.org/rightsforall/women/

[13] Morash and Schram, *The Prison Experience*, pp. 48–70.

[14] Barbara Owen, "Women and Imprisonment in the United States: The Gendered Consequences of the U.S. Imprisonment Binge," in Sandy Cook and Susanne Davies (eds.), *Harsh Punishment: International Experiences of Women's Imprisonment* (Boston, MA: Northeastern University Press, 1999).

[15] Morash and Schram, *The Prison Experience*, p. 59.

[16] *Ibid.*, pp. 55–57; Marian R. Williams, "Gender and Sentencing: An Analysis of Indicators," *Criminal Justice Policy Review*, 10(4) (1999): 471–90.

[17] Candace Kruttschnitt and Sharon Krmpotich, "Aggressive Behavior among Female Inmates: An Exploratory Study," *Justice Quarterly*, 7 (1990): 371–89.

[18] L. Goodstein and K. N. Wright, "Inmate Adjustment to Prison," in L. Goodstein and Doris L. Mackenzie (eds.), *The American Prison* (New York: Plenum, 1989).

[19] Barbara Owen, *"In the Mix": Struggle and Survival in a Women's Prison* (Albany: State University of New York Press, 1998).

[20] Morash and Schram, *The Prison Experience*, p. 72

[21] Elaine Lord, "A Prison Superintendent's Perspective on Women in Prison," *The Prison Journal*, 75(2) (1995): 257–69.

[22] Timothy F. Hartnagel and Mary Ellen Gillan, "Female Prisoners and the Inmate Code," *Pacific Sociological Review*, 23(1) (1980): 85–104.

[23] Esther Heffernan, *Making It in Prison: The Square, the Cool and the Life* (New York: Wiley, 1972).

[24] Dorothy S. McClellan, "Disparity in the Discipline of Male and Female Inmates in Texas Prisons," *Women and Criminal Justice*, 5(2) (1994): 71–97.

[25] Danielle Laberge, Daphne Morin and Victor Armony, "Gendered Construction of Expert Discourse: An Analysis of Psychiatric Evaluations in Criminal Court," *Critical Criminology*, 9(2) (2000): 22–38.

[26] Morash and Schram, *The Prison Experience*, p. 149.

[27] Kathleen Auerhahn and Elizabeth Dermody Leonard, "Docile Bodies? Chemical Restraints and the Female Inmate," *Journal of Criminal Law and Criminology*, 90(2) (2000): 599–634.

[28] Laberge, Morin and Armony, "Gendered Construction of Expert Discourse."

[29] Richard S. Jones, "Coping with Separation: Adaptive Responses of Women Prisoners," *Women and Criminal Justice*, 5(1) (1993): 71–97.

[30] Morash and Schram, *The Prison Experience*, pp. 162–89.

[31] *Ibid.*, p. 162.

[32] Mark S. Fleisher, Richard H. Rison and David W. Helman, "Female Inmates: A Growing Constituency in the Federal Bureau of Prisons," *Corrections Management Quarterly*, 1(4) (1997): 28–35.

[33] Kay Hayes and John T. E. Richardson, "Gender, Subject and Context as Determinants of Approaches to Studying in Higher Education," *Studies in Higher Education*, 20(2) (1995): 215–21.

[34] Patrick Griffin, "Painful Secrets: Helping Traumatized Girls in Pennsylvania's Juvenile Justice System," *Pennsylvania Progress*, 7(4) (2001): 1–8; Merry Morash, Timothy S. Bynum and Barbara A. Koons, *Women Offenders: Programming Needs and Promising Approaches* (Washington, DC: U.S. Dept. of Justice, National Institute of Justice, 1998), pp. 1–21; Allison Morris and Chris Wilkinson, "Responding to Female Prisoners' Needs," *The Prison Journal*, 75(3) (1995): 277–94.

[35] Morash and Schram, *The Prison Experience*, pp. 182–84.

[36] Amnesty International, "Mothers in Prison" in *Not Part of My Sentence.* (New York: AI-USA, 1999), available: http://www.amnestyusa.org/rightsforall/women/report/women-101.html#P275_37251

[37] "Inmate Health Care, Part II," *Corrections Compendium*, 23(11) (November 1998): 11.

[38] Amnesty International, *Abuse of Women in Custody: Sexual Misconduct and Shackling of Pregnant Women* (New York: AI-USA, Mar. 6, 2001), pp. 1–110.

[39] T. A. Ryan and James B. Grassano, "Taking a Progressive Approach to Treating Pregnant Offenders," *Corrections Today*, 54(6) (1992): 184–86.

[40] *Ibid.*

[41] Laura M. Maruschak, *HIV in Prisons, 2000* (Washington, DC: U.S. Dept. of Justice, Bureau of Justice Statistics, 2002), p. 4, NCJ-196023; Theodore M. Hammett, Patricia Harmon and Laura M. Maruschak, *1996–1997 Update: HIV/AIDS, STDs, and TB in Correctional Facilities* (Washington, DC: National Institute of Justice, 1999), p. 10, NCJ-176344.

[42] Maruschak, *HIV in Prisons, 2000*, p. 3.

[43] Morash and Schram, *The Prison Experience*, pp. 170–71.

[44] Judy Clark and Kathy Boudin, "Community of Women Organize Themselves to Cope with the AIDS Crisis: A Case Study from Bedford Hills Correctional Facility," *Social Justice*, 17(2) (1990): 90–109.

[45] Angela D. West and Randy Martin, "Perceived Risk of AIDS Among Prisoners Following Educational Intervention," *Journal of Offender Rehabilitation*, 32(2) (2000): 75–104.

[46] Christopher J. Mumola, *Incarcerated Parents and their Children* (Washington, DC: U.S. Dept. of Justice, Bureau of Justice Statistics, 2000), pp. 1–12, NCJ-182335.

[47] Carolyn Kleiner, "Breaking the Cycle: Can the Children of Convicts Learn Not to Be Like Their Parents?", *U.S. News & World Report*, 132(14) (April 29, 2002): 49; Susan Greene, Craig Haney and Aida Hurtado, "Cycles of Pain: Risk Factors in the Lives of Incarcerated Mothers and Their Children," *Prison Journal*, 80(1) (2000): 2–23.

[48] Gloria Logan, "Family Ties Take Top Priority in Women's Visiting Program," *Corrections Today*, 54(6) (1992): 160–61.

[49] Martha K. Wilson, Peggy Quinn and Barbara A. Beville, "Reducing Recidivism for Women Inmates: The Search for Alternatives," *Journal of Offender Rehabilitation*, 27(3-4) (1998): 61–76.

[50] *Ibid*; Greene, Haney and Hurtado, "Cycles of Pain."

[51] Wilson, Quinn and Beville, "Reducing Recidivism for Women Inmates"; Barbara Bloom, "Incarcerated Mothers and Their Children: Maintaining Family Ties," in American Correctional Association (eds.), *Female Offenders: Meeting Needs of a Neglected Population* (Laurel, MD: American Correctional Association, 1993), pp. 60–67; Judith Clark, "The Impact of the Prison Environment on Mothers," *The Prison Journal*, 75(3) (1995): 307–29

[52] Logan, "Family Ties Take Top Priority in Women's Visiting Program."

[53] Paula N. Rubin, *Civil Rights and Criminal Justice: Primer on Sexual Harassment* (Washington, DC: U.S. Dept. of Justice, 1995), pp. 1–7, citing *Meritor Savings Bank v. Vinson*, 477 U.S. 57, 40 FEP Cases 1822 (1986).

[54] Avery J. Calhoun and Heather D. Coleman, "Female Inmates' Perspectives on Sexual Abuse by Correctional Personnel: An Exploratory Study," *Women & Criminal Justice* 13(2/3) (2002): 101–24.

[55] LIS, Inc., *Sexual Misconduct in Prisons: Law, Remedies, and Incidence* (Longmont, CO: National Institute of Corrections, 2000), pp. 1–14.

[56] Julianne C. Taylor, "Vulnerable to Violence," *Amnesty Now*, 25(2) (2001): 19, citing Amnesty International, *Abuse of Women in Custody: Sexual Misconduct and Shackling of Pregnant Women* (New York: AI-USA, Mar. 6, 2001); Amnesty International, *Not Part of My Sentence*.

[57] LIS, Inc., *Sexual Misconduct in Prisons*, p. 5.

[58] James W. Marquart, Maldine B. Barnhill and Kathy Balshaw-Biddle, "Fatal Attraction: An Analysis of Employee Boundary Violations in a Southern Prison, 1995–1998," *Justice Quarterly*, 18(4) (2001): 877–910; Danny Burton, Eric Erdman, Geoffrey Hamilton and Kay Muse, "Women in Prison: Sexual Misconduct by Correctional Staff" (Washington, DC: U.S. General Accounting Office, 1999), pp. 1–31.

[59] Burton, Erdman, Hamilton and Muse, "Women in Prison."

[60] Kathleen Maguire and Ann L. Pastore, *Sourcebook of Criminal Justice Statistics 1996* (Washington, DC: U.S. Dept. of Justice, 1997), tables 1.106, 6.43, pp. 94, 541, NCJ-165361.

[61] See, generally, Kelly Hannah-Moffat, *Punishment in Disguise* (Toronto: University of Toronto Press, 2001); Kelly Hannah-Moffat and Margaret Shaw (eds.), *The Ideal Prison* (Halifax, Nova Scotia, Fernwood, 2000); Kelly Hannah-Moffat, "Feminine Fortresses: Woman-Centered Prisons?" *The Prison Journal*, 75(2) (1995): 135–64.

[62] American Correctional Association, *The American Prison: From the Beginning* (Laurel, MD: American Correctional Association, 1983), p. 175.

[63] James R. Davis, "Co-Corrections in the U.S.," *Corrections Compendium*, 23(3): 1–3 (Lanham, MD: American Correctional Association, March 1988).

[64] John O. Smykla and Jimmy J. Williams, "Co-Corrections in the United States of America, 1970–1990: Two Decades of Disadvantages for Women Prisoners," *Women and Criminal Justice*, 8(1) (1996): 61–76.

CHAPTER TEN

[1] Chadwick L. Shook and Robert Sigler, *Constitutional Issues in Correctional Administration* (Durham, NC: Carolina Academic Press, 2000), p. 9; Edgardo Rotman, "The Failure of Reform: United States, 1865–1965," in Norval Morris and David J. Rothman (eds.), *The Oxford History of the Prison* (Oxford University Press, 1995), p. 191.

[2] *Ruffin v. Commonwealth*, 62 Va. (21 Gratt) 790 (1871).

[3] *Ex Parte Hull*, 312 U.S. 546 (1941).

[4] *Johnson v. Avery*, 393 U.S. 483 (1969).

[5] Kenneth C. Haas and Geoffrey P. Alpert, "American Prisoners and the Right of Access to the Courts," in Haas and Alpert (eds.), *The Dilemmas of Corrections*, 4th ed. (Prospect Heights, IL: Waveland Press, 1999).

[6] *Ibid.*

[7] *Casey v. Lewis*, 43 F.3d 1261 (9th Cir., 1994).

[8] *Lewis v. Casey*, 116 S.Ct. 2174, 135 L.Ed.2d 606 (1996).

[9] *O'Sullivan v. Boerckel*, 119 S.Ct. 1728 (1999).

[10] *Holt v. Sarver*, 306 F Supp. 362 (1970), 442 F.2d 304 (8th Cir. 1971).

[11] *Newman v. Alabama*, 349 F. Supp. 278 (M.D.Ala. 1974).

[12] *Pugh v. Locke*, 98 S.Ct. 3144 (1976).

[13] *Hutto v. Finney*, 98 S.Ct. 2565 (1978).

[14] *Ruiz v. Estelle*, 503 F.Supp. 1265 (S.D. Texas, 1980).

[15] William A. Taggart, "Redefining the Power of the Federal Judiciary: The Impact of Court-Ordered Prison Reform on State Expenditures for Corrections," *Law and Society Review*, 23(2) (1989): 241–71.

[16] William C. Collins, *Correctional Law for the Correctional Officer* (Laurel, MD: American Correctional Association, 1993), pp. 10–11, citing *Jones v. North Carolina Prisoners Labor Union*, 433 U.S. 119 (1977); *Bell v. Wolfish*, 441 U.S. 529 (1979); *Rhodes v. Chapman*, 452 U.S. 337 (1981).

[17] Lynn S. Branham and Sheldon Krantz, *The Law of Sentencing, Corrections and Prisoners' Rights*, 5th ed. (St Paul: West, 1997), pp. 443–50, citing *Bell v. Wolfish*, 441 U.S. 520, 99 S.Ct. 1861, 60 L.Ed.2d 447 (1979).

[18] *Rhodes v. Chapman*, 452 U.S. 337, 101 S.Ct. 2392, 69 L.Ed.2d 59 (1981).

[19] Gary W. Deland, "Developing a 'Rationale' for Administrative Policies and Practices: The Key to Thriving in a Litigious Environment," *Corrections Managers' Report*, 1(1) (1995): 3–4, 14.

[20] John A. Fliter, *Prisoners' Rights: The Supreme Court and Evolving Standards of Decency* (Westport, CT: Greenwood Publishing Group, 2001), pp. 100–68; Jack E. Call, "The Supreme Court and Prisoners' Rights," *Federal Probation*, 59(1) (1995): 36–46.

[21] Shook and Sigler, *Constitutional Issues in Correctional Administration*, pp. 21–2, 146–49; Collins, *Correctional Law for the Correctional Officer*, p. 57.

[22] *Cooper v. Pate*, 378 U.S. 546, 84 S.Ct. 1733 (1964).

[23] *Cruz v. Beto*, 405 U.S. 319, 92 S.Ct. 1079 (1972).

[24] *O'Lone v. Estate of Shabazz*, 482 U.S. 342, 107 S.Ct. 2400 (1987).

[25] Julie C. Abril, "The Native American Identity Phenomenon," *Corrections Compendium*, 27(4) (2002): 1–4; James B. Waldram, *The Way of the Pipe: Aboriginal Spirituality and Symbolic Healing in Canadian Prisons* (Peterborough, Ontario: Broadview Press, 1997); Marianne O. Nielsen, "Canadian Correctional Policy and Native Inmates: The Control of Social Dynamite," *Canadian Ethnic Studies*, 22(3) (1990): 111–21; James B. Waldram, "Aboriginal Spirituality in Corrections: A Canadian Case Study in Religion and Therapy," *American Indian Quarterly*, 18(2) (1994): 194–214; Marianne O. Nielsen, personal communication, Jan., 17, 1996.

[26] See, for example, *Jones v. Bradley*, 590 F.2d 294 (9th Cir.,1979); *Theriault v. A Religious Office*, 895 F.2d 104 (2d Cir., 1990) and cases cited therein.

[27] Shook and Sigler, *Constitutional Issues in Correctional Administration*, pp. 62–66 citing *O'Lone v. Estate of Shabazz*, 107 S.Ct. 2400 (1987); *Turner v. Safley*, 107 S.Ct. 2254 (1987).

[28] *O'Lone v. Estate of Shabazz*, 107 S.Ct. 2400 (1987); *Standing Deer v. Carlson*, 831 F.2d 1525 (1987); *Turner v. Safley*, 107 S.Ct. 2254 (1987); *Benjamin v. Coughlin*, 708 F.Supp. 570 (1989).

[29] *Udey v. Kastner*, 805 F.2d 218 (5th Cir., 1986); *Benjamin v. Coughlin*, 708 F.Supp. 570 (1989).

[30] *Standing Deer v. Carlson*, 831 F.2d 1525 (1987); *Benjamin v. Coughlin*, 708 F.Supp. 570 (1989); *Scott v. Mississippi Department of Corrections*, U.S. App. (5th Cir., 1992).

[31] *Procunier v. Martinez*, 94 S.Ct. 1800 (1974).

[32] *Turner v. Safley*, 482 U.S. 78, 107 S.Ct. 2254, 96 L.Ed.2d 64 (1987); citing *Bell v. Wolfish*, 441 U.S. 529 (1979); *Jackson v. Elrod*, 881 F.2d 441 (7th Cir., 1989).

[33] *Thornburgh v. Abbott*, 109 S.Ct. 1874 (1989).

[34] *Harper v. Wallingford*, 877 F.2d 728 (9th Cir., 1989).

[35] *Procunier v. Martinez*, 94 S.Ct. 1800 (1974).

[36] U.S. 78, 107 *Turner v. Safley*, 482 S.Ct. 2254, 2254, 96 L.Ed.2d 64 (1987).

[37] *Thornburgh v. Abbott*, 109 S.Ct. 1874 (1989).

[38] *Shaw v. Murphy*, No. 99-1613 (2001).

[39] Collins, *Correctional Law for the Correctional Officer*, p. 65, citing *KQED v. Houchins*, 438 U.S. 1 (1978); *Mann v. Adams*, 846 F.2d 591 (9th Cir., 1988) and *Gaines v. Lane*, 790 F.2d 1299 (7th Cir., 1986).

[40] Collins, *Correctional Law for the Correctional Officer*, p. 66, citing *Jones v. North Carolina Prisoners' Labor Union*, 433 U.S. 119 (1977).

[41] *Hudson v. Palmer*, 104 S.Ct. 3194 (1984); *Bell v. Wolfish*, 441 U.S. 529 (1979).

[42] Collins, *Correctional Law for the Correctional Officer*, pp. 69–70.

[43] *Terry v. Ohio*, 1968, 392 U.S. 1, 88 S.Ct. 1868, 20 L.Ed.2d 889 (1968); *Brown v. Texas*, 443 U.S., 99 S.Ct. 2637, 61 L.Ed.2d 357 (1979).

[44] Collins, *Correctional Law for the Correctional Officer*, pp. 69–72.

[45] *Hudson v. Palmer*, 104 S.Ct. 3194 (1984); *Bell v. Wolfish*, 441 U.S. 529 (1979).

[46] *Hudson v. Palmer*, 104 S.Ct. 3194 (1984).

[47] *Brown v. Hilton*, 492 F.Supp. 771 (D.N.J., 1980); *Hudson v. Palmer*, 104 S.Ct. 3194 (1984); *Block v. Rutherford*, 104 S.Ct. 3227 (1984).

[48] Collins, *Correctional Law for the Correctional Officer*, pp. 70–75, citing *Goff v. Nix*, 803 F.2d 358 (8th Cir., 1986).

[49] *Griffin v. Wisconsin*, 483 U.S. 868 (1988).

[50] *Pennsylvania Board of Probation and Parole v. Scott*, 118 S.Ct. 2014 (1998).

[51] *U.S. v. Knights*, No. 00-1260 (2001); *Lee v. Kemna*, No. 00-6933 (2002).

[52] *U.S. v. Sullivan*, 625 F.2d 9, at 13 4th Cir. (1980); *New Jersey v. T.L.O.*, 469 U.S. 325, 83 L.Ed.2d 720, 105 S.Ct. 733 (1985); *U.S. v. Biswell*, 406 U.S. 311 (1972); Rolando V. del Carmen, *Criminal Procedure: Law and Practice*, 3d ed. (Belmont, CA: Wadsworth, 1995), pp. 203–4.

[53] *U.S. v. Knights*, No. 00-1260 (2001).

54 Jonathan D. Salant, "Court to Consider Inmate Visit Limits," Associated Press, Dec. 2, 2002, citing *Overton v. Bazetta*, 02-94. http://www.rr.com/v5/1/my/news/story/0,2050,1154_304596,00.html

55 *Trop v. Dulles*, 356 U.S. 86, 78 S.Ct. 590, 2d 630 (1958).

56 *Holt v. Sarver*, 306 F. Supp. 362 (1970), 442 F.2d.

57 *Estelle v. Gamble*, 429 U.S. 97, S.Ct. 285 (1976).

58 Collins, *Correctional Law for the Correctional Officer*, pp. 80–81.

59 *Ibid.*, pp. 82–85; *Trop v. Dulles*, 356 U.S.86, 78 S. Ct. 590, 2d 630 (1958); *Weems v. U.S.*, 217 U.S. 349, 30 S.Ct. 54454 L.Ed. 793 (1910); *Lee v. Tahash*, 352 F.2d 970 (8th Cir. 1965).

60 *Ruiz v. Estelle*, 503 F.Supp. 1265 (S.D. Texas, 1980); "Ruiz Dateline," *The Newsletter* (Huntsville: Texas Department of Criminal Justice, 1993), p. 4.

61 *Smith v. Wade*, 461 U.S. 30, 103 S.Ct. 1625 (1983).

62 Dan Eckhart, "Civil Actions Related to Prison Gangs: A Survey of Federal Cases," *Corrections Management Quarterly*, 5(1) (2001): 59–64; Brian Saccenti, "Preventing Summary Judgement against Inmates Who Have Been Sexually Assaulted by Showing That the Risk Was Obvious," *Maryland Law Review*, 59(3) (2000): 642–68.

63 *Davidson v. Cannon*, 474 U.S. 344, 106 S.Ct. 668 (1986).

64 *Daniels v. Williams*, 474 U.S. 327, 106 S.Ct. 662 (1986).

65 John Scalia, *Prisoner Petitions in the Federal Courts, 1980–1996* (Washington, DC: U.S. Dept. of Justice, 1997), p. 11; Collins, *Correctional Law for the Correctional Officer*, pp. 18–20.

66 *Estelle v. Gamble*, 429 U.S. 97, 97 S.Ct. 285 (1976).

67 *Wilson v. Seiter*, 501 U.S. 294, 111 S.Ct. 2321 (1991).

68 *Forbes v. Edgar*, 112 F. 3d 262 (7th Cir., 1997).

69 *Whitley v. Albers*, 475 U.S. 312, 106 S.Ct. (1986).

70 *Hudson v. Macmillian*, 503 U.S. 1, 112 S.Ct. 995 (1992). Justice Thomas, in a dissenting opinion, objected to this reasoning on the basis that "use of excessive force is (not always) accompanied by a 'malicious and sadistic' state of mind."

71 "Hitting a Moving Target While Avoiding Self-Inflicted Injury," *Corrections Managers' Report*, 1(3) (1995): 1–2, 14.

72 *Wolff v. McDonnell*, 418 U.S. 539 (1974).

73 *Wells v. Israel*, 629 F.Supp. 498 (E.D.Wisc., 1986); *McCollum v. Williford*, 793 F.2d 903 (7th Cir., 1986).

74 Collins, *Correctional Law for the Correctional Officer*, p. 48.

75 *Superintendent, Massachusetts Correctional Institution, Walpole v. Hill*, 472 U.S. 445, 105 S.Ct. 2768 (1985).

76 *Ponte v. Real*, 471, U.S. 491, 105 S.Ct. 2192 (1985).

77 *Ibid.*

78 Michael P. Hodge, "A Look at Some Recent Cases following *Sandin v. Connor*," *Corrections Managers' Report*, 1(5) (1996): 7–8, 12, citing *Bulger v. U.S. Bureau of Prisons*, 65 F.3d 48 (5th Cir, 1995); *Seltzer-Bey v. Delo*, 66 F.3d 961 (8th Cir., 1995); *Pratt v. Rowland*, 65 F.3d 802 (9th Cir., 1995); and *Gotcher v. Wood*, 66 F.3d 1097 (9th Cir., 1995).

79 Hodge, "A Look at Some Recent Cases Following *Sandin v. Connor*," pp. 7–8, 12, citing *Zanes v. Rhodes*, 64 F.3d 285 (7th Cir., 1995); *Mitchell v. Dupnik*, 67 F.3d 216 (9th Cir., 1995); and *Pratt v. Rowland*, 65 F.3d 802 (9th Cir., 1995).

80 Shook and Sigler, *Constitutional Issues in Correctional Administration*, citing *McCormack v. Stadler*, 105 F. 3d 1059 (5th Cir. 1997) and *Doby v. Hickson*, 120 F. 3d 111 (8th Cir. 1997).

81 *Washington v. Harper*, 110 S.Ct. 864 (1990).

82 Collins, *Correctional Law for the Correctional Officer*, p. 54, citing *David K. v. Lane*, 839 F.2d 1265 (7th Cir., 1988).

83 Dan Eckhart, "Civil Actions Related to Prison Gangs: A Survey of Federal Cases," *Corrections Management Quarterly*, 5(1) (2001): 59–64.

84 *Glover v. Johnson*, 478 F. Supp. 1075 (E.D. Mich., 1979).

85 Collins, *Correctional Law for the Correctional Officer*, p. 54, citing *French v. Owens*, 777 F.2d 1250 (7th Cir., 1985).

86 Scalia, *Prisoner Petitions in the Federal Courts, 1980–1996*, p. 11.

87 Shook and Sigler, *Constitutional Issues in Correctional Administration*, pp. 20–22, citing *O'Sullivan v. Boerckell* 119 S.Ct. 1728 (1999).

[88] "Frivolous Suits," *Jail and Prisoner Law Bulletin* (Chicago: Americans for Effective Law Enforcement, n.d.), pp. 3–4; Coalition Against STOP, Dec. 28, 1995.

[89] Jeffrey R. Maahs and Craig Hemmens, "The Prison Litigation Reform Act and Frivolous Section 1983 Suits," *Corrections Management Quarterly*, 2(3) (1998): 90–94.

[90] Shook and Sigler, *Constitutional Issues in Correctional Administration*, pp. 47–54; "New Law Curbs Lawsuits," *Corrections Digest*, 27(22) May 31 (1996): 1–2.

[91] Eric Tischler, "Supreme Court Decisions Stay the Course," *On the Line*, 21(4) Sept. (1998): 1–2, citing *Crawford-El v. Britton*.

[92] Shook and Sigler, *Constitutional Issues in Correctional Administration*, citing *Benjamin v. Jacobsen* (1997) and *Tyler v. Murphy* 135 F.3d 594, 1998.

[93] Shook and Sigler, *Constitutional Issues in Correctional Administration*, p. 52; William L. Selke, *Prisons in Crisis* (Bloomington: Indiana University Press, 1993), pp. 102–4; Texas Department of Criminal Justice, "About TDCJ's Ombudsmen," *Criminal Justice Connections*, Mar./Apr. (1997): 8.

[94] Giovanna Shay, "Sexual Abuse and Civil Rights: The Impact of the PLRA Physical Injury Requirement," *National Prison Project Journal*, 12(4) (1999): 1–5.

[95] Ken Armstrong and Maurice Possley, "The Verdict: Dishonor," *Chicago Tribune*, Jan. 10, 1999, Section 1, pp. 1, 12.

[96] *Booth v. Churner*, 532 U.S. ___ (2001).

[97] Shook and Sigler, *Constitutional Issues in Correctional Administration*, pp. 54, 150.

[98] Christopher E. Smith, "Governance of Corrections: Implications of the Changing Interface of Courts and Corrections," in Charles M. Friel (ed.), *Boundary Changes in Criminal Justice Organizations: Criminal Justice 2000*, Vol. 2 (Rockville MD: National Institute of Justice, 2000), pp. 113–66, NCJ-182409.

CHAPTER ELEVEN

[1] Robert A. Shearer, "Coerced Substance Abuse Counseling Revisited," *Journal of Offender Rehabilitation*, 30(3-4) (2000): 153–71.

[2] Peter Finn, *The Delaware Department of Correction Life Skills Program* (Washington, DC: National Institute of Justice, Office of Correctional Education, 1998), pp. 1–19, NCJ-169589; James A. Swartz, Arthur J. Lurigio and Scott A. Slomka, "The Impact of IMPACT: An Assessment of the Effectiveness of a Jail-Based Treatment Program," *Crime and Delinquency*, 42(4) (1996): 553–73; Yvonne Terry-McElrath, Duane McBride, Curtis J. Vander Waal and Erin Ruel, "Integrating Criminal Justice, Treatment, and Community Agencies to Break the Drugs/Crime Cycle," *Corrections Today*, August (2002): 78–83, 116–18.

[3] Mikail Muhammad, "Prisoners' Perspectives on Strategies for Release," *Journal of Offender Rehabilitation*, 23(2) (1996): 131–52.

[4] Caroline Wolf Harlow, *Education and Correctional Populations* (Washington, DC: Bureau of Justice Statistics, 2003), pp. 1, 2, NCJ-195670.

[5] Carol Strayhorn, *Blackboards behind Bars* (Austin: State of Texas, 2001), available: http://www.window.state.tx.us/comptrol/fnotes/fn0103/fn.html#blackboards

[6] Harlow, *Education and Correctional Populations*.

[7] Kirsten Rasmussen, Roger Almvik and Sten Levander, "Attention Deficit Hyperactivity Disorder, Reading Disability, and Personality Disorders in a Prison Population," *Journal of the American Academy of Psychiatry and the Law*, 29(2) (2001): 186–93; Judith A. Whichard, Richard W. Feller and Ruthanne Kastner, "The Incidence of Scotopic Sensitivity Syndrome in Colorado Inmates," *Journal of Correctional Education*, 51(3) (2000): 294–98.

[8] Alma I. Martinez, Michael Eisenberg and Nancy Arrigona, *Impact of Educational Achievement of Inmates in the Windham School District on Post-Release Employment* (Austin: Texas Criminal Justice Policy Council, 2000), pp. 1–30.

[9] T. A. Ryan and Kimberly McCabe, "Mandatory versus Voluntary Prison Education and Academic Achievement," *The Prison Journal*, 74(4) (1994): 450–61.

[10] Reginald A. Wilkinson, "Offender Reentry: A Storm Overdue," *Corrections Management Quarterly*, 5(3) (2001): 46–51; Jessie L. Krienert and Mark S. Fleisher, "Gang Membership as a Proxy for Social Deficiencies: A Study of Nebraska Inmates," *Corrections Management Quarterly*, 5(1) (2001): 47–58; Thomas P. Ryan and Joseph F. Desuta, "Comparison of Recidivism Rates for Operation Outward

Reach (OOR) Participants and Control Groups of Non-Participants for the Years 1990 through 1994," *Journal of Correctional Education*, 51(4) (2000): 316–19; David B. Wilson, Catherine A. Gallagher and Doris L. MacKenzie, "Meta-Analysis of Corrections-Based Education, Vocation, and Work Programs for Adult Offenders," *Journal of Research in Crime and Delinquency*, 37(4) (2000): 347–68; Kenneth Adams, Katherine J. Bennett, Timothy J. Flanagan, James W. Marquart, Steven J. Cuvelier, Eric Fritsch, Jurg Gerber, Dennis R. Longmire and Velmer S. Burton, Jr., "A Large-Scale Multidimensional Test of the Effect of Prison Education Programs on Offenders' Behavior," *Prison Journal*, 74(4) (1994): 433–49.

[11] Gennaro F. Vito and Richard Tewksbury, "Improving the Educational Skills of Inmates: The Results of an Impact Evaluation," *Corrections Compendium*, 24(10) (1999): 1–17; K. E. Needels, "Go Directly to Jail and Do Not Collect—A Long-Term Study of Recidivism, Employment, and Earnings Patterns among Prison Releasees," *Journal of Research in Crime and Delinquency*, 33(4) (1996): 471–96.

[12] Richard Tewksbury, "Literacy Programming for Jail Inmates: Reflections and Recommendations from One Program," *Prison Journal*, 74(4) (1994): 398–413; Anabel P. Newman, *Prison Literacy: Implications for Program and Assessment Policy* (Washington, DC: Office of Educational Research and Improvement, 1993); Peter Sutton, *Basic Education in Prisons: Interim Report* (Hamburg, Germany: United Nations Educational, Scientific, and Cultural Organization, Institute for Education, 1992).

[13] Stephen Duguid, "Confronting Worst Case Scenarios: Education and High Risk Offenders," *Journal of Correctional Education*, 48(4) (1997): 153–59.

[14] David B. Wilson, Catherine A. Gallagher and Doris L. MacKenzie, "A Meta-Analysis of Corrections-Based Education, Vocation, and Work Programs for Adult Offenders," *Journal of Research in Crime and Delinquency*, 37(4) (2000): 347–68.

[15] Dennis J. Stevens and Charles S. Ward, "College Education and Recidivism: Educating Criminals Is Meritorious," *Journal of Correctional Education*, 48(3) (1997): 106–11.

[16] Stephen Duguid, *Can Prisons Work? The Prisoner as Object and Subject in Modern Corrections* (Toronto, Ontario: University of Toronto Press, 2000).

[17] Stevens and Ward, "College Education and Recidivism."

[18] Michael G. Pass, "Race Relations and the Implications of Education within Prison," *Journal of Offender Counseling, Services and Rehabilitation*, 12(2) (1988): 145–51.

[19] Ahmad Tootoonchi, "College Education in Prisons: The Inmates' Perspectives," *Federal Probation*, 57(4) (1993): 34–40; Duguid, "Confronting Worst Case Scenarios: Education and High Risk Offenders."

[20] Mark R. Leary, Lisa S. Schreindorfer and Allison L. Haupt, "The Role of Low Self-Esteem in Emotional and Behavioral Problems," *Journal of Social and Clinical Psychology*, 14(3) (fall 1995): 297–314; Richard M. Gray, "Addictions and the Self: A Self-Enhancement Model for Drug Treatment in the Criminal Justice System," *Journal of Social Work Practice in the Addictions*, 1(2) (2001): 75–91.

[21] Brandon K. Applegate, "Penal Austerity: Perceived Utility, Desert, and Public Attitudes toward Prison Amenities," *American Journal of Criminal Justice*, 25(2) (2001): 253–68.

[22] Scott K. Smith, "Prison Literacy Programs Benefit from S. K. Smith's Colorful Writing Style," *Journal of Correctional Education*, 47(1) (1996): 14–19.

[23] Patricia Franklin, "Read to Succeed: An Inmate to Inmate Literacy Program in Washington State," *Journal of Correctional Education*, 51(3) (2000): 286–92.

[24] Gail C. Arnell, "Safety Net: A 24 Hour Educational Network," *Corrections Today*, July (2002): 88–91.

[25] Graham T. T. Molitor, "Should Prison Inmates Receive Education Benefits?" *On the Horizon*, 2(4) (1994): 9–10; Charles Pell and Kaye B. Hutchinson, "Should Inmates Get Student Aid? NO: Deserving Pupils Lose Out on Pell Grants. YES: Pell Grants Dramatically Reduce Recidivism," *USA Today*, Mar. 17, 1994, p. 13-A.

[26] Sam Walker, "Inmates Pay Debt to Society and Taxpayers—With Cash," *Christian Science Monitor*, Feb. 26, 1996, p. 1.

[27] Paul Sommers, B. Mauldin and S. Levin, *Pioneer Human Services: A Case Study* (Seattle: Northwest Policy Center, Daniel J. Evans School of Public Affairs, University of Washington, 2000), pp. 1–10; William G. Saylor and Gerald D. Gaes, "The Post-Release Employment Project: Prison Work Has Measurable Effects on Post Release Success," in Peter C. Kratcoski (, *Correctional Counseling and Treatment*, 3rd ed. (Prospect Heights, IL: Waveland Press, 1994).

[28] James W. Marquart, Steven J. Cuvelier, Velmer S. Burton, Jr., Kenneth Adams, Jurg Gerber, Dennis Longmire, Timothy J. Flanagan, Kathy Bennett and Eric Fritsch, "A Limited Capacity to Treat: Exam-

ining the Effects of Prison Population Control Strategies on Prison Education Programs," *Crime and Delinquency*, 40(4) (1994): 516–31.

[29] Randall Guynes and Robert C. Grieser, "Contemporary Prison Industry Goals," *A Study of Prison Industry: History, Components and Goals* (Washington, DC: U.S. Dept. of Justice, Jan. 1986), pp. 20–24.

[30] James Duffy, "Illiteracy, A National Crisis," *Corrections Today*, 50, Oct. (1988): 44–45; John A. Conley, "Prisons, Production, and Profit: Reconsidering the Importance of Prison Industries," *Journal of Social History*, 14(2) (1980): 257–75.

[31] "Prison Industries," *Corrections Compendium*, 25(3) (2000): 9–21.

[32] Guynes and Grieser, "Contemporary Prison Industry Goals," p. 24–26.

[33] Peter A. York, "Privatization of Prisons: A Look at the Issues Surrounding Private Sector Involvement in Prisons and Prison Industries within North America," *Security Journal*, 4(3) (1993): 129–38.

[34] Susan L. Clayton, "Weight Lifting in Corrections: Luxury or Necessity," *On the Line* (Lanham, MD: American Correctional Association, Nov. 1997), pp. 1, 3.

[35] Office of Correctional Job Training and Placement, "Report to the United States Congress," June 2001, available: http://www.nicic.org/pubs/2001/017080-old.pdf

[36] Sommers, Mauldin and Levin, *Pioneer Human Services: A Case Study*; Melinda M. Hohman, Richard P. McGaffigan and Lance Segars, "Predictors of Successful Completion of a Postincarceration Drug Treatment Program," *Journal of Addictions and Offender Counseling*, 21(1) (2000): 12–22; Thomas E. Hanlon, Kevin O'Grady and Richard W. Bateman, "Using the Addiction Severity Index to Predict Treatment Outcome among Substance Abusing Parolees," *Journal of Offender Rehabilitation*, 31(3-4) (2000): 67–79; Thomas E. Hanlon, Richard W. Bateman and Kevin E. O'Grady, "The Relative Effects of Three Approaches to the Parole Supervision of Narcotic Addicts and Cocaine Abusers," *Prison Journal*, 79(2) (1999): 163–81; James A. Inciardi, *A Corrections Based Continuum of Effective Drug Abuse Treatment* (Washington, DC: U.S. Dept. of Justice, 1996), pp. 1–2.

[37] Adam M. Bossler, Mark S. Fleischer and Jessie Krienert, "Employment and Crime: Revisiting the Resiliency Effect of Work on Crime," *Corrections Compendium*, 25(2) (2000): 1–2, 16–18.

[38] Mark Gornik, *Moving from Correctional Program to Correctional Strategy: Using Proven Practices to Change Criminal Behavior* (Washington, DC: National Institute of Corrections, 2001), available: http://www.nicic.org/pubs/2001/017624.pdf

[39] Dora Schiro, *Correcting Corrections: Missouri's Parallel Universe* (Rockville, MD: U.S. Dept. of Justice, Office of Justice Programs, 2000), pp. 1–8, NCJ-181414.

[40] Edwin Meese, III and Knut A. Rostad, "Prison Industries and Public Opinion: A Unique Opportunity to Redefine the Business of Corrections to Our Most Demanding Customer," *Corrections Management Quarterly*, 1(3) (1997): 36–43.

[41] D. J. Williams, "Fit to be Fit: Lowering Relapse Rates, Improving Thinking, and Curing Depression," *Corrections Technology and Management*, 5(1) (2001): 48–49; National Institute of Mental Health, *Child and Adolescent Violence Research at the NIMH* (Bethesda, MD: National Institute of Mental Health, National Institutes of Health, 2000), pp. 1–11, NIH 00-4706; Jiri Modestin, Andreas Hug and Roland Ammann, "Criminal Behavior in Males with Affective Disorders," *Journal of Affective Disorders*, 42 (1997): 29–38.

[42] D. J. Williams, "Exercise and Substance Abuse Treatment: Predicting Program Completion Using Logistic Regression," *Corrections Compendium*, 25(2) (2000): 3–7.

[43] Susan L. Clayton, "Weight Lifting in Corrections—Inmate Privileges: Jurisdictions Restrict Inmate Privileges in Response to Legislative Public Outcry," *Corrections Compendium*, 23(7) (Lanham, MD: American Correctional Association, July 1998), pp. 6–16.

[44] Dale K. Pace, "Dealing with the Whole Person," *American Jails*, 14(4) (2000): 41–47; Mede Nix, "Christian Group Makes Prison Bill," *Fort Worth Star-Telegram*, Aug. 2, 1998, p. B-4.

[45] "Religion Behind Bars," *Corrections Compendium*, 23(4) (1998): 8–21.

[46] Josiah N. Opata, *Spiritual and Religious Diversity in Prisons: Focusing on How Chaplaincy Assists in Prison Management* (Springfield, IL: Charles C Thomas, 2001); Rich Brown, "We Exist Primarily for Them," *The Joplin Globe*, Oct. 21, 1996, p. B-1.

[47] Diane Cook, "Prison Chaplain Services: A Hand to Hold Behind the Wall," *Corrections Technology & Management*, 5(5) (2001): 44–46.

[48] Todd R. Clear, Patricia L. Hardyman and Bruce Stout, "The Value of Religion in Prison: An Inmate Perspective," *Journal of Contemporary Criminal Justice*, 16(1) (2000): 53–74; James B. Waldram, *The Way of the Pipe: Aboriginal Spirituality and Symbolic Healing in Canadian Prisons* (Peterborough, Ontario: Broadview Press, 1997).

[49] Melvina T. Sumter, *Religiousness and Post-Release Community Adjustment Graduate Research Fellowship—Executive Summary* (Rockville, MD: U.S. Dept. of Justice, National Institute of Justice, 2000), pp. 1–17.

[50] George Cornell, "Study on Christian Ministry Bringing about Change," *Wilson Daily Times*, Dec. 1, 1990, available: http://www.prisonministry.org/stats.htm

[51] Finn, *The Delaware Department of Correction Life Skills Program*, pp. 1–19; "Adult Education: Functional Literacy and Life Skills Program for State and Local Prisoners," *Biennial Evaluation Report, FY 93–94* (Washington, DC: U.S. Dept. of Education, 1998), p. 1.

[52] James J. Stephan, *Census of State and Federal Correctional Facilities, 1995* (Washington, DC: U.S. Dept. of Justice, 1997), table 17, p. 14, NCJ-164266.

[53] Finn, *The Delaware Department of Correction Life Skills Program*; "Life Skills Training for Inmates Linked to Higher Employment Rate," *Criminal Justice Newsletter*, 28(1) (1997): 6.

[54] Jeremy Travis, *But They All Come Back: Rethinking Prisoner Reentry* (Washington, DC: National Institute of Justice, 2000), p. 2.

[55] Ted Palmer, "The Effectiveness Issue Today: An Overview," in Kenneth C. Haas and Geoffrey P. Alpert (eds.), *The Dilemmas of Corrections*, 4th ed. (Prospect Heights, IL: Waveland Press, 1999), pp. 339–54; Steven P. Lab and John T. Whitehead, "From 'Nothing Works' to 'the Appropriate Works': The Latest Stop on the Search for the Secular Grail," *Criminology*, 28(3) (1990): 405–17.

[56] Paul Gendreau and Robert R. Ross, "Correctional Treatment: Some Recommendations for Effective Intervention," in Haas and Alpert (eds.), *The Dilemmas of Corrections*, 4th ed., pp. 355–68.

[57] Richard P. Seiter, "The Rebirth of Rehabilitation: The Responsibility Model," *Corrections Management Quarterly*, 2(1) (1998): 89–92.

[58] Sally L. Satel, *Drug Treatment: The Case for Coercion* (Washington, DC: American Enterprise Institute for Public Policy Research, 1999), pp. 1–82; University of Alabama–Birmingham, Graduate School, *Breaking the Cycle* (U.S. Dept. of Justice, National Institute of Justice, 2001), pp. 1–19, NCJ-188087.

[59] Shearer, "Coerced Substance Abuse Counseling Revisited."

[60] See, generally, Stanton E. Samenow, *Inside the Criminal Mind* (New York: Random House, 1984); James Q. Wilson and Richard J. Herrnstein, *Crime and Human Nature* (New York: Simon and Schuster, 1985).

[61] Katurah D. Jenkins-Hall, "Cognitive Restructuring," in D. Richard Laws (, *Relapse Prevention with Sex Offenders* (New York: Guilford Press, 1988), pp. 207–15.

[62] Lawrence F. Travis, III, Martin D. Schwartz and Todd R. Clear, "Does Treatment Work?" in Travis, Schwartz and Clear (eds.), *Corrections: An Issues Approach*, 2nd ed. (Cincinnati: Anderson, 1983)

[63] Shearer, "Coerced Substance Abuse Counseling Revisited."

[64] *McKune, Warden, et al. v. Lile*, No. 00-1187 (2002).

[65] Shearer, "Coerced Substance Abuse Counseling Revisited."

[66] Diana Fishbein, "Violent Inmates: Matching Treatment to Offender Needs," *American Jails*, 14(5) (2000): 41–47.

[67] Faye S. Taxman, "Twelve Steps to Improved Offender Outcomes: Developing Responsive Systems of Care for Substance-Abusing Offenders," *Corrections Today*, 60(6) (1998): 114–17, 166.

[68] See, generally, Samenow, *Inside the Criminal Mind*; Glenn O. Walters, *The Criminal Lifestyle: Patterns of Serious Conduct* (Beverly Hills, CA: Sage, 1990).

[69] Seiter, "The Rebirth of Rehabilitation"; University of Alabama–Birmingham, Graduate School, *Breaking the Cycle*.

[70] See, generally, Kevin M. Correia, *Handbook for Correctional Psychologists: Guidance for the Prison Practitioner* (Springfield, IL: Charles C. Thomas, 2001).

[71] David Lester and Patricia Van Voorhis, "Cognitive Therapies," in Patricia Van Voorhis, Michael Braswell and David Lester (eds.), *Correctional Counseling and Rehabilitation*, 4th ed. (Cincinnati, OH: Anderson Publishing, 2000); Glenn D. Walters, "Short-Term Outcome of Inmates Participating in the Lifestyle Change Program," *Criminal Justice and Behavior*, 26(3) (1999): 322–37; Kris R. Henning and B. Christopher Frueh, "Cognitive-Behavioral Treatment of Incarcerated Offenders," *Criminal Justice and Behavior*, 23(4) (1996): 523–41; Jessica B. Konopa, "Recovery from the Inside Out," *Corrections Today*, August (2002): 56–58, 112.

[72] Danida Friedman-Baker, "Stress Management Training for State Prison Inmates," *Corrections Today*, Oct. (1997): 16–18; Jessica B. Konopa, "Recovery from the Inside Out," *Corrections Today*, Aug. (2002): 56–58, 112.

[73] Robert D. Morgan, Carrie L. Winterowd and Sean Ferrell, "A National Survey of Group Psychotherapy Services in Correctional Facilities," *Professional Psychology Research and Practice*, 30(6) (1999): 600–6.

[74] Douglas S. Lipton, "Treatment for Drug Abusing Offenders During Correctional Supervision: A Nationwide Overview," *Journal of Offender Rehabilitation*, 26(3-4) (1988): 1–45.

[75] Rudolph Alexander Jr., *Counseling, Treatment and Intervention Methods with Juvenile and Adult Offenders* (Belmont, CA: Brooks/Cole, 2000), pp. 161–89.

[76] Gerald Corey, *Theory and Practice of Counseling Psychotherapy*, 6th ed. (Belmont, CA: Brooks/Cole: 2001), pp. 297–309; Lester and Van Voorhis, "Cognitive Therapies."

[77] Corey, *Theory and Practice of Counseling Psychotherapy*, pp. 275, 276; Robert C. Berg and Garry L. Landreth, *Group Counseling: Concepts and Procedures,* 2nd ed. (Muncie, IN: Accelerated Development, 1990), pp. 1–17.

[78] Narcotics Anonymous World Services, *It Works How and Why: The Twelve Steps and Twelve Traditions of Narcotics Anonymous* (Van Nuys, CA: Narcotics Anonymous World Services, 1993); Delinda E. Mercer and George E. Woody, *Therapy Manuals for Drug Addiction Manual 3, An Individual Drug Counseling Approach to Treat Cocaine Addiction: The Collaborative Cocaine Treatment Study Model* (Washington, DC: U.S. Dept. of Health and Human Services, National Institute on Drug Abuse, 1999).

[79] Reid K. Hester and William R. Miller, *Handbook of Alcoholism Treatment Approaches*, 2nd ed. (Boston: Allyn and Bacon, 1995), pp. 160–75.

[80] *Ibid.*

[81] *Kerr v. Farrey* 95 F.3d 472 (7th Cir); *Griffin v. Coughlin* 88N.Y. 2d 674, and *Warner v. Orange County Department of Probation*, 115 F.3d 1068 (2d Cir) cited in Jessica B. Konopa, "Recovery from the Inside Out," *Corrections Today*, Aug. (2002): 56–58, 112.

[82] Shearer, "Coerced Substance Abuse Counseling Revisited"; Hester and Miller, *Handbook of Alcoholism Treatment Approaches,* 2nd ed., pp. 160–75.

[83] *NIJ Survey of Wardens and State Commissioners of Corrections* (Washington, DC: U.S. Dept. of Justice, USGPO, 1995), pp. 1–2.

[84] Office of National Drug Control Policy, *Drug Treatment in the Criminal Justice System* (Rockville, MD: Drug Policy Information Clearinghouse, Mar. 2001), pp. 1–5.

[85] Edward L. Zuckerman, *Clinician's Thesaurus*, 5th ed. (New York: Guilford Press, 2000), p. 191; Benjamin B. Wolman, *Dictionary of Behavioral Science*, 2nd ed. (New York: Academic Press, 1989), pp. 68, 238.

[86] Office of National Drug Control Policy, *Drug Treatment in the Criminal Justice System*, pp. 1–5; Lipton, "Treatment for Drug Abusing Offenders During Correctional Supervision."

[87] U.S. Dept. of Justice, Office of Justice Programs, "Reducing Offender Drug Use through Prison-Based Treatment," *National Institute of Justice Journal*, July (2000): 20–23, NCJ-83457.

[88] John Jung, *Psychology of Alcohol and Other Drugs: A Research Perspective* (Thousand Oaks, CA: Sage, 2001), p. 426.

[89] Dennise Orlando, *Sex Offenders* (Washington, DC: U.S. Federal Judicial Center, 1998), p. 1–20.

[90] Walter J. Meyer and Collier M. Cole, "Physical and Chemical Castration of Sex Offenders: A Review," *Journal of Offender Rehabilitation*, 25(3-4) (1997): 1–18; "Sex Offender Civil Commitments Expand in Wake of Court Ruling," *Criminal Justice Newsletter*, 28(24) Sept. (1997): 6; Gina Kolata, "The Many Myths about Sex Offenders," *New York Times*, Sept. 1, 1996, p. 10; B. Drummond Ayres, "California Child Molesters Face 'Chemical Castration,'" *New York Times*, Aug. 27, 1996, p. 1; Max Vanzi, "California to Inject Drugs to Castrate Repeat Molesters," *Seattle Times*, Aug. 31, 1996, p. 2.

[91] Howard Zonana, "Sex Offender Testimony: Junk Science or Unethical Testimony?" *Journal of the American Academy of Psychiatry and the Law*, 28(4) (2000): 386–88.

[92] *Kansas v. Hendricks,* 521 U.S. 346, 369 (1997).

[93] *Kansas v. Crane*, 00-957 U.S. (2002).

[94] Alexander, *Counseling, Treatment and Intervention Methods with Juvenile and Adult Offenders*, pp. 275; Jan Honea, "Validating Self-Report Through Technology," *Texas Journal of Corrections*, 18(6) Nov.-Dec. (1992): 8–11.

[95] Daniel T. Wilcox, "Application of the Clinical Polygraph Examination to the Assessment, Treatment and Monitoring of Sex Offenders," *Journal of Sexual Aggression*, 5(2) (2000): 134–52; Sydney Cooley-Towell, Diane Pasini-Hill and Diane Patrick, "Value of the Post-Conviction Polygraph: The Importance of Sanctions," *Polygraph*, 29(1) (2000): 6–19; J. Stephen Harrison and Bonnie Kirkpatrick, "Polygraph Testing and Behavioral Change with Sex Offenders in an Outpatient Setting: An Exploratory Study," *Polygraph,* 29(1) (2000): 20–25.

[96] Tracey M. Geer, Judith V. Becker, Steven R. Gray and Daniel Krauss, "Predictors of Treatment Completion in a Correctional Sex Offender Treatment Program," *International Journal of Offender Therapy and Comparative Criminology*, 45(3) (2001): 302–12.

[97] Howard E. Barbaree, Michael C. Seto, Calvin M. Langton and Edward J. Peacock, "Evaluating the Predictive Accuracy of Six Assessment Instruments for Adult Sex Offenders," *Criminal Justice and Behavior*, 28(4) (2000): 490–521; Gene G. Abel, Suzann S. Lawry, Elizabeth Karlstrom, Candice A. Osborn and Charles F. Gillespie, "Screening Tests for Pedophilia," *Criminal Justice and Behavior*, 21(1) (1994): 115–31.

[98] William Prendergast, *Treating Sex Offenders in Correctional Institutions and Outpatient Clinics* (Binghampton, NY: Haworth Press, 1991), pp. xiv–xv; Clark, "Missouri's Sexual Offender Program," pp. 84–89.

[99] Center for Sex Offender Management, *Recidivism of Sex Offenders* (Washington, DC: Center for Sex Offender Management, 2001), available: http://csom.org/pubs/recidsexof.html.

[100] Barry Anechiarico, "A Closer Look at Sex Offender Character Pathology and Relapse Prevention: An Integrative Approach," *International Journal of Offender Therapy and Comparative Criminology*, 42(1) (1998): 16–26.

[101] Gilles Launay, "Relapse Prevention with Sex Offenders: Practice, Theory and Research," *Criminal Behavior and Mental Health*, 11(1) (2001): 38–54.

[102] Ted D. Westerman and James W. Burfiend, *Crime and Justice in Two Societies: Japan and the United States* (Pacific Grove: Brooks/Cole, 1991), pp. 124–47.; see also Anechiarico, "A Closer Look at Sex Offender Character Pathology and Relapse Prevention."

[103] Launay, "Relapse Prevention with Sex Offenders"; Anechiarico, "A Closer Look at Sex Offender Character Pathology and Relapse Prevention"; Katurah Jenkins-Hall and G. Allan Marlatt, "Apparently Irrelevant Decision in the Relapse Process," in D. Richard Laws (, *Relapse Prevention with Sex Offenders* (New York: Guilford Press, 1988), pp. 47–55 (modified in conversation/lecture by Jan Honea, 6/29/92).

[104] Robert J. McGrath, "Sex-Offender Risk Assessment and Disposition Planning: A Review of Empirical and Clinical Findings," *International Journal of Offender Therapy and Comparative Criminology*, 35(4) (1991): 328–53; Fred S. Berlin and Martin H. Malin, "Media Distortion of the Public's Perception of Recidivism and Psychiatric Rehabilitation," *American Journal of Psychiatry*, 148(11) (1991): 1572–76; Vernon L. Quinsey, Grant T. Harris, Marnie E. Rice, Martin L. Lalumiere and W. L. Marshall, "Assessing Treatment Efficacy in Outcome Studies of Sex Offenders," *Journal of Interpersonal Violence*, 8(4) (1993): 512–23.

[105] John Irwin, "The Trouble with Rehabilitation," *Criminal Justice and Behavior*, 1(2) (1974): 139–49.

[106] Schiro, *Correcting Corrections: Missouri's Parallel Universe*.

[107] Westerman and Burfiend, *Crime and Justice in Two Societies*.

[108] Harlow, *Education and Correctional Populations*, table 4, p. 2.

CHAPTER TWELVE

[1] Jesse W. Doyle, "Six Elements That Form a Context for Staff Safety," *Corrections Today*, 63(6) (2001): 101–4.

[2] David Lovell and Ron Jemelka, "When Inmates Misbehave: The Costs of Discipline," *The Prison Journal*, 76(2) (1996): 165–79.

[3] "Violence/Riots/Escapes," *Corrections Compendium*, 27(5) May (2002): 6–19.

[4] James A. Lyons, *Inmate Escape Incidents 1993–1997* (Albany: New York State Dept. of Correctional Services, Division of Program Planning, Research and Evaluation, 1997), pp. 1–17.

[5] "Media Access," *Corrections Compendium*, 27(4) (2002): 6–18; Linda Postorino, "Identifying, Documenting and Managing Florida's High-Profile Inmates," *Corrections Today*, 63(6) (2001): 126–28; Robert M. Freeman, "Here There be Monsters: Public Perception of Corrections," *Corrections Today*, 63(3) (2001): 108–11; Ted Gest, "Behind Prison Walls: Restricting Media Access," *Corrections Today*, 63(3) (2001): 98–101.

[6] "Prisons in Virginia Set New Rules on Personal Items for Inmates," *Crime Prevention News*, 96(2) (1996): 7.

[7] Susan L. Clayton, "U.S. Prisons Experience Trend toward Smoking Bans," *On the Line* (Lanham, MD: American Correctional Association, November 2001), pp. 1–3.

[8] Anthony L. Guenther, "Compensations in a Total Institution: The Forms and Functions of Contraband," *Crime and Delinquency*, 21(3) (1975): 243–54.

[9] John M. Vanyur and J. T. O'Brien, "Reducing Drugs and Alcohol in Prisons: Moving Beyond the Basics," *Corrections Compendium*, 27(1) (2002): 1–5.

[10] Mary A. Finn, "Disciplinary Incidents in Prison: Effects of Race, Economic Status, Urban Residence, Prior Imprisonment," *Journal of Offender Rehabilitation*, 22(1-2) (1995): 143–56.

[11] Amy Craddock, "A Comparative Study of Male and Female Prison Misconduct Careers," *Prison Journal*, 76(1) (1996): 60–80.

[12] Ann Goetting and Roy Michael Howsen, "Correlates of Prisoner Misconduct," *Journal of Quantitative Criminology*, 2(1) (1986): 49–67.

[13] Thomas J. Reidy, Mark D. Cunningham and Jon R. Sorensen, "From Death to Life: Prison Behavior of Former Death Row Inmates in Indiana," *Criminal Justice and Behavior*, 28(1) (2001): 62–82; Leonore M. J. Simon, "Prison Behavior and the Victim-Offender Relationship among Violent Offenders," *Justice Quarterly*, 10(3) (1993): 489–506.

[14] John D. Wooldredge, "Inmate Experiences and Psychological Well-Being," *Criminal Justice and Behavior*, 26(2) (1999): 235–50.

[15] James A. Lyons, *Unusual Incident Reports, January–December 1997* (Albany: New York State Dept. of Correctional Services, Division of Program Planning, Research and Evaluation, 1998).

[16] John T. Whitehead, Charles A. Lindquist and John M. Klofas, "Correctional Officer Professional Orientation: A Replication of the Klofas-Toch Measure," *Criminal Justice and Behavior*, 14 (1987): 468–86.

[17] Mary-Ann Farkas, "Correctional Officer Attitudes toward Inmates and Working with Inmates in a 'Get Tough' Era," *Journal of Criminal Justice*, 27(6) (1999): 495–506; Mary Ann Farkas, "Correctional Officers: What Factors Influence Work Attitudes?" *Corrections Management Quarterly*, 5(2) (2001): 20–26.

[18] Jeanne B. Stinchcomb, "Developing Correctional Officer Professionalism: A Work in Progress," *Corrections Compendium*, 25(5) (2000): 1–4, 18.

[19] Sarah Ben-David, Peter Silfen and David Cohen, "Fearful Custodial or Fearless Personal Relations: Prison Guards' Fear as a Factor Shaping Staff-Inmate Relation Prototype," *International Journal of Offender Therapy and Comparative Criminology*, 40(2) (1996): 94–104.

[20] Marie L. Griffin, "Job Satisfaction Among Detention Officers Assessing the Relative Contribution of Organizational Climate Variables," *Journal of Criminal Justice*, 29(3) (2001): 219–32.

[21] Ruth Triplett, Janet L. Mullings and Kathryn E. Scarborough, "Examining the Effect of Work-Home Conflict on Work-Related Stress among Correctional Officers," *Journal of Criminal Justice*, 27(4) (1999): 371–85.

[22] David J. Srebalus and Duane E. Brown, *A Guide to the Helping Professions* (Boston: Allyn and Bacon, 2001), pp. 289–91; Barnett D. Elman and Edmund T. Dowd, "Correlates of Burnout in Inpatient Substance Abuse Treatment Therapists," *Journal of Addictions and Offender Counseling*, 17(2) (1997): 56–65.

[23] William D. Burrell, "How to Prevent PPO Stress and Burnout," *Community Corrections Report on Law and Corrections Practice*, 8(1) (2000): 1–14.

[24] Calvin Simmons, John K. Cochran and William R. Blount, "Effects of Job-Related Stress and Job Satisfaction on Probation Officers Inclination to Quit," *American Journal of Criminal Justice*, 21(2) (1997): 213–19.

[25] *Occupational Outlook Handbook, 2002–03 Edition* (Washington, DC: U.S. Dept. of Labor, Bureau of Labor Statistics), accessed 12/11/02: http://www.bls.gov/oco/ocos156.htm and http://www.bls.gov/oco/ocos265.htm

[26] Timothy J. Flanagan, W. Wesley Johnson and Katherine Bennett, "Job Satisfaction among Correctional Executives: A Contemporary Portrait of Wardens of State Prisons for Adults," *Prison Journal*, 76(4) (1996): 385–97.

[27] Dennis J. Stevens, "Correctional Officer Attitudes," *Corrections Compendium*, 23(70) July (1998): 19–20.

[28] Jeff Maahs and Travis Pratt, "Uncovering the Predictors of Correctional Officers' Attitudes and Behaviors: A Meta-Analysis," *Corrections Management Quarterly*, 5(2) (2001): 13–19.

[29] Richard G. Kiekbusch, "Looming Correctional Work Force Shortage: A Problem of Supply and Demand," *Corrections Compendium*, 26(4) (2001): 1–3, 24–25.

[30] Jo Ellen Rackleff, "Florida's Recruitment Methods," *Corrections Today*, June (2002): 76–79, 119; Glen Castlebury, "Correctional Officer Recruitment and Retention in Texas," *Corrections Today*, June (2002): 80–83; Reginald Wilkinson, "The Bureau of Staff Enrichment: Employees Are Our Most Valuable Resource," *Corrections Today*, 84–87.

[31] David Wilkening, "How Reform Came to 'Most Dangerous' Jail," *Corrections Technology & Management*, 5(4) (2001): 55–57; "Armed and Dangerous: Escapees' Spree Should Prompt Prison Reforms," *Dallas Morning News*, Dec. 27, 2000, p. 18-A; "Experts Say Lack of Staff Leading to Escapes," *Fort Worth Star-Telegram*, Oct. 23, 2001, p. 5-B.

[32] Patricia Van Voorhis, Frank T. Cullen, Bruce G. Link and Nancy T. Wolfe, "The Impact of Race and Gender on Correctional Officers' Orientation to the Integrated Environment," *Journal of Research on Crime and Delinquency*, 28 (1991): 472–500.

[33] *2001 Directory of Juvenile and Adult Correctional Departments, Institutions, Agencies and Paroling Authorities* (Lanham, MD: American Correctional Association, 2001), p. 30.

[34] Lynn Zimmer, "How Women Reshape the Prison Guard Role," *Gender and Society*, 1(4) (1987): 415–31; Camille G. Graham, "Women Are Succeeding in Male Institutions," *Women in Corrections* (College Park: American Correctional Association, 1981), pp. 27–36.

[35] Richard Lawrence and S. Mahan, "Women Corrections Officers in Men's Prisons: Acceptance and Perceived Job Performance," *Women and Criminal Justice*, 9(3) (1998): 63–86; Lynn Zimmer, "Solving Women's Employment Problems in Corrections: Shifting the Burden to Administrators," *Women and Criminal Justice*, 1(1) (1989): 55–79.

[36] Craig Hemmens and Mary K. Stohr, "Correctional Staff Attitudes Regarding the Use of Force in Corrections," *Corrections Management Quarterly*, 5(2) (2001): 27–40; Dana M. Britton, "Perceptions of the Work Environment among Correctional Officers: Do Race and Sex Matter?" *Criminology*, 35(1) (1997): 85–105.

[37] Mary Ann Farkas, "Inmate Supervisory Style: Does Gender Make a Difference?" *Women and Criminal Justice*, 10(4) (1999): 25–45.

[38] Maahs and Pratt, "Uncovering the Predictors of Correctional Officers' Attitudes and Behaviors"; Hemmens and Stohr, "Correctional Staff Attitudes Regarding the Use of Force in Corrections"; Britton, "Perceptions of the Work Environment among Correctional Officers."

[39] Denise L. Jenne and Robert C. Kersting, "Aggression and Women Correctional Officers in Male Prisons," *Prison Journal*, 76(4) (1996): 442–60.

[40] Mark R. Pogrebin and Eric D. Poole, "The Sexualized Work Environment: A Look at Women Jail Officers," *Prison Journal*, 78(1) (1998): 41–57; Lawrence and Mahan, "Women Corrections Officers in Men's Prisons."

[41] George R. Gross, Susan J. Larson, Gloria D. Urban and Linda L. Zupan, "Gender Differences in Occupational Stress among Correctional Officers," *American Journal of Criminal Justice*, 18(2) (1994): 219–34.

[42] Kathleen Maguire and Ann L. Pastore, *Sourcebook of Criminal Justice Statistics 1996* (Washington, DC: U.S. Dept. of Justice, 1997), tables 1.100–1.102, pp. 87–89, NCJ-165361.

[43] Gross, Larson, Urban and Zupan, "Gender Differences in Occupational Stress among Correctional Officers."

[44] Linda L. Zupan, "The Progress of Women Correctional Officers," in Imogene L. Moyer (ed.), *The Changing Roles of Women in the Criminal Justice System*, 2nd ed. (Prospect Heights, IL: Waveland Press, 1992), p. 326.

[45] Mary Ann Farkas and Kathryn R. L. Rand, "Sex Matters: A Gender-specific Standard for Cross-gender Searches of Inmates," *Women and Criminal Justice*, 10(3) (1999): 31–55.

[46] Katherine Bennett, "Constitutional Issues in Cross-Gender Searches and Visual Observation of Nude Inmates by Opposite-Sex Officers: A Battle between and within the Sexes," *Prison Journal*, 75(1) (1995): 90–112.

[47] Stephen Walters, "Changing the Guard: Male Correctional Officers' Attitudes toward Women as Co-Workers," *Journal of Offender Rehabilitation*, 20(1–2) (1993): 47–60.

[48] Kelly A. Cheeseman, Janet L. Mullings and James W. Marquart, "Inmate Perceptions of Security Staff Across Various Custody Levels," *Corrections Management Quarterly*, 5(2) (2001): 41–48.

[49] Van Voorhis, Cullen, Link and Wolfe, "The Impact of Race and Gender on Correctional Officers' Orientation to the Integrated Environment."

[50] Southern Poverty Law Center, "Behind the Wire," *Intelligence Report*, 100 (fall 2000): 24–29 (Montgomery, AL: Southern Poverty Law Center, 1999).

[51] *2001 Directory of Juvenile and Adult Correctional Departments, Institutions, Agencies and Paroling Authorities*, pp. xlii–xlv.

[52] Scott D. Camp, William G. Saylor and Kevin N. Wright, "Racial Diversity of Correctional Workers and Inmates: Organizational Commitment, Teamwork and Workers Efficacy in Prisons," *Justice Quarterly*, 18(2) (2001): 411–28.

[53] Britton, "Perceptions of the Work Environment among Correctional Officers."

[54] *Ibid.*

[55] Amitai Etzioni, *A Comparative Analysis of Organizations*, 2nd ed. (New York: Free Press, 1975), pp. 4–6.

[56] *Ibid.*, pp. 8–22.

[57] James Houston, "Correctional Management: Functions, Skills and Systems (Chicago: Nelson-Hall, 1995), pp. 74–75.

[58] *Ibid.*, pp. 259–65.

[59] Allen J. Beck, Jennifer C. Karberg and Paige M. Harrison, *Prison and Jail Inmates at Midyear 2001* (Washington, DC: U.S. Dept of Justice, Bureau of Justice Statistics, 2002), p. 6, NCJ-191702; James Austin and Garry Coventry, *Emerging Issues on Privatized Prisons* (Washington, DC: U.S. Dept. of Justice, Bureau of Justice Assistance, 2001), pp. ix–x, NCJ-181249; "Privatization: An Update," *Corrections Compendium*, 26(9) (2001): 8–14.

[60] Judith Greene, "Bailing Out Private Jails," *The American Prospect*, 12(16) (2001), available: http://www.prospect.org/print/V12/16/greene-ju.html

[61] *Ibid.*

[62] "Privatization: An Update"; Alex Singal, "The Private Prison Industry, Part II: Business Development," *Corrections Compendium*, 23(2) (1998): 1–3, 24–25.

[63] Austin and Coventry, *Emerging Issues on Privatized Prisons*.

[64] Alex Singal, "The Private Prison Industry: A Statistical and Historical Analysis," *Corrections Compendium*, 23(1) (1998): 1–3, 17–18, 20; Singal, "The Private Prison Industry, Part II."

[65] Austin and Coventry, *Emerging Issues on Privatized Prisons*, pp. iii.

[66] *Ibid.*, pp. x–xi.

[67] Eric Schlosser, "The Prison-Industrial Complex," *Atlantic Monthly*, 282(6) (1998): 51–77.

[68] "Alabama Could Send Inmates Out of State," *Corrections Compendium*, 26(8) (2001): 7.

[69] Greene, "Bailing Out Private Jails."

[70] Amy Cheung, *Prison Privatization and the Use of Incarceration* (Washington, DC: The Sentencing Project, January 2002), p. 2.

[71] Greene, "Bailing Out Private Jails"; "Privatization: An Update."

[72] Cheung, *Prison Privatization and the Use of Incarceration*, p. 3.

[73] Greene, "Bailing Out Private Jails."

[74] Cheung, *Prison Privatization and the Use of Incarceration*, p. 3.

[75] Greene, "Bailing Out Private Jails."

[76] Phil Mattera and Mafruza Khan, *Jail Breaks: Economic Development Subsidies Given to Private Prisons* (Washington, DC: Good Jobs First, 2001), chapter 1, p. 7, available: http://www.goodjobsfirst.org/pdf/jbch1.pdf

[77] Greene, "Bailing Out Private Jails."

[78] Judith Greene, Prison Privatization: Recent Developments in the United States. Paper Presented at ICOPA Toronto, Canada May 12, 2000, available: http://www.epinet.org/real_media/010111/materials/greene2.pdf

[79] Christy Hoppe, "2 Guilty in VitaPro Scandal—Company President, Ex-Prison Chief Took Part in Kickback Scheme," *Dallas Morning News*, Aug. 21, 2001, p. 1-A.

[80] Schlosser, "The Prison-Industrial Complex."

[81] Randall G. Shelden and William B. Brown, "Crime Control Industry and the Management of the Surplus Population," *Critical Criminology*, 9(2) (2000): 39–62; Thomas, "Making Crime Pay."

[82] Phillip Mattera and Mafruza Khan with Greg LeRoy and Kate Davis, *Jail Breaks: Economic Development Subsidies Given to Private Prisons* (Washington, DC: Institute on Taxation and Economic Policy, 2001), pp. 1–8.

83 Douglas C. McDonald, "Public Imprisonment by Private Means: The Re-Emergence of Private Prisons and Jails in the United States, the United Kingdom, and Australia," *British Journal of Criminology*, 34(1) (1994): 29–48.

84 *Richardson v. McKnight*, 117 S.Ct. 2100 (1997).

85 Frank D. Mylar, "Can Private Jails Survive *Richardson v. McKnight*?" *Corrections Managers' Report*, 3(5) (1998): 1, 4.

86 William C. Collins, *Correctional Law for the Correctional Officer* (Lanham, MD: American Correctional Association, 1993), pp. 114–15.

CHAPTER THIRTEEN

1 Brian K. Payne and Victoria Coogle, "Examining Attitudes about the Death Penalty," *Corrections Compendium*, 23(4) (1998): 1–5, 24–25.

2 United States Conference of Catholic Bishops, "A Good Friday Appeal to End the Death Penalty," available: http://www.nccbuscc.org/sdwp/national/criminal/appeal.htm, Apr. 2, 1999; American Bar Association, Section of Individual Rights and Responsibilities, *Report with Recommendations No. 107*, from ABA 1997 Midyear Meeting as Approved by The ABA House of Delegates Feb. 3, 1997, available: http://www.abanet.org/irr/rec107.html; Religious Tolerance, *Religious Groups' Policies about the Death Penalty*, available: http://www.religioustolerance.org/execut7.htm.

3 Robert M. Bohm, "The Future of Capital Punishment," *ACJS Today*, 22(4) (2000): 1, 4–6.

4 Pieter Spierenburg, "The Body and the State: Early Modern Europe," in Norval Morris and David J. Rothman (eds.), *The Oxford History of the Prison* (New York: Oxford University Press, 1995), pp. 49–77.

5 Lawrence M. Friedman, *Crime and Punishment in American History* (New York: HarperCollins, 1993), pp. 41–48, 73–75.

6 *Ibid.*, pp. 75–77, 168–69.

7 Perry T. Ryan, *The Last Public Execution in America* (1992), available: http://www.geocities.com/last publichang/

8 *Correctional Populations in the United States, 1997* (Washington, DC: U.S. Dept. of Justice, Bureau of Justice Statistics, 2000), table 7.26, NCJ-177613.

9 William J. Bowers, *Executions in America* (Lexington, MA: Lexington Books, 1974), pp. 40–69, 175.

10 Tracy L. Snell and Laura M. Maruschak, *Capital Punishment 2001* (Washington, DC: Bureau of Justice Statistics, 2002), appendix table 1, p. 13, NCJ-197020

11 Death Penalty Information Center, "Number of Executions by States since 1976."

12 Snell and Maruschak, *Capital Punishment 2001*, Appendix table 1, p. 13.

13 Death Penalty Information Center, "Number of Executions by States since 1976," accessed 12/31/02, available: http://www.deathpenaltyinfo.org/; Death Penalty Information Center, "Death Row Inmates by State," accessed 12/31/02, available: http://www.deathpenaltyinfo.org/DRowInfo.html#state; Death Penalty Information Center, "States without the Death Penalty," available: http://www.death penaltyinfo.org/firstpage.html; Maurice Possley and Steve Mills, "Clemency for All," *Chicago Tribune*, Jan. 12, 2003, pp. 1, 15.

14 James W. Marquart, Sheldon Ekland-Olson and Jonathan R. Sorenson, *The Rope, The Chair, and The Needle* (Austin: University of Texas Press, 1993), pp. 3–8.

15 *Furman v. Georgia*, 408 U.S. 238 (1972).

16 Thomas Keil and Gennaro Vito, "Race and the Death Penalty in Kentucky Murder Trials: An Analysis of Post-Gregg Outcomes," *Justice Quarterly*, 7 (1990): 189–207.

17 Death Penalty Information Center, "Number of Executions by States since 1976."

18 Death Penalty Information Center, "Death Row Inmates by State."

19 *Gregg v. Georgia*, 428 U.S. 153 (1976); *Coker v. Georgia*, 433 U.S. 583 (1977); *Woodson v. North Carolina*, 428 U.S. 280 (1976); *Godfrey v. Georgia*, 446 U.S. 420 (1980).

20 Robert Patrick, "New Challenge to Death Row Cases Could Stop Executions," Capital News Service, April 20, 2001, available: http://www.newsline.umd.edu/justice/specialreports/deathpenalty/deathrowchallenge042201.htm

21 Deon E. Brock, Jon Sorensen and James W. Marquart, "Tinkering with the Machinery of Death: An Analysis of the Impact of Legislative Reform on the Sentencing of Capital Murderers in Texas," *Journal of Criminal Justice*, 28(5) (2000): 343–49.

[22] Howard Zonana, "Sex Offender Testimony: Junk Science or Unethical Testimony?" *Journal of the American Academy of Psychiatry and the Law*, 28(4) (2000): 386–88; Maria Vouras, Ken Falkenstein, Liz Homoki, Larry Lewis and Jeffrey M. Summers, "Examination of Expert Witnesses" (Fairfax, VA: George Mason University, 2000), available: http://www.gmu.edu/departments/law/innofcourt/expert.pdf

[23] *Simmons v. South Carolina*, 512 U.S. 154 (1994); *Shafer v. South Carolina*, No. 00-5250 (2001).

[24] J. C. Greenburg, "Sentencing Laws Rejected," *Chicago Tribune*, June 25, 2002, pp. 1, 22.

[25] Northwestern Law, Center on Wrongful Convictions (Chicago: Center on Wrongful Convictions, 2002), available: http://www.law.northwestern.edu/wrongfulconvictions/; Talia Roitberg Harmon, "Predictors of Miscarriages of Justice in Capital Cases," *Justice Quarterly*, 18(4) (2001): 949–68; Judy Platania and Gary Moran, "Due Process and the Death Penalty: The Role of Prosecutorial Misconduct in Closing Argument in Capital Trials," *Law and Human Behavior,* 22(4) (1999): 471–86.

[26] Candace McCoy and Illya Lichtenberg. "Providing Effective Habeas Counsel for Indigents in Capital Cases," *Justice System Journal*, 21(1) (1999): 81–87; Max B. Baker, "Poor More Vulnerable to Death Penalty," *Fort Worth Star-Telegram*, Oct. 17, 2000, pp. 1-A, 23-A.

[27] Snell and Maruschak, *Capital Punishment 2001*.

[28] Rob Warden, "Texas's Exonerated: Randall Dale Adams" (Chicago: Center on Wrongful Convictions, May 2002), available: http://www.law.northwestern.edu/depts/clinic/wrongful/exonerations/RDAdams.htm

[29] James S. Liebman, Jeffrey Fagan and Valerie West, *Broken System: Error Rates in Capital Cases, 1973–1995* (New York: Open Society Institute Columbia University School of Law, 2000), pp. 1–174.

[30] Barry Latzer and James N. G. Cauthen, "State-by-State Information on State Capital Punishment," *Judicature,* 84(2) (2000): 64–71.

[31] James S. Liebman, Jeffrey Fagan and Valerie West, "Death Matters: A Reply to Professors Latzer and Cauthen," *Judicature*, 84(2) (2000): 72–99.

[32] *Innocence and the Death Penalty* (Washington, DC: Death Penalty information Center, 2001); Daphne Eviatar, "When DNA Releases the Innocent from Behind Bars," *Christian Science Monitor*, Feb. 17, 2000, p. 13; Sharon Cohen and Deborah Hastings, *For 110 Inmates Freed by DNA Tests, True Freedom Remains Elusive* (Associated Press, May 28, 2002), available: http://www.deathpenaltyinfo.org/AP-CohenDNA.html.

[33] The Justice Project, "Death Penalty Reform Takes Next Step toward Passage," accessed 12/31/02, available: http://justice.policy.net/ipa/; Jonathan Alter, "Death Penalty on Trial," *Newsweek*, 135(24), June 12, 2000, pp. 24–34; Clarence Page, "Bush Too Sure about Texas' Death Row," *Dallas Morning News*, Feb. 22, 2000, p. 17-A.

[34] Northwestern Center on Wrongful Convictions.

[35] *McCleskey v. Zant* 499 U.S. 467 (1991)

[36] McCoy and Lichtenberg, "Providing Effective Habeas Counsel for Indigents in Capital Cases."

[37] Richard C. Dieter, Remarks for Legislative Commission's Subcommittee to Study the Death Penalty and Related DNA Testing (Las Vegas, NV: Assembly and State of Nevada, April 2002), available: http://www.deathpenaltyinfo.org/RDcostTestimony.html

[38] Katherine Baicker, "The Budgetary Repercussions of Capital Convictions" (Cambridge, MA: National Bureau of Economic Research, 2001). Working paper #W8382.

[39] Mike Lee, "Trying Escapees May Cost $3 Million," *Fort Worth Star-Telegram*, Feb. 10, 2001, p. B-1.

[40] Report of the Governor's Commission on Capital Punishment (Springfield, IL: Preamble, April 15, 2002).

[41] Dieter, Remarks.

[42] *Ford v. Wainwright*, 477 U.S. 399 (1985).

[43] R. Lacayo, "Spared by Their Low IQ," *Time*, 160, July 1, 2002, p. 34.

[44] "A Long Way Since Horse Stealing," *Chicago Tribune*, June 21, 2002, p. 22.

[45] R. Simon, "Not a Suitable Punishment," *U.S. News & World Report*, 133, July 15, 2002, p. 9.

[46] J. C. Greenburg, "Executing Mentally Retarded Unconstitutional, Court Rules," *Chicago Tribune*, June 21, 2002, pp. 1, 13.

[47] *Ibid.*, p. 13.

[48] Simon, "Not a Suitable Punishment," p. 9.

[49] *Thompson v. Oklahoma*, 487 U.S. 815 (1988); *Wilkins v. Missouri*, 492 U.S. 937 (1989); *Stanford v. Kentucky*, 492 U.S. 361 (1989).

[50] Victor L. Streib, *The Juvenile Death Penalty Today: Death Sentences and Executions for Juvenile Crimes, January 1973–June 30, 2002* (Washington, DC: Death Penalty Information Center, 2002), available: http://www.law.onu.edu/faculty/streib/juvdeath.htm

[51] Streib, "Case Summaries for Current Death Row Inmates under Juvenile Death Sentences," from *The Juvenile Death Penalty Today: Death Sentences and Executions for Juvenile Crimes, Jan. 1, 1973–June 30, 2002*, available: http://www.deathpenaltyinfo.org/juvcases.html; Death Penalty Information Center, *Juveniles and the Death Penalty*, available: http://www.deathpenaltyinfo.org/juvchar.html

[52] Streib, *The Juvenile Death Penalty Today*; Death Penalty Information Center, *What's New?: Inter-American Commission Calls Nevada Juvenile Death Sentence a "Grave and Irreparable" Violation of Human Rights*, citing *Michael Domingues v. United States*, (case 12.285, Report No. 62/02, Inter-Am C.H.R., OEA/Ser./L/V/II.116 doc. 33 rev. at xx (2002)), available: http://www.deathpenaltyinfo.org/whatsnew.html#Domingues

[53] Eric Beauchemin, *Human Rights Violations by the Taliban* (Radio Netherlands, Dec. 13, 2000), available: http://www.rnw.nl/humanrights/afghanistan/html/rights001213.html

[54] Richard C. Dieter, *International Perspectives on the Death Penalty* (Washington, DC: Death Penalty Information Center, Oct. 1999), available: http://www.deathpenaltyinfo.org/internationalreport.html#efforts; *The Death Penalty: Facts and Figures* (London: Amnesty International, Oct. 1998), p. 2.

[55] Rick Halperin, "Lethal Injection First Introduced by Nazis," *Amnesty Now* (New York: Amnesty International-USA, 2002), p. 16.

[56] Death Penalty Information Center, *Facts about the Death Penalty: Methods of Execution*, available: http://www.deathpenaltyinfo.org/methods.html; Bill Rankin, "Chair's Demise Turns Challenge to Needle Lethal Injection Foes Face Harder Sell," *The Atlanta Journal and Constitution*, Oct. 7, 2001, p. D-1.

[57] Cary Federman and Dave Holmes, "Caring to Death: Health Care Professionals and Capital Punishment," *Punishment & Society*, 2(4) (2000): 444–51.

[58] Neil J. Farber, Brian M. Aboff, Joan Weiner, Elizabeth B. Davis, E. Gil Boyer and Peter A. Ubel, "Physicians' Willingness to Participate in the Process of Lethal Injection for Capital Punishment," *Annals of Internal Medicine*, 135(10) (2001): 884–88; William J. Wiseman Jr., "An 'Angel of Mercy's' Confession," *Amnesty Now* (New York: Amnesty International–USA, Fall 2001), pp. 16–17; Amnesty International, Death Penalty Facts: Cruel and Degrading Punishment, available: http://www.amnesty-usa.org/abolish/cruelanddegrading.html.

[59] Death Penalty Information Center, *Facts about the Death Penalty: Methods of Execution*.

[60] Michael A. Radelet, *Post-Furman Botched Executions* (Washington, DC: Death Penalty Information Center, Nov. 2001), pp. 1–5.

[61] "Special Housing," *Corrections Compendium*, 26(7) (2001): 6–15; Patricia Arriaga, "Managing Death Row," *Crime and Justice International*, 16(44) (2000): 5–6, 25–28.

[62] Patti Ross Salinas and Tana McCoy, "Management Issues Surrounding Women on Death Row," *Corrections Management Quarterly*, 3(1) (1999): 64–70.

[63] *Ibid.*, pp. 55–61.

[64] L. Scott Johnson, "The Bible and the Death Penalty: Implications for Criminal Justice Education," *Journal of Criminal Justice Education*, 11(1) (2000): 15–33.

[65] Frank G. Carrington, *Neither Cruel Nor Unusual* (New Rochelle, NY: Arlington House, 1978), pp. 92–100; Paul Passell, "The Deterrent Effect of the Death Penalty: A Statistical Test," *Stanford Law Review*, 28 (1975): 61–80.

[66] Isaac Erlich, "The Deterrent Effect of Capital Punishment," *American Economic Review*, 65 (1975): 397–98; Isaac Erlich, "Capital Punishment and Deterrence," *Journal of Political Economy*, 85 (1977): 741–42.

[67] Brian Forst, "The Deterrent Effect of Capital Punishment: A Cross-State Analysis of the 1960s," *Minnesota Law Review*, 61 (1977): 743–63; Hans Zeisel, "The Deterrent Effect of the Death Penalty: Facts v. Faiths," *Supreme Court Review* (1976): 317–40; Lawrence R. Klein, Brian Forst and Victor Filatov, "The Deterrent Effect of Capital Punishment: A Question of Life and Death," in *Deterrence* (Washington, DC: National Research Council, 1978), pp. 341–60.

[68] Stephen A. Layson, "Homicide and Deterrence: A Re-Examination of the United States Time-Series Evidence," *Southern Economic Journal*, 52 (1986): 68–69; Stephen A. Layson, "United States Time-Series Homicide Regressions with Adaptive Expectations," *Bulletin of the New York Academy of Medicine*, 62 (1986): 589–600.

[69] Samuel Cameron, "A Review of the Econometric Evidence on the Effects of Capital Punishment," *Journal of Socio-Economics*, 23(1-2) (1994): 197–214.

[70] Death Penalty Information Center, *Facts about Deterrence and the Death Penalty*, available: http://www.deathpenaltyinfo.org/deter.html (accessed 12/19/02).

[71] Payne and Coogle, "Examining Attitudes about the Death Penalty."

[72] John Sorenson, Robert Wrinkle, Victoria Brewer and James Marquart, "Capital Punishment and Deterrence: Examining the Expert of Executions on Murder in Texas," *Crime and Delinquency*, 45 (1999): 481–93, cited on http://www.deathpenalty.info.org.deter.html

[73] Jonathan R. Sorensen and Rocky L. Pilgrim, "Actuarial Risk Assessment of Violence Posed by Capital Murder Defendants," *Journal of Criminal Law and Criminology*, 90(4) (2000): 1251–70.

[74] Thomas J. Reidy, Mark D. Cunningham and Jon R. Sorensen, "From Death to Life: Prison Behavior of Former Death Row Inmates in Indiana," *Criminal Justice and Behavior*, 28(1) (2001): 62–82.

[75] Gary N. Howells, Kelly A. Flanagan and Vivian Hagan, "Does Viewing a Televised Execution Affect Attitudes Toward Capital Punishment?" *Criminal Justice and Behavior*, 22(4) (1995): 411–24.

[76] Andrew L. Shapiro, "State Killing: America's Newest Spectator Sport," *Salon Magazine*, July 1997, pp. 28–30.

[77] Karl Spence, "The Death Penalty Deters Murder," in Szumski and Bursell (eds.), *The Death Penalty: Opposing Viewpoints*, pp. 96–100.

[78] Ernest van den Haag, "The Death Penalty Is Moral," in Szumski and Bursell (eds.), *The Death Penalty: Opposing Viewpoints*, pp. 58–61; Donald D. Hook and Lothar Khan, *Death in the Balance: The Debate over Capital Punishment* (Lexington, MA: Lexington Books, 1989), pp. 79–88.

[79] Pat Bane, "Murder Victims' Families for Reconciliation," *The Voice*, winter 1997.

[80] Shapiro, "State Killing."

[81] American Bar Association, *Clemency and Consequences* (Chicago: ABA, July 2002), available: http://www.abanet.org/crimjust/juvjus/jdpclemeffect02.pdf

[82] See, for example, Craig J. Albert, "Challenging Deterrence: New Insights on Capital Punishment Derived from Panel Data," *University of Pittsburgh Law Review*, 60(2) (1999): 321–71

[83] Katherine Van Wormer and Chuk Odiah, "The Psychology of Suicide-Murder and the Death Penalty," *Journal of Criminal Justice*, 27(4) (1999): 361–70.

[84] Robert M. Bohm, "Understanding and Changing Public Support for Capital Punishment," *Corrections Now*, 1(2) (1996): 1–4.

[85] Donald P. Judges, "Scared to Death: Capital Punishment as Authoritarian Terror Management," *UC-Davis Law Review*, 33(1) (1999): 155–248.

[86] Neil J. Farber, Brian M. Aboff, Joan Weiner, Elizabeth B. Davis, E. Gil Boyer and Peter A. Ubel, "Physicians' Willingness to Participate in the Process of Lethal Injection for Capital Punishment," *Annals of Internal Medicine,* 135(10) (2001): 884–88.

[87] Russ Immarigeon, "When Restorative Justice Is Done within a Retributive Justice System, What Is Gained, What Is Lost, and What Lessons are Learned?" *Community Corrections Report*, 7(4) (2000): 55–59; *The Journey for Hope: From Violence to Healing* (San Antonio, TX: Benedictine Resource Center, 1998), pamphlet.

[88] Jack Douglas Jr., "Survivors Say Pain Endures: McVeigh's Death Meets Mostly Silence," *Fort Worth Star-Telegram*, June 12, 2001, p. 1-A.

[89] Bohm, "Understanding and Changing Public Support for Capital Punishment."

[90] Steven Stack, "Execution Publicity and Homicide in Georgia," *American Journal of Criminal Justice*, 18(1) (1994): 25–39.

[91] John K. Cochran, Mitchell B. Chamlin and Mark Seth, "Deterrence or Brutalization? An Assessment of Oklahoma's Return to Capital Punishment," *Criminology*, 32(1) (1994): 107–34.

[92] John K. Cochran and Mitchell B. Chamlin, "Deterrence and Brutalization: The Dual Effects of Executions," *Justice Quarterly*, 17(4) (2000): 685–706.

[93] Sam G. McFarland, "Is Capital Punishment a Short-Term Deterrent to Homicide?" *Journal of Criminal Law and Criminology*, 74 (1982): 61–68; William C. Bailey, "Murder, Capital Punishment and Television: Execution Publicity and Homicide Rates," *American Sociological Review*, 55(5) (1990): 628–33; David R. King, "The Brutalization Effect: Execution Policy and the Incidence of Homicide in South Carolina," *Social Forces*, 57(2) (1978): 683–87; Michael J. Godfrey and Vincent Schiraldi, "How Have Homicide Rates Been Affected by California's Death Penalty?" Report from the Center on Juvenile and Criminal Justice, April 1995; Raymond Bonner and Ford Fessenden, "States without Death Penalty Have Lower Homicide Rates," *San Francisco Chronicle*, Sept. 22, 2000, p. A3; Daniel P. Wirt, William C. Bailey and William J. Bowers, "Physicians' Attitudes about Involvement in Lethal Injection for Capital Punishment," *Archives of Internal Medicine*, 161(10) (May 28, 2001), available: http://archinte.ama-assn.org/issues/v161n10/ffull/ilt0528-4.html.

[94] William C. Bailey and Ruth D. Peterson, "Capital Punishment, Homicide, and Deterrence: An Assessment of the Evidence and Extension to Female Homicide," in M. Dwayne Smith and Margaret A. Zahn (eds.), *Homicide: A Sourcebook of Social Research* (Thousand Oaks, CA: Sage, 1999).

[95] *Furman v. Georgia*, 408 U.S. 238 (1972); Kristin D. Schaefer, James J. Hennessy and Joseph G. Ponterotto, "Race as a Variable in Imposing and Carrying Out the Death Penalty in the US," *Journal of Offender Rehabilitation*, 30(2) (1999): 35–45; *Race of Death Row Inmates* (New York: NAACP Legal Defense Fund, Oct. 1, 2002), available: http://www.naacp.org

[96] Richard C. Dieter, *The Death Penalty in Black & White: Who Lives, Who Dies, Who Decides* (executive summary) (Washington, DC: Death Penalty Information Center, June 1998); Death Penalty Information Center, *Race of Defendants Executed Since 1976*, available: http://www.deathpenaltyinfo.org/dpicrace.html, accessed 12/20/02.

[97] Frank J. Murray, "Reno Seeking More Executions among White Defendants," *Washington Times*, June 16, 1997.

[98] Matthew Eisley, "Study: Race of Victims Plays Role in Sentence: In N.C., Killing Whites Carries Harsher Penalty," *The News & Observer* (Raleigh, NC), Apr. 18, 2001, p. 18-A citing work in progress by Jack Boger and Issac Unah; Thomas Keil and Gennaro Vito, "Race and the Death Penalty in Kentucky Murder Trials: An Analysis of Post-Gregg Outcomes," *Justice Quarterly*, 7 (1990): 189–207; Raymond Paternoster, "Race of Victim and Location of Crime: The Decision to Seek the Death Penalty in South Carolina," *Journal of Criminal Law and Criminology*, 74 (1983): 754–85.

[99] *McCleskey v. Kemp*, 481 U.S. 279 (1987).

[100] Hans Zeisel, "Race Bias in the Administration of the Death Penalty: The Florida Experience," *Harvard Law Review*, 95 (1981): 456–68; Michael Radelet and M. Vandiver, "Race and Capital Punishment: An Overview of the Issue," *Crime and Social Justice*, 15 (1986): 94–113.

[101] Dieter, *The Death Penalty in Black & White*, pp. 1–6; David Baldus, George Woodworth, David Zuckerman, Neil Weiner and Barbara Broffitt, "Race Discrimination and the Death Penalty in the Post-Furman Era: An Empirical and Legal Analysis with Recent Findings from Philadelphia," *Cornell Law Review,* 83 (1998): 1630–770.

[102] Bohm, "Race and the Death Penalty in the United States," in Lynch and Patterson (eds.), *Race and Criminal Justice*, pp. 71–85.

[103] Jan Crawford Greenburg, "Condemned Killer Wins in Top Court," *Chicago Tribune*, June 4, 2002, Section 1, pp. 1, 20.

[104] American Bar Association, Section of Individual Rights and Responsibilities, *Report with Recommendations No. 107*, from ABA 1997 Midyear Meeting as Approved by The ABA House of Delegates, Feb. 3, 1997, available: http://www.abanet.org/irr/rec107.html.

[105] Dieter, *The Death Penalty in Black and White*, fig. 3.

[106] Bohm, "Understanding and Changing Public Support for Capital Punishment."

[107] *Texas Killing Spree Rivals Most Countries* (New York: Amnesty International, May 27, 1998); Roger Hood, *The Death Penalty: A World-Wide Perspective* (Oxford: Clarendon Press, 1989), pp. 7–31.

[108] *The Death Penalty: List of Abolitionist and Retentionist Countries* (London: Amnesty International, Nov. 2001).

[109] G. Robert Hillman, "Bush Draws Heat from Europeans," *Dallas Morning News*, June 13, 2001, p. 1-A; "Crime in America: Violent and Irrational—And That's Just the Policy," *The Economist*, June 8, 1996, pp. 23–24.

[110] "Court Bars Extraditing Suspects Facing Life," *Fort-Worth Star-Telegram*, Oct. 4, 2001, p. 17-A.

[111] "Spain Refuses to Extradite Al-Qa'eda Suspects," *U.S.A. Today*, Nov. 23, 2001, p. 2; Ed Johnson, "Death Penalty for Terrorists Debated," *Washington Post*, Dec. 12, 2001; Keith B. Richburg and T. R. Reid, "France Cautions U.S. Over Sept. 11 Defendant," *Washington Post*, Dec. 13, 2001, p. A-13.

[112] Angela Dolan, "U.S. Death Penalty Risk Is Obstacle in Kopp Extradition," *Seattle Post-Intelligencer*, Mar. 31, 2001, p. B-1; "Fugitive Einhorn Extradited from France," *U.S.A. Today*, Aug. 13, 2001, p. A-3.

[113] "Most Criminologists See No Deterrence from Imposing Death Penalty," *Crime Prevention News* (Washington, DC: CD Publications, Jan. 23, 1996), p. 14.

[114] *Facts about the Death Penalty* (Washington, DC: Death Penalty Information Center, Sept. 14, 1995), p. 4.

[115] Payne and Coogle, "Examining Attitudes about the Death Penalty."

[116] Possley and Mills, "Clemency for All," pp. 1, 15.

[117] George Ryan, excerpts from speech, *Chicago Tribune*, Jan. 12, 2003, p. 16.

[118] *Ibid.*

[119] Steve Mills and Maurice Possley, "Clemency Adds Fuel to Death Penalty Debate," *Chicago Tribune*, Jan. 13, 2003, p 20.

[120] The Gallup Organization, "The Death Penalty," August, 2002, available: http://www.gallup.com/poll/analysis/ia020830iv.asp; Death Penalty Information Center, *The Death Penalty in 2002: Year End Report* (Washington, DC: Death Penalty Information Center, December 2002), p. 6.

[121] John T. Whitehead and Michael B. Blankenship, "Gender Gap in Capital Punishment Attitudes: An Analysis of Support and Opposition," *American Journal of Criminal Justice*, 25(1) (2000): 1–13.

[122] Shaheen Halim and Beverly L. Stiles, "Differential Support for Police Use of Force, the Death Penalty, and Perceived Harshness of the Courts: Effects of Race, Gender, and Region," *Criminal Justice and Behavior*, 28(1) (2001): 3–23; Marian J. Borg, "Vicarious Homicide Victimization and Support for Capital Punishment: A Test of Black's Theory of Law," *Criminology*, 36(3) (1998): 537–67.

[123] Kimberly J Cook, "A Passion to Punish: Abortion Opponents Who Favor the Death Penalty," *Justice Quarterly*, 15(2) (1998): 329–46; John T. Whitehead, "'Good Ol' Boys' and the Chair: Death Penalty Attitudes of Policy Makers in Tennessee," *Crime and Delinquency*, 44(2) (1998): 245–56; John A. Arthur, "Proximate Correlates of Blacks' Support for Capital Punishment," *Journal of Crime and Justice*, 21(1) (1998): 159–72; Marian J. Borg, "The Southern Subculture of Punitiveness: Regional Variation in Support for Capital Punishment," *Journal of Research in Crime and Delinquency*, 34(1) (1997): 25–45.

[124] Whitehead and Blankenship, "Gender Gap in Capital Punishment Attitudes"; Mellisa M. Moon, John Paul Wright and Francis T. Cullen, "Putting Kids to Death: Specifying Public Support for Juvenile Capital Punishment," *Justice Quarterly*, 17(4) (2000): 663–84; John T. Whitehead, Michael B. Blankenship and John Paul Wright, "Elite Versus Citizen Attitudes on Capital Punishment: Incongruity between the Public and Policymakers," *Journal of Criminal Justice*, 27(3) (1999): 249–58; Whitehead, "'Good Ol' Boys' and the Chair."

[125] The Gallup Organization, "The Death Penalty."

[126] ABC News Poll, Press Release, Apr. 24, 2001, embargo May 2, 2001, available: http://deathpenalty-info.org/Polls.html#abc5/01.

[127] Benjamin D. Steiner, William J. Bowers and Austin Sarat, "Folk Knowledge as Legal Action: Death Penalty Judgments and the Tenet of Early Release in a Culture of Mistrust and Punitiveness," *Law and Society Review*, 33(2) (1999): 461–505.

[128] *Ibid.*, pp. 155–56.

CHAPTER FOURTEEN

[1] Alfred Blumstein and Joel Wallman (eds.), *The Crime Drop in America* (New York: Cambridge University Press, 2000).

[2] Jeremy Travis, "Invisible Punishment: An Instrument of Social Exclusion," in Marc Mauer and Meda Chesney-Lind (eds.), *Invisible Punishment: The Collateral Consequences of Mass Imprisonment* (New York: The New Press, 2002), p. 15.

[3] *Ibid.*, pp. 16–17.

[4] Todd R. Clear, "The Problem with 'Addition by Subtraction': The Prison-Crime Relationship in Low-Income Communities," in Marc Mauer and Meda Chesney-Lind (eds.), *Invisible Punishment: The Collateral Consequences of Mass Imprisonment* (New York: The New Press, 2002), p.184.

[5] *Ibid.*, p. 183.

[6] Donald Braman, "Families and Incarceration" in Marc Mauer and Meda Chesney-Lind (eds.), *Invisible Punishment: The Collateral Consequences of Mass Imprisonment* (New York: The New Press, 2002), p. 118.

[7] Peter Y. Sussman, "Media on Prisons: Censorship and Stereotypes," in Marc Mauer and Meda Chesney-Lind (eds.), *Invisible Punishment: The Collateral Consequences of Mass Imprisonment* (New York: The New Press, 2002), p. 275.

[8] *Ibid.*, p. 259.

[9] Cassia Spohn and David Holleran, "The Effect of Imprisonment on Recidivism Rates of Felony Offenders: A Focus on Drug Offenders," *Criminology*, 40(2) (2002): 329–57.

[10] Sasha Abramsky, "Breeding Violence," *Debt to Society: The Real Price of Prisons* (San Francisco, *Mother Jones*, July 10, 2001), available: http://www.motherjones.com/prisons/violence.html

[11] *Ibid.*

[12] Sussman, "Media on Prisons," p. 269.

[13] Braman, "Families and Incarceration," p. 134.

[14] Christopher J. Mumola, *Incarcerated Parents and Their Children* (Washington, DC: Bureau of Justice Statistics, August 2000), pp. 1, 2, 5, NCJ-182335.

[15] Abramsky, "Breeding Violence."

[16] Braman, "Families and Incarceration," p. 135.

[17] Sussman, "Media on Prisons," p. 259.

[18] Vince Beiser, "How We Got to Two Million," *Debt to Society: The Real Price of Prisons* (San Francisco, *Mother Jones*, July 10, 2001), available: http://www.motherjones.com/prisons/overview.html

[19] Eric Schlosser, "The Prison-Industrial Complex," *Atlantic Monthly*, 282(6) (1998): 51–77.

[20] Tracy Huling, "Building a Prison Economy in Rural America," in Marc Mauer and Meda Chesney-Lind (eds.), *Invisible Punishment: The Collateral Consequences of Mass Imprisonment* (New York: The New Press, 2002), p. 199.

[21] *Ibid.*, p. 212.

[22] Sussman, "Media on Prisons," p. 275.

[23] Jack Cowley, "Changing Public Opinion," *Corrections Today,* Feb. (1998): 38–40; Odie Washington, "Sex, Lies and Videotape," *Corrections Today,* Feb. (1998): 34–36.

[24] Mark Fishman, "Crime Waves as Ideology," in Gary W. Potter and Victor E. Kappeler (eds.), *Constructing Crime: Perspectives on Making News and Social Problems* (Prospect Heights, IL: Waveland Press, 1998).

[25] Vincent F. Sacco, "Media Constructions of Crime," in Potter and Kappeler (eds.), *Constructing Crime: Perspectives on Making News and Social Problems*.

[26] Beiser, "How We Got to Two Million."

[27] John Kass, "Truth of Matter Is Lies Are at Heart of Ryan's Reign," *Chicago Tribune*, Jan. 12, 2003, p. 2.

[28] Sussman, "Media on Prisons," p. 273.

[29] *Ibid.*, p. 274.

[30] Larry K. Gaines and Peter B. Kraska (eds.), *Drugs, Crime, & Justice*, 2nd ed. (Prospect Heights, IL: Waveland Press, 2003), p. 4.

[31] *Ibid.*, p. 11.

[32] Lawrence A. Greenfeld, *Alcohol and Crime* (Washington, DC: U.S. Dept. of Justice, 1998), pp. v, 1–3, NCJ-168632; Jeffery A. Roth, *Psychoactive Substances and Violence* (Washington, DC: U.S. Dept. of Justice, 1994), p. 1, NCJ-145534.

[33] Ryan King and Marc Mauer, *Distorted Priorities: Drug Offenders in State Prisons* (Washington, DC: The Sentencing Project, September 2002), p. 1.

[34] *Ibid.*, p. 2.

[35] *Ibid.*, p. 10.

[36] Patricia Allard, *Life Sentences: Denying Welfare Benefits to Women Convicted of Drug Offenses* (Washington, DC: The Sentencing Project, September 2002), pp. 1–2.

[37] King and Mauer, *Distorted Priorities,* p. 14.

[38] *Ibid.*, p. 2.

[39] James P. Gray, *Why Our Drug Laws Have Failed and What We Can Do about It: A Judicial Indictment of the War on Drugs* (Philadelphia: Temple University Press, 2001), p. 36.

[40] *Ibid.*, p. 36

[41] Allen J. Beck, Jennifer C. Karberg and Paige M. Harrison, *Prison and Jail Inmates at Midyear 2001* (Washington, DC: Bureau of Justice Statistics, Revised May 2002), table 1, p. 2, NCJ-191702.

[42] Lauren E. Glaze, *Probation and Parole in the United States, 2001* (Washington, DC: Bureau of Justice Statistics, August 2002), p. 1, NCJ-195669.

[43] Judith Greene and Vincent Schiraldi, *Cutting Correctly: New Prison Policies for Times of Fiscal Crisis* (Washington, DC: Justice Policy Institute, 2002), p. 1, available: http://www.justicepolicy.org/cutting/CuttingCorrectly.pdf

[44] *Cellblocks or Classrooms?: The Funding of Higher Education and Corrections and Its Impact on African American Men* (Washington, DC: Justice Policy Institute, 2002), available: http://www.justicepolicy.org/coc.pdf, p. 4.

[45] Greene and Schiraldi, *Cutting Correctly,* p. 1.

[46] *Cellblocks or Classrooms?,* pp. 1, 8, 10.

47 U.S. Dept. of Justice, *NIJ Survey of Wardens and State Commissioners of Corrections* (Washington, DC: USGPO, 1995), p. 1–2.

48 Michelle Gaseau and Carissa B. Caramanis, *Success of Inmate Fees Increases Their Popularity among Prisons and Jails* (The Corrections Connection Network, 1997), pp. 1–5, available: www.corrections.com/news/interview/interview.htm.

49 Richard G. Kiekbusch, "Why and How Sheriffs Must Lead Corrections into the 21st Century," *Correctional Managers' Report,* 4(4) Dec./Jan. (1999): 3–4, 11; Steve Aos, Robert Barnoski and Roxanne Lieb, "Preventive Programs for Young Offenders Effective and Cost-effective," *Overcrowded Times,* 9(2), Apr. (1998): 1, 7–11.

50 *Corrections Yearbook, 2001*, p. 16, available: http://www.cji-inc.com/cyb/download/01avg_los.pdf

51 Anne-Marie Cusac, "What's the Alternative?" *Debt to Society: The Real Price of Prisons* (San Francisco, *Mother Jones,* July 10, 2001), available: http://www.motherjones.com/prisons/alternatives.html

52 Greene and Schiraldi, *Cutting Correctly,* p. 1.

53 Cusac, "What's the Alternative?"

54 Samuel Walker, *Sense and Nonsense about Crime and Drugs,* 5th ed. (Belmont, CA: Wadsworth, 2001).

55 Beiser, "How We Got to Two Million."

56 Angela J. Davis, "Incarceration and the Imbalance of Power," in Marc Mauer and Meda Chesney-Lind (eds.), *Invisible Punishment: The Collateral Consequences of Mass Imprisonment* (New York: The New Press, 2002), p. 61.

57 Meda Chesney-Lind, "Imprisoning Women: The Unintended Victims of Mass Imprisonment," in Marc Mauer and Meda Chesney-Lind (eds.), *Invisible Punishment: The Collateral Consequences of Mass Imprisonment* (New York: The New Press, 2002), p. 94.

58 Gilbert Geis, "Victims," in David Shichor and Stephen Tibbetts (eds.), *Victims and Victimization: Essential Readings* (Prospect Heights, IL: Waveland Press, 2002), p. 30.

59 Marc Mauer and Meda Chesney-Lind (eds.), *Invisible Punishment: The Collateral Consequences of Mass Imprisonment* (New York: The New Press, 2002), p. 7.

60 Robert C. Davis and Barbara E. Smith, "The Effects of Victim Impact Statements on Sentencing Decisions: A Test in an Urban Setting," in Shichor and Tibbetts (eds.), *Victims and Victimization: Essential Readings*, p. 313.

61 Susan Herman and Cressida Wasserman, "A Role for Victims in Offender Reentry," in Shichor and Tibbetts (eds.), *Victims and Victimization: Essential Readings*, pp. 350–64.

62 Emilio C. Viano, "Stereotyping and Prejudice: Crime Victims and the Criminal Justice System," in Shichor and Tibbetts (eds.), *Victims and Victimization: Essential Readings*, p. 344.

63 *State and Federal Corrections Information Systems: Executive Summary* (Washington, DC: U.S. Dept. of Justice, 1998), pp. 1–12, NCJ-17186.

64 Gerald Berge, Jeffrey Geiger and Scot Whitney, "Technology Is the Key to Security in Wisconsin Supermax," *Corrections Today,* 63(4) (2001): 105–9.

65 Sanford Seymour, Richard Baker and Michael Besco, "Inmate Tracking with Biometric and Smart Card Technology," *Corrections Today,* 63(4) (2001): 75–77; Mike Bone and Carl Crumbacker, "Facial Recognition: Assessing Its Viability in the Corrections Environment," *Corrections Today,* 63(4) (2001): 62–64; Reginald A. Wilkinson and Peggy Ritchie-Matsumoto, "Collaborations and Applications," *Corrections Today* July (1997): 64–67.

66 Tommy Noris, "The Importance of Gang-Related Information Sharing," *Corrections Today,* 63(4) (2001): 96–99; John Moritz, "System Sought to Track Prison Gangs Nationally," *Fort Worth Star-Telegram,* July 18, 1998, p. 138; Brenda Vogel, "Ready or Not, Computers are Here," *Corrections Today,* July (1995): 160–62.

67 Ida M. Halasz, "Cyber Ed," *Corrections Today,* July (1997): 92–95, 124.

68 John Ward, Tom Barret and Lorraine Fowler, "South Carolina's Coordinated Response to Information Technology," *Corrections Today,* July (1995): 78–84.

69 Erin Dalton, "Leaders Convene to Assess Correctional Technology Needs," *Corrections Today,* July (1997): 82–85.

70 Gabrielle deGroot, "Hot New Technologies," *Corrections Today,* July (1997): 60–62.

71 Tony Fabelo, *"Technocorrections": The Promises, the Uncertain Threats* (Rockville, MD: U.S. Dept. of Justice, National Institute of Justice, 2000), pp. 1–8, NCJ-181411; Jasmine A. Tehrani and Sarnoff A. Mednick, "Genetic Factors and Criminal Behavior," *Federal Probation,* 64(2) (2000): 24–27.

[72] Eli Arquilevich, "Nowhere to Run, Nowhere to Hide," *Corrections Technology and Management*, 4(4) (2000): 42–44; Joseph Hoshen and George Drake, *Offender Wide Area Continuous Electronic Monitoring Systems: Project Summary* (Rockville, MD: U.S. Dept. of Justice, National Institute of Justice, 2000), pp. 1–18, NCJ-187102; Bill Siuru, "Tracking Down: Space-Age GPS Technology Is Here," *Corrections Technology and Management*, 3(5) (1999): 12–14.

[73] Doreen Geiger and Mark Shea, "The GENIE System," *Corrections Today*, July (1997): 72–75.

[74] Eric Tischler, "Does Technology Enhance or Hinder Community Supervision," *On the Line* (Lanham, MD: American Correctional Association, March 1998), pp. 1, 3.

[75] Dalton, "Leaders Convene to Assess Correctional Technology Needs."

[76] Tina Lam, "Extradited Businessman to Hear Today if He'll Serve More Time," *Detroit Free Press*, Feb. 8, 1999. Mr. Martin was sentenced to ten days for his escape in addition to his original sentence. The Virginia Department of Corrections calculated a release date of March 8, 1999, based on the time Martin served in jail awaiting sentencing.

[77] Associated Press, "Emergency Appeal Filed to Halt Execution," *The Dallas Morning News*, Jan. 30, 1999.

[78] "Eulogy: Bianca Jagger on Sean Sellers," *Time*, Feb. 15, 1999, 153(6): 21.

[79] David Miers, *International Review of Restorative Justice* (London, England: Great Britain Home Office, Research, Development and Statistics Directorate, 2001), pp. 1–113.

[80] Michael E. Smith, *What Future for "Public Safety" and "Restorative Justice" in Community Corrections* (Washington, DC: U.S. Dept. of Justice, Office of Justice Programs, 2001) pp. 1–8, NCJ-187773; David Shichor, "Penal Policies at the Threshold of the Twenty-First Century," *Criminal Justice Review*, 25(1) (2000): 1–30; Leena Kurki, "Restorative and Community Justice in the United States," *Crime and Justice: A Review of Research*, 27 (2000): 235–303.

[81] Commission for the Prevention of Youth Violence, *Youth and Violence: Medicine, Nursing, and Public Health: Connecting the Dots to Prevent Violence* (Chicago: American Medical Association, 2000), pp. 1–52.

[82] Melvin Stokes, "The First Program," *Corrections Today*, 63(5) (2001): 102–4; Catherine C. McVey, "Coordinating Effective Health and Mental Health Continuity of Care," *Corrections Today*, 63(5) (2001): 58–62; Rhode Island Dept. of Corrections, *Collaborative Development of Individual Discharge Planning for Incarcerated Women* (Cranston: Rhode Island Dept. of Corrections, 2000), pp. 1–5.

[83] Jane Nady Sigmon, M. Elaine Nugent, John Goerdt and Scott Wallace, *Key Elements of Successful Adjudication Partnerships* (Rockville, MD: U.S. Dept. of Justice, Bureau of Justice Assistance, 1999), pp. 1–11, NCJ-173949.

[84] Gordon Bazemore and C. T. Griffiths, "Conferences, Circles, Boards and Mediations: The 'New Wave' of Community Justice Decision-Making," *Federal Probation*, 61(2) (1998): 25–37.

[85] James F. Quinn, Larry A. Gould and Linda Holloway, "Meeting the Needs of Parole Officers: Texas' Community Partnership Councils," *Corrections Compendium*, 26(7) (2001): 1–5, 18–19; James F. Quinn, "Community Participation in the Parole Process: Texas' Community Participatory Councils," *Corrections Management Quarterly*, 3(2) (1999): 77–83.

[86] James F. Quinn, *Summary and Analysis of the Community Survey on the Tarrant County Criminal Justice Planning Process* (Fort Worth, TX: Tarrant County Criminal Justice Planning Group—Steering Committee, June 18, 2001).

[87] Faith E. Lutze, R. P. P. Smith and Nicholas P. Lovrich, "Premises for Attaining More Effective Offender Accountability through Community Involvement: Washington State's New Approach," *Corrections Management Quarterly*, 4(4) (2000): 1–9.

[88] John T. Whitehead and Michael C. Braswell, "Future of Probation: Reintroducing the Spiritual Dimension into Correctional Practice," *Criminal Justice Review*, 25(2) (2000): 207–33.

[89] *2002 Directory of Juvenile and Adult Correctional Departments, Institutions, Agencies and Parole Authorities* (Lanham, MD: American Correctional Association, 2002).

[90] Diane Blemberg, *Standards Committee Update*, American Correctional Association Accreditation & Standards, Aug. 2, 2002, available: http://www.aca.org/standards/revisions.htm

[91] Rod Miller, "Standards and the Courts: An Evolving Relationship," *Corrections Today*, (May 1992): 58, 60.

INDEX

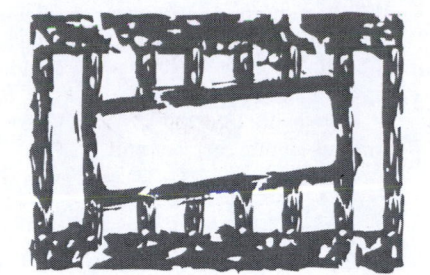